COUNSELING CHILDREN

SEVENTH EDITION

Charles L. Thompson
The University of Tennessee, Knoxville
Donna A. Henderson
Wake Forest University

THOMSON

BROOKS/COLE

Australia • Brazil • Canada • Mexico • Singapore • Spain
United Kingdom • United States

Counseling Children, Seventh Edition

Charles L. Thompson and Donna A. Henderson

Counseling Editor: Marquita Flemming
Assistant Editor: Jennifer Walsh
Editorial Assistant: Samantha Shook
Technology Project Manager: Inna Fedoseyeva
Marketing Manager: Meghan McCullough
Marketing Communications Manager: Tami Strang
Project Manager, Editorial Production: Trudy Brown
Creative Director: Rob Hugel
Art Director: Vernon Boes
Print Buyer: Linda Hsu

Permissions Editor: Joohee Lee
Production Service: Graphic World Publishing Services
Photo Researcher: Kathleen Olson
Copy Editor: Graphic World Publishing Services
Cover Designer: Lisa Henry
Cover Image: MaryBeth Thielhelm/Getty Images
Cover Printer: Phoenix Color Corp
Compositor: International Typesetting
   and Composition
Printer: R.R. Donnelley/Crawfordsville

Library of Congress Control Number: 2006925469

Student Edition
ISBN-13: 978-0-495-00775-3
ISBN-10: 0-495-00775-7

International Student Edition
ISBN-13: 978-0-495-17202-4
ISBN-10: 0-495-17202-2

Thomson Higher Education
10 Davis Drive
Belmont, CA 94002-3098
USA

For more information about our products, contact us at: **Thomson Learning Academic Resource Center 1-800-423-0563**

For permission to use material from this text or product, submit a request online at **http://www.thomsonrights.com.**

Any additional questions about permissions can be submitted by e-mail to **thomsonrights@thomson.com.**

Counseling Children, Seventh Edition, is dedicated to Charles L. Thompson, who died suddenly December 31, 2005, as this edition was being completed. The book mirrors his love for children and his skill in interacting with them. He devoted his working life to sharing that compassion and mastery with his students and to the people who read this book. His commitment reverberates across the many, many individuals who have learned from him.

Dr. Thompson received his Ph.D. in Counselor Education and Counseling Psychology at The Ohio State University. He was a professor of Counselor Education and Educational Psychology at the University of Tennessee for 39 years. He has written six books, published numerous professional articles, and was delighted to be the editor of the IDEA Exchange in the *Elementary School Guidance and Counseling Journal* from 1979 to 1997. However, he considered his greatest achievements those he saw in his students, and he took great pride in seeing us succeed. He was a mentor for life; an anchor, a welcoming, generous, supportive presence to all his current and former students. He shared the gifts of clear explanations, informative demonstrations, and constructive practice opportunities. He often described his teaching philosophy as "Tell me, show me, and let me try it." This book contains many examples of how he accomplished that in writing.

His humor, spirit, constancy, and wisdom have guided counselors across the world and changed the lives of those he encountered. He was a remarkable man who opened doors and helped you walk through them. He could always find the possibilities in situations and was masterful at balancing the challenge to do more and better and the support needed to accomplish the task. If you knew him, I know your world has been shaken too. If you didn't know him, perhaps reading the text will reveal the smiles and encouraging words that filled his days.

He was the quintessential teacher who lived what he taught and always looked for chances to deepen your understanding. And in that spirit I can say with confidence that he would want you to know that a joyful, significant component to living is being a reinforcing part of someone else's life, especially if that person is a child.

Donna A. Henderson

CONTENTS

PREFACE   xxii

AUTHOR BIOGRAPHIES   xxv

PART 1 | INTRODUCTION TO COUNSELING CHILDREN   1

CHAPTER 1   **Introduction to a Child's World   2**

Indicators of Well-Being   4
 What Causes Our Children's Problems?   4

A Changing World   5
 The American Home   6
 Societal Crises   7
 Changing Values   7
 Summary of Children's Difficulties   8

The Personal World of The Child   8
Child Development   11
A Child's Cognitive World   11
The Child's World of Social Development   15
 Resilience   19

What Is Counseling?   22
 How Does Counseling Differ from Psychotherapy?   23
 What Is an Appropriate Working Definition of Counseling?   23

What Counseling Can Do   24
What Specific Types of Assistance Can Be Expected from the Counseling Session?   24
Who Are the Mental Health Professionals?   27

Summary   29
Introduction to a Child's World Video   29
Websites for Understanding a Child's World   29
References   30

CHAPTER 2   **The Counseling Process**   33

Which Approaches to Counseling Are Effective?   33
Classifying Counseling Theories   36
Preparing for the Interview   39
What Are Some Things to Consider during the First Interview?   40
Children's Resistance to Counseling   40

Steps to Overcoming Children's Resistance   42
First Interview Goals and Observations   44

A General Model for Counseling   45
Step 1: Defining the Problem through Active Listening   45
Step 2: Clarifying the Child's Expectations   46
Step 3: Exploring What Has Been Done to Solve the Problem   46
Step 4: Exploring What New Things Could Be Done to Solve the Problem   47
Step 5: Obtaining a Commitment to Try One of the Problem-Solving Ideas   47
Step 6: Closing the Counseling Interview   47

Questions Counselors Ask   48
What Does the Counselor Need to Know about Counseling Records?   48
How Much Self-Disclosure Is Appropriate for the Counselor?   48
What Types of Questions Should the Counselor Use?   50
How Can Silences Be Used in Counseling?   52
Should Counselors Give Advice?   52
Should Counselors Give Information?   54
How Does the Counselor Keep the Client on Task during the Counseling Session?   54
What Limits Should Be Set in Counseling?   54
What about the Issue of Confidentiality?   55
Is This Child Telling Me the Truth?   56

What Can Be Done When the Interview Process Becomes Blocked? 56

When Should Counseling Be Terminated? 57

How Can Counseling Be Evaluated? 58

Goal Attainment Score Calculation: Level at Intake 59
Goal Attainment Score Calculation: Level at Follow-up 61

How Do Professional Counselors Work with Managed Health Care? 63

Step One: Problem Identification 67
Step Two: Problem Definition 67
Step Three: Goal Development 67
Step Four: Measurable Objectives 67
Step Five: Creating Interventions 68
Step Six: Diagnosing 68

Summary 69

The Counseling Process Video 69

Websites for the Counseling Process 69

References 70

PART 2 | COUNSELING THEORIES AND TECHNIQUES 73

CHAPTER 3 | **Psychoanalytic Counseling** 74

The Nature of People 76

Theory of Counseling 78
Structural Concepts 79

Id 79
Ego 79
Superego 80
Dynamic Concepts 81

Instinct 81
Cathexis 81
Anticathexis 81
Anxiety 81
Developmental Concepts 81

Defense Mechanisms 81
Psychosexual Stages and Erikson's Stages 84

Psychoanalytic Counseling and Development of Self-Esteem 86
Object Relations Theory 87

Counseling Methods 90
Catharsis 91

Free Association 92

Interpretation 92

Interpretation of Dreams   92
Parapraxia   94
Humor   94
Analysis of Transference   94
Analysis of Resistance   94
Analysis of Incomplete Sentences   95
Bibliocounseling   95
Storytelling   96
Psychoanalytic Play Therapy and the Expressive Arts   97
Case Studies   99

Cross-Cultural Applications of Psychoanalytic Counseling   104
Psychoanalytic Counseling, Accountability, and Managed
Health Care   105
Summary   105
Websites for Psychoanalytic Counseling   106
References   106

CHAPTER 4   **Reality Therapy: Counseling with Choice Theory**   109

The Nature of People   110
Choice Theory and the Nature of People   111

Theory of Counseling   115
Counseling Method   116
Reality Therapy Process   120
Case Study   123
The Ten-Step Reality Therapy Consultation Model   126
Cross-Cultural Applications of Reality Therapy   129
Reality Therapy, Accountability, and Managed Health Care   130
Summary   130
Introduction to Reality Therapy   131
Websites for Reality Therapy   131
References   131

CHAPTER 5   **Brief Counseling: Solution-Focused and Paradoxical
Counseling Strategies   133**

Background   133
Solution-Focused Brief Counseling   134
The Nature of People   134

Theory of Counseling   135

Counseling Method   137

Orientation Statement   137
Statement of the Problem   138

Setting Counseling Goals   138

The Skeleton Key Question/Statement for Goal Setting   139
Working with Unproductive Client Goals   139

Using the Miracle Question to Formulate Goals   140

Case Study   142

Reviewing the Steps in Solution-Focused Brief Counseling   146

Orientation to the Solution-Focused Brief Counseling Process   146
Setting Goals for Counseling   146
Active Listening   146
Working with Negative Goals   147
Working with Positive Goals   147
The Miracle Question   147
Relationship Questions   147
Exceptions to the Problem Situation   148
Positive Blame   148
Scaling Progress toward Goal   148
Ten Percent Improvements   148
Flagging the Mine Field   148
Closing the Session   148
Writing the Note   149

Ericksonian Play Therapy   150

Paradoxical Counseling Strategies   150

The Nature of People   150

Theory of Counseling   150

Counseling Method   151

Case Examples   152

Cross-Cultural Applications of Brief Counseling   153

Brief Counseling: Accountability and Managed Health Care   154

Summary   155

Introduction to Brief Counseling Video   156

Websites for Brief Counseling   156

References   156

CHAPTER 6   **Person-Centered Counseling   159**

The Nature of People   161

Theory of Counseling   161

Counseling Method   164
  Case Study   170

Person-Centered Counseling and the Development of Self-Esteem   172
  Integrating Self-Esteem–Building Activities with the Child's Life   173

Child-Centered Play Therapy   175

Cross-Cultural Applications of Person-Centered Counseling   176

Person-Centered Counseling, Accountability, and Managed Health Care   178

Summary   178
  Introduction to Person-Centered Counseling Video   180
  Websites for Person-Centered Counseling   180
  References   181

CHAPTER 7   **Gestalt Therapy**   183

The Nature of People   185

Theory of Counseling   187

Counseling Method   188
  Gestalt Techniques   189

    "I" Language   189
    Substituting *Won't* for *Can't*   190
    Substituting *What* and *How* for *Why*   190
    No Gossiping   190
    Changing Questions into Statements   190
    Taking Responsibility   190
    Incomplete Sentences   190
    Bipolarities   191
    My Greatest Weakness   193
    Resent, Demand, and Appreciate: The Integration of Opposing Thoughts, Feelings, and Beliefs   193
    Fantasy Games for Creating Awareness   194
    Dreamwork   195
  Gestalt Play Therapy   196

    Confidence Courses for Play Therapy   197
  Case Study   197

Cross-Cultural Applications of Gestalt Therapy   200

Gestalt Therapy, Accountability, and Managed Health Care   201

Summary   203
  Introduction to Gestalt Therapy Video   204

Websites for Gestalt Therapy 204

References 204

CHAPTER 8 **Rational-Emotive-Behavioral Therapy and Cognitive-Behavioral Therapy** 207

The Nature of People 208

Theory of Counseling 210

Counseling Method 214
  Rational-Emotive-Behavioral Education 219

Cognitive-Behavioral Therapy 220
  Case Study 223

Applications of Cognitive-Behavioral Therapy 226
  Aggression 226
  Anxiety 227
  Depression 227
  Attention-Deficit/Hyperactivity Disorder 228
  Obesity 228
  Children of Alcoholics 229
  Cognitive-Behavioral Play Therapy 229

Cross-Cultural Applications of Rational-Emotive-Behavioral Therapy and Cognitive-Behavioral Therapy 230

Rational-Emotive-Behavioral Therapy, Cognitive-Behavioral Therapy, Accountability, and Managed Health Care 231

Summary 232
  Websites for Rational-Emotive-Behavioral Therapy and Cognitive-Behavioral Therapy 234
  References 234

CHAPTER 9 **Behavioral Counseling** 238

The Nature of People 239

Theory of Counseling 240
  Behavior Analysis 241
    Why People Behave as They Do 241

Steps in Behavior Analysis   242

   Principles of Behavior   242

Schedules of Reinforcement   244

   Fixed Interval Schedule   244

   Variable Interval Schedule   244

   Fixed Ratio Schedule   244

   Variable Ratio Schedule   244

Counseling Goals   244

Counseling Methods   245

Contingency Contracts   245

   Example 1   246

   Example 2   247

Self-management   248

Shaping   249

Behavioral Momentum   249

Biofeedback   250

Modeling   250

Token Economies   251

Behavior-Practice Groups   251

Role-playing   252

   Role-playing to Define a Problem   252

   Role Reversal   252

   Role-playing Used as Behavior Rehearsal   253

Counseling Homework Assignments   253

Assertiveness Training   254

Classical Conditioning Methods   254

Ivan Pavlov (1849–1936)   254

Systematic Desensitization   255

Flooding   258

Hypnosis   259

Counterconditioning   259

Aversive Conditioning   259

Case Study   260

Applications of Behavioral Counseling   263

Response Cost   264

Eating Disorders   264

Multimodal Approaches   264

Cross-Cultural Applications of Behavioral Counseling   265

Behavioral Counseling, Accountability, and Managed Health Care   266

Summary   266

Introduction to Behavioral Counseling   267

Websites for Behavioral Counseling   267

References   267

CHAPTER 10   **Transactional Analysis**   269

The Nature of People and Theory of Counseling   270

Structural Analysis   271

Parent   271

Adult   272

Child   272

Transactional Analysis   273

Script Analysis   275

Game Analysis   276

Life Positions   277

Games Clients Play   278

The Pursuit of Strokes   280

Structuring Time   281

Rackets   283

Counseling Method   283

Case Studies   293

Cross-Cultural Applications of Transactional Analysis   295

Transactional Analysis, Accountability, and Managed Health Care   296

Summary   297

Websites for Transactional Analysis   297

References   297

CHAPTER 11   **Individual Psychology**   299

The Nature of People   301

The Need for Success   302

Goals of Behavior   302

Lifestyle   303

Social Interest   303

The Family Constellation   305
  Only Children   305
  Firstborn Children   305
  Second-Born Children   306
  Middle Children   306
  Youngest Children   306
The Family Atmosphere   307

Theory of Counseling   309
Goals of Misbehavior   311
  Attention   311
  Power   312
  Revenge   312
  Inadequacy or Withdrawal   312

Counseling Method   314
Early Recollections   317
Understanding   318
Confrontation   318
Stages   319
Interventions for the Four Goals of Misbehavior   319
  Sequence of the "Could It Be . . .?" Questions   321
  Encouragement   322
  Praise   323
  Bribery   323
Natural and Logical Consequences   323
  Natural Consequences   323
  Logical Consequences   324
Case Study   324

Adlerian Play Therapy   327
Adlerian Family Counseling   328
Cross-Cultural Applications of Individual Psychology   330
Individual Psychology, Accountability, and Managed Health Care   332
Introduction to Individual Psychology   333
Websites for Individual Psychology   333
References   333

CHAPTER 12   **Family Counseling**   335

How Does Family Counseling Differ from Individual Counseling?   335
What Defines a Family?   336
How Does General Systems Theory Relate to Families?   337

Systems Approach to Family Therapy   337
  Murray Bowen (1913–1990)   337
  The Spousal Relationship   338
  Differentiation of Self   339
  Detriangulation of Self from the Family Emotional System   340
  Nuclear Family Emotional Process   340
  Family Projection Process   340
  Multigenerational Transmission Process   341
  Sibling Position   341
  Emotional Cutoff   341
  Emotional Process in Society   341
  Emotional Systems of the Family   345
  Modeling Differentiation   345

Structural Family Therapy   346
  Salvador Minuchin's Contributions to Structural Family Therapy   347

Strategic Family Therapy   351
  Paradoxical Interventions   351
  Contributions of Milton Erickson, Jay Haley, and Cloé Madanes to Strategic Family Therapy   352

The Communications Approach to Family Therapy   357
  John Gottman's Behavioral Interview Method   357
  Virginia Satir's Conjoint Family Therapy   359
    The Nature of People   360
    Theory of Counseling   362
    Counseling Method   367
    An Example of Satir's Method   368
    The Importance of Including Children   368
    Three Keys to Satir's System   370
    Satir's Technique   370
    Simulated Family Game   371
    Systems Games   371
    Communication Games   372
    The Counselor's Role   372
  Case Studies   373

Play Therapy with Families   375
  Dynamic Family Play Therapy   376
  Filial Therapy   376
  Strategic Family Play Therapy   377
  Theraplay   378

Cross-Cultural Applications of Family Counseling   378

Family Counseling, Accountability, and Managed Health Care   379

Summary   380

   Introduction to Family Counseling   381

   Websites for Family Counseling   381

   References   381

CHAPTER 13   **Personality Types**   385

The Nature of People   386

Theory of Counseling   387

   Psyche   387

   Psychic Energy   387

   Consciousness   388

   The Personal Unconscious   388

   The Ego   388

   The Ego Gatekeeper   389

   Complexes   391

   Individuation   391

   Dreams   391

   Progression and Regression   392

   The Collective Unconscious   392

   Archetypes   392

      The Self   392

      The Anima and Animus   393

      The Shadow   393

      The Persona   393

   Word Association   394

   Psychological Types   394

   Myers Briggs Type Indicator (MBTI®)   397

   The Type Table™   402

   Dominance   402

   Temperament   402

   Preferences in Learning   403

   Psychological Diversity in Children   404

   Usefulness in Counseling   405

   Theory of Type Development   406

Counseling Method   406
  Case Study   407

Cross-Cultural Applications of Jung   411

Summary   411
  Websites for Jungian Counseling   411

  References   412

PART 3 | COUNSELING WITH CHILDREN: SPECIAL TOPICS   413

CHAPTER 14 | **Play Therapy**   414

Defining Play Therapy   414

Advantages of Play Therapy   415

Empirical Support for Play Therapy   417

Cross-Cultural Applications of Play Therapy   419

Play Therapy Approaches   420
  Applications of Play Therapy   420

  Group Play Therapy   420

  Prescriptive Play Therapy   422

  Play Therapy with Families   423

    Filial Therapy   423
    Parent-Child Interaction Therapy   425

Play Therapy with Specific Child Populations and Problems   427
  Children Experiencing Adjustment Difficulties in School   427

  Children Witnessing Domestic Violence   429

  Children Facing Persistent Illness and Children in the Hospital   429

  Autistic Children   430

  Children Experiencing Post-Traumatic Stress Disorder   431

Play Therapy in Combination with Other Interventions   432

Considerations in Play Therapy   433
  Therapist   433

Appropriate Clients   434

Play Stages   435

Play Therapy and Managed Health Care   436

Play Therapy Media and Strategies   436
  Basic Skills of Play Therapy   438

Art 439

Puppets 440

Sand 441

Case Study 443

Summary 445

Introduction to Play Therapy 446

Websites for Play Therapy 446

References 446

CHAPTER 15 **Cultural Factors in Counseling Children** 457

Competence 459

Multicultural Counseling Competencies 459

Awareness 460

Knowledge 461

Ethnic Identity Development 464

Acculturation 465

Skills 466

Children 468

African American Children 470

American Indian and Alaskan Native Children 473

Asian American Children 475

Latino Children 477

Multiracial Children 479

Summary 480

Websites for Cultural Factors in Counseling Children 480

References 480

CHAPTER 16 **Consultation and Collaboration** 487

Consultation 488

Models of Consultation 489

Mental Health Consultation 489

Process Consultation 489

Behavioral Consultation 491

Cross-Cultural Consultation 493

Consulting Process 494

Combinations   496

Consultation Interventions   497

  Role Shift   497

  Listing of Behaviors   497

  Logical Consequences   498

  Isolation Techniques   498

Collaboration   499

 Teaming   502

 Assessment as a Consulting and Counseling Intervention   502

  The Interview   502

  Case Histories   504

  Behavioral Observations   504

 Formal Psychological and Educational Tests   504

  Intelligence Tests   504

  Projective Techniques   505

  Achievement Tests   505

  Aptitude Tests   505

  Other Tests   505

Summary   506

 Websites for Consultation and Collaboration   507

 References   507

CHAPTER 17   **Group Counseling with Children**   510

Definition of Group   511

Types of Groups   511

Theoretically Oriented Group Counseling   513

Group Leadership Skills   515

Getting Started   516

 Group Focus   516

 Selecting Group Members   519

 Forming a Group   519

 Screening Interview   520

 Size of Group   521

 Group Setting   521

Group Stages   521

Group Counseling Process   523

 The First Session   523

Guidelines for the Remaining Sessions   524

Implications for Different Ages   525

Evaluation of Groups   527

Group Counseling Example   528

Classroom Meetings   530

Group Crisis Intervention   531

Summary   533

Websites for Group Counseling with Children   534

References   534

CHAPTER 18   **Counseling Children with Special Concerns**   538

Child Maltreatment   538

Physical Abuse and Neglect   541

Child Sexual Abuse   544

General Counseling Strategies for Working with Children Who Have Been Abused   545

Children's Memories of Abuse   547

Children in Chemically Dependent Families   548

Interventions for Children from Chemically Dependent Families   550

Death and Bereavement   551

Interventions for Children Who Are Grieving   553

Depression and Suicide   556

Interventions for Depression   557

Suicide   558

Interventions for Suicide   560

Postsuicide Interventions   561

Family Structures   562

Children of Divorce   562

Children in Stepfamilies   568

Children in Single-Parent Homes   570

Homeless Children   571

Children and Violence   573

Gangs   577

Summary   580

Websites for Counseling Children with Special Concerns   580

References   580

CHAPTER 19 **Counseling with Children with Special Needs 588**

The Situation 588

History 589

Categories of Exceptionality 590
  Methods for Counseling with Children Who Have Special Needs 593

Children with Behavioral-Emotional Disorders 593

The Child with a Learning Disability 595

Attention-Deficit/Hyperactivity Disorder and Attention Deficit Disorder 598

The Child with Mental Retardation 600

The Child with a Physical Disability 602

General Ideas 603

Counseling with Parents of Exceptional Children 604

Summary 605
  Websites for Counseling with Exceptional Children 605
  References 606

CHAPTER 20 **Legal and Ethical Considerations for Counselors 609**

Ethical, Professional, and Legal Issues 609
  Decision-Making Models 611
  Counseling Minors 612
  Competence 613
  Informed Consent 614
  Confidentiality 615
    Confidentiality of Files 618
    Breaching Confidentiality 620
    Duty to Protect 621
    Confidentiality in Groups 621
  Child Abuse Reporting 622

An Ethical Decision-Making Process 622

Summary 625
  Websites for Legal and Ethical Considerations for Counselors 625
  References 625

APPENDICES 629

NAME INDEX 695

TOPICAL INDEX 705

PREFACE

Counseling Children, Seventh Edition, maintains the focus of earlier editions—putting theory into the practice. We produced what we hope will be a valuable addition to this text. Video clips of counseling sessions with children accompany this volume. The counselors in those clips demonstrate some techniques, some relationship building skills, and the spirit of working with children. We hope you find these short segments instructive. As in previous editions, the book contains ideas that can be used by seasoned professionals as well as those who are just learning to work with children and their families. Counselors, psychologists, social workers, and teachers will discover ways to teach children how to meet their needs in ways that do not infringe on the rights of others. We synthesize the best ideas from research and practice and present practical, current interventions for helping children with specific developmental, educational, personal, social, and behavioral problems. The reader will find suggestions for working with children who have special needs; who are faced with crises such as death, violence, divorce, or substance abuse problems; and who may be victims of abuse, chronic illness, or other trying circumstances. Particular attention is given to both developmental and cross-cultural implications for the theories and interventions discussed.

The seventh edition of *Counseling Children* is based on the principle that people who work effectively with children adapt to the young people they serve. The helpers integrate and adapt interventions and techniques from a variety of theoretical systems into their counseling system. Therefore, one of our goals is to present accurate descriptions of a variety of theories from which readers can develop their own approaches to helping.

ORGANIZATION

Each chapter has been updated and many have been expanded. Several chapters have video clips that illustrate a concept from the theory. The sequence and changes in the book follow.

In Part 1, we consider barriers to children's healthy development as well as the resiliency that most children exhibit. We look at the world of the child by discussing some developmental theories—Piaget's stages of cognitive development, Erikson's theory of social development, Freud's psychosexual stages of development, Havighurst's developmental tasks, and Selman's descriptions of changes in perspective taking. We explore the practices most likely to contribute to effective counseling as well as the ways helping can be a remedial, preventive, or developmental activity. Next you will find definitions and dimensions of counseling as well as responses to frequently asked questions. The final section of Part 1 contains one way of evaluating progress in counseling and working with managed care companies.

In Part 2, we review counseling theories. This section of the book begins with psychoanalytic counseling theory, the stimulus for many other approaches to counseling. Chapters on reality therapy and solution-focused brief counseling follow because those counseling methods offer students some practical skills for work and field experiences. Those two models also meld with time restrictions faced in schools, agencies, and other mental health settings. Chapter 6 includes the discussion of person-centered counseling and active listening skills needed for that method of helping and for many other counseling approaches.

A primary objective of the theory and practice of counseling class is to provide our students with a basic counseling plan to prepare them for their work with children. Our experience has been that active listening in tandem with reality therapy and solution-focused counseling provides the basic skills counselors need to be successful in their early counseling practice.

Gestalt therapy is discussed for its unique interventions, which are helpful additions to the beginning counselor's repertoire. Rational-emotive-behavioral therapy, cognitive-behavioral therapy, and behavior therapy follow so that readers can add skills for working with people who respond well to cognitive and behavioral interventions. Transactional analysis is presented so that readers can investigate a way to help others understand how they communicate with other people, how their personality developed, and how life scripts can be rewritten. The Adlerian and family counseling chapter contains wide choices of ways to work with families, ranging from individual psychology and conjoint family therapy to structural, strategic, and systems approaches to family counseling. The chapter on personality types delivers a different view of personality development.

Part 3 begins with a chapter that includes points about play therapy that have not been covered in the other theories chapters. This section of the book also includes chapters on counseling children from different cultures, focusing on identity development and information on particular groups of children. Those who work with children often include parents, teachers, and other adults. The chapter on consultation, collaboration, and teamwork provides skills and models of conducting that work. The topic of the following chapter is working with children in groups. Legal and ethical guidelines for a counseling practice, based on the newly revised codes of ethics, are covered next. An extended discussion on working with children with special concerns rounds out the topics covered in Part 3.

ACKNOWLEDGMENTS

No project this big can be completed without encouragement and support. Thanks to those in our universities and communities who have helped in many ways. We also appreciate the people who gave us useful advice in their reviews: Susan Anzivino, University of Maine, Farmington; Steven Berman, Lewis & Clark College; John A. Casey, California State University, Bakersfield; Cher Edwards, Seattle Pacific University; Christie Eppler, Seattle Pacific University; Nadine Garner, Millersville University; Helen Wilson Harris, Baylor University; Catheleen Jordan, University of Texas, Arlington; Shannon H. Kim, University of Mississippi/Baddour Center; Sylvia Margolin, Governors State University; Carolyn Rollins, Albany State University; Linda Vanderbleek, Barry University; Deborah Watkins, York College of Pennsylvania; and Andrew Wenger, University of Miami. We are so grateful for the support from everyone at Thomson Arts and Sciences, especially our editor, Marquita Flemming; editorial assistant, Samantha Shook; and Phil Bugeau from Graphic World Publishing Services. They and many other fine people at Thomson Arts and Sciences shepherded this project to completion and were generous with their patience and expertise. A special thanks goes to Inna Fedoseyeva of Thomson, who came to North Carolina and helped with the video that now accompanies this text. That video project was developed and implemented by Trevor Buser with the help of Juleen Buser and Erin Brinkley, who are graduate students at Wake Forest University. They had the technical expertise of Henry Heidtman, a masterful producer, and of Summit School, which generously donated their space and equipment.

Finally we recognize the patience, support, understanding, and encouragement that our spouses, Harriet and J.D., and families have provided along the way. We love and appreciate all you do to help us and hope you know how much that matters.

Charles L. Thompson
Donna A. Henderson

AUTHOR BIOGRAPHIES

Charles L. Thompson was a professor of counselor education and in the Department of Educational Psychology & Counseling in the College of Education, Health, & Human Science at The University of Tennessee in Knoxville. He received his bachelor's and master's degrees in science education and educational psychology from The University of Tennessee and did his Ph.D. degree concentration in counselor education, developmental psychology, and counseling psychology at The Ohio State University, where he held NDEA and Delta Theta Tau fellowships. Charles was a former teacher and counselor in grades 7 to 12. He held memberships in the American Counseling Association and the American Psychological Association. He was licensed as a psychologist and school counselor and Board Certified by the National Board of Certified Counselors. His research interests included reality therapy and solution-focused brief counseling. Charles was a recipient of the American Mental Health Counselors Association's Counselor Educator of the Year Award and the Writer of the Year Award from the American School Counselor Association. He co-authored or authored seven books and over 100 articles in journals, including the *Journal of Counseling & Development*, *Professional School Counseling*, *Journal of Mental Health Counseling*, *Counselor Education & Supervision*, *Journal of Counseling Psychology*, *International Journal of Reality Therapy*, and the *International Journal for the Advancement of Counseling*. Charles was editor of The Idea Exchange Section of the *Elementary School Guidance & Counseling Journal* from 1979 to 1997. Charles always felt that all of the above would not have had much meaning in his life were it not for the time he and his wife, Harriet, were blessed to spend with their family. Charles Thompson passed away on December 31, 2005. His website can be accessed at http://web.utk.edu/~thompson/.

Donna A. Henderson is an associate professor of counselor education in the Department of Education at Wake Forest University in Winston-Salem, North Carolina. She received her bachelor's degree in English from Meredith College, her master's degree from James Madison University, and her Ph.D. degree in counselor education from the University of Tennessee, Knoxville. Donna is the recent Past-President of the Association for Counselor Education and Supervision. She is a former teacher and counselor in grades 7 to 12 and is a licensed school counselor and a licensed professional counselor. She holds memberships in the American Counseling Association and has been active in national, regional, and state counseling associations. Her research interests include counseling children, particularly in the school setting, and counselor education concerns. Donna has co-authored a book on school counseling and has written chapters on legal and ethical issues, developmental issues, creative arts and counseling, and other topics. She has had articles published in *The Journal for Specialists in Group Work, Arts in Psychotherapy, Journal of Family Therapy,* and *Elementary School Guidance and Counseling.*

Introduction to Counseling Children

I CHAPTER | INTRODUCTION TO A CHILD'S WORLD

The honor of one is the honor of all.
The hurt of one is the hurt of all.

Creek Indian Creed

According to the most recent census (Child Trends, 2005), in 2004 there were 73.3 million children under the age of 18 in the United States. That number represents 25 percent of the total population. By 2030, that number is projected to be 85.7 million.

We pride ourselves on being a child-oriented nation. Laws have been passed to prevent children from being misused in the workplace, to punish adults who physically or psychologically harm children, to provide means for all children to obtain an education regardless of their mental or physical condition, and to support programs for medical care, food, and clothing for children in need. Politicians continue to debate "save our children" issues such as educational reform, sex and violence on television, an adolescent girl's right to an abortion without parental consent, family-leave policies in the workplace, and ways of providing a more environmentally safe world for our children's future.

What could possibly be considered more precious than children? They enrich our lives and contribute to our delight. Certainly the unbounded joy of children frolicking on a playground brings smiles to the eyes of the beholder. Most teachers and other adults who interact often with young people have a storehouse of the humorous sayings and extraordinary wisdom of their charges. Children help us remember the wonder of the world. Many of us have had chances to refine our "mature" views after considering a careful answer to a question stemming from the curiosity of a younger one. Children bring us delight in these and so many other ways.

Furthermore, we know what children need to thrive. They need a place to live, adequate food and clothing, affordable health care, and safety. They need freedom from stress, caring relationships with family and friends, and positive role models. They also need opportunities to succeed in school and at other activities. Children need support and guidance as they move toward adulthood.

Yet forces that impede their opportunities for a childhood of manageable cares scar the days of too many children and adolescents, leading to difficulties that negatively complicate their lives. Data from the Children's Defense Fund (2005) delineate the difficulties in childhood. For example, according to the Children's Defense Fund:

MOMENTS IN AMERICA FOR ALL CHILDREN

Every 9 seconds a high school student drops out of school.*

Every 13 seconds a public school student is corporally punished.*

Every 20 seconds a child is arrested.

Every 23 seconds a baby is born to an unmarried mother.

Every 35 seconds a child is confirmed as abused or neglected.

Every 36 seconds a baby is born into poverty.

Every 37 seconds a baby is born to a mother who is not a high school graduate.

Every 42 seconds a baby is born without health insurance.

Every minute a baby is born to a teen mother.

Every 2 minutes a baby is born at low birth weight.

Every 4 minutes a baby is born to a mother who received late or no prenatal care.

Every 4 minutes a child is arrested for drug abuse.

Every 8 minutes a child is arrested for violent crimes.

Every 19 minutes a baby dies before his first birthday.

Every 41 minutes a child or teen dies in an accident.

Every 3 hours a child or teen is killed by a firearm.

Every 5 hours a child or teen commits suicide.

Every 6 hours a child is killed by abuse or neglect.

Every day a mother dies in childbirth.

Barriers to the well-being of young people contribute significantly to these grim statistics. Every adult could discover ways to ameliorate those difficulties—ways as distant as casting an informed vote, or as up close and personal as becoming a volunteer Big Brother or Big Sister. Mental health professionals have myriad possibilities for making the world healthier for children and more

---

*Based on calculations per school day (180 days of seven hours each)

supportive of positive, productive development. Counselors who work with children must learn to balance an appreciation for the gifts of childhood with the reality of a world of challenges.

Knowledge of indicators of well-being, supportive factors, healthy environments, and productive working alliances allows counselors to work for the mental health of children.

INDICATORS OF WELL-BEING

The behaviors of mentally healthy children include their functioning well at home, in school, and in their communities (Surgeon General, 2000). Children must be understood in the contexts of these social settings—with their family, peers, and others. Brazelton and Greenspan (2000), a pediatrician and a child psychiatrist, wrote about what they call the "irreducible needs" for a child to grow, learn, and thrive. They list the following components as fundamental for a child's health:

- Continuing, nurturing relationships
- Physical protection and safety with regulations to safeguard those needs
- Experiences tailored to individual differences for each child's optimal development
- Developmentally appropriate opportunities as building blocks for cognitive, motor, language, emotional, and social skills
- Adults who set limits, provide structure, and guide by having appropriate expectations
- A community that is stable, supportive, and consistent

Some children are born into warm and loving homes that provide excellent environments for growth and development. Many children pass successfully through the developmental stages of childhood and adolescence and become well-functioning adults. Other children overcome the adversities of their childhoods and go on to lead productive and meaningful lives. These children have the resilience to carry them through neglect, abuse, poverty, and other unfavorable home conditions. A later section in this chapter explains and explores that ability to ward off potentially negative forces. Next, we discuss some barriers that children face.

WHAT CAUSES OUR CHILDREN'S PROBLEMS?

While reading the following situations, consider whether they sound improbable or all too common.

Tommy is a fifth grader referred for counseling because of "lack of motivation." He is a loner who does not seem to want friends. He appears unenthusiastic about life—nothing interests or excites him. He has begun to exhibit signs of aggressiveness—increased fighting and abusive language. His teachers are concerned about this trend in his behavior.

Rochelle is a first grader whose parents have recently divorced. Her mother and father have found other partners, and in the excitement of their new lives, they have little time for Rochelle. She is very confused about whom she can rely on and trust. At this very crucial point in her school life, she is floundering in an unstable world. Her grades are falling, and she is withdrawing from interactions with adults and peers.

Stacie's family lives in abject poverty. Neither of her parents completed high school, and neither has been able to hold a steady job. Stacie's few clothes are too small for her and sometimes not clean. She often does not have lunch or lunch money, and she complains about being hungry at home. At school, she seems to be in her own dream world.

Carlos, a fourth grader, has been acting out since he was in the first grade, and no one has been able to work with him effectively. He comes from a family that has obvious wealth, and his parents have tried to provide him with care and loving support. Carlos is constantly in trouble for hitting, lying, and name-calling. He now has begun to fight in class, on the playground, and with children in his neighborhood. There are rumors about spousal abuse in his home, but Carlos refuses to discuss anything about his family life.

Mike has been diagnosed as having attention-deficit/hyperactivity disorder (ADHD), but his parents refuse to accept his diagnosis. They blame the school for Mike's learning and behavioral problems. Mike is two grades behind in reading and is a constant disruption in his classroom. His teacher has given up, saying that she cannot help Mike unless his parents cooperate with her educational plan.

A CHANGING WORLD

Parents often like to think that children are immune to the stressful complexities and troubles of the rapidly changing adult world. They see childhood as a carefree, irresponsible time, with no financial worries, societal pressures, or work-related troubles. Many adults who consider themselves child advocates do not understand children's perceptions. They do not believe a child's concerns matter significantly, and they see children as largely unaware of what is happening politically and economically.

Adults who underestimate children's awareness of the world may also misjudge children in other matters. Our experience in working with children has been that they are effective problem solvers and decision makers when they have the opportunity to be in a nonthreatening counseling atmosphere with a counselor who listens and provides guidance. Adults who help children discover their own strengths and practice their skills create the constructive environment needed for reaching their potential.

Normal child development involves a series of cognitive, physical, emotional, and social changes. Almost all children at some time experience difficulty in adjusting to the changes, and the accompanying stress or conflict can lead to learning or behavioral problems. Normal child development tasks include achieving independence, learning to relate to peers, developing confidence in self, coping with an ever-changing body, forming basic values, and mastering new ways of thinking and new information. Numerous factors in children's lives require them to adapt, including changes in home or school locations, death or divorce in the family, and major illnesses. A high degree of stress has been found to be strongly associated with behavior symptoms. Add the stresses and conflicts of a rapidly changing society—which even adults find difficult to understand—to normal developmental concerns, and the child's world does not look so appealing.

Several authors and organizations collect information on the condition of children in the United States. Weissberg, Walberg, O'Brien, and Kuster (2003) have compiled a study of the long-term trends in the well-being of children in the United States. These editors have produced an informative volume that details current issues in the lives of children and their families. In addition, the Children's Defense Fund (2004) published *The State of America's Children,* which considers the impact of many factors on youth development. An annual collection of trends for those factors can be found in the *Kids Count Data Book* (2005), produced by the Annie E. Casey Foundation. All these sources not only provide data related to children in the United States but also present summaries of successful intervention programs and action guides for child advocates.

Orton (1997) identifies many of those issues in her description of the world as having many faces of poverty, describing these deficiencies as a poverty of resources, a poverty of tolerance, a poverty of time, and a poverty of values. She discusses the poverty of resources, with more than 14 million U.S. children as victims. Hunger, poor housing, unemployment, and homelessness are evidence of this type of poverty. The impact is staggeringly dismal. Orton also writes about the poverty of tolerance for each other and for anyone who is dissimilar. Intolerance and the ignorance and fear it engenders reduce the quality of life for each individual in our society. The poverty of time relates to the widespread fatigue of a life moving too fast and of demands too great. Finally, Orton points out what she considers a poverty of values. Her examples include the high incidence of abuse, crime, and violence. Her explanation of these difficulties in the world helps us understand the stresses of childhood.

In summary, counselors need to be prepared to work with issues of separation, divorce, and differing family structures; increased stresses and differences among cultures; the effect of a changing world on the family and work environments; poor parenting and home conditions that lead to academic, social, and emotional problems in children; the need for sex education at increasingly younger ages to protect children from disease and early pregnancy; gangs and the violence that accompanies membership in them; and violence in general that results from societal influences such as abuse, alcohol and drug use, television, negative role modeling, anger, and other factors. Counselors and adults should pay attention to the particular vulnerabilities of many children in foster care or the juvenile justice systems, the difficulties facing teenage parents, and the dim future of those who do not complete their high school education.

THE AMERICAN HOME

According to developmental psychologists, children need warm, loving, and stable home environments to grow and develop in a healthy manner. Brazelton and Greenspan (2000) have emphasized that type of home environment as an irrevocable need. Hernandez (2003) reminds us that parents are the most important people in a child's world, not only because they provide the day-to-day care and nurturing needed but also because they supply the economic resources needed for shelter, food, health care, and other necessities.

In today's society, family constellations include intact families, single-parent homes, teen-parent families, intergenerational families, and blended families. Grandparents may live 3000 miles away and be almost unknown to their grandchildren. Aunts and uncles seldom live nearby; in any case, they are often busy pursuing individual interests and careers. Parents may work long hours to provide financial security for their families and also may be expected to attend meetings or other community events at night. Mothers still shoulder the primary responsibility for care of the home, so they are often occupied at night with washing, ironing, or cleaning. Single parents assume the roles of both mother and father, doubling the burden on the parent and too often leaving little free time to spend with their children. Garbarino (1997) reports estimates of a 50 percent decrease in the last 30 years of constructive parent–child time. Children may not be able to find someone to listen to them or provide the care and guidance they need, even though adults are present.

Societal Crises

Children in the United States are confronted by a conflict-ridden society. The media report the high cost of life's necessities—food, shelter, clothing—almost daily. The war on poverty has not been won, and children are some of the most vulnerable victims. In fact, in 2002, the families of 16.7 percent of children in the United States were classified as poor (Children's Defense Fund, 2004). Job markets change rapidly, and career planning is hampered by uncertainties about future demand for specific skills. Those adults with jobs may be dissatisfied, overworked, or stressed by an unpredictable market. Crime seems to be everywhere, and many neighborhoods are no longer safe for children or adults. The cost of vandalism to schools and other private and public property is astronomical. Many people are increasingly cynical and distrustful of local, state, and federal governments. Once-respected public figures, corporate leaders, and government agencies have engaged in criminal or highly unethical practices. Finally, we live in a world full of tension, war, and the threat of terrorism that can strike anywhere at any time.

Changing Values

Although change can be frightening or confusing, especially for a child, it can also be wondrous and exciting. It can bring new discoveries in medicine, new ideas for recreation, different jobs, and new ways of living; that is, all areas of life may be affected.

Children are forming values in a constantly and rapidly changing world. What is right or wrong seems to change daily or varies with the person. Who has the absolute answer concerning standards of sexuality, cohabitation, alternative lifestyles, or abortion? Are the various liberation movements good or bad? How does a person behave in a world with changing gender roles? Will drugs really harm a person? Should society condone mercy killing? Is capital punishment justified? Adults with mature thinking processes and years of life experience have difficulty making rational judgments on such ethical and moral issues.

SUMMARY OF CHILDREN'S DIFFICULTIES

No simple answer to what causes our children's problems has emerged. The home, society, and changing values contribute to the well-being and the difficulties of childhood. The impact of poverty may cause children to do without a home, food, or medical care. Family members under stress may abuse or neglect children, may not adequately supervise the young person, and may provide a dearth of learning opportunities. The most vulnerable children are those who face multiple risk factors. O'Brien, Weissberg, Walberg, and Kuster (2003) identify the most significant indicators of poor long-term outcomes for children as not living with both parents; household headed by a high school dropout; family income below poverty level; parents who do not have steady, full-time employment; family is receiving welfare benefits; and lack of health insurance (p. 23).

No one can deny that every child needs to feel loved and valued at home, at school, and in a community. Some children do enjoy secure childhoods that prepare them to meet the challenges of contemporary society, but many need additional support to navigate the confusing world around them. Although every adult was once a child, as early as the days of Socrates and Aristotle, adults have felt that the younger generation was "going to the dogs." However, past generations did not have to deal with a gap in understanding compounded by the complexities of today's society.

THE PERSONAL WORLD OF THE CHILD

The various social and cultural conditions discussed in this chapter can have a profound effect on a child's personal and psychological world. Maslow (1970) believed we all have certain basic needs that must be met for us to become "self-actualizing" and reach our potential in all areas of development (Figure 1-1). If our lower-level basic needs are not met, we will be unable to meet higher-order needs.

The first level of Maslow's hierarchy is physiological needs for food, shelter, water, and warmth. We might be tempted to pass these needs by and believe that children are fed well and have adequate shelter and clothes. However, we must consider the number of children who participate in breakfast and free lunch programs in schools, as well as the poor diets of some children who may consume an adequate quantity of food, but these foods do not satisfy their nutritional needs.

Maslow's second level is the need for safety. Some children feel afraid for their physical safety in their own homes and have cause for that concern. Parents who do not have their own needs adequately met may take out their frustrations on their child through physical or psychological abuse. Some

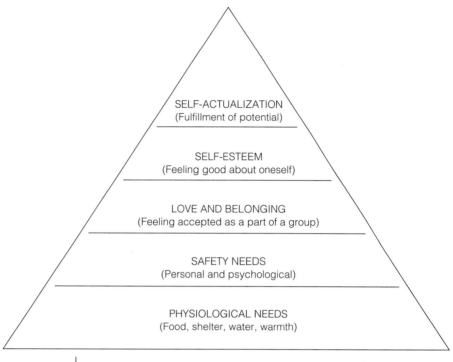

FIGURE 1-1 | MASLOW'S HIERARCHY OF NEEDS

adults who would not think of hurting children physically will psychologically abuse them with demeaning and damaging words. Children may receive similar treatment in school, where teachers may use children as a safe target for their personal or professional frustration.

Children are afraid not only of adults but also of their peers. Consider Antonio, who is small for his age, rather shy, and has few friends. As Antonio enters school one morning, several bigger boys tell him they will be waiting to get him this afternoon. Antonio cannot be expected to learn his multiplication tables with this problem weighing on his mind! Antonio's fear may not be limited to home and school. For some children, a high crime rate makes their neighborhood threatening. In addition, television news vividly portrays the dangers of natural disasters such as hurricanes, tornados, and earthquakes, as well as other all too prevalent acts of violence. Finally, the threat of war also seems ever present, and recent acts of terrorism threaten everyone's sense of personal safety.

Even if Antonio feels safe and protected, his learning or behavior may be influenced by the need to feel loved and to belong—the third-level need that emerges, according to Maslow, after physiological and safety needs have been met. Humans are social beings who want to feel part of a group, a need fulfilled by children's cliques, gangs, and clubs, as well as the family. Wherever we are, most of us want to be loved and accepted and to fit in with a group.

Antonio may not be getting positive attention from adults or peers, and he may think that no one likes him. Children sometimes hide their feelings of rejection or compensate for the rejection with antisocial behavior; either defense can hurt learning and personal relationships.

Perhaps children have the most trouble satisfying their need for self-esteem—the fourth need in Maslow's hierarchy. Children are ordered, directed, commanded, criticized, devalued, ignored, and put down. An adult treated like a child feels annoyance, inferiority, defensiveness, and anger and may rebel, fight, or leave the scene. Such responses are not considered acceptable in children. All people, adults and children, need to be respected as worthwhile individuals capable of feeling, thinking, and behaving responsibly. Children can be treated with the warmth and respect needed to encourage learning within firm guidelines and expectations. Adults can learn to avoid cruel and thoughtless remarks, reduce criticisms, and increase positive interactions with everyone.

Satisfaction of needs at the first four levels contributes to achievement of the fifth need in Maslow's hierarchy—self-actualization. Maslow (1970) states that a self-actualized person is moving toward the fulfillment of his or her inherent potential. Fulfilling this need implies that the child is not blocked by hunger, fear, lack of love or feelings of belonging, or low self-esteem. The child is not without problems, but has learned problem-solving skills and can move forward to become all that he or she can be.

According to Glasser (see Chapter 4), society is not meeting our children's needs, and thus children are failing in school and in life, unable to thrive academically and behaviorally. He lists five needs that both mirror and expand Maslow's work: (1) the need to survive and reproduce, (2) the need to belong and love, (3) the need to gain power, (4) the need to be free, and (5) the need to have fun. Glasser states that children's problems relate to their inability to fulfill these needs and emphasizes teaching reality, right and wrong, and responsibility.

Adlerian psychologists (see Chapter 11) believe that children often attempt to meet their needs in a mistaken direction. They suggest that adults examine the goals of misbehavior and redirect the behavior toward achieving more satisfying results.

Behavioral psychologists (see Chapter 9) see academic and behavioral problems as resulting from faulty learning; that is, the child has learned inappropriate ways of behaving through reinforcement or from poor models. Unlearning or extinguishing inappropriate patterns and learning more appropriate behaviors help the child succeed.

The interaction between the child and the world is obvious in all these approaches to the needs of children. Bronfenbrenner (1993) helps us understand that interaction with his proposal of an ecological systems theory of human development. This model categorizes the complex system within which a person exists and grows. Any person lives within nested systems that include an immediate environment with expanding connections beyond the home, school, and other settings. Bronfenbrenner calls the closest level of the environment the micro system, which is the activities and interactions in a child's immediate surroundings. He emphasizes that those interactions are bidirectional; for example, the parent's child-rearing practices affect the child, and the child's temperament affects parenting practices. The meso system refers to the connections between the immediate environment and other systems that support the child—for example, the parent's workplace. The exo system relates to social settings yet another step removed from the individual, such as health policy and unemployment. The outermost level of this model is the macro system, which is not a specific context but rather the laws, customs, and resources of the society in which the child lives. Bronfenbrenner delivers a comprehensive look at the many factors that influence childhood, as well as a way to categorize those variables.

Regardless of the factors contributing to children's learning, behavioral, and social problems, parents, counselors, and other professionals must assist and support children as they grow and develop in this complex, changing world. Understanding the process of development helps adults provide that support. The following section includes a review of developmental theories of cognitive, psychosocial, moral, and optimal development.

CHILD DEVELOPMENT

Children and adolescents bound through physical, cognitive, social, and emotional changes almost daily. A critical aspect in defining children's mental health is their successful movement through the normal developmental milestones. As noted earlier, other indicators of success are secure attachments, satisfying relationships, and effective coping skills. Development can be understood as periods of transition and reorganization—a lifelong process of growing, maturing, and change. One challenge in working with children is the different interpretations of behaviors according to different ages. LeVine and Sallee (1992) explain that one child may display certain symptoms at one stage of development and completely different symptomatic behavior at another stage. They cite an example of a child expressing anger with a temper tantrum at age 3 and with drug abuse at 13. Counselors must be steeped in knowledge of normal development to understand mental health in children. The following sections review just a few of those important concepts.

A CHILD'S COGNITIVE WORLD

Cognitive development refers to the thinking skills of the child. According to Jean Piaget (Piaget & Inhelder, 1969), children move to increasingly sophisticated thought processes as they progress through four stages (Table 1-1). These distinct patterns of thought occur in the stages of sensorimotor (birth to age 2), preoperational (ages 2–7), concrete operations (ages 7–11), and formal operations (after age 11).

The work of Piaget and Inhelder (1969) establishes that children from ages 5 to 12 may function in as many as three stages of cognitive development. Although age is no guarantee of a child's stage of development, 5- and 6-year-old children are on the verge of moving from the preoperational to the concrete

TABLE 1-1 | PIAGET'S FOUR STAGES OF COGNITIVE DEVELOPMENT

Stage	Type of Development	Age	Cognitive Traits
Infancy	Sensorimotor	0–2	Children: • Learn through their senses by touching, hitting, biting, tasting, smelling, observing, and listening • Distinguish between "me" and "not me" world • Learn about invariants in their environment, e.g., chairs are for sitting • Form language • Develop habits • Begin to communicate symbolically • Can distinguish self and other objects • Have the ability to think about things, and engage in purposeful behavior • Achieve a sense of object permanence • Begin trial-and-error problem solving
Childhood	Preoperational	2–7	Children: • Are not able to conserve in problem solving • Have greatest language growth • Are trial-and-error problem solvers who focus on one stimulus at a time • Can classify objects more than one way (i.e., by shape, color, size, texture) • Have trouble with reversible thinking • Prefer to learn things in ascending rather than descending order • Are egocentric thinkers • Are able to use mental images, imagination, and symbolic thought • Are capable of understanding simple rules—regarded as sacred and unchangeable

TABLE 1-1 | PIAGET'S FOUR STAGES OF COGNITIVE DEVELOPMENT *continued*

Stage	Type of Development	Age	Cognitive Traits
Preadolescence	Concrete	7–11	Children: • Have conversation skills • Can do reversible thinking • Have difficulty with abstract reasoning • Can appreciate views of others • Need concrete aids for learning • Move toward logical thought • Are less egocentric • See rules as more changeable • Can distinguish reality from fantasy • Have greater capacity for concentration, attention, and memory • Are capable of understanding that distance equals rate times time
Adolescence through adulthood	Formal	11+	Children: • Have no need to manipulate objects to solve problems • Are capable of abstract thought and scientific experimentation • Are capable of understanding and applying ethical and moral principles • Are capable of self-reflective thought and high levels of empathic understanding • Have a sense of what is best for society

stage of cognitive development, and 11-year-old children are moving into the formal stage. The counselor must know the child's level of cognitive development, particularly the degree to which a child is able to engage in abstract reasoning, a characteristic of the formal thinking stage. Children in the concrete thinking stage need explicit examples, learning aids, and directions. For example, the concrete thinker can walk through a series of directions but cannot draw a map of the same route.

Counseling methods need to be matched with the child's cognitive ability if counseling is to be effective. Piaget characterized the preoperational child's behavior and thinking as egocentric; that is, the child cannot take the role of or see the viewpoint of another (see Wadsworth, 1989). Preoperational children believe that everyone thinks the same way and does the same things they do.

As a result, preoperational children never question their own thoughts; as far as they are concerned, their thoughts are the only thoughts possible and consequently must be correct. When they are confronted with evidence that is contradictory to their thoughts, they conclude that the evidence must be wrong because their thoughts cannot be wrong. Thus, from the children's point of view, their thinking is always logical and correct. This egocentrism of thought is not egocentric by intent; children remain unaware that they are egocentric, and consequently see no problem in need of resolution.

Wadsworth (1989) adds that not until about age 6 or 7, when children's thoughts and those of their peers clearly conflict, do children begin to accommodate others and their egocentric thoughts begin to give way to social pressure. Peer group social interaction and the repeated conflict of the child's own thoughts with those of others eventually jar the child to question and seek verification of his or her thoughts. The very source of conflict—social interaction—becomes the child's source of verification. Thus, peer social interaction is the primary factor that acts to dissolve cognitive egocentrism.

Elkind (1984, 1994) explains ways abstract thought affects the adolescent. As they move into Piaget's stage of formal operations, young people can think logically, rationally, and abstractly (Paisley & Hubbard, 1994). Teenagers can combine facts and ideas to build an argumentative case, as well as multiple reasons to invalidate any contradictions. Elkind also discusses adolescent egocentrism. This self-centered nature of adolescent thinking may make communication processes difficult. One characteristic of adolescent thinking is the "imaginary audience," a concept involved in teenagers' self-consciousness that results from their belief that they are always at the center of everyone's attention. Public criticism can be devastating to a teenager. Another characteristic is the "personal fable"; that is, the belief that leads teenagers to feel invincible and immune from harm. That may lead to exaggerated expectations for self and unwise risk taking. Adults need to recognize these tendencies when working with adolescents.

Other theorists (Selman, 1976; Selman & Bryne, 1974) also offer explanations of a child's and an adolescent's perspective taking; that is, the capacity to imagine what someone else may be thinking and feeling. This ability supports important social skills needed to build and maintain relationships. In the first stage (ages 3–6), children have undifferentiated perspective taking. They may recognize that other people can have different thoughts and feelings than their own, but they confuse the separation. In social-informational perspective taking (ages 4–9), children comprehend that other people may have different information and therefore different perspectives. Self-reflective perspective taking (ages 7–12) involves children being able to step into another person's views and see their own thoughts, feelings, and actions from the other person's perspective. They also recognize that other people have the same ability. For third-party perspective taking (ages 10–15), children move beyond the two-person situation and can imagine how they and others are seen from the view of a third, impartial party. With the last type, societal perspective taking (age 14 to adult), people understand that third-party perspective taking can be influenced by systems of societal values. Thus, children move from a limited idea of what others might be thinking to a more differentiated view of the thoughts and feelings of others.

Hunt (1978) considers both the cognitive and the interpersonal dimensions of development in his work on conceptual level. He defines conceptual level as the increasing complexity of thought and the increasing interpersonal maturity indicated by defining one's self and others. A person in the earliest stage would have an impulsive, negative, and unsocialized world view and be centered on self. In Stage 1, a person is characterized by concrete, stereotypical thinking and personal motivation would be focused on what is socially acceptable or is dictated by authority figures. The conceptual level of someone in Stage 2 reflects being open to other people's ideas, being able to evaluate alternatives, having some tolerance of uncertainty, and possessing an increased awareness of emotions. Finally, a person who is in Stage 3 has a greater capacity for weighing alternatives, has concern for one's own ideas and for the ideas of other people, and can consider the effects of actions. An individual who is in Stage 3 also possesses enhanced problem-solving ability and is willing to accept responsibility. As they work with children, counselors should consider these developmental issues and be attuned to the stages of thought and perspective taking through which children move.

THE CHILD'S WORLD OF SOCIAL DEVELOPMENT

Psychosocial development relates to the attitudes and skills needed to become a productive member of society. Erikson (1963, 1968) and Havighurst (1961) have written extensively about these stages of human development. Erikson describes eight stages of human development from birth through adulthood beyond the age of 50. Havighurst, in a similar vein, describes expectations and developmental tasks over the life span. Effective counselors are well informed about human development and know how to incorporate this knowledge into their methods.

Using Erikson's (1963, 1968) and Havighurst's (1961) systems as a frame of reference, counselors can compare expectations, human needs, and developmental tasks across the childhood years. Table 1-2 shows developmental tasks and necessary interventions for each of the eight stages of human development. The two basic tasks are: (1) coping with others' demands and expectations that conflict with an individual's own needs, and (2) meeting these demands with the limited abilities individuals have in each developmental stage. Newman and Newman (2003) have extended Erikson's eight stages of human development to include three additional stages: prenatal, from conception to birth; later adolescence, from ages 18 to 22; and old age, from age 75 until death. They point out that theories of human development emerge and change because development is shaped by biological and psychosocial evolution within the context of cultural, environmental, and genetic influences.

To become a contributing member of the world, a person must build relationships. A way of understanding that ability has been provided by some other developmental theorists. John Bowlby (1969) introduced the concept of attachment when studying the bond between a mother and her

TABLE 1-2 | **DEVELOPMENT TASKS AND INTERVENTIONS FOR THE EIGHT STAGES OF HUMAN DEVELOPMENT**

STAGE I: BIRTH TO AGE 1$^1/_2$
Basic Trust versus Basic Mistrust

Task:
- Develop trust in their parents and environment
- Learn the world is safe, consistent, predictable, and interesting

Interventions:
- Children need responsive, affectionate, consistent caregivers who meet their basic needs in order to bond with others

STAGE II: AGES 1$^1/_2$ TO 3
Autonomy versus Shame and Doubt

Task:
- Gain a sense of self-control as well as control over their environment

Interventions:
- Children have gained trust, need to experience success in doing things for themselves
- Overly restrained or overly punished children develop a sense of shame and doubt

STAGE III: AGES 3 TO 6
Initiative versus Guilt

Task:
- Develop a sense of initiative as opposed to feelings of guilt about never doing anything right

Interventions:
- Children begin to set goals and take leadership roles in carrying out projects
- Parent should empower children by giving them choices and allow them to participate in family activities
- Unacceptable behavior is corrected in a loving, caring manner
- Discipline is based on logical consequences
- Expectations are realistic in order to prevent guilt and anxiety

STAGE IV: AGES 6 TO 12
Industry versus Inferiority

Task:
- Learn range of academic, social, physical, and practical skills needed in an adult world

Interventions:
- Encouragement and praise will help children achieve competence and be productive
- Nurturing can help children develop special talents and abilities

STAGE V: AGES 12 TO 18
Identity versus Role Confusion

Task:
- Develop a self-image, know who they are and how their roles will fit into their future

Interventions:
- Adults should make teens feel accepted as they develop their identity through group activities, work, or play
- Key questions are: "Who am I?" and "Where am I going?"
- period of exploration for further education, training, jobs, career, and marriage

TABLE 1-2	DEVELOPMENT TASKS AND INTERVENTIONS FOR THE EIGHT STAGES OF HUMAN DEVELOPMENT *continued*

STAGES VI, VII, AND VIII
Adult Stages

Tasks:
- Achieve intimacy through sharing a close friendship or love relationship in young adulthood
- Middle adulthood tasks are proper care of children and productive work life
- Older adults are concerned with ego integrity— acceptance of past life, a search for meaning in the present, and continued growth and learning in the future

Interventions:
- Must match young adult's counseling to learning style
- Adults may use concrete or abstract thinking in problem solving
- Issues in counseling often center on relationships, careers, and the search for meaning and purpose in life

infant. Bowlby states that the pattern of early attachment forms the basis for later relationships. Attachment relates to secure ties of affection. Attachment to another gives us pleasure and joy when we interact, as well as comfort in their nearness when we are stressed. Out of the experiences infants have with their caretakers, children build a set of expectations about the availability of attachment figures and the likelihood that those figures will provide support. Those expectations guide close relationships through childhood, adolescence, and the adult years (Bretherton, 1992). Bowlby (1988) suggests that a therapist becomes an attachment figure who inspires trust in a client. That relationship then would become a secure base for clients to explore themselves and their relationships with others. Lopez and Brennan (2000) suggest that counseling provides a place to learn ways to lessen negative attachment patterns and cope more effectively. Using those ideas, Corcoran and Mallinckrodt (2000) reports that, when clients experienced success, their functioning improved. Ainsworth (1989) discusses attachments beyond infancy and related care giving relationships to future friendships, kinship bonds, and intimate relations. Berk (2004) summarizes support for the importance of attachment relationships. Researchers (Bartholomew & Horowitz, 1991; Kirkpatrick & Davis, 1994; Shaver & Brennan, 1992) asked adults to discuss their early bonds with parents, their attitudes toward intimate relationships, and their actual experiences with romantic partners. Consistent with Bowlby's (1969) premise, the memories and interpretations of childhood attachment indicated relationship experiences. Three models explain different types of attachments. People who reported secure attachment had parents they described as warm, loving, and supportive. The adults considered themselves likable and easy to get to know. They were comfortable with intimacy and rarely worried about being abandoned or about someone getting too close to them. They talked about loving relationships in terms of trust, happiness, and friendship. Peers of people with secure attachments talked about competent, charming, cheerful, and likable young adults (Kobak & Sceery, 1988).

The two types of insecure attachments are avoidant and resistant. People who reported avoidant attachment described their parents as demanding, disrespectful, and critical. As adults, they mistrusted partners and had anxiety about people getting too close to them. They believed that others did not like them and that love is elusive. Their intimate relationships were apt to include jealousy, emotional distance, and lack of acceptance. Finally, adults who discussed resistant attachment characterized their parents as unpredictable and unfair. Those adults wanted to merge with their significant others. They worried about intense feelings overwhelming them and about being abandoned by those they love. Their relationships included jealousy, emotional highs and lows, and desperation (Berk, 2004).

Children must build relationships with siblings and peers, as well as with adults. These bonds also change over time. Toddlers have few social skills. Time with others involves playing side by side. As children mature, they learn the give-and-take of relationships. Children who can form close friendships have highly developed social skills. They can interpret and understand other children's nonverbal cues. They can respond appropriately to what other children say. They use eye contact and the other person's name and may touch the other person to get attention. If they disagree with a peer, they can explain why their plan is a good one. They are willing to forgo their desires to reach a compromise and may even change their stated belief. When they are with strange children, they observe until they have a sense of the group. Children without these skills tend to be rejected. They are withdrawn, do not listen well, and give few reasons for their wishes. They rarely praise others and have trouble participating in cooperative activities (Dodge, 1983; Dodge & Feldman, 1990; Putallaz, 1983).

Children with these relationship difficulties may have a negative sense of self. Broderick and Blewitt (2003) explain two main domains of self-concept: academic and nonacademic. Academic self-concept is divided into specific school subjects such as math, science, social studies, and English. Nonacademic self-concept includes a person's sense of self in the social, emotional, and physical realms. Different areas of self-concept emerge at different times in life. For children, the scholastic competence, athletic ability, physical appearance, peer acceptance, and behavioral conduct are the most important dimensions. Harter (1990) finds that people who have great discrepancies between their adequacy in a dimension and the importance of that domain experience a negative impact on their self-concept.

These brief descriptions of a child's cognitive, personal, and interpersonal development illustrate the multiple factors that must be taken into account in constructing healthy environments. Developmental psychology also provides a base for understanding the range of normal and abnormal behaviors at various times in life. Many professionals in the mental health field rely on those areas of knowledge as they work with children.

The Surgeon General (2000) discusses principles necessary for understanding children's mental health. First, professionals must acknowledge the complexity of all of these dynamics: the interactions within the child (biological, psychological, and genetic factors), the child's environment (parents, siblings, family relations, peers, as well as neighborhood, school, community, and national factors), and the way these factors interact. Therefore, the history of the child is crucial. Second, the report identifies the child's innate abilities to adapt. These "self-righting" and "self-organizing" tendencies allow a child to cope with the world. Third, the importance of age and timing in a professional's understanding of normality is stressed. Crying after separation from a caretaker seems normal for a 2-year-old and perhaps a disturbing symptom in a 10-year-old child. A final point is that the difference between mental health and mental illness often involves only differences in degrees. These guidelines help professionals by identifying factors for recovery, thus reducing a tendency to oversimplify. The guidelines also offer perspectives of multiple targets for intervention and highlight windows of opportunity during a child's development. Counselors will be well served to take advantage of those possibilities.

RESILIENCE

A promising line of research in child counseling revolves around the concept of resiliency. Rak (2001) explains that counselors often question whether to help clients overcome problems or instead focus on clients' strengths and resiliency. He provides some guidelines for focusing on resilience. In a comprehensive article, Rak and Patterson (1996) define resiliency in children as the ability "to continue to progress in their positive development despite being 'bent,' 'compressed,' or 'stretched' by factors in a risky environment" (p. 368). Benard (2004) summarizes this concept as the capacity all young people have for healthy development and successful living. Masten (2001), who has extensively researched the concept of resiliency, explains:

> What began as a quest to understand the extraordinary has revealed the power of the ordinary. Resilience does not come from rare and special qualities, but from the everyday magic of ordinary, normative human resources in the minds, brains, and bodies of children, in their families and relationships, and in their communities (p. 235).

According to Benard (2004), Werner and Smith (2001), and Masten (2001), our focus needs to be on the strength of people. They consider resilience as a natural drive, a self-righting tendency toward health not limited to any ethnicity, social class, or geographic boundary.

Benard (2004) states four categories of personal strengths are the positive developmental outcomes of resilience. She then describes the attributes within those groupings. Her explanation coincides with and summarizes the descriptions of other researchers (Rak & Patterson, 1996; Berry, Shillington, Peak, & Hohman, 2000; Canino & Spurlock, 1994). The four categories Benard (2004) proposes are social competence, problem solving, autonomy, and a sense of purpose. Characteristics of these qualities are discussed below.

Social competence involves the characteristics, skills, and attitudes needed to form positive relationships and to become attached to other people. The socially competent person has a friendly nature, the ability to elicit positive responses from others, and good verbal skills. These young people can communicate their personal needs in an appropriate way. They show empathy, compassion, altruism, and forgiveness toward others. In addition, resilient children receive affection and support from caregivers.

These young people have "good intellectual functioning" (Masten & Coatsworth, 1998) and are active problem solvers. They are proactive, intentional, and flexible. Resilient children use critical thinking skills and have the capacity to develop meaningful insight.

According to Benard (2004), autonomy concerns developing one's sense of self, one's sense of positive identity, and one's sense of power. Acting independently and having a sense of control over the environment are other characteristics of the autonomous child. Benard also lists the concepts of internal locus of control, initiative, self-efficacy, mastery, adaptive distancing, mindfulness, and humor in this category of personal strengths.

The fourth identified category relates to the sense that life has meaning (Benard, 2004). Resilient youngsters believe in a positive and strong future. That faith in the future has a direct correlation with academic success, positive self-identity, and fewer risky behaviors. Other distinctive attributes within this category are goal direction, creativity, special interest, optimism, and hope.

Benard (2004) argues these resilient characteristics are developmental possibilities of every individual. She supports her line of reasoning in a summary of research from several theoretical models that support these concepts as critical life skills. For example, she has connected the attributes of resilience to the basic needs described by Maslow (1970), to emotional intelligence (Goleman, 1995), to multiple intelligences (Gardner, 1993), and to Erikson's developmental stages (1963).

Resiliency tendencies can be augmented. Some authors (Benson, 1997; Garmezy, 1991; Hauser, 1999; Lowenthal, 1998; Werner & Smith, 1982) have studied resiliency and developed lists of protective factors or variables that act as buffers for the many children who overcome their difficulties to grow and lead well-adjusted lives. Families who enhance resilience have ties with caregivers and associations with friends and others in stable households. Young people in these families are helpful with appropriate domestic responsibilities. In addition, families who support resilient behavior have a faith that gives them a sense of coherence, meaning, and compassion. Communities enhance resilience when young people are able to make and keep friends, when the community values education, when there is structure and clear limits, and when there is positive mentoring at school and beyond (Lewis, 2006). The environmental characteristics in families and communities that support positive development can be summarized as caring and support, high expectations, and opportunities for participation (Benard, 2004). Lewis (2006) further describes these qualities as follows:

- *Caring and support*: A connection with at least one caring adult is the most important variable in fostering positive youth development. Those relationships provide stable care, affection, attention, social networks across generations, a sense of trust, and climates of care and support.
- *High expectations*: Adults recognize the strengths and assets of young people more than the problems and deficits. Adults see a youngster's potential for maturity, responsibility, self-discipline, and common sense. Adults provide structure, order, clear expectations, and cultural traditions. They value young people and promote their chances for social and academic success.
- *Opportunities for participation*: Young people have chances to connect to other people, to their interests, and to valuable life experiences. Youth can participate in socially and economically useful tasks. They have responsibilities for decision making, planning, and helping others as meaningful participants (p. 44).

Rak and Patterson (1996) provide a set of questions to guide counselors in uncovering the patterns of helpful habits that children have. Rak (2001) proposes that the counselor use this set of questions with follow-up responses to develop "an assessment that minimizes judgment, enhances salutogenesis [origins of health], and evaluates the client's life space, support systems, and capacity to endure and overcome" (p. 229). With this understanding of the child's historical pattern of resilience, counselors can provide interventions to reinforce those patterns. Counselors can also teach or model self-management and effective coping skills for problems and stressors. Rak notes that counselors who work with resilience in mind do not focus on arriving at solutions or resolving conflicts. Rather, that type of counseling emphasizes the "client's reservoir" of resilient behavior. Some possible ways for counselors to provide support to young people include: (1) role plays that help young people learn to express themselves; (2) conflict resolution techniques to help young people through interpersonal difficulties; (3) nurturing, empathy, authenticity, realistic reinforcement, and genuine hope from the counselor; (4) models of healthy interactions; (5) peer support interventions; (6) creative imagery; and (7) bibliotherapy (Rak & Patterson, 1996).

The resiliency approach to understanding children provides one example of looking at the positive attributes of human beings. Identifying coping mechanisms that lead to buffers for stress helps counselors promote healthy lifestyles. Likewise, the work of Rogers and Maslow (see Chapter 6) contributes to a view on positive, healthy development that allows counselors to take a perspective focused on strength when working with children, concentrating on what they can rather than what they cannot do (Nystul, 2003). Attachment theory (Bowlby, 1988; Ainsworth, 1989) also contributes insights into ways counselors can help children move toward full psychosocial development.

A thorough understanding of these strengths-based approaches will support effective counseling practices.

Although some children do have the resiliency to survive a poor home environment, a growing number have emotional, behavioral, social, and other problems that warrant mental health treatment. Resources for counselors and others who work with children are increasing; however, clinical, agency, and school professionals have felt frustrated because information about specific counseling procedures for developmental, learning, and behavioral problems has been limited and difficult to obtain. This book provides people in clinical, agency, school, and other counseling situations with suggestions for counseling children with specific learning or behavioral problems, as well as ways to support the mental health of children.

WHAT IS COUNSELING?

The American Psychological Association, Division of Counseling Psychology, Committee on Definition (1956), defines *counseling* as a process "to help individuals toward overcoming obstacles to their personal growth, wherever these may be encountered, and toward achieving optimum development of their personal resources" (p. 283). The following definitions have been adopted by both the American Counseling Association (ACA) and the National Board for Certified Counselors (NBCC):

> *The Practice of Professional Counseling:* The application of mental health, psychological, or human development principles, through cognitive, affective, behavioral, or systemic intervention strategies, that address wellness, personal growth, or career development as well as pathology.

> *Professional Counseling Specialty:* A Professional Counseling Specialty is narrowly focused, requiring advanced knowledge in the field founded on the premise that all Professional Counselors must first meet the requirements for the general practice of professional counseling.

These definitions were adopted by the ACA Governing Counsel in October 1997 and by the NBCC Board of Directors in November 1997 (more information is available via the Internet at www.nbcc.org/definition).

Atkinson (2002) summarizes other explanations of counseling. He identifies counseling as a profession that deals with personal, social, vocational, empowerment, and educational concerns. It is for people who are within the normal range of functioning. Counseling is theory based and structured. In counseling, people learn to make decisions and to find new ways to behave, feel, and think. Counseling includes subspecialties. Counselors may have roles in prevention, remediation, and positive development. The focus is on intact personalities, personal assets, strengths, and positive mental health regardless of the severity of the disturbance. Counseling is relatively brief and emphasizes person–environment interactions and the educational and career development of individuals.

TABLE 1-3 | COMPARISON OF COUNSELING AND PSYCHOTHERAPY

Counseling is More for	Psychotherapy is More for
1. Clients	1. Patients
2. Mild disorders	2. Serious disorders
3. Personal, social, vocational, educational, and decision-making problems	3. Personality problems
4. Preventive and developmental concerns	4. Remedial concerns
5. Educational and developmental settings	5. Clinical and medical settings
6. Conscious concerns	6. Unconscious concerns
7. Teaching methods	7. Healing methods

HOW DOES COUNSELING DIFFER FROM PSYCHOTHERAPY?

Distinctions between counseling and psychotherapy may be superficial in that both processes have similar objectives and techniques. Nystul (2003) suggests the main difference involves counseling exploring the conscious and psychotherapy examining unconscious processes. In addition, Nystul discusses more specific distinctions between counseling and psychotherapy, underscoring a differentiation in focus, client problems, treatment goals, and treatment approaches. Table 1-3 contains further information about these variations. Although this table summarizes some differences, those features are often lost in the common ground they share. The key question about each process rests with counselors and therapists, who must restrict their practice to their areas of competence.

WHAT IS AN APPROPRIATE WORKING DEFINITION OF COUNSELING?

Counseling involves a relationship between two people who meet so that one person can help the other resolve a problem. One of these people, by virtue of training, is the counselor; the person receiving the help is the client. The terms *counselor* and *client,* which some view as dehumanizing, can be replaced by words such as *helper* and *helpee, child, adolescent, adult,* or *person.* In fact, Carl Rogers (see Chapter 6) refers to his client-centered counseling approach as *person-centered.*

We see counseling as a process in which people learn how to help themselves and, in effect, become their own counselors. Counseling may also be a group process, in which the role of helper and helpee can be shared and interchanged among the group members. The group counselor then functions as a facilitator as well as a counselor.

Coleman, Morris, and Glaros (1987) credit David Palmer of the Student Counseling Center at UCLA with one of the best definitions of counseling we have found:

To be listened to & to be heard.
To be supported while you gather your forces & get your bearings.

A fresh look at alternatives & some new insights; learning some needed skills.
To face your lion—your fears.
To come to a decision—& the courage to act on it & to take the risks that living demands (p. 282).

WHAT COUNSELING CAN DO

Mental health incorporates the way we think, feel, and act; how we look at ourselves, our lives, and other people; how we evaluate and make choices; and how we handle stress, relate to others, and make decisions. Mental health exists along a continuum from good to not so good to poor. A person may be mentally healthier at some times than at other times. At certain times an individual may seek help for handling specific problems. A young person's performance on schoolwork, his or her success in relationships, and his or her physical health may suffer during difficult times. Mental health problems in children and adolescents may lead to school failure, violence, suicide, family distress, drug abuse, and a host of other difficult situations.

Counseling with children is a growing area of interest for mental health professionals. Developmental theorists have studied children's growth and development and the effect of childhood experiences on the adult, whereas child psychiatry has focused on seriously disturbed children. However, children with learning, social, or behavioral problems who are not classified as severely disturbed have been largely overlooked. Counseling can prevent "normal" problems from becoming more serious and resulting in delinquency, school failure, and emotional disturbance. Counselors can work to create a healthy environment to help children cope with the stresses and conflicts of their growth and development. Counseling can also help children in trouble through appraisal, individual or group counseling, parent or teacher consultation, or environmental changes.

The principles of counseling with children are the same as those used with adults; however, as discussed throughout this chapter, the counselor needs to be aware of the world as the child sees it and adjust his or her counseling procedures to suit the child's cognitive level, emotional and social development, and physical abilities. Each child is a unique individual with unique characteristics and needs. Childhood should be a time for healthy growth, for establishing warm and rewarding relationships, for exploring a widening world, for developing confidence in oneself and others, and for learning and experiencing. It should contain some fun and carefree times, and it should also provide a foundation and guidance for the maturing person.

What Specific Types of Assistance Can Be Expected from the Counseling Session?

Counseling generally involves three areas: (1) the client's thoughts and feelings about life at present, (2) where the client would like to be in life, and (3) plans to reduce any discrepancy between the first and second areas.

The emphasis given to each area varies according to the counseling approach used. Nevertheless, most counseling approaches seem to share the ultimate goal of behavior change, although they may differ in the method used to attain that goal.

Perhaps the most important outcome for counseling occurs when clients learn how to be their own counselors. By teaching children the counseling process, we help them become more skilled in solving their problems and, in turn, they become less dependent on others. In our view, counseling is a process of re-education designed to replace faulty learning with better strategies for getting what the child wants from life. Regardless of the counseling approach, children bring three pieces of information to the counseling session: (1) their problem or concern, (2) their feelings about the problem, and (3) their expectations of the counselor. Failure to listen for these points makes further counseling a waste of time.

Most problems brought to the counselor concerning children can be classified in one or more of five categories:

1. *Interpersonal conflict, or conflict with others:* The child has difficulty in relating with parents, siblings, teachers, or peers and is seeking a better way to relate to them.
2. *Intrapersonal conflict, or conflict with self:* The child has a decision-making problem and needs some help with clarifying the alternatives and consequences.
3. *Lack of information about self:* The child needs to learn more about his or her abilities, strengths, interests, or values.
4. *Lack of information about the environment:* The child needs information about what it takes to succeed in school or general career education.
5. *Lack of skill:* The child needs to learn a specific skill, such as effective study methods, assertive behavior, listening, or how to make friends.

In summary, counseling goals and objectives can range from becoming one's own counselor to positive behavior change, problem solving, decision making, personal growth, remediation, and self-acceptance. The counseling process for children often includes training in communication, relationship skills, and effective study; however, counselors choose the focus that seems most appropriate for the child and the child's situation. Some counselors prefer to work on developing meaning and purpose in everyday living, whereas others work toward solving specific problems (Figure 1-2). Of course, many counselors try to accomplish both ends. Conceivably, Child A could start at point −5 on both the x-axis and the y-axis and move toward +5 on both axes.

In counseling children in their middle childhood years (ages 5–12), for example, counselors may choose to work with problem areas in any or all of the quadrants represented in Figure 1-2. Some counselors prefer to work with the developmental and personal growth concerns found in Quadrant 1. The children in Quadrant 1 are solving their problems and seem to be finding purpose in living. They are sometimes referred to as stars because they get along

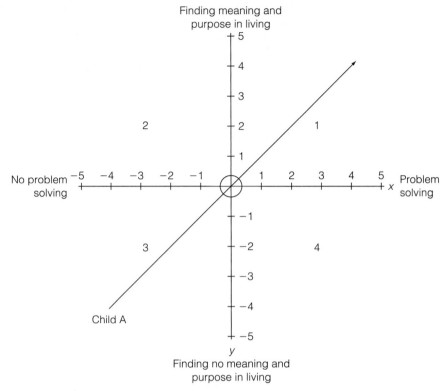

FIGURE I-2 | COUNSELING FOCUS SCALE

well with their friends, teachers, and family. Children in Quadrant 1 seem to have a winner's script for achieving their goals in academic, athletic, social, and artistic endeavors. Working with these children is often a matter of staying out of their way, helping them develop their full potential, and ensuring that they receive the appropriate teaching and parenting necessary for the development of their gifts and talents. This developmental model, emphasizing problem prevention over remediation, was pioneered by Herman J. Peters (Peters & Farwell, 1959), who encouraged counselors to focus on their clients' strengths as a way to facilitate their next steps up the developmental ladder. The developmental emphasis continues to be popular in counseling literature.

Children in Quadrant 2 find purpose in life but are not able to solve many of their problems. The counselor's role with these children is remedial in that counseling is directed toward establishing problem-solving strategies. Frequently, these children have good interpersonal relationships but experience problems with academic achievement and self-concept. They lack the success identity found in children in Quadrant 1.

Children in Quadrant 4 do very well with their everyday problem solving but do not seem to find life exciting or challenging. Frequently, these introverted children have little fun and few high points in their lives. A recent fourth-grade classroom discussion led by one of our authors on the topic "My High Points from Last Week" revealed that 20 percent of the class had difficulty finding one high point. Counseling plans for this group are more developmental than remedial in that they are directed toward building high points for each day of the child's life.

Children in Quadrant 3 represent the toughest counseling cases. They are not solving their problems, and they find little value in living their lives. Children in this group suffer from depression, have a very poor self-concept, and may be potential suicides. Frequently, no one really loves and cares about these children, and they have no one to love and care for in return. These children have experienced a world of failure at home and at school. Counseling with these children is a highly remedial process directed toward encouragement and, as in all counseling, establishing a positive, caring relationship between counselor and child. Once a helpful relationship has been established, the counseling focus can be directed toward building success experiences in the child's life.

WHO ARE THE MENTAL HEALTH PROFESSIONALS?

Those seeking help for children need to choose the counselor best suited to the child's and family's needs and the particular type of problem. Various people trained in the helping professions—counselors, school counselors, school psychologists, social workers, marriage and family counselors, counseling psychologists, clinical psychologists, rehabilitation counselors, child development counselors—work with children (Table 1-4). Their duties may include individual counseling, group counseling, and/or consultation in a school, agency, clinic, hospital, criminal justice facility, or other institutional setting. These counseling and consulting roles focus on assisting children with their personal, social, developmental, educational, or vocational concerns; collecting and analyzing data (personality, interests, aptitude, attitudes, intelligence, and so on) about an individual through interviews, tests, case histories, observational techniques, and other means; and using statistical data to carry out evaluative functions, research, or follow-up activities. A counselor can serve in an administrative role as the director of a school guidance unit or the head of an institutional counseling division or can be engaged primarily in teaching or research. The various types of helpers, the different licensure and degree requirements, the range of skills and responsibilities, as well as the diverse work settings can be found in Table 1-4.

Accreditation standards and state laws governing the certification and licensure of counselors and psychologists are moving toward requiring at least a 2-year master's degree, including a supervised practicum or internship. Doctoral programs also require additional supervised practicum and internship

TABLE 1-4 | MENTAL HEALTH PROFESSIONALS

Professional	Minimum Degree Requirement	Work Setting
Human service worker	Baccalaureate	Human service agencies
Juvenile justice counselor	Baccalaureate	Juvenile justice system
Child-development specialist	Master's	Community agencies
Clinical social worker	Master's	Private practice Community agencies Hospitals
Community agency counselor	Master's	Private practice Community agencies
Marriage and family therapist	Master's	Private practice Community agencies
Mental health counselor	Master's	Private practice Community agencies
Pastoral counselor	Master's	Churches Counseling centers Private practice
Rehabilitation counselor	Master's	Rehabilitation agencies Hospitals
School counselor	Master's	Elementary, middle, and secondary schools
Social worker	Master's	Community agencies Hospitals Schools
School psychologist	Educational specialist/doctorate	Schools
Child psychologist	Doctorate	University Private practice Community agencies Hospitals
Clinical psychologist	Doctorate	University Private practice Community agencies Hospitals
Counseling psychologist	Doctorate	University Private practice Industry Community agencies Hospitals
Counselor educator	Doctorate	University Private practice Industry
Psychiatrist	Medical degree	Private practice Hospitals

experiences. Doctoral programs generally require 5 years of study beyond the baccalaureate degree.

Many professionals use counseling skills in their jobs (for example, teachers use behavior-modification procedures; ministers and nurses use active listening), but using these skills does not make them professional counselors who have completed degree and credentialing requirements in their counseling specialty. Many states define and regulate the practice of counseling, psychology, and social work through certification (protection of title) and licensure (protection of practice).

The Council for Accreditation of Counseling and Related Educational Programs (CACREP), an accrediting body associated with the ACA, recommends a graduate training program including 48 semester hours of master's degree–level training and competency in such areas as human growth and development, social and cultural foundations, helping relationships, group work, lifestyle and career development, appraisal, research and evaluation, and professional orientation. Its recommendations for doctoral training build on these competencies and include additional internship experiences.

The NBCC administers the National Counselor Examination (NCE) as a component of the NBCC national professional counselor certification program. Special credentialing associations provide information about the recognition of counselors in many specialties, and state licensing boards regulate practice parameters.

SUMMARY

Children thrive when adults understand their world and respond appropriately. Recognizing the stresses of everyday life and acknowledging the impact of those problems will allow families, communities, and helping professionals to interact in supporting the mental health and optimal development of all young people.

INTRODUCTION TO A CHILD'S WORLD VIDEO

To gain a more in-depth understanding of the concepts in this chapter, visit www.thomsonedu.com/counseling/thompson to view short clips of an actual therapist-client session demonstrating a counselor relating to child's world.

WEBSITES FOR UNDERSTANDING A CHILD'S WORLD

Internet addresses frequently change. To find the sites listed here, visit www. thomsonedu.com/counseling/ thompson for an updated list of Internet addresses and direct links to relevant sites.

Annie E. Casey Foundation

Children's Defense Fund

Child Welfare League of America

Resiliency in Action, Bouncing Back from Risk and Adversity: Ideas for Youth, Families, and Communities

REFERENCES

Ainsworth, M. D. (1989). Attachments beyond infancy. *American Psychologist, 44,* 709–716.

American Psychological Association, Division of Counseling Psychology, Committee on Definition. (1956). Counseling psychology as a specialty. *American Psychologist, 11,* 282–285.

Annie E. Casey Foundation. (2005). *Kids count data book.* Baltimore, MD: Author.

Atkinson, D. R. (2002). Counseling in the 21st century: A mental health profession comes of age. In C. L. Juntunen & D.R. Atkinson (Eds.), *Counseling across the lifespan* (pp. 3–22). Thousand Oaks, CA: Sage Publications.

Bartholomew, K., & Horowitz, L. M. (1991). Attachment styles among young adults: A test of a four-category model. *Journal of Personality and Social Psychology, 61,* 226–244.

Benard, B. (2004). *Resiliency: What we have learned.* San Francisco, CA: WestEd.

Benson, P. L. (1997). *All kids are our kids.* Minneapolis, MN: Search Institute.

Berk, L. E. (2004). *Development through the lifespan* (3rd ed.). Boston: Allyn & Bacon.

Berry, E. H., Shillington, A. M., Peak, T., & Holman, M. M. (2000). Multi-ethnic comparison of risk and protective factors for adolescent pregnancy. *Child and Adolescent Social Work, 17,* 79–96.

Bowlby, J. (1969). *Attachment and loss: Vol. 1. Attachment.* London: Hogarth.

Bowlby, J. (1988). Attachment, communication, and the therapeutic process. In J. Bowlby (Ed.), *A secure base: Clinical applications of attachment theory* (pp. 137–157). London: Routledge.

Brazelton, T. B., & Greenspan, S. I. (2000). *The irreducible needs of children: What every child must have to grow, learn, and flourish.* Cambridge, MA: Perseus.

Bretherton, I. (1992). The origins of attachment theory: John Bowlby and Mary Ainsworth. *Developmental Psychology, 28,* 759–775.

Broderick, P. C., & Blewitt, P. (2003). *The life span: Human development for helping professionals.* Upper Saddle River, NJ: Merrill.

Bronfenbrenner, U. (1993). The ecology of cognitive development: Research models and fugitive findings. In R. H. Wozniak & K. W. Fischer (Eds.), *Development in context* (pp. 3–44). Hillsdale, NJ: Erlbaum.

Canino, I.A., & Spurlock, J. (1994). *Culturally diverse children and adolescents: Assessment, diagnosis, and treatment.* New York: Guilford.

Child Trends. (2005). Demographic characteristics. Retrieved August 23, 2005, from http://www. childtrendsdatabank.org/indicators/53NumberofChildren.cfm

Children's Defense Fund. (2004). *The state of America's children 2004.* Washington, DC: Author.

Children's Defense Fund. (2005). Moments in America for all children. Retrieved August 25, 2005, from http://www.childrensdefense.org/data/moments.aspx

Coleman, J., Morris, C., & Glaros, A. (1987). *Contemporary psychology and effective behavior.* Glenview, IL: Scott, Foresman.

Corcoran, K. O., & Mallinckrodt, B. (2000). Adult attachment, self-efficacy, perspective-taking, and conflict resolution. *Journal of Counseling and Development, 78,* 473–483.

Dodge, K. A. (1983). Behavioral antecedents of peer social status. *Child Development, 54,* 1386–1399.

Dodge, K. A., & Feldman, E. (1990). Issues in social cognition and sociometric status. In S. R. Asher & J. D. Coi (Eds.), *Peer rejection in childhood* (pp. 119–155). Cambridge, MA: Cambridge University Press.

Elkind, D. (1984). *All grown up and no place to go.* Reading, MA: Addison-Wesley.

Elkind, D. (1994). *A sympathetic understanding of the child: Birth to sixteen* (3rd ed.). Boston: Allyn & Bacon.

Erikson, E. (1963). *Childhood and society.* New York: Norton.

Erikson, E. (1968). *Identity, youth, and crisis.* New York: Norton.

Garbarino, J. (1997). Educating children in a socially toxic environment. *Educational Leadership, 54,* 12–16.

Gardner, H. (1993). *Multiple intelligences: The theory in practice.* New York: Basic Books.

Garmezy, N. (1991). Resiliency and vulnerability to adverse developmental outcomes associated with poverty. *American Behavioral Scientist, 34,* 416–430.

Goleman, D. (1995). *Emotional intelligence. Why it can matter more than I.Q.* New York: Bantam Books.

Harter, S. (1990). Causes, correlates, and the functional role of global self-worth: A life-span perspective. In R. Sternberg & J. Kolligian, Jr., (Eds.), *Competence considered* (pp. 67–98). New Haven, CT: Yale University Press.

Hauser, S. T. (1999). Understanding resilient outcomes: Adolescent lives across time and generations. *Journal of Research on Adolescence, 9,* 1–24.

Havighurst, R. (1961). *Human development and education* (2nd ed.). New York: David McKay.

Hernandez, D. J. (2003). Changing family circumstances. In R. P. Weissberg, H. J. Walberg, M. U. O'Brien, & C. B. Kuster (Eds.), *Long-term trends in the well-being of children and youth: Issues in children's and families' lives* (pp. 155–180). Washington, DC: Child Welfare League of America.

Hunt, D. E. (1978). Theorists are person, too: On preaching what you practice. In C. Parker (Ed.), *Encouraging student development in college.* Minneapolis, MN: University of Minnesota Press.

Kirkpatrick, L. A., & Davis, K. E. (1994). Attachment style, gender, and relationship stability: A longitudinal analysis. *Journal of Personality and Social Psychology, 66,* 502–512.

Kobak, R. R., & Sceery, A. (1988). The transition to college: Working models of attachment, affect regulation, and perceptions of self and others. *Child Development, 88,* 135–146.

LeVine, E., & Sallee, A. (1992). *Listen to our children: Clinical theory and practice* (2nd ed.). Dubuque, IA: Kendall-Hunt.

Lewis, R. E. (2006). Resilience: Individual, family, school, and community perspectives. In D. Capuzzi & D. R. Gross (Eds.), *Youth at risk: A prevention resource for counselors, teachers, and parents* (4th ed., pp. 35–68). Upper Saddle River, NJ: Pearson.

Lopez, R. G., & Brennan, K. A. (2000). Dynamic processes underlying adult attachment organization: Toward an attachment theoretical perspective on the healthy and effective self. *Journal of Counseling Psychology, 47,* 283–300.

Lowenthal, B. (1998). The effects of early childhood abuse and the development of resiliency. *Early Child Development and Care, 142,* 43–52.

Maslow, A. (1970). *Motivation and personality* (2nd ed.). New York: Harper & Row.

Masten, A. (2001). Ordinary magic: Resilience processes in development. *American Psychologist, 56,* 227–238.

Masten, A., & Coatsworth, D. (1998). The development of competence in favorable and unfavorable environments: Lessons from research on successful children. *American Psychologist, 53,* 205–220.

Newman, B. M, & Newman, P. R. (2003). *Development through life: A psychosocial approach* (8th ed.). Belmont, CA: Thomson.

Nystul, M. S. (2003). *Introduction to counseling: An art and science perspective.* Boston: Allyn and Bacon.

O'Brien, M. U., Weissberg, R. P., Walberg, H. J., & Kuster, C. B. (2003). Contributions and complexities of studying trends in the well-being of children and youth. In R. P. Weissberg, H. J. Walberg, M. U. O'Brien, & C. B. Kuster (Eds.), *Long-term trends in the well-being of children and youth: Issues in children's and families' lives* (pp. 3–26). Washington, DC: Child Welfare League of America.

Orton, G. L. (1997). *Strategies for counseling with children and their parents.* Pacific Grove, CA: Brooks/Cole.

Paisley, P. O., & Hubbard, G. T. (1994). *Developmental school counseling programs: From theory to practice.* Alexandria, VA: American Counseling Association.

Peters, H., & Farwell, G. (1959). *Guidance: A developmental approach.* Chicago: Rand McNally.

Piaget, J., & Inhelder, B. (1969). *The psychology of the child.* New York: Basic Books.

Putallaz, M. (1983). Predicting children's sociometric status from their behavior. *Child Development, 54,* 1417–1426.

Rak, C. F. (2001). Understanding and promoting resilience with our clients. In E. R. Welfel & R. E. Ingersoll (Eds.), *The mental health desk reference* (pp. 225–231). New York: Wiley.

Rak, C. F., & Patterson, L. E. (1996). Promoting resilience in at-risk children. *Journal of Counseling and Development, 74,* 368–373.

Selman, R. L. (1976). Social-cognitive understanding: A guide to educational and clinical practice. In T. Lickona (Ed.), *Moral development and behavior: Theory, research, and social issues* (pp. 299–316). New York: Holt, Rinehart and Winston.

Selman, R. L., & Bryne, D. F. (1974). A structural-developmental analysis of levels of role taking in middle childhood. *Child Development, 45,* 803–806.

Shaver, P. R., & Brennan, K. A. (1992). Attachment styles and the "big five" personality traits: Their connections with each other and with romantic relationship outcomes. *Personality and Social Psychology Bulletin, 18,* 536–545.

Surgeon General. (2000). Children and mental health (pp. 124–220). In *Mental health: A report of the Surgeon General.* Retrieved August 6, 2002 from www. surgeon-general.gov/library/mentalhealth/toc.html.

Wadsworth, B. (1989). *Piaget's theory of cognitive and affective development.* New York: Longman.

Weissberg, R. P., Walberg, H. J., O'Brien, M. U., & Kuster, C. B. (Eds.). (2003). *Long-term trends in the well-being of children and youth: Issues in children's and families' lives.* Washington, DC: Child Welfare League of America.

Werner, E. E., & Smith, R. S. (1982). *Vulnerable but invincible: A longitudinal study of resilient children and youth.* New York: McGraw-Hill.

Werner, E. E., & Smith, R. S. (2001). *Journeys from childhood to the midlife: Risk, resilience, and recovery.* New York: Cornell University Press.

THE COUNSELING PROCESS

CHAPTER 2

We shall not cease from exploration
And the end of all our exploring
Will be to arrive where we started
And know the place for the first time.

—T.S. Eliot, *Four Quartets*

The type of help counselors offer children may vary according to the model of counseling used. In simple terms, theories provide a way to organize and use information. Theories help counselors understand patterns of personalities and causes of difficulties. Theories explain behavior change and provide details about relationship factors, counseling goals, techniques, process, and hoped-for outcomes. Counselors use theory to make sense of their observations and to organize information (Gladding, 2000). The following chapters provide an overview of counseling theories, the foundation of a helping relationship.

Counseling theories often differ more in name and description than in actual practice. However, some counseling situations and some children are better suited to one approach than to another. Counseling is basically a learning situation, and individuals have their own favorite ways of learning.

WHICH APPROACHES TO COUNSELING ARE EFFECTIVE?

According to Seligman (2006), 350 counseling and psychotherapy forms have been described. However, these myriad systems can generally be classified in four intervention categories: thoughts, actions, emotions, and some combination of categories, referred to as eclectic or integrative systems. In comparison studies of the different systems of counseling and psychotherapy, no one system has emerged as consistently most effective. Rather, various counseling approaches based on different theories and emphasizing different methods have been found to be effective for a wide range of people and their problems.

How do we know if counseling is working? We know because the client changes. What contributes to that change occurring? Seligman (2006) states that all successful treatments have the following common ingredients:

- A helping relationship that is based on collaboration, trust, a mutual commitment to the counseling process, respect, genuineness, positive emotions, and a holistic understanding of the client
- A safe, supportive, therapeutic setting
- Goals and direction
- A shared understanding of the concerns that will be addressed and the process to be used in working on them
- Learning
- Encouragement
- Clients' improved ability to name, express appropriately, and change their emotions
- Clients' improvement in identifying, assessing the validity of, and changing their thoughts
- Clients' increased ability to gauge and change their actions, as well as acquire new, more effective behaviors to promote coping, impulse control, positive relationships, and sensible emotional and physical health (p. 11)

Seligman also notes that effective counseling promotes feelings of mastery, self-efficacy, realistic hope, and optimism.

Kazdin (2000) reviewed meta-analyses of child and adolescent therapy. He concludes that treatment appears to be better than no treatment, and the positive effects with children and adolescents are equivalent to the benefits obtained with adults.

Based on their review of counseling effectiveness, Lambert and Cattani-Thompson (1996) likewise found that counseling is more effective than no treatment, that the positive effects are lasting, and that improvement can occur relatively quickly. Those and other authors (Kazdin, 1994; Sexton & Whiston, 1996; Smith, Glass, & Miller, 1980) have found little evidence for specific techniques being consistently more effective than others. In fact, Sexton (2001), like Seligman (2006), supports the notion that common factors across counseling approaches contribute to effectiveness. Those factors can be grouped as support factors, learning factors, and action factors (Lambert & Cattani-Thompson, 1996). Support factors include variables such as a positive relationship with the counselor, a working alliance, warmth, empathy, and trust. Some of the learning factors are corrective emotional experiencing, affective experiencing, and assimilating problem experiences. Some examples of the third category, action factors, are gaining cognitive mastery, facing fears, and regulating behaviors. The understanding of those common factors can help counselors build essential skills. Their theoretical knowledge will allow them to use those skills wisely.

Training counselors in a variety of approaches has considerable support. Thompson and Campbell (1992), in a phenomenological study, surveyed 500 people on what type of self-help interventions they chose to alleviate mild depression. These interventions were spread fairly equally across affective, behavioral, cognitive, and eclectic categories, with a slight but significant preference for affective remedies. The authors attributed these results to the preponderance of women in the sample and to their expressed preference for affective interventions. Men, by contrast, tended to favor cognitive interventions. The study indicates that effective counselors should be able to adapt to the client's preferred learning style rather than expecting the client to adapt to the counselor's preferred counseling style.

An individualized counseling plan is usually superior, but it is possible only when the counselor can draw on a vast array of theories and techniques, an eclectic approach, and is not bound by any single approach. Lazarus (1989, 1997, 2000) recommends a multimodal, or comprehensive, eclectic framework for counseling that can be adapted to meet the needs of individual children. Lazarus developed his BASIC ID model based on a social learning model to describe seven ways people experience their world and some of the problem areas often treated in counseling related to his categories. The BASIC ID model is as follows:

> *Behavior:* This includes habits, responses, and reactions that can be observed. Examples of counseling problems in this modality would be concerns such as fighting, crying, inappropriate talking, stealing, and procrastination
>
> *Affect:* This arena refers to a variety of emotions and moods. Some of the resulting counseling concerns would be expressions of anger, anxiety, phobias, depression, loneliness, and feelings of helplessness.
>
> *Sensation/School:* This includes the basic senses of seeing, hearing, touching, tasting, and smelling. The negative aspects include things such as headaches, backaches, dizziness, and stomachaches; perceptual or motor difficulties; and for children, concerns about school failure or lack of achievement.
>
> *Imagery:* This category incorporates fantasies, mental pictures, and dreams, as well as images from auditory or other senses. Related counseling problems would be things such as nightmares, low self-esteem, negative body image, fear of rejection, and excessive daydreaming and fantasizing.
>
> *Cognition:* This category incorporates thoughts, ideas, values, and opinions. Children may come to counselors with problems such as irrational thinking, difficulty in setting goals, decision-making problems, problem-solving difficulties, or thoughts of worthlessness.

Interpersonal relationships: An area devoted to the way one interacts with family, friends, peers, teachers, and others. Related counseling concerns may be withdrawing from others (shyness), conflict with adults, conflict with peers, family problems, or difficulties with others.

Drugs/Diet/Biology: The final category focuses on health and medical concerns. Examples of problems counselors may work with include hyperactivity, weight-control problems, drug abuse, and addictions.

The Lazarus BASIC ID model covers most of the problems that counselors working with children, adolescents, or adults are likely to encounter and provides a well-defined eclectic approach to understanding and working with people seeking help.

Gerler (1990) and Gerler, Drew, & Mohr (1990) reviewed multimodal research, applications, and changes and cited considerable research support for this eclectic counseling method. Keat (1990a,b) specialized his multimodal writing on counseling children. He converted the BASIC ID model into the acronym HELPING:

H refers to *health* issues (pain and sickness).

E stands for *emotions* (anxiety, anger, feeling down).

L is for *learning* problems (deficiencies, failing, and sensory shallowness).

P stands for *personal relationships* (adult and peer relationships).

I refers to *imagery* (low self-worth and poor coping skills).

N is the *need* to know (despair, faulty thinking, lack of information).

G stands for *guidance* of actions, behaviors, and consequences (behavior and motivation problems).

After identifying the problem areas, counselors design interventions to strengthen weak areas before those areas become more serious problems. The counseling approaches presented in this book offer possibilities for helping counselors work with one or more of the seven areas presented in the BASIC ID model and/or the HELPING model.

CLASSIFYING COUNSELING THEORIES

One way to classify counseling theories is to examine how the practitioners of each theory encounter their clients. Some counselors focus on the client's feelings, whereas others intervene with thinking or behavior. Change in any one of these three areas is likely to produce change in the other two. Therefore, rather than a two-dimensional continuum, we propose a model showing the integrative relationship that exists among thoughts, feelings, and behaviors (Figure 2-1).

Counselors may also choose to work beyond the individual on a systemic level. At that level counselors may intervene with families, institutions, teachers, health care professionals, communities, or other systems that have an

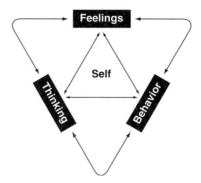

FIGURE 2-1 | CLASSIFICATION OF COUNSELING APPROACHES

impact on the lives of children. This book focuses on the point of intervention, classifying the theories and interventions presented in this book as follows:

Affective (feeling)

Person-centered counseling

Gestalt therapy

Behavior (behaving)

Behavioral counseling

Reality therapy

Brief counseling

Individual psychology

Cognitive (thinking)

Rational-emotive behavioral therapy

Cognitive behavioral therapy

Psychoanalytic counseling

Transactional analysis

Systemic interventions

Family therapy

Consultation, collaboration, teamwork

Our intention is not to isolate feeling, thinking, and behaving or systems. Failure to integrate feelings, thoughts, and behaviors is a symptom of schizophrenia, a diagnosis that describes a loss of contact with the environment, a split from reality, and a disintegration of personality. Rather, we attempt to describe how effective intervention in one of the three areas helps the individual integrate the other two areas into a more fully functioning lifestyle.

Counseling theories can also be classified as belonging to one of two broad categories. The first category focuses on observable events and data: behavior,

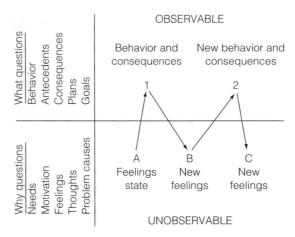

FIGURE 2-2 | FOCUS POINTS FOR COUNSELING INTERVENTIONS

antecedents to behavior, consequences of behavior, behavioral goals, and plans. The second category focuses on the unobservable events and data surrounding counseling: feelings, thoughts, motivation, and causes of behavior (Figure 2-2).

Category 1 counselors believe that if you feel bad at Point A (see Figure 2-2), the only way to feel better at Point B is to make a positive change in your behavior, which, in turn, leads to better feelings at Point B. Additional positive change in behavior leads to even better feelings at Point C.

Category 2 counselors believe just the opposite. If you feel bad at Point A, you need to work through these feelings and/or thoughts with your counselor until you have sufficient strength to make a behavioral change at Point A. You then examine the resulting thoughts and feelings at Point B for meaning and significance, which helps you to gather sufficient strength to tackle the next behavioral change.

Classifying the various approaches to counseling creates a framework for examining their similarities and differences. These approaches have a variety of techniques adaptable to learning style differences. The cognitive, affective, and behavioral classifications should help counselors provide children with appropriate counseling methods.

Attending to the points of intervention helps counselors make treatment plans. Counselors also need to pay attention to particular skills to allow the counseling process to succeed. Erdman and Lampe (1996) have identified critical adaptations to basic counseling skills when working with children. They urge for counselors to attend to the following issues:

- The child's developmental level of cognitive and emotional understanding
- The presentation of information that matches that understanding
- The utilization of concrete examples, hands-on activities, clear interpretation of rules, and careful explanation of consequences
- The recognition that the egocentric child will be unable to see another point of view and will not question his or her own thoughts or reasons
- The lack of a child's clarity about time, amount, and frequency

- The knowledge that recollections and expectations of the child may be distorted
- The reality that children often lack control over many aspects of their existence
- The acknowledgment that reluctance to change may be expected and may involve crying, silence, laughing, fidgeting, and fighting

To address these characteristics in counseling settings, counselors work to establish appropriate physical environments, build trust in the relationship, maintain a helpful attitude, and use questions appropriately (Erdman & Lampe, 1996). Additional information about these practices follows.

PREPARING FOR THE INTERVIEW

Effective counselors create a relaxed counseling environment and build rapport with their clients. The counseling environment should contribute to a client's feelings of comfort and ease. A cluttered, stimulating, busy room can distract children, whose attention is easily drawn to interesting objects in the room and away from the counseling interaction. Restless, distractible children may be affected by brightly colored objects, mobiles, ticking clocks, outside noise, or even darting fish in an aquarium. Inasmuch as counselors are part of the environment, you should also check yourself for distracting jewelry, colorful ties, or patterns in clothing that may affect children.

The furniture in the counseling room should be comfortable for both adults and children. We suggest that the counselor not sit behind a desk or table that can act as a barrier between child and counselor. Children see people sitting behind desks as authority figures, such as teachers, principals, and caseworkers. Keep in mind that children prefer chairs that are low enough to allow them to keep their feet on the floor.

Counseling seems to work better if children can control the distance between themselves and the counselor. Adults are often too aggressive in trying to initiate conversations with children. Children prefer to talk with adults at the same eye level; thus, some care needs to be given to seating arrangements that allow for eye-to-eye contact and feet on the floor. Of the various possible seating arrangements (Figure 2-3), two seem to be *least* effective: (1) having a desk between the counselor and child, and (2) having no barrier at all between counselor and child. The third arrangement, which uses the corner of a desk or table as an optional barrier that allows the child to retreat behind the desk or table corner or to move out around the corner when he or she feels comfortable doing so, is the preferred seating arrangement.

A thick carpet, comfortable chairs, floor pillows, puppets, dollhouses, and other toys to facilitate communication are also recommended for the counseling room. Many counselors conduct all of their interviews with children on the carpet in a play therapy room (see Chapter 14). Play media have developed a relaxed atmosphere with younger children, and some counselors employ large, friendly dogs as icebreakers, with child and counselor sitting on a rug and playing with the dog during the session (Burton, 1995; O'Brien, 1993; Trivedi & Perl, 1995).

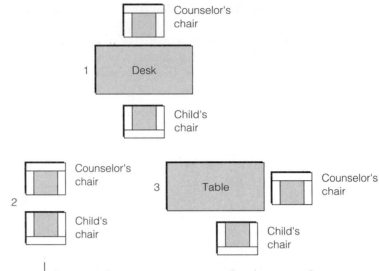

FIGURE 2-3 | SEATING ARRANGEMENTS FOR COUNSELING CHILDREN

Counselors should be models of promptness for scheduled sessions. Children (and adult clients) dislike being kept waiting. Tardiness may be interpreted as lack of interest or cause restlessness, fatigue, or irritability. The counselor should be free from distracting worries and thoughts and ready to devote full attention to the child. Children are extremely sensitive to adult moods and can recognize insincerity or lack of concern quickly. Many counselors reschedule appointments when they do not feel well rather than risk hurting the counseling relationship. If you have a cold, headache, or other minor ailment, you may want to admit to the child that you are not feeling up to par rather than have the child misinterpret your behavior as a lack of interest.

WHAT ARE SOME THINGS TO CONSIDER DURING THE FIRST INTERVIEW?

CHILDREN'S RESISTANCE TO COUNSELING

Children who are clients are still children, with their own feelings, behaviors, problems, and expectations of counselors. Like adults, children have fear of the unknown. To be frightened of new faces in new places with new activities and mystery outcomes is very natural. Children may not know why they are being taken to a counselor's office. In fact, parents or teachers may have given them misinformation that could result in mistrust of the counselor who does not meet a child's expectations. Questions children may have about counseling include:

- What is counseling, and why do I have to go there?
- Did I do something wrong? Am I being punished?

- Is something wrong with me?
- Do Mom and Dad think something is wrong with me? Do they love me?
- Will my friends think something is wrong with me? Will they make fun of me if they find out?
- Will it hurt? Is it like going to the doctor?
- How long does it take? When will I get to go home?
- If I don't like it, will I have to come back?
- What am I supposed to say and do? What if I say something wrong?
- Should I tell bad things about my family?
- Will the counselor tell anybody what I say?

Effective counselors understand the full range of fears, concerns, and questions children might have about visiting a counselor's office for the first time. In addition, children, as well as adults, naturally resist situations in which they might lose their autonomy or freedom to choose what they would like to say and do. When children are forced to do things, they become angry, resistant, and oppositional in an attempt to regain control. Children may also get angry because they view the trip to the counselor's office as unfair. They may think they are being blamed for the family's problems.

Children generally are not motivated to seek counseling. Children are drawn to pleasurable thoughts, feelings, and behavior and tend to avoid negative feelings, thoughts, and activities. A first visit to the counselor would ordinarily not be a favorite activity. The exception to the rule occurs in those elementary and middle schools that are fortunate enough to have talented counselors who lead regular group meetings with all of the students. Often in those inviting environments children refer themselves to these trusted counselors.

Children do many of the same things adult clients do to resist counseling, such as:

- Refuse to talk, refuse to share anything of importance, deny there is a problem, and/or talk about irrelevant topics
- Avoid any type of connection with the counselor such as eye contact
- Come late for or miss their appointments
- Exhibit negative body language and make hostile verbal comments
- Act out and refuse to cooperate (for example, hide behind the furniture)

The above list is certainly not exhaustive. People can be very creative in devising ways to resist anything, and counselors should rely on their own feelings as indicators of client resistance. Frustration and anger are common reactions counselors have toward uncooperative clients. Counselors need considerable patience and high levels of frustration tolerance to work with difficult children. Their major task is to get on the same team with their child clients and try to help these children find better ways to get what they want and need. Remember that resistant children are reacting normally, as anyone would do, to a strange situation and to someone who is trying to change them. Many children are not self-referred, and counselors are often viewed as extensions of the system that has been unhelpful and even painful to them. Resistant children are protecting themselves from the counselor's agenda, which they are unwilling or too scared to follow.

STEPS TO OVERCOMING CHILDREN'S RESISTANCE   The first step in the successful application of all counseling theories is the development of a good counseling relationship, a therapeutic alliance between counselor and client. The relationship-building process begins with the counselor as a person. *Friendly, warm, interested, genuine,* and *empathic* are the key descriptive words used to define successful counselors. For children, such a person truly listens and understands how they think and feel about things. Children view effective counselors as caring, protective, safe, and on their side. "On the child's side" means being the child's advocate rather than best friend. However, taking the role of a child's advocate does not excuse the counselor from maintaining the empathy/objectivity balance necessary for successful counseling. Effective counselors are also able to strike a healthy balance between adult–adult and parent–child activities in the counseling session. From transactional analysis (see Chapter 10), adult–adult activities are the problem-solving and decision-making parts of counseling; the parent–child activities are the nurturing and relationship-building parts of counseling. Finally, the counselor should offer children as many choices as possible to restore to them some of the control children might have thought they lost by coming to counseling; for example, allowing them to choose where to sit or what to discuss gives them a sense of mastery.

As a second step, as mentioned earlier, the counselor's office should seem like a friendly, comfortable, relaxed, safe place to be. Children find security in consistency, limits, and predictability. Counseling appointments should be regularly scheduled for the same time and day. Counseling time is the child's time. The appointment should begin on time and not be interrupted by phone calls or knocks on the door or any other disruption. Attention to these scheduling details makes children feel worthy and important. Counselors should set behavioral limits that can be enforced with logical consequences; for example, "the sand must stay in the sandbox, and sand play has to stop until the sand is swept up and put back in the box." Misbehavior is handled best by redirecting it to appropriate activity; for example, "People are not for hitting; punching bags are for hitting."

Third, children need to understand what counseling is and what they can expect from it. Some counselors prefer to ease the anxiety of the initial meeting by engaging in general conversation with the child for a few minutes. After initial introductions, the counselor may start to talk with the child about home, school, friends, hobbies, or other interests. For nonverbal or extremely anxious children, the first session or two may include play therapy. Through these methods the counselor can begin to build a good relationship with the child while learning something about the child's world. Other counselors prefer to go directly to the problem; for example, "Would you like to tell me why you have come to see me?" During the initial interview, the counselor should explain to the child the process of counseling and the counselor's expectations. The following is sample dialogue between a counselor and a child of middle school age:

COUNSELOR: Do you know what counseling is?

CHILD: No. [If the child answers yes, the counselor might say, "Tell me your ideas about what counseling is."]

COUNSELOR: Well, at some time during our lives, most of us have things that worry or upset us—things we would like to talk to someone about. It could be something that's going on at school, like another student in our class or our teacher; or it could be something at home, brothers or sisters, or maybe parents who don't really understand how we feel. It could be that we are having trouble with friends or we're confused about how things are going. We may have some thoughts or feelings that would be helpful to discuss with someone. A counselor listens and tries to help the other person work out these things. A counselor tries to think with that person about ways to solve these worries. Your job is to tell me whatever is bothering you. My job is to listen carefully and try to help you find ways to solve these problems.

The preceding statement is too long and wordy for children younger than 7. Counselors should adjust their explanations of the process to the developmental level of the child and use sentences with fewer words.

For children whom others have referred for counseling, the counselor can begin with a statement such as "Mrs. Jones told me that you were very unhappy since you moved here and that you might want to talk to me about it," or "Mr. Clifford told me that you would be coming by," and wait for the child to respond to tell what the trouble is.

In the first example, the counselor has informed the child that he or she is aware of the problem and is ready to discuss it. In the second example, the counselor is less directive, provides less structure, and allows the child to explain the problem, which may or may not be the one for which the child was referred. The counselor will want to consider the child's age, culture, and cognitive, social, and emotional development, as well as the type of presenting problem, before deciding which type of opening statement to use. The younger the child, chronologically and developmentally, and the more specific the problem, the greater the probability that the child will respond more readily to a structured approach.

Carlson (1990) prefers a direct approach for counseling "other-referred" children. For example, a counselor might say, "Let me tell you what your teacher shared with me that led to your being asked to see me." The counselor states the teacher's concern in a way that lets the child know that the counselor is there to help and not to punish. The counselor could say, for example, "Mr. Thompson is concerned about your behavior in class. He is afraid you will not learn all you need to know if you don't change what you are doing." Carlson (1990) also believes that counseling needs to be defined for "other-referred" children in language they can understand. For example, "Counseling is a time when you can talk to me about things that bother you. We can also talk about what we need to do to make things better."

Children need to know how much of what they say in counseling is confidential and what is not. Counselors are required by law to report any evidence of homicidal or suicidal ideation, child sexual or physical abuse, and child neglect. Counselors may say something such as "What we talk about is confidential or just between you and me unless I have to stop someone from getting hurt. I'll tell you if I have to talk to someone if you say something like that, and I will not tell anybody about anything else unless you say it is okay to tell something." These examples of what counselors might say can be modified to fit the situation, the age and maturity level of the child, and the counselor's personality. Of course, counselors may divulge any of the content of counseling that clients give them permission to report.

FIRST INTERVIEW GOALS AND OBSERVATIONS   Defining the counselor's role and the child's expectations provides the structure for an ongoing counseling relationship. During the first session, the counselor's main task is to build bridges between the child's world and the counseling office. Friendly, confident counselors who seem in control help children feel safe and secure in the new counseling environment. Counselors can begin by asking children what name they want to be called. Fun activities are helpful in getting the first session off to a relaxing start. A child who feels anxious about separating from a parent can have the parent join the activity. Serving a snack, reading a favorite story, and playing a game are good ways to reach the child. A parent may be included in all of these introductory activities. Some children, having been told not to speak to strangers, need assurance from their parents that the counselor can be trusted and that it is all right to speak to him or her.

If parents oppose counseling, children may feel disloyal if they participate in it or cooperate with the counselor. These children need reassurance that it is all right for them to work with the counselor. Children differ from adults in several ways that affect counseling and play therapy. For example:

1. Children, lacking elaborate adult defenses, regress quickly and easily into spontaneous and revealing play activities.
2. Children have rich fantasy lives that reveal their thoughts, feelings, and expectations.
3. Lacking adult formal thinking skills, insight, and verbal skills, children communicate through acting out their fantasies.

Once the relationship is established, the counselor can focus on how children conduct themselves in the counseling session. The counselor's work is to evaluate the climate of each counseling session. Was it happy, sad, pleasant, neutral, stormy, or productive? What seemed to set the tone? Next, counselors should look for patterns in the child's behavior or play. Children with attention-deficit/hyperactivity disorder (ADHD) act out their disorganization and impulsive behavior. Obsessive-compulsive children, by contrast, are rigid and structured in their play activities.

Children's choices of toys provide another rich area of data for counselors. Toys can be classified as passive or aggressive, masculine or feminine, and constructive or destructive; however, many toys may be neutral. Observe what the child does with each toy. Counselors search for themes and patterns in children's behavior and play therapy activities in the effort to learn the motivation directing their behavior.

More important than the themes uncovered in counseling is the intensity with which these themes are played out in the sessions. The play themes of unstable or disturbed children are more variable and unreliable.

Counselors' accurate reflection of content, feelings, expectations, and behavior helps focus children's attention on their actions and stimulates the self-observation needed to gain insight about their lifestyle and incentive to change. Play therapy methods are presented in detail in Chapter 14. The following six-step counseling model combines the best of reality planning with person-centered, active listening for children receiving general counseling or a combination of counseling and play therapy.

A GENERAL MODEL FOR COUNSELING

Counselors work to create an environment in which helping relationships can be formed. The work of Rogers (1957), Egan (1994), and Truax and Carkhuff (1967) support the concept of core conditions that set the stage for effective counseling. Those conditions include empathic understanding, respect and positive regard, genuineness and congruence, concreteness, warmth, and immediacy. Capuzzi and Gross (1999) also include cultural awareness as a critical condition of counseling. Empathic understanding refers to the ability to understand a child's feelings, thoughts, ideas, and experiences through the child's frame of reference. Respect and positive regard concern the counselor's unwavering belief in the innate worth and potential of each person and the counselor's ability to communicate that belief. Genuineness and congruence refer to the ability to be authentic rather than artificial in the relationship. Concreteness refers to the counselor's ability to infer complete pictures from a child's incomplete view of the situation. This ability helps clarify vague issues, focus on specific topics, and reduce ambiguity (Capuzzi & Gross, 1999). Warmth relates to being able to demonstrate caring and concern for the young person. Another core condition, immediacy, refers to dealing with things that emerge in the helping relationship, such as the child being angry at the counselor. Finally, cultural awareness relates to counselors being open and motivated to understand their own cultural, as well as the cultural diversity young people bring to their relationships. Using these core conditions will increase the likelihood of success for the counseling process that is outlined below.

STEP 1: DEFINING THE PROBLEM THROUGH ACTIVE LISTENING

The way the counselor listens to the child is important in building rapport. An open, relaxed body posture is the best way to invite a child to talk. It is often helpful to suggest a time limit for your interview, which should vary according to the attention span of the child. For example, saying, "Jimmy, we have 20 minutes today to talk about anything you'd like to discuss" sets an open tone and clear expectation. In fact, several 20-minute periods might be used to build a friendship with Jimmy. Individualizing the counseling process to fit each child you counsel is important.

When the child wishes to discuss a concern or problem with you, it is necessary to listen for three significant points: (1) a problem that has not been solved, (2) feelings about the problem, and (3) expectations of what the counselor should do about the problem. The counselor can assume the role of student and let the child teach these three topics, because people learn best when they teach something to another person.

Counselors have the responsibility of letting the child know what they have heard and learned as their clients teach them. For example, the counselor should periodically respond with a statement, such as "In other words, you are feeling _____ because _____, and you want _____." This feedback to the child is referred to as *active listening;* it promotes better communication and lets the child know you are paying attention. The active listening process continues throughout the interview, but it is most important in helping to clarify the nature of the child's problem. When the child confirms your response as an accurate understanding of the problem, counseling can move to the next phase (see Chapter 6 for a detailed explanation of the active-listening process).

STEP 2: CLARIFYING THE CHILD'S EXPECTATIONS

Counselors also need to let children know whether they can meet their expectations for counseling. The counselor probably cannot have an unpopular teacher fired, for example. However, counselors can inform children and their parents what they are able to do and let them determine whether they want to accept or reject the service available. If the service is rejected, the counselor may want to explore other alternatives with the family about where or how the child can obtain the service.

STEP 3: EXPLORING WHAT HAS BEEN DONE TO SOLVE THE PROBLEM

Counselors need to know about past attempts to solve the problem. Open-ended questions generally elicit the best responses. Counselors should avoid closed questions that yield one-word answers such as *yes, no,* and *maybe.* As noted in this text, many approaches to counseling avoid heavy questioning, and others rely on a predetermined series of questions. Statements often work better than questions; they empower the client by letting the client maintain the pace and direction of the interview. For example, rather than asking the child, "What have you done to solve the problem?" the counselor would say, "Tell me what you have already tried to solve the problem." Counselors may ask the client to list what has already been tried; if the child cannot write, he or she can dictate the answers to the counselor. The list becomes important if we want the child to make a commitment to stop behaviors that are not helping to solve the problem. It is helpful to explore the possible rewards or payoffs the child derives from ineffective or unhelpful behaviors. Change is facilitated when both the pluses and the minuses are examined. A profit and loss statement can be prepared to determine whether the behavior is actually worth the cost the child is paying. If it is not, the child may discard the behavior in favor of a more productive alternative.

STEP 4: EXPLORING WHAT NEW THINGS COULD BE DONE TO SOLVE THE PROBLEM

The next step could be a brainstorming session in which the counselor encourages the child to develop as many problem-solving alternatives as possible. Counselors encourage children to generate as many alternatives as possible and to withhold judgment until the list is finished. Quantity of ideas is more important than quality in this first step. Thompson and Poppen (1992) recommended drawing empty circles on a sheet of paper and then seeing how many circles the child can fill with ideas. If children are blocked from thinking of possible new ideas, the counselor can fill two circles with ideas as a way of encouraging the child to get started. After the brainstorming list is complete, children are asked to evaluate each alternative in light of its expected success in helping them get what they want.

STEP 5: OBTAINING A COMMITMENT TO TRY ONE OF THE PROBLEM-SOLVING IDEAS

After the possibilities have been listed and their viability considered, the client can decide on a plan of action. Building commitment to try a new plan may be difficult because the child may be quite discouraged by his or her previous failures to solve the problem. We suggest that the child not set impossible goals in this first attempt; the first plan should be achievable. Children do better if they are asked to report the results of their plan to the counselor. When plans do not work, the counselor helps the child write new ones until the child achieves success.

STEP 6: CLOSING THE COUNSELING INTERVIEW

A good way to close the interview is to invite the child to summarize or review what was discussed in the session; for example, the summary might include what progress was made and what plans were developed. Summarizing by the child is also helpful when the interview becomes mired and the child cannot think of anything to say. Because the process seems to stimulate new thoughts, summarizing at the close of the interview should be limited to 2 to 4 minutes. We also recommend asking the child to summarize the last counseling interview at the start of each new interview.

These counselor requests to summarize teach children to pay attention in the session and to review counseling plans between sessions; they have the effect of an oral quiz without the threat of a failing grade. The summary also helps counselors evaluate their own effectiveness. Finally, the counselor and the child make plans for the next counseling interview or for some type of maintenance plan if counseling is to be terminated.

QUESTIONS COUNSELORS ASK

WHAT DOES THE COUNSELOR NEED TO KNOW ABOUT COUNSELING RECORDS?

Most counselors keep some record of interviews with their clients. Notes that summarize the content of sessions and observations the counselor makes can assist in recalling previous information. Before deciding on a method of taking notes, counselors are wise to become knowledgeable about their state's laws regarding privileged communication and the regulations contained in the Buckley Amendment (the federal Family Rights and Privacy Act of 1974), which gave parents and young people of legal age the right to inspect records, letters, and recommendations about themselves. Personal notes do not fall under these regulations; however, for their own protection, counselors in institutional settings should become aware of the full requirements of the law.

Videotaping or audio taping counseling sessions is also common practice. This procedure not only provides a record of the interview but also aids counselors in gaining self-understanding and self-awareness. Counselors can listen to or watch their tapes with another counselor and continue to grow and learn by evaluating their own work. In addition, listening to and discussing some sessions with the client may promote growth. Written permission to record counseling sessions should be obtained from the child and the parents before any taping is done. Regarding use and storage of these records, reading state laws pertaining to privileged communication and the Buckley Amendment is advised.

When introducing a recording system to children, show them the recorder, perhaps allow them to listen to themselves for a minute, and then place the equipment in an out-of-the-way place. Occasionally, children are unable to talk when they are being recorded; most, however, quickly forget the equipment. Should a child resist being recorded, the counselor may wish to pursue the reasons for this resistance. If circumstances indicate that recording is inhibiting the counseling process, the counselor may choose to remove the equipment. At the other extreme, some children become so excited and curious about the taping equipment that counseling becomes impossible. Again, the counselor may prefer to remove the equipment, or a contract may be made with the child, such as "After 30 minutes of the counseling work, Mickey may listen to the tape for 5 minutes." It is usually best to give as little attention to the recorder as possible after a brief initial explanation of its purpose and uses.

HOW MUCH SELF-DISCLOSURE IS APPROPRIATE FOR THE COUNSELOR?

Children are often interested in their counselors as people. They ask their age, where they went to school, where they live, and whether they have children, and counselors are faced with the perplexing problem of how much personal information to share. Counselors who refuse to answer any personal questions run the risk of hurting the counseling relationship or being viewed as a mysterious figure, bringing forth more questions. If counselors answer all personal questions, however, the interview time may center on the counselor rather than the client.

A general guideline might be to share some personal information (favorite sport or TV show, number of children) and, when the questions become too personal or continue too long, reflect to the child, "You seem to be very interested in me personally," and explore the child's curiosity. Understanding the child's interest in the counselor could promote understanding of the child as a person. Questioning the counselor can be a defense for children who wish to avoid discussing their own problems.

A second problem concerning self-disclosure relates to the counselor's feelings and emotions. Counselor training programs are founded on the assumption that people are unique, capable of growth, and worthy of respect. These programs focus on listening and responding to clients with empathic understanding and respect. The programs also emphasize being genuine; however, genuineness is often interpreted as showing only genuine *positive* emotions and feelings. Counselor trainees are sometimes quite surprised when their supervisors encourage them to admit to the client their negative feelings, such as frustration or anger. Obviously, admitting emotions does not mean attacking and degrading the client; rather, it means admitting that the counselor is a person with feelings and is frustrated or angry over what is occurring ("I am really frustrated that we seem to be talking about everything except what happened with your friend today").

The counselor's proper level of self-disclosure is a controversial issue in the profession. Some feel comfortable being completely open and honest about their feelings (high levels of self-disclosure); others think such openness interferes with the counselor–client relationship and prefer low levels of self-disclosure. However, most counselors agree that self-disclosure is not "true confessions." Poppen and Thompson (1974) have summarized the arguments on both sides of the issue. The principal arguments in favor of high levels of self-disclosure are as follows:

1. Counselors who are open and honest about their thoughts and feelings encourage similar behavior by their clients.
2. Knowing that the counselor has had similar adjustment problems helps clients feel more at ease to discuss their own problems.
3. Children learn by imitation and can learn to solve their own problems through hearing about the experiences of others.
4. Counselors could be models for behavior.

On the other side of the issue, those opposing high levels of self-disclosure claim the following:

1. Clients are in the counselor's office for help with their problems, not to hear about the counselor's problems.
2. Counseling could become a time for sharing gripes or problems, rather than a working session for personal growth.
3. Counselors can lose objectivity if they identify too strongly with the child's concerns.

According to Poppen and Thompson (1974), self-disclosure is more beneficial when it takes a here-and-now focus—that is, when self-disclosure becomes an open and authentic expression of the counselor's or student's (child's) thoughts and feelings experienced at a particular time. Self-disclosure, when examined in the here-and-now context, means much more than dredging up the dark secrets of the past (p. 15).

WHAT TYPES OF QUESTIONS SHOULD THE COUNSELOR USE?

Adults often think they must ask children several questions to get the "whole story." Usually, these questions are of the "who," "what," "when," "where," and "what did you do next" variety. These questions may or may not be asked for the purpose of helping the child or for clarification; too often they arise out of general curiosity. Some questions may even be irrelevant and interrupt or ignore the child's thoughts and expressions. Questions can also be used to judge, blame, or criticize. For example:

CHILD: The teacher called me a dummy in front of the whole class today!

ADULT: (sarcastically) What did you say this time to make him call you that?

At that particular moment, the important fact is not what the child said, but that the child was embarrassed, hurt, and possibly angered. By listening and understanding feelings and expressions rather than probing for details of who said what and when, the adult will get the whole story eventually and maintain a much friendlier relationship with the child. Counselors who listen and respond with understanding often learn the child's important thoughts or problems. In other words, questions rephrased as statements work better. Some counselors, in their efforts to help the child, take over the counseling interview.

Counselors who direct the interview risk missing important feelings and thoughts. The counselor may guide the conversation in a totally meaningless direction. For example:

CHILD: I hate my brother.

COUNSELOR: Why do you hate your brother?

CHILD: Because he's mean.

COUNSELOR: How is he mean?

CHILD: He hits me.

COUNSELOR: What do you do to make him hit you? [accusation]

CHILD: Nothing.

COUNSELOR: Come on, now. Tell me about when he hits you—and what your mother does when he hits you.

This example sounds more like an inquisition than a counseling session. The hitting and what the mother does may or may not be what is really troubling the child. What could be more important is the feeling that exists between the child and her brother. Is it really "hate" because he hits her, or could there be other problems in the relationship that the counselor will miss by focusing on hitting rather than listening to the child tell about her relationship with her brother? It is also possible that "hating her brother" could have been a test problem to determine whether the counselor really would listen and be understanding. A counselor who guides the interview by questions could overlook the true problem entirely.

In the preceding example, the child answered the counselor's questions but offered no further information. Children easily fall into the role of answering adults' questions and then waiting for the next question. Rather than being a listener and helper, the counselor assumes the role of inquisitor. Once this pattern has been established, the interview may die when the counselor runs out of questions.

Obviously, there are times in counseling when direct questions should be asked. The counselor may need factual information or clarification. However, counselors can probably get more information from children with open-ended questions. An open-ended question does not require a specific answer. It encourages the child to give the counselor more information about the topic, but does not restrict replies or discourage further communication in the area. Suppose a counselor was interested in learning about a child's social relationships. Rather than asking the direct, closed question "Do you have friends?" the counselor might elicit more information about the child's social relationships by saying, "Tell me what you like to do for fun—things that you enjoy doing in your free time." In this way, the counselor could learn not only about friends but possibly also about the child's sports interests, hobbies, and other activities (or lack of activities).

Another open-ended question that might help the counselor understand what is going on in the child's life is "Tell me about your family," out of which could come answers to such unasked questions as "Do both your mother and father live in the home?" "How many people live in the household?" "What are your feelings about various members of the household?" One further point should be made about questioning in counseling. Adults should be careful about the use of "why" questions with youth because they are associated with blame; "Why did you do that?" is often interpreted in the mind of a child as "Why did you do a *stupid thing* like that?" These questions put people on the defensive; when asked why we acted a certain way, we feel forced to find some logical reason or excuse for our behavior. Glasser (see Chapter 4) suggests that a better question might be a "what" question. Most of us are not really sure *why* we behaved a certain way, but we can tell *what* occurred. A "what" question does not deal with possible unconscious motives and desires, but rather focuses on present behavior; the client and counselor can look at what is happening now and what can be done.

Garbarino and Stott (1989) remind counselors that effective questions must be appropriate for the developmental level of their clients. They make the following suggestions for interviewing preschoolers and probably most elementary school-aged children:

- Use sentences that do not exceed by more than five words the number of words in a sentence the child uses.
- Use names rather than pronouns.
- Use the child's terms.
- Do not ask, "Do you understand?" Ask the child to repeat your message.
- Do not repeat questions children do not understand because they may think they have made errors and attempt to "correct" their answers. Rephrase the question instead.
- Avoid time-sequence questions.
- Preschoolers, being very literal, may give us answers that are easy to over-interpret.
- Do not respond to every answer with another question. A short summary or acknowledgment encourages the child to expand on his or her previous statement.

In summary, counselors learn more by listening and summarizing than by questioning. The habit of questioning is difficult to break. When tempted to question, counselors might first ask themselves whether the questions they ask will (1) contribute therapeutically to understanding the child and the child's problems, or (2) inhibit the further flow of expression.

How Can Silences Be Used in Counseling?

Most of us are uncomfortable with silences. We have been socially conditioned to keep the conversation going; when conversation begins to ebb, we search through our thoughts for a new topic of interest to introduce to the group. Although silences can be very productive in a counseling interview, counselors may rush to fill the pauses. However, a child may need a few moments of silence to sort out thoughts and feelings. The child may have related some very emotional event or thought and may need a moment of silence to think about this revelation or regain composure. The child or the counselor may have behaved or spoken in a confusing manner, and sorting things out may take time and silence.

Silences can be used for problem solving, and therefore be productive, but how long should the counselor allow the silence to last? Obviously, an entire session of silence between child and counselor is not likely to be helpful. The child may spontaneously begin to speak again when ready. Children's nonverbal behavior may provide counselors with clues that they are ready to begin. The counselor may test the water by making a quiet statement reflecting the possible cause of the silence; for example, "You seem a little confused about what you just told me." The child's response to this reflection should indicate whether he or she is ready to proceed.

Should Counselors Give Advice?

The role of a counselor has often been interpreted as an advice giver, and some counseling theorists advocate giving advice to clients. Their rationale is that the counselor, who is trained in helping and is more knowledgeable, should advise the less knowledgeable client.

We prefer to view the role of the counselor as using skills and knowledge to assist another person in solving his or her own problems or conflicts. Counselors who believe in the uniqueness, worth, dignity, and responsibility of the individual and who believe that, given the right conditions, individuals can make correct choices for themselves are reluctant to give advice on solving life's problems. Instead, they use their counseling knowledge and skills to help clients make responsible choices of their own and, in effect, learn how to become their own counselor. An illustration of the difference between giving advice and assisting in problem solving may clarify the point. Consider the following example: Tony was threatened by neighborhood bullies who were going to beat him up on the way home from school. Tony confided his fear of fighting to the counselor, who advised him to talk this over with his parents. Even though Tony was reluctant to talk to his parents, the counselor persuaded him they would understand and help. Tony returned later to relate that his father lectured him for being a "sissy" and instructed him to "go out and fight like a man." Tony was more terrified than ever because neither his parents nor the counselor understood his dilemma or could be counted on to support him. In this case, the counselor, not considering the client's home and culture, gave advice that intensified the problem. The counselor might have been more helpful by assisting Tony to think of ways of solving the problem—ways that Tony would choose.

Another possible disadvantage of counselors' advice is the problem of dependency. Counselors want their clients to become responsible individuals capable of solving their own problems. Children have a multitude of adults telling them how and when to act, but only a few assist them to learn responsible problem-solving behavior. In counseling, children learn the problem-solving process; they learn that they do not have to depend entirely on adults to make all their decisions for them. The process can develop confident, mature, and independent individuals moving toward self-actualization.

This conflict is analogous to the typical adolescent struggle for independence. Because many people see the counselor's role as that of advice giver, some clients may become frustrated and angry when counselors will not give advice. Talking about the role of the counselor and working with the client to negotiate realistic expectations may ease the tension and assist in building a working alliance with the client.

When asked what they think they could do to work out the conflict or problem, children typically are unable to think of possible solutions. It is a new experience for many children to be involved in solving their own problems. When pressed to give advice, a counselor could reflect the feeling that the child is not sure what to do and would like to have an answer, and then suggest again that they explore possibilities together. If the child is persistent and demands an answer, the counselor may wish to explore the reasons for this demand.

We need to point out, however, that counselors have a duty to protect their clients from any harm they might do to themselves, as well as to prevent them from harming others. Therefore, counselors may need to give advice in emergency situations and to act on the advice they give.

SHOULD COUNSELORS GIVE INFORMATION?

Beginning counselors, believing that giving information is the same as giving advice, often give neither. Clients need good information to make good decisions, and counselors help clients by sharing what good information they have. For example, counselors should inform their clients of community and school resources where clients can receive assistance. The decision to seek assistance should be the client's. In other words, advice often takes the form of a suggestion to perform a certain behavior or to take some course of action. Giving information, however, means providing data, facts, general knowledge, and to some extent, alternatives.

Two primary causes of problems are lack of information about oneself and the environment. The counselor's role is to help clients find the information they need to solve their problems. Once again, we believe the more actively that clients seek their own information, the better their learning experience.

HOW DOES THE COUNSELOR KEEP THE CLIENT ON TASK DURING THE COUNSELING SESSION?

Children soon discover that the counselor is a good listener who gives them undivided attention. Because many children are not listened to by adults, they often take advantage of the counseling situation to talk about everything except the reason for coming to counseling. With the least suggestion, the counselor may find the child rambling on about a TV show, last night's ball game, a current movie, tricks a pet dog can do, or any number of other irrelevant topics. Children, like adults, can ramble excessively when they wish to avoid a problem. Talkativeness then becomes a diversionary tactic either to avoid admitting what is troubling them or to avoid coping with the conflict. The conflict could be too traumatic or painful to face.

Another possible reason for losing focus in a counseling session is that children do not understand their role in the counseling interview. If the purpose of counseling and expectations of the people involved are clearly defined in the initial interview, pointless chatting is less likely.

Counselors who discover themselves being led into superficial or rambling conversations may want to bring the conversation back to the problem at hand by reflecting to the child, "We seem to be getting away from the reason for our time together. I wonder if you could tell me more about . . ." If a child consistently wanders, state that you notice the wandering and then explore possible reasons for the avoidance. A tape recorder can be an excellent means of determining when, how, and why the distractions occur. A contract might be drawn up, such as [The counselor] and I will work on [the problem] for 25 minutes. I can talk to [the counselor] about anything else for the last 5 minutes."

WHAT LIMITS SHOULD BE SET IN COUNSELING?

In training, most counselors are taught to be empathic, respectful, genuine, accepting, and nonjudgmental—characteristics that writers such as Carl Rogers and Robert Carkhuff define as essential for a facilitative counseling relationship. Counselors may follow many other theories during the counseling process, but most believe that establishing a therapeutic relationship based on these ingredients is a necessary first step for effective counseling. Based on their synthesis of outcome literature, Orlinsky, Grawe, and Parks (1994) conclude that the counseling relationship is the best predictor of counseling outcome and is critical to its success. The characteristics of empathy, respect, and genuineness have been operationally defined by Carkhuff (1969), and many training institutions teach counselors these behaviors according to his model.

Being accepting and nonjudgmental can be difficult for some counselors, especially regarding moral and ethical issues. Counselors are human beings with their own attitudes, values, and beliefs. Remaining open-minded enough to really hear the client's entire story is difficult if the client's values and those of the counselor conflict.

Being nonjudgmental does not mean that anything goes. Rather, it is withholding those judgments we ordinarily make and allowing clients to tell the whole story without the young person being threatened by the counselor's condemnation. Counselors attempt to refrain from blaming, accusing, criticizing, and moralizing, but they also attempt to teach responsible, reality-oriented behavior to their child clients. The counselor does not tell children they are wrong; the counselor's job is to help children explore the consequences, advantages, and disadvantages of their choices and, perhaps, discover better methods of resolving the conflict. For instance, rather than sermonizing to Tony that fighting is wrong, the counselor might be more helpful by thinking with him about what would happen if he challenged the bully to a fight and whether he could gain his father's acceptance and respect in other ways.

In summary, accepting and nonjudgmental attitudes are essential for good counseling, but they must be combined with respect for the rights of others, the reality of the situation, and responsibility for one's own behavior.

WHAT ABOUT THE ISSUE OF CONFIDENTIALITY?

Most counselors have been taught that whatever is said in a counseling interview should remain confidential unless there is danger to the client or to another person or if there is suspicion of child abuse. As noted earlier, counselors explain the principle of confidentiality to their clients during the first interview. If information indicating danger to a person is revealed during later interviews, counselors remind children of the counselor's obligation to report such danger to the proper authorities. Counselors do not have privileged communication in their counselor–client relationships unless they are licensed by a state regulatory board. Counselors' records can be subpoenaed, and counselors can be called to testify in court proceedings should the information they possess be deemed necessary for a court decision. If counselors think that revealing the information required in their testimony could harm the child, they can request a private conference with the judge to share both the information and their reasons for wanting to keep the information confidential. See Chapter 20 for more information on confidentiality and privileged communication.

Some counselors maintain that children and adults should be encouraged to communicate more openly and that the counselor can facilitate this process in the family counseling interview. They further contend that parents and other adults can provide insight and needed information about the child; the significant adult in the child's life can become a cocounselor. A signed contract with the parents to protect the confidentiality of the child's counseling sessions, although not legally binding, may establish the privacy of the communication. Talking with the parent about the counseling relationship may also allow the counselor opportunities to involve the parent in the out-of-session activities of the client, such as homework assignments or information gathering.

Careful evaluation of the child's presenting problem and the adults involved may help the counselor decide whether strict confidentiality should be maintained or others should be included. The decision to include others or share information should always be discussed with the child to avoid misunderstandings and to maintain the trust necessary for the counseling relationship. The child may agree and, in fact, lead the discussions.

IS THIS CHILD TELLING ME THE TRUTH?

Another counseling problem is whether the child is telling the counselor the truth or enhancing or exaggerating to get attention or sympathy. Children may tell their counselors about extraordinary events such as seeing people shoot one another, raging fires, and robberies. Unfortunately, many of these stories are true; however, children have vivid imaginations, and it is sometimes difficult to know how much to believe. Children may feel they have to tell of major difficulties to keep the counselor interested. Counselors can ask for more details of the incident (for example, by saying, "Tell me more"), which might clarify whether the story is truth or fiction. When asked to give specifics, children may admit they were "only kidding" or "making it up." Counselors might also admit their genuine concerns: "I am really having trouble with this because I have never heard anything like it." An admission of this sort by a counselor expresses a genuine feeling and avoids labeling the child a liar or possibly denying a true story. It also provides the child with an opportunity to change the story while saving face.

WHAT CAN BE DONE WHEN THE INTERVIEW PROCESS BECOMES BLOCKED?

In some counseling sessions the child does not feel like talking. It is possible that things have been going well for the past few days and the child really has nothing to discuss. There may be a lull before new material is introduced. One way to avoid these unexpected empty periods is to be prepared for a session. Some counselors have general goals for their client (for instance, to increase social skills) and also define specific short-term goals for each session as counseling proceeds. Regardless of whether the counselor prefers to define objectives, notes of the previous session can be reviewed and a tentative plan made for the coming interview. Obviously, this plan is subject to change according to the content of the interview.

When the child seems highly distracted, a short summary by the counselor or child of the previous conversation may stimulate further communication. If the child does not seem to want to talk, the techniques of play therapy (drawing, clay, games) may be beneficial. At certain times (for example, because of illness, extreme excitability, or apathy) ending the session short of the designated time is best. The length of counseling sessions can vary from a few minutes to an hour, depending on the client's age and presenting problem.

When sessions become blocked, evaluate what is happening. Again, the tape recorder assists in assessing the lack of progress. Blocking may be a sign that the child is ready for the counseling to conclude. It could be resistance on the part of the child. It could come from the counselor's inadequate skills or lack of planning.

Unproductive sessions occur occasionally with all counselors, but frequent periods of nonproductivity should signal the counselor to investigate what is happening.

WHEN SHOULD COUNSELING BE TERMINATED?

How does a counselor decide when to end counseling? Does the counselor or the client decide? How does either party know the client is ready to stand alone? If the counselor and client have clearly defined the problem brought to counseling and the goal to be accomplished, the termination time will be evident—when the goal is accomplished. The counselor may also want to look for any of the following signs:

- Is the child more open?
- Does the child accept responsibility for feelings and actions?
- Is the child more tolerant of self and others?
- Is the child more independent and self-directing?
- Is the child less fearful, less unhappy, and less anxious than when the counseling relationship began?

Termination may be difficult for children, who usually find the sessions to be a time when a caring adult gives them undivided attention. Mutual attachments may be formed between counselor and child, and the child (and possibly the counselor) does not wish to end this pleasant relationship. To ease the break, client and counselor can discuss a possible termination date several weeks ahead of time. Plans can be made and rehearsed about how the child will react should problems recur. The child learns that the counselor still cares and will be available should trouble arise. Counselors may even consider building in a follow-up time when they ask their child clients to drop them a note or call to let them know how things are going. The counselor may want to schedule a brief follow-up visit. Any informal method of showing the child that a counselor's caring does not end with the last interview can signal the counselor's continued interest in the child's growth and development. Most successful counselors use a plan for maintaining the gains their clients have achieved during counseling. Such maintenance plans require periodic follow-up contacts, for example, 30 days or 6 months.

How Can Counseling Be Evaluated?

Currently, as accountability has become a high priority because of budgetary pressures, counselors are being asked to demonstrate their effectiveness in specific and measurable outcomes. In addition, providers of mental health services working with clients enrolled in managed care plans are under pressure to deliver services in the most cost-effective way possible (Steenbarger & Smith, 1996).

Consumer Reports (cited in Seligman, 1995) conducted a survey to determine the efficacy of therapy and concluded that no single measure of effectiveness sufficed. However, three areas for assessment were suggested: (1) "How much did treatment help with the specific problem?" (2) "How satisfied was the consumer with services received?" and (3) overall, "How much did the client improve?"

Steenbarger and Smith (1996) recommend using similar measures. They propose a measure evaluating the degree to which clients feel they have received services that are convenient and useful. These authors recommend several scales designed to measure satisfaction. Unfortunately, most scales that have been validated and have established reliability are constructed for adults. They would have to be adapted for the developmental age of the child client, and validity and reliability would need to be re-established.

A second measure suggested by Steenbarger and Smith (1996) is outcome measures taken at two or more points. Outcome measures are related to the goals of counseling and are statements about the counselors' and clients' expected outcomes from counseling written in measurable terms. Measures could be evaluated by both client and counselor. Again, most published measures are for adults and usually assess symptoms that are indicative of pathology, rather than growth and development, and may not be individualized to the clients' particular goals. Steenbarger and Smith (1996) and Ahn and Wampold (2001) also report that standards of care can be used as measures of effectiveness if professionals agree on the *best practices* of the profession and *common factors* including the healing context, working alliance, and rationale of the treatment. Counselors would be required to document in their notes how and when they engaged in these practices. The writers conclude that professionals in counseling need to assess and document client satisfaction, outcomes, and counselor performance on selected criteria to demonstrate effectiveness. The challenge for counselors working with children is to develop age-appropriate satisfaction scales, to develop outcome measures from initial goals set early in counseling, and to work with other professionals to establish *best practices* and *common factors* for highly effective care.

Goal attainment scaling is another method of evaluation designed for evaluating counseling outcomes. Goal attainment scaling (Kiresuk, Smith, &

Cardillo, 1994; Yarbrough & Thompson, 2002) allows counselor and client the opportunity to establish counseling goals cooperatively. The counselor's task is to help the child clarify these goals in measurable terms as a way of evaluating the distance between "What I have." and "What I would like to have." The tabulation and calculation of the data are the counselor's responsibility. Generally one to five goals are set, with five levels of attainment defined for each goal (Table 2-1). In addition, each goal is given a weight to represent its importance to the client. Clients establish priorities for their goals and assign weights to the most important and least important. For instance, Goal 1 may be three times more important than Goal 2. Intermediate goals are assigned weights representing their relative importance to the client. For example, if the most important goal is three times as important as the least important goal, it would receive a weight of 30 compared with a weight of 10 for the least important goal. Goals are then weighed on a scale of 10, 20, or 30, depending on their relative importance to the client.

Levels of attainment for each goal range from a "+2" for the best anticipated success to a "−2" for the least favorable outcome. A "0" value is assigned for the middle level or expected outcome success. Values of "+1" and "−1" represent "more than" and "less than" expected levels of success, respectively.

The goals are defined in measurable and observable terms, with the level of entry checked on the goal attainment follow-up guide. After counseling, an asterisk is placed on the guide indicating where the client is after counseling. Follow-up data can also be recorded periodically on the chart.

Goal attainment scores can be calculated for both the intake and follow-up levels. A follow-up goal attainment score of 50 or better is considered successful. Kiresuk and Sherman (1968) adopted a conventional *T*-score scale with the mean set at 50 and a standard deviation set at 10 for their goal attainment scale. The following formulas are used to derive the goal attainment scores for the guide in Table 2-1 (Kiresuk & Sherman, 1968). Using the numbers from the guide in Table 2-1, the reader will find that the formula is not as difficult to use as it initially may appear to be. However, *T*-score tables are provided for those who wish to avoid calculating the scores (see pages 000–000 in the Appendix).

GOAL ATTAINMENT SCORE CALCULATION: LEVEL AT INTAKE

$\overline{X}$ = mean $\qquad\qquad\qquad\qquad$ $\overline{X} = 50$

s = standard deviation $\qquad\qquad$ $s = 10$

ρ (rho) = probability of $\qquad\quad$ $\rho = 0.3$ $(1 - \rho = 0.7)$
$\qquad\qquad$ inter-scale correlation

w_1 = weight value $\qquad\qquad\quad$ $w_1 = 10$ to 30

x_1 = scale value $\qquad\qquad\qquad$ $x_1 = -2$ to $+2$

Goal attainment score (T) $= 50 + \dfrac{10\Sigma w_1 x_1}{\sqrt{(0.7\Sigma w_1{}^2) + 0.3(\Sigma w_1)^2}}$

$50 + 10\,[(20 \times -2) + (30 \times -1) + (10 \times -2) + (30 \times -2) + (10 \times -2)]$

TABLE 2-1 | GOAL ATTAINMENT SCALE

Scale attainment level	Scale 1: on task $W_1 = 20$	Scale 2: behavior $W_2 = 30$	Scale 3: punctuality $W_3 = 10$	Scale 4: relationships $W_4 = 30$	Scale 5: grade improvements $W_5 = 10$
a. Most unfavorable counseling outcome expected (−2)	Daydreams, leaves desk; ignores assignments [	Breaks classroom rules 4 or more times/day	Late to class 4 times/week [	Child gets into three fights per week [	Child continues to fail [
b. Less than expected success with counseling (−1)	Completes one assignment per day	Breaks rules 3 times/day [	Late to class 3 times/week	Child gets into at least one fight per week	Child demonstrates D work
c. Expected level of counseling success (0)	Completes two assignments per day	Breaks rules 2 times/day	Late to class 2 times/week	Child avoids all fights	Child demonstrates C work
d. More than expected success with counseling (+1)	Completes three assignments per day φ	Breaks rules 1 time/day φ	Late to class 1 time/week	Child develops one new friend φ	Child demonstrates B work φ
e. Most favorable counseling outcome expected (+2)	Completes four assignments per day	Follows all rules	Late to class 0 time/week φ	Child develops three new friends	Child demonstrates A work

NOTE: Level at intake: [; level at follow-up: φ.

$$50 + \cfrac{10\,(-\,170)}{\sqrt{0.7(20^2 + 30^2 + 10^2 + 30^2 + 10^2) + 0.3(20 + 30 + 10 + 30 + 10)^2}}$$

$$50 + \cfrac{-1700}{\sqrt{0.7(2{,}400) \;+\; 0.3(10{,}000)}}$$

$$50 + \cfrac{-1700}{\sqrt{4{,}680}}$$

$$50 + \cfrac{-1700}{68.41}$$

$$50 + \cfrac{-1700}{68.41}$$

$$50 + (-24.9)$$

$$T = 25.1$$

$$Z \text{ score} = \cfrac{50 - 25.1}{10} = 2.49 \text{ standard deviations below the mean}$$

GOAL ATTAINMENT SCORE CALCULATION: LEVEL AT FOLLOW-UP

$\overline{X}$ = mean	$\overline{X} = 50$
s = standard deviation	$s = 10$
ρ (rho) = probability of inter-scale correlation	$\rho = 0.3\ (1 - \rho = 0.7)$
w_1 = weight value	$w_1 = 10$ to 30
x_1 = scale value	$x_1 = -2$ to $+2$

$$\text{Goal attainment score (T)} = 50 + \cfrac{10\Sigma w_1 x_1}{\sqrt{(0.7\Sigma w_1{}^2) + 0.3(\Sigma w_1)^2}}$$

$$50 + 10\,[(20 \times 1) + (30 \times 1) + (10 \times 2) + (30 \times 1) + (10 \times 1)]$$

$$50 + \cfrac{10(110)}{\sqrt{0.7(20^2 + 30^2 + 10^2 + 30^2 + 10^2) + 0.3(20 + 30 + 10 + 30 + 10)^2}}$$

$$50 + \cfrac{1100}{\sqrt{0.7(2{,}400) \;+\; 0.3(10{,}000)}}$$

$$50 + \cfrac{1100}{\sqrt{4{,}680}}$$

$$50 + \cfrac{1100}{68.41}$$

$$50 + \cfrac{1100}{68.41}$$

$$50 + (16)$$

$$T = 66$$

$$Z \text{ score} = \cfrac{66 - 50}{10} = \cfrac{16}{10} = 1.6 \text{ standard deviations above the mean}$$

FIGURE 2-4 | WEEKLY GOAL ATTAINMENT SCALE

Goal attainment scaling (Dowd & Kelly, 1975) can be graphed to show weekly progress (Figure 2-4). The graph also can be used to chart the results of periodic follow-up checks on the maintenance of counseling gains.

Martin and Thompson (1995) also find the goal attainment scale effective in helping student athletes balance their responsibilities between school, sports, and other areas to fulfill their expectations of success. Yarbrough and Thompson (2002) use goal attainment scales in tracking elementary school students improving their on-task behaviors.

T-scores and average scale scores may be obtained from the conversion tables in the Appendix C if you wish to avoid doing the arithmetic required to work the T-score formula. Both before and after treatment scores can be obtained from the conversion tables. Simply sum the individual scale scores before treatment and enter the conversion table corresponding to the number of scales on the goal attainment scale. For example, the goal attainment scale in Figure 2-4 has five scales and a sum of −9 on the individual pretreatment scale scores $((-2) + (-1) + (-2) + (-2) + (-2) = -9)$. Thus, entering conversion Table 5 from Appendix C, we find that the pretreatment T-score is 22.86 with an average scale score of −1.8 for the five scales. After treatment, the scale scores totaled +6 found by summing the individual scale score of $(1 + 1 + 2 + 1 + 1)$. Again, checking conversion Table 5, we find the post-treatment scale score to be 68.09 with an average scale score of 1.2. Therefore, with a mean T-score of 50 and a standard deviation of 10, the client on the goal attainment scale improved from $(50 − 22.86)/10 = 2.7$ standard deviations *below* the mean to $(68.09 − 50)/10 = 1.8$ standard deviations *above* the mean. Improvements of at least one step on a scale are considered to be significant gains. In the above case, the child improved 4.5 standard deviations on his full scale score.

How Do Professional Counselors Work with Managed Health Care?*

In both the private and public sectors, changes continue to involve significantly more counseling services for children and youth managed by specialized behavioral health insurance organizations (Stein & Orlando, 2001). The following brief overview may serve to further understand the structure of managed care.

Many managed behavioral health organizations (MBHOs) oversee and manage only the behavioral health benefits of those insured by the contracting health maintenance organization (HMO). This separates the management of medical benefits and frees the HMO to delegate the more specialized behavioral health issues to its contracted MBHO. During the 1990s, competition among the MBHOs for the increasingly shrinking health care dollar resulted in many buyouts and consolidations of MBHOs. Currently, there are now three major MBHOs that manage behavioral health care for more than half of all managed behavioral health in the United States. These MBHOs or carve-outs are dominating the management of counseling services currently in the private and public sectors of the United States.

Several important trends in mental health care have emerged with the growth of managed care. Ringel and Sturm (2001) found major changes in the delivery of care since previous 1986 figures, namely, a much higher use of outpatient mental health services (57 percent of the total 1998 cost). Not surprisingly, the authors conclude that the majority of children who could respond favorably to mental health care do not receive the needed services. Lastly, they found primary care medical settings provide a substantial amount of mental health care for children (Ringel & Sturm, 2001). In a policy statement made by the American Academy of Pediatrics, this last trend is seen as a barrier because "pediatricians often are professionally unprepared and usually have inadequate appointment time to address the mental health needs of children and adolescents" (Taras & Young, 2004, p. 1839).

The public sector also has seen significant changes as a result of managed care. In its fortieth year, Medicaid is the primary insurer of 52 million low-income, elderly, and disabled citizens and provides insurance for approximately one in four children in the United States (Heflinger & Saunders, 2005). The turn of the century witnessed extensive MBHO contracting for Medicaid-covered individuals in the public sector; 56 percent of Medicaid enrollees have been transitioned into managed care (Kaiser Commission on Medicaid and the Uninsured, 2001). Each state determines how Medicaid services are administered by the selected MBHOs, and numerous problems have occurred with contract administration. Recently, a steep downward trend shows many commercial insurers exiting the market terminating public sector contracts (Kaiser Commission on Medicaid and the Uninsured, 2001). In addition, minimal research examining the effectiveness of managed care related to mental health services exists, especially regarding the public sector.

---

*We appreciate Dr. Laura Veach, Wake Forest University, for contributing this section.

In one critical multisite study (Cook, Heflinger, Hoven, Kelleher, Mulkern, & Paulson, 2004) found that when compared with traditional fee-for-service care, three of four levels of care (inpatient/residential, psychiatric medication, and nontraditional services) in Medicaid-funded managed care were much less utilized. The authors cite that less utilization of these levels of care contributed to reducing the probability for children to receive "the full spectrum of services comprising the system of care approach" (p. 401). The major findings also cite "factors other than children's service needs are influencing their receipt of mental health-care, which may be cause for concern if needed services are denied because of attempts to control costs" (p. 399). Even projects aimed at prevention of serious mental health problems in young children met with significant frustration when trying to work with a managed care approach and Medicaid (Hocutt, McKinney, & Montague, 2002). Continued research into the impact of managed mental health care is greatly needed, especially involving children and adolescents, because major changes and economic pressures continue to occur in the managed care industry with significant impact on the counseling children now receive.

Increased penetration by managed care into community and school counseling settings has complicated how counseling is provided for children and adolescents throughout the continuum of care. Based on their extensive case study, Heflinger and Northrup (2000) conclude that a clash of philosophy between containing costs and best care for the client often contaminates authorizations for the type, level, and duration of counseling and stresses the need for independent review of MBHO practices and authorization patterns (Heflinger & Northrup, 2000). In addition, Coffey, Olson, and Sessions (2001) report that managed care has greatly compromised systemic family therapy. Even though much has been written about the efficacy of counseling the whole family, the majority of MBHOs do not provide coverage for family counseling. These restrictions placed on counselors and their clients regarding dollar amounts and time limits for certain types of therapy complicate care. It is helpful for counselors in today's managed care environment to use this new awareness of potential challenges to better advocate for the client faced with restrictions or barriers.

Murphy (1998) raises the questions of whether managed care is ethical and whether counselors can engage in ethical practice within the managed care system. Her response to both questions is that counselors have the responsibility to ensure that they practice within the codes and laws that govern the counseling profession and within the limits of their training and competence regardless of managed care restrictions. She points out that the answer to the question of how to be an ethical practitioner within the context of managed care lies in our ability to hold the line—what we consider to be "good enough" counseling. She recommends that counselors work as a group to advocate change of those aspects of managed care that breach the limits of our ethical codes.

English and Marino (1998) provide a thorough update and analysis of how professional counselors were letting managed health care influence their practice. Somewhat surprising is the finding that counselor attitude toward managed care ranged from enthusiasm to outright hostility and opposition. Some counselors, having adapted to managed care, were actually thriving within the limits and restrictions placed on their practice. Other counselors, though, completely frustrated with the paperwork, restrictions, and guidelines posed by managed care, have chosen to exempt their practice from managed care.

English and Marino (1998) cite a survey conducted by Howard Smith, chair of the ACA Professionalization Committee. Sixty-five percent of 1200 counselors surveyed received one quarter or less of their income from managed care. Several complaints about managed care were registered in the survey. These included lower fees, delays in payments, and concerns about possible breaches of clients' confidentiality. It was reported that fees paid by managed care programs have failed to keep pace with the rather low rate of inflation and have, in some cases, actually decreased in the range of 10 to 15 percent over the past 4 years of the survey for all nonphysician mental health professionals. Other complaints listed include difficulty in getting authorization for treatment, excessive paperwork, and the expense involved in purchasing software to generate claim forms and record forms for tracking patient outcomes. Since the mid 1980s, the authors have recommended that all counselors find a system for tracking their clients' progress and outcomes. We have found no better instrument than the goal attainment scale for documenting one's success as a counselor, whether with managed health care or school administrators. Even without calculating the z-scores for each client, which can be done with simple arithmetic, the chart is quite effective in showing client change from the first to the last counseling session.

Some counselors are choosing to develop private practice without participating in MBHO panels. O'Hara (1996) wrote a very positive article on how she has been successful in her practice outside managed care. We strongly recommend her article for all who currently are doing or contemplating private practice. O'Hara believes the key to her success is marketing her services outside the medical model for treating mental illness. Her focus, much like the focus of our entire book, is to further personal growth and development through concentrating on fostering mental health rather than treating mental illness. People come to her for self-improvement and education rather than for curing an illness. Campbell (personal communication, 1999) has followed a similarly successful plan since the 1980s. Her office, an attractive, refurbished, small house, contains a waiting room, counseling office, and play-therapy room. The sign in the front yard reads "Educational Development Center." Her counseling philosophy defines counseling as an educational process directed toward helping her clients find better ways to meet their needs. Campbell's philosophy is quite compatible with ours: Counselors support the optimal development of all human beings. This philosophy guides each chapter in this book.

Not all the data on counseling and managed care are negative. Definite benefits for the profession have accrued from managed care. First, professional counselors have been recognized as viable providers of mental health services. The number of MBHOs recognizing counselors continues to increase each year. The ACA office of Public Policy and Information was successful in achieving recognition of professional counselors by managed health care's leading accrediting body, the National Committee for Quality Assurance (NCQA). NCQA is also the developer of the primary assessment instrument used by the government and businesses to measure the quality of care provided by medical care organizations (MCOs). The American Mental Health Counselors Association (AMHCA) also has been successful in increasing recognition of professional counselors by MCOs.

Second, the Balanced Budget Act of 1997 stipulates that Medicare managed care administrators cannot discriminate against providers on the basis of their type of license. The Mental Health Parity Act of 1998 prohibits health plans from using annual or lifetime dollar limits on coverage for mental health services that are different or less than those provided for medical services. These two acts represent significant first steps in bringing parity to counselors as recognized providers of mental health services. Senate Bill 1754, the Health Professions Education Partnership, included mental health counselors among the list of health service providers that could be trained under their legislation. In addition, the bill recognized professional counselors as "core mental health professionals" by the Health Resources and Services Administration, thereby making professional counselors eligible for participation in the National Health Service Corps scholarship and loan repayment program. The program was established to ensure that an adequate supply of health professionals, including mental health professionals, exist in areas designated as health professional shortage areas (Powell, 1998).

Third, MCOs have helped counselors make their practices more time- and cost-effective with their demands for quality care documentation. Studies are increasingly finding that counselors and therapists are cost-effective. For example, Stein and Orlando (2001), using data from United Behavioral Health (UBH), the third largest MBHO in the United States, report in a study of youths younger than 15 being treated for ADHD that the least number of counseling sessions (7.6) was provided by therapists and the duration of counseling was the shortest when the counselor was the only mental health practitioner working with the young person. The current trend is to offer consumers more choices from which they can select for their mental health care providers.

English and Marino (1998) suggest several ways counselors can work successfully with MBHOs. First, counselors need to be good marketers, distinguishing themselves and what they do from other providers. English and Marino interviewed Brett Steenberger, executive director of Prime Care, a multispecialty group practice in Syracuse, NY, on the question of how to succeed in working with MBHOs. Steenberger emphasized the importance of having a specialty such as solution-focused brief counseling or group psychotherapy, which are favored by MBHOs. Any therapy with time-limited and goal-directed foci is quite popular with the MBHOs. It appears that competing on cost is a good way to work within managed care and also a good way to compete outside of it. Steenberger also recommended that counselors consider joining a group practice or network to increase their chances of being appointed to MBHO panels. Steenberger also recommended that counselors keep their MBHOs appraised of their specialties and any new training obtained in performing one of their approved specialties. Counselors may find it helpful to try and develop rapport with the network case managers, especially if one or two can be consistently contacted. This can be particularly helpful when dealing with a difficult client case for which the counselor needs to advocate for increased authorizations for care. Most important, mental health providers' success in remaining on panels will be determined by report card records on such factors as customer service, documented outcome success, and length of client time in treatment. It is also important to be fully informed regarding the appeal process within the MBHO and the Department of Insurance in one's state in case the option of appeal is needed for the client. In summary, professional counselors need to be highly accountable for quality and cost, whether they choose to work with or without the managed health care systems.

Davis (1998) summarizes six steps for developing effective treatment plans that meet MCO specifications. These steps are explained in the next section. The steps are taken from a presentation by Judy Stone, manager of training and development for Value Behavioral Health. Stone echoed the treatment philosophy of today: "Treatment is very focused on solutions and doing it in the shortest amount of time."

STEP ONE: PROBLEM IDENTIFICATION   Concentrate on those problems that are within the realm of managed care's short-term treatment focus. Describe client problems with descriptor words for behaviors that occur with excessive or deficient intensity, frequency, and duration. Examples include the terms *acting out, compulsive drinking,* and *physically assaultive.* Descriptor words for frequency and duration include *prolonged excitement, daily worry,* and *consistent dread.* Examples of behavioral deficits include the terms *social withdrawal* and *lack of concentration.*

STEP TWO: PROBLEM DEFINITION   After identification of the problem, the counselor needs to define the problem in terms that are consistent with the *Diagnostic and Statistical Manual, Fourth Edition, Text Revision* (DSM-IV-TR). Definitions should include the cognitive process that motivates the problem behaviors of the client and a description of the history of the problem. For example, for an anger management problem, the report could read that the client has a history of explosive, aggressive behaviors disproportionate to any precipitating stressors leading to assaultive acts and destruction of property.

STEP THREE: GOAL DEVELOPMENT   Write broad goals that are more general in scope and may be long term. For example, "stabilized mood" or "sustained abstinence" are broad goals that help focus on the overarching, larger picture for which the client aims.

STEP FOUR: MEASURABLE OBJECTIVES   As mentioned earlier, substeps or objectives need to be developed for each goal with projected time lines for meeting them. Objectives help the client and counselor have specific, brief, measurable steps to reach the broad goal. For example, if a client had attempted suicide, objectives leading to the overall goal of preventing future attempts could be the development of future plans to build relationships with others and to find a job. These steps could be broken down into joining an organization such as a church to meet people and the development of a résumé to use in job applications. Again, the goal attainment scale described in this chapter is an excellent instrument for meeting managed care guidelines. It is important to have goals for which small steps in progress can be charted.

STEP FIVE: CREATING INTERVENTIONS   Develop at least one intervention for every outcome objective. Regardless of one's personal orientation to counseling, it is important that treatment plans include specific, well-defined steps that are understood by MBHO personnel. For example, a counselor practicing reality therapy would list how the reality therapy steps were to be used to get the client to explore better alternatives to meet personal needs, the intervention frequency, and the duration of the intervention. For example, "individual counseling once per week for 8 weeks" and re-evaluate as needed.

STEP SIX: DIAGNOSING   Diagnoses must fit the DSM-IV-TR system if treatment is to be reimbursed by MBHOs. Decisions to certify the treatment provided will be based on what is written for the five DSM-IV-TR axes.

We also found that MBHOs are not especially interested in having the public know about the differential rates given to various groups and individuals. We found the best way to collect data on companies was to survey individuals on the particular plan under which they are covered or contact the related state Department of Insurance. The following figures represent some typical limits placed on mental health coverage by various MBHOs. Many MBHOs have a 30-day limit per benefit period for inpatient care. Mental health parity continues to be a legislative and administrative challenge, but in 2003 President Bush's New Freedom Commission on Mental Health urged full mental health parity on the federal level to help improve the delivery of mental health care in the U.S. (ACA, 2006). One company we researched had no limit on psychological therapy, whereas others did not cover marriage counseling. Outpatient visits may be limited as follows: visits 1 to 26 are covered with a co-payment by the client ranging from $10 to $30. Some MBHOs may require more extensive utilization reviews of outpatient care that requires the counselor to contact the MBHO for authorizations for additional visits or more intensive levels of care. Although some MBHO panels may be closed in general to additional counselors, meeting with a representative from the MBHO provider relations department may reveal a need for services in specialized areas, especially in counseling services for children or in rural areas. Also, although you may be building a private practice, it probably is a good idea to keep your salaried position as a counselor in one of your community agencies. It is our contention that professional counselors have overlooked a viable resource in developing their practice.

SUMMARY

In summary, we have noted the positive and negative implications managed health care has for the mental health profession in general and professional counselors in particular. Disadvantages to counselors included limitations placed on treatment, time, and cost. Some of the advantages to counselors included efficiency, more accountability, professional recognition, and for some counselors, the challenge to succeed outside the traditional medical model and managed health care.

The Counseling Process Video

To gain a more in-depth understanding of the concepts in this chapter, visit www.thomsonedu.com/counseling/thompson to view a short clip of an actual therapist–client session demonstrating the counseling process.

Websites for the Counseling Process

Counseling is a challenging field because the world is changing so rapidly. The need for new information about how to handle counseling cases confronts counselors on an almost daily basis. There are hundreds of websites with specific kinds of information available to help counselors with these challenges. Internet addresses frequently change. To find the sites listed here, visit www.thomsonedu.com/counseling/thompson for an updated list of Internet addresses and direct links to relevant sites.

American Counseling Association

American Psychological Association

American School Counselor Association

Clinical Social Work Federation, Inc.

Counselor Net

National Alliance for the Mentally Ill

National Mental Health Association

Web Resources for Counselors

Websites for Information on Managed Care

At Health, Inc.

Managed Care—Medscape

Mental Health Patient's Bill of Rights

Clinical Social Work Federation (CSWF)

National Coalition of Mental Health Professionals and Consumers

References

Ahn, M., & Wampold, B. (2001). Where oh where are the specific ingredients? A meta analysis of component studies in counseling and psychotherapy. *Journal of Counseling Psychology, 48,* 251–257.

American Counseling Association. (2006). Parity of insurance for mental health treatment. Retrieved March 7, 2006 from http://www.counseling.org/PublicPolicy/ Position Papers.aspx?AGuid=72f8b242-7ee7-446c-9cbf-bad609859690

Burton, L. (1995). Using a dog in an elementary school counseling program. *Elementary School Guidance and Counseling, 29*(3), 236–240.

Capuzzi, D., & Gross, D. R. (1999). *Counseling and psychotherapy: Theories and interventions* (2nd ed.). Upper Saddle River, NJ: Merrill.

Carkhuff, R. (1969). *Helping and human relations* (2 vols.). New York: Holt, Rinehart & Winston.

Carlson, K. (1990). Suggestions for counseling "other-referred" children. *Elementary School Guidance and Counseling, 24,* 222–229.

Coffey, E. P., Olson, M. E., & Sessions, P. (2001). The heart of the matter: An essay about the effects of managed care on family therapy with children. *Family Process, 40*(4), 385–399.

Cook, J. A., Heflinger, C. A., Hoven, C. W., Kelleher, K. J., Mulkern, V., & Paulson, R. I. (2004). A multi-site study of Medicaid-funded managed care versus fee-for-service plans' effects on mental health service utilization of children with severe emotional disturbance. *Journal of Behavioral Health Services & Research, 31*(4), 384–402.

Davis, J. (1998). Managed care forum offers counselors advice on how to gain the competitive edge. *The Advocate, 21,* 5, 9, 12.

Dowd, E., & Kelly, F. (1975). The use of goal attainment scaling in single case study research. *Goal Attainment Review, 2,* 11–21.

Egan, G. (1994). *The skilled helper* (5th ed.). Pacific Grove, CA: Brooks/Cole.

English, S., & Marino, T. (1998). Update: Professional counselors and managed care. *Counseling Today, 40,* 11(1), 18–19.

Erdman, P., & Lampe, R. (1996). Adapting basic skills to counsel children. *Journal of Counseling and Development, 74,* 374–377.

Garbarino, J., & Stott, F. (1989). *What children can tell us?* San Francisco: Jossey-Bass.

Gerler, E. (1990). Multimodal approaches to counseling in schools. *Elementary School Guidance and Counseling, 24,* 242.

Gerler, E., Drew, N., & Mohr, P. (1990). Succeeding in middle school: A multimodal approach. *Elementary School Guidance and Counseling, 24,* 263–271.

Gladding, S.T. (2000). *Counseling: A comprehensive profession.* Upper Saddle River, NJ: Merrill.

Heflinger, C., & Northrop, D. (2000). What happens when capitated behavioral health comes to town? The transition from the Fort Bragg Demonstration to a capitated managed behavioral health contract. *Journal of Behavioral Health Services and Research, 27,* 390–406.

Heflinger, C. A., & Saunders, R. C. (2005). Physical and behavioral health of Medicaid children in two southern states. *Southern Medical Journal, 98*(4), 429–435.

Hocutt, A. M., McKinney, J. D., & Montague, M. (2002). The impact of managed care on efforts to prevent development of severe emotional disturbance in young children. *Journal of Disability Policy Studies, 13*(1), 51–60.

Kaiser Commission on Medicaid and the Uninsured. (2001, December 14). Fast facts. Retrieved September 15, 2005, from http://www.kff.org/medicaid/206803-index.cfm

Kazdin, A. E. (2000). *Psychotherapy for children and adolescents: Directions for research and practice.* New York: Oxford University Press.

Kazdin, A. E. (1994). Psychotherapy for children and adolescents. In A. E. Bergin, & S. L. Garfield (Eds.), *Handbook of psychotherapy and behavior change* (pp. 543–594). New York: John Wiley.

Keat, D. (1990a). Change in child multimodal counseling. *Elementary School Guidance and Counseling, 24,* 248–262.

Keat, D. (1990b). *Child multimodal therapy.* Norwood, NJ: Ablex.

Kiresuk, T., & Sherman, R. (1968). Goal attainment scaling: A general method for evaluating comprehensive community mental health programs. *Community Mental Health, 4,* 443–453.

Kiresuk, T., Smith, A., & Cardillo, J. (1994). *Goal attainment selling: Applications, theory, and measurement.* Hillsdale, NJ: Erlbaum.

Lambert, M. M., & Cattani-Thompson, K. (1996). Current findings regarding the effectiveness of counseling: Implications for practice. *Journal of Counseling and Development, 74,* 601–608.

Lazarus, A. (1989). *The practice of multimodal therapy.* Baltimore: Johns Hopkins University Press.

Lazarus, A. (1997). *Brief but comprehensive therapy: The multimodal way.* New York: Springer.

Lazarus, A. (2000). Multimodal therapy. In R. J. Corsini & D. Wedding (Eds.), *Current psychotherapies* (6th ed., pp. 340–374). Itasca, IL: Peacock.

Martin, S., & Thompson, C. (1995). Reality therapy and goal attainment scaling: A program for freshman student-athletes. *Journal of Reality Therapy, 14* (2), 45–54.

Murphy, K. (1998). Is managed care unethical? *International Association of Marriage and Family Counselors, 11*(1), 3.

O'Brien, M. (1993). Pets as counselors. *Elementary School Guidance and Counseling, 4,* 308.

O'Hara, M. (1996). Divided we stand. *The Family Therapy Networker, 20*(5), 46–53.

Orlinsky, D. E., Grawe, K., & Parks, B. K. (1994). Process and outcome in psychotherapy-Noch einmal. In A. E. Bergin & S. L. Garfield (Eds.), *Handbook of psychotherapy and behavior change* (pp. 270–378). New York: John Wiley.

Poppen, W., & Thompson, C. (1974). *School counseling: Theories and concepts.* Lincoln, NE: Professional Educators.

Powell, B. (1998). Professional counselors included in Federal Health Professionals Training Bill. *The Advocate, 21,* 5, 1, 8.

Ringel, J. S., & Sturm, R. (2001). National estimates of mental health utilization and expenditures for children in 1998. *Journal of Behavioral Health Services and Research, 28,* 319–334.

Rogers, C. R. (1957). The necessary and sufficient conditions of therapeutic personality change. *Journal of Consulting Psychology, 21,* 95–103.

Seligman, L. (2006). *Theories of counseling and psychotherapy: Systems, strategies, and skills* (2nd ed.). Upper Saddle River, NJ: Merrill.

Seligman, M. (1995). The effectiveness of psychotherapy. *American Psychologist, 50*(12), 965–974.

Sexton, T. L. (2001). Evidence-based counseling intervention programs. In D. C. Locke, J. E. Myers, & E. L. Herr's (Eds.), *The handbook of counseling* (pp. 499–512). Thousand Oaks, CA: Sage.

Sexton, T. L., & Whiston, S. C. (1996). Integrating counseling research and practice. *Journal of Counseling and Development, 74,* 588–589.

Smith, M. L., Glass, G. V., & Miller, T. I. (1980). *The benefits of psychotherapy.* Baltimore, MD: Johns Hopkins University Press.

Steenbarger, B., & Smith, H. (1996). Assessing the quality of counseling services: Developing accountable helping systems. *Journal of Counseling & Development, 75*(2), 145–150.

Stein, B., & Orlando, M. (2001). ADHD Rx in a behavioral health care carve-out: Medications, providers, and service utilization. *Journal of Behavioral Health Services and Research, 28*(1), 30–42.

Tares, H. L. & Young, T. L. (2004). Policy statement: School-based mental health services. *Pediatrics, 113*(6), 1839–1845.

Thompson, C., & Campbell, S. (1992). Personal intervention preferences for alleviating mild depression. *Journal of Counseling and Development, 71*(1), 69–73.

Thompson, C., & Poppen, W. (1992). *Guidance activities for counselors and teachers.* Knoxville, TN.

Trivedi, L., & Perl, J. (1995). Animal facilitated counseling in the elementary school: A literature review and practical considerations. *Elementary School Guidance and Counseling, 29*(3), 223–234.

Truax, C. B., & Carkhuff, R. R. (1967). *Towards effective counseling and psychotherapy: Training and practice.* Chicago: Aldine.

Yarbrough, J., & Thompson, C. (2002). Using single-participant research to assess the efficacy of two brief counseling approaches on children's off-task behavior. *Professional School Counseling, 5,* 308–314.

COUNSELING THEORIES AND TECHNIQUES

Adaptations for Children

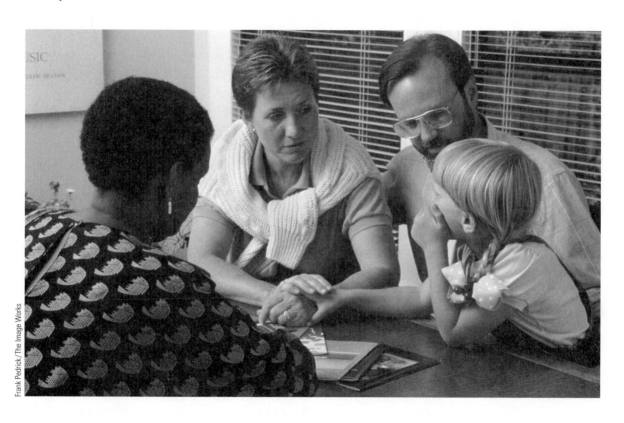

PART 2

Frank Pedrick/The Image Works

3 CHAPTER | PSYCHOANALYTIC COUNSELING

A moment's insight is sometimes worth a life's experience.

—Oliver Wendell Holmes

Sigmund Freud (1856–1939)

Sigmund Freud was born in Freiberg, Moravia, in 1856 and died in London in 1939. However, he is considered to have belonged to Vienna, where he lived for nearly 80 years. Freud was the first of his mother's eight children; he also had two half brothers more than 20 years his elder.

Freud graduated from the gymnasium at 17 and, in 1873, entered the medical school at the University of Vienna. He became deeply involved in neurological research and did not finish his M.D. degree for 8 years. Never intending to practice medicine because he wanted to be a scientist, Freud devoted his next 15 years to investigations of the nervous system (Hall, 1954). However, the salary of a scientific researcher was inadequate to support the wife and the six children he had at that time. In addition, the anti-Semitism prevalent in Vienna during this period prevented Freud from achieving university advancement. Consequently, Freud felt forced to take up the practice of medicine.

Freud decided to specialize in the treatment of nervous disorders; at the time, not much was known about this particular branch of medicine. First, he spent a year in France learning about Jean Charcot's use of hypnosis in the treatment of hysteria (Stone, 1971). Freud (1963) was dissatisfied with hypnosis because he thought its effects were only temporary and did not get at the center of the problem. Freud then studied with Joseph Breuer, learning the benefits of the catharsis (or "talking out your problems") form of therapy.

Noticing that his patients' physical symptoms seemed to have a mental base, Freud probed deeper and deeper into the minds of his patients. Hall

(1954) notes, "His probing revealed dynamic forces at work which were responsible for creating the abnormal symptoms that he was called upon to treat. Gradually there began to take shape in Freud's mind the idea that most of these forces were unconscious" (p. 15). According to Stone (1971), this finding was probably the turning point in Freud's career. To substantiate some of his ideas, Freud decided to undertake an intensive analysis of his own unconscious forces in order to check on the material he had gathered from his patients. Hall (1954) further notes, "On the basis of the knowledge he gained from his patients and from himself he began to lay the foundations for a theory of personality" (p. 17).

Freud's early support of Charcot and his new and revolutionary ideas cost him the support of most scholars and doctors. Eventually, however, Freud was accepted as a genius in psychotherapy. Many influential scientists, including Carl Jung, Alfred Adler, Ernest Jones, and Wilhelm Stekel, recognized Freud's theory as a major breakthrough in the field of psychology; however, these scientists broke with Freud early on. Freud's academic career with the University of Vienna began in 1883; however, he did not receive the rank of full professor until 1920. Freud's recognition in academic psychology came in 1909, when he was invited by G. Stanley Hall to give a series of lectures at Clark University in Worcester, Massachusetts. According to Fancher (2000), Hall single-handedly made Freud's name a household word in the United States by ensuring full press coverage for all of Freud's lectures on psychoanalysis. It was Clark University's twentieth anniversary, and Hall marked it by bringing Freud to the United States for his first and only trip. Freud's name began to appear in popular songs, and *Time* magazine featured him on the cover.

Freud's writing career spanned 63 years, during which he authored more than 600 publications. His collected works have been published in English in 24 volumes as *The Standard Edition of the Complete Psychological Works of Sigmund Freud* (1953–1964). Among his more famous works are *The Interpretation of Dreams* (1900/1965a), *The Psychopathology of Everyday Life* (1901/1971), and *New Introductory Lectures in Psychoanalysis* (1933/1965b).

Freud seemed never to think his work was finished. "As new evidence came to him from his patients and his colleagues, he expanded and revised his basic theories" (Hall, 1954, p. 17). As an example of his flexibility and capability, at age 70, Freud completely altered a number of his fundamental views: He revamped motivation theory, reversed the theory of anxiety, and developed a new model of personality based on id, ego, and superego.

Freud developed his psychoanalytic model of people over five decades of observing and writing. The major principles were based on the clinical study of individual patients undergoing treatment for their problems. Free association became Freud's preferred procedure after he discarded hypnosis.

Just as Sigmund Freud was the father of psychoanalysis, he was the grandfather of child psychoanalysis. His therapy with adults conducted at the Vienna Psychoanalytic Institute was continuous and lengthy, often requiring several years to complete. A school for children was established adjacent to the institute. Anna Freud, Sigmund Freud's daughter, began to take great interest in these children and eventually devoted herself almost exclusively to the study of psychoanalysis in children. She stands today as the outstanding pioneer in the field. The institute also trained other prominent child analysts, most notable among them Peter Blos, Marianne Kris, and Erik Erikson. Erikson is best known for his theory of sequenced tasks as the means to develop one's identity.

Psychoanalysis includes theories about the development and organization of the mind, the instinctual drives, the influences of the external environment, the importance of the family, and the attitudes of society. As useful as psychoanalysis is, as a therapeutic tool, its impact and value reach far beyond medical applications. It is the only comprehensive theory of human psychology. Psychoanalytic theory has proved helpful to parents and teachers in the upbringing and education of children.

Although psychoanalytic theory has been modified in some areas, its basic concepts remain unchanged. The fact that almost all counseling theories include some of the basic premises from the psychoanalytic method shows the influence and durability of the theory.

THE NATURE OF PEOPLE

The concept of human nature in psychoanalytic theory found its basis in psychic determinism and unconscious mental processes. Psychic determinism implies that mental life is a continuous manifestation of cause-related relationships. Mental processes are considered the causative factors of human behavior. Mental activity and even physical activity may be kept below the conscious level. Analysis on the basis of unconscious determinism is the foundation of psychoanalytic counseling. Counseling leading to catharsis then leads to confronting the unconscious mind in ways that promote learning, understanding, and growth in mental development and coping skills.

Freud viewed people as basically evil and victims of instincts that must be balanced or reconciled with social forces to provide a structure in which human beings can function. To achieve balance, people need a deep understanding of the forces that motivate them to action. According to Freud, people operate as energy systems, distributing psychic energy to the id, ego, and superego; human behavior is determined by this energy, by unconscious motives, and by instinctual and biological drives. Psychosexual events during the first 5 years of life are critical to adult personality development.

Sugarman (1977), believing that Freud's concept of human nature is often misinterpreted, presented a contrasting view of Freudian theory in which a humanistic image of people is recognized in the following eight ideas:

1. People have a dual nature, biological and symbolic.
2. People are both individuals and related to others simultaneously.
3. People strive for goals and values.
4. One of the strongest human needs is meaning in life.
5. One's internal world, including the unconscious, is more important than overt behavior.
6. People are social creatures whose need for interpersonal relationships is supreme.
7. People are always evolving, always in process.
8. People have a certain amount of autonomy within the constraints of reality.

In summary, according to psychoanalytic theory, the basic concepts of human nature revolve around the notions of psychic determinism and unconscious mental processes. Psychic determinism simply implies that our mental function or mental life is a continuous logical manifestation of causative relationships. Nothing is random; nothing happens by chance. Although mental events may appear unrelated, they are actually closely interwoven and depend on preceding mental signals. Closely related to psychic determinism are unconscious mental processes, which exist as fundamental causative factors in the nature of human behavior. In essence, much of what goes on in our minds, and hence in our bodies, is unknown, below the conscious level; thus, people often do not understand our feelings or actions. The existence of unconscious mental processes is the basis for much of what is involved in psychoanalytic counseling.

Freud believed that unresolved conflict, repression, and free-floating anxiety often go together. Painful and stressful conflicts that cannot be resolved in the conscious may be buried and forgotten in the unconscious. Later on, a person may experience anxiety that cannot be readily traced to any ongoing situation in the person's life. Relief from such anxiety may come only from accessing the unconscious and uncovering and resolving the original conflict. Recall and integration of repressed memories into one's conscious functioning often provide symptom relief from free-floating anxiety.

Freud also was interested in how people handled the tension of being pulled in opposite directions by the polarities in life. He saw people as born with the pleasure principle, or the will to seek pleasure; however, people are confronted with an opposite force, the reality principle, which demands that the will to pleasure be bridled. The tension that results from being pulled in opposite directions by the pleasure principle and by the reality principle becomes the essential, motivating force in one's life. People can either find productive ways to reduce the tension or give in to the tension and be destroyed by it. The task of humankind is to find a way to integrate the polarities into synergistic choices that neither compromise nor deny the opposing polarities. For example, taking your textbook to the beach on spring break may be an attempt to find a middle ground between doing what you want and what you should. A synergistic solution might be completing the work before leaving on the trip, which would probably result in higher quality work and play. Living becomes a process of either mastering or succumbing to the tension resulting from life's polarities.

As noted in Figures 3-1 and 3-2, the *unconscious* holds about 85% of the material in our minds. The concept of the unconscious is the foundation of psychoanalytic theory and practice. It holds that, in a part of the mind that we are not aware of, drives, desires, attitudes, motivations, and fantasies exist and exert influence on how people think, feel, and behave in the conscious area of functioning. The *conscious* refers to the part of mental activity that we are aware of at any given time. The *preconscious* refers to thoughts and material that are not readily available to the conscious but can be retrieved with some effort. Students may struggle to find an answer to a test

FIGURE 3-1 | FREUD'S PSYCHOANALYTIC MODEL

question lost in the preconscious. The *subconscious* refers to those involuntary bodily processes such as digestion and breathing that have been with the person since birth. Carl Jung's *collective unconscious* refers to the vast reservoir of inherited wisdom, memories, and insights that individuals share with all humankind (see Figure 3-2).

THEORY OF COUNSELING

Freud's concepts of personality form the basis of a psychoanalytic counseling theory. The principal concepts in Freudian theory can be grouped under three topic headings: structural, dynamic, and developmental. The structural

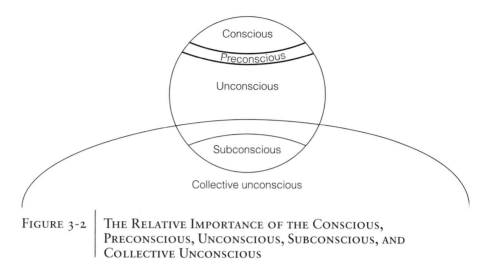

FIGURE 3-2 | THE RELATIVE IMPORTANCE OF THE CONSCIOUS, PRECONSCIOUS, UNCONSCIOUS, SUBCONSCIOUS, AND COLLECTIVE UNCONSCIOUS

concepts are id, ego, and superego. The dynamic concepts are instinct, cathexis, anticathexis, and anxiety. The developmental concepts are defense mechanisms and psychosexual stages.

STRUCTURAL CONCEPTS

Freud believed human behavior resulted from the interaction of three important parts of the personality: id, ego, and superego.

ID   The id contains our basic instinctual drives, including thirst, hunger, sex, and aggression. These drives can be constructive or destructive. Constructive, pleasure-seeking (sexual) drives provide the basic energy of life (libido). In Freud's system, anything pleasurable is labeled sexual. Destructive, aggressive drives tend toward self-destruction and death. Life instincts are opposed by death instincts. The id, working on the pleasure principle, exists to provide immediate gratification of any instinctual need, regardless of the consequences. The id is not capable of thought, but can form, for example, mental pictures of hamburgers for a hungry person. The formation of such images and wishes is referred to as *fantasy* and *wish fulfillment* (the *primary process*).

EGO   Often called the "executive" of the personality, the ego strives to strike a balance between the needs of the id and the reality of the external world and transforms the mental images formed by the id (the hamburgers, for example) into acceptable behavior (purchasing a hamburger). These reality-oriented, rational processes of the ego are referred to as the *secondary process*. The ego, operating under the *reality principle,* is left with the task of mediating a balance among the demands of the id, superego, and reality.

Dependency–autonomy continuum

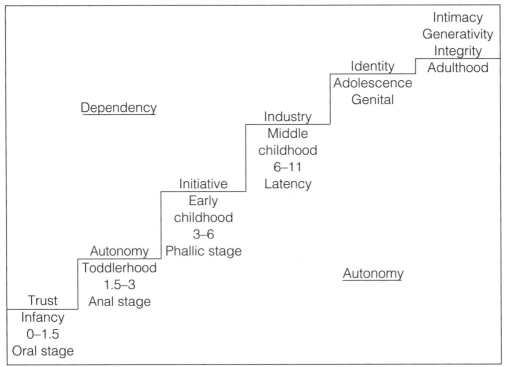

FIGURE 3-3 | DEVELOPMENTAL STAGES AND THE DEPENDENCY–AUTONOMY CONTINUUM

SUPEREGO   Composed of two parts—the *ego ideal* (developed from the child's idea of what parents and significant others thought was good) and the *conscience* (what parents and significant others thought was bad)—the superego is, in essence, a personal moral standard. Often thought of as the judicial branch of the personality, the superego can act to restrict, prohibit, and judge conscious actions.

In summary, the id, the basic unit in Freud's personality structure, contains the basic human instincts plus each person's genetic and constitutional inheritance. As a result of interacting with reality, the id developed a liaison between itself and the environment that Freud labeled the ego. The ego's primary mission is self-preservation, which is accomplished by mediating the demands of the id (instinctual demands) with the realities of the environment. The well-functioning ego is able to achieve the right balance between seeking pleasure and avoiding the consequences of immoderate infringement on the societal rules and mores. As noted in Figure 3-3, children are generally dependent on their parents to a large extent during their first two decades of life. During this time, the ego develops a superego that continues the parents' influence over the remainder of the person's lifetime.

DYNAMIC CONCEPTS

INSTINCT   An instinct is an inborn psychological representation, referred to as a *wish*, that stems from a physiological condition referred to as a *need*. For example, hunger is a need that leads to a wish for food. The wish becomes a motive for behavior. Life instincts serve to maintain the survival of the species. Hunger, thirst, and sex needs are served by life instincts. Freud believed that human behavior is motivated by basic instincts. *Libido* is the energy that permits life instincts to work.

CATHEXIS   Cathexis refers to directing one's libidinal energy toward an object, person, or idea that will satisfy a need.

ANTICATHEXIS   Anticathexis refers to the force the ego exerts to block or restrain the impulses of the id. The reality principle or superego directs this action of the ego against the pleasure principle emanating from the id.

ANXIETY   Anxiety refers to a conscious state in which a painful emotional experience is produced by external or internal excitation; that is, a welling up of autonomic nervous energy. Closely akin to fear, but more encompassing, is the anxiety that originates from internal and external causes. Freud believed there were three types of anxiety: reality, neurotic, and moral. Reality anxiety results from real threats from the environment. Neurotic anxiety results from the fear that our instinctual impulses from the id will overpower our ego controls and get us into trouble. Moral anxiety results from the guilt a person feels when he or she fails to live up to his or her own standards.

DEVELOPMENTAL CONCEPTS

DEFENSE MECHANISMS   The ego protects itself from heavy pressure and anxiety with defense mechanisms. Patton and Meara (1991) point out that defenses are any operations of the mind that aim to ward off anxiety and depression. The healthy, high-functioning ego attempts to cope with anxiety, depression, and stress with effective, reality-based, task-oriented, coping skills. When the load becomes too heavy, the ego may resort to defense-oriented coping methods that provide short-term relief but deny or distort reality and generally cause more problems in the long term.

Clark (1991) defines *defense mechanisms* as unconscious distortions of reality that reduce painful affect and conflict through automatic, habitual responses. Defense mechanisms are specific, unconscious, adjustive efforts used to resolve conflict and provide relief from anxiety. Counselors are generally able to detect their clients' defense mechanisms. Borrowing from Clark, this chapter provides examples of how a child might express a preference or lifestyle built around one, two, or a combination of defense mechanisms.

Identification   Identification is the development of role models that people identify with or imitate. They may choose to imitate either a few traits of the model or the total person. Identification often occurs with the same-sex parent and may be borne out of love or power; for example, "I love Dad so much I want to be just like him," or "If I can't beat him, I'll join him until I get big, too." Adolescents may be at the point where they are challenging all issues raised by their parents. The underachieving student might say, "I know a high school student who dropped out and is making a lot of money. He says school is a waste of time."

Displacement   Displacement means redirecting energy from a primary object to a substitute when an instinct is blocked. For example, anger toward a parent may be directed toward a sibling or another object because of the fear of reprisal from the parent. The underachieving child might say, "The stuff we study is so boring I'll never make good grades." The child may be redirecting hostile feelings from the teacher to the subject matter.

Repression and Suppression   Repression forces a dangerous memory, conflict, idea, or perception out of the conscious into the unconscious and places a lid on it to prevent the repressed material from resurfacing. In repression, the person unconsciously bars a painful thought from memory. Suppression is a conscious effort to do the same thing. An underachieving child might have repressed painful memories about failure in a prior school experience.

Projection   Projection is attributing one's own characteristics to others or to things in the external world. For instance, a teacher may find it uncomfortable to admit he does not like the children in his class, so instead he says the children do not like him. In this way, he projects his dislike for his students onto the students. An underachieving child may say, "My teacher doesn't like me; he thinks I'm stupid."

Reaction Formation   Reaction formation refers to the development of attitudes or character traits exactly opposite to ones that have been repressed. Anxiety-producing impulses are replaced in the conscious by their opposites; for example, "I would love to drink" is replaced by "Liquor should be declared illegal." An underachieving child may say, "I don't want to be a nerd; nerds suck up to the teacher just to make good grades."

Rationalization   Rationalization is an attempt to prove that one's behavior is justified and rational and is thus worthy of approval by oneself and others. When asked why they behaved in a certain manner, children may feel forced to think up logical excuses or reasons. An underachieving child may say, "I could finish my homework if my little brother would stop bothering me."

Denial   Denial is a refusal to face unpleasant aspects of reality or to perceive anxiety-provoking stimuli. Children may deny the possibility of falling while climbing high trees. An underachieving child may say, "Things are going fine; my grades will be much higher this time." Counselors need to remember that denial is common in young children, but is maladaptive for adolescents.

Fantasy   Fantasy is a way of seeking gratification of needs and frustrated desires through the imagination. A fantasy or imagined world may be a more pleasant place than a child's real world. An underachieving child may say, "Just wait, one of these days I'll become a doctor and show that teacher. She'll be sorry she made fun of my bad test score."

Withdrawal   Withdrawal means reducing ego involvement by becoming passive or learning to avoid being hurt; examples of withdrawn children include the shy child or school-phobic child. A withdrawn, underachieving child will probably not say much as he or she tries to avoid "risky" situations.

Intellectualization   Intellectualization is the act of separating the normal affect, or feeling, from an unpleasant or hurtful situation; for example, a child whose dog has been hit by a car might soften his or her grief by saying, "Our dog is really better off dead; he was feeble and going blind." An underachieving child may say, "I learn best from doing things outside school," or "I don't learn from the boring things we do at school."

Regression   Regression is a retreat to earlier developmental stages that are less demanding than those of the present level. An older child may revert to babyish behavior when a baby arrives in the family. An underachieving child may say, "All we do is work; recess and lunch should be longer."

Fixation   Fixation differs from regression in that the individual does not always regress to a more pleasant stage of development to avoid the pain or stress in a current developmental stage, but instead might decide to remain at the present level of development rather than move to the next stage, which poses more difficulties and problems to solve. The tendency is to stay with a situation that is pleasurable and comfortable and in which the person has been successful. Counselors often are confronted with dependent, underachieving students who have a difficult time, first, in developing alternative problem solutions and, second, in making commitments to try their new alternatives.

Undoing   Undoing is engaging in some form of atonement for immoral or bad behavior or for the desire to participate in such behavior; for instance, after breaking a lamp, a child may try to glue it back together. An underachieving child may say, "I get in a lot of arguments with my teacher, but I always try to do something to make up for it." Adolescents may become fixated on trying to repair a relationship that is beyond mending.

Acting Out   Acting out means reducing the anxiety aroused by forbidden desires by expressing them. The behavior of a revenge-seeking child is one example. An underachieving student may engage in violence, vandalism, or theft to express forbidden hurt feelings.

Compensation   Compensation is covering up a weakness by emphasizing some desirable trait or reducing frustration in one area of life by overgratification in another area; for example, the class clown may compensate for poor academic performance by engaging in attention-getting behavior. An underachiever may be an attention-getting clown of the first order or may overachieve in another area (for example, sports, hobbies, or gang activities) to compensate for low grades.

Sublimation   Sublimation often has been referred to as the backbone of civilization. Through it, people redirect their libidinal desires and energy into productive and acceptable activities and outlets. Often the products of this redirected energy have resulted in significant advances in the arts, sciences, quality of life, and civilization in general. We might speculate that surgeons and butchers found more useful and acceptable outlets for their libidinal desires than did Jack the Ripper. Parents and teachers would do well to help children find productive outlets for their great energy. Underachieving students do not need a lot of unstructured time to fill with negative addictions such as television, gang activity, overeating, and drugs.

PSYCHOSEXUAL STAGES AND ERIKSON'S STAGES   Freud (1940/1949) viewed personality development as a succession of stages, each characterized by a dominant mode of achieving libidinal pleasure and by specific developmental tasks. How well one adjusts at each stage is the critical factor in development. Freud believed that personality characteristics are fairly well established by the age of 6. Gratification of need during each stage is important if the individual is not to become fixated at that level of development. The key to successful adjustment in each stage is how well parents help their child adjust to that stage and make the transition to the next stage. The difficulty with Freud's system comes when counselors emphasize the extremes rather than the normal range of behaviors. The key seems to lie in maintaining a balance between extremes. The five developmental stages are oral, anal, phallic, latency, and genital.

Oral Stage (Birth to 2 Years Old): Trust versus Mistrust   The oral-erotic substage is characterized by the sucking reflex, which is necessary for survival. The child's main task in the oral-sadistic substage is to adjust to the weaning process and learn to chew food. The mouth is characterized as an erogenous zone because one obtains pleasure from sucking, eating, and biting. Adult behaviors, such as smoking, eating, and drinking, and the personality traits of gullibility, dependency (oral-erotic), and sarcasm (oral-sadistic) originate in the oral period.

Winnicott (1971, 1977, 2001) and Piaget and Inhelder (1969) believe that children at 12 to 18 months old begin to form an identity based on their "me" and "not me" worlds during this oral or trust-building stage. The process of developing an identity begins when infants see their image reflected in their mothers' expression as they look at their babies. Mothers who are depressed or under stress and have difficulty expressing their love by their looks and expressions send a disturbing message to their infants. The infant begins to sense, "If Mother seems not to love me or be pleased with what she sees, I may be unlovable."

Anal Stage (2 to 3 Years Old): Autonomy versus Shame and Doubt   During the anal stage, the membrane of the anal region presumably provides the major source of pleasurable stimulation. There are anal-expulsive and anal-retentive substages. The major hurdle is the regulation of a natural function (bowel control). Toilet training requires the child to learn how to postpone immediate gratification. Again, the manner in which the parents facilitate or impede the process forms the basis for a number of adult personality traits. Stubbornness, stinginess, and orderliness (anal-retentive) and generosity and messiness (anal-expulsive) are among the adult traits associated with the anal stage.

Phallic Stage (3 to 6 Years Old): Initiative versus Guilt   Self-manipulation of the genitals provides the major source of pleasurable sensation at this age. The Oedipus complex also occurs during this stage; the female version is sometimes referred to as the Electra complex. Sexual and aggressive feelings and fantasies are associated with the genitals. Boys have sexual desires for their mothers and aggressive feelings toward their fathers; girls develop hostility toward their mothers and become sexually attracted to their fathers. Attitudes toward people of the same sex and the opposite sex begin to take shape. Criticisms of Freud's castration complex concepts range from labeling them ridiculous to calling his ideas projections of his own fears. In any case, Freud believed that boys are afraid that their fathers will castrate them for loving their mothers. Girls' castration complexes were thought to take the form of penis envy; compensation for lacking a penis came with having a baby. The key question for healthy development in the phallic stage is, "How does the child handle competition with the same-sex parent for the affection of the opposite-sex parent?" The answer lies within whether the child has chosen to identify with the same-sex parent as a power figure or love object. In other words, Dad has the power, so if you cannot beat him, join him; or, Dad is a great guy and I would like to be like him.

Latency Stage (6 to 11 Years Old): Industry versus Inferiority   Sexual motivations presumably recede in importance during the latency period as the child becomes preoccupied with developmental skills and activities. Children generally concentrate on developing same-sex friendships. Sexual and aggressive impulses are relatively quiet during this phase. (As for aggression, Freud obviously never worked with a group of children in this age group.)

Genital Stage (Adolescence): Identity versus Role Confusion   After puberty, the deepest feeling of pleasure presumably comes from heterosexual relations. The major task of this period is developing opposite-sex relationships, a risky task involving rejection and fear of rejection that has a tremendous impact on future heterosexual relationships.

Oral, anal, and phallic stages are classified as narcissistic because children derive pleasure from their own erogenous zones. During the genital stage, the focus of activity shifts to developing genuine relationships with others. The goal for the young person is to move from a pleasure-seeking, pain-avoiding, narcissistic child to a reality-oriented, socialized adult.

In summary, overgratification of the child's needs could result in the child's fixation at a particular stage; deprivation may result in regression to a more comfortable developmental stage. For example, a 3-year-old only child suddenly finding a rival for his parents' attention in the form of a new baby sister regresses to his pre–toilet-training period in an effort to compete. Too much frustration in coping with a particular developmental stage also could result in fixating the child at that stage. Residue from regression and fixation may reappear in adult personality development.

Finding the healthy balance between unhealthy extremes is the key to mental health and a theme that runs throughout this book. Parents always have the difficult task of walking the thin line between too much and too little gratification of their child's needs. How much is too much or too little help in assisting a child in advancing to a new developmental stage? Perhaps the answer lies in the nurturing and preservation of the child's self-esteem, confidence, and trust.

PSYCHOANALYTIC COUNSELING AND DEVELOPMENT OF SELF-ESTEEM

Psychoanalytic counselors often search for repressed, traumatic events in the lives of their clients as possible causes for the symptoms and problems brought to counseling. Severe trauma is often associated with damaged egos, low self-esteem, and anxiety disorders; however, counselors can overlook the devastating effects on self-esteem of the daily onslaught of negative criticism heaped on some children throughout their developing years. Because such behavior falls short of legally being abuse and because it occurs in relatively small doses, it often goes unnoticed and unchecked. Therefore, we are presenting two systems for evaluating how well a child's self-esteem, mental health, and other personal needs are being supported by the family and, to a great extent, by the school.

Simon (1988) presents six conditions for nurturing and maintaining self-esteem and mental health in children and adults. Self-esteem is a by-product of our productive activity and our relationships. It is not a goal that can be attained through self-affirmation activities. Programs designed to build self-esteem tend to fall short unless the participants take steps to improve their productivity and relationships. Freud believed that love and work are the keys to mental health. For children, the keys to mental health are their schoolwork and their relationships with family, peers, and other significant people. Simon's (1988) six conditions complement the productivity and relationship equation for self-esteem. These conditions are as follows:

Belonging: Children need to feel connected to their family or to a family of their own creation if the family of origin did not work out. As children grow older, they need to feel connected to a peer group.

Child advocacy: Children need at least one advocate who can be trusted to help them through crisis periods.

Risk management: Self-esteem increases as children are able to take risks and master challenging tasks. The difficulty is finding tasks that are challenging, yet not impossible. Children need to believe that they are successful if they have given a task their best effort and that it is all right to take risks and fail.

Empowerment: Children need to exercise developmentally appropriate amounts of control over their own lives. Opportunities to make choices and decisions contribute to empowerment.

Uniqueness: Children need to feel they are special. Simon (1988) suggests that we work with children in constructing lists of 100 sentences validating their unique and positive qualities, which he calls "anti-suicide" lists.

Productivity: As children get things done, they feel better. Encouragement and reinforcement of productive activity can move children toward finding intrinsic rewards in accomplishment.

Simon's six conditions are as relevant for adults as they are for children and adolescents. Adding more risk to one's life can improve one's mental health, providing the risk falls within rational limits. Closely related to self-esteem is the degree to which children are meeting their other human needs.

Counseling children through Freud's five stages of development often requires an assessment of how well their basic needs are being met. A rating scale of 0 to 10 (0 for unmet needs and 10 for fully met needs) can be used to assess the child's progress in each level of Maslow's (1970) hierarchy, including self-esteem (Table 3-1).

Problems in adult development are often traced to childhood frustration from failure to meet basic human needs during the developmental years. Psychoanalytic counseling can focus on the child's level of human needs attainment in past years, as well as in the present. Questions of how children handle the pain of not getting what they want can be treated in psychoanalytic counseling. Are conflict and stress repressed in the unconscious or handled in the conscious area of functioning? Are depression and anxiety handled in task-oriented or defense-oriented ways? Both are good questions for psychoanalytic counselors to address.

OBJECT RELATIONS THEORY

As mentioned earlier, love and work are important concepts in Freud's system. He believed that a quick assessment of mental health could be based on how well people were managing their relationships and careers. Object relations theory is

TABLE 3-1 | CHILD'S NEEDS ASSESSMENT

Physiological needs			
Nutrition, sleep, exercise, general	0	5	10
Safety needs			
Safety within the family and peer group settings	0	5	10
Love and belonging needs			
Affection shown to the child	0	5	10
Promises made and kept to the child	0	5	10
Someone listens to the child	0	5	10
Family follows a dependable schedule	0	5	10
Child has own space, possessions, and a right to privacy	0	5	10
Someone is there when the child arrives home	0	5	10
Child is loved unconditionally	0	5	10
Child has a place and role in the family	0	5	10
Child has found acceptance and a place in his/her peer group	0	5	10
Self-esteem needs			
Someone affirms the child's worth	0	5	10
Child is given the opportunity to achieve and accomplish tasks	0	5	10
Child is given the opportunity to make choices	0	5	10
Self-actualization needs			
Child is not blocked by unmet needs in the previous four levels	0	5	10
Child is developing potential abilities, strengths, and skills	0	5	10
Problem-solving skills enable the child to engage in developmental rather than remedial activities	0	5	10

a natural progression from his earlier work on how well children resolved the conflict surrounding competition with the same-sex parent for the love and attention of the opposite-sex parent. Object relations theory focuses on how the early family relationships affect the type of relationships formed outside the family. For example, missing a solid father figure during her childhood years may motivate a woman to seek the love and attention she did not get from her father from older, fatherly types of men. Object relations theorists use the word *object* to refer to people other than the self. Family relationships that model appropriate and healthy models for future relationship development are the best assistance children can have in learning to build relationships outside the family. Children who receive proper nurturing during their dependent years do not seek parent figures in their adult relationships. Parents who facilitate their children's movement through the developmental stages toward the achievement of independence and identity provide them with blueprints for fulfilling and healthy adult relationships. As children begin differentiating themselves from their families, they carry their internalized view of how relationships operate to their peer group and eventually to their adult world. For example, a woman might carry a repressed image of her father as a hostile and rejecting person who did not provide the love and nurturing she needed and project this image of her father on all men in general. Seeing this hostile father image in her husband, she reacts accordingly, causing him to act out the hostile role of her father. Treatment for children educates parents to be better models of how to provide the right amount of love and nurturing. Treatment for adults accesses the unconscious to find the history of the unresolved conflicts with their parents and to find out how the repressed conflicts contribute to their difficulties in establishing and maintaining the relationships they would like to have.

Donald Woods Winnicott (1896–1971) was a British psychoanalyst who, through his clinical experience as a pediatrician and child psychiatrist, came to believe that the first few months of a child's life were critical to the development of good mental health and adjustment in the future life of the child. He strongly emphasized the mother's role in her child's development. Winnicott's view was that mothers did not have to be extraordinary in their duties, and that the "good enough mother" would be sufficient in facilitating the development of good mental health in her children. He believed that most mothers instinctively know how to meet their children's needs through providing the love, caring, and support needed to get their children started on the road to mature independence, providing they do not let themselves become misguided by child-rearing books. Winnicott (1971, 1977, 2001) recognized the importance of physical holding by the mother when the child is totally dependent and the "holding environment" mothers create through their empathy, which meets the child's physiological and emotional needs in reliable and consistent ways. He viewed holding as a form of ego support that is needed for children, adolescents, and adults when they are under stress. Well-cared-for infants do not experience the anxieties produced by environmental failure that some children experience during their stage of total dependence. These anxieties include feelings of falling, depersonalization, and generalized insecurity. To handle these intolerable feelings and anxieties, children create elaborate defenses such as repression to avoid having to face these difficulties on a day-to-day basis. Splitting themselves from reality (schizophrenia) would be an extremely costly, but not uncommon, measure for developing a position of invulnerability to defend against these anxieties. Winnicott believed that the analyst should "stand in" for the important people (objects) in a person's psychological history who literally let the person down. He used these transference relationships in treatment to help people relive and re-evaluate their pasts. The analyst assumes the "holding" role the child never experienced, including the environmental support or holding that was lacking in the person's past. Such environmental support was the forerunner of case management, which includes helping people meet their basic survival needs so that they can benefit from counseling.

What about father? Two recent reports in the press have caught our attention. Although we do not believe animal psychology always translates to human behavior, we noted that in Pilansberg National Park in South Africa, park rangers have reported that young bull elephants have become increasingly violent, especially to white rhinos. They attack the rhinos, knock them over, kneel, and gore them to death. This has not previously been typical elephant behavior. Apparently, according to the game wardens, the aggressiveness is the result of a government program to reduce the elephant population by killing the older animals, including the dominant, older male animals that kept the young bulls in line and served as role models (Dobson, 2002). The question is: Are boys reared without the influence of a strong and positive father figure more likely to become violent teenagers and adults?

The second news report focuses on a past Mother's Day project by a greeting card company to furnish free cards and postage to all of the male inmates who wanted to send their mothers a card. The response was overwhelming, and the sponsor had to bring in additional cards. Because the Mother's Day project was so successful, the company decided to repeat it for Father's Day. You guessed right: Nobody showed up for the free cards. Approximately 2 million people in the United States are serving time in jail; 94% of them are men. Again, the question is: How much influence does a father-absent home have on violent behavior in men? Westen (1998) notes that childhood experiences are critical to the development of the adult personality. Children must have stability in their relationships to develop stable, mature personalities as adults. Children lacking healthy interactions with a stable family will have to look no further than their childhood to find their source of pain and suffering. Mental representations formed in childhood of self, others, and relationships, for better or worse, may determine our interactions with others throughout the adult years unless corrective adjustments are made.

COUNSELING METHODS

The primary goal of counseling within a psychoanalytic frame of reference is to make the unconscious conscious. All material in the unconscious was once in the conscious. Once brought to the conscious level, repressed material can be dealt with in rational ways by using any number of methods discussed in this book.

Several methods are used to uncover the unconscious. Detailed case histories are taken, with special attention given to the handling of conflict areas. Hypnosis, although rejected by Freud, is still used to assist in plumbing the unconscious. Analyses of resistance, transference, and dreams are frequently used methods, as are catharsis, free association, interpretation, and play therapy. All these methods have the long-term goal of strengthening the ego. The principal counseling methods discussed in this chapter are catharsis, free association, interpretation, analysis of transference, analysis of resistance, analysis of incomplete sentences, bibliocounseling, storytelling, and play therapy.

Much of what is practiced in psychoanalytic counseling depends on the spirit and process of play therapy. Successful outcomes depend on voluntary engagement and participation. By definition, play is voluntary; when it is not, it ceases to be play. Free association rests on spontaneous, uncensored engagement in a type of voluntary play. If censorship occurs in the free-association game, an important rule is broken, and progress in counseling stops. Rather than admonishing clients for censoring their thoughts, the counselor makes an interpretation of why the censorship might have occurred, which helps the client gain insight.

Play in counseling helps the child, as well as the adult, suspend reality, thus allowing children to direct a make-believe gratification for those areas found wanting in their lives. In cases where fantasy has become delusion, totally detached from reality, the client may be experiencing the results of failed attempts to play. If counseling is to work for these clients, they will have to be taught how to play. In addition to being taught how to play, some clients will have to be taught how to trust, and others will need to be taught about the limits to be observed in play therapy. Working through transference is an exercise in fantasy and imagination requiring a form of role-playing.

Psychodrama with older children and adolescents who have lived in chaotic and dysfunctional families can be an effective counseling play method. Successful psychodrama for these clients depends on providing structured directions stated clearly in an exact manner, with as little room for misinterpretation as possible. The counselor has to take charge of the session with confidence and leadership. The drama should be kept in the first person to be effective in working through personal concerns. Do not terminate the drama until the important objectives have been achieved. Provide ample time for sharing what the group learned from the drama. Both play and the expressive arts, including psychodrama, allow thoughts and feelings in the unconscious to return to the conscious, where they can be treated, especially in children who have limited skills and ability to reason by nature of their stage of cognitive development, be it the preoperational or concrete stage. Some blocks to cognitive development can be overcome in psychoanalytic counseling by using metaphors to explain how the unconscious works.

CATHARSIS

Freud, along with Breuer, first discovered the benefits of catharsis through hypnosis. Freud found that if, under hypnosis, hysterical patients were able to verbalize an early precipitating causal event, the hysterical symptoms disappeared. Freud soon discarded hypnosis because he was not able to induce in every patient the deep hypnotic sleep that enabled the patient to regress to an early enough period to disclose the repressed event. Freud discovered that for many people the mere command to remember the origin of some hysterical symptom worked quite well. Unfortunately, many of his patients could not remember the origin of their symptoms even on command. Freud thus decided that all people were aware of the cause of their illness, but that for some reason certain people blocked this knowledge. Freud believed that unless this repressed traumatic infantile experience could be retrieved from the unconscious, verbalized, and relived emotionally, the patient would not recover. Because not everyone had the ability to find this unconscious material, the analyst had to use more indirect means to gain access to the unconscious mind. Freud developed free association and interpretation to bring everyone to the emotional state of catharsis he believed was necessary for cure.

FREE ASSOCIATION

In traditional psychoanalysis, the client lies on a couch and the analyst sits at the head of the couch beyond the client's line of vision. The analyst then orders the client to say whatever comes to mind. Through this method, the unconscious thoughts and conflicts are given freedom to reach the conscious mind. A great struggle takes place within the client to keep from telling these innermost thoughts to the analyst. The analyst must constantly struggle against this resistance. The fundamental rule of psychoanalytic counseling requires clients to tell the counselor whatever thoughts and feelings come into their minds, regardless of how personal, painful, or seemingly irrelevant.

While the client is trying to associate freely, the counselor must remain patient and nonjudgmental and insist that the client continue. The counselor must also look for continuity of thoughts and feelings. Although the client may appear to be rambling idly, psychoanalytic counselors believe there is a rational pattern to this speech. To interpret what the client is saying, the counselor must pay attention to the affect, or feeling, behind the client's verbalization, noting the client's gestures, tone of voice, and general body language during free association. At this point, the counselor offers some interpretations of the client's statements to try to open another door for free association.

INTERPRETATION

Free association, in turn, leads to another important technique: interpretation. Three major areas of interpretation are dreams, parapraxia, and humor.

INTERPRETATION OF DREAMS   Freud (1901/1952, 1965a) believed dreams expressed wish fulfillment. To correctly interpret the power of the id, the analyst must learn about and interpret the client's dreams. There are three major types of dreams: those with meaningful, rational content (almost invariably found in children); those with material very different from waking events; and those with illogical, senseless episodes. All dreams center on a person's life and are under the person's psychic control. Every dream reveals an unfulfilled wish. In children's dreams, the wish is usually obvious. As the individual matures, the wish, as exposed in the dream, becomes more distorted and disguised. The ego fights the initial conscious wish, which thus is pushed back to the unconscious mind; it brings itself back into the conscious mind by means of a dream. The dream guards against pain. When people are sleeping, repressive defenses are weaker, and forbidden desires and feelings can find an outlet in dreams. Freud referred to dreams as the royal road to the unconscious. The counselor's role is to listen to the client's dream and help the client interpret the dream's symbolism.

Freud's method of dream interpretation was to allow the client to free-associate about the dream's content. Certain objects in dreams were universal symbols for Freud. For example, a car in someone's dreams usually represented analysis. Car dreams also may refer to one's direction in life or how one treats his or her body and takes care of his or her personal health. The number 3 represented male genitals; jewel cases and purses were vaginas; peaches and twin sisters were female breasts; woods were pubic hair; trees and steeples were penises; and dancing, riding, and flying were symbols for sexual intercourse. Dreams about falling are related to fears about falling from one's moral standards. Dreams about teeth were associated with lying, as in lying through your teeth. Dreams about a person may relate to positive or negative traits that person has that the dreamer may wish to emulate or discard. The same may be true for animal dreams that symbolize the dreamer's own negative traits or behaviors he or she should discard. House and building dreams may refer to specific concerns in one's life; for example, dreams in a kitchen may relate to one's eating habits. Dreams about children may indicate one's need for fun, happiness, spontaneity, and doing something new and different; in contrast, they may signify indulging in childish behavior. Clothing dreams could relate to changing one's mood or state of mind. Death dreams could refer to anxiety about significant changes in one's life. The key for understanding one's dream is identifying the basic theme being communicated in the dream. This is done by stripping away such details as names, places, and things, leaving only the action. For example, a dream about someone drowning could be reduced to the theme that something bad is happening to a person the dreamer cares about and his or her help is needed. Next match the bare-bones theme to an ongoing part of the dreamer's life and give full attention to the feelings and emotions that are generated. One's feelings are the best indicators of what needs attention in one's life or the unfinished business that needs to be completed (see the Dream Central Web page for one method of interpretation: www. sleeps.com/analysis.html).

Freud (1901/1952) believed every dream to be a confession and a by-product of repressed, anxiety-producing thoughts. He thought that many dreams represented unfulfilled sexual desires and expressed the superego's guilt and self-punishment. Nightmares result from the desire for self-punishment. Because we are consciously and unconsciously aware of those things that we fear most, we put these things into our nightmares to punish ourselves.

PARAPRAXIA   Parapraxia, or "Freudian slips," are consciously excused as harmless mistakes, but through them the id pushes unconscious material through to the conscious. The counselor must be aware of any slips of the tongue while dealing with a client. The Freudians also believe there are no such things as "mistakes" or items that are "misplaced." According to psychoanalytic thinking, everything we do—for example, forgetting a person's name, cutting a finger while peeling potatoes—has unconscious motivation. The analyst must take all these unconscious mistakes and arrange them into a conscious pattern.

HUMOR   Jokes, puns, and satire are all acceptable means for unconscious urges to gain access to the conscious. The things we laugh about tell us something about our repressed thoughts. One of the fascinations of humor, according to psychoanalytic theory, is that it simultaneously disguises and reveals repressed thoughts. Repressed thoughts, released by humor, usually generate from the id or superego. Because sexual thoughts are usually repressed, many jokes are sexually oriented; because aggressive thoughts are usually repressed, they are expressed in humor by way of satire and witticisms.

Again, the counselor must watch for patterns and themes. What does the client think is funny? How does the client's sense of humor fit into a pattern from the unconscious?

ANALYSIS OF TRANSFERENCE

Transference occurs when the client views the counselor as someone else. Freud was genuinely surprised when his patients first regarded him as someone other than an analyst, helper, or adviser. During the course of psychoanalytic counseling, clients usually transfer their feelings about some significant individual from their past to the therapist. Transference generally is a product of unfinished business with a significant person from the client's childhood. Clients commonly transfer their feelings, thoughts, and expectations about the significant other to the counselor. Counseling provides a stage for re-enacting unresolved conflicts with the counselor, who can help clients deal with them in more effective and functional ways. Transference relationships can become a real battleground when love feelings directed toward the counselor are rejected and the client, in turn, rejects the counselor by resisting the counselor's every effort to be helpful. Both transference and resistance can be analyzed for cause-and-effect implications for the client's life. Countertransference occurs when the counselor begins to view a client as someone other than a client. Referral to another competent professional is recommended for a counselor who loses his or her balance on the objectivity–empathy continuum.

ANALYSIS OF RESISTANCE

Freud also was surprised by the amount of resistance his patients mounted against his attempts to help them. Resistance took the form of erecting barriers to free association, thus breaking Freud's rule against censoring or holding back material; Freud's patients were often unwilling or unable to talk about some of their thoughts during free association or descriptions of their dreams. Resistance prevents painful and irrational content from reaching the conscious, and it must be eliminated for the person to have the opportunity to face and react to these repressed conflicts in realistic and healthy ways. Therefore, the essential task of any counselor is building a trusting relationship with each client that undermines the client's need to resist the counselor's attempts to be helpful. Analysis of resistance can also provide valuable information regarding the client's need to withhold information from the counselor.

ANALYSIS OF INCOMPLETE SENTENCES

Psychoanalytic counselors often use projective techniques such as the House/Tree/Person or Children's Apperception Test in an attempt to understand their clients' thoughts, behaviors, and feelings. Ecker and Hulley (1995) recommend asking children to complete stimulus statements about likes, dislikes, family, friends, goals, wishes, and things that make the child happy or sad to help counselors understand children and find problem areas. This procedure may be especially useful in acquainting counselors with children and in establishing better rapport with those who are anxious, fearful, or reluctant to talk.

EXAMPLES

The thing I like to do most is _____.

The person in my family who helps me most is _____.

My friends are _____.

I feel happiest (or saddest) when _____.

My greatest wish is _____.

The greatest thing that ever happened to me was _____.

I wish my parents would _____.

When I grow up, I want _____.

Brothers are _____.

Sisters are _____.

Dad is _____.

Mom is _____.

School is _____.

My teacher is _____.

BIBLIOCOUNSELING

Bibliocounseling—that is, reading and discussing books about situations and children similar to themselves—can help clients in several ways. Children unable to verbalize their thoughts and feelings may find them expressed in books. From selected stories, children can learn alternative solutions to problems and new ways of behaving; by reading about children similar to themselves, clients may not feel so alone or different.

In an article citing the benefits of bibliocounseling for abused children, Watson (1980) suggests that children may become psychologically and emotionally involved with characters they have read about. Vicarious experiences through books can be similar to the child's own thoughts, feelings, attitudes, behavior, or environment. Directed reading can lead to expression of feelings or problem solving. Watson lists the goals of bibliotherapy as: (1) teaching constructive and positive thinking, (2) encouraging free expression concerning problems, (3) helping clients analyze their attitudes and behaviors, (4) looking at alternative solutions, (5) encouraging the client to find a way to cope that is not in conflict with society, and (6) allowing clients to see the similarity of their problems with those of others.

With bibliocounseling, discussion focused around characters' behaviors, feelings, thoughts, relationships, cause and effect, and consequences is more effective than just asking the child to relate the story. Discussion also clears up questions that arise from the reading. Counselors can guide children to see how the story applies to their own lives.

Bibliocounseling is also a means of educating children about certain areas of concern such as sex, physical disabilities, divorce, and death. Once children have enough information about a problem, their attitudes and behaviors tend to change.

STORYTELLING

Richard Gardner developed the mutual storytelling technique as a therapeutic means for working with children (Schaefer & Cangelosi, 1993). It uses a familiar technique to help children understand their own thoughts and feelings and to communicate meaningful insights, values, and standards of behavior to children. The counselor sets the stage and asks the child to tell a story, which is recorded on tape. The counselor instructs the child that the story should have a beginning, a middle, and an ending, and that the child will be asked to tell the moral (lesson) of the story at the end. The counselor may need to clarify some points of the story after the child has finished. The counselor then prepares a story using a similar theme and setting and including the significant figures from the child's story. The counselor's story, however, provides the child with better alternatives or responses to the situation.

We have found storytelling to be an excellent counseling technique to help children cope with feelings, thoughts, and behaviors they are not yet ready to discuss in a direct manner with the counselor. Storytelling also has been useful in helping children realize possible consequences of their behavior. (See the Case Study of Pete later in this chapter.)

In examining mutual storytelling as a viable therapeutic method, Kestenbaum (1985) presents three cases. In two cases, the child dictated the stories and the teacher wrote them down. In the third case, the child spoke into a tape recorder as though an original radio play was being produced. Transcripts from each case were typed, and together the client and the counselor listened to the tapes during subsequent sessions. Story plots and characters were found to parallel events in the children's lives. The children's answers to questions about the characters, their backgrounds, and their motives were recorded for use in future sessions.

Lawson (1987) presents a helpful method of using a story within a story in working with an overweight 8-year-old girl who was acting out in an attempt to handle rejection by her peers. The therapist told a story about a similar girl who had no friends. No name was used in the story, but the counselor mentioned the client's name in nearly every sentence; for example, the counselor would say, "Ann, I once knew a little girl . . ." Next, the counselor began another story within a story with the same theme: "Ann, this little girl had a dream about a little brown, black, and white puppy who had no friends because she was different than the other puppies who were all white, all black, or all brown." The second story worked out a solution around the theme that being different and special is good. When the girl wakes from her dream about the puppy, she is excited about being special and can hardly wait to take her new feelings to school because, as in the puppy story, what the other children thought about her did not matter as long as she felt special.

PSYCHOANALYTIC PLAY THERAPY AND THE EXPRESSIVE ARTS

Anna Freud (1926) adapted psychoanalysis for the treatment of children by incorporating play activities into therapy. She used toys and games to put the child at ease, create an alliance with the child, and discover clues about the child's inner life. The therapist engages the child, entering the fantasy, dramatization, or free play by going along with the child's make-believe world. Thus, Anna Freud used play to enhance the relationship and as a diagnostic tool. Melanie Klein (1932) also recognized the value of play in understanding the child's wishes, fears, and fantasies. She saw children's play as significant symbolic communication and interpreted the meaning of play in sessions with children (Lyness-Richard, 1997). Klein used play to accomplish with children the effect of free association used with adults (Fall, 1994).

Neubauer (1987) lists ways that play can affect therapy. Play involves a mental act, unconscious or conscious, that contains a fantasy and a wish. It has a physical component that is an observable enactment. Finally, play is an exploration, a "trying on"; play is pretending. The role of the therapist is to establish and maintain an alliance by interpreting, empathizing with, and understanding the child. Frankel (1998) examines processes essential in psychoanalytic play therapy. Play is the first process. The interrelated aspects of play include the emergence and integration of the dissociated self states, symbols, and recognition. The second process proposed is renegotiation of relationships with self and others. The goals of psychoanalytic play therapy are to resolve fixations, regression, developmental deficiencies, and other impediments to the child's normal development (Lee, 1997).

Play is a universal activity that people of all ages need. Both spectator and participative play and recreation activities fill important human needs. Play provides needed change from our daily school or work routines. Play provides opportunities to work through emotional problems and release pent-up emotions in ways that are acceptable to society. It also allows rest for our bodies and minds. Play has been identified as preparation for adulthood in that it provides children with a medium in which to act out the roles they will live, or hope to live, as adults: spouse, parent, hero, doctor, lawyer, and star athlete. The theory has even been advanced that play provides a theater for children to re-enact the drama of the development of civilization. Young children begin learning about the "not me" world by biting, hitting, and pushing anything and anyone they can without regard to consequences and rules. Gradually, as children move through the socialization process, they do approximate, in brief form, the steps humankind took in moving from primitive to advanced civilizations.

From a Freudian view, play provides the medium for moving through the five psychosexual stages and the corresponding development of the ego and superego superstructures from the id structure. Exercise of the pleasure principle, such as hitting, biting, pushing others, and doing what the child pleases, gradually comes up against the reality principle, which tells the child that games have rules and that sometimes it is necessary and even best to postpone pleasurable activities. Play is useful in working through healthy identification with the same-sex and opposite-sex parent. The development of relationships with same-sex peers and, eventually, with opposite-sex friends is facilitated through play activities.

For children, play therapy is the treatment of choice for bringing both conscious and unconscious material into the counseling session. Play is the natural mode of communication for children. Limited verbal ability prevents children from being able to verbally express their thoughts, feelings, and behavior. Play is the natural way for children to express themselves and learn about their world. Many counseling techniques, including the expressive arts of painting, drawing, playing and singing music, and dancing, can be used with play therapy to adapt the process to a particular child's developmental level. Self-portrait drawings are good indicators of how children see their world. See Figure 3-4 for a drawing done by a 10-year-old girl who has love and support from her family, does well in school, makes friends easily, and excels in her sport of gymnastics. Contrast this drawing with Pete's drawing later in this chapter (see Figure 3-5).

Winnicott (1971, 1977, 2001), in his extensive work with children from the 1920s through the early 1960s, developed a squiggle game play technique that combined drawing and storytelling. He would begin by drawing a few neutral lines (a "squiggle"), and then passed the paper to the child to make it into a picture. Next, the child would start a squiggle for Winnicott to finish. Each time a drawing was finished, the "artist" made up a story about the completed picture. Through the storytelling and conversation surrounding the squiggle game, children were able to express thoughts, feelings, and ideas from their unconscious that previously were not accessible to them.

Of course, most general theories of counseling can be adapted to fit the play therapy setting. Some counselors use dogs and other pets in their play therapy and regular sessions (Burton, 1995; Levinson, 1962; O'Brien, 1993; Trivedi & Perl, 1995).

FIGURE 3-4
SELF-PORTRAIT
DRAWING BY A
10-YEAR-OLD
GIRL (REPRINTED
BY PERMISSION
OF JESSICA MARIE
MARTIN.)

FIGURE 3-5
PETE'S DRAWING

As is true with the counselor's office, children must perceive the play therapy room as a safe place to discuss anything they wish without fear of criticism or punishment. The counselor's role is to interpret the child's symbolic play in words that are meaningful to the child. Successful play therapy should result in higher levels of self-esteem, communication, trust, confidence, and problem-solving ability. (See Chapter 14 for a full discussion and presentation of play therapy.)

In summary, Freud (1930) viewed the personal unconscious as the repository of the primitive, the antisocial, and the evil within us. Repressed below the conscious area of functioning, these three forces tend to cause anxiety and tension through conflicts that affect our behavior in negative ways. The solution is to bring these three forces into conscious awareness.

Psychoanalytic counselors are interested in accessing the personal unconscious to bring these repressed conflicts into conscious awareness, where they can be treated. The most common means of returning unconscious content to the conscious are dream interpretation, free association, analysis of resistance, analysis of transference, hypnosis, meditation, journal writing, reflection, and analysis of slips of the tongue, selective remembering and forgetting, and accidents. Play therapy, in combination with the expressive arts, provides the preferred treatment modality for any theoretical orientation for younger children.

CASE STUDIES

Identification of Problem I[1]

Dennis, age 9, was considered a disturbed, slow, resistant boy who had to be pushed into doing everything he was supposed to be doing. He rarely participated in any family activities and had no friends in the neighborhood. His school records listed such problems as regression, playing with much younger children, thumb sucking, daydreaming, soiling, bullying, and tardiness. An excerpt from the first counseling session begins with Dennis entering the playroom.

Transcript

DENNIS: Well, what are we going to do today?

COUNSELOR: Whatever you'd like. This is your time.

DENNIS: Let's talk.

COUNSELOR: All right.

DENNIS: Let's go back in history. We're studying about it in school. I'm going to be studying about Italy next week. I can't think of anything to talk about. I can't think of one thing to say. Can you?

---

[1]The case of Dennis was contributed by Michael Gooch, and is reprinted by permission.

COUNSELOR: I'd rather discuss something you suggest.

DENNIS: I can't think of a thing.

COUNSELOR: We can just sit here if you like.

DENNIS: Good. Do you want to read?

COUNSELOR: Okay.

DENNIS: You be the student, and I'll be the teacher. I'll read to you. Now you be ready to answer some questions. I don't like spelling. I like social studies, and I like history more than any other subject. I'd like being the teacher for a change. [Dennis asks the counselor questions from a reading text.]

COUNSELOR: You like to ask questions you think I'll miss.

DENNIS: That's right. I'm going to give you a test next week. A whole bunch of arithmetic problems, and social studies, and other questions.

COUNSELOR: You like getting to be the teacher and getting to be the boss.

DENNIS: Yeah, I never get to be the boss.

COUNSELOR: You would like to have a chance to tell people what to do.

DENNIS: Yeah, I hate getting bossed around all the time.

COUNSELOR: It would be nice if you got to be your own boss sometimes and not have to take orders from your teacher and your parents.

DENNIS: Right, I never get to do anything I want to do.

COUNSELOR: It would be really nice if your teacher or parents would let you choose some things to do.

DENNIS: Yeah, but they don't let me.

COUNSELOR: It's hard for you to get your own way at school and home.

DENNIS: Sometimes I do.

COUNSELOR: How were you able to do that?

DENNIS: I raised a fuss.

COUNSELOR: You mean you got what you wanted by making a lot of noise.

DENNIS: I cried, kicked, and screamed.

COUNSELOR: So one time you got what you wanted.

DENNIS: I got punished, too; I couldn't play video games for a week.

COUNSELOR: So you need a better way to get to do something you want to do.

DENNIS: I don't know what to do.

COUNSELOR: Well, we can practice in here on how to get things you want.

DENNIS: How?

COUNSELOR: Kind of like you are doing now, when you are the teacher and I am the student.

DENNIS: Okay. Now, I'm going to read like my friend does. [Dennis imitates his friend's reading style.] Notice how he reads?

COUNSELOR: He seems to read fast without pausing.

DENNIS: Yes.

COUNSELOR: You'd like to be able to read like that.

DENNIS: Not much. Let's name the ships in the books. [Dennis names each type of boat.] I have so much fun making up those names. That's what we'll do next week. [Dennis begins reading again.] Stop me when I make a mistake or do something wrong.

COUNSELOR: I'd rather you stop yourself.

DENNIS: The teacher always stops me.

COUNSELOR: I'm a listener, not a teacher.

DENNIS: Be a teacher, all right? [Dennis begins reading again.] That reminds me, I have three darts at home. The set cost me three dollars. Two have been broke. [The session is about to end. The counselor examines some darts and a board.] Oh boy, darts. Maybe we can play with them next week.

COUNSELOR: You're making lots of plans for next time.

DENNIS: Yeah.

Several counseling sessions followed this one. Dennis showed marked improvement at school and at home. Dennis's mother and teacher spoke more positively of him. The counselor gave Dennis his complete, undivided attention, participating in his games, tasks, projects, and plans. The counselor was someone with whom Dennis could talk and share his interests and ideas at a time when no one else would understand and accept him. He needed someone who would let him lead the way and be important in making decisions and plans. Dennis played the role of the initiator, the director, the teacher. He needed to have someone else know how it felt to be the follower who is told what to do, ordered into activity, and made to meet expectations. He needed to gain respect, as well as confidence, in his ability to face tasks and problems and see them through successfully. In short, he used the therapy experience to improve his relationships and skills. He became a competent, self-dependent person by practicing behavior that gave him a sense of adequacy and self-fulfillment.

Identification of Problem II[2]

A family sought therapy for problems with Pete, their rebellious 12-year-old son. The boy and his younger sister had been adopted 5 years earlier after a series of foster care arrangements. The adopting couple had no children before the adoption.

---

[2]The case of Pete was contributed by Robert Lee Whitaker, Ph.D., and is reprinted by permission.

A history-gathering first session with the adoptive parents revealed that Pete had been physically abused by his biological mother and by at least one subsequent foster mother. The parents described Pete as rebellious and disrespectful, especially toward his mother. During the second session, the counselor met separately with Pete to establish rapport and continue assessing the context of the presenting problem. Although the boy was 12 years old, his social and emotional development appeared to be more like that of a 6- or 7-year-old child. The counselor wanted to help Pete feel comfortable, as well as elicit more information about his inner thoughts. With these objectives in mind and in view of Pete's apparent developmental stage, the counselor asked him to draw a picture of a person. Pete drew a hyper-muscular, threatening-looking young adult (Figure 3-5). Then the counselor asked Pete to make up a story about the picture. Pete then told the following story. Note how the story's themes metaphorically describe Pete's experiences and his frustrated efforts to cope with them.

Pete's Story

He was born in a hollow tree. His mom was a dog; his dad was a cat. He was green, and he was the strongest person who ever lived. People called him Starman. He could throw a car, and it wouldn't come down for a week.

Then one day he met a baby. The baby had a race with him in the Olympics and beat him. The baby asked if he thought he could beat him again. For 2 years, they competed, and the baby always won. So the guy trained for 2 more years to beat the baby, but by that time, the baby was so big his head went out of the earth. He could jump out the earth. The guy knew he couldn't do anything about it, so he retired and went off to be a wimp and was never seen again. There were stories that he was beat up, killed, shot. And that was the last they saw of him.

A week later, the counselor asked Pete to tell the story of Starman's early life.

He lived in a jungle and helped his dad fight off the beasts that tried to attack his family. He's been alive 300 billion years. He was a god and a very powerful prince of the world then. His dad was the king. The prince made up the rules for the kingdom (which was communist). People could only work when the prince wanted them to work, and no family could have over $700. If so, they had to see him, and they couldn't leave the country.

The queen was named Laura. She was as skinny as a toothpick, and she was so powerful she could make it rain or snow or any kind of weather when she wanted. She could make people feel like they were dying and could make them grow old real fast. She could make them have nine lives or make them look ugly. She could change their bodies into beasts. She was very wicked.

The prince didn't like her because she was trying to overrule him and get all the power he had. So, the prince got all the other gods in all the world or universe and his dad and formed all their powers together and killed her. When she died, she turned into a planet called Saturn (her remains). The queen is dead now.

The prince grew up, and his dad died because of Zeus. Zeus gave him poison, and the prince was in charge from then on, except for Zeus (the god over all). The prince enforced all the laws the same way the lady did, and Zeus threatened to kill him. The lady had enforced the laws because Zeus threatened to kill her. The prince killed her because he didn't like the rules and what she was doing to the people, but he didn't know Zeus was making her do it by threatening to kill her.

The prince went on doing things the way Zeus wanted until he died. Now he is just a strong person.

Interpreting the Story This story suggested to the counselor a need to explore issues of anger and powerlessness with Pete. "Starman," or "the prince," felt powerless against the exceptional power and influence of the queen and the baby. Queen "Laura" had absolute control over the environment and could make whatever kind of weather she wanted (usually bad), make people grow old quickly, make them experience a feeling of death, make them ugly, and even turn them into beasts. Leadership, no matter who was in power, was always threateningly authoritarian. The prince's battle for power or control is described as a violent act against the leader, made possible by combining the power of all oppressed victims.

The story appears to reflect the trauma of Pete's upbringing and the particularly negative feelings he has toward female individuals with power over him. Furthermore, the story seems to parallel closely his history of abuse and development into an aggressive person involved in a power struggle with his adoptive mother. The information elicited from the story alerted the counselor to Pete's experience of the reported historical events. It is unlikely that Pete could have conveyed the impact of his history and its present relevance to his life in a form more insightful and descriptively meaningful than the story he told.

Intervention From the initial assessment interview with Pete's parents and the issues identified within the story, the counselor chose the following initial interventions: First, he decided to continue combining direct assessment procedures with picture-drawing and storytelling strategies to identify additional problematic areas for Pete. Second, the counselor began formulating a story to be used later about an abused person or animal who learned to adapt to a new environment by gradually learning to trust. Third, he asked Pete's permission to share with Pete's parents the story and the counselor's impressions of it. He then used the story to show the parents the relationship between Pete's present behavior and the trauma of his early experiences. The parents appeared to expect Pete to behave like any normal 12-year-old boy and not manifest any significant behavioral deficits related to the care he received during the first 7 years of his life. The counselor suggested that Pete was attempting to cope with these early experiences and that his parents might be able to help him and themselves by reconsidering the long-range impact of such an experience, adjusting their expectations, mutually deciding on and concentrating on just a few rules, giving Pete choices within limits they could accept, and selecting the roles each of them wanted to serve in Pete's life in light of what the story might suggest. Finally, the counselor suggested they try an experiment to begin their exploration of the new roles they wished to assume in Pete's life by letting the mother have a vacation from her job as the primary disciplinarian.

Rationale The therapeutic intentions of this plan were: (1) to reinforce consistency in the parents' rules and expectations; (2) to empower Pete with choices his parents

could accept; (3) to empower Pete's mother by providing more involvement and support from his father in parenting; (4) to foster an expectation of trust rather than distrust ("I know he'll do the right thing," instead of "I know he'll do the wrong thing");
(6) to focus less on punishment and more on logical consequences for Pete's misbehavior; and (7) to do away with any "mystery" rules or consequences.

CROSS-CULTURAL APPLICATIONS OF
PSYCHOANALYTIC COUNSELING

Many of the adaptations psychoanalytic counselors are making to meet managed care guidelines will also assist them in adapting the system to a wider
variety of clients representing *many different cultures*. Long-term treatment
focused on attainment of intrapsychic insight to bring more of the unconscious
into conscious awareness does not hold much appeal for clients from cultures
that have neither the resources, patience, nor desire for such treatment and
outcomes. However, being the oldest treatment approach and having been
developed in Austria, it has a classical acceptance worldwide that many U.S.
counseling theories do not. As psychoanalytic counselors move toward treating families, their acceptance among other cultures should increase (see
Chapter 15). Likewise, moving from stressing the individual to focusing on the
welfare of the family and community should appeal to those cultures where
group needs are considered over individual needs.

Catharsis, the process of talking out painful feelings and emotions, does
not enjoy universal appeal across all cultures. The use of the analysis of transference and countertransference is rendered impossible when counselors lack
awareness of the cultural realities of their clients. These cultural realities are
presented in Chapter 15 with some guidelines on how to use the information
in counseling.

Yi (1998) points out that psychoanalytic counseling had its birth in
European culture and has been shaped by values such as a bounded, autonomous self with an affect-filled inferiority; assertiveness of personal needs;
personal achievement; personal identity; democracy; introspection; and interpersonal equality. Practitioners of psychoanalytic counseling traditionally hold
that the truths on which psychoanalysis was founded are objective and universally applicable to all cultures. However, as Imber-Black (1997) note, this view
is being modified by the realization that, to be effective, counselors need to
understand differing cultural constructs and decenter themselves from their
own cultural values.

Kirsner (2004), reporting on the decline of psychoanalytic counseling in
the United States, writes that, unlike the United States, some countries such as
Argentina and France incorporate psychoanalysis into their culture.
Psychoanalytic counseling in these countries is cheaper and readily available to
university students.

PSYCHOANALYTIC COUNSELING, ACCOUNTABILITY, AND MANAGED HEALTH CARE

For psychoanalytic counselors to meet the managed care guidelines presented in Chapter 2, they will have to move toward briefer treatment periods. Such a move will necessitate a clearer focus on problems with the setting of definite, measurable goals and the development of definite counseling strategies and treatment plans. Attention will shift from the past and unconscious conflicts to current environmental stresses. More attention will be given to children and adolescents and how they interact with their families. There will also be a shift from interpretation of intrapsychic mechanisms to reliance on the counselor–client relationship as the main treatment agent. The use of play therapy and the expressive arts will continue to increase in counseling children. Alexander (2004) writes that psychoanalytic counselors would do well to incorporate other counseling interventions such as behavioral methods into their practices.

Mander (2000), in agreement with Alexander (2004), details a psychodynamic approach to brief therapy that can be adapted to working with children and adolescents within the school setting. Several other publications have appeared under the title "brief psychoanalytic counseling." Laor (2001) notes that brief psychoanalytic psychotherapy can be adapted to individual clients by varying time limits, therapist's activity, and the therapeutic focus.

King and Randall (2003), editors of a book on the future of psychoanalytic psychotherapy, include several chapters on finding an identity for brief psychoanalytic psychotherapy that is different from traditional psychoanalysis and also different from the nonanalytic modalities. This identity crisis appears to leave brief psychoanalysis somewhere in the middle of the two extremes. However, several of that book's authors point to the value of short-term gains the approach offers to people for whom extended psychoanalysis is neither available nor appropriate.

SUMMARY

Freud (1918) identified the task of analysts as bringing to patients' knowledge their unconscious, repressed material and uncovering the resistances that oppose this extension of their knowledge about themselves. He believed that frustration made his patients ill, and that their symptoms served them as substitute satisfactions. Freud (1918) clearly noted the harm that may come to patients who receive too much help and consolation from their therapists, but also pointed out that many patients lack the strength and general knowledge to handle their lives without some mentoring and instruction, in addition to analysis, from their therapists.

Freud's theory continues to be criticized for its lack of sound research support. Freud considered his theory of repression to be the cornerstone of the entire structure of psychoanalysis. However, Grünbaum (1993) notes that more research is needed to validate the link between such things as repressed childhood molestation and adult neurosis. He points out that a first event followed by a second event does not prove causality between the events. The theories of dreams and parapraxia also suffer from lack of hard data to prove causality.

In Freud's defense, much of his data collecting was similar to what passes today for acceptable, phenomenological research. In fact, data collecting through free association has many similarities to the open-ended, phenomenological interviewing method in which participants are encouraged to free-associate about the topic under study. In addition, Morgan and Morgan (2001) make a strong case for using single-participant designs in counseling research. Freud used a single-participant design method in his case study research. Finally, much of what is being done in counseling today has its roots in Freud's many contributions to the current theory and practice of counseling.

Websites for Psychoanalytic Counseling

Internet addresses frequently change. To find the sites listed here, visit www.thomsonedu.com/counseling/thompson for an updated list of Internet addresses and direct links to relevant sites.

D. W. Winnicott

National Psychological Association for Psychoanalysis

Dream Central's Unique Method of Dream Analysis

Sigmund Freud Museum, Vienna

References

Alexander, F. (2004). A classic in psychotherapy integration revisited: The dynamics of psychotherapy in light of learning theory. *Journal of Psychotherapy Integration, 14,* 347–359.

Burton, L. (1995). Using a dog in an elementary school counseling program. *Elementary School Guidance and Counseling, 29,* 236–240.

Clark, A. (1991). The identification and modification of defense mechanism in counseling. *Journal of Counseling and Development, 69,* 231–236.

Dobson, J. (2002, June 29). If father wasn't there, life probably isn't full, happy. *Knoxville News Sentinel,* p. C-3.

Ecker, B., & Hulley, L. (1995). *Depth-oriented brief therapy.* New York: Jossy-Bass, Inc.

Fall, M. (1994). Physical and emotional expression: A combination approach for working with children in small areas of a school counselor's office. *The School Counselor, 42,* 72–77.

Fancher, R. (2000). Snapshots of Freud in America. *American Psychologist, 55,* 1025–1028.

Frankel, J. B. (1998). The play's the thing: How the essential processes of therapy are seen most clearly in child therapy. *Psychoanalytic Dialogues, 8,* 149–182.

Freud, A. (1926). *Psychoanalytic treatment of children.* London: Imago.

Freud, S. (1918). *Lines of advance in psychoanalytic therapy.* Paper presented at the fifth International Psychoanalytic Congress, Budapest, Hungary.

Freud, S. (1930) The question of God. Sigmund Freud: Civilization and Its Discontents from Program Two. Retrieved March 6, 2006 from http://www.pbs.org/wgbh/questionofgod/transcript/civilization.html

Freud, S. (1949). *An outline of psychoanalysis* (J. Strachey, Trans.). New York: Norton. (Original work published 1940)

Freud, S. (1952). *On dreams* (J. Strachey, Trans.). New York: Norton. (Original work published 1901)

Freud, S. (1963). *An autobiographical study* (J. Strachey, Trans.). New York: Norton. (Original work published 1925)

Freud, S. (1965a). *The interpretation of dreams* (J. Strachey, Trans.). New York: Norton. (Original work published 1900)

Freud, S. (1965b). *New introductory lectures in psychoanalysis* (J. Strachey, Ed. & Trans.). New York: Norton. (Original work published 1933)

Freud, S. (1971). *The psychopathology of everyday life* (A. Tyson, Trans.). New York: Norton. (Original work published 1901).

Grünbaum, A. (1993). *Validation in clinical theory of psychoanalysis*. Madison, CT: International Universities Press.

Hall, C. (1954). *A primer of Freudian psychology*. New York: Mentor.

Imber-Black, E. (1997). From the literature: Developing cultural competence: Contributions from recent family therapy literature. *American Journal of Psychotherapy, 51,* 607–610.

Kestenbaum, C. J. (1985). The creative process in child psychotherapy. *American Journal of Psychotherapy, 39,* 479–489.

King, L., & Randall, R. (Eds.) (2003). *The future of psychoanalytic psychotherapy*. London: Whurr Publishers.

Kirsner, D. (2004). Psychoanalysis and its discontents. *Psychoanalytic Psychology, 21,* 339–352.

Klein, M. (1932). *The psychoanalysis of children*. London: Hogarth.

Laor, I. (2001). Brief psychoanalytic psychotherapy: The impact of its fundamentals on the therapeutic process. *British Journal of Psychotherapy, 18*(2), 169–183.

Lawson, D. (1987). Using therapeutic stories in the counseling process. *Elementary School Guidance and Counseling, 22,* 134–142.

Lee, A. C. (1997). Psychoanalytic play therapy. In K. O'Connor & L. M. Braverman (Eds.), *Play therapy theory and practice: A comparative presentation* (pp. 46–78). New York: Wiley.

Levinson, B. (1962). The dog as co-therapist. *Mental Hygiene, 46,* 59–65.

Lyness-Richard, D. (1997). Play and perfectionism: Putting fun back into families. In H. G. Kaduson, D. Cangelosi, & C. E. Schaefer (Eds.), *The playing cure: Individualized play therapy for specific childhood problems* (pp. 29–60). Northvale, NJ: Jason Aronson.

Mander, G. (2000). *A psychodynamic approach to brief therapy*. London: Sage Publications.

Maslow, A. (1970). *Motivation and personality* (2nd ed.). New York: Harper & Row.

Morgan, D., & Morgan, R. (2001). Single-participant research design: Bringing science to managed care. *American Psychologist, 56,* 119–127.

Neubauer, P. (1987). The many meanings of play. *Psychoanalytic Study of the Child, 42,* 193–203.

O'Brien, M. (1993). Pets as counselors. *Elementary School Guidance and Counseling, 4,* 308.

Patton, M., & Meara, N. (1991). *Psychoanalytic counseling*. New York: Wiley.

Piaget, J., & Inhelder, B. (1969). *The psychology of the child*. New York: Basic Books.

Schaefer, C., & Cangelosi, D. (Eds.). (1993). *Play therapy techniques*. Northvale, NJ: Aronson.

Simon, S. (1988, June). *Six conditions for nurturing self-esteem*. Paper presented at the American School Counselors Association convention, Breckenridge, CO.

Stone, I. (1971). *Passions of the mind*. New York: Doubleday.

Sugarman, A. (1977). Psychoanalysis as a humanistic psychology. *Psychotherapy: Theory, Research, and Practice, 14*, 204–211.

Trivedi, L., & Perl, J. (1995). Animal facilitated counseling in the elementary school: A literature review and practical considerations. *Elementary School Guidance and Counseling, 29*, 223–234.

Watson, J. (1980). Bibliotherapy for abused children. *School Counselor, 27*, 204–208.

Westen, D. (1998). The scientific legacy of Sigmund Freud toward a psychodynamically informed psychological science. *Psychological Bulletin, 124*, 333–371.

Winnicott, D. W. (1971). *Playing and reality*. London: Tavistock.

Winnicott, D. W. (1977). *The piggle: An account of the psychoanalytic treatment of a little girl*. New York: International University Press.

Winnicott, D. W. (2001, February 16). D.W. Winnicott 1896–1971: His life and work. Retrieved August 15, 2002, from www.hjem.sol.no/vals/winni.html

Yi, K. (1998). Transference and race: An intrasubjective conceptualization. *Psychoanalytic Psychology, 15*, 245–261.

REALITY THERAPY: COUNSELING WITH CHOICE THEORY

Nothing strengthens the judgment and quickens the conscience like individual responsibility.

—Elizabeth Cady Stanton

Restlessness and discontent are the first necessities of progress.

—Thomas A. Edison

Fritz William Glasser (b. 1925) graduated from Case Institute of Technology as a chemical engineer in 1944, at the age of 19. He enrolled at Case Western Reserve University and, at 23, earned a master's degree in clinical psychology. At 28, he received a medical degree from the same institution. While serving his last year of residency at the University of California at Los Angeles School of Psychiatry and in a Veterans Administration hospital, Glasser discovered that traditional psychotherapy was not for him. Glasser voiced reservations about psychoanalysis to his last teacher, who reputedly responded, "Join the club"; however, such an attitude was not common or popular among his colleagues. Denied a promised teaching position because of his rebellion against Freudian concepts, Glasser said he would have made about $8,000 in the first 16 years of his practice if he had relied on referrals from his alma mater, as most beginning psychiatrists do.

In 1956, Glasser became head psychiatrist at the Ventura School for Girls, an institution operated by the State of California to treat seriously delinquent adolescent girls. For 12 years, Glasser conducted a successful program at the Ventura School; the theory and concepts of reality therapy evolved out of this program. In his first book, *Mental Health or Mental Illness?* (1961), he laid the foundation for the techniques and concepts that became reality therapy.

William Glasser

Glasser used the term *reality therapy* for the first time in April 1964 in a manuscript, "Reality Therapy: A Realistic Approach to the Young Offender." His widely read *Reality Therapy* was published in 1965. In 1966, Glasser began consulting in California public schools for the purpose of applying reality therapy in education. These new ideas for applying reality therapy to teaching later became his third book, *Schools without Failure* (1969).

In 1968, Glasser founded the Institute for Reality Therapy in Los Angeles. It offers training courses for physicians, probation officers, police officers, nurses, lawyers, judges, teachers, and counselors. Introductory and advanced courses and programs are offered on a regular and continuing basis. After the publication of *Schools without Failure,* the Educator Training Center, a special division of the Institute for Reality Therapy, was established in Los Angeles in 1971. In 1970, the William Glasser La Verne College Center was established at the University of La Verne in southern California to provide teachers with an off-campus opportunity to gain graduate and in-service credits while working within their own schools to provide an exciting educational environment for children.

The Schools without Failure Seminars, sponsored by the Educator Training Center, drew large followings across the country. Glasser's other books include *The Identity Society* (1972), *Positive Addiction* (1976), *Stations of the Mind* (1981), *Control Theory* (1984), *Control Theory in the Classroom* (1986), *The Quality School: Managing Students without Coercion* (1990), *The Quality School Teacher* (1993), *Staying Together* (1995), *Choice Theory: A New Psychology of Personal Freedom* (1998), *Getting Together and Staying Together* (2000b), *Reality Therapy in Action* (2000c), *Every Student Can Succeed* (2000a), *Unhappy Teenagers: A Way for Parents and Teachers to Reach Them* (2002), *Warning: Psychiatry Can Be Dangerous to Your Health* (2004), and *Treating Mental Health as a Public Health Problem: A New Leadership Role for the Helping Professions* (2005). Glasser has averaged about 75 speaking appearances a year in addition to television interviews, writing, and videotaping.

THE NATURE OF PEOPLE

Glasser believes that, despite varying manifestations, psychological problems are the result of one factor: the inability to fulfill one's basic needs. Glasser (1965) sees a correlation between people's lack of success in meeting their needs and the degree of their distress and unhappiness. He is interested in the symptoms people choose to ease the pain of not getting what they want. He maintains that psychological problems can result from people's denial of the reality of the world around them. *Denial of reality* in the reality therapy system refers to the tendency of people to try to avoid the unpleasant natural and logical consequences of their irresponsible behavior. People also are viewed as getting into trouble when they behave in irresponsible ways. In Glasser's system, *irresponsible behavior* is defined as attempts by people to satisfy their own basic needs in ways that infringe on the rights of others to meet their needs. Glasser believes that people have five basic needs: survival, freedom, power, fun, and love and belonging. Joining reality and responsibility is the third *R*: right and wrong. As is true with the other two *R*s, the issue of following the right behavior is addressed in the practice of reality therapy. Glasser struggled more with the definition of the right behavior than he did when defining behavior in touch with reality and responsible behavior. For Glasser,

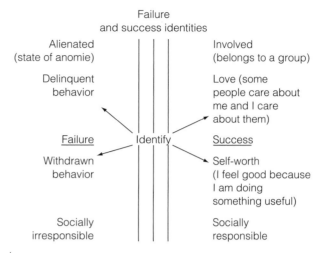

FIGURE 4-1 | FAILURE AND SUCCESS IDENTITIES

feelings are the one indicator that our behavior is on the right track; that is, if people feel good about their behavior and if others also feel good about it, chances are they are doing the right thing. More recently, in his incorporation of choice theory into reality therapy, Glasser (1998) states that all problems brought to counseling have a relationship component. Behavior in opposition to the three *R*s is likely to lead to an abundance of relationship problems.

Similar to Maslow's hierarchy of human needs, Glasser focused his early treatment plans on teaching people to love and be loved and to feel valued by themselves and others through success in their careers. Successful attainment of these two needs leads to a success identity (Figure 4-1). In fact, success in these two important areas can be a quick index for evaluating one's mental health. Both are keys to healthy self-esteem. Building a network of friends and supportive people puts children and adolescents on the road to achieving a healthy sense of self-esteem, a journey to be completed through success in the classroom. "Schools without failure" has been a principal theme throughout Glasser's work, which has been continued in his writing on quality schools and quality schoolteachers. More recently, he has authored *Warning: Psychiatry Can Be Dangerous to Your Health* (2004) and *Treating Mental Health as a Public Health Problem: A New Leadership Role for the Helping Professions* (2005). These two publications present alternatives to the medical model for helping people achieve mental health through finding better ways to meet their needs. Glasser also attacks prescribing drugs to treat symptoms where no pathology exists.

CHOICE THEORY AND THE NATURE OF PEOPLE

Choice theory is based on the proposition that the only behavior we can control is our own. Glasser (1998) points out that people get into trouble when they try to control other people. He believes that the practice of control psychology is responsible for the widespread belief that people and their behaviors can be controlled. Consequently, people waste considerable energy and time trying to get other people to do things they do not want to do. Equal amounts of time and energy are expended on resisting the efforts of others to get you to do things you do not want to do. Glasser (1998) sees these efforts to get others to do things they do not want to do as responsible for the breakdown of good relationships. In fact, Glasser believes that all long-lasting psychological problems brought to counseling are relationship problems resulting from attempts to get people to do things they do not want to do. The remedy for fixing the damage done by the practice of control psychology is to teach choice theory psychology to as many people as possible. Choice theory psychology practitioners teach their clients that they can control only their own behavior and that they have the freedom to make choices that lead to better-quality lives. Glasser (1998) holds that each person maintains mental images of what and whom we would like to have in our quality world. The best way to bring reality to our quality world image is to make the changes in our lives that help us find better ways to meet our needs.

Glasser believes that all we can give or get from other people is information. What we do with that information is our choice, as are the type and amount of information we give to others. We are responsible only for what we choose to do with our behavior. Relationships become progressively better as people focus on changing their own behavior, as opposed to trying to get other people to change their ways.

Glasser (1998, 2000c) points out that relationship problems are at least partial causes of many other problems, such as pain, fatigue, weakness, and some chronic diseases commonly referred to as autoimmune diseases. He believes that people choose misery and depression rather than facing the problem of what they are doing to destroy an important relationship that is not working the way they want. Petersen and Thompson (2005), finding that adolescents were significantly less well-informed than adults about the differences in personal relationships between real love, having a person permanently in your quality world, and romantic love or the period of falling in love and being infatuated with another. The researchers concluded that this information gap could be related to the failure rate of relationships and marriages where unrealistic expectations prevent adolescents from fulfilling their need for love.

Consistent with reality therapy philosophy, Glasser states that problem relationships are part of a person's present life. Although past painful events and relationships have significant influence on a person's present life, Glasser believes that to revisit the past is not nearly as productive as focusing on what needs to be done to improve a current important relationship.

As mentioned previously, reality therapists practicing choice theory psychology believe that people are driven by five genetic needs: survival, freedom, power, fun, and love and belonging. Glasser did not define his list of needs in a Maslow-like hierarchy. That is, filling a particular need does not depend on filling a prerequisite lower level need. It could be argued that filling the survival need would necessarily always precede filling other needs, with the exception of a person who chooses suicide over survival. Glasser believes all five needs have to be satisfied. Failure to satisfy a particular need often results in choosing a symptom behavior such as depression. These needs are satisfied only by satisfying an image or picture we have included in our quality world. Hence, we see the importance of being able to visualize ourselves achieving the important and realistic goals we have set for ourselves. The amount of freedom we have in our lives is directly proportional to the success we have in satisfying the pictures and images we hold in our quality worlds. We give up freedom when we put pictures in our quality worlds that we cannot satisfy. Glasser (1998) views all behavior as total behavior consisting of four integrated components: acting, thinking, feeling, and physiology. Interventions with any one of the four components will affect the others. Glasser believes that all behavior is chosen, but that direct control is limited to acting and thinking. Feelings and physiology can be controlled indirectly by how people choose to think and act.

Glasser has been influenced by W. Edwards Deming's (1966) philosophy that high-quality work is dependent on eliminating the fear that prevents people from getting along well with each other. You cannot get good work from people when there is an adversarial relationship between management and labor, teachers and students, and counselors and clients. To be successful, managers, teachers, and counselors must become a part of the quality worlds of the people with whom they work. Glasser believes that the practice of control psychology—that is, punishing wrong behavior and rewarding right behavior—is responsible for most of the human misery and adversarial relationships that exist worldwide. The problem is compounded by the fact that those who have power—government agencies, parents, teachers, business managers, and religious leaders who define right and wrong—totally support the practice of control psychology.

In *Choice Theory* (1998), Glasser describes methods for taking control of one's life. The theory is based on the idea that people are responsible for their own choices, decisions, goals, and the general degree of happiness in their lives. Individuals are not controlled by external events and other people unless they choose to let them take over. To a person who said, "Mary Sue hurt me when she rejected me, and I am too depressed to want to continue my life," Glasser would point out that the person is "depressing" (using *depression* as a verb) as a last, desperate, ineffective effort to regain control of a large part of his life that seems to be slipping away. Glasser would recommend reframing the mental image of life to include something more than a relationship with Mary Sue as a *raison d'être*. This concept is similar to the methodology used in rational-emotive-behavior therapy and cognitive therapy, which focus on reframing thoughts, self-talk, and visualization as ways of treating undesired emotional states such as depression. In fact, many points that Glasser raises are similar to those of Gestalt and existential theory regarding self-responsibility for living life. For example, rather than saying, "I have a cold," one would say, "I am doing a cold." Presumably, taking control over having a cold enables one to take control over stopping it. Two themes run through *Choice Theory*. First, we control our mental images or pictures. We can put them in, exchange them, add to them, or throw them out. We can also choose which picture or goal we can and want to satisfy. Second, whenever we choose to depress or develop a psychosomatic illness, we have the option of choosing something more satisfying. The chapter on choice theory and rearing children, in which Glasser integrates his choice theory points into the standard steps of reality therapy, is particularly relevant for counseling children and adolescents. Perhaps the greatest help to parents, counselors, and teachers is the idea that we need to empower rather than overpower children to win their cooperation when they grow too big to overpower.

The notion of empowering children is central to *Control Theory in the Classroom* (1986). In his best work for educators since *Schools without Failure* (1969), Glasser makes a strong case for the teacher as manager, who motivates students by empowering them with the responsibility for learning. Note that Glasser now uses choice theory rather than control theory. The principal motivation method is two- to five-member learning teams designed to meet student needs for belonging, power, friendships, and achievement. The team idea has been presented elsewhere (Thompson & Poppen, 1972) and found to be successful. Glasser draws a parallel between successful managers in business and successful managers (teachers) in education and presents examples of how lead managers connect with people. He has been highly critical of stimulus–response learning; however, the team-learning approach, if well designed, appears to be an excellent example of creating the proper stimulus conditions to foster the desired learning response. Much of the research and writing on reality therapy is related to the school environment because counselors and teachers find the theory and practice of reality therapy useful in working with student problems.

Glasser continued his educational model in four other books: *The Quality School: Managing Students without Coercion* (1990), *The Quality School Teacher* (1993), *Every Student Can Succeed* (2000a), and *Unhappy Teenagers: A Way for Parents and Teachers to Reach Them* (2002). These books emphasize the business metaphor derived from Deming's work with Japanese factories. The message is that managers and teachers have a lot in common in that the results depend on how people are treated. The book presents two managerial models: the boss manager and the lead manager. Boss managers motivate by punishment rather than encouragement and reinforcement, tell rather than show, overpower rather than empower, and rule rather than cooperate. Lead managers do the reverse. In short, Glasser makes a case for cooperative teachers rather than controlling ones. Glasser (2002, 2005) believes that teachers can connect with their students if they give up the seven deadly habits that destroy all relationships. These are criticizing, blaming, complaining, nagging, threatening, punishing, and rewarding to control. The model works equally well in personal relationships, homes, schools, businesses, community agencies, and government because, regardless of setting, we are all in the business of managing people. The seven deadly habits should be replaced by the seven caring habits of encouraging, listening, negotiating, supporting, trusting, accepting, and respecting.

In summary, Glasser's views on the nature of people are based on the following principles.

1. The only person whose behavior we can control is our own. Behavioral psychologists would disagree, pointing out that we can control the behavior of others with reinforcement, punishment, and extinction. Glasser's response would be that the practice of behavioral methods to control the behavior of others will cost you a positive working relationship with the person whose behavior you are trying to control.

2. All long-lasting psychological problems are relationship problems that result from attempts of people to control other people. Disagreement comes from those who point out that problems also originate from inner conflicts with the self, lack of information, and lack of skill.

3. Past events have everything to do with what we are today, but we can satisfy our basic needs only in the present and make plans for the future. Psychodynamic theorists disagree, stating that insight into how we became the people we are is helpful in bringing about change.

4. Satisfying the needs represented by the pictures in our quality world is the way we meet our needs for survival, freedom, power, fun, and love and belonging. Failure to meet these needs often results in choosing a symptom as a way of rationalizing or excusing this failure. Huffstetler, Mims, and Thompson (2004) developed an informal inventory for helping people prioritize their needs by comparing the strength of one need over another. For example, which of the following best describes you? (a) Having a savings account equal to five month's salary is important to me (Survival). (b) Having a good time is very important to me (Fun).

5. Total behavior is all that we do, including acting, thinking, feeling, and physiology. We have direct control over acting and thinking; however, we can control our feelings and physiology indirectly by how we choose to act and think. That is, if we feel bad on Monday, we will feel bad on Tuesday unless we change our behavior or thinking. Disagreement would come from those counselors who believe that exploration of feelings precedes changes in thinking and behavior.

THEORY OF COUNSELING

Glasser was reacting against some of the principles of psychoanalytic theory when he developed reality therapy. Choice theory reality therapy differs from traditional psychoanalytic therapy in six ways.

First, reality therapists discard the concept of mental illness in favor of the concept of responsibility. Traditionally, people behave irresponsibly because they are mentally ill, whereas Glasser believes that people become mentally ill because they behave irresponsibly. Glasser (2005) is critical of the diagnostic categories of the *Diagnostic and Statistical Manual of Mental Disorders, Fourth Edition* (DSM-IV), which he believes violate a basic principle of medical science by presenting diagnostic descriptions of mental illness from symptoms alone with no supporting pathology. Exceptions, of course, would be Parkinson's disease, Huntington's chorea, Alzheimer's disease, and brain injury where pathology does exist.

Second, reality therapists focus on the moral issue of right and wrong—an issue often ignored in counseling because many believe that people already feel too guilty about various unresolved conflicts. In Freud's time, everyone talked about doing the right thing, so Freud thought it best to make psychotherapy a sanctuary free of moral judgments to avoid increasing his patients' feelings of guilt. In reality therapy, moral issues are addressed head-on when clients are asked to evaluate their own behavior.

Third, reality therapists largely ignore the past in favor of dealing with the present and future. Most discussion in reality therapy evaluates how present behavior is helping to meet one's needs. If present behavior is not working, future alternatives are examined and commitments to change are made.

A fourth difference involves transference. In traditional psychoanalytic practice, transference is frequently used as a therapeutic mechanism for working through unresolved conflicts. In reality therapy, the counselor relates to the client on a person-to-person basis and does not encourage the client to relate to the counselor as someone else; for example, the child does not relate to the counselor as a parent, teacher, or other authority figure (objects).

Fifth, reality therapists largely ignore the unconscious, whereas it is generally the primary focus in psychoanalytic practice. According to Glasser, the unconscious is a fertile ground for excuses for misbehavior; the counselor is advised to look at *what* is going on rather than *why*.

The sixth and perhaps most significant feature of reality therapy distinguishing it from traditional practice is the aspect most dear to educators, whose philosophy is that the counseling is primarily a teaching–learning situation. Glasser said about reality therapy that it is a teaching process, not a healing process. Counselors are in the business of teaching people better ways to meet their needs. From the reality therapy point of view, counseling is a matter of learning how to solve problems, teaching people, in effect, to become their own counselors.

COUNSELING METHOD

The biggest challenge counselors face in the practice of reality therapy based on choice theory is to teach their clients that control psychology will not work for them any better than it has worked for the rest of the world. Glasser (1998, 2000c) believes that our attempts to control others are largely responsible for the misery in so many people's lives. When other people do not do what we want them to do, humankind has a long history of turning to coercion and control to get others to follow our wishes.

The primary focus of choice theory in reality therapy is to prevent problems before they happen. Regardless of the skill of the counselor, it is often impossible to rescue failing students who have never been willing to put school and teachers in their quality world vision. People do not admit those who try to control them to their quality world. Glasser (1998, 2000a) believes that a good way to learn choice theory is to treat others in your life like you treat your best friend, your boss, and most strangers. You rarely try to force these people to do anything. Ownership contributes to the problem of trying to control others. People tend to believe that they own their spouses, children, students, and employees. For example, I have a right to control the people I own, and when they do not do what I want, I have a right to force them to do it. Consequently, we often have better relationships with those not so close to us because we do not try to own them and force them to do things they do not want to do. Glasser (1998, 2002) recommends that parents treat their children like the grandparents do, but he recognizes that there must be limits; natural or logical consequences should result when limits are breached.

In concert with Albert Ellis's rational-emotive-behavior therapy, Glasser (1998, 2000c) has identified three faulty beliefs that undergird the control psychology that essentially rules the world.

First belief: Much of my behavior is a response to an external signal, such as answering a ringing phone.

Second belief: I can make people do what I want them to do even if they do not want to do it, and other people can control how I think, act, and feel.

Third belief: I have a right and a duty to punish those who do not do what I tell them to do and to reward those who do.

Therefore, reality therapy based on choice theory now includes an examination of the client's belief system. Clients will be challenged to prove the rationality of what they believe, as well as the utility of what they do when they act on their beliefs. It is Glasser's contention that acting on the faulty beliefs of control psychology will make every situation or problem immediately worse.

Each person has a quality world vision made up of the pictures of the people he or she want to be with, the things he or she wants to own and experience, and the ideas or belief systems that govern his or her behavior. The closer a person's reality world approaches his or her quality world, the happier he or she will be. The farther apart a person's reality and quality worlds are, the more pain the person experiences from not getting what he or she wants. Choice theory and reality theory treatment plans are directed toward helping people handle the pain from not getting what they want. Treatment often involves changing strategies to help people get what they want and/or reviewing the pictures in their quality world. In all cases, counseling is focused on changing the client rather than how the client should try to change others. However, it must be noted that change in the client's behavior often influences change in others. The idea is to place one's quality world totally in one's hands and not have quality world objectives under the control of others. Choice theory reality therapy focuses on improving present relationships through personal change while disregarding past relationships. The success of the counseling process depends on creating a good relationship between the client and the counselor. The trust level between client and counselor needs to be high enough to handle confrontations, such as the following example:

COUNSELOR: What do you think caused the problem?

CLIENT: It's hard to say. It's really hard to say.

COUNSELOR: [In a friendly tone of voice] Well, say it anyway. This is the place to say hard-to-say things.

Clients sometimes choose to depress themselves when they do not get what they want. When this happens, counselors should confront them with the following four choices:

1. Continue to depress yourself.
2. Change what you are doing to get what you want.
3. Change what you want.
4. Both (2) and (3).

Glasser holds that choosing to depress, no matter how strongly or how long the duration, is not a mental illness. Like all behavior, it is a choice.

The practice of reality therapy follows eight steps. Step 1 is building good relationships with clients. Glasser calls this first step becoming involved, although *involvement* may not be the best word to describe this stage of counseling because it implies entangled or complex rather than positive, honest, open, unencumbered relationships. All approaches to counseling include building a trusting climate in which clients feel free to express their innermost fears, anxieties, and concerns.

In Step 2, children describe their present behavior. In Step 3, children evaluate what is going on in their lives and how they are helping themselves. In other words, Is their behavior helping them get what they want from life? If not, the counselor asks, "Do you want to change what is going on?" However, people do not change old behaviors until they are convinced that they are either not helping themselves or are actually harming themselves. In fact, people are more likely to change their behavior if they are thoroughly disgusted with their current behavior. Therefore, if in Step 3 clients do not give counselors negative evaluations about their current behaviors, counseling is not likely to generate any behavioral changes. Some helpful evaluation questions to ask in Step 3 include:

- How does this behavior help you?
- How does this behavior hurt you?
- How does this behavior help you learn math?
- How does this behavior improve your grade?
- Is your behavior getting you what you want?

Glasser believes that the only way for a person who feels bad to feel better is to make a positive change in behavior (see Figure 2-2). Reality therapy focuses on working with observable content, including behavior, plans, and goals. "What" questions are preferred to "why" questions, because why questions encourage people to find excuses for their irresponsible behavior.

In Step 4, the counselor and child begin to look at possible alternatives for getting what the child wants in life. A brainstorming format is used in which the child looks at better ways of meeting his or her needs. If the child has difficulty selecting new things to try, he or she might focus on stopping something that is not working. However, the counselor will want to have clients plan for what they will be doing to fill the free time resulting from stopping ineffective behaviors. Counselors also can draw five idea circles, filling two with suggestions and leaving the rest empty for the child to fill. Children, preferring not to leave the circles empty, generally fill them. Counselors can ask children who their best friends are and what they might tell them to do. In Step 5, children select alternatives for reaching their goals and commit to trying them. A key process in counseling children is helping them make commitments. When they are able to fulfill their commitments, they can build on these successes to achieve bigger goals.

In Step 6, the counselor and client examine the results of the commitment. Children returning for a second interview often say, "Well, I made a commitment to turn in one homework paper a day, and I did not meet my commitment," and then begin to list all the reasons why they failed. Reality therapists do not dwell on rationalizing "why." At this point, the counselor and child discuss writing a new contract the child can handle; maybe one homework paper per day is too much for now and a less demanding contract is needed. Counselors do not accept excuses if children do not meet the commitments they made. Excuses are designed to avoid punishment, and when children learn they will not be punished for not meeting a commitment, they have no need for excuses.

Step 7 applies logical consequences—for example, a lower grade for failing to turn in a homework paper. Additional penalties that are not logical or natural consequences of failing to turn in the paper, such as paddling, are considered neither effective nor humane; however, logical and natural consequences are not removed.

In Step 8, perseverance is required. How long should counselors stick with children who seem bent on destroying their self-esteem? Glasser recommends working with such children three or four times longer than they expect. "Never give up" does not mean a lifelong commitment but rather building on whatever relationship has been established in Step 1 and continuing to build this relationship through the entire eight-step process.

To review, three key terms in reality therapy are *reality, responsibility,* and *right and wrong.* The question becomes: How should these three concepts be treated in counseling children, adolescents, and adults? Piaget (1973) has described three broad stages of moral development, which match his stages of cognitive development:

1. Preconventional (preoperational stage, ages 2–7)
2. Conventional (concrete stage, ages 7–11)
3. Postconventional (formal stage, ages 11 to adulthood)

Kohlberg (1981) expands Piaget's three stages to six by defining two substages within each of Piaget's stages. The questions on which people make their moral judgments, choices, and decisions are listed for each substage.

PRECONVENTIONAL MORALITY

Stage 1: Will I get caught?

Stage 2: What is in it for me?

CONVENTIONAL MORALITY

Stage 3: What will the neighbors think?

Stage 4: What is the rule or law?

POSTCONVENTIONAL MORALITY

Stage 5: What is best for society?

Stage 6: What is best for humankind? Is human life at risk?

A strong case can be made that most problems brought to counseling are actually disorders of responsibility. Neurotic individuals assume too much responsibility; people with character disorders assume too little. Most people find themselves, at times, doing a little of both, depending on the situation. Sometimes knowing how much responsibility to take is difficult. Perhaps Glasser's answer would be to consult your brain first; then, second, evaluate the feelings you are getting as indicators of whether you are expressing the right behavior. Right behavior could be like the Golden Rule: behavior you would like done to you or for you. Feelings are often the product of your brain's attempt to communicate with you when you fail to consult it.

REALITY THERAPY PROCESS

The first step—one that must continue throughout the counseling process—is to build a warm relationship. Glasser refers to building a relationship as having the counselor work toward becoming included in the client's quality worldview of what is important in his or her life. Development of a warm and trusting relationship is also referred to as establishing a therapeutic alliance between counselor and client, when both join forces to help the client meet those needs he or she is having difficulty meeting. For example, when resistant clients are sent for counseling or are court-ordered to attend counseling, the alliance between counselors and clients would work toward meeting the conditions for termination of counseling.

Next, a series of five questions often is asked in reality therapy: (1) What are you doing? (2) Is what you are doing helping you get what you want? (3) If not, what might be some other things you could try? (4) Which idea would you like to try first? (5) When? The following dialogue is an example:

COUNSELOR: Mary, can you tell me a little bit about your life right now here at school?

MARY: What do you mean?

COUNSELOR: Well, Mary, it seems as though you get sent to the office a lot to talk to me about problems you're having with your teachers. Tell me what you're doing and let's talk about it.

MARY: Well, I guess I talk out of turn in class too much sometimes. But my classes are so boring.

COUNSELOR: Okay, so you talk a lot in class and the teachers don't like what you're doing. Do you do anything else that seems to get you in trouble with Mr. Thompson and Mrs. Rudolph?

MARY: No, I don't think so.

COUNSELOR: Are you happy with what happens to you when you do these things?

MARY: I do the same old things that keep getting me in trouble, but I feel good for the moment.

COUNSELOR: I know you do feel better for a while. Are the good feelings worth the price you have to pay for them?

MARY: I guess not, because I'm sure tired of spending so much time in the office.

COUNSELOR: Would you like to work on a better plan?

MARY: Okay. Why not?

COUNSELOR: Let's start by thinking of some things you could do to get along better in your classes and some ways to make them less boring as well.

MARY: Well, I could stop talking out of turn! I know the teachers would like that.

COUNSELOR: Stopping unhelpful things is usually a good way to start. What about some things you could begin doing in class?

MARY: Doing more assignments would please the teachers, but I don't like all the work.

COUNSELOR: Your two suggestions will probably help you with the teachers, but they won't do much to make the class more enjoyable for you. Can you think of something to help you like school more?

MARY: Some of the kids get free time or get to go to the library when they turn in their work. Could I do this, too?

COUNSELOR: We can ask your teachers about that today. That might be a way to please both you and the teachers. Can you think of other ideas to try?

MARY: I guess that's about all for now.

COUNSELOR: Okay, Mary, how many of these ideas do you want to try?

MARY: I think I can do all of them if I can get free time too.

COUNSELOR: When do you want to start?

MARY: Today, if I can.

COUNSELOR: We can try. Can you go over these with me one time before we leave?

MARY: I think so. No more talking out of turn, and do enough work to earn some free time.

COUNSELOR: That sounds good to me. Do you want to shake hands and make this an agreement between you and me?

MARY: Okay.

COUNSELOR: Good. I'd like to talk with you a little each day to see how your plan is working. If it doesn't work, we'll have to make another plan. See you tomorrow?

MARY: Okay, see you tomorrow.

This is a typical reality therapy interview. Identifying and evaluating present behavior are followed by making a plan and building a commitment to follow through on it. Each step in the reality therapy process is supported by a relationship of trust, caring, and friendship between the counselor and the child.

As mentioned in Chapter 2, the counseling process works better when the counselor uses statements rather than questions. Questioning moves the interview from a dialogue toward a teacher–student question-and-answer session that develops the counselor's plan rather than one for which the child feels ownership. More important, statements by the counselor allow the client more options in shaping the direction of the interview. As Carl Rogers noted, given the opportunity to take charge of the counseling interview, clients may gradually begin to take charge of their lives outside the counseling session as well. Following are examples of questions changed to reality therapy statements:

1. What are you doing to solve the problem? *Changed to statement:* If you are ready to do this, we can begin by looking at what you have been doing to solve the problem.
2. How is what you have been doing helping? Is your behavior getting you what you want? *Changed to statement:* It might be helpful to think about your behavior to see how each method is working for you if you feel ready to move to the next step.
3. If what you have been trying is not working, what are some things you could do that would help? *Changed to statement:* We could look at some new ideas to try when you are more comfortable about moving toward a plan.
4. Which of these new alternatives would you like to try? *Changed to statement:* You have several possibilities listed. Tell me what you think about trying any of them.
5. When can we meet again to find out how well your plan worked out? *Changed to statement:* It might be helpful to schedule a time for a follow-up of your plan. (Shake hands and sign a written plan if necessary.) (I've changed to some "child friendly language—your additions are fine)

A second transcript from a case brought to a counselor follows as a way of demonstrating how reality therapy can be put into practice.

CASE STUDY

Identification of the Problem

Wendy is a 12-year-old girl in the seventh grade at White Oak School. She was referred to the counselor because she cheated on a mathematics test.

Individual and Background Information

Academic School records indicate that Wendy is a high achiever, with an overall A average on her elementary school record. She also has an A average for the first two grading periods in the seventh grade. During the third grading period, which is almost over, Wendy has had some erratic test scores in mathematics. She was caught cheating on an important test that would have brought up her low grades had she done well on it.

Family Wendy is the only child of older parents, both of whom are professionals. Teachers have indicated that the parents seem to expect Wendy to make the highest grades in her class.

Social According to teachers' reports on cumulative records, Wendy was well liked by most of the children in her classes in elementary school. She did not seem to have a close friend then, but this year she has developed a close friendship with a girl in her class. A sociogram done in her sixth-grade class indicated she was well accepted by her peers.

Counseling Method

The counselor uses the reality therapy counseling method to help Wendy evaluate her behavior and identify some things she could do to meet more of her needs socially and emotionally without creating problems in other areas of her life.

The five basic steps followed by the counselor in this case are: (1) establishment of a relationship, (2) identification of present behavior (What is being done or has been done?), (3) evaluation of present behavior (Is it helping the client get what he or she wants?), (4) development of plans that will help, and (5) commitment from the client to try at least one of the plans.

Transcript

COUNSELOR: Wendy, I understand that there has been a problem in your math class. Would you like to talk about it?

WENDY: I guess so.

COUNSELOR: You're feeling somewhat embarrassed about the problem and uncomfortable about talking with me.

WENDY: Yes, I am, but I know I need to talk about it.

COUNSELOR: Would you like to tell me what happened?

WENDY: Miss Waters caught me cheating on my math test. I have some bad grades in math this period. I knew I had to do well on this test, but I wasn't ready for it.

COUNSELOR: How did you see cheating as helping you?

WENDY: I was feeling a lot of pressure because I wasn't prepared and my parents expect me to do well.

COUNSELOR: Can you tell me what you've been doing that kept you from being prepared for the test?

WENDY: I'm just getting to know Susan, and I've been spending a lot of time talking with her and not enough time studying.

COUNSELOR: Susan's friendship is very important to you.

WENDY: Yes, I've never had a really close friend before.

COUNSELOR: What might be some ways you could still be friends with Susan and also keep up with your studies?

WENDY: Well, I guess I could spend less time talking to her and more time studying.

COUNSELOR: You believe that you can spend less time with Susan and still be close friends?

WENDY: Yes, I'm sure she'd understand.

COUNSELOR: What are some other things you could do that might help?

WENDY: Maybe we could spend time together studying instead of talking so much.

COUNSELOR: Would you like to try one of these plans for the next week and see how it works?

WENDY: Okay. I'd like to try studying with Susan.

COUNSELOR: All right. Let's meet next Tuesday at one o'clock and see how well your plan worked.

As pointed out in Chapter 1, counselors must adapt their counseling style and language to their clients' developmental levels. A suggested reality therapy format for counseling younger children is as follows:

1. What did you do?
2. What is our rule about this?
3. Was what you did against our rule?
4. What were you supposed to do?
5. What are you going to do next time?
6. Do you want to write your plan for next time, or do you want me to write it?
7. Let's check tomorrow to see if your new plan is working. (Shake hands and sign names.)

Following is an outline of basic reality therapy for older children and teenagers who are capable of formal reasoning and abstract thinking.

1. Let's begin by talking about what you have been doing to solve the problem.
2. It would be helpful if you could give me an idea of how what you have been doing has been helping you or the situation. We may want to consider some questions: Is your behavior in touch with *reality*? Is your behavior the *responsible* thing to do? Is your behavior the *right* thing to do? From a cost-analysis point of view, is your behavior cost-effective? (These questions would be addressed one at a time.)
3. If your behavior is not getting you what you want, what would you like to do differently?
4. What plan would you like to develop?
5. When can we follow up on your plan?

As suggested in these questions, much of reality therapy becomes a cost-analysis procedure of helping clients determine whether their behavior is giving them fair value for the price they are paying. A good question to investigate is, "Are you getting your money's worth?"

For example, in counseling children and their parents going through divorce, Oz (1994) presented a reality-based intervention that can facilitate discussion during any stage of the divorce process. In brief, her method provides a cost-analysis system of the benefits and costs of each alternative related to a particular problem. Following a brainstorming session for generating a list of alternatives for solving a problem, clients move to evaluate each alternative in light of the costs they are willing and prepared to pay. How costs can be reduced for selected alternatives is considered. After narrowing the choices to the most cost-effective alternative, clients may be asked to role-play the situation with the chosen alternative. Likely impediments and worst-case scenarios are considered in the client's implementation plan. A secondary advantage accrues to the clients in reframing "difficult to do" alternatives as the least expensive and most cost-effective choices.

In summary, reality therapy is such a straightforward approach to counseling that some of our students question its utility for counseling difficult cases. Glasser's *Reality Therapy in Action* (2000c) is a strong answer to those who believe that, although reality therapy may be the treatment of choice for regular problems of adjustment, it is not sufficient for treating people with major disturbances in their lives. In *Reality Therapy in Action,* Glasser presents eighteen of his most challenging cases from his 50-year career as a psychiatrist. These cases range from chronic depression to an extreme obsessive-compulsive disorder. Regardless of the various symptoms presented by these clients, they all had some things in common. Each of the clients had problems with establishing and maintaining relationships. All of them also lacked meaning in their careers or in their lives. Glasser believes that when people have difficulty meeting their basic needs of survival, freedom, power, fun, and love and belonging, they often choose a symptom as a way of compensating for failure to meet one or more of these basic needs. Choosing a symptom has the reinforcing effect of excusing the person for living an unproductive or even irresponsible life. After all, what can be expected from a person who has problems or who is "mentally ill"? If the symptom is sufficiently severe, further reinforcement for keeping the symptom is provided if the person receives total care for the disability. The road back to living a responsible life begins with a reality therapy type of plan to commit to doing those tasks or homework assignments the client can do and gradually increasing the tasks until the client decides, "I do not need my symptom anymore, and there are better ways to meet my basic needs." Therefore, treatment, via choice theory reality therapy, is geared toward taking the steps needed to put clients on track to finding better ways to meet their needs. The core of life is building loving relationships and a solid career or other meaningful activities that contribute to society. For students, academic progress is their career. Likewise, the foundation of choice theory reality therapy is building and maintaining relationships and improving academic or career performance to meet one's basic needs. Glasser presents a blueprint for how to use reality therapy to treat the most difficult cases you will ever face in your counseling career, and yes, it is the same basic choice theory reality therapy that you use with children and adolescents who are not completing their math assignments.

THE TEN-STEP REALITY THERAPY CONSULTATION MODEL

The ten-step reality therapy consultation model is an effective tool for counselors to use with teachers and parents who seek the counselor's assistance with their children's behavioral and motivation problems. Glasser (1998, 2000a, 2002) no longer endorses his own version of the ten-step model. He believes his version to be an application of the control psychology he now views as a harmful attempt to get people to do things they do not want to do. We believe our current model to be more consistent with Glasser's choice theory model. The ten steps are divided into three phases, each with a special objective. Phase I, consisting of three steps, is designed to assist a teacher or parent in building a better relationship with the child.

Step 1. List what you have already tried that does not help. Stopping these ineffective interventions often stimulates a positive change in the child's behavior.

Step 2. If Step 1 is unsuccessful, make a list of change-of-pace interventions to disrupt the expected interactions between the adult and the child. For example, catch the child behaving appropriately, act surprised when the child repeats the same old aggravating behavior, ask yourself what the child expects you to do, and then do *not* do it, or try a paradoxical counseling strategy, such as asking the child to increase the behavior you would like to eliminate (see Chapter 5).

Step 3. If Step 3 is necessary, make a list of things you could and would do to help the child have a better day tomorrow. For example, give the child at least three 20-second periods of your undivided positive attention, ask the child to run an errand for you, give the child some choices in how to complete a task or an assignment, ask the child's opinion about something relevant to both of you, give the child an important classroom or household chore, or negotiate a few rules (fewer than five) that you and the child think are fair to both of you.

Phase II, consisting of three steps, is devoted to counseling the child. In most cases, we find that successful interventions happen in the first phase. When this does not occur, we ask the adult to move to Step 4.

Step 4. Try one-line counseling approaches such as the following:

- Ask the child to stop the undesirable behavior. Use as few words as possible, relying instead on nonverbal gestures. Do not use threats.
- Try the "Could it be?" questions recommended by the practitioners of individual psychology (see Chapter 11).
- Acknowledge the child's cooperative efforts, but do not thank the child for behaving responsibly as if this behavior is a favor to you.

Step 5. Use reality therapy questions that emphasize the rules on which agreement was reached in a previous negotiation. For example:

- What did you do?
- What is our rule?
- What were you supposed to do?
- What will you do?

Step 6. Use the standard reality therapy questions that end with a written contract or a handshake. For example:

- What did you do?
- How did it help you?
- What could you do that would help you?
- What will you do?

Have the child dictate or write and sign a contract; have a follow-up meeting. If the contract is broken, have the child write or dictate a contract that he or she can meet. Eliminate punishment in favor of letting the child experience the logical consequences of appropriate and inappropriate behavior.

Phase III, consisting of four steps, is designed for children whose behavior makes teaching and learning difficult for everyone else in the classroom. In the home setting, Phase III is used when the child's behavior infringes on the rights of other family members. The hope is to solve the consultant problems in the six steps before Phase III, in which the primary intervention is isolation.

Step 7. In-class time-out is recommended. A quiet corner, study carrel, or private work area may be used. Time-out should not be in a punishment area or a "dunce's corner." The child has two choices: be with the group and behave, or be outside and sit. When the misbehavior occurs, send the child to the quiet area firmly with no discussion. The rest of the group does not have to be aware of the intervention. Have the child make a plan before returning to the group. The child's room may be used for time-out at home.

Step 8. Some children may require a time-out outside the classroom. The procedure is basically the same one described in Step 7. Some schools use a time-out room; others use an in-school suspension room. Contracts or plans for making a successful return to the classroom group can follow the questions used in the reality therapy method.

Step 9. Some children have difficulty getting through the entire school day without disrupting the class. Individual educational plans (IEPs) for these students may list four or five expectations or rules that the school has for all students. If the child does not meet one of these rules, have the child's parents remove the child from school for the remainder of the day. Allow the child to return the next day and remain as long as he or she follows the rules. Community agencies have been used when home isolation was not possible. Once again, no punishment in addition to the logical consequence of isolation needs to be administered. Such IEPs require the input of teachers, parents, administrators, the child, and the counselor.

Step 10. Step 10 often involves taking the child on a field trip to juvenile court to observe the probable consequences of continuing his or her present behavioral patterns. Interviews with the judge, other court officials, counselors, teachers, and inmates increase the child's awareness of logical consequences existing outside the home and school settings. Failure to meet consultation goals with a child who has not reacted positively to the ten-step method may mean that the child should be referred to a community agency better equipped to solve the child's problems.

The basic consultation model can be adapted to any situation in which the counselor is consulting with a client about how to work with a third person or is working directly with a client.

Yarbrough and Thompson (2002), using Step 6 in the ten-step consultation model with an underachieving student, were able to help the student significantly increase the number of school assignments from nearly 0 to 100 percent in five counseling sessions. (See Chapter 16 for more information about consultation.)

Consultation may be done in groups. McFadden (1991) uses several principles of reality therapy to teach students how to train the teacher *not* to pick on you. She begins by discussing with the student how the student has managed to train the teacher to look his or her way whenever there is a disturbance in the classroom. Next, McFadden points out that when teachers get a new group of students, they tend to classify them in one of two groups: the workers and the disturbers. "How did you train your teacher to put you in the disturbers group?" is the question. Finally, after a good discussion of how one gets in the disturbers group, the topic turns to how to get into the workers group that the teacher has pictured in his or her quality world. The following clues are given.

1. Does the student make eye contact with me when I am teaching?
   Inference: The student is listening.
2. Does the student answer and ask questions on the topic?
   Inference: The student is interested.
3. Does the student get to class on time with all of the right equipment and books?
   Inference: The student cares about the class and subject.
4. When work is assigned, does the student begin before I count to ten?
   Inference: The student wants to learn and cares about success.

5. Does the student complete quality work?
   Inference: The student wants to succeed.
6. Does the student treat me and others well?
   Inference: The student is a nice person who behaves well.
7. Does the student find something to do when finished working or when disturbed by others?
   Inference: The student is responsible.

The message is that the students who are in the teacher's "workers" group get more privileges and "get away" with more things than the students in the "disturbers" group do. And, to be in the workers group, you do not have to do all seven things all of the time.

Donato (2004) recommends a maintenance program for students identified as proceeding through a school's discipline program too quickly. The program is for homeroom teachers to help these students meet their five basic needs by connecting students with peers or groups (belonging), providing opportunities for students to make choices (freedom), giving students jobs and leadership roles to perform (power), and incorporating enjoyable activities into the day (fun).

CROSS-CULTURAL APPLICATIONS OF REALITY THERAPY

Glasser (1965) has always held the view that all humans have the same basic needs; these needs do not vary with age, sex, or race. A Chinese infant girl has the same basic needs as a Swedish king. Reality therapy was designed to help all types of people meet two basic needs: the need to love and be loved, and the need to feel worthwhile to ourselves and others. Glasser (1998, 2000c, 2005) has revised his list of human needs to include the needs for survival, freedom, power, fun, and love and belonging. However, we need to keep in mind that different cultures shape different images in the quality worldview of the people growing up in those cultures. We are not suggesting that cultural influence destroys the freedom to choose, only that different values and philosophies are part of these different cultures. Even within cultures, individuals hold different quality worldviews. Therefore, for each client we counsel, we must examine the individual's spiritual values, oral traditions, nonverbal behaviors and communication, family values, and healing practices. Counseling has always been based on treating each client as a unique individual. Cunningham (1995) points out that counseling theories originating in Western culture may contain inherent cultural biases that are not always appropriate for culturally dissimilar clients. However, reality therapy can be adapted for clients from most cultures, providing the counselor is familiar with the values and traditions of the cultures in question. Wubbolding and Brickell (2000) point out that reality therapy has been well received in Asia, the Middle East, and South Africa. Reality therapy is currently taught and successfully practiced in a diversity of countries including Canada, Korea, Japan, China, India, Singapore, United Kingdom, Norway, Israel, Ireland, Egypt, Germany, France, Slovenia, Croatia, Italy,

Columbia, Kuwait, South Africa, Russia, and in a diversity of cultures here in the United States (Wubbolding, Brickell, Imhof, Kim, Lojk, & Al-Rashidi, 2004). See Chapter 15 for descriptions of differences and similarities within and between cultures.

REALITY THERAPY, ACCOUNTABILITY, AND MANAGED HEALTH CARE

Reality therapy, based on choice theory, fits well into the managed care framework. It is goal directed and easily evaluated for progress. The process generally can be terminated successfully in ten or fewer sessions. Building current, trusting relationships with others is the focus of reality therapy, with little attention given to the past. The focus remains on what the client is choosing to do now. Practitioners of choice theory reality therapy do not deny their clients have real pain, but very little time is allowed for clients to complain about their symptoms. Counselors teach clients that the only people they can control are themselves. Glasser (2004, 2005) believes that it is no kindness to treat unhappy people as helpless, hopeless, or inadequate, no matter what has happened to them. Glasser sees kindness as having faith that people can handle the truth and to do so is to their benefit. True compassion is helping people help themselves.

In opposition to Freud, Glasser (2004, 2005) believes that counseling should always move forward, never backward. He believes there are more than enough problems in the present to keep the counselor and client busy. The managed care section in Chapter 2 confirms that reality therapy fits managed care guidelines.

SUMMARY

Perhaps the best validation of choice theory reality therapy is Glasser's success at the Ventura School for Girls. Before his tenure, the school's recidivism rate approached 90 percent; in a relatively short time, this rate fell to 20 percent. What was the secret of changing the orientation of these young women into success identities? Glasser gave them the experience of personal responsibility and success by assigning them tasks they could handle and by making each girl responsible for her own behavior. He discarded punishment in favor of logical consequences, gave generous amounts of praise, and showed sincere interest in each girl's welfare. Glasser's approach at the Ventura School included individual and group counseling conducted within the reality therapy model and framework presented in this chapter. Regardless of one's theoretical outlook, it would be difficult to argue with Glasser's formula for success. In fact, most counseling approaches are effective under Glasser's conditions, as described earlier in this chapter.

Reality therapy is simple and easy to understand, but difficult and demanding to implement. The key is helping people accept responsibility for what they are doing now. A pessimistic counselor cannot be a successful reality therapist. Considerable effort, persistence, and optimism are required from both the client and the counselor to make the reality therapy process work. The definition of behavior should expand to include feelings and thoughts, as well as what we actually do. The focus remains on what we can change about these three behavior components. Basically, according to Glasser (2005), the purpose of counseling is not to talk about the problem, but to straighten out one's life and one's day by focusing on meeting the five basic needs.

As is true with all counseling approaches, reality therapy has its supporters and critics. As might be expected, Glasser continues to find his greatest supporters among counselors, educators, psychologists, and social workers.

INTRODUCTION TO REALITY THERAPY

To gain a more in-depth understanding of the concepts in this chapter, visit www.thomsonedu.com/counseling/thompson to view a short clip of an actual therapist-client session demonstrating reality therapy.

WEBSITES FOR REALITY THERAPY

Internet addresses frequently change. To find the sites listed here, visit www.thomsonedu.com/counseling/thompson for an updated list of Internet addresses and direct links to relevant sites.

What Is Reality Therapy?

REFERENCES

Cunningham, L. (1995). Control theory, reality therapy and cultural bias. *Journal of Reality Therapy, 15*, 15–22.

Deming, W. E. (1966). *Some theory of sampling.* New York: Dover.

Donato, T. (2004). Maintenance for the CT/RT student in the classroom. *International Journal of Reality Therapy, 24*, 38–42.

Glasser, W. (1961). *Mental health or mental illness?* New York: Harper & Row.

Glasser, W. (1965). *Reality therapy.* New York: Harper & Row.

Glasser, W. (1969). *Schools without failure.* New York: Harper & Row.

Glasser, W. (1972). *The identity society.* New York: Harper & Row.

Glasser, W. (1976). *Positive addiction.* New York: Harper & Row.

Glasser, W. (1981). *Stations of the mind.* New York: Harper & Row.

Glasser, W. (1984). *Control theory.* New York: Harper & Row.

Glasser, W. (1986). *Control theory in the classroom.* New York: Harper & Row.

Glasser, W. (1990). *The quality school: Managing students without coercion.* New York: Harper & Row.

Glasser, W. (1993). *The quality school teacher.* New York: HarperCollins.

Glasser, W. (1995). *Staying together.* New York: HarperCollins.

Glasser, W. (1998). *Choice theory: A new psychology of personal freedom.* New York: HarperCollins.

Glasser, W. (2000a). *Every student can succeed*. Chatsworth, CA: Author.

Glasser, W. (2000b). *Getting together and staying together*. New York: HarperCollins.

Glasser, W. (2000c). *Reality therapy in action*. New York: HarperCollins.

Glasser, W. (2002) *Unhappy teenagers: A way for parents and teachers to reach them*. New York: Harper Collins.

Glasser, W. (2004). *Warning: Psychiatry can be dangerous to your health*. New York: Harper Collins.

Glasser, W. (2005). *Treating mental health as a public health problem: A new leadership role for the helping professions*. Chatsworth, CA: William Glasser Inc.

Huffstetler, B., Mims, S., & Thompson, C. (2004). Getting together and staying together: Testing the compatibility of the need-strength profile and the basic needs inventory. *International Journal of Reality Therapy, 23*, 4–12.

Kohlberg, L. (1981). *The philosophy of moral development: Moral stages and the idea of justice*. New York: Harper & Row.

McFadden, J. (1991). Behavior lotto or how to train the teacher not to pick on you. *Journal of Reality Therapy, 10*, 16–19.

Oz, S. (1994). Decision making in divorce therapy: Cost-cost comparison. *Journal of Marital and Family Therapy, 20*, 77–81.

Petersen, J., & Thompson, C. (2005). Perceptual differences between adolescents and adults in meeting their need for love. *International Journal of Reality Therapy, 24*(1), 16-21 .

Piaget, J. (1973). *The moral judgment of children*. New York: Free Press.

Thompson, C., & Poppen, W. (1972). *For those who care: Ways of relating to youth*. Columbus, OH: Merrill.

Wubbolding, R., & Brickell, J. (2000). Misconceptions about reality therapy. *International Journal of Reality Therapy, 19*, 64–65.

Wubbolding, R., Brickell, J., Imhof, L., Kim, R., Lojk, L., & Al-Rashidi, B. (2004). Reality theory: A global perspective. *International Journal for the Advancement of Counseling, 26*, 219–228.

Yarbrough, J., & Thompson, C. (2002). Using single-participant research to assess counseling approaches on children's off-task behavior. *Professional School Counseling, 5*, 308–314.

BRIEF COUNSELING: SOLUTION-FOCUSED AND PARADOXICAL COUNSELING STRATEGIES

If you want truly to understand something, try to change it.
—Kurt Lewin

BACKGROUND

Brief counseling could be labeled "counseling for the millennium." Quicker and faster—the watchwords for the past several decades—have now moved from fast foods, faxes, and faster computers into the world of managed health care. Counseling is one of the health care services. However, the recent popularity of brief counseling cannot be attributed solely to the insurance company underwriters who seem to be running the U.S. health care systems. Deviations from long-term, analytic therapy have been developing since the 1950s, beginning with Rogers's person-centered counseling, which was followed by a number of new therapies designed to help people reach their counseling goals in shorter and more efficient ways. Even Freud himself, the architect of long-term analysis, described several single-session therapy cases that resulted in successful outcomes. As noted in Chapter 4, in addition to advocating shorter term therapy, Glasser (1965) is one of the first psychiatrists to take a stand against psychotherapy and counseling as being a cure for emotional problems. Instead, he views counseling and psychotherapy as an educative process directed toward helping people find better ways to meet their psychological needs of being successful and loved. Behavioral counseling methods have been directed toward these same goals. The case can be made that brief counseling has been evolving since the beginning of the twentieth century and is well positioned to take its place in the twenty-first century. To date, two types of brief counseling have emerged.

First came the paradoxical counseling strategies focusing on symptom reduction, introduced by Dunlap (1928, 1932) in the 1920s and 1930s, developed by Viktor Frankl (1975) in the 1930s, and refined and popularized by Milton Erickson, Jay Haley (1973, 1976, 1984), and Watzlawick, Weakland, and Fisch (1974). Then came the work of de Shazer (de Shazer, 1985, 1988, 1994; de Shazer & Molnar, 1964), which focuses on solutions rather than on the client's problem. Both types of brief counseling are discussed in the next section, beginning with the most recent form of brief counseling, solution-focused brief counseling (SFBC).

SOLUTION-FOCUSED BRIEF COUNSELING

The Nature of People

Counselors practicing SFBC fall into the top half of the chart presented in Chapter 2 (see Figure 2-2). They believe that people feeling bad at Point A on the chart will continue to feel bad if they do not make positive behavioral changes in their lives. Merely discussing "why" people feel as they do will not help, neither will focusing on such unobservable elements as feelings, thoughts, and motivations. The key to feeling better is to focus on "what" people are doing that seems to be helpful and to set goals with plans on how to accomplish these goals. SFBC counselors believe that their clients will do better with a present and future orientation. In fact, SFBC may be the only counseling theory in which a future orientation takes precedence over a present orientation. The SFBC philosophy appears to be that clients can become mired in their past unresolved conflicts and failures and blocked when focusing on present problems rather than on future solutions.

SFBC counselors view their clients as being free to make choices and not victimized by their heredity or environment. They hold a positive view of people that rivals that held by followers of Rogers's theories. People are seen as being basically good, with the power to overcome evil and to make good behavioral choices. SFBC counselors believe that people are also basically rational, having the capacity to solve their own problems and overcome the irrational influences in their culture. It would be difficult to find an approach to counseling holding a more humanistic view of nature than that embodied in SFBC. The biggest exception to the humanistic philosophy in SFBC is in the high activity level of the counselor in directing the client's thoughts toward building on the positive things that are happening in formulating counseling goals and plans for reaching them. Even then, the client's input is always sought, with most of the counselor's activity directed to holding the counseling focus on the positive, rather than the negative, side of the client's situation.

The tremendous faith SFBC practitioners have in their clients' ability to work through their own problems is highlighted in the words of the old song "AC-Cent-Tchu-Ate the Positive": "Accentuate the positive, eliminate the negative, and say no to Mr. In-Between." In other words, people do better when they concentrate on their successes rather than on their failures. Positive and helpful changes are more likely to grow from exploring strengths rather than weaknesses or deficits. It is human nature for clients to prefer talking about what is going right in their lives over what is going wrong.

SFBC counselors cater to whatever common sense is found in their clients' thinking. For example, the test of any good idea is whether it will work for the client. Legum (2005), Sklare (2005), Lipchik (2002), Bruce (1995), Walter and Pellar (1992), Berg and Miller (1992), and de Shazer (1986) emphasize the appeal to their clients' common sense in the following pragmatic points stated in colloquial, if not overused, everyday language:

1. "If it ain't broke, don't fix it."
2. "If it works a little, build on it and try to do more of the part that is working."
3. "If it is broke, do something different to fix it."

In other words, once you know what works and what does not, do more of what works and stop doing what does not work.

In summary, SFBC practitioners base their work on the following concepts about the nature of people:

1. People are viewed as basically good, capable of rational thought, able to implement positive change, and free to make choices. However, without direction from the counselor, people appear by nature to want to focus on the negative aspects of their lives.
2. Once the counseling focus has shifted from the negative to the positive, people prefer to talk about what is going well in their lives. No problem happens all of the time.
3. People have the capacity to act on common sense if given the opportunity to identify commonsense problem-solving strategies.
4. People respond better to counseling when they make positive changes in their behavior as opposed to working on the cognitive and affective components of their situation. For children who may have difficulty in handling some of the abstract thinking involved in cognitive and affective counseling, the behavior change focus is most useful.
5. People will respond better to a present and future counseling orientation than they will to a past orientation focused on why they have a problem they cannot solve.

THEORY OF COUNSELING

SFBC practitioners might well adopt the 4-H club motto: "Make the best better." The method is based on the theory that people will respond better to building up the positive aspects of their lives. Every problem is viewed as having identifiable exceptions that can be transformed into solutions. For example, a child who is having trouble making friends in her classroom might be asked to look at those times when she was able to initiate some contact. She may say, "Well, one day Jane Ann asked me to eat lunch with her, and that made me feel good." The counselor would build on that by asking how that happened and how she could make it happen more often.

SFBC is based on the theory that small solutions can lead to big changes. Small behavior changes build momentum in a person's life, much like the momentum defined in Newton's laws of motion. A body at rest tends to remain at rest, and a body in motion tends to remain in motion. Many of our clients come for counseling because they are bodies at rest. Small behavioral changes are used to get them moving. For example, John might be asked to complete a small portion of his math assignment rather than the entire assignment, based on the theory that he needs encouragement and success to get some momentum started in his life. In addition, SFBC methods are helpful to counselors wanting to capitalize on role-shift theory. Small shifts in role by one person in a relationship will cause a role shift by others in that relationship. For example, Mary notices that when she says something nice to her brother, he is more likely to be nice to her. George may notice that his parents are more cooperative with him when he does his homework and chores without being nagged.

SFBC is also based on the theory that goals need to be stated in positive and observable terms to be effective. People do better in attaining goals that are quantifiable and specific. For example, the goal of "completing one homework assignment per day at school" is far superior to the goal "to study harder." Behavioral counselors and reality therapists would concur that clients respond better to accomplishments they can observe and record. Goals stated as "Thou shalt not" have less chance for success than goals stated positively. For example, the goal of "I will not cause anybody to become angry with me" is better stated as "I will say something nice to one person each day." "Thou shalt not" goals may have the paradoxical effect of making clients want to do the things they are trying to quit doing. For example, the worst goal a dieter could have would be the self-admonition "Don't think about food!" Former President Clinton's initiative to curb teenage smoking by making smoking the forbidden fruit may have been responsible, in part, for the sudden upsurge in teenage smoking that occurred at that time. Bruce (1995) has identified the following four main components of SFBC:

1. Development of a working alliance in which the counselor and client work together in attacking the problem and its causes.
2. Identification of clients' strengths and assets as foundations on which to build their confidence in their ability to make positive changes in their lives.
3. Implementation of active, eclectic counseling strategies and interventions, including role-playing, homework assignments, confrontations, interpretations, visualization, and reframing, to help clients achieve their goals.
4. Establishment of clear, concrete, measurable goals that serve to help counselors and clients evaluate their progress.

The emphasis in SFBC counseling is on creating concrete word pictures to describe the problem and the problem setting. Clients are asked to describe exactly what happens, who is there, and what is said and done. Bruce (1995) has detailed four useful intervention tasks:

1. "Do something different" for the client who tends to repeat the same ineffective reaction in problem situations.
2. "Pay attention to what you do when you overcome the urge to . . ." for the client who has trouble controlling impulsive behaviors.
3. "Tell me about a time when you had a good day at school" for clients who have taken on the victim mentality of believing that nothing good ever happens to them.
4. "Observe and take notes" for clients who have trouble avoiding problem situations and interactions. The observations help the client identify the good and bad things that happen in the problem setting; however, the most beneficial outcome is the client's role shift from someone who interacts to someone who observes. A role shift by one person in a group leads to role shifts by the other interacting members.

Finally, the SFBC method is based on the theory that more (counseling) is not better. Better is better—that is, counseling works best when the focus shifts from the number of counseling sessions to increasing or expanding the best parts of clients' lives. The current status of managed health care is certainly favorable to the SFBC philosophy, and SFBC practitioners might even owe a debt of gratitude to insurance companies and health maintenance organizations (HMOs) for promoting brief counseling. However, we caution that many clients require longer term counseling than what is generally implied by brief counseling. Such cases include clients who are suicidal or psychotic and those with schizophrenia, manic-depression, and various addictions. This is not to say, however, that SFBC strategies could not be incorporated into longer term counseling and psychotherapy.

COUNSELING METHOD

ORIENTATION STATEMENT   Brief counseling generally requires more structuring than most methods because it differs radically in counselor activity and the number of sessions required. Although it is of prime importance to clarify any counseling process to new clients and to children, it is mandatory as a first step in doing SFBC. The SFBC focus and goal-setting strategies begin to take shape with the counselor's orientation statement about how the process works. For example, your opening statement to your client might be:

> Our purpose in talking together will be to help you find out what you need to do to solve a problem. We will look at some things you do well and see if we can use them to figure out what you want to do and what steps you should take next. I will be asking you several questions. Some of these questions will be hard to answer. I will be writing things down about what we are talking about. After we finish our talk, I will leave for a few minutes and write you a message from the notes I have been taking. I will make a copy for you and keep a copy for me. Does all of this sound okay with you?

STATEMENT OF THE PROBLEM   As is true with any other approach to counseling, we recommend that counselors use active listening from person-centered counseling before embarking on the preferred counseling interventions. Failure to use active listening often results in the counselor and client working on the wrong problem; therefore, we suggest that counselors remain in the active listening mode until clients agree that their counselors understand four important things about their situation:

1. The problem.
2. The feelings associated with the problem.
3. The intensity of those feelings on a 0 to 10 scale (10 is the best feeling [high]; 0 is the worst feeling [low]).
4. The client's expectations of what he or she would like to happen in counseling and the goals the client would like to accomplish.

Regarding the third point, rating intensity of feelings on a ten-point scale, this activity can result in a goal statement. When the client says, "I am about a six on a ten-point scale in feeling good," the counselor can focus the interview on those good things the client is doing and the things that are happening in the client's life that make the client's rating as high as a 6. Then, the interview can be directed toward discovering how the client can make more of these good things happen.

As noted in Chapter 1, children in the upper range of the preoperational stage of cognitive development will need visual presentations of such a rating scale. Five smiley faces ranging from a very happy smile to a deeply frowning, unhappy face help younger children identify how good or bad they are feeling. Some counselors use a "feel-o-meter" constructed like a regular outdoor thermometer and let the child color in how high the mercury level has risen on the feelings scale. Smiling and frowning faces also can be used on the feel-o-meter to depict how the child is feeling. The same rating scale can be used throughout the SFBC process for setting goals and measuring the child's progress. Note that many children set behavioral goals to jump all the way from a low rating of a 3 to a high rating of 10 in just a day or two. Counselors will do well to focus on helping children move from a 3 to a 4 on behavioral goals (what the child will actually be doing at level 4) to ensure early success with the SFBC process. Gains of 10 percent are good when they are defined in observable, positive behavioral changes.

SETTING COUNSELING GOALS

The heart of many counseling methods is to set good or productive goals. Good goals have some of the following common properties:

1. Goals owned or set by the client work best because clients are more likely to achieve the goals for which they hold ownership.
2. If clients need assistance in goal setting—and they probably will with SFBC—be sure that the goals are cocreated and are not the counselor's goals.

3. Set goals that are behavior oriented. Goals work best when they are positive, concrete, and reduced to small steps.
4. State a goal in terms of what behavior will occur, how often it will occur, and under what conditions it will occur.

For example, Frank's goal is to earn an A grade in English. To earn an A, Frank has agreed to request that his seat be moved to the front row, attend class every day, complete each day's homework assignment, and answer at least one question per day during class discussion.

THE SKELETON KEY QUESTION/STATEMENT FOR GOAL SETTING De Shazer (1985) and Berg & Shilts (2005) recommend starting goal setting by asking clients to think about the good things rather than the bad things that have been happening in their lives; for example, "I would like to have you think about your life recently and the things that have happened to you that you would like to have happen more often in the future," or "Please think about what you would like to get done in counseling and how you will know if counseling is helping." The client's thoughts on either of these statements will help the counselor determine what the client's goals might be. Berg & Shilts (2005) use what they call the "woww" approach, which is working on what works.

WORKING WITH UNPRODUCTIVE CLIENT GOALS Unproductive goals will scuttle the SFBC approach before it leaves the harbor. The three most common unproductive client goals are negative goals, harmful goals, and "Beats me, I don't know" goals. Sklare (2005) has done an excellent job in describing how each of these three types of unproductive goals can be reframed into productive, positive goals. Remember that SFBC focuses on the solutions, not the problem.

Negative Goals. Negative goals are stated as "Thou shalt not . . ." goals—that is, goals to "stop doing things" and goals to get others to stop doing things; for example, "I would like to stop getting so many detentions." All of the preceding goals need to be reframed to describe what it is the client will be doing rather than not doing; for example, "I need to raise my hand in class to get permission to speak and that will lower the number of detentions I have been getting."

Negative goals need to be refocused on what clients *will* be doing instead of what they *will not* be doing. The refocused goal can be derived from the things the client will be doing; for example, "If you stop doing all those things you said caused you to fail English, what will you be doing instead?" Nature abhors a vacuum, and something is sure to rush in and fill the void in a person's life when an activity is stopped. Therefore, clients should be asked how they plan to fill the free time they will have when they stop doing an unproductive behavior such as arguing excessively with their parents.

Harmful Goals. Harmful goals are those goals that, when achieved, will bring either harm to the client or to others. More often than not, these goals also will lead to violations of the law or school rules, such as selling drugs or engaging in other criminal acts. The counselor can approach harmful goal statements by exploring with clients how achieving such goals would get the clients what they want. For example:

COUNSELOR: So, dropping out of school and selling drugs to make a living is what you really want. How will this help you?

CLIENT: Well, I hate school because I don't do the work and I get Fs.

COUNSELOR: So you are saying if you did the work, you would get better grades and then you might like school a little better?

CLIENT: Maybe.

COUNSELOR: Maybe a goal for you would be to find out how you could do the work and do better on your grades.

Finally, in discerning harmful counseling goals, it is incumbent on the counselor to inform their clients about the conditions under which counselor-client confidentiality cannot be maintained. Harming self or others, property damage, and other violations of the law must be reported, and the counselor will have to take whatever steps possible to prevent the client from doing harmful acts.

I Don't Know Goals. "I don't know goals" are most likely ploys by the client to engage the counselor in some type of resistance activity. The client usually has been sent for counseling by parents, teachers, or judges and is determined to resist any effort by the counselor to help in any way. As noted in Chapter 2, to overcome a child's resistance, the counselor can begin with the following dialogue:

COUNSELOR: What would have to happen to get your parents off your back and say you don't need counseling?

CLIENT: They want me to try harder at school.

COUNSELOR: What would I be seeing you do at school that would let your parents know that you were trying harder?

By following this script, the counselor becomes an ally who is working on the same team with the client to figure out how to help her or him avoid the need for counseling.

Legum (2005), in working with involuntary clients, recommends finding out whose idea it was to come for counseling and is this what the client wants. If not, ask what the client might like to have happen in counseling and explain how counseling could help with the presenting problem.

USING THE MIRACLE QUESTION TO FORMULATE GOALS

The miracle question, developed by de Shazer (1990) in his frustration with some clients' inability to form good, behavioral goals, is used to help clients visualize and hypothesize what their problems would be like if suddenly they were solved. For example, the counselor could say, "suppose a miracle occurs one night and the problem you brought to counseling is solved while you were sleeping. What would be different the next morning? How would you know that the miracle had happened? What would you be doing that would indicate to you that the miracle had taken place?"

Children may respond better to the question stated in magic terms (Sklare, 2005); for example, "If I were to wave a magic wand or rub a magic lamp and wish all your problems away, what would we see you doing if we could video you for a day?" Older children, teenagers, and adults might respond better with a visualization about what their life would look like 6 months or a year from now if the problem brought to counseling was solved; for example, "If the problem you brought to counseling was solved in the next 6 months, how would you know things were okay, and what would you be doing differently?" Again, active listening is a good way to help clients put their hypotheses about their problem-free futures in good, behavioral goal language. This is where the future orientation parts of SFBC stand out. The counselor's job is to keep the focus on what the client *will* be doing when the problem is solved.

Frequently, clients still use ineffective goal statements and generalizations in stating their hypotheses about their problem-free futures, such as, "Well, I would feel good, I would be happy, or my parents would be nicer to me." When this happens, the counselor tries to identify the client's specific behavior: "When you are feeling this good feeling, what are you doing that will let you know that you are feeling good, or that you are happy?" Other examples are: "What are your parents doing that would let you know that they are treating you nicer?" and "What are you doing that would cause your parents to be nicer to you?" Again, visualization of the "new" behavior in the client's future, problem-free environment can be assisted with the video recording metaphor of what the video would show the client doing and by asking what others would see him or her doing. Others who would be observing the client could be the counselor, family members, classmates, teachers, and friends. For example, you could ask, "What would your friends see you doing differently, and what would they say?"

Sklare (2005) points out that clients often respond to the miracle question with improbable (if not impossible) miracles and "I want others to be different" miracles. For the former, the counselor's job is to reframe the improbable answer into what might be probable. For example, in the case of a divorce, the child may say:

CLIENT: I want my Mom and Dad to get married again.

COUNSELOR: How would that help you?

CLIENT: I would feel like I was part of a real family.

COUNSELOR: So, feeling a part of your family would be a goal for you.

CLIENT: Yes, because now it doesn't seem like I am.

COUNSELOR:	What would you be doing to let you know that you were a part of your family?
CLIENT:	I would like to be doing things that would help Mom and Dad out, like I did before they got divorced.
COUNSELOR:	So, finding out how you could help both your Mom and Dad could be another goal for you.

For the latter "I want others to be different" goal, the counselor would continue to keep the focus on what the client will be doing to cause others to behave differently. For example:

CLIENT:	I would like other kids in my class to be friends with me.
COUNSELOR:	Well, if that miracle occurred, what would we see on a video of what was going on in your classroom?
CLIENT:	Other kids would choose me to work with them on stuff.
COUNSELOR:	So, if the other kids were choosing you for a work partner, what would you start doing differently?
CLIENT:	I guess I would be nice about sharing my stuff with them.
COUNSELOR:	That sounds like a good goal for you to have. What else would you be doing?
CLIENT:	I would be working hard to do my share of the work.
COUNSELOR:	That sounds like a better goal, because you would know right away if you did at least your share of the work.

CASE STUDY

Identification of the Problem

George is an 8-year-old boy in the second grade at Mountain Springs School. He was brought to private counseling by his parents, who were concerned because of his anxiety about going to school.

Individual and Background Information

Academic. George's school records were a small road map of low achievement beginning midway through the first grade, when he began to fall behind the others in reading and mathematics concepts. Testing by the school psychologist did not reveal any learning disabilities, and his verbal and performance IQ was calculated to be within the 110 to 120 range. The school psychologist concluded that George's poor academic progress was more of a case of not wanting to do the school work rather than not being able to do it.

Family. George is the middle child between an older sister, age 10, and a younger brother, age 5. His parents indicated that George's older sister had always made top grades, and that his younger brother enjoyed going to kindergarten.

Social. George's first-grade teacher had reported in his records that he had some difficulty in making friends with most of the other children. He seemed to gravitate toward two boys who were causing most of the classroom discipline problems, and George frequently had to be disciplined because of his own misbehavior, as well as misbehavior with the other two boys. The pattern has continued in the second grade.

Counseling Method

The counselor used SFBC to help George identify some specific behavioral goals for himself. After identification of the goals, the counselor had periodic follow-up sessions with him to coordinate his progress with the school counselor, who was working with George's teachers in reinforcing progress on his goals. Behavioral contingency contracts and reality therapy used by the school counselor had not been successful with George.

Transcript

After about 5 minutes of getting to know each other and giving the structuring speech about what the SFBC counselor does, the counselor begins:

COUNSELOR: Well, George, do you know why your parents wanted you to see me?

GEORGE: I don't know.

COUNSELOR: That is one of the hard questions I told you I would be asking. So, I would like to have you pretend for a moment that you do know why your parents brought you here.

GEORGE: Well, it's probably about school, isn't it?

COUNSELOR: That was a good guess. What do you think they want to have happen to you in school?

GEORGE: Probably make better grades on my schoolwork.

COUNSELOR: George, I have a thermometer-type thing here that goes from a low of zero to a high of five. The zero would be for very low grades, like all Fs, and the five would be for very high grades like all As. Which number on my thermometer is most like your grades?

GEORGE: I think I am about a two, because my grades are Cs and Ds.

COUNSELOR: I wonder how good your grades will have to be to get your parents to stop bringing you here for counseling.

GEORGE: Bs and Cs might make Mom and Dad happier with me, and that would be about a three on your scale.

COUNSELOR: So raising your grade one level would be a good goal for you. I would like to do another "let's pretend" with you. Suppose I had a magic lamp like in the genie story, and I could rub it and make a wish and a miracle happened. Imagine that your parents said, "George, your grades are good enough, and you don't have to go back to see the counselor." What would you be doing in your classroom the next day?

GEORGE:	I would be really happy, and so would my teacher and Mom and Dad.
COUNSELOR:	If I could videotape you in your classroom, what would I see you doing that would let me know you were happy about your grades?
GEORGE:	I wouldn't be getting into trouble.
COUNSELOR:	That's right, George, but what would you be doing instead?
GEORGE:	I would be doing my schoolwork at my desk and raising my hand before talking in class.
COUNSELOR:	These things sound like two good goals for you to work on this week. What else would you be doing that we could see on a videotape?
GEORGE:	I would be finishing nearly all of my work at school so I wouldn't have to bring it home.
COUNSELOR:	These goals are getting better all the time. Do you think this would be a good goal that you could do?
GEORGE:	Yes, I could if I could sit away from some guys who always get me into trouble.
COUNSELOR:	So changing your seat might be another goal for you. Where do you see yourself sitting?
GEORGE:	I think I would do better in the front row.
COUNSELOR:	What else would we see you doing?
GEORGE:	Making mostly B grades and no more than two C grades.
COUNSELOR:	What would that videotape show you doing to make mostly B grades and just two Cs?
GEORGE:	Well, like I said, I would be getting nearly all my work done at school, and I would be working away from the troublemakers.
COUNSELOR:	Okay, George, it looks like you have two good goals to work on this week. Would it be okay if I talked to the school counselor about getting your seat moved so that you can get your work done at school, or do you want to talk this over with your teacher?
GEORGE:	I'll ask my teacher.
COUNSELOR:	What if she asks you why you want to move?
GEORGE:	I'll tell her that it will help me get my work done.
COUNSELOR:	Well, George, I have asked you about all the questions I have for you, and you have given me some really smart answers. I am wondering if you have any questions for me. [Pause] If not, I have one last questions: What other things do I need to know that might help you reach your goals? [Pause] If there isn't anything else, we need to look at what might happen to stop you from meeting your goals. [Pause] If there is nothing you can think of, I need to leave you for a few moments to think about my notes and all the answers you gave me and to write you a message that you can take

with you. You can play with any of the toys in the room and read any of the magazines while I am gone for a few minutes.

While they write these messages, some counselors prefer to remain in the room with younger children. Sklare (2005) recommends that messages should contain at least three compliments, with each compliment bridged to a task that will indicate that the child has met his or her goal. In George's case, the counselor would refer to the notes taken during the session.

George's Goals

1. Raise his grades to all Bs and Cs.
2. Improve his classroom behavior.
3. Do well enough in school to get out of having to go to counseling.

Miracle

- I would be completing most of my homework at school and finishing the rest of my assignments at home.
- My grades would be all Bs and Cs.
- My classroom behavior would be good.
- My parents would be happy with my school behavior and grades, and I would not have to have more counseling.

First Sign(s) the Miracle Had Happened

- I would be doing my work in a front row seat away from the guys who got in trouble with me.
- I would be completing all of my school assignments, and my teacher would notice that I am doing better.
- I would be raising my hand for permission to speak in class, and that would make my teacher happy.

Instances or Exceptions When the Miracle Has Happened a Little Bit

- When I ignore the two boys who try to get me to break the rules.
- When I do my assignments during work periods.

Scaling

- Currently at a 2 because grades are all Cs and Ds.
- To get to a 3 on a five-point scale, all grades have to be a C or better.
- To get a 5, all grades will have to be at least half Bs and half As.
- Classroom behavior is at a 2, because George had to go to three time-outs for disrupting class last week. To get to a 4, he would have to be sent to no more than one time-out each week.

The counselor's written message to George was as follows:

[Compliment] I think you were really smart in coming up with some good ways to let your parents know that you won't need to come in here for more counseling. You figured out a good way to stay out of trouble and an even better way to raise your grades. Getting your seat moved to the front row, doing most of your homework assignments at school, turning in all of your assignments, and raising your hand to get permission to speak are four excellent ideas that should help you meet all your goals. [Bridges] Because of your promise to do your four ideas at school, [Task] I would suggest that you begin by asking the teacher if she would move your seat to the front and tell her why you want to do this. Then I would suggest that you start doing the three other ideas and move up to a 3 on your five-point scale for grades and a 4 for classroom behavior.

George may have trouble reading the message, so the language may need to be simplified for him to understand the compliments and how those are bridged to the tasks he needs to do. Sklare (2005) recommends having children draw pictures of their miracles, showing what will be happening when the miracle occurs. Discussion of the events depicted in these miracle drawings provides an excellent review of the session and leads into the counselor's message. For children who are not able to read the counselor's message, it might also be a good idea to draw a picture of their messages showing the complimented behaviors and the tasks to be done. Pictures help children visualize outcome goals being met, and hence contribute to the child's ability to meet these goals.

REVIEWING THE STEPS IN SOLUTION-FOCUSED BRIEF COUNSELING

No theory of counseling has more steps or interventions than SFBC. In fact, the prudent approach to using SFBC would be to select from the menu those interventions you think will take your clients where they want to go. Our purpose here is to present a menu of SFBC interventions discussed by several key authors on the subject, including Berg and Shilts (2005), Legum (2005), Sklare (2005), Daughhtree and Grant (2002), Littrell (1998), Fleming and Rickford (1997), Murphy and Duncan (1997), Selekman (1997), and Cade and O'Hanlon (1993). All have contributed steps and questions typically used in conducting SFBC counseling interviews.

ORIENTATION TO THE SOLUTION-FOCUSED BRIEF COUNSELING PROCESS   Tell the child that you will be asking some hard questions and that you will be taking notes so that you can remember the answers. Explain that the answers will help you write a note to the child at the end of the talk.

SETTING GOALS FOR COUNSELING   Begin by asking, "What is your goal in coming in for counseling?" or "What would you like to have happen from our counseling?" The focus is on goals and positive information, rather than on problems and negative aspects of the problem.

ACTIVE LISTENING   Use active listening to help clients.

1. Clarify: (a) "What my goal is and what I will be doing when my goal is reached"; (b) "My feelings about my situation"; and (c) "How strongly I feel about my situation."
2. Scaling: For example, "On a ten-point scale where ten is very good and zero is very bad, where are you on the scale of zero to ten?" If clients indicate they are a 4, ask what is happening that keeps their bad feelings from being a 0. Focus on how they can make more of these good things happen.

WORKING WITH NEGATIVE GOALS   Negative goals are an absence of something, as in:

CLIENT: I don't want to . . .

COUNSELOR: So, what would you be doing instead?

Or

CLIENT: I want others to stop . . .

COUNSELOR: What difference would this make? [Or] How will that help you? [Or] What will you do if they don't change?

WORKING WITH POSITIVE GOALS   Positive goals are the presence of something, as in:

CLIENT: I would like to make better grades.

COUNSELOR: What would you be doing that would show you have gotten what you want?

THE MIRACLE QUESTION

1. "If a miracle happened overnight and your problem was solved but you didn't know it, what would you be doing differently that would let you know the problem was solved?"
2. "If we videotaped you after the miracle happened, what would we see you doing?"
3. "Who would be the first to notice the difference in your behavior?"

    a. "What would they notice?"
    b. "How would they respond to you?"
    c. "How would you respond to them?"
    d. "What would be different/happening after this miracle?"

Repeat this question three or four times to get more indicators of what the counseling goals should be for your client. The counseling agenda can be set from the miracle question.

RELATIONSHIP QUESTIONS

1. "What will your [parents, brother or sister, teacher, friend] say that will be different after the miracle?"

a.   "How will they act when they see you are different after the miracle?"
b.   "When they act differently toward you, what will you do differently in response to them?"

EXCEPTIONS TO THE PROBLEM SITUATION

1.   Ask about some instances when some of the miracle has already happened a little bit.
2.   Encourage and reinforce these exceptions to the problem situation.
3.   Fleming and Rickford (1997) recommend the EARS approach—which stands for Elicit, Amplify, Reinforce, and Start again—when exceptions to the problem, other positive thoughts, and positive behaviors are mentioned.

POSITIVE BLAME   Use positive blame when exceptions to the problem situation are identified. For example, say, "How in the world were you able to make that happen?"

SCALING PROGRESS TOWARD GOAL

1.   "On a scale of 0 to 10, where 0 is the worst that things could be and 10 is the day after the miracle, where are you right now?"
2.   Again, if the client says 4, ask what is going on that keeps it from being a 0.
3.   Focus on talking about how to make more of these good things happen.
4.   Again, reinforce any indicators that the client is already doing some helpful things that can be increased.

TEN PERCENT IMPROVEMENTS

1.   Ask clients what they need to do to go up one step, or 10 percent, on the scale.
2.   Develop a plan for making the 10 percent improvement. Operational goals work best because they can be documented; for example, complete mathematics homework the next 5 days.

FLAGGING THE MINE FIELD

1.   Ask clients what things might prevent them from moving up 10 percent on the scale or what might sabotage their plan.
2.   Ask your clients what they could do to prevent their plan from being sabotaged.

CLOSING THE SESSION

1.   Ask clients to draw a picture of what will be happening after the miracle occurs (visualization).
2.   Ask clients if they have any questions or if there is anything else you (the counselor) should know.

WRITING THE NOTE   Write the client a message with at least three compliments and a bridging statement from each compliment to one of the tasks the client needs to accomplish to raise the scale score 10 percent, or one level from a 4 to a 5. The counselor has the option of drawing a picture of what the client will be doing the day after the miracle occurs.

In summary, additional SFBC sessions can follow the same pattern of interventions and questions to build on progress made or to recycle the process if little or no progress has occurred.

O'Hanlon, Wiener-Davis and O'Hanlon (2003) recommend beginning each counseling session by asking, "What happened in the past week that you would like to continue to see happen?"; this question focuses on and amplifies the positive actions toward change. Most SFBC sessions will not require all of the steps mentioned in this chapter. In fact, Daughhtree and Grant (2002) use only five questions or steps in their practice of SFBC.

1. Ask clients, "How do you experience the problem?"
2. Ask clients, "When do (or did) you not experience the problem? What were you doing then?"
3. Have clients rate their current progress on solving the problem on the 0 to 10 scale.
4. Ask the miracle question.
5. Set goals based on increasing what works for the client.

Campbell, Elder, Gallagher, Simon, and Taylor (1999) present five SFBC statements that assist clients in moving away from the problem impasse toward solutions.

1. *Normalizing statements.* These statements let clients know they are not alone in experiencing their problem; for example, "No wonder you are feeling . . ." Although this statement appears to be in conflict with our philosophy of not using "level one, discount of feelings" statements in person-centered counseling, it does have the possibility of offering clients the hope that others have worked their way out of similar difficulties and that they are not "crazy" for experiencing the feelings they are having.
2. *Restructuring statements.* These statements are used to rephrase the impasse as directions for the future; for example, "You have reached a decision point in your life."
3. *Affirmation statements.* These statements reinforce the positive steps the client has already taken and attributes the client can marshal to achieve personal goals.
4. *Bridging statements.* These statements connect client attributes with the next steps in achieving goals.
5. *Between-session homework statements.* These statements of what the client will be doing serve to connect the sessions and remind students of when times are better. Homework will also move clients toward their goals.

ERICKSONIAN PLAY THERAPY

Marvasti (1997) discusses the characteristics of Ericksonian play therapy in the following terms: This therapy relies on the child's strengths rather than weaknesses. It focuses on the present and future rather than the past. The child's potential is utilized, and the current symptoms are transformed into solutions. The therapy uses trance without the child's awareness. The counselor communicates through metaphor and storytelling, not interpreting play and not necessarily searching for insight. The counselor uses a doll or puppet to play the role of an older, wiser self, telling a therapeutic story that includes suggestions, metaphors, and happy endings.

The type of play therapy is modified for each child and relies on the flexibility and creativity of the counselor for success. Diagnosis is used to determine the child's potential, resources, assets, interpersonal issues, and favorite hero. The solution-oriented aspect of this therapy requires well-defined goals focusing on the present and the future. The recognition that change is constant and inevitable, often a ripple effect, is a crucial principle. The counselor searches for exceptions, times when the problem was not present. The counselor uses the miracle question (de Shazer, 1988), as well as reframing and positive connotations to the problem situation, in the Ericksonian approach to play therapy.

PARADOXICAL COUNSELING STRATEGIES

THE NATURE OF PEOPLE

Practitioners of paradoxical brief counseling (PBC) strategies differ in one significant way from practitioners of SFBC in how they view the nature of people. They view people as having a drive toward independence that makes them want to resist compliance with counselors' suggestions and directives. Not only do people resist cooperating with their counselors but they also often do the opposite. The resistance can be either passive or active. Working on this principle, practitioners of PBC methods try to harness this resistance and make it work for the client rather than against the counselor. Actually, this drive toward independence is viewed as a positive trait in human nature. It becomes difficult in counseling only when the client is resisting just for the sake of resisting, much like the 2-year-old who says "no" to all requests. In other words, these are times when resistance is the right choice based on the logic that not to resist would result in an undesirable outcome. Also, there are times when resistance is an attempt to impede progress toward making changes that would lead to a good outcome.

THEORY OF COUNSELING

The goal of all brief counseling methods is to help clients resolve a problem that is preventing them from moving on in their lives. There is a slight shift in focus when comparing SFBC with PBC methods. In SFBC, the focus is on solutions; in the PBC method, the focus is on problem formation and elimination. PBC methods are as specific and eclectic as the particular client requires. Counseling is focused, with the counselor taking an active role in initiating brief counseling interventions. However, the clients are still responsible for making behavioral changes in their lives. Positive outcome is valued over the counseling process. Counseling is designed to make each session productive and to end counseling as soon as possible. Clients can return for additional sessions when they are needed.

PBC practitioners believe that they will perform best by staying out of conflict with their clients. Such power struggles are not helpful to the client, counselor, counseling process, or counseling outcome. Rather, the client's resistance can be used as a source of energy that can be redirected, helping the client make positive behavioral changes. Not using the client resistance as an energy resource would be viewed as inefficient, as well as ineffective, in helping clients change their behavior. Clients seem to respond best when they can show the counselor that they know more about their lives than their counselors do. Therefore, given the opportunity to prove their counselors wrong, clients often will take the path opposite to that directed by the counselor.

PBC practitioners have two basic ways to approach their clients. One way is to take a "one-down" position, which elevates the client to the expert and drops the counselor to the "less than expert" role. For example, the counselor might say to a resistant, underachieving, bright adolescent, "I'd like to put you into the College Prep English class for a while to see how it goes, but I'm afraid you might have trouble understanding some of the things they are reading in there. They have a spot open in third period. Do you know anybody who might like to give it a shot?" Given a golden opportunity to prove the counselor wrong, many highly resistant students will beg for the chance. The counselor's role is to remain skeptical and show utter amazement (positive blame) when the student actually does well in the class. Another way the PBC counselor may choose to approach the client is from a "one-up" frame of reference, where the counselor, as expert, prescribes the behavior the client is to follow. For example, the counselor might prescribe the client to do more of his symptomatic behavior, which puts the resistant client into the double bind of having to obey the counselor or choose to do the appropriate behavior. The resistant client will nearly always choose to disobey the counselor. For example, the clients having difficulty in losing weight can be directed by the counselor to gain 20 pounds just to see if they have control of their bodies. Resistant clients will often lose weight under the directive to gain weight.

COUNSELING METHOD

In addition to prescribing symptoms from the "one-up" position and pleading a "less than expert knowledge" solution from the "one-down" position, PBC counselors use several variations on the same paradoxical theme. Problems are often reframed as opportunities. For a person who has trouble sleeping, the counselor might reframe the problem as an opportunity to get those extra household chores done. Because the client is sleeping only 2 hours per night, she is only giving up about 14 hours per week to sleep, and that would be a small price to pay for curing the sleep problem and getting so much work done. Of course, the counselor would emphasize the point that the intervention would be for 1 week only. In any case, it would be important for the client not to sleep for the next 7 nights; she was to continue to do whatever she ordinarily did during the day. Shifting the emphasis from "I must sleep" to "I must not sleep" generally has the desired effect of returning people to their normal sleep routine without the aid of medication. Tantrum-throwing children can be instructed to schedule their tantrums, for example, at 2 P.M. in a time-out area.

Performance anxiety can be successfully treated by de-reflection. Students with test anxiety can be instructed to fail their next six examinations to get used to taking tests. However, the counselor would not do the intervention without working with the student's teachers to ensure that the student would not suffer during the intervention period.

Students who are afraid to make speeches in their speech classes for fear of showing how nervous they are can be instructed to actually show the class how scared they are by sweating and trembling during their next speech. Of course, students find that they can show the symptoms only when they try *not* to show them. It is similar to trying to blush on cue—the only time you can do it is when you try not to blush.

Case Examples

In a recent consultation, a high school teacher of a computer class described how one of her senior girls liked to get up and walk out of class without permission. She did this two or three times each class period. When asked how the problem was handled, the teacher said that she would go after her and bring her back. Detention was threatened, the bluff was called, and detention was served. Worst of all, the student–teacher relationship had become quite adversarial, and the teacher herself realized that she could not get quality work under such conditions. Power struggles such as this one are right up the PBC counselor's alley. The solution was to assign errands for the girl to run when she had the urge to walk out of class. The first day when the student started to leave, the teacher said, "Would you please drop this note off to Ms. Brown in Room 303?" The girl looked puzzled but did the errand, which took her to one of the building's farthest points from the classroom. When she returned, the teacher said, "Let me know when you need to leave again because I always have several errands you can help me do." After the third "errand," which did not happen until the next day, the girl complained that she should not be the only errand person in the class. The teacher responded that everybody else was too busy with their work to go. That marked the end of the problem. Not every symptom can be prescribed, but leaving class was one that worked especially well.

Some time ago, we had the opportunity to replicate a case reported many years ago by Viktor Frankl (1975). A sixth-grade boy discovered that he could keep his entire class and the teacher in a minor uproar all day long by selectively staring at individual students until they reported him to the teacher. The teacher would tell him to quit staring at the student; then he would select another student, and the sequence would be repeated. Various punishments and a behavior modification program had not helped the situation. Our PBC intervention was to have the teacher make out a staring schedule for our student. The schedule was presented to him with instructions that he was to spend the day staring at the students on his list. He was to switch students every 20 minutes, and if he forgot to stare or switch students, the teacher was to remind him. Placed in the double bind of doing the appropriate behavior or obeying his teacher, he chose the appropriate behavior and refused to stare at the students. He said if he did the staring, he would not get his work done. He still refused to stare even when his teacher offered him a day off from his work.

Our next brief case study involved a third-grade boy who refused to stay in his seat. Rather than labeling him as having attention-deficit/hyperactivity disorder and sending him to a special education resource room, the teacher had his desk removed. When he came in the next day and reported his desk missing, the teacher explained there was a shortage of desks in another room and because his was not being used, she donated it to the other teacher. The flabbergasted boy sputtered a protest, to which the teacher replied that she could not keep moving desks back and forth between rooms all year, so he would have to make a commitment that the desk would be occupied at all the appropriate times for the rest of the year. The boy readily agreed to sign a "desk lease" under those terms.

CROSS-CULTURAL APPLICATIONS OF BRIEF COUNSELING

Brief counseling will work most effectively with cultures and individuals with preferences for engaging in direct behavioral change rather than interventions focusing more on cognitive or affective material. Thompson and Campbell (1992) report that people in U.S. culture were equally divided in preferences for behavioral, cognitive, affective, and integrative self-help interventions to deal with depression. It could be that similar findings regarding preferences for counseling interventions might be found in all cultures. Keeping in mind the dangers involved in generalizing from cultural norms to all individuals within that cultural setting, we refer the reader to Chapter 15 for a more complete description of what counseling methods work best in certain cultures.

Brief counseling methods appeal to cultures and individuals who prefer their counselors to act as consultants who dispense useful information on what is needed to solve the presenting problem. Brief counseling has a present-time orientation with little, if any, time given to talking about the past. In fact, little time is given to discussing the presenting problem itself. Rather, attention centers on the problem's solution and how the client can do more of the behaviors that will make the solution happen. Brief counseling, true to its name, is just that. It is generally completed in less than ten sessions and appeals to those cultures and individuals who want their counseling to be a down-to-earth, all-business approach to making things better as soon as possible. As such, brief counseling should have wide appeal for African, Hispanic, and Asian clients, as well as African American, Latino, Asian American, and European American clients. However, Native American clients could have difficulty with the practice in brief counseling of de-emphasizing the past. Practitioners of brief counseling should be aware of clients who want their counselors to function as expert advisers and guard against the possibility that they could exert too much control over what these clients decide to do about their presenting problems.

Brief counseling enjoys wide appeal among cultures and clients who emphasize individual responsibility over the family and the community. Sue and Sue (2003) point out that in Western cultures when one does something wrong, the most common reaction is guilt, yet in non-Western cultures, the emotion most often expressed is shame. Sue and Sue hold that guilt focuses on the individual, whereas shame appears to focus on the group, as in "I did something wrong and let down my family." Once again, the authors believe that it is dangerous to overgeneralize such statements on guilt and shame across cultures to all individuals within them. Western cultures have not cornered the market on guilt, and non-Western cultures have not cornered the market on shame. Although brief counseling does take an individual approach, considerable attention is given to how the client's family, friends, and colleagues will be reacting when the problem's solution is achieved. In fact, brief counseling is being used to counsel families. Park (1997) reports success in using the SFBC model to provide counseling for families in a teaching hospital in Seoul, Korea.

BRIEF COUNSELING: ACCOUNTABILITY AND MANAGED HEALTH CARE

Fleming and Rickford (1997) observe that managed care organizations (MCOs) want to do business with providers who can deliver high-quality care with the lowest possible cost to them and to their clients. In summary, MCOs want to reduce recidivism, as well as time spent on treatment waiting lists, whereas increasing client satisfaction with their treatment. Brief counseling methods practiced by trained counselors are well positioned to meet all of these MCO preferences. In fact, brief counseling practitioners are eagerly sought out for panel membership by MCOs that fund mental health services. As mentioned in Chapter 2, MCOs prefer to work with counselors who limit their treatment to ten or less sessions; who identify short-term, behaviorally stated counseling goals; and who are able to measure session-by-session progress by their clients. Accountability of counselors to their clients and to third-party payers is the watchword of the day. Therefore, we are confident in stating that competent practitioners of brief counseling should do well in the current MCO system. Brief counseling methods infused into the other approaches presented in this book can provide counselors with the tools they need to be successful in helping their clients meet their goals in the least number of sessions. Fleming and Rickford (1997) point out that an additional benefit accruing to brief counseling practitioners is witnessing their clients discover what they need to do more often to improve their lives, and then watching them do it.

Levenson and Evans (2000), concerned that training in the brief therapies was not keeping pace with the demand for their use, surveyed 1250 psychologists across the nation on their training and use of brief therapy. With a response rate of 87 percent, the authors state that 90 percent of the psychologists reported using brief therapy in their practice; however, 50 percent of the respondents had not had any coursework in brief therapy. The authors also surveyed 165 training directors of clinical psychology programs and 370 training directors of internship programs on the number of programs providing brief therapy training. Only 59 percent of the graduate programs offered training in brief therapy; however, 85 percent of the professional schools of psychology offered brief therapy training. In summary, the good news is that a majority of training programs are providing brief therapy training. The bad news is that 40 percent are not providing any training. With 90 percent of the psychologists in private practice using brief therapy, more training and continuing education in brief therapy needs to be made available to students and practitioners.

Myrick (2003) and Lines (2002) stress the importance of accountability in the school counseling program. Documentation of the counselor's success can provide support for the program and meet the compliance requirements of local, state, and federal laws. Brief counseling is particularly strong in setting specific goals and documenting progress in meeting these goals. Littrell (2002), using three variations of brief counseling ranging from problem-focused to solution-focused methods, reports all three to be effective in single-session counseling with high school students.

SUMMARY

Solution-focused brief counseling and paradoxical counseling have much to offer counselors who are working under the constraints of managed health care and who are working with large client loads in kindergarten through twelfth grade (K-12) school systems and community agencies. Numerous studies on the efficacy of SFBC with children and adolescents have been reported. Corcoran and Stephenson (2000), Franklin, Biever, Moore, Clemons, and Scamardo (2001), Williams (2000), and Yarbrough and Thompson (2002) have used SFBC successfully in a school setting with children. Singleton and Pope (2000) have found SFBC to be effective in successful smoking cessation by adults and adolescents. We are not suggesting brief counseling as the recommended treatment for all clients and all problems, but we do think the method is a valuable addition to our scope of practice, which is built on the philosophy that counselors should adapt to their clients' learning styles and not force clients to adapt to the counselor's preferred counseling and learning styles.

The brief counseling approaches appear to be deceptively easy to master; however, this is not the case. As is true with any other approach to counseling, therapists and counselors of all orientations need to study and practice brief counseling under expert supervisors if they are to do it well and not harm their clients. Although organizational demands from MCOs may be forcing therapists into shorter term counseling, this does not absolve therapists who practice outside their area of competence and training.

INTRODUCTION TO BRIEF COUNSELING VIDEO

To gain a more in-depth understanding of the concepts in this chapter, visit www.thomsonedu.com/counseling/thompson to view a short clip of an actual therapist-client session demonstrating brief counseling.

WEBSITES FOR BRIEF COUNSELING

Internet addresses frequently change. To find the sites listed here, visit www.thomsonedu.com/counseling/thompson for an updated list of Internet addresses and direct links to relevant sites.

What Is Possibility Therapy?

REFERENCES

Berg, I., & Miller, S. (1992). *Working with the problem drinker.* New York: Norton.

Berg, I., & Shilts, L. (2005). Keeping solutions inside the classroom. *ASCA School Counselor, 42*(6), 30–35.

Bruce, M. (1995). Brief counseling: An effective model for change. *The School Counselor, 42,* 353–364.

Cade, B., & O'Hanlon, W. (1993). Negotiating the problem. *A brief guide to brief therapy* (pp. 49–63). New York: Norton.

Campbell, J., Elder, J., Gallagher, D., Simon, J., & Taylor, A. (1999). Crafting the "tap on the shoulder": A compliment template for solution-focused therapy. *American Journal of Family Therapy, 27,* 35–47.

Corcoran, J., & Stephenson, M. (2000). The effectiveness of solution-focused therapy with child behavior problems: A preliminary report. *Families in Society, 81,* 468–474.

Daughhtree, C., & Grant, D. (2002). Stress management. *ASCA School Counselor, 39,* 17–19.

de Shazer, S. (1985). *Keys to solutions in brief therapy.* New York: Norton.

de Shazer, S. (1986). Minimal elegance. *Family Therapy Networker, 59,* 57–60.

de Shazer, S. (1988). *Clues! Investigating solutions in brief therapy.* New York: Norton.

de Shazer, S. (1990). What is it about brief therapy that works? In J. K. Zeig & S. G. Gilligan (Eds.), *Brief therapy: Myths, methods, and metaphors* (pp. 90–99). New York: Brunner/Mazel.

de Shazer, S. (1994). *Words were originally magic.* New York: Norton.

de Shazer, S., & Molnar, A. (1964). Four useful interventions in brief family therapy. *Journal of Marital and Family Therapy, 10,* 297–304.

Dunlap, K. (1928). A revision of the fundamental law of habit. *Science, 671,* 360–362.

Dunlap, K. (1932). *Habits: Their making and unmaking.* New York: Liveright.

Fleming, J., & Rickford, B. (1997). Solution-focused brief therapy: One answer to managed mental health care. *Family Journal, 5,* 286–294.

Frankl, V. (1975). Paradoxical intention and de-reflection. *Psychotherapy: Theory, Research, and Practice, 12,* 226–237.

Franklin, C., Biever, J., Moore, K., Clemons, D., & Scamardo, M. (2001). The effectiveness of solution-focused therapy with children in a school setting. *Research on Social Work Practice, 11,* 411–434.

Glasser, W. (1965). *Reality therapy.* New York: Harper & Row.

Haley, J. (1973). *Uncommon therapy: The psychiatric techniques of Milton H. Erickson, M.D.* New York: Norton.

Haley, J. (1976). *Problem-solving therapy.* New York: Norton.

Haley, J. (1984). *Ordeal therapy: Unusual ways to change behavior.* San Francisco: Jossey-Bass.

Legum, H. (2005). Finding solutions. *School Counselor, 42(5),* 33–37.

Levenson, H., & Evans, S. (2000). The current state of brief therapy training in American psychological association-accredited graduate and internship programs. *Professional Psychology: Research and Practice, 31,* 446–452.

Lines, D. (2002). *Brief counseling in schools.* London: Sage Publications.

Lipchik, E. (2002). *Beyond technique in solution-focused therapy.* New York: Guilford.

Littrell, J. (1998). *Brief counseling in action.* New York: Norton.

Littrell, J. (2002). Single-session brief counseling in a high school. *Journal of Counseling & Development, 73,* 451–459.

Marvasti, J. A. (1997). Ericksonian play therapy. In K. O'Connor & L. M. Braverman (Eds.), *Play therapy theory and practice: A comparative presentation* (pp. 285–309). New York: Wiley.

Murphy, J., & Duncan, B. (1997). *Brief interventions for school problems: Collaborating for practical solutions.* New York: Guilford.

Myrick, R. (2003). Accountability: Counselors count. *Professional School Counseling, 6,* 174–179.

O'Hanlon, W.H., Weiner-Davis, M., & O'Hanlon, B. (2003). *In search of solutions: A new direction in psychotherapy,* (2nd Ed). New York: Norton.

Park, E. (1997). An application of brief therapy to family medicine. *Contemporary Family Therapy, 19,* 81–88.

Selekman, M. (1997). *Solution-focused therapy with children: Harnessing family strengths for systematic change.* New York: Guilford.

Singleton, M., & Pope, M. (2000). A comparison of successful smoking cessation interventions for adults and adolescents. *Journal of Counseling and Development, 78,* 448–453.

Sklare, G. (2005). *Brief counseling that works: A solution-focused approach for school counselors and administrators.* Thousand Oaks, CA: Corwin.

Sue, D., & Sue, D. (2003). *Counseling the culturally diverse: Theory and practice.* New York: Wiley.

Thompson, C., & Campbell, S. (1992). Personal intervention preferences for alleviating mild depression. *Journal of Counseling and Development, 71,* 69–73.

Walter, J., & Pellar, J. (1992). *Becoming solution-focused in brief therapy.* New York: Brunner/Mazel.

Watzlawick, P., Weakland, J., & Fisch, R. (1974). *Change: Principles of problem formation and problem resolution.* New York: Norton.

Williams, G. (2000). The application of solution-focused brief counseling in a public school setting. *Family Journal, 8,* 76–78.

Yarbrough, J., & Thompson, C. (2002). Using single-participant research to assess counseling approaches on children's off-task behavior. *Professional School Counseling, 5,* 308–314.

Person-Centered Counseling

If you bring forth what is within you, what you bring forth will save you. If you do not bring forth what is within you, what you do not bring forth will destroy you.

—Saint Thomas

I'm looking for the angel within.

—Michelangelo

Carl Rogers was born in Illinois, the fourth of six children. His early home life was marked by close family ties, a strict religious and moral atmosphere, and an appreciation of the value of hard work. During this period, Rogers thought his family was different from others because they did not mix socially. In fact, Rogers had only two dates during his high school years.

Carl Rogers (1902–1987)

When Rogers was 12, his parents moved to a farm to remove the young family from the "temptations" of suburban life. From raising lambs, pigs, and calves, Rogers learned about matching experimental conditions with control conditions and about randomization procedures; he also acquired knowledge and respect for the methods of science. Rogers's thinking was influenced by teachers who encouraged him to be original.

Rogers started college at the University of Wisconsin to study scientific agriculture. After 2 years, however, he switched his career goal to the ministry as a result of attending some emotionally charged religious conferences. In his junior year, he was chosen to go to China for 6 months for an international World Student Christian Federation conference. During this period, two things greatly influenced his life. First, at the expense of great pain and stress within his family relationships, he freed himself from the religious thinking of his parents and became an independent thinker, although he did not abandon religion entirely. Second, he fell in love with a woman he had known most of his life. He married her, with reluctant parental consent, as soon as he finished college so they could attend graduate school together.

Rogers chose to go to graduate school at Union Theological Seminary, where Goodwin Watson's and Marian Kenworthy's courses and lectures on psychology and psychiatry interested him. He began to take courses at Teachers College, Columbia University, across the street from Union, and found himself drawn to child guidance while working at Union under Leta Hollingworth. He applied for a fellowship at the Institute for Child Guidance and was accepted; he was well on his way to a career in psychology.

At the end of his internship at the Institute for Child Guidance, Rogers accepted a job in Rochester, New York, at the Society for the Prevention of Cruelty to Children. He completed his Ph.D. at Columbia Teachers College and spent the next 12 years in Rochester. His son and daughter grew through infancy and childhood there. Rogers once said that his children taught him far more about the development and relationships of individuals than he ever learned professionally.

Rogers spent his first 8 years in Rochester immersed in his work, conducting treatment interviews, and trying to be effective with clients. Gradually, he began teaching in the sociology department at the University of Rochester. He was also involved in developing a guidance center and writing a book, *The Clinical Treatment of the Problem Child* (1939). At this time, Otto Rank's work influenced Rogers's belief in people's ability to solve their own problems, given the proper climate.

In 1940, Rogers accepted a full professorship at Ohio State University. Realizing he had developed a distinctive viewpoint, he wrote the then-controversial book *Counseling and Psychotherapy* (1942), in which he proposes a counseling relationship based on the warmth and responsiveness of the therapist. Rogers believed that in such a relationship clients would express their feelings and thoughts. This first truly American system of psychotherapy was a radical change in a field that had been dominated by psychoanalysis and directive counseling. He and his students at Ohio State University made detailed analyses of counseling sessions and began to publish cases in "client-centered therapy." The theory developed as Rogers and his colleagues began to test the hypotheses they formed from their case studies.

In 1945, Rogers moved on to the University of Chicago, where he organized the counseling center and spent the next 12 years doing research. While he was associated with the University of Chicago, he wrote his famous work *Client-Centered Therapy*, published in 1951. Rogers described his years at Chicago as very satisfying, but he accepted an opportunity at the University of Wisconsin, where he was able to work in both the departments of psychology and psychiatry; he had long wanted to work with psychotic individuals who had been hospitalized.

Rogers moved to the Western Behavioral Science Institute in La Jolla, California, in 1966. In 1968, he and several colleagues formed the Center for Studies of the Person, also in La Jolla. Through the 1970s and into the 1980s, Rogers spent most of his time working with and writing about person-centered therapy with groups. Rogers came to prefer the term *person-centered* to *client-centered* in writing about his approach.

THE NATURE OF PEOPLE

Carl Rogers, with his person-centered school of thought, viewed people as rational, socialized, forward-moving, and realistic beings. He contended that negative, antisocial emotions are only a result of frustrated basic impulses; this idea is related to Maslow's hierarchy of needs. For instance, extreme aggressive action toward other people results from failure to meet the basic needs of love and belonging. Once people are free of their defensive behavior, their reactions are positive and progressive.

People possess the capacity to experience—that is, to express rather than repress—their own maladjustment to life and move toward a more adjusted state of mind. Rogers believed that people move toward actualization as they move toward psychological adjustment. Because people possess the capacity to regulate and control their own behavior, the counseling relationship is merely a means of tapping personal resources and developing human potential. People learn from their external therapy experience how to internalize and provide their own psychotherapy.

In summary, a person-centered counselor believes that people:

- Have worth and dignity in their own right and therefore deserve respect
- Have the capacity and right to self-direction and, when given the opportunity, make wise judgments
- Can select their own values
- Can learn to make constructive use of responsibility
- Have the capacity to deal with their own feelings, thoughts, and behavior
- Have the potential for constructive change and personal development toward a full and satisfying life (self-actualization)

Rogers (1994) provided perhaps the best description of his view of human nature:

> One of the most satisfying experiences I know—is just fully to appreciate an individual in the same way that I appreciate a sunset. When I look at a sunset . . . I don't find myself saying, "Soften the orange a little on the right hand corner, and put a bit more purple along the base, and use a little more pink in the cloud color . . . ." I don't try to control a sunset. I watch it with awe as it unfolds. (p. 189)

THEORY OF COUNSELING

Rogers (1992), in a reprint of his classic 1957 article, addressed the question, "Is it possible to state in clearly definable and measurable terms what is needed to bring about personality change?" Accepting the behaviorists' challenge, Rogers proceeded to answer in descriptive terms. His six *core* conditions for personality change have become the classic conditions for person-centered counseling. These conditions are:

1. Two people are in psychological contact.
2. The client is in a state of incongruence.

3. The therapist is congruent and involved in the relationship.
4. The therapist experiences unconditional positive regard for the client.
5. The therapist experiences empathetic understanding of the client's frame of reference.
6. The communication of empathetic and positive regard is achieved.

Rogers believed that each core condition is necessary to create optimal opportunity for personality change. The sixth condition, the basis for trust between counselor and client, is especially vital to the therapy process. We agree with Rogers that the six conditions, which need not be limited to the person-centered method of counseling, provide a sound foundation for most standard methods of counseling children and adults.

Rogers first called his process *nondirective therapy* because of the therapist's encouraging and listening role. Later, he adopted the term *client-centered*, because of the complete responsibility given to clients for their own growth, and then *person-centered*, in hopes of further humanizing the counseling process.

To maintain himself in the nondirective role of the person-centered counselor, Rogers refrained from giving advice, asking questions, and making interpretations of the client's message, thoughts, feelings, and behaviors. All three of these counselor behaviors tend to shift the counseling process from a person-centered to counselor-centered focus. When pressed for advice, a common Rogers response would be, "I would like to know the advice you would like to hear from me." Rogers believed that one way people get themselves into trouble is letting other people direct their lives, and that a counselor who does likewise makes the client's problem situation worse. Therefore, Rogers believed he could facilitate his clients' progress if he put them in the position of charting the direction of their counseling interviews. He was successful in doing so by replacing advice, interpretations, and questions with the active listening process of limiting his responses to summaries and clarifications of the content, feelings, and expectations for counseling presented in his clients' interviews. Hence, the direction of person-centered interviews is left to the client. Visualize two people riding side by side in a horse-drawn carriage with the reins lying on the floor of the driver's seat. Each rider is waiting for the other to pick up the reins and drive the horse. Finally, out of clear frustration, if not fear, one of the riders picks up the reins and guides the horse. Rogers will not be the one to pick up the reins unless possible bodily injury demands it. Some scholars are not all that sure that he would have done it even then. Rogers believed that directing the counseling interview would be an important first step for clients to begin directing their lives outside the counseling interview. A second important benefit accrued from person-centered counseling that escaped even Rogers's awareness. That is, the person-centered approach puts clients in the role of teachers as they teach counselors about their situations in life. As all teachers know, when you teach something you learn more about it in greater depth than you have ever previously known. Clients receiving person-centered counseling learn more about themselves and their unsolved problems than they have ever known before because they are in the teaching role of trying to help counselors understand their situations. The task of person-centered counselors is to take periodic oral quizzes on how much they are learning and understanding their clients' teaching. Person-centered counselors do not need a script or list of questions to follow because all of their "lines" come from listening to their clients. As Myers (2000) draws an important conclusion from her phenomenological study on the experience of being heard. She says that even though it would be comforting for counselors to have a perfect model or recipe for empathic listening, the experience of being heard requires an interpersonal, relational context.

Reflecting Rogers's view of human nature, if the counselor creates a warm and accepting climate in interviews, people trust the counselor enough to risk sharing their ideas about their lives and the problems they face. During this sharing with a nonjudgmental counselor, people feel free to explore their feelings, thoughts, and behaviors as they relate to their personal growth, development, and adjustment. Such explorations should, in turn, lead to more effective decision making and to productive behavior. Rogers (1951) wrote that the counselor operates from the point of view that people have the capacity to work effectively with all aspects of their lives that come into conscious awareness. Expansion of this conscious awareness occurs when the counseling climate meets Rogers's standards and clients realize that the counselor accepts them as people competent to direct their own lives.

Person-centered counseling deals primarily with the organization and function of self. The counselor becomes an objective, unemotional "mirror" who reflects the person's inner world with warmth, acceptance, and trust. This mirroring allows people to judge their thoughts and feelings and to begin to explore their effects on behavior. Thus, people are enabled to reorganize their thoughts, feelings, and behaviors and function in a more integrated fashion.

The Rogerian model for helping, as modified by Carkhuff (1973), involves three general stages through which the client proceeds. In the first phase, self-exploration, people examine exactly where they are in their lives, including a type of self-searching in which they question themselves concerning their status at the present moment. In the second phase, people begin to understand the relationship between where they are in life and where they would like to be. That is, they move from a type of discovery in self-exploration to an understanding. The third phase involves action. In this context, action is goal directed; people engage in some program or plan to reach the point where they want to be. The only exception to the logical order of these three stages might be in helping children; their movement through the process may be more meaningful if action is followed by understanding and then self-exploration. Children problem-solve better when they can move from concrete to abstract thinking. Self-exploration is the most abstract area of the process in Rogers's system.

Person-centered counseling can be thought of in two dimensions: responsive and facilitative, which includes attending, observing, and listening, and initiative, which includes initiating, personalizing, and responding. The counselor is the "expert" in creating the nonthreatening environment vital to the counseling process. Empathy, respect, warmth, concreteness, genuineness, and self-disclosure all facilitate change in client behavior. As mentioned previously, the process works best when counselors let clients direct the interviews—a first step in teaching clients how to direct their lives. Clients are the experts whose task is to teach the counselor about their life situation. Clients thereby learn more about themselves, because teaching also generally helps the teacher learn. The teaching factor may be the main reason that person-centered therapy helps many people.

The main goal of person-centered therapy is assisting people in becoming more autonomous, spontaneous, and confident (Rogers, 1983). As people become more aware of what is going on inside themselves, they can cease fearing and defending their inner feelings. They learn to accept their own values and trust their own judgment, rather than live by the values of others. Expectations of person-centered therapy include the discussion of plans, behavioral steps to be taken, and the outcome of the steps; a change from immature to mature behavior; less present defensive behaviors; more tolerance for frustration; and improved functioning in life tasks.

The ultimate goal of person-centered therapy is for the client to be a fully functioning person who has learned to be free and who can counsel himself or herself. According to Rogers, learning to be free is the essential goal of education "if the civilized culture is to survive and if individuals in the culture are to be worth saving" (1983). People who have learned to be free can confront life and face problems; they trust themselves to choose their own way and accept their own feelings without forcing them on others. Such individuals prize themselves and others as having dignity, worth, and value.

COUNSELING METHOD

The counselor as a person is vital to person-centered counseling. The conditions the counselor models become the ultimate counseling goals for all clients. Optimally, effective person-centered counselors must possess openness, empathic understanding, independence, spontaneity, acceptance, mutual respect, and intimacy. After clients move through the immediate counseling goals of self-exploration and subgoals, such as improving a math grade or making a new friend, they begin to work toward achieving the ultimate counseling goals for the effective person-centered counselor: developing the same traits modeled by person-centered counselors.

Perhaps the strongest techniques in the person-centered counselor's repertoire are attitudes toward people: *congruence* (genuineness), *unconditional positive regard* (respect), and *empathy.* Congruence implies that the counselor can maintain a sense of self-identity and can convey this identity to clients. In other words, the counselor is not playing an artificial role. Unconditional positive regard implies that the counselor accepts clients as people who have the potential to become good, rational, and free. Because people have self-worth, dignity, and unique traits as individuals, they require individualized counseling approaches. Thus, people direct their own counseling sessions. For the process to succeed, clients must believe they can reveal themselves to the counselor in an atmosphere of complete acceptance. Empathy is the attitude that holds the counseling process together. By attempting to understand, the counselor helps convince people that they are worth hearing and understanding. Rogers (1995), in a reprint of a 1956 speech, identified six principles he believed helped him become more effective in understanding and showing empathy in counseling. He believed that acceptance and understanding of his clients kept him from trying to fix their problems. Once he came to believe that people have a basic positive direction, he wanted his clients to discover their own paths to resolving their problems. Rogers's six principles are as follows:

First principle: "In my relationships with people I have found that it does not help, in the long run, to act as though I am something I am not." Rogers found it harmful to pretend to be feeling a certain way with a client if he actually felt differently. Constructive relationships cannot be built on pretense.

Second principle: "I have found it effective in my dealings with people to be accepting of myself." He learned to trust his reactions to clients, which he thought made his relationships with clients much more authentic. He believed that real relationships were always in the process of change and never static.

Third principle: "I have found it to be of enormous value when I can permit myself to understand another person." This principle became the cornerstone for his theory of person-centered counseling. He believed a therapist should be completely open to hearing exactly what the client is trying to relate. He believed that most people had an opinion formed before hearing what another person was trying to communicate. Consequently, Rogers thought the best thing that counselors could do was listen. He placed great value on learning from his students' reactions to each of his classes. Any success he enjoyed as a teacher was attributed to understanding each student's point of view.

Fourth principle: "I have found it to be of value to be open to the realities of life as they are revealed in me and in other people." He believed there was balance to life, the fragile as well as the tough.

Fifth principle: "The more I am able to understand myself and others, the more that I am open to the realities of life and the less I find myself wishing to rush in." That is, he was less likely to try to manipulate people into meeting certain goals or conforming to certain modes of living. Rogers did not believe clients should learn what a therapist thought they should learn, but did hold that other people change as the therapist changes.

Sixth principle: "It has been my experience that people have a basically positive direction." He believed that the more individuals felt they were being understood and well received, the more they would drop false pretenses. Having seen the negative side of human behavior—immaturity, destructiveness, regression, and antisocial behavior—he still maintained that people in general were positive and constructive, moving forward toward self-actualization and growing toward maturity. Most rewarding to Rogers were the times when his clients discovered their positive directions in life.

In summary, the person-centered counselor refrains from giving advice or solutions, diagnosing, interpreting, moralizing, and making judgments, which would defeat the plan for teaching clients how to counsel themselves and imply that the counselors know and understand their clients better than the clients know themselves—an assumption totally out of line with Rogers's view. Instead, person-centered counselors use the methods of (1) active and passive listening, (2) reflection of thoughts and feelings, (3) clarification, (4) summarization, (5) confrontation of contradictions, and (6) general or open leads that help client self-exploration.

The major technique for person-centered counseling is active listening, which lets the client know that the counselor is hearing and understanding correctly what the client is saying. As discussed in Chapter 2, active listening is especially important for counseling children. If the counselor fails to receive the correct message, the child attempts to reteach it to the counselor. Once counselor and child agree that the counselor has the story straight and that the counseling service will be helpful, counseling can continue.

Carkhuff (1973, 1981) systematized Rogers's concept of active listening (reflection) into a highly understandable, usable model (Table 6-1). Carkhuff believes that counselors typically respond on any one of five levels relating to the three phases of counseling: Phase I is where you are now in your life; Phase II is where you would like to be; and Phase III is planning how to get from Phase I to Phase II. He classified Levels 1 and 2 as harmful, Level 3 as break even, and Levels 4 and 5 as helpful. It is often assumed that the worst thing that can happen in counseling is that clients show no change. However, this is not true. The conditions of clients who receive a preponderance of Level 1 and 2 responses could grow worse as the result of counseling.

Level 1 and 2 responses in Carkhuff's model also appear in Gordon's (1974) "dirty dozen" list of responses that tend to close or inhibit further communication: (1) ordering, directing; (2) warning, threatening, stating consequences; (3) moralizing, shoulds, oughts; (4) advising, giving suggestions and solutions; (5) messages of logic, counterarguments; (6) judging, criticizing; (7) praising, buttering up; (8) name-calling, ridiculing; (9) psychoanalyzing; (10) reassuring, giving sympathy, consoling; (11) probing: "who, what, when, where, why?"; and (12) humor, distracting, withdrawing.

Level 1 responses tend to discount what a person is feeling and thinking with statements such as:

- "Oh, don't worry about that. Things will work out."
- "If you think you have a problem, listen to this."
- "You must have done something to make Mrs. Jones treat you that way."

Level 1 responses may also be an indication that the counselor simply was not listening. As such, Level 1 responses do not help with any of the three counseling phases in Table 6-1.

Level 2 responses are messages that give advice and solutions to problems. These responses are relevant in Phase III, but they are not considered helpful because they do not allow the counselor and the client to fully explore the

TABLE 6-1 | FIVE LEVELS OF COMMUNICATION

Levels	Phase I	Phase II	Phase III
	Thoughts and feelings about where you are now	Thoughts and feelings about where you would like to be	Plans for getting from where you are to where you would like to be
1			
2			X
3	X		
4	X	X	
5	X	X	X

NOTE: The X's indicate which phases of counseling is treated by each of the five levels of communication.

problem situation. Ignoring the active listening process deprives clients of the opportunity to work out their own solutions to their problems. Level 2 responses keep clients dependent on the counselor's authority and prevent clients from learning to counsel themselves. Typical Level 2 responses include the following:

- "You need to study harder."
- "You should eat better."
- "You should be more assertive."
- "Why don't you make more friends?"
- "How would you like your brother to treat you the way you treat him?"

Even though the advice may be excellent, the client—child or adult—may not have the skills to do what you suggest. The advice clients seek may often be something they already know but wish they did not. Moreover, rebellious children and adolescents may work especially hard to show that your advice is ineffective, just to receive the satisfaction of knowing that an "expert" counselor is no more successful than they are in solving day-to-day problems. We do, however, want to distinguish between giving advice and giving information. Information could be news about a job opening. Advice, in contrast, could be, "I think you need to quit your job." In summary, Levels 1 and 2 are ill-advised attempts to fade or fix the client's problem.

Level 3 responses are classified as break-even points in the counseling process; they are neither harmful nor helpful. However, these responses provide

Strong	Happy	Sad	Angry	Scared	Confused	Weak
____	____	____	____	____	____	____
____	____	____	____	____	____	____
____	____	____	____	____	____	____

FIGURE 6-1 | SYNONYMS FOR FEELING WORDS

bridges to further conversation and exploration in the counseling process; they are the door openers and invitations to discuss concerns in more depth.

Level 3 responses reflect what the client is thinking and feeling about the present status of the problem; for example, "You are feeling discouraged because you haven't been able to make good grades in math." Such responses are checkpoints for counselors in determining whether they are hearing and understanding the client's problem. Either the client acknowledges that the counselor has understood the message correctly, or the client makes another attempt to relate the concern to the counselor. At this point in counseling, clients are teaching the counselors about their problems and are thereby learning more about their problems themselves.

According to Carkhuff's model, an aid to counselors in making Level 3 responses is to ask themselves whether the client is expressing pain or pleasure. The next task is to find the correct feeling word to describe the pain or pleasure. Seven feeling words are listed in Figure 6-1. To build your counseling vocabulary, add three synonyms of your own under each word. In reflecting the client's feeling and thoughts, do not parrot the exact words of the client. Time used for a summary is often helpful; say to your client, "Let's see if I understand what you have told me up to now."

Remember that the focus on feelings is to help clients to recognize and be aware of their feelings so that they can use them as indicators of whether they are making good decisions and doing the behaviors they need to be doing. To ignore feelings is much like driving a car without paying attention to the red lights and gauges on the car's dashboard. Feelings are one of the best indicators that people have for helping them find direction in their lives. Children may prefer to discuss their feelings by selecting one of the faces on the feelings chart in Figure 6-1. In fact, they may prefer to draw a face that represents how they feel.

Level 4 responses reflect an understanding of Phases I and II in Carkhuff's model; for example, "You are feeling discouraged because you haven't been able to make good grades in math, and you want to find a way to do better." Rephrase the responses in your own words as you summarize the client's thoughts and feelings.

Level 5 responses are appropriate when the client agrees that the counselor understands the problem or concern. Now it is time to assist the client in developing a plan of action. Reality therapy provides a good framework for planning after person-centered counseling has helped the client relate the concern to the counselor. Following is an example of a combined Level 5 response:

Person-centered therapy: You feel _____ because _____, and you want _____.

Reality therapy: Let's look at what you have been doing to solve your problem.

Combined person-centered and reality therapies: You feel discouraged because you haven't been able to make good grades in math, and you want to find a way to do better. Let's look at what you have been trying to do to make better grades in math.

The entire counseling interview cannot be accomplished in one response. Several sessions of Level 3 and 4 responses may be necessary before the problem is defined well enough to solve.

Because the success of the person-centered approach to counseling depends so much on the relationship between counselor and client, this approach may be unsuccessful with young children. Not every adult is capable of establishing true empathy with children or even of liking children. Children, to a greater degree than adults, are sensitive to the real feelings and attitudes of others. They intuitively trust and open up to those who like and understand them. Phony expressions of understanding may not fool children, and certainly not adolescents, for very long. Virginia Axline's *Dibs: In Search of Self* (1964) presents a good example of a person-centered counseling method used with play therapy.

To help children effectively, the counselor must provide a warm, caring environment in which children can explore their emotions and verbally act out the consequences of alternative means of expressing them. Together, the counselor and the child—or the child alone if he or she possesses sufficient maturity—can evaluate the alternatives and select the one most likely to be appropriate and productive.

In using the person-centered approach with young children, the counselor may have to assume a more active role. Still, even young children can distinguish between positive and negative behaviors and are able to choose the positive once the counselor has established an open dialogue in which feelings and emotions can be aired and conflicts resolved.

Again, the counselor uses active listening to give children an opportunity to release emotions without feeling threatened by the counselor. Listening carefully and observing the child increase the counselor's ability to understand what the child is trying to communicate. All clients convey both verbal and nonverbal messages, and the counselor needs to be alert to these messages. Because a child's verbal skills may be limited, nonverbal messages may be the most important clue to what the child is really feeling and trying to communicate.

Once again, the person-centered approach is most successful when clients take the role of teaching their counselors about their problem situations. The counselor's job, as the "student" being taught, is to take periodic oral quizzes (counseling summary or reflection statements) to let the client (teacher) know how well the subject matter is being understood. The subject matter consists of the problem, type and depth of feelings about the problem, and expectations the client has for its solution. Clients learn by teaching their counselors about themselves and their lives. In addition, through active listening, the counselor also helps clients clarify problems clouded by the *overgeneralizations, distortions,* and *deletions* commonly brought to counseling. The focus on feeling is done to help clients learn how to recognize and use their feelings as indicators of whether they are making good choices and decisions in their lives. Lacking the verbal skills of most adults, children can benefit from bibliocounseling, storytelling, and play therapy (see Chapter 14) as aids to teaching about and communicating their problem situations.

CASE STUDY[1]

Identification of the Problem

Ginger Wood, an 11-year-old girl in the sixth grade at Hill Middle School, was referred to the school counselor because her grades recently had fallen and she seemed depressed.

Individual and Background Information

Academic School records show that Ginger is an A student who was chosen to be in an advanced group in third grade. On her last report card, however, her grades dropped to a C average.

Family Ginger is the elder of two children; her younger brother is 9. Her mother is an elementary school teacher, and her father is a systems analyst; they recently have separated.

Social Ginger is approximately 30 pounds overweight. She has a friendly personality, and teacher reports do not show that she has a problem relating to her peers.

Counseling Method

The counselor chose to use Rogers's (1965) person-centered counseling method. The counselor believes that Ginger's problem originates from emotional blocks. Her goal is to establish a warm relationship with Ginger, aid her in clarifying her thoughts and feelings, and enable her to solve her problems.

---

[1]The case of Ginger was contributed by Anne Harvey.

In this method, the counselor uses five basic techniques: (1) unconditional positive regard, (2) active listening, (3) reflection, (4) clarification, and (5) summarization.

Transcript

COUNSELOR: Hi, Ginger. I'm Susan Morgan. Your teacher, Ms. Lowe, told me that you might come to talk to me.

GINGER: Yeah, I decided to.

COUNSELOR: Do you know what a counselor's job is?

GINGER: Yeah, Ms. Lowe told me that you help people with their problems.

COUNSELOR: That's right. I try to teach people how to solve their own problems. Do you have something on your mind that you'd like to talk about?

GINGER: Well, I haven't been doing so well in school lately.

COUNSELOR: Yes, Ms. Lowe said you are normally an A student.

GINGER: I used to be, but not now. I made Cs on my last report card. My mom was really upset with me; she yelled at me and then grounded me.

COUNSELOR: It sounds as though she was angry with you because your grades went down.

GINGER: Well, not so much angry as unhappy. [Ginger looked ready to cry.]

COUNSELOR: So she was disappointed that you weren't doing as well in school as you usually do, and this made you feel bad too.

GINGER: I guess so. She probably blamed herself some, too, and that could have made her feel worse.

COUNSELOR: You mean that she felt responsible for your grades going down.

GINGER: Well, maybe. Things aren't going so well at home. Mom and Dad aren't living together right now, and they may get a divorce. She hasn't had a lot of time for us lately. I guess she's really been worried.

COUNSELOR: The problem at home has made it tougher for you to do well at school because you're worried about what's happening.

GINGER: Yeah, I think about it a lot. It's harder to study when I'm worrying about it.

COUNSELOR: It would be for me too. This must be a very hard situation for you to go through.

GINGER: It sure is; everybody's mad. My little brother doesn't understand what's going on, and he cries a lot. Mom does too.

COUNSELOR: So the whole family is upset.

GINGER: Well, I guess so. My dad doesn't seem to be, but why should he be? It's all his fault. He's getting what he wants.

COUNSELOR: I guess he's the one who wants the divorce. It doesn't seem fair to the rest of you.

GINGER: Yeah. He's got a girlfriend. My mom didn't even know anything about her until Daddy said he was leaving. I hate him! [Ginger starts to cry.] And that makes me feel even worse cause I know I shouldn't hate my father. I wish he were dead!

COUNSELOR: [Handing her a tissue] So you're all torn up between the way you feel and the way you think you should feel.

GINGER: Yeah, it's so hard to sort everything out. Do you think that makes me a bad person for me to hate my father?

COUNSELOR: I think you are a good person who doesn't know what to do with all of her feelings right now. I'm wondering if you think you are a bad person.

GINGER: No, I guess not. I mean, I think most of my friends would feel about the same way I do if they were in my shoes.

COUNSELOR: Sure, it's a tough thing to handle.

GINGER: And I guess they're not all bad people. Thanks, Ms. Morgan. I'm glad we talked about it. I feel a little better now.

COUNSELOR: I'm glad, Ginger. It sounds like you're beginning to work out your problems. Would you like to make another appointment to talk with me?

GINGER: Okay. Could I come back during free time next week?

COUNSELOR: That will be fine. You can see me any day when you want to talk.

GINGER: Bye, Ms. Morgan, and thanks.

COUNSELOR: You're welcome.

PERSON-CENTERED COUNSELING AND THE DEVELOPMENT OF SELF-ESTEEM[2]

Self-esteem development has been a centerpiece of person-centered counseling. Building self-esteem in children is receiving increasing emphasis. Our position is that self-esteem is a by-product of achievements and relationships and can be increased by helping clients improve these two important areas in their lives.

Radd (2005) developed a process to integrate self-esteem development into life skills education, a theme consistent with the application of person-centered theory to education. The process includes a series of activities that focus on teaching children about self-esteem and ways of applying that information to daily living.

---

[2]Tommie R. Radd, Professor in the College of Education, University of Nebraska at Omaha, contributed this section.

The activities each have three steps. The counselor may choose to teach these statements in the first person or in the format given. The counselor begins by saying:

1. "All people are special and valuable because they are unique." This statement is discussed to teach the concept of unconditional valuing of people simply because they are people. For children in kindergarten through fourth grade, the words *special* and *different* are effective. "No matter what you do, you are still special because you are a person." For children in grades 5 through 8, variations of the words *unique* and *valuable* are effective. "If everyone were the same, it would be boring." "It is impossible for people to be better than other people because everyone is unique." In other words, "I'm the best me there is." The counselor continues with the second step.

2. "Because people are special and unique, they have a responsibility to *help* and *not hurt* themselves. People *show* if they remember that they are important by the way they *choose* to act. If people choose to hurt themselves or others, they are forgetting that they are special. Likewise, if people choose to help themselves or others, they are remembering that they are special. What is special to you? How do you treat it? Do you help or hurt the things you think are special? Are your toys and computer games more important to you than people? Toys and games can be replaced, but people are different and irreplaceable. If you are remembering that you are as special as your toys, will you help or hurt yourself? When people help others, they are helping themselves. People hurt themselves when they hurt other people by forgetting that all people are special and unique. What people give is generally what they receive. The point we want to teach is that, if we like ourselves, we do not hurt ourselves or others." The counselor continues with the third step.

3. "People are responsible for 'watching' their actions to see if they are remembering the *truth* that they are special. People are 'with' themselves at all times and are accountable for remembering to treat themselves as important people. When people blame others for their actions, they are forgetting their responsibility to others. Who is with you all the time? Who will live with you forever? Who decides what happens to you? Who is the only one you can change?"

INTEGRATING SELF-ESTEEM–BUILDING ACTIVITIES WITH THE CHILD'S LIFE

After the self-esteem activities are introduced into all environments children experience, the concepts are related to the children's daily life experiences and are associated with various situations, interactions, and other skills, such as decision making, self-control, and group cooperation.

The continuing process of relating self-esteem activities to a child's life is the *self-esteem series weave.* After this information is taught and processed, the children experience the integration of these concepts into their daily life experiences. The weaving process makes the concepts about self alive and relevant for children.

The self-esteem series weave process is implemented consistently, regardless of the counseling approach or setting. The self-esteem activities and weave can become the core of classroom group guidance, small-group counseling, individual counseling, and positive behavior management. The self-esteem activities are introduced and taught. Then, each subsequent session begins with a brief review of the self-esteem activities and a weave of the self-esteem activities into the process of the group or individual session.

An example of the self-esteem series weave process follows. Although it is part of the second individual counseling session with a third-grade student, the same process is used in classroom group guidance, in small-group counseling, and within the classroom behavior plan.

In the first session, the self-esteem activities were introduced and woven throughout the session. Bill was referred to counseling because of his problems with work completion. Following is an extract from Bill's counseling session:

BILL: I'm still in trouble with my teacher this week.

COUNSELOR: You are not feeling very good about this.

BILL: I think my teacher doesn't like me. She thinks I'm dumb.

COUNSELOR: Your bad feelings come from what your teacher thinks about you. I'm wondering how this fits in with what we talked about last week.

BILL: You said that I am special, no matter what I do, because no one else is like me anywhere in the world.

COUNSELOR: It seems this week you are feeling as though you're not special.

BILL: I don't know. My teacher doesn't think so.

COUNSELOR: So you think you are not important or special because you think your teacher does not think you are special.

BILL: Yeah. I know you think I'm special, but it is hard for me to think so when my teacher doesn't like me.

COUNSELOR: You may be showing that you forget you are special by the way you have been acting in your class. You and your teacher told me you have been deciding not to complete your work. I'm wondering if you have been hurting yourself with your choices.

BILL: I've been hurting myself because I'm not doing my work. But other people aren't doing their work and they don't get picked on.

COUNSELOR: It sounds as though you feel cheated because the teacher likes the other children better than you and does not treat you fairly. Let's see if we can figure this out with the ideas we learned last week.

BILL: Okay.

COUNSELOR: I wonder if you remember what we said about whom children hurt when they choose not to do their work.

BILL: I think they are hurting themselves.

COUNSELOR:	So, we could take a look at what happens to you when you don't do your work.
BILL:	I guess it hurts me.
COUNSELOR:	If you want to, we can think of some ways to help you stop hurting yourself.
BILL:	Okay. Maybe I can ask the teacher for help when I get lost on my work, or I can get a friend to help me. I can ask for help remembering the homework too.
COUNSELOR:	These ideas might help you. We need to know which ones you want to try.
BILL:	I guess I just need to do what it takes to turn in all my assignments.
COUNSELOR:	Next week we can see if you've been remembering to do all those things you need to do to help yourself. Maybe you could show me the work you get done each day.
BILL:	Okay.

The process of integrating self-esteem building with life skill development is most effective if it becomes the focus and foundation of group guidance, group counseling, behavior management, and individual counseling (Radd, 2005). The consistent exposure of children to self-concept activities related to life experiences clarifies and personalizes these difficult concepts so they become part of the children's knowledge base. Once again, however, self-esteem development is best served by helping children improve their academic performance and develop more friendships.

CHILD-CENTERED PLAY THERAPY

Virginia Axline translated the nondirective counseling approach of Carl Rogers to work with children. Her book *Dibs: In Search of Self* (1964) describes this play therapy model. Landreth (2002) provides further details on the child-centered approach to play therapy. This model is based on beliefs in the child's innate desire for growth and capacity for self-direction. In child-centered play therapy, the child leads. The counselor focuses on the child's strengths, reflects the child's feelings, and recognizes the power of a warm, accepting, and empathic relationship. Basic principles of the child-centered relationship are as follows:

1. The counselor has a genuine interest in the child and builds a warm, caring relationship.
2. The counselor accepts the child unconditionally, not wishing the child were different.
3. The counselor institutes a feeling of safety and permissiveness in the relationship, allowing the child freedom to explore and express.
4. The counselor maintains sensitivity to the child's feelings and reflects them in a way that increases the child's self-understanding.
5. The counselor strongly believes in the child's capacity to act responsibly and solve personal problems, and allows the child to do so.
6. The counselor trusts the inner direction of the child, allowing the child to lead the relationship and refusing to override the child's direction.

7. The counselor does not hurry the therapeutic process.
8. The counselor uses only the limits necessary for helping the child accept personal and appropriate responsibility (Axline, 1947; Landreth, 2002).

The counselor who practices child-centered play therapy expresses an attitude of being completely with the child, an emotional and verbal participant. The process involves the counselor being open to the child's experience by living out these messages: I am here (nothing will distract me), I hear you (I am listening carefully), I understand you, and I care about you (Landreth, 2002). *Play Therapy: The Art of the Relationship* (Landreth, 2002) contains details about accomplishing these goals.

Moustakas (1998) explains relationship play therapy as the creation of play dramas. Within the relationship, the counselor demonstrates acceptance, receptiveness, and openness, together with the skills of "listening and hearing, teaching and learning, directing and receiving, participating actively and quietly observing, confronting and letting be" (p. 2). He discusses the use of play therapy as a prevention strategy in which parents and teachers participate. The brief therapy—one to four play sessions—is supportive. The relationship and counseling process encourage self-disclosure, expression of feelings, and limits.

Johnson, McLeod, and Fall (1997) studied client-centered play therapy with children who had special needs. Six children were identified in two rural Midwestern elementary schools. Six weekly 30-minute play therapy sessions were held. The transcripts and videotapes of the sessions were analyzed for expression of feelings and of control. These authors concluded that nondirective child-centered play therapy was effective in allowing the children chances to express feelings, experience control, and develop coping skills. They also noted that therapists' perceptions were altered more favorably toward the children. Griffith (1997) discusses a client-centered empowerment model of play therapy for working with children who had been sexually abused. Her report also documents the effectiveness of child-centered play therapy.

CROSS-CULTURAL APPLICATIONS OF PERSON-CENTERED COUNSELING

Counselors following the person-centered model make no prior assumptions about how clients from different cultures will react to counseling. Rogers prized the individuality and uniqueness of every person. He treated all persons as having their own culture and was willing to spend the time to let his clients teach him about their cultural proclivities and world views. Cardemil and Battle (2003) recommend suspending preconceptions about a client's race/ethnicity and suggest that counselors should engage clients in an open dialogue on these facts. Moodley, Lago, and Talahite (2004) agree that person-centered counseling is based on understanding the uniqueness of the individual through empathic understanding, genuineness, and unconditional positive regard by the therapist. Because clients experience their environment in their own unique way, the person-centered counselor's role is to perceive the client unlike any client seen before.

Historically, person-centered counseling has been accepted across most cultures within the United States and across the world. These cultures include African, African American, Puerto Rican, Anglo American, Japanese, Chinese, Canadian, white and black South Africans, and Austrian. Several researchers (Follensbee, Draguns, & Danish, 1986; Hayashi, Kuno, Osawa, Shimizu, & Suetake, 1998; Hill-Hain & Rogers, 1988; Jenni, 1999; Spangenberg, 2003; Stipsits & Hutterer, 1989; and Waxer, 1989;) have provided information relative to person-centered counseling in these cultures.

Europe is currently the most active continent involved in the research and practice of person-centered theory. Currently, in Britain and Austria (the birth place of Freud's psychoanalysis, Adler's Individual Psychology, and Frankl's Logo therapy), the largest therapeutic discipline is person-centered therapy (Mearns, 2003). Approximately 200 organizations and training centers located around the world are dedicated to the research and application of principles developed by Rogers (Kirschenbaum & Jourdan, 2005).

Kincade and Evans (1996) point out that person-centered counseling can be problematic for clients from cultures that expect their "counselors" to be experts who will advise and guide them regarding decisions to be made and problems to be solved. In other words, when expectations are not met, clients are likely to become frustrated with the person-centered process and drop out of counseling. Asian and Native American clients, operating from a value system that stresses seeking help from older, wiser adults, are likely to become frustrated with the nondirective quality of person-centered counseling. However, we know from experience that similar expectations are held by some clients from the U.S. culture who work mightily to move counseling from an adult–adult encounter to a parent–child relationship in which the counselor advises the client on what decisions should be made. Clients with an entitlement world view are likely to push for a parent–child counseling relationship through which they can avoid the responsibilities that come from an adult–adult counseling relationship. Counseling theorists, dating back to the establishment of person-centered counseling, are in agreement that counseling relationships other than adult–adult will fail to help clients become the inner-directed, independent people they have the potential to be. As mentioned in Chapter 2, clients from all cultures may need orientation by the counselor on how counseling will be conducted and why it is done that way.

Regarding working with clients from all cultures, a strong point in favor of the person-centered approach is the therapeutic conditions established by the counselor. These conditions of genuineness, unconditional positive regard, accurate empathic understanding, and nonjudgmental interest in the client show the respect for others that is important in many cultures (see Chapter 15). People in action-oriented cultures who are frustrated with the person-centered process will need to be told that person-centered counseling is designed to solve immediate problems by teaching clients how to be their own counselors. Clients from cultures that value group interests over individual interests find the individual freedom offered by competent, person-centered counselors very appealing. The emphasis on individual freedom and self-directed thinking and behavior featured in person-centered counseling is quite popular with people who, because of their cultures, have not always been free to make choices and speak their minds.

Combs (1988) summarizes Rogers's work in cross-cultural settings by pointing out how people from groups with supposedly irreconcilable differences and prejudices apparently learned to appreciate and communicate with one another in Rogers's encounter groups. Rogers was working actively on world peace projects at the time of his death in 1987. Soloman (1990) points out that Rogers devoted the last 15 years of his life to working on ways to bring emotional honesty and personal congruence into international dialogue. Rogers firmly believed that the methodology of person-centered theory could be successfully applied to the negotiation process needed to achieve peace between people and nations.

PERSON-CENTERED COUNSELING, ACCOUNTABILITY, AND MANAGED HEALTH CARE

Person-centered counselors will be hard-pressed to meet some of the managed care guidelines presented in Chapter 2. Having less counseling sessions, establishing behavioral goals, and monitoring goal attainment progress tend to work against clients proceeding at their chosen rate or clients who have rather indefinite or undefined goals. Key to the person-centered process is letting clients structure the sessions to meet their own needs. That is, the person-centered process typically does not initiate moving into the third stage of counseling, which is initiating a plan to help clients move from where they are to where they would like to be. Such a move will not occur until the client makes a move toward putting a plan together. Perhaps the problem can be solved by ensuring that clients know the limitations of their health coverage and then adjusting person-centered methods to fit the plan. To that end, some counselors are cutting cost to their clients through the following practices: (1) conducting 25-minute sessions rather than 50-minute sessions; (2) doing more group counseling; (3) informing their clients about the necessity to set and work toward meeting counseling goals; (4) offering reduced fees to self-paying clients or those who choose to continue after their coverage lapses; and (5) supporting medical savings account legislation that rewards people for being proactive in maintaining their medical and physical health.

SUMMARY

Criticisms of person-centered counseling call it too abstract for young children and for adults who have not attained the ability to do formal thinking. The perfect clients for person-centered counseling often have been described as having the YAVIS syndrome; that is, they are *young, attractive, verbal, intelligent,* and *sensitive.* Such people may not need much counseling. Who, then, we might ask, will counsel tough, nonverbal children and adolescents? Others criticize the approach as becoming mired in feelings and not moving quickly enough into planned behavioral change. Another criticism is Rogers's distaste for diagnostic tools and tests. Critics argue that valuable data may be lost to counselors who do not use diagnostic methods. Rogers also had a strong aversion to diagnosis, prognostication, and prescription. Critics of person-centered counseling hold that counselors are experts who can dispense valuable advice, as well as predict future behavioral patterns and personality development in their clients. In rebuttal, Rogers (1977) pointed out how person-centered counseling relates to a wide variety of individual and group concerns that span diverse populations, including the areas of family counseling, couple relationships, education, politics, government, and business administration.

Quinn (1993) challenges the person-centered approach of Carl Rogers as being too soft to provide the motivation clients often need to move ahead in their lives. Furthermore, he contends that it does not allow the confrontation needed to help clients see the contradictions and inconsistencies in their thinking and behavior. Quinn states that people develop best when they interact with and confront their environment, and that counselors should provide the same opportunities. Person-centered counselors, he argues, avoid interactive confrontation with their clients. We believe that Quinn misses the point that Rogers was trying to create a counseling environment in which clients felt safe and could begin directing their own lives within the context of the therapy setting. Rogers's hope was that, given this opportunity, the inner-directed behavior would generalize to life outside the counseling interview. Counselors who take an active and directive role in counseling deprive their clients of the opportunity to practice directing their own lives. In a response to Quinn, Graf (1994) writes that Quinn did not understand Rogers's approach to genuineness. Graf argues that Quinn's recommendation on what genuineness should be was actually what Rogers intended it to be: counselor and client communicating their thoughts and feelings honestly and openly. According to Graf, Rogers never intended to restrict person-centered counseling to active listening and expression of empathy. However, Myers (2000) has found that clients in her phenomenological study on the experience of being heard put high values on their therapists' active listening, feedback, and expressions of empathy. They reported that these methods gave them room for self-exploration, the opportunity to move further and deeper into their own experience, and the feelings of safety, trust, and being understood, all of which were reported as being necessary to give them the freedom to examine their personal experiences. In a similar vein, Siebert (2000) studied the efficacy of empathy on the "recovery" of an 18-year-old woman who had been diagnosed as an "acute paranoid schizophrenic" on her commitment to a hospital by her parents. She was telling her parents that God told her she was to have his baby. Her physician and the hospital staff thought she should be committed to the state psychiatric hospital, where they predicted she would spend the rest of her life. Siebert viewed this as an opportunity to try something different in his interview with her, because she was headed to what he termed "the snake pit" anyway. It was definitely a "What have you got to lose?" situation for him. Before his interview with the patient, he developed a game plan of four questions for himself. What would happen if:

1.   I just listened to her and did not allow my mind to put any psychiatric labels on her?
2.   I talked to her believing that she could turn out to be my best friend?
3.   I accepted everything she reports about herself as being the truth?
4.   I questioned her to find out whether there is a link between her self-esteem, the workings of her mind, and the way others have been treating her?

Siebert, following the person-centered counseling model he designed for himself, brought about dramatic improvement in his patient, and she was not committed to the state hospital. Several days after that first session, she mentioned to Siebert that she had been doing a lot of thinking about what they had talked about. She asked, "I've been wondering, do you think I imagined God's voice to make myself feel better?" This case led Siebert to do a lot of thinking also.

In conclusion, Rogers (1985) was an early supporter of using phenomenological research methods and hermeneutics to answer the difficult questions about the inexact human science of the person. He believed these approaches would require researchers to indwell the perceptions, attitudes, feelings, experiences, and behaviors of the participants, whom he referred to as coresearchers. We concur with Rogers on the value of phenomenological research.

Kirschenbaum and Jourdan (2005), reviewing the history and current status of person-centered counseling, note that Rogers was the first to record entire transcripts of therapy for research and teaching. He was the first psychotherapist to receive both the APA's Distinguished Scientific Contribution Award and its Distinguished Professional Contribution Award. Currently, 141 books, 174 book chapters, and 462 journal articles have been written about Rogers's work. Between 1987 (the year of Rogers's death) and 2004, 777 books, chapters, and articles have been published about Rogers's work.

INTRODUCTION TO PERSON-CENTERED COUNSELING VIDEO

To gain a more in-depth understanding of the concepts in this chapter, visit www.thomsonedu.com/counseling/thompson to view a short clip of an actual therapist–client session demonstrating person-centered counseling.

WEBSITES FOR PERSON-CENTERED COUNSELING

Internet addresses frequently change. To find the sites listed here, visit www.thomsonedu.com/counseling/thompson for an updated list of Internet addresses and direct links to relevant sites.

Association for the Development of the Person-Centered Approach (ADPCA)
Carl Rogers

REFERENCES

Axline, V. (1947). *Play therapy: The inner dynamics of childhood*. Boston: Houghton Mifflin.

Axline, V. (1964). *Dibs: In search of self*. Boston: Houghton Mifflin.

Cardemil, E., & Battle, C. (2003). Guess who's coming to therapy? Getting comfortable with conversations about race and ethnicity in psychotherapy [Electronic version]. *Professional Psychology: Research and Practice, 34,* 278–286.

Carkhuff, R. (1973, March). Human achievement, educational achievement, career achievement: Essential ingredients of elementary school guidance. Paper presented at the National Elementary School Guidance conference, Louisville, KY.

Carkhuff, R. (1981, April). Creating and researching community based helping programs. Paper presented at the American Personnel and Guidance Association convention, St. Louis, MO.

Combs, A. W. (1988). Some current issues for person-centered therapy. *Person-Centered Review, 3,* 263–276.

Follensbee, R. W. Jr., Draguns, J. G., & Danish, S. J. (1986). Impact of two types of counselor intervention on Black American, Puerto Rican, and Anglo-American analogue clients. *Journal of Counseling Psychology, 33,* 446–453.

Gordon, T. (1974). *Teacher effectiveness training*. New York: Wyden.

Graf, C. (1994). On genuineness and the person-centered approach: A reply to Quinn. *Journal of Humanistic Psychology, 34,* 90–96.

Griffith, M. (1997). Empowering techniques of play therapy: A method for working with sexually abused children. *Journal of Mental Health Counseling, 19,* 130–143.

Hayashi, S., Kuno, T., Osawa, M., Shimizu, M., & Suetake, Y. (1998). Client-centered therapy in Japan: Fujio Tomoda and Taoism. *Journal of Humanistic Psychology, 38,* 103–124.

Hill-Hain, A., & Rogers, C. (1988). A dialogue with Carl Rogers: Cross-cultural challenges of facilitating person-centered groups in South Africa. *Journal for Specialists in Group Work, 13,* 62–69.

Jenni, C. (1999). Psychologists in China: National transformation and humanistic psychology. *Journal of Humanistic Psychology, 39,* 26–47.

Johnson, L., McLeod, E. H., & Fall, M. (1997). Play therapy with labeled children in the schools. *Professional School Counseling, 1,* 31–34.

Kincade, E., & Evans, K. (1996). Counseling theories, process, and interventions within a multicultural context. In J. Delucia-Waack (Ed.), *Multicultural counseling competencies: Implications for training and practice* (pp. 89–112). Alexandria, VA: Association for Counselor Education and Supervision.

Kirschenbaum, H., & Jourdan, A. (2005). The current status of Carl Rogers and the person-centered approach [Electronic version]. *Psychotherapy: Theory, Research, Practice, Training, 42,* 37–51.

Landreth (2002). *Play therapy: The art of relationship*. New York: Brunner-Routledge.

Mearns, D. (2003). The humanistic agenda: articulation. *Journal of Humanistic Psychology, 43*(3), 53–56.

Moodley, R., Lago, C., & Talahite, A. (2004). *Carl Rogers counsels a black client: Race and culture in person-centered counseling*. Ross-on-Wye, UK: PCCS Books Ltd.

Moustakas, C. (1998). Relationship play therapy. Retrieved August 26, 2002, from http://www.aronson.com/ppp/relation.htm

Myers, S. (2000). Empathic listening: Reports on the experience of being heard. *Journal of Humanistic Psychology, 40,* 147–173.

Quinn, R. (1993). Confronting Carl Rogers: A developmental-interactional approach to person-centered therapy. *Journal of Humanistic Psychology, 33,* 6–23.

Radd, T. R. (2005). *Teaching and counseling for today's world: Pre-K-12 and beyond.* Omaha, NE: Grow with Guidance.

Rogers, C. R. (1939). *The clinical treatment of the problem child.* Boston: Houghton Mifflin.

Rogers, C. R. (1942). *Counseling and psychotherapy.* Boston: Houghton Mifflin.

Rogers, C. R. (1951). *Client-centered therapy.* Boston: Houghton Mifflin.

Rogers, C. R. (1965). *Client-centered therapy: Its current practice, implications, and theory.* Boston: Houghton Mifflin.

Rogers, C. R. (1977). *Carl Rogers on personal power: Inner strength and its revolutionary impact.* New York: Delacorte.

Rogers, C. R. (1983). *Freedom to learn for the 80's.* Columbus, OH: Merrill.

Rogers, C. R. (1985). Toward a more human science of the person. *Journal of Humanistic Psychology, 25,* 7–24.

Rogers, C. R. (1992). The necessary and sufficient conditions of therapeutic personality change. *Journal of Consulting and Clinical Psychology, 60,* 827–832.

Rogers, C. R. (1994). Rogers's quote. *Journal of Humanistic Education and Development, 32,* 189.

Rogers, C. R. (1995). What understanding and acceptance mean to me. Illinois Personnel and Guidance Association Meeting (1956, Urbana, Illinois). *Journal of Humanistic Psychology, 35,* 7–22.

Siebert, A. (2000). How non-diagnostic listening led to a rapid "recovery" from paranoid schizophrenia: What is wrong with psychiatry? *Journal of Humanistic Psychology, 40,* 34–58.

Soloman, L. N. (1990). Carl Rogers' efforts for world peace. *Person-Centered Review, 5,* 39–56.

Spangenberg, J. (2003). The cross-cultural relevance of person-centered counseling in post-apartheid South Africa. *Journal of Counseling & Development, 81,* 48–54.

Stipsits, R., & Hutterer, R. (1989). The person-centered approach in Austria. *Person-Centered Review, 4,* 475–487.

Waxer, P. H. (1989). Cantonese versus Canadian evaluation of directive and non-directive therapy. *Canadian Journal of Counseling, 23,* 263–271.

Gestalt Therapy

Making mental connections is our most crucial learning tool, the essence of human intelligence: to forge links; to go beyond the given; to see patterns, relationship, context.

—Marilyn Ferguson

I learned to make my mind large, as the universe is large, so that there is room for paradoxes.

—Maxine Hong Kingston

Fritz Perls (1893–1970)

Fritz Perls's estranged wife, Laura, once referred to him as half prophet and half bum, and Perls considered this description accurate. In his autobiography, *In and Out the Garbage Pail* (1971), Perls wrote that, at the age of 75, he liked his reputation of being both a dirty old man and a guru. Unfortunately, he continued, the first reputation was on the wane and the second ascending.

Born in a Jewish ghetto on the outskirts of Berlin on July 8, 1893, Friedrich Salomon Perls was the third child of Amelia Rund and Nathan Perls. He later Anglicized his first name to Frederick but is remembered more commonly as Fritz.

Perls disliked his eldest sister, Else. He thought of her as a clinger and was uncomfortable in her presence. Else also had severe eye trouble, and Perls disliked the thought that he might have to take care of her someday. He did not mourn greatly when he heard of her death in a concentration camp. Shepard (1975) speculates that Perls resented the extra attention and favors his mother offered Else because of her partial blindness. He did seem to like his second sister, Grete.

After a difficult first few weeks of life, Perls seems to have led a happy and healthy life for his first 9 years. About the age of 10, Perls became rebellious. His parents were having bitter fights, and his father was away from home quite often. Perls described himself as loving his mother, ambitious, loving the arts, and hating his father. He described his father as hating Amelia and loving other women. Perls began to doubt his paternity and suspected that his biological father was a much-respected uncle; this question remained open for Fritz until his death. His marriage was not much happier than his childhood, although he and Laura remained married and worked together in the development of Gestalt therapy. Perls came to realize that the roles of husband and father gave him little satisfaction.

Perls first attended school at the Humanistic Gymnasium in 1910. From his late teens through his university schooling, Perls studied and acted with the Reinhard School of Drama, earning money to pay for most of his education. He earned his M.D. degree from the Friedrich Wilhelm University in 1921. He was in psychoanalysis with Karen Horney, Clara Happel, and Wilhelm Reich and studied with Helene Deutsch at the Psychoanalytic Institute in Vienna.

After some hard times in Europe, Perls found success as a training analyst in Johannesburg, South Africa. In 1934, he founded the South African Institute for Psychoanalysis in Johannesburg. He learned to fly and got his pilot's license. In 1936, Perls flew to Czechoslovakia to deliver a paper to the Psychoanalytic Congress. He met with his hero, Sigmund Freud, but was given only a cool reception—a brief 4-minute audience while he stood in Freud's doorway. Perls experienced another disappointment when most of the other analysts gave his paper an icy reception. From then on, Perls challenged the assumptions and directions of Freud and the psychoanalysts. In his final years, many people began to listen. Perls thought he had four main "unfinished situations" in his life: not being able to sing well, never making a parachute jump, never trying skin diving, and never having the opportunity to show Freud his mistakes.

Perls spent 12 years in South Africa, during which he formulated all the basic ideas underlying what he would later call Gestalt therapy. At 53, he moved his family to New York, where the "formal birth" of Gestalt therapy took place. The people involved debated what to call the new theory. Perls held out for *Gestalt,* a German term that cannot be translated exactly into English, but the meaning of the concept can be explained as:

> A form, a configuration or a totality that has, as a unified whole, properties which cannot be derived by summation from the parts and their relationships. It may refer to physical structures, to physiological and psychological functions, or to symbolic units. (English & English, 1958, p. 225)

In late 1951, Perls's book *Gestalt Therapy: Excitement and Growth in the Human Personality* was published. Perls is listed as one of the authors, although Ralph Hefferline wrote nearly all of the first half of the book and Paul Goodman the second. Perls's other writings include *Ego, Hunger, and Aggression: The Beginnings of Gestalt Therapy* (1969a), *Gestalt Therapy Verbatim* (1969b), *The Gestalt Approach and Eye Witness to Therapy* (1973), *Gestalt Is: A Collection of Articles about Gestalt Therapy and Living* (1975), and, with Patricia Baumgardner, *Gifts from Lake Cowichan and Legacy from Fritz* (1975).

At first, the new therapy had almost no impact. Perls began traveling to cities such as Cleveland, Detroit, Toronto, and Miami to run groups for professionals and laypeople interested in the new idea. As he traveled throughout the United States, he discovered that he was received far better on the road than he was in New York. After 10 years in New York, Perls decided to leave the city—and his wife—for the warmth of Miami. Laura Perls's interpretation of Fritz's reason for leaving was that he was not the leading psychotherapist—or even the leading Gestaltist—in New York.

Miami was important to Perls because there he met "the most significant woman in my life," Marty Fromm. In Florida, he also found LSD and became involved in the drug subculture. He then moved to California in 1964, eventually Big Sur, where he became widely known. At the Esalen Institute, he had to compete with people such as Virginia Satir, Bernard Gunther, and Will Schutz. Perls contended that the techniques Gunther and Schutz employed used other people's ideas and offered "instant joy." Perls, who opposed quick cures and respected only originality, established his own Gestalt Institute of Canada at Cowichan on Vancouver Island in British Columbia in 1969.

Nine months after the center in Canada was begun, Fritz Perls died. An autopsy disclosed advanced cancer of the pancreas. Perls died as he had lived. On the last evening of his life, March 14, 1970, Perls was sitting on the edge of his bed in the intensive care unit getting ready to light a cigarette. His nurse rushed in, took his cigarettes and lighter, and said, "Dr. Perls, you can't smoke in here." Fritz glared at her, said "Nobody tells Fritz Perls what to do," fell back on his bed, and died.

Perls viewed Gestalt theory as being in progress at the time of his death. He thought that theory development, like human development, was a process of becoming. He was not one to close the book on his theory and treat it as gospel. Rather, Perls revised the theory to fit his observations of human behavior.

THE NATURE OF PEOPLE

According to Gestalt theory, the most important areas of concern are the thoughts and feelings people are experiencing at the moment. Normal, healthy behavior occurs when people act and react as total organisms. Many people fragment their lives, distributing their concentration and attention among several variables and events at one time. The results of such fragmentation can be seen in an ineffective living style, with outcomes ranging from low productivity to serious accidents. The Gestalt view of human nature is positive: People are capable of becoming self-regulating beings who can achieve a sense of unity and integration in their lives.

Perls (1969b) saw the person as a total organism—not just as the brain. His saying that people would be better off losing their minds and coming to their senses meant that our bodies and feelings are better indicators of the truth than our words, which we use to hide the truth from ourselves. Body signs such as headaches, rashes, neck strain, and stomach pains may indicate that we need to change something in our lives. Perls believed that awareness alone can be curative. With full awareness, a state of organismic self-regulation develops, and the total person takes control.

Mentally healthy people can maintain their awareness without being distracted by the various environmental stimuli that constantly vie for their attention. Such people can fully and clearly experience their own needs and the environmental alternatives for meeting them. Healthy people still experience their share of inner conflicts and frustrations, but, with their higher levels of concentration and awareness, they can solve their problems without complicating them with fantasy elaborations. They likewise resolve conflicts with others when it is possible; otherwise, they dismiss the conflicts. People with high levels of awareness of their needs and their environment know which problems and conflicts are resolvable and which are not. In Perls's theory, the key to successful adjustment is the development of personal responsibility—responsibility for one's life and response to one's environment. Much of the Perls doctrine is summarized in his famous Gestalt Prayer:

> I do my thing and you do your thing.
> I am not in this world to live up to your expectations,
> And you are not in this world to live up to mine.
> You are you and I am I
> And if by chance we find each other, it's beautiful.
> If not, it can't be helped. (Perls, 1969b, p. 4)

The healthy person focuses sharply on one need (the figure) at a time, thereby relegating other needs to the background. When the need is met—or the Gestalt is closed or completed—it is relegated to the background and a new need comes into focus (becomes the figure). The smoothly functioning figure–ground relationship characterizes the healthy personality. The dominant need of the organism at any time becomes the foreground figure and the other needs recede, at least temporarily, into the background. The foreground figure is the need that presses most sharply for satisfaction, whether the need is to preserve life or is related to less physically or psychologically vital areas. For individuals to be able to satisfy their needs, close the Gestalt, and move on to other things, they must be able to determine what they need, and they must know how to manipulate themselves and their environment to get it. Even purely physiological needs can be satisfied only through the interaction of the organism and the environment (Perls, 1975).

Perls defined neurotic people as those who try to attend to too many needs at one time and, as a result, fail to satisfy any one need fully. Neurotic people also use their potential to manipulate others to do for them what they have not done for themselves. Rather than running their own lives, they turn them over to those who will take care of their needs. In summary, people cause themselves additional problems by not handling their lives appropriately in the following six categories:

1. *Lacking contact with the environment:* People may become so rigid that they cut themselves off from others or from resources in the environment.
2. *Confluence:* People may incorporate too much of themselves into others or incorporate so much of the environment into themselves that they lose touch with who and where they are. Then the environment takes control.
3. *Unfinished business:* People may have unfulfilled needs, unexpressed feelings, or unfinished situations that clamor for their attention. (This situation may manifest itself in dreams.)

4. *Fragmentation:* People may try to discover or deny a need, such as to show aggression. The inability to find and obtain what one needs may be the result of fragmenting one's life.

5. *Top dog/underdog:* People may experience a split in their personalities between what they think they "should" do (top dog) and what they "want" to do (underdog).

6. *Polarities (dichotomies):* People tend to flounder at times between existing, natural dichotomies in their lives, such as body-mind, self-external world, fantasy-reality, infantile-mature, biological-cultural, poetry-prose, spontaneous-deliberate, personal-social, think-feeling, and unconscious-conscious. Much of everyday living seems to be involved in resolving conflicts posed by these competing polarities.

Assagioli (1965) has identified five types of polarities:

1. *Physical:* masculinity-femininity and parasympathetic-sympathetic nervous system
2. *Emotional:* pleasure-pain, excitement-depression, love-hate
3. *Mental:* parent-child, eros (feeling)-logos (reason), top dog-underdog
4. *Spiritual:* intellectual doubt-dogmatism
5. *Interindividual:* man-woman, black-white, Christian-Jew

THEORY OF COUNSELING

An adaptation of Perls's system to counseling children should incorporate the five layers of neuroses proposed by Perls (1971). Perls devised these five layers to depict how people fragment their lives and prevent themselves from succeeding and maturing. The five layers form a series of counseling stages, or benchmarks, for the counseling process; in fact, they could be considered as five steps to a better Gestalt way of life. These five layers are:

1. *The phony layer:* Many people are trapped in trying to be what they are not. The phony layer is characterized by unresolved conflicts and failure to find integration of competing polarities.

2. *The phobic layer:* As people become aware of their phony games, they become aware of their fears that maintain the games. This experience is often frightening.

3. *The impasse layer:* This is the layer people reach when they shed the environmental support of their games and find they do not know a better way to cope with their fears and dislikes. People often become stuck here and refuse to move on.

4. *The implosive layer:* People become aware of how they limit themselves, and they begin to experiment with new behaviors within the safe confines of the counseling setting.

5. *The explosive layer:* If experiments with new behaviors are successful outside the counseling setting, people can reach the explosive layer, where they find much unused energy that had been tied up in maintaining a phony existence.

Perls believed that progress through the five layers of neuroses is best achieved by observing how psychological defenses might be associated with muscular position, or what he called *body armor*. He believed the client's body language would be a better indicator of the truth than the client's words, and that awareness of hidden material could be facilitated by acting out feelings. Perls asked people to project their thoughts and feelings on empty chairs representing significant people in their lives. People were often asked to play several roles in attempting to identify sources of personal conflict. Perls expanded on Rogers's idea of feedback as a therapeutic agent by including body posture, voice tone, eye movements, feelings, and gestures.

Gestalt therapists emphasize direct experiences. They focus on achieving awareness of the here and now and block the client in any attempt to break out of this present awareness by talking about the past or future. As an experiential approach, Gestalt therapy is not concerned with symptoms and analysis, but rather with total existence and integration. Integration and maturation, according to Perls, are never-ending processes directly related to a person's awareness of the here and now. A "Gestalt" is formed in a person as a new need arises. If a need is satisfied, the destruction of that particular Gestalt is achieved, and new Gestalts can be formed. This concept is basic in Gestalt therapy. Incomplete Gestalts are referred to as "unfinished business."

Perls (1969b) wrote that the aim of his therapy was to help people help themselves to grow up—to mature, take charge of their lives, and become responsible for themselves. The central goal in Gestalt therapy is deeper awareness, which promotes a sense of living fully in the here and now. Other goals include teaching people to assume responsibility for themselves and facilitating their achievement of personal integration. These goals are consistent with those of most counseling systems.

The aim of integration is to help people become systematic, whole persons whose inner state and behavior match so that little energy is wasted within the system. Such integration allows people to give their full attention and energy to meeting their needs appropriately. The ultimate measure of success in Gestalt therapy is the extent to which clients grow in awareness, take responsibility for their actions, and move from environmental support to self-support.

COUNSELING METHOD

The function of the Gestalt counselor is to facilitate the client's awareness in the "now." Awareness is the capacity to focus, to attend, and to be in touch with the present. The Gestalt counselor is an aggressive therapist who frustrates the learner's attempts to break out of the awareness of here and now. The counselor stops client's attempts to retreat into the past or jump into the future by relating the content to the immediate present.

Miller (1989) points out that Perls often used sarcasm, humor, drama, and shock to rouse people from neurosis. For Perls, Gestalt therapy was a search for a workable solution in the present. The counselor's job is to assist the client in experimenting with authentic new behaviors, rather than to explain and maintain the unhelpful or harmful behaviors of the past. Dolliver (1991), attacking "inconsistencies" in Perls's philosophy and style in the often-reviewed *Three Approaches to Psychotherapy* (Shostrom, 1965), concludes that none of the counselor's objectives in Miller's statement was met with Gloria. Actually, after viewing the Gloria interviews with Rogers, Perls, and Ellis, it is fairly obvious that Perls is the only one of the three therapists who is successful in getting Gloria to deal with her core issue of trying to please others by being the person she thinks others want her to be. Her lifestyle was an excellent example of a phony layer of neuroses. Perls, confronting Gloria with the inconsistencies in her verbal and nonverbal behavior, was able to penetrate her well-defended lifestyle of playing roles she thought others would prefer to the actual person she was trying to conceal. Basically, the point of Gestalt therapy is to treat the client's lifestyle rather than fragments of the client's life. To Perls, spending time talking with Gloria about her daughter, father, ex-husband, boyfriends, and transference issues would be like trying to put a jigsaw puzzle together, one piece at a time, without looking at the picture of the completed puzzle before starting. Perls wanted to work with the whole Gestalt person, not fragments of the person's life.

The general reaction students have to watching Perls working with Gloria is, first, they cannot visualize themselves counseling a client in the same confrontational manner. Second, they do not see a counseling framework or guideline, such as those provided in reality therapy, solution-focused brief counseling, and rational-emotive behavior therapy. However, they do become interested in various Gestalt methods that help clients work through impasses in their personal development. In many ways, these Gestalt interventions are breakthrough mechanisms that help clients reframe their problems into manageable projects, resolve decision-making conflicts, and find a reasonable balance between taking too much or too little responsibility in their lives. Descriptions of these and other Gestalt interventions follow. Miller and others, no doubt, disagree, and the controversy over the film will most likely continue well into the twenty-first century. Fritz Perls—in person or on film—never left anyone feeling neutral; he made everyone think and react.

GESTALT TECHNIQUES

Several language, game, and fantasy methods may be used to maintain the present-time orientation of the counseling interview. We have used some of the following techniques with 5- to 12-year-old children, as well as with adolescents and adults.

"I" LANGUAGE Encourage use of the word *I* when the client uses a generalized *you* when talking; for example, "*You* know how it is when *you* can't understand math and the teacher gets on *your* back." When *I* is substituted for *you*, the message becomes, "*I* know how it is when *I* can't understand math and the teacher gets on *my* back." The client tries on such substitutions of I for you like a pair of shoes to see how they fit. "I" language helps children take responsibility for their feelings, thoughts, and behaviors.

SUBSTITUTING *WON'T* FOR *CAN'T*   Again, the client tries on the "shoes" for comfort, substituting "I *won't* pass math" for "I *can't* pass math." How much of the responsibility the child will own is the question to be answered.

SUBSTITUTING *WHAT* AND *HOW* FOR *WHY*   Substituting *what* and *how* for *why* is another technique; for example, "*How* do you feel about what you are doing?" "*What* are you doing with your foot as we talk about your behavior?"

NO GOSSIPING   If the client must talk about someone who is not present in the room, let the talk, all in the present tense, be directed to an empty chair. For example, a student might say, "I think you treat me unfairly, Ms. Clark. I wish you would be as nice to me as you are to the other kids." The student can then move to the other chair and answer for Ms. Clark, "Joan, I would find it easier to like you if you would be more helpful to me during the day." The dialogue between Joan and Ms. Clark would continue until the child finished her complaint and the anticipated responses from her teacher. Person-to-person dialogues not only update the material into the present but also increase Joan's awareness of the problem. Side benefits include a better picture of the situation for the counselor and rehearsal time for Joan, who may wish to discuss the problem later with her teacher. Some empathy on Joan's part for the teacher's side of the conflict may also emerge from the dialogue.

CHANGING QUESTIONS INTO STATEMENTS   The method of changing questions into statements has the effect of helping children to be more authentic and direct in expressing their thoughts and feelings. For example, rather than asking, "Don't you think I should stop hanging around those guys?" the child should say, "I think I should stop hanging around those guys" or "I think you want me to stop hanging around those guys." Perls believed that most questions are phony in that they are really disguised statements.

TAKING RESPONSIBILITY   Clients are asked to fill in sentence blanks as another way of examining personal responsibility for the way they manage their lives. For example, "Right now I'm feeling _____, and I take _____ percent responsibility for how I feel." The exercise is quite an eye opener for those clients who tend to view outside sources as the total cause of their good and bad feelings.

INCOMPLETE SENTENCES   Incomplete sentence exercises, like the exercise on taking responsibility, help clients become aware of how they help and hurt themselves. For example, "I help myself when I _____," or "I block or hurt myself when I _____."

BIPOLARITIES   Perls applies the term *differential thinking* to the concept of thinking in terms of opposites. Much of everyday life appears to be spent resolving conflicts posed by competing polarities, such as "I should" versus "I want" when one is confronted with a difficult decision.

Top Dog versus Underdog   One of the most common bipolarities is what Perls (1969) labeled *top dog* and *underdog*. The top dog is righteous, authoritarian, and knows best. The top dog is a bully and works with "you should" and "you should not." The underdog manipulates by being defensive or apologetic, wheedling, and playing crybaby. The underdog works with "I want" and makes excuses such as "I try hard" and "I have good intentions." The underdog is cunning and usually gets the better of the top dog because the underdog position appeals to the pleasure-seeking side of our personality.

Two chairs can be used to help clients resolve "I want" versus "I should" debates. Label one chair top dog (I should) and the other chair underdog (I want). Clients are asked to present their best "I should" argument while sitting in the top dog chair and facing the empty underdog chair. On completion of the first "I should" point, the client moves to the underdog chair to counter with an "I want" argument. The debate continues back and forth until the client completes all arguments from both points of view. Processing the activity often reveals in which chair (or on which side of the argument) the client feels and thinks the greatest integration of shoulds and wants occurs, thus allowing the client to have the best of both sides.

The top dog–underdog technique works for individuals and groups. To use the technique in a group, the counselor can divide the clients into two subgroups, the top dogs and the underdogs. The top dog group members list reasons they *should* do a certain thing, whereas the underdog group members think of reasons they *want* to do something. The lists generally lead to much discussion. Children and adolescents respond well to this activity.

The best outcomes from the top dog–underdog debate occur when clients can identify areas in their lives where the shoulds and wants agree; for example, "I love to read, and I should read." These synergistic solutions help children and adolescents integrate the polarities in their lives.

The Empty Chair Technique   The Gestalt technique of the empty chair often is used to resolve a conflict between people or within a person (Greenberg & Malcolm, 2003; Paivio & Greenberg, 1995). The child can sit in one chair, playing his or her own part; then the child can sit in the other chair, playing out a projection of what the other person is saying or doing in response. Similarly, a child may sit in one chair to discuss the pros of making a decision, and then argue the cons of the decision while sitting in the opposite chair.

For example, Sharon was having trouble deciding whether to tell of her friend's involvement in destruction of property. She thought her friend had behaved wrongly and should not let other children take the blame for the incident, yet she was reluctant to tattle on the friend and get her in trouble.

The counselor suggested that Sharon sit in one chair and talk about what would happen if she did tell on her friend, and then move to the other chair to describe what would happen if she did not. The technique helped Sharon to look at the consequences of both acts and make her decision. In this instance, Sharon decided to talk with her friend to give her the opportunity to confess and make amends for the damaged property.

The empty chair technique is a powerful intervention for working with clients of all ages who are in conflict with a third party who is not present in the session. For example, the conflict might be with a spouse, sibling, teacher, parent, friend, or boss. Rather than having clients talk on and on about how awful this other person is, the client is asked to speak directly to the offending person as if she or he were sitting in the empty chair. Then, because the client knows this person well, the client is asked to sit in the empty chair and reply the way the offending person would respond. The back-and-forth dialogue continues until clients finish expressing all of their thoughts and feelings on the subject.

Three productive things happen with this version of the empty chair technique. First, the counselor gets a better, firsthand account of the dynamics of the relationship. Second, the client may develop some empathy for the offending party's position. Third, the client receives some rehearsal practice for confronting the absent person. The counselor might even model some possible methods of confronting the third party by taking the client's role and having the client play the part of the other person. Then, the client can practice confronting the offending third person, with the counselor taking the role of that person. This method has been particularly useful in helping students protest effectively to their teachers when they have questions about their grades.

The empty chair method also has been useful with clients of all ages who have "unfinished business" with a departed loved one. They talk to their lost loved one as though that person were sitting in the chair and, in many cases, sit in the empty chair and reply as they "know" this person would reply. For example, a son might say to his deceased father, "Dad, I always wanted to tell you how much I loved you, and I was never able to do this." Speaking for his father from the other chair, the reply is almost always, "Son, you didn't have to say it. I knew all along that you loved me." Counselors have only to witness such an event one time to "see" the heavy burden of guilt lift from the shoulders of their client.

Alexander and Harman (1988) report a successful application of a Gestalt approach to group counseling with middle school classmates of a student who committed suicide. Using the empty chair, writing, and artwork, children said good-bye and discussed their own fears and anxieties about suicide.

In a variation of the empty chair method, a problem can be explored in an individual or group situation by introducing the empty chair as a hypothetical person with behaviors and characteristics similar to those of the child and his or her particular problem. It is sometimes easier for children to discuss a hypothetical child and how this child feels or could change than to discuss their own feelings and behaviors. While discussing an imagined person, children learn about themselves.

The empty chair method is useful for angry children, who can talk to the angry self in another chair and find out why they are so upset. It can also serve as projection for the child who is afraid of an ugly monster. The child can become the monster and allow that creature to explain its motives for scaring children. Retroflection also may be used to help students express difficult or frightening thoughts and feelings. Retroflection is giving voice to that part of the body that is exhibiting muscular tension. The counselor may ask a child who tightens up his or her mouth to say what the mouth would like to say.

Engle and Holliman (2002) write that the expression of emotional experiences allows for the formation of a new Gestalt when people are in conflict over opposing values or over what they should do versus what they want to do. Experiments such as the empty chair dialogue are useful in developing new schematic structures for bringing the conflict into focus so that it can be integrated into a workable solution. Greenberg and Malcolm (2003) present a six-step method for using the empty chair. The intervention begins with clients addressing an individual with whom they have unfinished business, followed by clients responding as they believe the other person would respond. The dialogue continues until clients reach a point of resolution in completing the unfinished business, which, in effect, moves the issue of "unfinished" business from figure to ground in the client's field of awareness.

Wagner-Moore (2004) points out that the two-chair method has been shown to be superior to person-centered, empathic responding in resolving inner conflicts. Kellogg (2004) presents an update on the various Gestalt methods involving "chairwork" in saying "good-bye" when a client is holding on to a relationship that no longer exists, in working with dreams, and in finding integrations of bipolar opposites in a person's life.

My Greatest Weakness   In another exercise, clients are asked to name their greatest weakness and write a short paragraph on how this weakness is really their greatest strength; for example, "My greatest weakness is procrastination, but I'll never give it up because by putting things off I create the motivation I need for completing unpleasant tasks." Once clients realize that their greatest weakness may, in fact, be the greatest strength they have going for them, they begin to realize that they control the weakness rather than vice versa. Clients also realize that the counselor who uses this technique is not pushing them to fix their "weakness." Maybe all that is needed is to just manage the weakness more efficiently, such as by not procrastinating too long.

Resent, Demand, and Appreciate: The Integration of Opposing Thoughts, Feelings, and Beliefs   Have your clients list the three people to whom they are closest and, for each of them, write one thing they resent about the person, one thing they demand, and one thing they appreciate. Such an exercise helps clients become more aware of the mixed feelings they have about others, how it is possible to resent and appreciate a person at the same time, and how opposing thoughts and feelings can be integrated.

The purpose of working with these bipolarities, or splits in the personality, is to bring each side into awareness so reorganization that does not exclude either side can take place. Gestalt therapy is directed toward making life easier by integrating the splits in existence; each side is necessary and has its place in the well-integrated personality.

Name	Something You Resent	Something You Demand	Something You Appreciate
John	I resent that you don't spend enough time with me.	I demand more time.	I appreciate your company and friendship.
Mary			
Sue			

FANTASY GAMES FOR CREATING AWARENESS Fantasy games can be great fun for children of all ages while enabling them to become aware of their present feelings. As a group activity, the children choose an animal they would like to be, and then move around as they think this animal would. The children sit down in pairs and discuss what they would feel if they were this particular animal. As a culmination of the activity, they write stories about how they would feel, think, and behave if they were actually the animal. By the end of the exercise, children should have a real awareness of how they feel and think and be able to discuss this with their counselor, teacher, or parents.

Fantasy games can be devised from almost any object or situation. The rosebush and wise-person fantasies are two favorites. In the first fantasy, the client pretends to be a rosebush and then considers the following points:

1. Type of bush—strong or weak?
2. Root system—deep or shallow?
3. Number of roses—too many or too few?
4. Number of thorns—too many or too few?
5. Environment—bad or good for growing?
6. Does your rosebush stand out?
7. Does it have enough room?
8. How does it get along with the other plants?
9. Does it have a good future?

The wise-person fantasy involves asking a fantasized source of wisdom one question, which the wise person ponders for a few minutes before answering—speaking through the client, of course. Both question and answer should add some awareness and understanding to the client's life. For example, a client may ask, "What should I do with my life?"; then he or she answers, as the wise person, "Develop all your talents and skills as much as you can."

Clients are asked to discuss their fantasies in depth with the counselor in individual sessions and with groups of two to four if a group is meeting. A good follow-up procedure for clients is to complete the statement "I learned that _____" after each exercise. The fantasy games are enhanced if clients lie down and participate in relaxation exercises before the experience and continue to lie down and relax in a comfortable spot during the fantasy exercises.

Heikkinen (1989) wrote a helpful article on reorienting clients from altered states of consciousness (ASCs), used in Gestalt and other therapies, in a way that avoids uncomfortable aftereffects, such as unusual cognitive or emotional functioning and atypical body reactions. Because clients may experience an ASC during activities such as the rosebush or wise-person fantasies, these activities should end with the counselor counting backward slowly from ten or in the direction opposite to that used to reach the ASC. Imagining a climb up steps, a swim to the top of the lake, or a return from a journey is a useful method for reorienting clients. Directing clients in a group setting to look slowly around the area and become reacquainted with their environment also is effective.

DREAMWORK   Dreaming is a way of becoming aware of the world in the here and now. Because awareness is the dominant theme of Gestalt, dreaming and Gestalt seem to work well together. Dreaming is a guardian of one's existence because the content of dreams always relates to one's survival, well-being, and growth; therefore, Gestalt therapists have helped clients overcome impasses in their lives through serious consideration of dreams. The Gestalt approach to dreams is helpful not only to people experiencing dilemmas in their lives but also to the average "healthy" person. Most people spend many of their waking hours out of touch with the here and now because they are worrying compulsively about the future or doting on memories of failure or past pleasures.

Spontaneity is an important feature of Gestalt therapy, and according to Perls, dreams are the most spontaneous expression of the existence of the human being. The Gestalt approach is concerned with integration rather than analysis of dreams. Such integration involves consciously reliving a dream, taking responsibility for being the objects and people in the dream, and becoming aware of the messages the dream holds. According to Perls, all parts of the dream are fragments of the dreamer's personality that must be pieced together to form a whole. These projected fragments must be reowned; thus, hidden potential that appears in the dream also is to be reowned. As clients play the parts of all the objects and persons in the dream, they may become more aware of the message the dream holds. They may act out the dream until two conflicting roles emerge—for instance, the top dog and the underdog. This want-should conflict is essentially the conflict from which the dreamer suffers. Gestaltists believe that dreams have hidden existential messages that, once discovered, can fill the voids in people's personalities. In the Gestalt system, dreamwork holds many possibilities for solving the problems of life or for developing a better self-awareness.

Basically, the Gestalt method for working with dreams requires clients to describe the dream and then list all the parts of the dream, including people, objects, animals, buildings, rooms, and trees. Clients are asked what, if anything, the dream might mean to them. Interpretation is left to the client, based on the philosophy that to interpret the client's dream for the client would suggest that the counselor would know the client better than the client knows himself or herself. Next, the client is asked to speak or give voice to each part of the dream, much like an animated movie in which trees and animals talk. Each object in the dream offers clients the opportunity to project parts of their personality onto that object. For example, a client may say, "I am the bedroom in Harriet's house and I like being her bedroom. She is very particular about keeping me clean, neat, and orderly." These projections are done for all of the things in the client's dream. The counselor may suggest that Harriet's bedroom have a conversation with Harriet's house and ask the client to role-play the dialogue for such a conversation. Following the talking exercise for each object in the dream, the client is again asked for an interpretation of the dream. It may come in the form of a best guess. Regardless of the interpretation or best guess about the dream's meaning, the client is not likely to have this dream again. This method has a way of finishing up unfinished business that retires the dream to the background of the client's experience. We have found this method to yield spectacular results in ending unpleasant recurring dreams and nightmares. The therapist's task in the integration of dreams is to concentrate on what clients are avoiding in their present existence and to help them act out painful situations and reintegrate the alienated parts of their personality into their lives.

GESTALT PLAY THERAPY

Carroll and Oaklander (1997) explain that Gestalt therapy is a humanistic and process-oriented approach. The concern of the therapy is the integrated functioning of all aspects of the person so that senses, body, emotions, and intellect are well coordinated in a creative adjustment. They state that the child's capacity to represent experiences in symbolic fashion allows a self-reflective manner that helps the child develop a greater sense of self. Oaklander describes (Campbell, 1993) the process of Gestalt play therapy as like a dance that sometimes the counselor leads and other times the child leads. Meeting the child where she or he is and suggesting, but not pushing, are Oaklander's admonitions for the counselor.

She also explains the important concept of *contact* in Gestalt play therapy. Contact is having the ability to be completely present in a situation by using one's senses that connect with the environment, such as looking, listening, and smelling. Being aware of feelings and using the intellect are also part of making contact. Recognizing what is being done and how it is being done is the contacting process. When children are anxious or troubled, they do not use their senses fully. They block emotions and inhibit contact. Gestalt play therapy includes exercises and experiences that involve the senses and the expression of feelings. Oaklander's book *Windows to Our Children: A Gestalt Therapy with Children and Adolescents* (1988) contains examples of these exercises in which she uses various creative activities and explains how they work. Enhancing the self increases a person's ability to be in contact. The goal of the therapy is to restore the child's natural functioning and self-regulatory processes. Experiencing the contacting process leads to integration, choice, and change. Oaklander (1978, 1993) also adapted several Gestalt techniques for children. She recommends projection through art and storytelling as a way of increasing the child's self-awareness and cites fantasy and imagery, such as the wise-person fantasy, as good ways to tap intuitive thought in children and adults. Oaklander has also frequently used the empty chair method as a helpful way to handle unfinished business, frustration, and anger.

Wheeler and McConville (2002), in agreement with Oaklander, point out that Gestalt techniques in working with children are focused on the development of inner strength and confidence in the child through opportunities to make choices, achieve mastery, own their projections, participate in imaginative play, and expel aggressive energy appropriately.

CONFIDENCE COURSES FOR PLAY THERAPY   This gentle form of obstacle course, designed to build confidence, uses combinations of pit jumps, incline balances, boxes, barrels, ladder climbs, rope slides, and other similar objects. (Children also can be involved in constructing such a course.) As children attain better motor coordination and balance, they form better self-images, a feeling of mastery, and an "I can do it" attitude about themselves. They begin to feel they can solve problems and deal with their world competently. The same holds true for adolescents who negotiate tougher ropes courses.

CASE STUDY

Many short-term counseling sessions with children can be conducted using the empty chair technique. For example, consider the following method for working with anger:

CHILD: I hate my dad. He's mean. I hate his guts.

COUNSELOR: Let's pretend your dad is sitting in that empty chair. What do you want to say to him? You can walk over there and say whatever you want.

CHILD: Get off my back! Leave me alone! I cleaned my room just as good as I could.

COUNSELOR: Now sit in the other chair. Pretend to be your dad.

CHILD: I've told you and told you that this room looks like a pigpen.

COUNSELOR: Now be yourself again.

CHILD: I cleaned my room good, Dad! Then you came in and said it still isn't good enough. Nothing was left out in the room but my toys!

COUNSELOR:	Now be your dad.
CHILD:	This is the last time I'm telling you, Son. The room better be finished when I get back. That means toys too.
COUNSELOR:	Now be you.
CHILD:	You don't care about me! You don't care about how I feel. You just worry about the house being messed up. You get mad when I get out my toys. Kids are supposed to have toys! It's MY ROOM! Quit buggin' me! [This outburst is accompanied by much nonverbal expression of anger, as well as the overt angry verbal content.]

The child has expressed his strong thoughts that his room should be his territory, that it should be all right to have his toys out. A global "hatred" for the father has been reduced to anger about a specific recurring problem (the differing standards for the room held by the parent and the child). After release of the built-up anger, some problem-solving could achieve a compromise about the room situation.

Another sample counseling session involves the top dog–underdog debate, using an empty chair for each "dog." This technique is useful when the child has a decision-making problem. Most decision-making problems involve a debate between the inner voice of "I should do . . ." (top dog) versus "Yes, but I want to do . . ." (underdog). An empty chair is assigned to each point of view.

Identification of the Problem

Susan is experiencing a conflict whether to live with her mother or her father when their divorce is final.

Individual and Background Information

Susan Adams is a 10-year-old girl in the fourth grade. Her mother and father are getting a divorce, and she has to decide whether to live with her mother or her father. Susan is the second of three children. This was the second marriage for Susan's mother and the first marriage for Susan's father. Her elder brother is not her father's son. Both parents work in factory jobs, but their income seems to be limited by the fact that Susan's father spends most of his paycheck on alcohol. Susan is an average student in school; she is quiet and has never had behavioral problems. She gets along well with her peers at school. Susan's physical health is good, but she has a vision problem that requires a new pair of glasses, which her parents claim they do not have the money to buy.

Transcript

COUNSELOR:	Susan, we have the next thirty minutes for our talk. Where would you like to start?
SUSAN:	Well, you know my problem about having to decide whether to live with Mom or Daddy after their divorce is final. I just don't know what I'm going to do.
COUNSELOR:	I know that when we talked about this the other day, you were feeling really upset about this situation of having to choose between your mom and dad. I can tell you still feel this way.

SUSAN: Yes, I do. I did all the things we talked about—like talking to both of them. That made it even harder to decide because they both want me. I still don't know what to do. I wish they would stop the divorce.

COUNSELOR: Well, it's a good feeling to know that they both want you, but a bad feeling to know you have to choose. You would really like to have them stay together.

SUSAN: Yes, I really would, but that's impossible! I've tried every way I can to keep them together.

COUNSELOR: Susan, would you try an exercise with me that might help clarify your thinking about this decision?

SUSAN: I'll try anything to help.

COUNSELOR: [explains and demonstrates the top dog–underdog technique] So, when you are in the top dog chair, you say, "I should . . .," and when you are in the underdog chair, you say, "I want . . ." Okay?

SUSAN: Okay. [goes to the top dog chair first]

TOP DOG: I should go with Daddy because he'll be all alone.

UNDERDOG: Yes, but I want to stay with Mom because I hate to give up my room, and I want to stay with my sister.

TOP DOG: What is Daddy going to do without anyone to cook for him and clean house?

UNDERDOG: Why can't he hire a maid, and I can visit him a lot too?

TOP DOG: If I don't live with Daddy, he won't have anybody, because he doesn't want Jake, and Sally is too young to move away from Mom.

UNDERDOG: Well, Daddy goes out and drinks a lot with his friends, and sometimes he gets sick and is not nice to be around when he gets drunk.

TOP DOG: I think I should take care of him when he gets sick.

UNDERDOG: I think it is better not to be near him when he drinks. I would like to visit him when he is not drinking.

TOP DOG: How can I live with Mom and help Daddy too?

UNDERDOG: I just know things will be better if I live with Mom in my room and see Daddy as often as I can.

COUNSELOR: Do you think you've finished with this argument, Susan?

SUSAN: Yes, I've said all I can think of.

COUNSELOR: I'm wondering what you learned from doing this exercise.

SUSAN: Well, I think things will be better if I stay where I am with Mom. But I'll need to see a lot of Daddy—as much as I can. I love them both so much. [starts to cry]

COUNSELOR: I know this has to be a sad and rough time for you. It really hurts, doesn't it?

SUSAN: It sure does. I need to be brave about this and not let it make me so sad.

COUNSELOR: Its okay to feel sad about this. You can always come in here to talk to me when you want to.

[Counselor terminates the interview and schedules another session for the next day.]

CROSS-CULTURAL APPLICATIONS OF GESTALT THERAPY

Gestalt therapy has certain aspects that appeal to some cultures and others that the same cultures might find offensive. Gestalt therapy is directed more toward total lifestyle change than it is to individual problems that are mere pieces of the total puzzle that represents a person's life and style of interacting with the environment. Most people from all cultures coming to counseling for the purpose of getting help for specific problems are frustrated when they find the Gestalt counselor taking a global focus of examining the total picture rather than its fragments that define the presenting problem. In summary, Gestalt counselors believe that teaching clients how to behave in an authentic, honest, and open manner will be sufficient for handling any problem that might arise. After studying Chapter 15, you should be better prepared to meet the cultural expectations of each client.

Gestalt therapy is the most present-oriented therapy discussed in this book; however, old, unfinished business can be updated to the present by having clients confront their "problem" people in the empty chair. Even unfinished business with deceased people can be addressed with the empty chair method. Techniques such as the empty chair may present problems for clients from cultures where emotions are not expressed.

Gestalt therapy practitioners do not believe that a victimhood or entitlement worldview is a healthy way to live. People are viewed as being responsible for how well they are handling their lives. The focus on individual responsibility may be more difficult for some cultures than it is for others. Gestalt therapists would argue that no matter how difficult personal circumstances might be, people are still responsible for finding ways to lift themselves out of the oppressive situation in which they might find themselves. Gestalt therapists would not quarrel with the concept of organizing a group or using any legal resource available for getting oneself out of the ditch. All of these issues raise the ethical question of the counselor's role when a client brings the baggage of some individual cultural ideas to counseling—and every culture has these. Does preservation of irrational cultural ideas take precedence over helping a client who might be suffering from trying to live by such ideas?

Specifically, people suffering from oppression may be put off by the Gestalt emphasis on individual responsibility. For instance, Native American clients may not like discounting the past. Asian clients may not appreciate the emphasis on confrontation and the expression of honest feelings. Clients from African cultures may appreciate the emphasis on the expression of true and honest feelings. Hispanic clients, like Asian clients, may not appreciate the emphasis on expression of feelings that could happen in Gestalt therapy.

Saner (1989) has voiced concerns about possible cultural bias in U.S. Gestalt therapy methods. He suggests several ways to make Gestalt therapy valid across cultures: Drop the ethnocentric emphasis on the individual in favor of stressing reciprocal interaction by all participants in a social setting, use psychodrama in group therapy rather than the hot-seat method of individual therapy within the group setting, and incorporate contributions from other disciplines in Gestalt theory and practice.

In the end, it is the counselor's responsibility to be aware of possible difficulties clients from other cultures may have with the interventions and theories the counselor practices. Each client, regardless of cultural background, should be respected and treated as a unique individual.

Practitioners of Gestalt therapy and other methods of counseling would do well to adapt their counseling approach to fit the particular learning styles and worldviews of their clients. The traditional approaches to counseling have always been focused on the uniqueness of each client. This unique quality of each client is not to be lost in groups and cultural stereotyping. However, as Bingham, Porche-Burke, James, Sue, and Vasquez (2002) point out, counselors must avoid disrespecting the worldview of their clients, either from ignorance of their cultural norms or from insensitivity to their values. They remind us that there is no one way to conceptualize human behavior, no all-inclusive theory that captures and explains the experience of all diverse cultures, and no counseling method that has proved efficacy across all cultures.

GESTALT THERAPY, ACCOUNTABILITY, AND MANAGED HEALTH CARE

Managed health care administrators might have difficulty accepting the rather general goals of Gestalt therapy—general, that is, to the novice and layperson points of view that focus on counseling interventions with behavioral, measurable, and concrete goals, such as getting and holding a job, having one social date per week, running a mile each day, and earning a B average in school. These goals, although quite laudable, represent to the Gestalt therapist just pieces of the complicated jigsaw puzzle that makes up a person's life and lifestyle. Rather than examining each individual piece in a person's jigsaw puzzle, the Gestalt therapist prefers to work with the total person. What this means is that discussion of how to get a job or make better grades could take a backseat to interacting with the counselor with the goal of teaching the client to interact with people in an open, authentic manner, whereas discarding phony behavior designed to portray a personality different from the one the client is trying to cover up. However, the common sense of needing to administer to survival needs first should take priority over other goals. The Gestalt counselor does believe the key to solving day-to-day problems is to relate to others in an open, honest manner and to invest their energy, formerly used to play phony roles, into more productive activities, such as getting and maintaining employment and earning better grades. In addition, the Gestalt counselor trains clients to trust the feelings their brains are sending to their bodies. In other words, people need to give their attention to those feelings that are indicators they are about to do the right or wrong thing, make the right or wrong decision, stay in the right or wrong job, or stay in the right or wrong relationship. These global counseling outcome goals are more difficult to sell to managed care organizations. However, Harman (1996) writes that there is definitely a future for the here-and-now approach to personal development as practiced by Gestalt counselors.

Because Gestalt techniques facilitate discovery, confrontation, and resolution of the client's major conflict, often in a dramatically short time, the inexperienced therapist, observer, or client might assume that Gestalt therapy offers an "instant cure." Even experienced counselors are tempted to push the client to a stance of self-support too fast, too soon. Group Gestalt therapy is common, but frequently it amounts to individual counseling in a group setting. Another hazard is the counselor's assumption of excessive responsibility for the direction of the group by too much activity, thus fostering client passivity and defeating the goal of client self-support. Extensive experience with Gestalt therapy may actually make clients less fit for or less adjusted to contemporary society; at the same time, however, they may be motivated to work toward changing the world into a more compassionate and productive milieu in which human beings can develop, work, and enjoy their full humanness.

As noted in Chapter 2 and by Anderson (2000), the key terms defining preferred treatments by managed care organizations include *brevity, accountability, low cost, quantifiable outcomes,* and *client satisfaction.* Gestalt counseling generally can compete well for cost and client satisfaction, but not as well as other therapies for accountability, quantifiable outcomes, and brevity. To that end, Brief Gestalt Therapy (BGT) was created to adapt the practice of Gestalt therapy to managed care restrictions (Houston, 2003). There are some significant differences between BGT and Brief Therapy (BT). BGT counselors adapt the counseling process to fit the individual needs of clients and their presenting problems. There is greater emphasis on developing a working relationship between the counselor and client. Methods and assumptions from other systems of counseling are used. Solution-focused methods of expanding the positive aspects of one's life and scaling progress toward goals are two examples. Homework assignments or between-session experiments are used as they are in reality therapy and rational-emotive behavior therapy. Burley and Freier (2004), in a related article, point out that people get into difficulty when there are interruptions of the process of Gestalt formation and resolution, which may have developed in the early childhood years. They refer to this as a procedural memory problem that prevents people from retaining learned connections between stimuli and response (habits). It may not be long until we find behavioral methods finding their way into BGT.

SUMMARY

We urge caution regarding the misuse of popular Gestalt techniques with fragile children, adolescents, and adults who cannot handle the emotional intensity some of the methods generate. Additional caution, patience, and sensitivity also are recommended regarding Gestalt counseling with severely disturbed or psychotic clients. Therapeutic activity should be limited to procedures that strengthen clients' contact with reality, their self-confidence, and their trust in the counselor and the counseling process. With trust established between the counselor and the client, Gestalt counseling can be directed toward working with the painful, unfinished business of past and current conflicts.

Greenberg (1989) echoes similar concerns about using traditional Gestalt therapy with people who have borderline personality disorder. He recommends interactive group therapy over talking to a dead parent in an empty chair and hot-seat confrontations. Therefore, the question of who should receive Gestalt therapy is as important as the skills, training, experience, and judgment of the therapist. A counselor who uses this approach must be neither afraid nor inept in allowing the client to follow through and finish the experience of grief, rage, fear, or joy. Without such skill, the counselor may leave the client vulnerable.

Another issue hinges on the questions of when, with whom, and in what situations Gestalt therapy should be used. In general, Gestalt therapy is most effective with overly socialized, restrained, constricted individuals. Less organized, more severely disturbed clients may require longer-term counseling. Limiting activities at first to those that strengthen a client's contact with reality is preferable to role-playing situations further removed from the here and now. Individuals whose problems lie in lack of impulse control, acting out, and delinquency require a different approach. For these people, Gestalt therapy could reinforce the activities that are causing the problems.

Misconceptions surround the use of Gestalt methods for quick and exciting results, whereas Gestalt therapy was developed as a lengthy, time-consuming process. Effective practitioners of Gestalt therapy use small steps to help clients heighten their own awareness. Too much awareness too soon can have an adverse effect on clients. Clients cannot be expected to drop elaborate defenses and "walk without these crutches" after just a few sessions. Living without defenses requires considerable rehearsal and practice within the therapy session.

Laura Perls (1992) has discussed her concerns about the misconceptions surrounding Gestalt therapy. She notes that many therapists who had attended Fritz's workshops began to attach Gestalt therapy to whatever they happened to be working on at the time. People began holding workshops on such topics as sensitivity training and transcendental meditation with Gestalt therapy. Laura Perls notes that Gestalt therapy has been useful in working with a variety of subject areas and client treatment programs; however, she points out that Fritz Perls realized that Gestalt methods were not effective in working with every type of disorder and would not work with people who had paranoid or schizoid disturbances.

Laura Perls has discussed other misconceptions about Gestalt therapy. Contrary to popular belief, Gestalt therapy is not limited to treating the here-and-now aspects of the client's life. The focus of Gestalt therapy is on the here-and-now present occurring within the therapy session; however, a person's past and present life outside therapy also is valued by Gestalt therapists. Fritz Perls believed that the past is very real in defining our life experiences and memories. Laura Perls also reminds her readers that Fritz Perls thought that tension was too valuable to waste. Tension is an indicator that something in a person's life is not working or that some unfinished business needs attention. Yet, many therapists use Gestalt methods to rid their clients of tension. Tension, as a resource, can provide the motivation and energy to make adjustments and changes in one's life.

Perls appears to have done well in his attempt to establish the philosophy and practice of Gestalt therapy. The approach is well grounded in and consistent with the principles of human behavior. By removing the mystique of professional jargon, he made Gestalt therapy comprehensible to the general public. Many counselors, although choosing not to become true believers or disciples of Gestalt therapy, use many of the procedures reported in the Gestalt literature. Most notable among these techniques are the two-chair dialogue, visualization, fantasy, and projection.

Introduction to Gestalt Therapy Video

To gain a more in-depth understanding of the concepts in this chapter, visit www.thomsonedu.com/counseling/thompson to view a short clip of an actual therapist-client session demonstrating Gestalt therapy.

Websites for Gestalt Therapy

Internet addresses frequently change. To find the sites listed here, visit www.thomsonedu.com/counseling/thompson for an updated list of Internet addresses and direct links to relevant sites.

A Life Chronology of Fritz Perls

American Association of Gestalt Therapy (AAGT)

Behavior OnLine: An Introduction to Gestalt Therapy

Gestalt Theory: Society for Gestalt Theory and Its Applications (GTA)

The Gestalt Therapy Page

References

Alexander, J., & Harman, L. (1988). One counselor's intervention in the aftermath of middle school student's suicide: A case study. *Journal of Counseling and Development, 66,* 283–285.

Anderson, C. (2000). Dealing constructively with managed care: Suggestions from an insider. *Journal of Mental Health Counseling, 22,* 343–353.

Assagioli, R. (1965). *Psychosynthesis.* New York: Viking.

Baumgardner, P., & Perls, F. (1975). *Gifts from Lake Cowichan and legacy from Fritz.* Palo Alto, CA: Science and Behavior Books.

Bingham, R. P., Porche-Burke, L., James, S., Sue, D. W., & Vasquez, M. J. T. (2002). Introduction: A report on the National Multicultural Conference and Summit II [Electronic version]. *Cultural Diversity and Ethnic Minority Psychology, 8,* 75–87.

Burley, T., & Freier, M. (2004). Character structure: A gestalt-cognitive theory. *Psychotherapy: Theory, Research, Practice, Training, 41,* 321–331.

Campbell, C. A. (1993). Interview with Violet Oaklander, author of *Windows to Our Children. Elementary School Guidance and Counseling, 28,* 52–61.

Carroll, F., & Oaklander, V. (1997). Gestalt play therapy. In K. O'Connor & L. M. Braverman (Eds.), *Play therapy theory and practice: A comparative presentation* (pp. 184–203). New York: Wiley.

Dolliver, R. (1991). Perls with Gloria re-reviewed: Gestalt techniques and Perls's practices. *Journal of Counseling and Development, 69,* 299–304.

Engle, D., & Holliman, M. (2002). A Gestalt-experiential perspective on resistance. *Journal of Clinical Psychology, 58,* 175–183.

English, H., & English, A. (1958). *A comprehensive dictionary of psychological terms.* New York: Longmans, Green.

Greenberg, E. (1989). Healing the borderline. *Gestalt Journal, 12,* 11–55.

Greenberg, L. S., & Malcolm, W. (2003). Resolving unfinished business: Relating process to outcome. *Journal of Consulting and Clinical Psychology, 70,* 406–416.

Harman, R. (1996). Is there a future for the here and now? *Journal of Gestalt, 19,* 101–108.

Heikkinen, C. (1989). Reorientation from altered states: Please, more carefully. *Journal of Counseling and Development, 67,* 520–521.

Houston, G. (2003). *Brief Gestalt therapy.* Thousand Oaks, CA: Sage.

Kellogg, S. (2004). Dialogical encounters: contemporary perspectives on "chairwork" in psychotherapy. *Psychotherapy: Theory, Research, Practice, Training, 41,* 310–320.

Miller, M. (1989). Introduction to Gestalt therapy verbatim. *Gestalt Journal, 7,* 5–24.

Oaklander, V. (1978). *Windows to our children.* Moab, UT: Real People Press.

Oaklander, V. (1988). *Windows to our children: A Gestalt therapy approach to children and adolescents.* Highland, NY: Center for Gestalt Development.

Oaklander, V. (1993). From meek to bold: A case study of Gestalt therapy. In T. Kottman & C. Schaefer (Eds.), *Play therapy in action: A casebook for practitioners* (pp. 281–300). Northvale, NJ: Aronson.

Paivio, S., & Greenberg, L. (1995). Resolving "unfinished business": Efficacy of experimental therapy using empty chair dialogue. *Journal of Consulting and Clinical Psychology, 63,* 419–425.

Perls, F. (1969a). *Ego, hunger, and aggression: The beginnings of Gestalt therapy.* New York: Vintage.

Perls, F. (1969b). *Gestalt therapy verbatim.* Moab, UT: Real People Press.

Perls, F. (1971). *In and out the garbage pail.* New York: Bantam.

Perls, F. (1973). *The Gestalt approach and eye witness to therapy.* New York: Bantam.

Perls, F. (1975). *Gestalt is: A collection of articles about Gestalt therapy and living.* Moab, UT: Real People Press.

Perls, F., Hefferline, R., & Goodman, P. (1951). *Gestalt therapy: Excitement and growth in the human personality.* New York: Julian Press.

Perls, L. (1992). Concepts and misconceptions of Gestalt therapy. *Journal of Humanistic Psychology, 32,* 50–56.

Saner, R. (1989). Culture bias of gestalt therapy: Made-in-U.S.A. *Gestalt Journal, 12,* 57–71.

Shepard, M. (1975). *Fritz.* New York: Saturday Review Press.

Shostrom, E. (Producer). (1965). *Three approaches to psychotherapy* [Film]. Orange, CA: Psychological Films.

Wagner-Moore, L. (2004). Gestalt therapy: Past, present, theory, and research. *Psychotherapy: Theory Research, Practice, Training, 41,* 180–189.

Wheeler, G., & McConville, M. (2002). *The heart of development: Gestalt approaches to working with children, adolescents, and their worlds.* Hillsdale, NJ: Gestalt Press.

RATIONAL-EMOTIVE-BEHAVIORAL THERAPY AND COGNITIVE-BEHAVIORAL THERAPY

Our civilization is still in a middle stage, no longer wholly guided by instinct, not yet wholly guided by reason.

—Theodore Dreiser

Nothing is so terrible as activity without thought.

—Johann Wolfgang von Goethe

We do not see things as they are; we see things as we are.

—The Talmud

Albert Ellis (b. 1913) is currently president of the Institute for Advanced Study in Rational Psychotherapy in New York, a community agency chartered by the regents of the State University of New York. He is widely known as the founder or developer of rational-emotive therapy, which he has renamed rational-emotive-behavioral therapy (REBT) (A. Ellis, personal communication, 1994).

Since the 1950s, Ellis has given individualized remedial instruction—what he calls *emotional education*—to several thousand adults, adolescents, and children. In addition, he has conducted group therapy with more than 3000 adults and adolescents.

Ellis was born in Pittsburgh in 1913 and grew up in New York City. Despite a difficult childhood, he earned a degree in Business Administration from the City University of New York in 1934. During the Depression, he earned his living first by working with his brother in a business that located matching pants for still-usable suit coats, then as the personnel manager in a gift and novelty firm.

Albert Ellis

Ellis's ambition was to write, which he did in his spare time. He collected material for two books on sexual adjustment that were eventually published, *The American Sexual Tragedy* (1954) and *The Case for Sexual Liberty* (1965). His friends began to regard him as an expert on the subject and often asked his advice. He discovered he enjoyed counseling people as much as writing and decided to return to school. In 1942, Ellis entered the clinical psychology program at Columbia University; in 1947, he was awarded his doctorate.

Ellis's early professional work as a therapist in state institutions in New Jersey applied classical psychoanalytic methods, but he has since set psychoanalysis aside completely. His change in philosophy came about when he discovered that clients treated once a week or even every other week progressed as well as those he treated daily. Ellis found that a more active role, interjecting advice and direct interpretation, yielded faster results than passive psychoanalytic procedures. His own theory of counseling, however, did not emerge until after he had received his doctorate from Columbia and later received training as a traditional psychoanalytic therapist. Consequently, some of the origins of REBT can be traced to Freud and others to disillusionment with Freudian psychoanalysis.

After discovering that rationalist philosophy fit his temperament and taste, Ellis began concentrating on changing people's behavior by confronting them with their irrational beliefs and persuading them to adopt more rational ones. He now considers himself a philosophical or educational therapist and sees REBT as uniquely didactic, cognition oriented, and explicative. He believes that REBT places people at the center of the universe and gives them almost full responsibility for their fate.

More than 400 books and articles, in addition to his Institute for Rational Living, have proceeded from Ellis's conceptualization of REBT. From its early days to the present, he has modified REBT. Writing in 1977, Ellis noted that REBT, once a limited rational-persuasive therapy, had grown into a therapy that consciously used cognitive, emotive, and behavioral techniques to help clients (Ellis, 1977). In 1957, he published his first REBT book, *How to Live with a "Neurotic"* (1957/1975), and in 1960, his first successful book, *The Art and Science of Love* (1960/1969) was published. Other books by Ellis include *Reason and Emotion in Psychotherapy* (1994), *Better, Deeper, and More Enduring Brief Therapy* (1996), *The Practice of Rational Emotive Behavior Therapy* (1996) (with W. Dryden), *Rational Emotive Behavior Therapy: A Therapist Guide* (1998) (with C. MacLaren), and *Overcoming Destructive Beliefs, Feelings, and Behaviors* (2001b).

THE NATURE OF PEOPLE

Ellis based REBT on the philosophy of Epictetus (ca. A.D. 55–135): "What disturbs men's minds is not events, but their judgment of events." Generally speaking, very young children have limited emotional repertoires and tend to express emotions in a quick, unsustained manner. When children grow old enough to use language effectively, they acquire the ability to sustain their emotions and possibly keep themselves emotionally upset. Rather than concentrating on past events, REBT practitioners emphasize present events and how we react to them. The theory of REBT stresses that, as human beings, we have choices. We control our ideas, attitudes, feelings, and actions, and we arrange

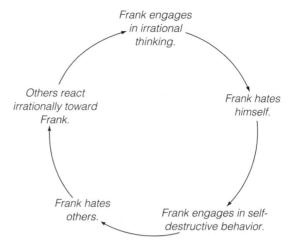

FIGURE 8-1 | THE CIRCLE OF IRRATIONAL THINKING

our lives according to our own dictates. We have little control over what happens or what actually exists, but we do have both choices and control over how we view the world and how we react to difficulties, regardless of how we have been taught to respond.

People are neither good nor bad, according to REBT theory, if they respond to others with a rational belief system. If individuals react with irrational beliefs, however, they view themselves and others as evil, awful, and horrible whenever they or others fall short of their expectations. Ellis (1987, 1997) views people as naturally irrational, self-defeating individuals who need to be taught to be otherwise. They think crookedly about their desires and preferences and escalate them in a self-defeating manner into musts, shoulds, oughts, and demands. In assimilating these irrational beliefs, people become emotionally disturbed and feel anger, anxiety, depression, worthlessness, self-pity, and other negative feelings that lead to destructive behavior. However, Ellis also states that people can be "naturally" helpful and loving *as long as they do not think irrationally.* In other words, Ellis describes a circular process, as depicted in Figure 8-1. Irrational thinking leads to self-hate, which leads to self-destructive behavior, and eventually to hatred of others, which, in turn, causes others to act irrationally toward the individual, thus beginning the cycle again.

In the early years of the development of civilization, our very survival undoubtedly depended on our ability to face the environment, always expecting and preparing for the worst to happen. Although it was a good way to survive, it was not a happy way to live. We may carry on this pessimistic way of life inherited from the Stone Age when we tend to "catastrophize" the events that happen to us as a defense against being unprepared or caught off guard when the next "disaster" strikes. However, Ellis believes that we do have the potential to think rationally if we can master the ABCDE steps of REBT.

Ellis (2001b) writes that some of our irrational thoughts are biological in origin, but the majority stem from our upbringing (parents, teachers, and clergy). Ellis has described three areas in which people hold irrational beliefs: They must be perfect, others must be perfect, and the world must be a perfect place to live. The following examples summarize what people tell themselves when they interpret events with an irrational belief system. A more rational replacement thought follows each irrational self-message.

1. Because it would be highly preferable if I were outstandingly competent, I absolutely should and must be; it is awful when I am not, and I am therefore a worthless individual. *Alternative:* It would be nice if I were outstanding in whatever I do, but if I am not, it is okay, and I will try my best anyway.
2. Because it is highly desirable that others treat me considerately and fairly, they absolutely should and must, and they are rotten people who deserve to be utterly damned when they do not. *Alternative:* I would prefer people to treat me considerately. However, I realize they will not always, so I will not take it personally when they do not, *and* I will make it my business to be considerate.
3. Because it is preferable that I experience pleasure rather than pain, the world should absolutely arrange this outcome, and life is horrible and I can't bear it when the world doesn't. *Alternative:* I realize that in life there are both pleasurable moments and painful moments. Therefore, I will try to make the painful moments positive learning experiences so I can endure trials and even benefit from them.

THEORY OF COUNSELING

Ellis (1998) postulated a system of inherently irrational beliefs or philosophies common to our culture that are conducive to maladjustment. When interpreting daily events with one or more irrational philosophies, the individual is likely to feel angry or hostile toward others or to internalize these feelings, with resulting anxiety, guilt, or depression. In essence, REBT theory holds that people are primarily responsible for their feelings about themselves, others, and the environment, and whether they want to be perpetually disturbed by them.

In their *Guide to Rational Living*, Ellis and Harper (1975) write that, because humans naturally and easily think crookedly, express emotions inappropriately, and behave in a self-defeating manner, it seems best to use all possible educational modes dramatically, strongly, and persistently to teach them how to do otherwise. Ellis and Harper compiled the following list of irrational beliefs that cause people trouble:

1. It is a dire necessity for people to be loved or approved by almost everyone for virtually everything they do.
2. One should be thoroughly competent, adequate, and achieving in all possible respects.

3. Certain people are bad, wicked, or villainous, and they should be severely blamed and punished for their sins.
4. It is terrible, horrible, and catastrophic when things are not going the way one would like them to go.
5. Human unhappiness is externally caused, and people have little or no ability to control their sorrows or rid themselves of their negative feelings.
6. If something is or may be dangerous or fearsome, one should be terribly occupied with and upset about it.
7. It is easier to avoid facing many life difficulties and self-responsibilities than to undertake more rewarding forms of self-discipline.
8. The past is all-important, and because something once strongly affected one's life, it should do so indefinitely.
9. People and things should be different from the way they are, and it is catastrophic if perfect solutions to the grim realities of life are not immediately found.
10. Maximum human happiness can be achieved by inertia and inaction or by passively and noncommittally enjoying oneself.
11. My child is delinquent (or emotionally disturbed or mentally retarded); therefore, I'm a failure as a parent.
12. My child is emotionally disturbed (or mentally retarded); therefore, he or she is severely handicapped and will never amount to anything.
13. I cannot give my children everything they want; therefore, I am inadequate.

Consequences resulting from irrational or "stinking thinking" can be quite costly in the stress added to one's life. These include:

- Work or career-related problems
- Relationship problems
- Low self-esteem
- Depression over not getting what one wants
- Anxiety from irrational fears
- Overreacting to daily inconveniences
- Negative addictions to overeating, drugs, and other useless behaviors
- Physical illness

Crawford and Ellis (1989) provide further information on irrational beliefs and their consequences in their dictionary of thirty-six self-defeating feelings, accompanied by their corresponding rational and irrational beliefs. In the listing, the rational beliefs appear first and often are followed by sequential irrational beliefs to form a chain of irrational beliefs. Crawford and Ellis classify each irrational belief into one of five categories: (1) *self-defeating* beliefs that interfere with basic goals and drives, (2) highly rigid and *dogmatic* beliefs that lead to unrealistic preferences and wishes, (3) *antisocial* beliefs that cause people to destroy their social groups, (4) *unrealistic* beliefs that falsely describe reality, and (5) *contradictory* beliefs that originate from false premises.

In his article "What Rational-Emotive Therapy Is and Is Not," Ellis (1974) makes the following points:

1. Anxiety is not "irrational," but an inappropriate feeling that stems largely from irrational ideas. Feelings should not be confused with ideas.
2. Clients have almost full or complete responsibility for their ideas, and consequently for their feelings.
3. Clients mainly—not early environment or conditioning or contemporary conditions—choose to create their irrational ideas and consequent feelings. They can choose to change their ideas.
4. Do not blame, damn, denigrate, or condemn people for choosing irrational ideas, inappropriate feelings, or defeating behaviors.
5. Discourage absolutes, such as *must, should, always, never,* and *ought,* in clients' thinking. There are no absolutes (pun intended).
6. Therapists definitely do not determine whether clients' ideas or behaviors are rational or irrational.

Waters (1982; V. Waters, personal communication, 1998) examined differences among the irrational beliefs of children, adolescents, and parents. Although she found some similarities among the three age-groups, she also found some beliefs more prevalent in one group or another. The biggest commonality among groups is the resulting self-defeating emotions stimulated by the irrational beliefs leading to depression, anxiety, anger, and guilt. Gonzalez, Nelson, Gutkin, Saunders, Galloway, & Shwery (2004) point out that REBT has been an effective treatment for a variety of problems presented by children and adolescents. However, they did find children more responsive to REBT than adolescents.

COMMON IRRATIONAL BELIEFS OF CHILDREN

1. It is awful if others don't like me.
2. I am bad if I make a mistake.
3. Everything should go my way; I should always get what I want.
4. Things should come easily to me.
5. The world should be fair, and bad people should be punished.
6. I should not show my feelings.
7. Adults should be perfect.
8. There's only one right answer.
9. I must win; it's awful to lose.
10. I should not have to wait for anything.

COMMON IRRATIONAL BELIEFS OF ADOLESCENTS

1. It would be awful if other kids did not like me, and if I were a loser.
2. I should not make mistakes, especially social mistakes.
3. It's my parents' fault that I'm so miserable.
4. I cannot help being the way I am. I'll always have to be this way.
5. The world should be fair and just.
6. It is awful when things do not go my way.
7. It's better to avoid challenges than to risk being a failure.

8. I must conform to my peers.
9. I cannot stand being criticized.
10. Others should always be responsible.

COMMON IRRATIONAL BELIEFS OF PARENTS

1. It would be awful if my children did not like me.
2. I cannot stand it if others criticize my parenting.
3. I'm totally responsible for everything my children do, and if they behave obnoxiously, I must feel awful.
4. I must be a perfect parent and always know the right thing to do in every situation.
5. My children should always do what I want them to.
6. If my child has a problem, then I have to feel terrible too.
7. Children should not disagree with their parents.
8. My children make me angry, depressed, and anxious.
9. If my children do not turn out the way I think they should, then I am a failure.
10. Parenting should be fun all the time.

Ellis (1998) recommends that people would do better to resist the tendency to rate themselves in favor of limiting themselves to rating only their deeds, traits, acts, characteristics, and performances. Therefore, if a student earned a bad grade on a math test, it would be acceptable to say, "I did poorly on the test," but *not* to say, "I am a stupid person." Ellis favors rating the effectiveness of how people think, feel, and behave. He also supports rating our progress toward goals we have set. Global, all-over ratings of the "self" or "ego" almost always create self-defeating, neurotic thoughts, feelings, and behaviors.

Ellis quarrels with the practice followed by the majority of psychotherapy systems that appear directed toward strengthening people's self-esteem. He took issue with Rogers's practice of trying to increase clients' self-esteem by providing them with vast amounts of unconditional positive regard. Ellis points out that self-acceptance would still be conditional on the therapists' uncritical acceptance of their clients. Ellis believes that we are more than our behavior and performances, and to rate ourselves bad because we had a bad performance would lead to an unhappy life. Ellis's goal for the people of the world is what he termed unconditional self-acceptance—that is, we are worthwhile individuals regardless of how we did on the last test or in the last game. Unconditional self-acceptance works better when it includes what Ellis called unconditional other acceptance, or acceptance of others. Ellis's (1998, 2004) view of healthy personalities is one that accepts others *and* ourselves with our virtues and our failings, with our important accomplishments and our nonachievements, simply because we are alive and because we are human.

The goal of REBT is to teach people to think and behave in a more personally satisfying way by making them realize they have a choice between self-defeating, negative behavior and efficient, enhancing, positive behavior. It teaches people to take responsibility for their own logical thinking and the consequences or behaviors that follow it.

COUNSELING METHOD

In the past, counselors concentrated on either the developmental events in one's life or one's feelings about these events. Ellis does not believe these two main methods to be totally erroneous, but he did not find either approach effective. Neither approach explained why some people are rather well adjusted (that is, not too unhappy too much of the time, regardless of the passage of events) and others are emotionally dysfunctional much of the time with the same passage of events.

Ellis hypothesizes that individuals' belief systems predicate their responses or feelings toward the same events. These individual belief systems are what people tell themselves about an event, particularly an unfortunate incident. For example, 100 people may be rejected by their true loves. One of these people may respond, "I can't go on; I've lost my purpose in life. Because I've been rejected by such a wonderful person, I must really be a worthless slob. My only solution for getting rid of the unbearable pain I feel is to kill myself." Another person may respond, "What a pain in the neck! I had dinner reservations and tickets for the show. Now I have to get another date for Saturday night. This surely sets me back. What an inconvenience!" Between these two extreme reactions are several other degrees of bad feelings growing from the various self-messages of the 100 rejected people. Such a wide variety of reactions to the same basic event suggests that one's view of the event and consequent self-message provide the key to the counseling strategy. The same process happens to children who experience bad feelings from school failure, peer conflicts, conflicts with adults, or rejection.

Thebarge (1989), in differentiating REBT from behavior modification, systematic desensitization, and traditional psychoanalysis, points out that REBT practitioners treat underlying causes (irrational beliefs) of symptoms and not the symptoms themselves. Therefore, successful REBT generates none of the symptom substitution that may occur when treatment focuses only on symptoms. Behavior modification and systematic desensitization are two therapies that are directed toward symptom removal.

DiGiuseppe (1990) has detailed a method for using inference chaining as a technique for helping children re-evaluate their automatic irrational beliefs. Children were asked to imagine or think about what would happen next if the automatic thought (for example, "I am stupid") were true and what it would mean to them. DiGiuseppe also recommends deductive interpretation with children. In this method, the counselor and the child form and test hypotheses concerning the irrational belief. Both methods allow self-discovery by the child.

The main goal of REBT is to increase happiness and decrease pain. REBT has two main objectives to achieve a prevailing happier state. The first is to show the emotionally disturbed client how irrational beliefs or attitudes create dysfunctional consequences. These consequences might include anger, depression, or anxiety. The second objective is directively and intellectually teaching clients how to dispute or crumble their irrational beliefs and replace them with rational beliefs. Once counselors lead the clients to dispute the irrational ideas, they guide them into adopting new expectations for themselves, others, and the environment. Ellis reasons that if the irrational, absolute philosophies and resultant feelings are replaced with more rational, productive thoughts, clients will no longer be trapped in a repetitious cycle of negative feelings. When children are no longer incapacitated by dysfunctional feelings, they are free to choose behaviors that eliminate the problem or at least lessen its disappointing impact.

REBT is often referred to as the "A, B, C, D, and E" approach to counseling. A, B, and C show how problems develop; D and E are the treatment steps:

A is the activating event: "I failed my math test."

B is how you evaluate the event: (1) irrational message: "I failed the test; therefore, I'm a total failure as a person; (2) rational message: "I failed the test. This is unpleasant and inconvenient, but that is all it is. I need to study more efficiently for the next exam."

C represents the consequences or feelings resulting from your self-message at the B stage. The irrational message (B1 stage) will cause you to feel very depressed. The rational message (B2 stage) will not make you feel great, but it will not be so overwhelming as to inhibit your performance on the next test.

D represents the disputing arguments you use to attack the irrational self-messages expressed in the B1 stage. The counselor's function is to help you question these irrational self-messages once they have been identified.

E represents the answers you have developed to the questions regarding the rationality of your B1 stage self-messages.

For example, counseling would proceed through the following steps:

A—Something unpleasant happens to you.

B—You evaluate the event as something awful, something that should not be allowed to happen.

C—You become upset and nervous.

D—You question your B self-message:

1. Why is it awful?
2. Why shouldn't it be allowed to happen?

E—You answer:

1. It is a disappointment.
2. It is a setback but not a disaster.
3. I can handle it.
4. I would like things to be better, but that doesn't mean I'm always supposed to get things done my way.

Ellis (1972) provides another example of REBT in action in "Emotional Education in the Classroom." A student named Robert is so anxious about reciting in class, even though he knows the material, that he anticipates the event (A) and already feels the blocking and nervousness (C) just by anticipating the event (A). At point B2, he tells himself, "It would be unfortunate if I did not recite well because the other children might think I did not know my lesson. They might even think I am a dummy, and I would not want that." At B1, however, Robert usually adds another statement to his rational message: "It would be awful if I failed. No one would like me, and I would be a bum." The great anxiety felt at C caused by the B1 message would sabotage Robert's efforts to recite in class the next time the teacher called on him.

REBT is direct, didactic, confrontational, and verbally active counseling. Initially, the counselor seeks to detect the irrational beliefs that are creating the disturbance. Seven factors help to detect irrational thinking and galloping inferentialism:

1. Look for *overgeneralizations:* "I made an F on the first math test; therefore, I always will do poorly on math tests."
2. Look for *distortions*: sometimes referred to as all-or-nothing thinking or black-and-white categorizing of things as all good or all bad. "I did not make all As on my report card; therefore, I will never be a good student."
3. Look for *deletions:* the tendency to focus on negative events or disqualifying positive events. "I struck out two times and got one hit; therefore, I will probably strike out the next time I bat."
4. Look for *catastrophizing*: mistakes are exaggerated, and achievements are minimized. "I was just lucky to get that A on my last test."
5. Look for the use of absolutes such as *should, must, always, ought,* and *never*: "I should not make mistakes."
6. Look for statements *condemning* something or someone clients think they cannot stand: "He should be punished and should not be allowed to get away with that!"
7. Look for *fortune-telling* or future predictions: "I just know my friends will not have fun at my party."

Once the irrational beliefs are recognized, the counselor disputes and challenges them. Ultimately, the goal is for children and adolescents to recognize irrational beliefs, think them through, and relinquish them. As a result of this process and therapy, clients, it is hoped, reach three insights. First, the present neurotic behavior has antecedent causes. Second, original beliefs keep upsetting them because they keep repeating these beliefs. Third, they can overcome emotional disturbances by consistently observing, questioning, and challenging their own belief systems.

People hold tenaciously to their beliefs, rational or not; consequently, the counselor vigorously attacks the irrational beliefs in an attempt to show the children how illogically they think. Using the Socratic method of questioning and disputing, the counselor takes a verbally active part in the early stages of counseling by identifying and explaining the child's problem. If counselors guess correctly, which often happens, they argue with and persuade the child to give up the old irrational view and replace it with a new, rational philosophy.

Waters (1980, 1982; V. Waters, personal communication, 1998) writes on how to help children build tease tolerance that works for children who do not handle teasing well. She recommends that counselors begin by teaching children there are two types of responses to being teased. One is what they *think* and *feel,* and the other is how they *behave.* Children are told they are in control of both things. Counseling is focused on these two points. First, children are taught that they can change what they tell themselves about being teased, and that will change how they feel about it. Second, when they feel less bad about being teased, they will be able to do things that will help them handle the teasing better. In other words, the immediate goal is to move from being angry, depressed, or anxious to irritated, displeased, or concerned. Children are taught that to continue with "stinking thinking" will result in more bad feelings and responses that encourage the teaser to keep on teasing. Also, the teaser will get the payoff he or she is after—that is, causing the child to feel angry or depressed. Waters (1982; V. Waters, personal communication, 1998) points out how irrational beliefs or stinking thinking exacerbates the resulting emotions of anger, depression, and anxiety.

ANGER

"I can't stand to be teased!"

"He shouldn't tease me."

"It's absolutely awful if others tease me."

"She should be punished for teasing me."

DEPRESSION

"If others tease me, I must be a total loser."

ANXIETY

"I'll always be teased forever, and I can't stand it."

Next, the irrational or stinking thinking responses are disputed or challenged and then answered with more rational responses.

ANGER

"How does Jim's teasing make your life terrible?"

"What do you think Jim wants you to do when he teases you?"

Answer: "Well, I don't like it when Jim teases me, but that does not have to ruin my life. I need to figure out a way to stop the payoff he gets from teasing me."

DEPRESSION

"How does Sally's teasing you make you totally worthless?"

Answer: "Well, it does make me feel sad when someone wants to make me feel that way, but that does not mean I am totally worthless. It just means that for the present, I don't have Sally's goodwill and that is just a minor pain, because I like myself. I do want to work on ignoring Sally's teasing."

ANXIETY

"How does teasing by those two girls mean you will always be teased?"

Answer: "Well, I guess their teasing doesn't mean that I will always be teased. But I still don't like it, and I want to find out how to make teasing me no fun for them."

To the usual psychotherapeutic techniques of exploration, ventilation, excoriation, and interpretation, REBT therapists add techniques of confrontation, indoctrination, and re-education. Counselors are didactic in that they explain how children's beliefs (which intervene between an event and the resultant feelings), rather than events themselves, cause emotional disturbances. Because the counselor honestly believes that children and adolescents do not understand the reason for their disturbance, the counselor enlightens and teaches. Counselors frequently assign homework—reading, performing specific tasks, and taking risks—for the child as an integral part of therapy.

There is little transference in REBT. Contrary to classical psychoanalysis, the counselor serves as a model of rational thinking and behavior and urges children to resolve problems with significant people in their lives. In addition, the counselor sometimes uses conventional methods, such as active listening, with the end result that the child's irrational thinking—which has led to irrational behavior—is destroyed, and a saner belief system replaces it.

REBT counselors believe that the development of a person's belief system (which is defined as the meaning of facts) is analogous to the acquisition of speech. Just as children learn language by imitation and modeling, they learn a belief system. Therefore, the belief system and attitudes children acquire are largely a reflection of the significant people in their lives. Furthermore, the belief systems incorporated into children's minds determine whether they think rationally about facts. Continuing the analogy, just as one continues to build one's vocabulary and modify one's speech, one also can change or replace one's belief system.

For children, REBT is modified because its style depends so much on verbal and abstract conceptualization skills. Working on the premise that people feel the way they think, the therapist attempts to change overt behavior by altering internal verbalization. A major disadvantage in using REBT with children is that children do not generalize well from one situation to another; that is, the improved behavior is limited to the specific circumstances. Furthermore, Piaget's research indicates that children in the preformal stages of cognitive development (see Chapter 1) might have difficulty relating to the REBT counseling method.

Role reversal is an effective technique with children. In this technique, the child describes the activating event and the emotional consequences. Next, the counselor explains that thoughts are upsetting the child. Then, they role-play the activating event, with the counselor playing the child. While acting out the event, the counselor demonstrates the appropriate behavior while uttering rational self-statements aloud. The roles are reversed again, with the child trying new thoughts and being rewarded, preferably with social approval, as reinforcement for rational statements and behaviors. The child may need successive approximations of the appropriate REBT behaviors reinforced before the concept is learned. Adolescents with abstract reasoning ability and an understanding of cause and effect may be more comfortable with REBT.

RATIONAL-EMOTIVE-BEHAVIORAL EDUCATION

An offspring of REBT is rational-emotive-behavioral education (REBE). Its objectives are to teach how feelings develop, how to discriminate between valid and invalid assumptions, and how to think rationally in "antiawful" and "antiperfectionist" ways.

REBE programs have been effective in reinforcing rational verbal expressions with disturbed children. Children become more rational not only in their verbal expressions and belief systems but also in their behaviors. Following are examples of beliefs that can be reinforced by writing statements:

I don't like school, but I can stand it.

I did something bad, but I'm not a bad person.

I don't like being called insulting names, but being insulted is not awful.

Just because someone calls you "stupid" does not mean you are.

Ellis claims that all children act neurotically simply because they are children. He states that childish behavior cannot be differentiated from neurosis until the age of 5. At this point, many children have integrated into their belief system the irrational belief that one should be thoroughly competent, adequate, and achieving in all possible respects to be considered worthwhile. Strategies for undermining this philosophy in children can be summarized as follows:

1. Teach children the joy of engaging in games that are worthwhile because they are fun. De-emphasize the importance of winning at all costs by teaching children that you do not have to win to have fun and be a worthwhile person.
2. Teach children that significant achievements rarely come easily and that nothing is wrong with working long and hard to achieve their goals.
3. Teach children that they are not bad people when they do not meet their goals. Children must like themselves during periods of failure, even when they may not be trying their best to achieve their goals. Children also need to learn the difference between wants and needs. Wanting something we cannot get is not the same as not getting what we absolutely need.
4. Teach children that, although striving for perfectionism in performance is good, perfection is not required to be a worthwhile person. Making mistakes is not only allowed but also is a good way to learn why certain things happen and how to prevent them from happening again.

5. Teach children that popularity and achievement are not necessarily related, that to be liked by all people at all times is difficult, and that being a worthwhile person does not require 100 percent popularity.

6. In summary, teach children not to take themselves and situations too seriously by turning minor setbacks into catastrophes. Balance corrective feedback with positive reinforcement in evaluating children's performances.

COGNITIVE-BEHAVIORAL THERAPY

The movement toward integrative approaches to counseling is documented in the literature. These integrative approaches often involve the combination of two or more standard approaches into one treatment modality. We suggest that this has been happening in practice since the beginning of the counseling movement, and only now are some theorists willing to admit that they have been integrative all along. One such integrative combination is represented by the unification of cognitive and behavioral approaches into cognitive-behavioral therapy (CBT). The practice of CBT combines behavior-change methods with thought-restructuring methods to produce behavior and feeling change in clients. Such a marriage between two approaches results from deficiency in one or both of the methods in bringing about the desired counseling outcomes. The terms *cognitive restructuring, cognitive behavior modification,* and *stress inoculation* all represent current descriptions of Ellis's original work and some related work by Beck (1976), Maultsby (1984), and Meichenbaum (1977, 1985). These techniques combine various cognitive and behavioral approaches (Bernard, 1990).

Stress-inoculation methods combined with role-playing provide an example of a cognitive-behavioral technique. In cases of test anxiety, the client might be asked to practice the following examples of self-talk: (1) "Tests are no fun, but all I want is to do the best I can." (2) "Though it would be nice to make an A, it is not required for me to be a good and worthwhile person." (3) "All I need to do is prepare for the test and do the best I am able to do. If I fail, it will be inconvenient and no fun at all, but that is all it will be. For the moment, I just will not be getting what I want." Combining the self-talk with taking practice tests and visualization practice of the steps in the client's test-taking stimulus hierarchy (systematic desensitization) represents a typical CBT treatment plan.

Other stress-inoculation techniques include relaxation training, deep-breathing exercises, and reframing exercises that help children replace their anxiety with relaxation. Such reframing exercises help children perceive anxiety-provoking situations in a less threatening light. Rather than having the child focus on school as a place of potential failure and frightening teachers, for example, the counselor teaches the child to focus on the friends and fun available at school.

Stress-inoculation training programs, such as those designed by Meichenbaum (1977, 1985), have four categories of self-talk designed to help people master difficult and highly stressful situations and events. There categories are:

1. *Preparation for a stressor:* "What is it you have to do? You can develop a plan to deal with it. Don't worry."
2. *Confrontation and management of a stressor:* "One step at a time; you can handle the situation. Relax, you are in control. Take a slow, deep breath."
3. *Coping:* "Don't try to eliminate fear totally; just keep it manageable. Keep the focus on the present; what is it you have to do?"
4. *Reinforcing self-statements:* "It worked; you did it. It wasn't as bad as you expected. It's getting better each time."

CBT treatment programs for such things as childhood depressive disorders are often quite elaborate. CBT models often consist of four levels of treatment: (1) behavioral procedures, such as contingent reinforcement, shaping, prompting, and modeling, to increase social interaction; (2) CBT interventions, which include pairing successful task completion with positive self-statements and reinforcement for those self-statements; (3) cognitive interventions, which are used with social-skills training, role-playing, and self-management; and (4) self-control procedures, such as self-evaluation and self-reinforcement.

McGinn and Sanderson (2001) make the case that CBT belongs to the family of brief therapies. CBT sessions are formatted in a fashion similar to the time-efficient methods of solution-focused brief counseling, reality therapy, and behavioral counseling. CBT sessions follow a four-step process:

1. Review progress to bring counselor and client up to date on how much has been accomplished toward meeting the client's goals. Homework assignments are checked for completion. We like to use a four-quadrant structure that asks clients to review their past 7 days by listing high points in Quadrant 1, low points in Quadrant 2, how the week could have been better in Quadrant 3, and plans for next week in Quadrant 4.
2. Set the agenda for the current session based on the information gleaned from the high points/low points survey. For example, high points occur most often when plans are made in advance. Low points can often be avoided with similar planning.
3. Complete the current session by clarifying and setting specific behavioral goals for the next week.
4. Summarize the session (preferably done by the client) to provide a bridge to the next session by: (a) reviewing next week's homework, (b) anticipating obstacles that might scuttle the client's plans, and (c) evaluating the current session.

Watkins (1983) adapted Maultsby's (1976) rational self-analysis format to fit the developmental level of children (Table 8-1). In Step 1, children write down what happened ("Jimmy called me a name because he doesn't like me."). In Step 2, children are asked to write, from the vantage point of a digital

TABLE 8-1 | RATIONAL SELF-ANALYSIS FOR CHILDREN

Step 1. Write down what happened.	Step 2. Be a video camera. If you were a video camera and recorded a videotape of what happened, what would you see and hear?	Step 3. Write down your thoughts about what happened. What did you think? A. B. C.
Step 4. A. How did you feel? B. What did you do?	Step 5. Decide if your thoughts are "smart." To do this, look at each thought you had an ask yourself the five questions in Step 6. Answer yes or no to each question and write your answers below. A. 1.　　B. 1.　　C. 1. 　　2.　　　　2.　　　　2. 　　3.　　　　3.　　　　3. 　　4.　　　　4.　　　　4. 　　5.　　　　5.　　　　5.	Step 6. How do you know if you're thinking "smart" thoughts? Ask 1. Is my thought really real, say if I were a video camera, what would I see? 2. Does the thought help me stay alive and in good physical shape? 3. Does the thought help me get what I want? 4. Does the thought help me stay out of trouble with others? 5. Does the thought help me feel the way I want to?
Step 7. How do you want to feel?	Step 8. Write down thoughts you could have that would be "smarter" than those listed. A. B. C.	Step 9. What do you want to do?

SOURCE: Watkins, 1983; adapted from Maultsby, 1976.

camera, what they would see and hear ("Jimmy didn't like it when I didn't choose him for my team."). With the increased objectivity obtained in Step 2, children are then asked in Step 3 to write down their thoughts about what happened ("It's terrible when people talk mean to me," or "If people get angry at me, I'm a bad person."). In Step 4, children are asked to write how they felt (hurt, angry) and what they did ("I hit him."). In Step 5, children are asked to find out if they have been thinking "smart" thoughts by testing their thoughts with the five questions listed in Step 6 (for example, "Does my thought help me stay out of trouble with others?"). The answers are tabulated in the Step 5 box. If "no" wins, the children go to Step 7 and list some of the feelings they want to feel (for example, a child may prefer to feel sad or disappointed instead of hurt, irritated, or angry). In Step 8, children are asked to write "smarter" thoughts that would help them feel better feelings ("I don't like it when others get upset with me, but things could be worse, and I don't have to let others control how I act."). Step 9 is reserved for a plan of action children can use the next time somebody does something to make them feel bad. Watkins's adaptation of Maultsby's model makes use of visualization in Step 2. Ellis (2001a) endorses visualization as a way of experiencing the negative consequences of telling ourselves irrational messages and the positive consequences of telling ourselves rational messages about the events in our lives. In addition, goals that are not visualized as attainable are seldom achieved.

Case Study

Jeff is a quiet, serious, 12-year-old seventh-grade student at Smith County Middle School. He was referred to the counselor because a failing grade on a language arts test left him very upset. After the test, Jeff seemed to be firmly convinced that he would fail the class.

Individual and Background Information

Academic. School records indicate that Jeff is a high achiever. He had excellent grades (B and above) in all his classes for the first two grading periods of the year. Except for an F on the last test, he has also maintained an above-average grade in language arts this grading period.

Family. Jeff is the youngest of three sons. His father is retired, and his mother works as a grocery store cashier. Both of Jeff's older brothers, one a high school senior and the other a college sophomore, are excellent students. The family expects (or appears to expect) Jeff to excel also.

Social. Jeff seems to get along well with his peers. He participates in group efforts and is especially good friends with one other student John, who is also a good student with a quiet personality.

Counseling Method

The school counselor used REBT as a counseling method to help Jeff recognize and evaluate the erroneous messages he was giving himself (and which upset him) about his low grade in language arts. The counselor also taught Jeff to replace the erroneous messages with "sane" messages and to recognize "insane" messages when he encountered them again. The basic steps the counselor used included having Jeff examine each step along the way to becoming upset and look at the real message he was telling himself at each step.

Transcript*

COUNSELOR	Jeff, why do you think you're going to fail language arts?
JEFF:	Because I failed the last test.
COUNSELOR:	You mean if you fail one test, you're bound to fail the next one?
JEFF:	Well, I failed that test, and I'm stupid!
COUNSELOR:	What are you telling yourself about your performance on that test?
JEFF:	I remember thinking it was a really bad grade—not at all the kind I was used to getting. Then I thought how terrible it would be if I failed language arts and how my mom and dad and brothers would hate me and would think I was lazy and dumb!
COUNSELOR:	It would be unpleasant and inconvenient if you failed language arts, but would this make you a hateful and dumb person?
JEFF:	It makes me really worried about passing the next test that's coming up. . . .
COUNSELOR:	I can understand how you would be worried about the next test, but does a bad grade make someone a bad or hated person?
JEFF:	No, but it's not the kind of grade I usually get.
COUNSELOR:	Okay, so a bad grade is unpleasant, and you don't like it, but it does not make you a bad person.
JEFF:	My grade was an F and most of the other kids made A's, so it made me look dumb.
COUNSELOR:	Okay, it *was* a bad grade compared with the rest of the class, but does this mean you are the dumbest kid around?
JEFF:	No, I make mostly A's, a few B's. One bad grade does not make me a dumb kid.
COUNSELOR:	So, compared with your usual grade and the class's grades, this *was* a bad grade, and that is all it is, right?
JEFF:	Yeah.
COUNSELOR:	What else are you telling yourself about the low test grade?
JEFF:	Well, like I said, I immediately thought how terrible it would be if I failed language arts, and—
COUNSELOR:	Stop there for just a minute, Jeff. Suppose you did fail language arts, even with your other high grades. It would be a bad experience, but would it be the end of the world?
JEFF:	No, I guess I'd have to repeat the class, that's all.

*The case of Jeff was contributed by Sharon Simpson.

COUNSELOR: Right, it would be inconvenient and maybe embarrassing. It would not be pleasant, but you would go on living.

JEFF: Well, I guess that's right.

COUNSELOR: Are you beginning to see what you told yourself about the consequences of *one* bad grade?

JEFF: Yeah, I guess I believed that one bad grade was awful—the end of the world—and that I shouldn't even try anymore because I would fail the class anyway.

COUNSELOR: Was that the correct information to give yourself about your grade?

JEFF: No!

COUNSELOR: Okay! Let's look at the rest of the message you gave yourself after you got that bad grade. Remember what was next?

JEFF: I think I thought my family would hate me and think I was dumb and lazy because I failed that test and would probably fail language arts.

COUNSELOR: Do you think your family's love depends on your grades?

JEFF: No, Jimmy made an F on a chemistry test the first part of the school year, and nobody hated him.

COUNSELOR: What did your parents do?

JEFF: Let's see. Oh yeah, they got him a tutor—a friend of Dad's knew a student who was majoring in chemistry.

COUNSELOR: What did your brother in college do when Jimmy failed the test?

JEFF: He offered to help Jim on weekends. He's a brain—a physics major!

COUNSELOR: So when your brother failed a test, your family helped him out. They didn't say he was "dumb" or "lazy" or that they hated him for it!

JEFF: No, they didn't. And I guess they wouldn't say it to me, either; in fact, Dad and Jim ask every night if I need help with my homework. I can usually do it okay by myself.

COUNSELOR: Okay. Let's go back over some of these bad messages you've been giving yourself about your bad grade.

JEFF: I got a bad grade. I thought I would fail language arts no matter what I did. I decided my family would hate me and think I was dumb and lazy.

COUNSELOR: Do you *still* believe those "crazy" messages you told yourself about failing and the way your family would react?

JEFF: No!

COUNSELOR: Next time you mess up on something—maybe a ball game, maybe a test—what message will you give yourself?

JEFF: Well, I'm not exactly sure what I'll say, but I *won't* tell myself that it's a disaster and I'll never be able to do anything else. I'll probably say that I don't like what happened and that I'm not happy about it. That's all. Now I guess I'll go study and try to ace that next language arts test. Thanks a lot!

APPLICATIONS OF COGNITIVE-BEHAVIORAL THERAPY

Kendall (1993) has addressed the issue of how best to intervene to reduce or remediate cognitive, behavioral, and emotional difficulties in childhood that are associated with present psychological distress and later psychopathology. Specifically, Kendall presents a status report on the effectiveness of CBTs in treating children in four diagnostic categories: aggression, anxiety, depression, and attention-deficit/hyperactivity disorder (ADHD).

AGGRESSION

Kendall (1993) emphasizes that aggressive children suffer from both distortions and deficiencies in their cognitive processing. Cognitive distortions result from dysfunctional thinking. Cognitive deficiencies result from insufficient cognitive activity in situations requiring cause–effect reasoning or the ability to visualize consequences of behavior. Kendall has found support for the effectiveness of CBT treatments with aggressive psychiatric children in reducing their aggressive behavior. The treatments included problem-solving skills training and self-monitoring with self-instruction for monitoring their arousal states.

Lochman (1992) has studied the effects of CBT on the behavior of 145 aggressive 10- to 12-year-old boys. The CBT interventions, ranging from watching video training tapes to role-playing social problem-solving situations, had a long-term effect on some behaviors of aggressive boys. The most notable area of change was lower levels of substance abuse over a 3-year follow-up period. It did not prove to have as strong an impact on decreasing deviant behavior, however.

Davis and Boster (1993) proposed using CBT in combination with expressive interventions in working with aggressive and resistant adolescents. They viewed the combined approach as a way to modify the dysfunctional cognitive, affective, behavioral, and problem-solving skills seen in aggressive youth and considered several multimodal treatment interventions. Logbooks of perceptions were recommended as helpful for recording thoughts and reinforcing nonviolent appraisals. Art therapy techniques such as cartoons without captions helped to frame nonviolent appraisals. Art therapy, as well as the other expressive arts of music and movement, was also effective with violent clients, who are likely to be limited in requisite verbal skills and creative resources for expressing and testing alternative appraisals of life events. Instruction in social skills and conflict resolution was also recommended for the multimodal package for treating aggressive youth.

ANXIETY

Kendall (1993) has found support for using muscle relaxation, deep breathing, and cognitive imagery (systematic desensitization) to reduce anxiety in anxious children. Anxious children exceed the norm by a significant margin with thoughts of being scared, hurt, and in danger. The same is true for self-critical thoughts.

Jay, Elliot, Woody, and Siegel (1991) have investigated the effectiveness of CBT in combination with diazepam (Valium) for children undergoing painful medical procedures. The study was done with eighty-three children ages 3 to 12 who had leukemia. The purpose of the study was to find ways to reduce the anxiety and distress caused by the medical tests and procedures required for treatment. One group received CBT and one group received CBT plus Valium. The CBT techniques included modeling, breathing exercises, imagery, positive incentives, and behavior rehearsal. The results showed that Valium did not increase the efficacy of CBT as hypothesized. In fact, the data, though not statistically significant, supported the possibility that Valium might impair the learning process of CBT. Used alone, CBT was found to decrease distress and to increase the children's rate of reporting their fears.

Beck, Sokol, Clark, Berchick, and Wright (1992) have found that cognitive therapy is more effective than person-centered therapy for helping clients with panic disorders. Cognitive strategies were used to break down the panic cycle. Person-centered strategies were nondirective and did not focus on the panic symptoms. Cognitive therapy resulted in a 71 percent rate of effectiveness in ending panic attacks, whereas only 25 percent of the person-centered participants succeeded. Clients could elect to cross over to the other treatment group. Cognitive therapy was successful for 79 percent of the crossover clients.

Two treatments, CBT and CBT plus family therapy (FAM), were used with children suffering from anxiety disorders. In a 5- to 7-year follow-up of these children, Barrett, Duffy, Dadds, and Rapee (2001) report that 86 percent of the children no longer met the diagnostic criteria for any anxiety disorder. CBT and CBT plus FAM were equally effective at long-term follow-up. In a similar study comparing parent involvement in children's CBT treatment with no parent involvement, Spence, Donovan, and Brechman-Toussaint (2000) report that both groups improved significantly more than a wait list group in the reduction of general and social anxiety and that there were no significant differences between the two CBT groups.

DEPRESSION

Depressed children and adolescents experience distortions in attributions, self-evaluation, and perceptions of past and present events. Silverman and DiGiuseppe (2001) have found a significant correlation between self-reported depression and negative automatic thoughts in a study of 126 students in grades 4 through 8. Depressed children exhibit more external locus of control (an indication that they feel less capable) and low self-esteem resulting from a perceived inability to succeed academically and socially. Effective help for depressed children included training in self-control, self-evaluation, assertiveness, and social skills. Social skills training included initiating and maintaining interactions and conflict resolution; specific CBTs included relaxation, imagery, and cognitive restructuring. Succeeding academically and socially are the two cornerstones of Glasser's (2005) choice theory reality therapy. He believes helping children and adolescents do better in making good grades and friends will solve a host of problems ranging from school violence to depression.

Attention-Deficit/Hyperactivity Disorder

Children with ADHD show deficiencies in the mechanisms that govern (1) sustained attention and effort, (2) inhibitory controls, and (3) the modulation of arousal levels to meet situational demands. Kendall (1993) proposes CBT with medication to treat ADHD. Stimulant medication should improve attention, and CBT should improve cognitive functioning. Ronen (1992) discusses cognitive therapy with children and its suitability for children's needs and ability levels. She lists the most frequent behavior problems of children (from most common to least common): loss of temper, hyperactivity, fears, restlessness, sleep disorders, enuresis, food intake, nail biting, tics, and stuttering. Her review of the literature revealed that children with behavior problems such as hyperactivity, impulsivity, and aggression tend to (1) generate fewer alternative solutions to interpersonal problems, (2) focus on ends or goals rather than on the intermediate steps toward obtaining them, (3) see fewer consequences associated with their behavior, (4) fail to recognize causes of others' behavior, and (5) be less sensitive to interpersonal conflict. Ronen then outlines some successful applications of CBT, such as self-assessment, self-instruction, self-reinforcement, and self-punishment. Cognitive treatments require children's active participation in learning to identify irrational thoughts, initiate internal dialogues, halt automatic thinking, change automatic thoughts to mediated ones, and use CBT to change unwanted behavior. Ronen responds to the question of whether children have developed sufficient cognitive skills to benefit from a cognitive approach by citing the similarity in difficulty between early childhood tasks and understanding CBT; she compares changing one's behavior with learning to ride a bicycle, use computers, read, and write. Ronen identifies three keys to such learning: (1) the knowledge of how to do it, (2) the desire to learn and practice, and (3) time to practice. Basically, our position is that good counselors should be able to teach children and adolescents almost any CBT skill that can be broken down into mediating steps that they can understand and find meaningful to the events in their everyday lives.

Obesity

Duffy and Spence (1993) have researched the effectiveness of cognitive self-management as an adjunct to behavioral interventions for childhood obesity. The study was done with twenty-nine children and adolescents ages 7 to 13. The traffic light system, which classified foods into three categories—green (eat freely), amber (eat in moderation), and red (stop, danger)—was used in behavioral therapy. The behavioral therapy group also received training in exercise, and their parents were trained to use goal-setting and positive reinforcement strategies for facilitating behavior change. The CBT component included monitoring negative thoughts, restructuring negative or maladaptive thoughts, problem-solving skills, self-instructional training, and self-reinforcement. The results of the study confirmed the effectiveness of behavioral programs in the reduction of obesity in some children. The addition of the CBT component did not add significantly to the behavioral therapy approach.

As we have noted throughout this book, counseling clients who do not view themselves as having a problem is difficult. Such was true with the participants in that obesity reduction study.

CHILDREN OF ALCOHOLICS

Webb (1993) endorses CBT as a valuable method for school counselors to use with children of alcoholics. The principal benefit of CBT for children of alcoholics was help in dealing with situations beyond their control, and thus help in avoiding responsibility for family issues that are, in reality, the responsibility of other family members. Moreover, CBT practitioners also provide their clients with the means for taking control of their lives and for improving those areas that are in the clients' control.

COGNITIVE-BEHAVIORAL PLAY THERAPY

Cognitive-behavioral play therapy is an adaptation of cognitive and behavioral therapies. Knell (1997) explains that cognitive-behavioral play therapy provides structured, goal-directed activities, allowing the child to engage in an unstructured, spontaneous way. The therapy is brief, directive, and problem oriented. In cognitive-behavioral play therapy, the therapeutic relationship is educational and collaborative. The positive relationship is based on rapport and trust, with play activities being means of communication. Play techniques, as well as verbal and nonverbal communication, are used to help children change their behavior and participate in the therapy. The active intervention involves the child and the counselor working together to establish goals. Both choose play materials and activities. New skills are taught to the child. The counselor uses praise and interpretation to help the child learn new behaviors and increase understanding. The counselor focuses on the child's thoughts, feelings, fantasies, and environment. The counselor also provides strategies for developing more adaptive thoughts and behaviors. The behavioral techniques used by the counselor may include systematic desensitization, contingency management, self-monitoring, and activity scheduling. Cognitive techniques include recording thoughts, cognitive change strategies, coping self-statements, and bibliotherapy. To accomplish the educative process, counselors use techniques such as modeling, role-playing, and using behavioral contingencies (Knell, 1996, 1998; Ellis, 2001c).

The counselor emphasizes the issues of control, mastery, and responsibility for the client's own behavior change. Knell (1996) believes that combining cognitive and behavioral interventions increase the potency of the intervention. The change proceeds first in calming the child through the counselor's empathy and acceptance. Relaxation techniques and verbal approval also are appropriate. In the second stage, children are given opportunities to experience and test the thoughts that are associated with their emotions. Next, the children examine those distortions and learn to discern rational and irrational ideas to shift their perceptions. The counselor uses modeling tailored to the needs of the children to demonstrate adaptive coping skills. Cognitive change and adaptive behaviors are communicated indirectly (Knell, 1998).

The success of cognitive-behavioral play therapy has been discussed in work with children who have excessive anger problems (Wilde, 2001), who are depressed (Briesmeister, 1997), who have ADHD (Kaduson, 1997), who express perfectionistic tendencies (VanFleet, 1997), and who have anxiety (Lyness-Richard, 1997). Friedberg (1996) have given some specific suggestions for using cognitive-behavioral games and workbooks with distressed children in schools. He states that the flexibility and creativity of incorporating games and workbooks can promote the counseling relationship and augment the traditional counseling process. Utay and Lampe (1995) present a cognitive-behavioral group counseling game designed to increase the social skills of children with learning disabilities. Their study supports the effectiveness of the cognitive-behavioral approach to play therapy.

CROSS-CULTURAL APPLICATIONS OF RATIONAL-EMOTIVE-BEHAVIORAL THERAPY AND COGNITIVE-BEHAVIORAL THERAPY

REBT and CBT are especially appealing to those cultures and to those individuals in all cultures who prefer strong, directive counseling and an active counselor who favors dispensing information about the "A, B, C, D, and E" philosophy and approach to helping people think, feel, and behave better. REBT and CBT counselors are not shy in telling clients what they are doing wrong and what they need to do to correct their behavior. REBT and CBT are education or re-education methods that teach clients what they are doing to themselves to make themselves feel bad and what to do to make themselves feel better. Both therapies are especially effective with those individuals who prefer to focus on reason and thinking rather than on affect or behavior to bring about a positive change in their lives. Likewise, these approaches are favored by cultures and individuals who want their counselor to be a strong and active consultant. In other words, these clients prefer reason over emotion and reason over behavior in solving their problems and resolving conflicts. As mentioned in Chapter 2, Thompson and Campbell (1992) report that 25 percent of their surveyed population of 500 people in U.S. culture selected cognitive methods over affective, behavioral, and integrative counseling interventions when working through their own bad feelings. Again, it might be inaccurate to assign a specific learning or problem-solving style to a culture that will be true for all groups and individuals within that culture. However, in general, we might expect REBT and CBT to be most accepted in cultures where people want their teachers and advisers to supply a strong, authoritative, and active presence in their lives. As noted in Chapter 15, African Americans, Hispanics, and Asian Americans are among those cultures favoring the direct approach offered by CBT and REBT. These same cultural groups appreciate the direct and immediate attention that cognitive-behavioral counselors give to their presenting problems. Asian Americans and Asians seem to prefer the CBT and REBT focus on thinking rather than on feelings. CBT and REBT practitioners offer an array of techniques and methods that can be taught to people from cultures favoring education and training that will, in turn, lead to empowering clients to solve problems and resolve conflicts more efficiently. All three cultural groups respond well to learning new skills (Kincade & Evans, 1996; Pinderhughes, 1989; Sue & Sue, 2003). CBT and REBT methods include relaxation and stress reduction techniques, assertiveness training, anxiety management, modeling, role-playing, and goal setting. The counseling interview offers a "safe" environment for the counselor to explain and demonstrate each technique before giving clients a choice of which methods they would like to try. Clients feel safe in experimenting with the new methods they have been taught before using them in real-life situations. As for any client from any culture, the CBT or REBT counselor will want to be sure that the client's belief system is examined in the bright light of reality to see which beliefs are truly rational and irrational. For example, for a minority client, the belief that "I can't get a job" could very well be a rational belief in situations where discrimination against certain groups is practiced (Fuertes, Bartolomeo, & Nichols, 2001; Lega & Ellis, 2001).

RATIONAL-EMOTIVE-BEHAVIORAL THERAPY, COGNITIVE-BEHAVIORAL THERAPY, ACCOUNTABILITY, AND MANAGED HEALTH CARE

As noted in the managed care guidelines presented in Chapter 2, any type of CBT, including REBT, fits nicely into the type of counseling treatments and interventions managed care organizations (MCOs) support (Cohen, 2003; Dobson & Khatri, 2000). CBT and REBT are relatively short-term treatments that can be administered successfully in twenty or fewer sessions. They both have specific behavioral objectives that can be tracked on a weekly basis and specific goals marking the end of treatment. CBT and REBT counseling outcomes and client satisfaction generally receive positive ratings. In addition, both types of treatment are generally near the top of the list when counseling outcomes are reported in comparative studies with other therapies. In summary, counselor accountability to the client and to the MCO are both high, the cost is reasonable, the treatment is one of the shorter term interventions, the client's present-day conflicts and problems are addressed, considerable benefit is derived from homework assignments done by the clients on their own time, the treatment can be done well in groups, and the success rate is high. All of these characteristics make CBT and REBT quite compatible with managed healthcare guidelines. CBT and REBT training delivered in psychoeducational groups could be one of the best preventive measures counselors have for addressing adjustment disorders before they become severe mental illness problems.

SUMMARY

Replying to articles critical of REBT, Ellis (1981, 1984, 1998) writes that REBT remains within the field of science while resting on some evaluative assumptions. For example, the REBT concept of unconditional humanistic self-acceptance is still valid, even though it requires an operational definition. The REBT concept of self-acceptance means that a person is more than a set of behaviors; that is, people are better off negating specific behaviors without labeling their entire selves as good or bad. Albert Ellis (1993a) traced the development of his REBT from 1955 to 1993, and he suggests directions where REBT may be taken in the future. He points out that, in 1955, REBT, the first of today's CBTs, was highly cognitive, largely positivist, and very active directive. Its ABC theory of human disturbance held that people experience undesirable activating events (A), that they have rational and irrational beliefs (B) about these events, and that they create *appropriate* emotional and behavioral *consequences* (aC) with their *rational beliefs* (rB) or they create *inappropriate* and dysfunctional *consequences* (iC) with their *irrational beliefs* (iB). Thus, REBT is directed to the client's belief system, which is the cause of the problem, not the activating event.

Ellis found support for his theory in the 1970s from Berkowitz's (1970; Berkowitz & Alioto, 1973) work on aggression, which pointed out the danger and futility of "acting out" aggressive impulses as a way of relieving and treating aggression. Aggression begets more aggression. Therefore, treatment of aggression needs to be directed to the client's belief system that directs him or her to act on often irrational thinking, which leads to inappropriate aggressive acts.

Ellis makes a distinction between general REBT, which he views as synonymous with general CBT, and preferential REBT, which he describes as a unique type of cognitive therapy that is distinctly constructivist and humanistic. He lists ten points defining the unique style of preferential REBT (Ellis, 1994, 1996, 2003):

1. People, learning their expectations, preferences, and goals for success and culture, feel appropriately frustrated and disappointed when they fail and receive disapproval. People make themselves neurotic by their innate tendencies to construct absolutist "musts" and demands on themselves, others, and their environments.

2. People make themselves more disturbed by creating exaggerated derivatives of their "musts" and demands. For example, "She absolutely must

like me!" When she ignores me, I rashly conclude and devoutly believe that (a) "She hates me!" (b) "It's awful that she hates me!" (c) "I'm worthless because she hates me!" and (d) "No decent person will ever like me!"

3. REBT contains the information to prevent people from making themselves neurotic.

4. REBT is multimodal and used in conjunction with a variety of cognitive, emotive, and behavioral methods, including imagery, shame-attacking exercises, coping statements, role-playing, encouragement, and humor.

5. People are biologically predisposed to hold on strongly to their irrational beliefs. Therefore, REBT is designed to teach clients to think, feel, and act against these beliefs.

6. REBT tends to be more heavily behavioral than some of the other CBTs. Behavioral methods used in REBT include behavioral homework with reinforcements and penalties, in vivo desensitization, implosive counterphobic procedures, and response prevention.

7. REBT has always been psychoeducational, and consequently includes a number of instructional and teaching methods to help people learn to survive within a dysfunctional system and change that system.

8. People are faced with two opposing creative tendencies: (a) to make themselves disturbed and dysfunctional; or (b) to change and actualize themselves to reduce their self-disturbing tendencies, and thus enjoy happier lives.

9. REBT opposes dogma, rigidity, "musturbation," and one-sidedness in favor of science, empiricism, and logic in constructing a healthy, rational belief system. The preceding statement defines *mental health* for Ellis.

10. Once people upset themselves, their emotional reactions of panic, depression, and self-hatred are so strong that they require an active-directive REBT approach to provide the instruction and guidance people need to pull themselves out of the hole they have dug.

In summary, Ellis's objective for all people is that they rate their performance in relation to the goals they have set. It is *healthy* to believe "It is good when I succeed and am loved" or "It is bad when I fail and am rejected." It is *unhealthy* to believe "I am good for succeeding" and "I am bad for getting rejected." Regarding unconditional positive regard, Ellis points out that REBT therapists try to give this type of acceptance to all clients, but also teach them how to give it to themselves. Ellis (1993b) envisioned the main future of REBT in psychoeducational applications for the millions of people who do not have access to counseling services. Despite some contradictory evidence, REBE still has promise as a preventive intervention for children, adolescents, and adults inclined to exaggerate negative events. REBT and CBT training may be the only hope for adding rationality to the emotion-driven culture in which we find ourselves living. Even in his later years Albert Ellis continues to be tolerant of irrationalities, loving his work, and working at his loving. That, he says, is the secret of his present unusually happy state.

Websites for Rational-Emotive-Behavioral Therapy and Cognitive-Behavioral Therapy

Internet addresses frequently change. To find the sites listed here, visit www.thomsonedu. com/counseling/thompson for an updated list of Internet addresses and direct links to relevant sites.

Albert Ellis Institute

Cognitive-Behavior Therapy

Rational Emotive Behavior Therapy

REFERENCES

Barrett, P., Duffy, A., Dadds, M., & Rapee, R. (2001). Cognitive-behavioral treatment of anxiety disorders in children: Long-term (6-year) follow-up. *Journal of Consulting and Clinical Psychology, 69,* 135–141.

Beck, A. (1976). *Cognitive therapy and emotional disorders.* New York: International Universities Press.

Beck, A., Sokol, L., Clark, D., Berchick, R., & Wright, F. (1992). A crossover study of focused cognitive therapy for panic disorder. *American Journal of Psychiatry, 149,* 778–783.

Berkowitz, C. (1970). Experimental investigations of hostility catharsis. *Journal of Consulting and Clinical Psychology, 35,* 1–7.

Berkowitz, L., & Alioto, J. (1973). The meaning of an observed event as a determinant of its aggressive consequences. *Journal of Personality and Social Psychology, 28,* 206–217.

Bernard, M. (1990). Rational-emotive therapy with children and adolescents: Treatment strategies. *School Psychology Review, 19,* 294–303.

Briesmeister, J. M. (1997). Play therapy with depressed children. In H. G. Kaduson, D. Cangelosi, & C. E. Schaefer (Eds.), *The playing cure: Individualized play therapy for specific childhood problems* (pp. 3–28). Northvale, NJ: Jason Aronson.

Cohen, J. (2003). Managed care and the evolving role of the clinical social working in mental health. *National Association of Social Work, 48*(1), 34–43.

Crawford, T., & Ellis, A. (1989). A dictionary of rational-emotive feelings and behaviors. *Journal of Rational-Emotive & Cognitive Behavior Therapy, 7,* 3–28.

Davis, D., & Boster, L. (1993). Cognitive-behavioral expressive interventions with aggressive and resistant youth. *Residential Treatment for Children and Youth, 10,* 55–67.

DiGiuseppe, R. (1990). Rational-emotive assessment of school aged children. *School Psychology Review, 19,* 287–293.

Dobson, K. & Khatri, N. (2000). Cognitive therapy: looking backward, looking forward. *Journal of Clinical Psychology, 56*(7), 907–922.

Duffy, G., & Spence, S. (1993). The effectiveness of cognitive self-management as an adjunct to a behavioral intervention for childhood obesity: A research note. *Journal of Child Psychology and Psychiatry, 34,* 1043–1050.

Ellis, A. (1954). *The American sexual tragedy.* New York: Twayne.

Ellis, A. (1965). *The case for sexual liberty.* Tucson, AZ: Seymour Press.

Ellis, A. (1969). *The art and science of love* (2nd ed.). New York: Lyle Stuart/Bantam.

Ellis, A. (1972). Emotional education in the classroom. *Journal of Clinical Child Psychology, 1,* 19–22.

Ellis, A. (1974). What rational-emotive therapy is and is not. *Counselor Education and Supervision, 14*, 140–144.

Ellis, A. (1975). *How to live with a "neurotic"* (Rev. ed.). New York: Crown. (Original work published 1957)

Ellis, A. (1977). *How to live with and without anger.* New York: Reader's Digest Press.

Ellis, A. (1981). Science, religiosity and rational emotive psychology. *Psychotherapy: Theory, Research, Practice, 18*, 55–58.

Ellis, A. (1984). Rational-emotive therapy and pastoral counseling: A reply to Richard Wessler. *Personnel and Guidance Journal, 62*, 266–267.

Ellis, A. (1987). The impossibility of achieving consistently good mental health. *American Psychologist, 42*, 364–375.

Ellis, A. (1993a). Reflections on rational-emotive therapy. *Journal of Consulting and Clinical Psychology, 61*, 199–201.

Ellis, A. (1993b). Rational emotive therapy. Paper presented at the convention of the American Psychological Association, Toronto, Ontario, Canada.

Ellis, A. (1994). *Reason and emotion in psychotherapy* (Rev. ed.). New York: Birch Lane.

Ellis, A. (1996). *Better, deeper, and more enduring brief therapy.* New York: Brunner/Mazel.

Ellis, A. (1997). Must musterbation and demandingness lead to emotional disorders? *Psychotherapy, 34*, 95–98.

Ellis, A. (1998). *REBT diminishes much of the human ego.* New York: Institute for Rational-Emotive Therapy.

Ellis, A. (2001a). The relationship of rational emotive behavior therapy (REBT) to social psychology. *Journal of Rational-Emotive & Cognitive Behavior Therapy, 21*(1), 5–20.

Ellis, A. (2001b). *Overcoming destructive beliefs, feelings, and behaviors.* New York: Prometheus Books.

Ellis, A. (2001c). Rational-emotive imagery. Retrieved August 23, 2002, from www.rational.org.nz

Ellis, A. (2003). Early theories and practices of rational emotive therapy and how they have been augmented and revised during the last three decades. *Journal of Rational-Emotive & Cognitive Behavioral Therapy, 21*, 219–234.

Ellis, A. (2004). Why rational emotive behavior therapy is the most comprehensive and effective form of behavior therapy. *Journal of Rational-Emotive & Cognitive Behavior Therapy, 82*, 439–442.

Ellis, A., & Dryden, W. (1996). *The practice of rational emotive behavior therapy* (Rev. ed.). New York: Springer.

Ellis, A., & Harper, R. (1975). *Guide to rational living.* Englewood Cliffs, NJ: Prentice-Hall.

Ellis, A., & MacLaren, C. (1998). *Rational emotive behavioral therapy: A therapist guide.* Atascadero, CA: Impact Publications.

Friedberg, R. D. (1996). Cognitive-behavioral games and workbooks: Tips for school counselors. *Elementary School Guidance & Counseling, 31*, 11–19.

Fuertes, J., Bartolomeo, M., & Nichols, C. (2001). Future research directions in the study of counselor multicultural competency. *Journal of Multicultural Counseling & Development, 29*(1), 3–10.

Glasser, W. (2005). *Treating mental health as a public health problem: A new leadership role for helping professions.* Chatsworth, CA: William Glasser, Inc.

Gonzalez, J., Nelson, J., Gutkin, T., Saunders, A., Galloway, A., & Shwery, C. (2004). Rational emotive therapy with children and adolescents: A meta-analysis. *Journal of Emotional and Behavioral Disorders, 12*(4), 222–235.

Jay, S., Elliot, C., Woody, P., & Siegel, S. (1991). An investigation of cognitive-behavior therapy combined with oral Valium for children undergoing painful medical procedures. *Health Psychology, 10,* 317–322.

Kaduson, H. G. (1997). Play therapy for children with attention-deficit hyperactivity disorder. In H. G. Kaduson, D. Cangelosi, & C. E. Schaefer (Eds.), *The playing cure: Individualized play therapy for specific childhood problems* (pp. 197–228). Northvale, NJ: Jason Aronson.

Kendall, P. (1993). Cognitive-behavior therapies with youth: Guiding theory, current status, and emerging developments. *Journal of Consulting and Clinical Psychology, 61,* 235–247.

Kincade, E., & Evans, K. (1996). Counseling theories, process, and interventions within a multicultural context. In J. Delucia-Waack (Ed.), *Multicultural counseling competencies: Implications for training and practice* (pp. 89–112). Alexandria, VA: Association for Counselor Education and Supervision.

Knell, S. M. (1996). Cognitive-behavioral play therapy. *The Hatherleigh guide to child and adolescent therapy* (pp. 129–152). New York: Hatherleigh.

Knell, S. M. (1997). Cognitive-behavioral play therapy. In K. O'Connor & L. M. Braverman (Eds.), *Play therapy theory and practice: A comparative presentation* (pp. 79–99). New York: Wiley.

Knell, S. M. (1998). Cognitive-behavioral play therapy. *Journal of Clinical Child Psychology, 27,* 28–33.

Lega, L., & Ellis, A. (2001). Rational emotive behavior therapy (REBT) in the new millennium: A cross-cultural approach. *Journal of Rational-Emotive & Cognitive Behavior Therapy, 19*(4), 201–222.

Lochman, J. (1992). Cognitive behavioral intervention with aggressive boys: Three-year follow-up and preventive effects. *Journal of Consulting and Clinical Psychology, 60,* 426–432.

Lyness-Richard, D. (1997). Play and perfectionism: Putting fun back into families. In H. G. Kaduson, D. Cangelosi, & C. E. Schaefer (Eds.), *The playing cure: Individualized play therapy for specific childhood problems* (pp. 29–60). Northvale, NJ: Jason Aronson.

Maultsby, M. (1976). *Rational self-analysis format.* Lexington, KY: Center for Rational Behavior Therapy and Training, University of Kentucky.

Maultsby, M. (1984). *Rational behavior therapy.* Englewood Cliffs, NJ: Prentice-Hall.

McGinn, L., & Sanderson, W. (2001). What allows cognitive behavioral therapy to be brief: Overview, efficacy, and crucial factors facilitating brief treatment. *Clinical Psychology: Science and Practice, 8,* 23–36.

Meichenbaum, D. (1977). *Cognitive behavior modification: An integrative approach.* New York: Plenum.

Meichenbaum, D. (1985). *Stress-inoculation training.* New York: Pergamon.

Pinderhughes, E. (1989). *Understanding race, ethnicity, and power: The key to efficacy in clinical practice.* New York: Free Press/Macmillan.

Ronen, T. (1992). Cognitive therapy with children. *Child Psychiatry and Human Development, 23,* 19–30.

Silverman, S., & DiGiuseppe, R. (2001). Cognitive-behavioral and emotional problems. *Journal of Rational-Emotive & Cognitive-Behavioral Therapy, 19,* 119–134.

Spence, S., Donovan, C., & Brechman-Toussaint, M. (2000). The treatment of child-hood social phobia: The effectiveness of a social skills training based cognitive-behavioral intervention with and without parent involvement. *Journal of Child Psychology and Psychiatry, 41,* 713–726.

Sue, D., & Sue, D. (2003). *Counseling the culturally different: Theory and practice.* New York: Wiley.

Thebarge, R. (1989). Symptom substitution: A rational-emotive perspective. *Journal of Rational-Emotive & Cognitive-Behavior Therapy, 7,* 93–97.

Thompson, C., & Campbell, S. (1992). Personal intervention preferences for alleviating mild depression. *Journal of Counseling and Development, 71,* 69–73.

Utay, J. M., & Lampe, R. E. (1995). Use of a group counseling game to enhance social skills of children with learning disabilities. *Journal of Specialists in Group Work, 20,* 114–121.

VanFleet, R. (1997). Play and perfectionism: Putting fun back into families. In H. G. Kaduson, D. Cangelosi, & C. E. Schaefer (Eds.), *The playing cure: Individualized play therapy for specific childhood problems* (pp. 61–82). Northvale, NJ: Jason Aronson.

Waters, V. (1980). *Rational stories for children.* New York: Albert Ellis Institute.

Waters, V. (1982). Helping children build tease tolerance. *RETwork, 1,* 1.

Watkins, C. E. (1983). Rational self-analysis for children. *Elementary School Guidance and Counseling, 17,* 304–306.

Webb, W. (1993). Cognitive behavior therapy with children of alcoholics. *School Counselor, 40,* 170–177.

Wilde, J. (2001). Interventions for children with anger problems. *Journal of Rational-Emotive & Cognitive Behavioral Therapy, 19,* 191–197.

9 CHAPTER | BEHAVIORAL COUNSELING

Not everything that can be counted counts, and not everything that counts can be counted.

—Albert Einstein

When all else fails, I become a behaviorist.

—Howard Gardner

B. F. Skinner (1904–1990)

Behavioral therapy is rooted in the work of Ivan Pavlov's experiments in respondent or classical conditioning. Behavior modification stems from B. F. Skinner's work on instrumental or operant conditioning. Both scholars shared a common interest in using experimental methods to research abnormal behavioral patterns. The field of behavioral psychology has had numerous other contributors over the years. The 1920s marked the time when the basic concepts of behavioral therapy were first used. It was not until the 1950s and 1960s, though, that systematic and comprehensive forms of behavioral therapy emerged. Primary contributors were Joseph Wolpe in South Africa, M. B. Shapiro and Hans Eyseneck in Britain, and B. F. Skinner in the United States. The name best known to the general public, as well as the most controversial, is B. F. Skinner. Although he did not develop new principles of behaviorism, Skinner did the most to translate the theories and ideas of other behaviorists into the methods currently used by counselors and therapists around the world.

Burrhus Frederic Skinner was born in Susquehanna, Pennsylvania. He majored in literature at Hamilton College in Clinton, New York, with the goal of becoming a writer. After a few years with little success, Skinner regarded himself a failure as a writer. Reflecting later on this time in his life, Skinner commented that he failed because he had nothing to say. Skinner then entered Harvard University to study psychology. The behavior of humans and animals was of special interest to him. He received a master's degree in 1930 and a Ph.D. in experimental psychology in 1931. After graduation, Skinner began his most productive career as a teacher and researcher, first at Harvard and then at the University of Minnesota in 1936. While in Minnesota he married Yvonne Blue. They had two daughters, the younger of which became famous for being reared in Skinner's air crib, a combination playpen and crib with a plastic mattress cover, glass sides, and air conditioning. In short, it resembled an aquarium for babies. It never caught on with crib-buying shoppers.

He was appointed chairman of the Psychology Department at Indiana University in 1945. He later returned to Harvard in 1948 to accept a professorship, which he held until his death. As he began to generate things to say in the field of behaviorism, Skinner's flair for writing returned. His numerous books include *The Behavior of Organisms* (1938), *Walden Two* (1948), *The Technology of Teaching* (1968), *Beyond Freedom and Dignity* (1971), *A Matter of Consequences: Part III of an Autobiography* (1983), and *Upon Further Reflection* (1987). R. Epstein also edited the book *Skinner for the Classroom* (1980).

Skinner's contribution to knowledge is not strictly confined to the laboratory. He made considerable contributions to solving educational problems. He developed and advanced the concepts of programmed instruction, operant conditioning in classroom management, and the teaching machine (first developed by Sidney Pressey in 1923). Perhaps the most controversial of Skinner's works is *Beyond Freedom and Dignity* (1971), which pictures a society where behavior is shaped and controlled by a planned system of rewards. His most helpful contributions to classroom management are found in *The Technology of Teaching* and *Skinner for the Classroom*.

Skinner (1990a), in an article he completed the evening before his death, attacked those who would use introspection or brain analysis as methods for analyzing behavior. He asserted that behavior is the product of three types of variation and selection: natural selection, operant conditioning, and modeling. Skinner had little use for cognitive psychology because he contended that it had not contributed, as behavior analysis, to the design of better environments for solving existing problems and preventing future problems. Summing up his 60 years in the profession, Skinner (1990b) said that the point he tried to make is that it can be demonstrated that people choose behavior based on anticipated consequences. According to Skinner, this selection by consequences has negative implications for the world and its future unless some vital changes are made. He concluded by saying that he would like to be remembered as fostering the needed changes.

Skinner's death in 1990 ended six decades of significant contributions to behavioral psychology that began with the publication of his first article in 1930. During his career, citations of Skinner's name in the literature exceeded those of the previous leader, Sigmund Freud (Banks & Thompson, 1995).

THE NATURE OF PEOPLE

A broad statement of the behaviorist view of the nature of people is Skinner's (1971) belief that things that happen to children influence and change them as biological entities. He believed that the idea that the child of our past is still contained within us is a form of animism that serves no useful purpose in explaining present behavior. Behaviorists view human beings as neither good nor bad but merely products of their environment. People are essentially born neutral (the blank slate or tabula rasa idea), with equal potential for good or evil and for rationality or irrationality.

Behaviorists view people as responders. They reject self-directing, mentalistic concepts of human behavior. Behaviorists contend that people can make only those responses they have learned, and they make them when the stimulus conditions are appropriate.

Behavioral counselors, therefore, view individuals as products of their conditioning. The stimulus–response paradigm is the basic pattern of all human learning. People react in predictable ways to any given stimulus according to what they have learned through experience. Humans react to stimuli much as animals do, except that human responses are more complex and organized on a higher plane.

Skinner regarded the human being as an organism who learns patterns of behavior, catalogs them within a repertoire, and repeats them at a later date. More specifically, the organism learns a specific response when a satisfying condition follows an action. The number of these responses mounts as time passes and satisfying conditions are repeated. The behaviorist's interest is in the science of behavior as it relates to biology. Skinner believed:

> A person is a member of a species shaped by evolutionary contingencies of survival, displaying behavioral processes which bring him under the control of the environment in which he lives, and largely under the control of a social environment which he and millions of others like him have constructed and maintained during the evolution of a culture. The direction of the controlling relation is reversed: a person does not act upon the world, the world acts upon him. (1971, p. 211)

Because human behavior is learned, any or all behavior can be unlearned and new behavior learned in its place. The behaviorist is concerned with observable events that, when they become unacceptable behaviors, can be unlearned. The behavioral counselor is concerned with this unlearning or re-education process. Behavioral counseling procedures can be developed from social learning theory.

THEORY OF COUNSELING

Behavioral counseling is an action therapy in much the same way that reality therapy, solution-focused brief counseling, and cognitive-behavioral therapy are. Clients do something about their behavior rather than trying to understand it by talking about it. Clients learn to monitor their behavior, practice coping skills, and complete homework assignments to help them reach their goals.

Behavioral counseling is a re-education or relearning process. Counselors help clients develop plans to reinforce adaptive or helpful behavior and extinguish maladaptive or unhelpful behavior. The counselor's role is, through reinforcement principles, to help clients achieve the goals they have set for themselves.

Behavioral counseling includes several techniques based on principles of learning used to manage maladaptive behavior. Currently, behavioral counseling

	Present	Withhold
Positive stimuli: Praise Tangible rewards	Positive reinforcement	Extinction

Negative stimuli:
Criticism
Unpleasant
  consequences
  and tasks
	Punishment	Negative reinforcement

FIGURE 9-1 | EXAMPLES OF OPERANT CONDITIONING

is used with covert processes (cognitions, emotions, obsessive ideation), as well as with traditional overt behavior problems. Behavioral counseling involves two types of behavior: operant and respondent.

In operant conditioning, *operant behavior* refers to behavior that operates on and changes the environment in some manner. It is also referred to as *instrumental behavior* because it is instrumental in goal achievement. People who use operant conditioning wait until the desired behavior or an approximation of the desired behavior occurs, and then reinforce it with a rewarding stimulus known as *positive reinforcement* (for example, praise, money, candy, free time, and attention). *Negative reinforcement* (different from punishment) occurs when the operant behavior is reinforced by its capacity to stop an aversive stimulus. For example, rats learn to press a bar to shut off an electric shock, and children take their seats at school to shut off the aversive sound of their teacher's scolding. *Punishment,* like positive reinforcement, occurs after the behavior is emitted but tends to decrease its occurrence. *Extinction* is the process of eliminating a learned behavior by ignoring the behavior or by not reinforcing it by withholding attention and other rewards. Figure 9-1 compares positive reinforcement, negative reinforcement, punishment, and extinction.

BEHAVIOR ANALYSIS

WHY PEOPLE BEHAVE AS THEY DO   People behave in ways that maintain or enhance their self-images. They also behave in ways to achieve goals that meet the following hierarchy of needs developed by Maslow (1970):

- Self-fulfillment (the need to develop skills, interests, and talents)
- Self-esteem (feeling worthwhile)
- Social (belonging to a group, giving and receiving love)
- Security (safety, shelter)
- Physiological (food, sleep, oxygen, water)

Steps in Behavior Analysis

Principles of Behavior

1. Behavior consists of three phases:

   - *Antecedents:* the stimuli or cues that occur before behavior that leads to its occurrence
   - *Behavior:* what the person says or does (or not does)
   - *Consequences:* what the person perceives happens to him or her (positive, neutral, and negative) as a result of his or her behavior

2. Behavioral problems are usually rooted in antecedents or consequences.
3. People usually prefer behavior for which the consequences are known to behavior for which the consequences are uncertain.

A behavior analysis designed to determine causes of and solutions to performance problems requires four steps:

1. Identify the problem category. Is it a problem of *performing a task,* or is it a problem of *dealing with people?*
2. Identify the problem type. Is it the person *unable* to do the task, or is the person *unwilling* to do the task? The acid test is whether the person could do the task if his or her life depended on it (not that we would go that far).
3. Determine the problem cause if the person is unable to do the task. Is it due to a *lack of knowledge* about what, when, and how the task should be done, or is there an *obstacle* in the environment that is preventing accomplishment of the task? If the person is *unwilling* to do the task, is it because there is a *lack of knowledge* about why something needs to be done, or is it simple *refusal?* Behavioral methods often fail because of their tendency to assume that all problems with people are rooted in someone's refusal to do certain things.
4. Select a problem solution that is appropriate for the problem at hand. If the person is *unable* to perform the task and needs to know how to do it, *provide training.* If there is an *obstacle in the environment* (for example, the student cannot see the marking board), fix the problem (move the student closer to the board) or *remove the obstacle.* If a person is refusing to do a task (for example, shows up late every day), the counselor needs to determine what is reinforcing the *undesired* behavior and what is punishing the *desired* behavior. Then, the counselor must find a way to *decrease* or *eliminate* both of the things that maintain the undesired behavior and find a way to reinforce the desired behavior (showing up on time). Note that punishment of the undesired behavior is a last-resort option because it carries a possible side effect of damaging the relationship you are trying to build with your client. The behavior analysis process is outlined in Table 9-1 and Figure 9-2.

| Table 9-1 | Determining Causes of and Solutions to Performance Problems |

What category of problem?	Is it a problem of:	Is it due to:	Approach it by:
Performing a task Dealing with people	Being unable*	Lack of knowledge about what, when, how	Providing training
		Obstacle in the environment	Removing the obstacle
	Being unwilling*	Lack of knowledge about why something needs to be done	Providing information/ feedback
		Simple refusal	Changing the balance of positive and negative consequences

*Could he or she do it if his or her life depended on it? No = unable; yes = unwilling.

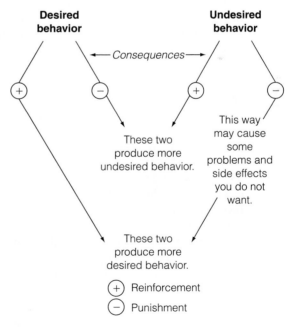

FIGURE 9-2 | BALANCING CONSEQUENCES

SCHEDULES OF REINFORCEMENT

Changing the balance of positive and negative consequences requires selecting an appropriate schedule of reinforcement. There are two schedules of reinforcement for the acquisition and establishment of a new behavior: continuous and intermittent. *Continuous reinforcement,* the reinforcement of each successful response, is best when the new behavior is first being learned. Once the new behavior has been learned, continuous reinforcement has the effect of extinguishing the behavior by satiating the learner. Reinforcement should be switched to one of four intermittent schedules: fixed interval, variable interval, fixed ratio, or variable ratio.

FIXED INTERVAL SCHEDULE   Reinforcement is provided on the first response after a fixed time has elapsed. The interval could be set at, for example, 30 seconds. Hourly wages paid weekly and weekly tests given in a class each Friday are other examples of fixed interval schedules. Reinforced behavior increases before the reinforcement and decreases dramatically after reinforcement. Study behavior increases before the test and decreases after the test.

VARIABLE INTERVAL SCHEDULE   Reinforcement is provided on the first response after some average time period. For instance, intervals could range from 15 to 45 seconds, averaging 30 seconds over several successful responses. Unannounced pop quizzes given in class are excellent examples of an application of the variable interval schedule. Study behavior is highest for classes where pop quizzes are given, but the teacher's popularity may suffer. Study behavior increases as the time between quizzes increases.

FIXED RATIO SCHEDULE   The participant is reinforced for every five, ten, or twenty correct responses made. The reinforcement rate is fixed at the same rate (for example, every fifth correct response is reinforced). Piecework in a factory where people are paid according to the number of products produced is a good example of a fixed ratio schedule.

VARIABLE RATIO SCHEDULE   Participants are reinforced on a schedule varying, for example, from five to twenty-five correct responses, with an average number of responses between reinforcements falling somewhere in midrange between five and twenty-five. Playing slot machines is a good example of both how variable ratio reinforcement is applied and how strongly this method maintains the gambling addictions people have. Fishing is another good example of variable ratio reinforcement. An occasional bite will keep a fisherman "hooked" for hours.

COUNSELING GOALS

As with most counseling, the ultimate goal of behavioral counseling is teaching children and adolescents to become their own counselors by changing their behavior to better meet their needs. All behavior change, internal and external, can be attempted through behavioral counseling. Specific techniques reduce and eliminate anxiety, phobias, and obsessive thoughts, as well as reduce inappropriate, observable behaviors.

After the problem has been identified and the desired behavior change agreed on by the counselor and the client, the behavioral counselor is apt to use a variety of counseling procedures to help the client acquire the behaviors necessary to solve the problem. The ultimate outcome of behavioral counseling is to teach people to become their own behavior-modification experts—that is, to program their own reinforcement schedules (self-management). Encouraging people to move from extrinsic to intrinsic reinforcement—to please themselves with their behavior rather than constantly seek the approval of others—is even more desirable. The success of behavioral counseling lies in the client's success in transferring from an extrinsic reward system to an intrinsic reward system for maintaining the target behavior. For example, a child who receives extra privileges at home for completing homework assignments reaches the intrinsic level when she realizes that her life is better when she does well at school and then continues the target behavior, reinforced only by the realization that her life is more pleasant. As her grades improve, she finds her parents more cooperative and nicer to be around, and she finds her teachers praising her efforts rather than nagging her about the missed homework assignments.

Because behavioral counseling differs from traditional counseling principally in terms of specificity, the behavioral counselor prefers to state goals as overt changes in behavior rather than hypothetical constructs. The basic counseling function involved in behavioral counseling is defined as discrimination—differential responding to different situations (individuals, groups, institutions, and environmental settings). In behavioral counseling, continuing assessment of the effects on outcomes of each counseling intervention determines effectiveness of the procedure.

COUNSELING METHODS

When using behavioral counseling methods with children, the counselor needs to match reinforcement to the child's developmental level and reward preferences. Social development is one good predicator of effective reinforcers. Egocentric children in the preoperational stage of development probably do not find sharing toys with siblings or friends to be a priority reward. Preoperational-stage children find playing alone with favorite toys or playing a game in which they can make up all the rules much more reinforcing. Adolescents, in contrast, find the social contact involved in sharing and team activities reinforcing.

CONTINGENCY CONTRACTS

Contracts are effective for children if they have a voice in writing the terms. Contract language must be simplified for understanding, and the goals should be quite clear, with as few steps as possible to meet the goals. Reinforcement should be immediate when the target behavior is being established. Readily available cost-free and developmentally appropriate rewards are preferable—being first in line, doing a favorite classroom job, being a student helper, running errands, tutoring a classmate—if they are reinforcing to the child. Learning-enrichment activities are reinforcing for older students.

The contingency contracting process can be broken down into six steps:

1. The counselor and the student identify the problem to be solved.
2. The counselor collects data to verify the baseline frequency rate for the undesired behavior.
3. The counselor and the student set mutually acceptable goals.
4. The counselor develops a contingency plan that identifies the target behaviors and the number of times the target behavior has to be performed to earn the reward for the client. For example, completion of one homework paper per day in math earns 20 minutes of playing a favorite video game at home. The counselor selects counseling interventions for attaining the goals.
5. The counselor evaluates the plan for observable and measurable change in the target behavior.
6. If the plan is not effective, the counselor repeats Step 4. If the techniques prove effective, the counselor develops a maintenance plan to maintain the new behavior and move the client from extrinsic rewards to the intrinsic reward of learning that life is better when math assignments are completed.

EXAMPLE 1   Jerry completed none of his assignments in any of his school subjects. His teachers are lowering his grades because of his unwillingness to complete these assignments. He is referred to the counselor.

Step 1. The counselor talks with Jerry about the problem. Jerry is not happy with his grades but still has trouble concentrating on completing his work. He would like to do better on these assignments and make better grades.

Step 2. Jerry's past 10-day record is reviewed to determine the exact amount of work Jerry has been completing. The record verifies the teacher's report that Jerry does not complete many assignments, even though he starts about half of them.

Step 3. Jerry and the counselor agree that a good goal for a start would be to complete one assignment each day.

Step 4. For each assignment completed, Jerry will receive 10 points to be applied toward a total of 100 points, which can be exchanged for 30 minutes of free-time learning activities during the school day.

Step 5. Evaluation of the contingency contract indicates that Jerry completed 4 assignments the first week, earning 40 points, and 6 assignments the second week, for a total of 100 points. He then received his 30 minutes of free time. The following week, he earned 100 points and received a second 30 minutes of free-time learning activities. He was also successful during Week 3.

Step 6. The counselor and Jerry agree that continuing with the point system is not necessary. Jerry's grades are improving, and everyone seems happier—the

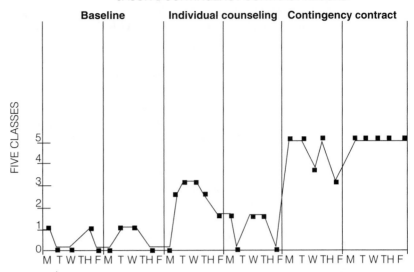

FIGURE 9-3 | Jason's Contingency Contract Record

teacher, Jerry, and his parents. As a maintenance procedure, Jerry agrees to check in with the counselor each Friday afternoon for reports on his completed assignments for the week, which he records on a pocket-size scorecard. Of course, a good teaching procedure would be to continue to allow Jerry and his classmates to earn free time when they complete assigned work. It would also be helpful if Jerry's parents would award more privileges at home as Jerry's work improves.

EXAMPLE 2 Jason, a ninth grade student, was referred to the counselor for not completing assignments in his five classes. He was taking a "college-bound" curriculum that required completion of daily school and work assignments. Jason's prior work in middle school and his test scores were indicative of a student who was clearly underachieving. His parents were punishing him for his inattention to school work by taking away his computer games and game system privileges. Baseline data collected over the past 2 weeks indicated that Jason was completing work in only one class, and that was done on 4 of 10 school days. Individual counseling appeared to be somewhat effective during the first week it was tried; but at the conclusion of the second week, Jason's performance had nearly retreated to its baseline rate. The counselor met with Jason and his parents for the purpose of designing a contract where he could be in charge of time for his game system and computer game. An illustration of the plan and its progress can be found in Figure 9-3. Contingency contracts have a "Let's make a deal" focus. The "deal" was that for each day of completed work in all five of his classes, Jason would earn 1 hour of game time that could be shared with his friends.

For a perfect week of completed work, he would earn a bonus of 3 hours. Jason's performance was a dramatic improvement over his baseline and counseling intervention record. He had 3 days with all work completed during the first week and a perfect week during the second week, in which he earned 8 hours of game time. After the behavior has been established, the goal would be to help Jason move from a dependence on extrinsic reinforcement to intrinsic reinforcement, where Jason would realize that life works better for him when he completes his work. His grades are going up. His parents and teachers are off his back, and he controls the time he gets to spend on computer games. Eventually, the record-keeping and reinforcement schedule can be dropped, and as long as his grades remain high, Jason can monitor his free-time activities. However, it is important to have a maintenance plan in place. One such plan would have Jason check in with his counselor at the end of the school day on each Friday with an index card, checked and signed by his teachers, indicating the days when all work was completed. The counselor would reinforce and encourage Jason to keep up his good work and place his card in a card file under his name.

SELF-MANAGEMENT

An adaptation of the six-step contingency contract method, the self-management plan, is for people who can take more responsibility for their behavior. These plans also follow a step-by-step process: defining a problem in behavioral terms, collecting data on the problem, introducing a treatment program based on behavioral principles, evaluating the effectiveness of the program, and appropriately changing the program if the plan is not working. The major difference between self-management and other procedures is that clients assume the major responsibility for carrying out their programs, including arranging their own contingencies or reinforcement when they have the skills to do so.

Steps in developing a self-management plan are as follows:

1. Choose an observable and measurable behavior you wish to change, for example, completing daily home assignments.
2. Record the following for at least 1 week: (a) your target behavior, (b) the setting in which it occurs, (c) the antecedent events leading to the behavior, and (d) the consequences resulting from the behavior.
3. Set a goal you can achieve.
4. Change the setting and the antecedent events preventing the target behavior from occurring.
5. Change the consequences that reinforce the target behavior.
6. Keep accurate records of your target behavior—your successes and failures.
7. Develop a plan for rewarding yourself when you meet your daily goal and a plan to punish or levy a fine on yourself when you fail to meet your daily goal.
8. Arrange a plan to maintain the goals you have reached.

Self-management contracts are generally not effective for younger children unless the plan is managed by both the child and an older person. Self-tracking and self-rewarding usually are difficult for children younger than 11. Children can set goals and choose consequences, but they need an adult to monitor for tracking and reinforcing behavior. Training in self-management skills has been one of the best applications of behavioral principles to counseling children and adolescents.

SHAPING

The basic operant technique of shaping is a general procedure designed to induce new behaviors by reinforcing behaviors that approximate the desired behavior. Each successive approximation of the behavior is reinforced until the desired behavior is obtained. To administer the technique, the counselor must know how to skillfully use (1) looking, (2) waiting, and (3) reinforcing. The counselor looks for the desired behavior, waits until it occurs, and reinforces it when it does occur. In essence, the counselor is catching the child in good behavior—a much more difficult task than catching the child in bad behavior. Shaping of successful approximations of the target behavior works well with children if the program is administered correctly. Small steps need to be reinforced immediately each time they occur. Shaping offers a method for teaching complex behaviors to children because mediating steps are identified and rewarded. Extrinsic reinforcers are more likely to be effective with children. Sugar-free candy, stickers, trinkets, and "good behavior" ink stamps on the hand all work well. Pairing intrinsic rewards with extrinsic rewards is always good practice to help children move away from the need for extrinsic rewards.

BEHAVIORAL MOMENTUM

Behavioral momentum is a relatively new concept in behavioral counseling. It operates on much the same principle of Newton's law of motion, which states that a body in motion tends to remain in motion. Behavioral momentum has been used mostly to reduce noncompliant behavior in children and adults. Momentum is established by making three to five short, easy requests with a high probability of compliance administered to a person just before a request having a low probability of compliance. Each high-probability request is reinforced by verbal praise on compliance. The theory is that the reinforcement gained from doing the easy tasks builds momentum that carries over to completion of the more difficult or low-compliance task. Romano and Roll (2000) have researched the level of compliance needed on the easy tasks to carry over for completion of the difficult task. High-probability tasks are generally defined as those having an 80 percent compliance rate. Romano and Roll have investigated the momentum effect that requests with medium levels of compliance probability might have. Medium levels of compliance probability were set at

50 to 70 percent of the time. The researchers found that both high and medium levels of compliance probability were effective in increasing compliance to low-probability requests.

Ray, Skinner, and Watson (1999), in a related study on behavioral momentum, found that momentum could be established by having parents of an autistic child administer the easy tasks, followed by the teacher administering the difficult task. Before the intervention, the student had consistently displayed noncompliant behavior toward the teacher. In this case, stimulus control did transfer from the parents to the teacher.

BIOFEEDBACK

In biofeedback, a machine accomplishes the three behaviors of looking, waiting, and reinforcing. Brain waves, muscle tension, body temperature, heart rate, and blood pressure can be monitored for small changes and fed back to the client by auditory and visual means. Biofeedback methods have been successful in, for example, teaching hyperactive children to relax. The more the child relaxes, the slower and lower is the beeping sound on the monitor. The equipment may provide feedback with electric trains and recorded music. Both stop when the child stops relaxing and restart when the child takes the first small step toward relaxing again. An understanding of cause and effect by the children enhances biofeedback methods but is not a necessity.

MODELING

Modeling consists of exposing the child to one or more individuals, either in real life or in film or tape presentations, who exhibit behaviors to be adopted by the child. Counselors may be the models to demonstrate certain behaviors to the child, or peers of the child may be used.

Peers are an important part of a child's world, and their influence can help children change. Children usually imitate the behaviors of people they like. A model may be presented to the child through the use of television, films, videotapes, or books. Other models include friends, classmates, adults, and the counselor.

For example, Charlene mentioned a friend, Patty, a number of times during the counseling sessions. She indicated that she would like to be like Patty because Patty had a lot of friends, made good grades, and got along well with her parents and teachers. The counselor asked Charlene to observe Patty's behaviors closely for 1 week and to write on an index card those behaviors she particularly liked and wanted to imitate. The next week, Charlene brought back her list of six behaviors. The counselor and Charlene selected the most important one for Charlene (giving compliments) and began to work on that behavior. Role-playing and behavior rehearsal were included in the counseling to help Charlene learn the new behaviors. The observed behaviors were practiced and modified until they were appropriate for Charlene. As counseling progressed, Charlene continued to observe her model and to practice new behaviors until she became more like her ideal self.

Modeling is a process for teaching children voluntary behaviors through observation and replication of desired behaviors. Modeling and shaping could be done in combination for younger children. Negative reinforcement is effective in this process if a new behavior is learned to avoid a consequence such as peer ridicule.

TOKEN ECONOMIES

Token economies are used on a group basis, as in a school classroom. The children earn tokens or points for certain target behaviors. These behaviors are classified as either on task or socially appropriate. Children also lose tokens or points for off-task and socially inappropriate behaviors. Children may periodically cash in tokens or points earned for rewards such as learning-enrichment activities, game time, trinkets, and sugarless candy. Some teachers use token economies for their classroom groups. An empty jar sits on the teacher's desk. Every time something good happens in the classroom, the teacher drops some marbles in the jar. The marble noise becomes an auditory reinforcement to go with the visual image of the jar filling up. A full jar means all students get free popcorn during the lunch period. The Case Study describing Sue that appears later in this chapter is an example of how to use a token economy contract.

BEHAVIOR-PRACTICE GROUPS

Behavior-practice groups have some advantages in counseling children. They provide a relatively safe setting for the child to practice new behaviors before trying them out in real-life situations. These groups are also useful in supporting and reinforcing children as they attempt new behaviors and reach goals. Behavior-practice groups may focus on any of several behavior changes, including the following:

- Weight loss
- Study habits
- Assertiveness training
- Communication skills
- Negative addictions such as drugs, alcohol, and smoking

In working with behavior-practice groups, the counselor needs to develop a lesson plan with behavioral objectives, instructional methods, reinforcement, and evaluation. A good lesson plan maintains a balance among three teaching strategies: (1) tell me, (2) show me, and (3) let me try it. For example, a lesson plan in assertiveness training might have the following objective: After ten weekly group meetings, each child in the group will have demonstrated in at least three real-life settings the ability to do the following:

1. Make an effective complaint
2. Give negative feedback
3. Give positive feedback

4. Make a reasonable request
5. Say no to an unreasonable request

ROLE-PLAYING

Role-playing is a counseling technique that is not restricted to one theory. Many counseling professionals use it. Behavioral counselors often find that role-playing facilitates their clients' progress in self-management programs; for example, it can help clients see their behaviors as others see them and obtain feedback about these behaviors. Role-playing also can provide practice for decision making and exploring consequences.

Negative role-playing or rehearsal can be helpful in identifying what *not* to do. Role-playing negative behaviors and their consequences may help children evaluate objectively what is happening and the consequences of their behavior.

Role-playing can help children learn about cause and effect and experience the consequences of their behavior in a relatively safe setting. Role-playing is useful to children who are working toward developing a sense of empathy and beginning to modify their egocentric views of the world. Children usually can act out a problem scenario better than they can describe it.

ROLE-PLAYING TO DEFINE A PROBLEM   Children often have trouble describing exactly what occurred in a particular situation, especially one involving interpersonal problems with parents, teachers, or peers. Moreover, they may be unable to see clearly how certain behaviors have evoked an unwanted response or consequence. For example, suppose Jason tells the counselor that he and his mother are in constant conflict. She is unfair and never allows him to do *anything* he asks. Role-playing could provide some insight into what occurs when Jason asks for permission.

COUNSELOR: I'll be your mother, and you show me exactly how you ask her to allow you, for instance, to have a birthday party. Talk to me exactly as you would to your mother if you were to ask her for the party.

JASON: Mom, you never let me do anything! You always say no to anything I want. I want a birthday party, and you'll be mean if you don't let me have one this year!

The counselor can now readily see that if a conflict already exists between mother and child, this demand will increase the conflict and is unlikely to get Jason his birthday party.

Children having trouble with peers might be asked to describe what happened, and then to role-play one or more persons in the incident. Verbal and nonverbal behaviors not adequately described in relating the incident often become more apparent when they are demonstrated through role-playing.

ROLE REVERSAL   When conflicts occur between children, adults frequently ask one child, "How would you feel if he hit you like that [said that to you, bit you, and so on]?" The purpose of this admonition is to have the child empathize with the other. However, many cognitive theorists, especially Piaget, emphasize that young children up through the preoperational stage (2–7 years old) lack the cognitive development to be able to put themselves in another person's place. Because children better understand what they see, hear, or experience directly, role-playing other children's positions could promote a better understanding than a verbal admonition.

COUNSELOR: Barbara, I understand from your sister that you hit her on the head quite often. Would you agree that this is what happens?

BARBARA: Yeah, I can really make her move if I threaten to hit her on the head!

COUNSELOR: Would the two of you describe to me what happened the last time you hit Judy? [The girls describe the incident.] Now, Barbara, I wonder if you would mind playing Judy and saying and doing exactly what Judy did. I would like Judy to say and do exactly what you did. [Remind the girls that hitting hard is not allowed during role-playing because people are not for hitting.]

The purpose of this role reversal is to help Barbara experience Judy's feelings when Barbara hit her, with the hope that Barbara will then want to explore better methods of relating to Judy.

Role reversal can be effective when communication breaks down between parents and children, between teachers and children, between peers, or between counselors and their clients. Each player can gain increased knowledge of the other's point of view.

Role-playing Used as Behavior Rehearsal   To refine a speech and ensure a smooth delivery, most adults rehearse a speech before presenting it to an audience. Children also may feel more comfortable about trying a new behavior if they can practice it before actually facing the real world.

Dave is a shy child who has no friends. In an effort to help Dave make friends, the counselor may want to help him decide exactly how to approach another child and what to say to the child after the opening "Hello." To build confidence, the counselor could first role-play another child and allow Dave to practice his new behaviors in a safe atmosphere. When Dave feels secure in role-playing with the counselor, another child can be involved in the role-playing to help Dave gain more realistic experiences in meeting other children.

Counseling Homework Assignments

Homework assignments may be given to children in counseling for a variety of reasons. Homework can build continuity between sessions and facilitate counseling by encouraging "work" on the child's problems between sessions. A homework assignment could be a commitment by the child to keep a record of some particular feeling or behavior, to reduce or stop a present behavior, or to try a new behavior. Homework assignments provide the child with an opportunity to try out new or different behaviors and discuss the consequences with the counselor. For example, after Dave (see preceding example) has rehearsed approaching a new person within the counseling session, the counselor might ask him to approach one new person during the coming week and try out this new behavior. Dave could evaluate whether the new behavior was effective for him and discuss the results with the counselor; if it was not effective, they could explore other methods.

ASSERTIVENESS TRAINING

Some children's typical response to everyday interactions is withdrawal. Some of these children may have low self-esteem or feelings of inferiority that inhibit them; others, having experienced negative consequences as a result of speaking out, are inhibited from doing so by their anxiety. Children who are withdrawn and passive need to be encouraged to recognize their rights as people, as well as accept the rights of others.

Tim and Charles were close friends. However, Tim always took from Charles whatever he wanted or needed—toys, pencils, food, and so on. Charles responded passively, always allowing Tim to have his way. The counselor asked Charles to describe in detail the latest incident, in which Tim had taken Charles's new bike, ridden it all afternoon, and brought it back scratched. The counselor encouraged Charles to formulate an assertive statement, such as "I want to ride my new bike. Would you go and get your bike to ride?" Charles and the counselor took several incidents from the past, and Charles was encouraged to state (1) his needs and (2) what he would like to have happen in each situation. They then used behavior rehearsal to give Charles an opportunity to practice his assertiveness.

After several sessions, Charles made a commitment to try out his new response. He reported that he told Tim, "I want to use my colored markers now. Would you get your own?" and that it had worked. The counselor worked for several months on helping Charles learn how to become appropriately assertive. Each new situation was discussed and practiced in the counseling sessions before Charles actually tried it in daily living.

A word of caution is necessary to counselors teaching assertiveness to children. The adults in the child's life must be prepared for the child's new behavior. Parents may not tolerate assertiveness on the part of their child. To avoid unpleasant consequences, the counselor has to determine the effect of the child's behavioral change on the child's significant others and on the child's culture and environment before teaching the child this new skill.

CLASSICAL CONDITIONING METHODS

IVAN PAVLOV (1849–1936)

Classical conditioning has its roots in the work of the Russian physiologist Ivan Pavlov. Born in 1849, Pavlov began his education in a seminary school but abandoned his pursuit of the priesthood for his fascination with science. He received his M.D. in 1883 from the University of St. Petersburg and was made director of several research facilities, including the Imperial Institute of

Experimental Medicines (Windholtz, 1997). Pavlov was awarded the Nobel Prize in 1904 for his book *Lectures on the Work of the Digestive Glands.*

Reminded that he had studied all the digestive juices of the body with the exception of saliva, Pavlov came out of retirement to research how saliva contributed to the digestive process, if at all. In collecting saliva from dogs, he made several observations. He noted that dogs salivated when they were fed and when they heard any noise that accompanied it, such as the click of opening the dog pen gate. This observation led to further experiments with Pavlov's classical, or respondent, conditioning model and to more efficient methods for collecting saliva for his research.

Classical, or respondent, conditioning can be defined as a form of learning that occurs when a neutral stimulus (the conditioned stimulus) elicits a response after multiple pairings with another stimulus (the unconditioned stimulus). In other words, respondent behavior is associated with classical conditioning, in which learning occurs when a stimulus that already elicits a response (an unconditioned stimulus) is presented together with a neutral stimulus that elicits no response or a different response. With repeated pairings of the two stimuli, the neutral stimulus begins to elicit the same response as the unconditioned stimulus. In the case of Pavlov's dogs, for example, Pavlov paired the unconditioned stimulus of food with the neutral stimulus of a bell. The response to the unconditioned stimulus was salivating. The neutral stimulus (the bell) became the conditioned stimulus, and the response to the conditioned stimulus became the conditioned response (salivating).

Wolpe and Plaud (1997) present an overview of the development of behavior therapy, which feature the contributions of Pavlov through his work on animal conditioning. Pavlov and his students discovered experimental neurosis, which could be produced and eliminated in animals through conditioning and counterconditioning. Many of his counterconditioning techniques are in use today to treat neurotic and anxiety reactions. Pavlov found he could eliminate undesirable conditioned responses and reduce associated anxieties by manipulating conditioned stimuli. As a footnote to history, Pavlov's Nobel Prize work on digestive juices has since been proved to be erroneous. The portion of his work that has withstood the test of time is his classical conditioning method first used to collect saliva from dogs.

SYSTEMATIC DESENSITIZATION

Systematic desensitization, developed by Wolpe (1958, 1969) from earlier work by Jacobsen (1938), is a procedure used to eliminate anxiety and fear. A response incompatible with anxiety, such as relaxation, is paired with weak and then progressively stronger anxiety-provoking stimuli. The approach is based on the principles of counterconditioning; that is, if all skeletal muscles are deeply relaxed, one cannot experience anxiety at the same time.

A student may be experiencing anxiety related to specific stimulus situations such as taking tests, performing in front of a group, being in high places, or seeing some animal. The first step is to develop a hierarchy of scenes related to the fear or phobia, with mildly aversive scenes at the bottom and progressively more aversive scenes at the top. The counselor then teaches the student the process of deep muscle relaxation and asks the relaxed child to visualize the various scenes in the hierarchy.

The relaxation exercises are successively tensing and relaxing nineteen different muscle groups at 6-second intervals until a high level of relaxation is achieved. The process usually is performed with the student in a recliner chair or stretched out on a soft rug. The student is asked to go as high as possible on the hierarchy without feeling anxiety. When the student feels anxiety, he or she signals the counselor by raising one finger, and the counselor reverts to a less anxiety-provoking scene. Behavior practice facilitates the process. A student may successively practice giving a short speech in front of a mirror, with an audio tape recorder, with a video recorder, in front of a best friend, in front of a small group, and so on, until the student can give the speech in front of twenty-five classmates. The student's stimulus hierarchy might look like this:

0.   Lying in bed in your room just before going to sleep—describe your room
1.   Thinking about the speech alone in your room 1 week before you give it
2.   Discussing the upcoming speech in class 1 week before it's due
3.   Sitting in class while another student gives a speech 1 week before your speech
4.   Writing your speech at home
5.   Practicing your speech alone in your room or in front of your friend
6.   Getting dressed the morning of the speech
7.   Eating breakfast and thinking about the speech before going to school
8.   Walking to school on the day of your speech
9.   Entering the classroom on the day of the speech
10.   Waiting while another student gives a speech on the day of your presentation
11.   Standing in front of your classmates and looking at their faces
12.   Presenting your speech before the class

The technique consists of asking the student to relax, imagine, relax, stop imagining, relax, and so on until, after repeated practice, the student learns to relax while visualizing each stage of the stimulus hierarchy.

Several relaxation exercises can be used with clients. Following are two types of exercises frequently used.

1.   Consciously "let go" of the various muscle groups, starting with your feet and moving to your legs, stomach, arms, neck, and head as you make yourself as comfortable as you can in a chair or lying down.

a. Stop frowning; let your forehead relax.
b. Let your hands, arms, and so on relax.
c. Tighten 6 seconds, relax; tighten again 6 seconds, relax.

2. Form mental pictures.

   a. Picture yourself stretched out on a soft bed. Your legs are like concrete, sinking down in the mattress from their weight. Picture a friend coming into the room and trying to lift your concrete legs, but they are too heavy and your friend cannot do it. Repeat with arms, neck, and so on.

   b. Picture your body as a big puppet. Your hands are tied loosely to your wrists by strings. Your forearm is connected loosely by a string to your shoulder. Your feet and legs are also connected with a string. Your chin has dropped loosely against your chest. All strings are loose; your body is limp and sprawled across the bed.

   c. Picture your body as consisting of a bunch of rubber balloons. Two air holes open in your feet, and the air begins to escape from your legs. Your legs begin to collapse until they are flat rubber tubes. Next, a hole is opened in your chest, and the air begins to escape until your entire body is lying flat on the bed. Continue with your head, arms, neck, and so on.

   d. Imagine the most relaxing, pleasant scene you can remember—a time when you felt really good and peaceful. If you remember fishing in a mountain stream, pay attention to the little things, such as quiet ripples on the water and leaves on the trees. What sounds were present? Did you hear the quiet rustling of the leaves? Is your relaxing place before an open fireplace with logs crackling, or is it the beach, with a warm sun and breezes?

Continued practice facilitates achievement of these mental pictures and relaxation levels.

Systematic desensitization, a classical conditioning technique, could be too complex for younger children, who are not always capable of handling sequential behaviors. Conscious relaxation and visualization may also be difficult for younger children, who benefit more by actual practice of the steps in the stimulus hierarchy. For example, the following systematic desensitization program could be used to help a 6-year-old child who is experiencing school phobia: The child indicates that he would like to work toward getting a favorite video game. A chart is drawn up with spaces to star each day he followed the program and earned a dollar toward the purchase price of his video game. Steps in the hierarchy were small enough not to overwhelm the child. Each session lasted 30 minutes.

Step 1. Child and his mother working together alone in the schoolroom, the child reading or talking to his mother

Step 2. Child, mother, and friend of the child in the schoolroom, with the child talking to his friend

Step 3. Child, mother, friend, and familiar adult (not on the school staff) together in the schoolroom, with child talking while playing

Step 4. Child, mother, friend, and teacher in the schoolroom, the child talking with the teacher; mother leaves them; friend leaves

Step 5. Child and teacher together in the schoolroom, talking to each other

Step 6. Child and teacher move to the classroom and talk to each other

Step 7. Child joins the classroom for half a day

Step 8. Child spends an entire day in the classroom

In extreme cases of anxiety, desensitization methods may need to be paired with appropriate reinforcers such as sugar-free candy to help the child relax. Performing the task becomes the final step in the hierarchy.

Classical conditioning and operant conditioning usually occur at the same time. A student is given after-school detention for disrupting her class. Detention has the operant effect of preventing the child's disruptive behavior; however, detention may also cause a classical conditioned response of hating school because more school is used as punishment. School time becomes associated with punishment. Associating being in school with a privilege would be much better. When the student misbehaves, she loses the privilege of being in class and has to spend her class time working in a time-out area or in the in-school suspension room. Additional school time (detention) would not be used as a punishment or consequence.

In summary, the technique of desensitization is based on a principle of learning referred to as *reciprocal inhibition*—that is, an organism cannot make two contradictory responses at the same time. If we assume that all responses are learned, relearning or reconditioning can extinguish them. Therefore, relaxation, being more rewarding than anxiety, can gradually replace anxiety as the response to the anxiety-evoking situation.

Wolpe (1989), attacking those who practiced cognitive therapy, makes the point that if a habit has been acquired by learning, the logical approach is to treat it by a method based on learning principles. He writes that the real difference between true behavioral therapy and cognitive therapy is the cognitivists' failure to deny the possibility that some fears may be immediately triggered by a particular stimulus without the mediation of an idea of danger. Wolpe also criticizes cognitive therapists for dispensing with the behavior analysis required for successful treatment of neurotic suffering.

FLOODING

Flooding, the opposite of desensitization, begins with the most feared stimulus in the stimulus hierarchy rather than the weakest or least feared. It is diving into cold water rather than getting used to it gradually. The clients are exposed to their strongest fears by putting themselves into the situation repeatedly over a short period of time. For example, a client might make several public speeches over a period of 2 weeks. The constant, concentrated approach has the effect of literally wearing out the stimulus. Flooding conducted during visualization exercises is referred to as *implosion*.

Flooding, also referred to as *reactive* or *internal inhibition,* is a process in which an anxiety-evoking stimulus is presented continuously, leading to fatigue and eventual unlearning of the undesirable response. When a parent told you to get back on your bike after a crash, you were exposed to the flooding technique. Another application might involve taking a child with a fear of riding in cars on a 4-hour trip. The initial response would be high anxiety or panic, which would, after a while, wear itself out as a stimulus. For example, the next time you find your eyelid blinking involuntarily when you are under too much stress, try blinking your eyelid 100 times without stopping (flooding). If the blinking continues, try again with 200 blinks of your eyelid.

HYPNOSIS

A technique that incorporates deeper forms of relaxation, hypnosis has long been controversial; however, researchers have found that it can be a useful tool for working with children and adolescents. Children seem to be fascinated with the procedure and, therefore, are usually easier to hypnotize than adults. Hypnotherapy has been used successfully with clients experiencing anxiety, high blood pressure, asthma, and psychosomatic pain and to overcome such habits as nail biting, thumb sucking, tics, insomnia, and sleepwalking.

The danger of hypnotherapy, of course, comes when untrained individuals attempt to use the procedure. Counselors may wish to investigate the availability of training in this area. Hypnotherapy appears to be a highly effective counseling tool for working with repressed conflicts, including memories of childhood sexual abuse. However, questions have been raised about hypnosis eliciting false memories of such abuse. Therefore, we suggest that counselors proceed with caution in selecting their training in hypnosis and in their practice of hypnosis after completing their training.

COUNTERCONDITIONING

In counterconditioning, a stronger pleasant stimulus is paired with a weaker aversive stimulus as a procedure for overcoming the anxiety the aversive stimulus evokes. For example, a child may be given his or her favorite candy while sitting in the classroom. If the candy is sufficiently rewarding to the child, the anxiety evoked by the classroom should be diminished.

AVERSIVE CONDITIONING

Aversive conditioning is the application of an aversive or noxious stimulus, such as a rubber-band snap on the wrist, when a maladaptive response or behavior occurs. For example, children could wear rubber bands around their wrists and snap them each time they found themselves daydreaming instead of listening to the teacher. Opportunity for helpful behavior to occur and be reinforced is recommended with this technique.

The following diagrams represent each of the four classical conditioning methods presented earlier ($\oplus$ = pleasant stimulus; $\ominus$ = aversive stimulus):

1. Desensitization—where $\ominus$ is giving a speech. The aversive stimulus is handled in small steps by visualization or relaxation and by practice until increasingly larger steps can be handled.
2. Flooding (internal inhibition)—where $\ominus$ is getting back on the bike after falling off. The aversive stimulus is continually repeated until the fear response wears itself out.
3. Counterconditioning—where $\oplus$ is a candy bar and $\ominus$ is going to school. The larger pleasant stimulus overcomes the anxiety or fear evoked by the smaller aversive stimulus.
4. Aversive conditioning—where $\ominus$ is a snap of a rubber band on the wrist and $\oplus$ is daydreaming during class. The more painful stimulus overcomes the smaller reward gained from daydreaming in class.

CASE STUDY

Identification of the Problem

Sue is a 9-year-old girl in the fourth grade. She has exhibited some behavior problems in her classroom. She does not complete her classroom assignments, tells lies about her work and about things she does at home and at school, and is reported to be constantly out of her seat.

Individual and Background Information

Academic. Sue has an above-average IQ. She is an excellent reader and has the ability to do any fourth-grade assignment.

Family. Sue is an only child. Her parents are in their 30s. Sue comes from an upper-middle-class family; her father and mother manage their own business.

Social. Sue seems to get along relatively well with the other children but has only one close friend, Marie. Sue has been caught telling lies by the other children, and they tell her they do not like her lies. She brings money and trinkets to share with Marie and lets her wear her nice coats, sweaters, and jewelry. Sue has no other children to play with and is mostly around adults who let her have her own way.

Counseling Method

The counselor in this case used a behavioral counseling technique to help Sue evaluate her behavior and make better decisions. When using this method, counselors have to determine how much they are going to influence the client's choices in modifying behavior. The criteria for determining when to use behavioral counseling are based on the frequency of the maladaptive behavior and the degree to which it hinders the child's healthy development and that of other children in the class.

In this case, the counselor used the following steps:

1. Establish a warm, talking relationship (therapeutic alliance) with the child.
2. List the problem behaviors on paper.
3. List rewards and consequences for doing appropriate and inappropriate behavior.
4. Obtain a commitment from the client on the plan of action that would be most likely to help.
5. Use a behavior contract with positive reinforcement in the form of a social reward (praise) for desirable behavior and token reinforcement (points to exchange for learning-enrichment activities). Positive reinforcers are withdrawn (by loss of points) when undesirable behavior occurs.
6. Draw up plans for a behavior contract. These plans are discussed with, agreed on, and signed by the client, counselor, teacher, and parents because the child was exhibiting some of the undesirable behavior at home by not completing assigned tasks and telling her parents lies.

Transcript

COUNSELOR: Sue, your teacher sent you to me because you seem to be having some problems in class. Would you like to tell me what kind of problems you are having? I'll write them down in a list so we can see what could be done to help you here and at home.

SUE: I just can't seem to get my work done or turned in on time.

COUNSELOR: How do you stop yourself from doing this?

SUE: I just can't seem to be able to sit in my seat long enough to finish, and then time is always up before I finish.

COUNSELOR: Who else is affected by your getting out of your seat?

SUE: I guess I'm keeping the others from working when I go to their seats, and it bothers my teacher because she stops what she is doing and tells me to sit down and get busy.

COUNSELOR: What happens when you don't finish your work?

SUE: Well, nothing really happens, except I try to get out of being fussed at and being kept in during play period for not doing my work.

COUNSELOR: What do you mean, Sue?

SUE: I make up stories about I can't find my paper or somebody took it when I really hadn't even started it, or I hide what I have started in my desk or notebook and take it home and do it and then turn it in the next day and say I found it.

COUNSELOR: What do you tell your mom and dad about your work for the day when they ask you?

SUE: Well, I tell a story to them too. I tell them I did all my work, and usually the same things I tell the teacher I tell them too.

COUNSELOR:	How do you feel about telling untrue stories?
SUE:	I don't really feel good about it, but I want Mom and Dad to be proud of me and I really do want to do my work, but I just can't seem to do it, so I just tell a story.
COUNSELOR:	Okay, Sue, you say you want to change, so let's look at the list of things you want to change and see what you and I can work out together.
SUE:	Okay, I'd like that.
COUNSELOR:	Let me read your contract terms to you. If you think there is anything you can't live with, we'll change it until we get it the way we think will help you the most. This contract tells you what will happen when you are able to finish your work. Your teacher, your mom and dad, you, and I will all sign it to show you we are all willing to help you live up to the terms. Will you go over it with your mother and father and see if there is anything that needs to be changed?
SUE:	I think it's okay just the way it is.
COUNSELOR:	Okay, you and I will sign first, and I will send copies to your teacher and your parents to sign. We will try this for a week, and then you and I will meet at the same time next week to see how you are doing and if any changes need to be made.
SUE:	Okay.

Contract for Behavior and Learning

POSITIVE BEHAVIORS	**TOKENS**
1. Bringing needed materials to class	5
2. Working on class or home assignment until finished	5
3. Staying in seat	5
4. Extra credit (reading assignments or laminated task sheets)	1, 2, 3, 4, 5

You may exchange tokens earned for positive behavior for time to do learning-enrichment activities.

LEARNING-ENRICHMENT ACTIVITIES	**TOKENS**
1. Writing on the small chalkboards	15
2. Playing phonic rummy	15
3. Playing with the tray puzzles	15
4. Getting to be the library aide for a day	15
5. Getting to use the computer	15
6. Playing Old Maids with classmates	10
7. Using the headphone and tape recorder to hear a story from video or audio tapes	15
8. Using clay, finger paints, and other art supplies	10

I, _____, agree to abide by the terms set forth in this contract. It is my understanding that tokens earned will depend on my classroom work and behavior.

Signature

We, your teacher, your parents, and your counselor, agree to abide by the conditions specified in the contract. It is our understanding that we will assist you in any way we can with your work and problems.

Teacher

Parents

Counselor

Behavioral counseling helps individuals look at what they are doing and what happens when they do it. The contract helps children try different behaviors to see which ones work for them. It encourages parents to adhere to the terms of the contract and positively reinforce all desirable behaviors at home. If the child continues to receive positive reinforcement for socially desirable and classroom-adaptive behavior, the counselor gradually implements a self-reinforcement system and maintenance plan to help the child develop a sense of intrinsic reinforcement where he or she realizes that life is better at school and home when he or she makes good decisions about his or her school work and general behavior.

APPLICATIONS OF BEHAVIORAL COUNSELING

Behavioral counselors have more supporting research data available than counselors practicing other counseling approaches. As noted previously, behavioral counselors must collect accurate data if their procedures are to operate with maximum efficiency. Therefore, they have done a thorough job of validating their successful outcomes.

The purpose of behavioral counseling is to change the client's overt and covert responses (cognitions, emotions, physiological states). Bandura (1974) reacted to the oft-repeated dictum, "Change contingencies and you change behavior," by adding the reciprocal side: "Change behavior and you change the contingencies . . . since in everyday life this two-way control operates concurrently" (p. 866). Behavioral counselors work with behavior that is objective and measurable. Behavioral counseling methods, not confined to one stimulus–response theory of learning, are derived from a variety of learning principles.

The distinguishing features of behavioral counseling include the functional analysis of behavior and the development of the necessary technology to bring about change. Thus, behavioral counseling is the application of specified procedures derived from experimental research to benefit individuals, groups, and organizations.

RESPONSE COST

Introducing response cost into behavioral programs often is necessary to modify difficult and well-established behavior patterns. One example is the treatment of enuretic children, in which a waking schedule is often a first-step method in solving the bed-wetting problem. When the first step fails, response cost is introduced as a second-step intervention. When the bed is wet, the child is required to change bed linens, clean urine-alarm pads, remake the bed, and reset the alarm after each wetting. The child receives monetary rewards for success in postponing urination. After 14 dry days, overlearning is started by having the child drink 16 ounces of water before bedtime. Fourteen dry days after overlearning is defined as successful completion of the program. Treatment of encopresis is also successfully treated by response cost methods combined with reinforcement and punishment. Typical response cost contracts include washing dirty clothes, bathing immediately after soiling, doing extra chores, losing privileges, or a combination of such tasks. Reinforcement includes spending time in favorite activities with parents or receiving a toy, money, or both.

EATING DISORDERS

Behavioral counseling has been effective in treating eating disorders. Response prevention has been used to treat bulimia, in which eating is followed by vomiting or purging, which relieves the anxiety produced by eating and sustains the habit of binge eating because it removes the consequence of feeling guilty. The treatment plan is designed to allow the client to eat but not purge. The client is forced to tolerate the resulting anxiety and guilt by locking all nearby bathroom doors and remaining in the presence of other people, in front of whom the client is ashamed to vomit. This rather harsh treatment should be accompanied by plans to teach the client how to eat in moderation until it produces less anxiety and the client can eat normal amounts of food without vomiting.

Anorexic clients need positive reinforcement (social activities and visiting privileges) and punishment (isolation, bed rest, and tube feeding) to encourage eating and gaining weight. Friends and family often reward undesired behaviors with their attention and sympathy and need to be instructed how to reward the helpful and lifesaving behaviors of eating and gaining weight.

MULTIMODAL APPROACHES

Multimodal treatment plans are recommended for aggressive and violent youths, who present a wide range of learning styles and complex personalities that cannot be treated effectively with a single approach for everyone. We believe that the same argument holds true for all people. Suggested interventions for aggressive and resistant youths include cognitive-behavioral counseling, the expressive arts, stress management, modeling of social skills, and the conflict resolution skills of negotiation and compromise. Interventions for unwilling clients include: (1) frequent group therapy with individual therapy as a contingency for refusal to participate in the group, (2) options for clients to terminate therapy after certain behavioral goals have been met, and (3) allowing them to know as much as possible about their cases by sharing case records and tapes of their counseling sessions, together with the privilege of sitting in on their own case conferences. Many of the recommendations rest on the assumption that aggressive and violent people are fascinated with themselves and that sharing their case data with them may draw them into the treatment process by making them active participants.

CROSS-CULTURAL APPLICATIONS OF BEHAVIORAL COUNSELING

Behavioral counseling is most compatible with cultures that prefer behavioral interventions over working with the cognitive and affective parts of the problems brought to counseling. Behavioral counseling focuses on present behavior and on achieving short-term behavioral changes leading to the attainment of specific, measurable goals. The behavioral counselor functions more as a directive, expert consultant than as a nondirective, active listener and facilitator for personal reflection. As noted in Chapter 15, with all of these characteristics, clients from African American, Latino, Asian American, African, Hispanic, and Asian cultures are likely to find behavioral counseling to be compatible with their preference for directive approaches focusing on current problems. Counselors using an active, direct, and expert approach should be cautious about exerting too much influence over the lives of clients from cultures that place a high premium on seeking advice from recognized experts.

Lee (1999) suggests that behavioral counselors beginning a counseling relationship would do well to be aware of the shame and guilt often felt by Asians, Native Americans, Latinos, and African Americans. Lee recommends selecting counseling techniques that focus on the positive things these clients bring to counseling rather than their maladaptive behaviors. Lee also points out that behavioral counseling might work well with Asian clients, who commonly believe that hard work, effort, and character development are the best cures for mental disorders (Christopher, 2003).

However, Diller (2004) and Ivey, D'Andrea, Ivey, & Simek-Morgan (2002) point out that counseling approaches, such as behavioral counseling, often put a major focus on individual responsibility for changing one's life, whereas neglecting cultural influences favoring an external locus of control in how people run their lives. These authors believe that directive approaches can still be effective if they are tailored to fit the cultural expectations of the clients.

BEHAVIORAL COUNSELING, ACCOUNTABILITY, AND MANAGED HEALTH CARE

As noted in Chapter 2, managed care organizations (MCOs) favor counseling treatments that hold the counselor accountable for session-to-session progress, culminating in reaching definite and specific goals in the shortest possible time. Behavioral counseling practitioners are well established to meet MCO requirements for third-party reimbursement. Treatment plans with specific, measurable goals generally can be implemented during the first session. Treatment periods are relatively brief, and client progress can be tracked on a daily or weekly basis. Costs for behavioral counseling treatments are relatively inexpensive, and client satisfaction with behavioral methods is generally high. Behavioral counseling, with accurate recording of baseline and post-treatment data, is well documented as an effective way to achieve rather impressive outcomes. In summary, behavioral counselors are apt to find themselves courted by MCOs for panel membership on their lists of approved and recommended counselors.

Lambert and Hawkins (2004) recommend three instruments for validating the counseling outcomes important to health maintenance organizations (HMOs): *Behavior and Symptom Identification Scale, Brief Symptom Inventory,* and *Outcome Questionnaire.* Each instrument has its strengths in being brief, easy to administer, and easy to score. Weaknesses include validity issues and weakness in constructs. We prefer using goal-attainment scales that are individualized for each client (see Chapter 2).

SUMMARY

The same eclectic theme that runs through the current literature on behavioral counseling is found in all approaches to counseling. Behavioral counseling methods by themselves are inadequate to treat the full range of human problems. A more eclectic approach, such as multimodal counseling, which is discussed elsewhere in this book, may be preferable. However, behavioral methods are valuable tools in the counselor's repertoire.

Reinforcement methods may serve to extinguish desired behavior when the reward or token replaces any intrinsic reward a person might receive from engaging in the desired behavior. For example, if parents reward or reinforce a child's piano practice, the message to the child may be that piano playing is not worth doing without pay, and therefore is not worthwhile in and of itself.

Children prefer independent group contingencies over interdependent and dependent group contingencies. Independent group contingencies require the same response of all individuals in the group, but access to reinforcement is based only on each individual's response (for example, everyone scoring 90 percent gets a reward). Interdependent contingencies depend on the collective performance of the group (for example, the entire group receives a reward if the group mean equals 90 percent or better). Dependent group contingencies are based on the performance of a selected member or selected members of the group (for example, if a paper drawn at random from a box containing all group members' test papers has a score of 90 percent or better, everyone receives a reward). Considerable evidence exists in the literature to support behavioral methods that use self-control, self-determination, and personal responsibility as motivators and reinforcers.

Behavioral counseling, like most other counseling methods, is moving toward multimodal or integrative approaches that use it in combination with other counseling approaches. However, behavioral counselors do share several commonalities. Their work is based on research in experimental and social psychology. Like most of the other counseling orientations presented in this book, behavioral counseling focuses more on present than past concerns and more on actions than on personality. Behavioral counselors operationalize terms referring to subjective states listed under such diagnostic categories as depression, anxiety, paranoia, shyness, obsession, and compulsion by describing these conditions as specific patterns of observable actions. For example, depression might be defined as loss of adequate reinforcement. Behavioral counselors are committed to defining problems precisely by breaking them down into observable and countable components of behavior. Behavioral goals are set in advance and systematically evaluated throughout the treatment process and follow-up period. Behavioral counselors view their work as re-educative rather than healing and reject diagnostic labels for behavior analysis. Often, behavioral counseling begins with a written contract outlining what the client is going to do and what outcomes are to be expected. Counseling begins with the behavior that is easiest to change, with accurate records maintained throughout the counseling experience. Behavioral counselors follow the scientific method in discarding ineffective interventions in favor of new intervention plans based on data collection and analysis.

INTRODUCTION TO BEHAVIORAL COUNSELING

To gain a more in-depth understanding of the concepts in this chapter, visit www.thomsonedu.com/counseling/thompson to view a short clip of an actual therapist-client session demonstrating behavioral counseling.

WEBSITES FOR BEHAVIORAL COUNSELING

Internet addresses frequently change. To find the sites listed here, visit www.thomsonedu.com/counseling/thompson for an updated list of Internet addresses and direct links to relevant sites.

Behavior OnLine: The Mental Health and Behavioral Science Meeting Place

Positive Reinforcement

REFERENCES

Bandura, A. (1974). Behavior therapy and the models of man. *American Psychologist, 29,* 859–869.

Banks, S., & Thompson, C. (1995). *Educational psychology: For teachers in training.* St. Paul, MN: West.

Christopher, M. (2003). Albert Ellis and Buddha: Rational soulmates? A comparison of rational emotive behavior therapy and Zen Buddhism. *Mental Health, Religion, and Culture, 6,* 283–293.

Diller, J. (2004). *Cultural diversity: A primer for the human services.* Belmont, CA: Brooks/Cole.

Epstein, R. (Ed.). (1980). *Skinner for the classroom.* Champaign, IL: Research Press.

Ivey, A., D'Andrea, M., Ivey, M., & Simek-Morgan, L. (2002). *Theories of counseling and psychotherapy: A multicultural perspective* (5th ed.). Boston: Allyn and Bacon.

Jacobsen, E. (1938). *Progressive relaxation.* Chicago: University of Chicago Press.

Lambert, M., & Hawkins, E. (2004). Measuring outcome in professional practice: Considerations in selecting and using brief outcome instruments. *Professional Psychology, Research, and Practice, 35,* 492–499.

Lee, W. (1999). *An introduction to multicultural counseling.* Philadelphia: Taylor & Francis.

Maslow, A. (1970). *Motivation and personality* (2nd ed.). New York: Harper & Row.

Ray, K., Skinner, C., & Watson, T. (1999). Transferring stimulus control via momentum to increase compliance in student with autism: A demonstration of collaborative consultation. *School Psychology Review, 28,* 622–628.

Romano, J., & Roll, D. (2000). Expanding the utility of behavioral momentum for youth with developmental disabilities. *Behavioral Interventions, 15,* 99–111.

Skinner, B. F. (1938). *The behavior of organisms.* New York: Appleton-Century-Crofts.

Skinner, B. F. (1948). *Walden two.* New York: Macmillan.

Skinner, B. F. (1968). *The technology of teaching.* Englewood Cliffs, NJ: Prentice-Hall.

Skinner, B. F. (1971). *Beyond freedom and dignity.* New York: Knopf.

Skinner, B. F. (1983). *A matter of consequences: Part III of an autobiography.* New York: Knopf.

Skinner, B. F. (1987). *Upon further reflection.* Englewood Cliffs, NJ: Prentice-Hall.

Skinner, B. F. (1990a). Can psychology be a science of mind? *American Psychologist, 45,* 1206–1210.

Skinner, B. F. (1990b, August). *Cognitive science: The creationism of psychology.* Keynote address presented at the meeting of the American Pyschological Association, Boston.

Windholtz, G. (1997). Ivan P. Pavlov: An overview of his life and psychological work. *American Psychologist, 52,* 941–945.

Wolpe, J. (1958). *Psychotherapy by reciprocal inhibition.* Stanford, CA: Stanford University Press.

Wolpe, J. (1969). *The practice of behavior therapy.* New York: Pergamon.

Wolpe, J. (1989). The derailment of behavior therapy: A tale of conceptual misdirection. *Journal of Behavior Therapy and Experimental Psychiatry, 20,* 3–15.

Wolpe, J., & Plaud, J. (1997). Pavlov's contributions to behavior therapy: The obvious and the not so obvious. *American Psychologist, 52,* 966–972.

Transactional Analysis

CHAPTER 10

The hardest thing to learn in life is which bridge to cross and which to burn.

—David L. Russell

We do not grow absolutely, chronologically. We grow sometimes in one dimension, and not in another, unevenly. We grow partially. We are relative. We are mature in one realm, childish in another. The past, present, and future mingle and pull us backward, forward, or fix us in the present. We are made up of layers, cells, constellations.

—Anaïs Nin

Eric Berne (1910–1970)

Eric Lennard Bernstein was born May 10, 1910, in Montreal, Canada. His family consisted of his father, a general practitioner; his mother, a professional writer and editor; and a sister 5 years younger than he. Eric respected his father a great deal and was permitted to make house call rounds with him. He was 10 years old when his father died from tuberculosis, at which time his mother assumed responsibility for supporting the two children.

After receiving his medical degree from McGill University at the age of 25, Bernstein moved to the United States and began a psychiatric residency at Yale University. He became a U.S. citizen in 1938 and shortly thereafter changed his name to Eric Berne. After service with the armed forces from 1943 to 1946, he began working to earn the title of psychoanalyst. His first book, *The Mind in Action,* was published in 1947. That same year, Berne began analysis with Erik Erikson.

One of the major rejections of his life occurred when, in 1956, the Psychoanalytic Institute denied his application for membership and recommended that he continue through 4 more years of personal analysis and then reapply for the coveted title. This action greatly discouraged Berne, but at the same time motivated him, and he immediately began work on a new approach to psychotherapy.

Although Berne first published on the topic of the three ego states in his article "The Nature of Intuition" (1949), he formed the core of transactional analysis (TA) in 1954. At that time, Berne was involved in the psychoanalysis of a successful middle-aged lawyer he was treating by applying classic Freudian principles. During a session, the patient suddenly said, "I'm not a lawyer, I'm just a little boy," sparking the idea that each of us contains a child ego state accompanied by parent and adult ego states. After listening to his patients relating "games" for some 30 years, Berne decided to gather some of these into a catalog. Three years after its publication, *Games People Play* (1964) had been on the nonfiction best-seller list for 111 weeks—longer than any other book that decade. Some reviewers called the book psychiatric gimmickry, emphatically denying that it would ever be regarded as a contribution to psychological or psychiatric theory. Other reviewers found the book a real contribution to psychology and suggested that Berne had offered a thesaurus of social transactions with explanations and titles. In 1967, Berne attributed the book's success to the recognition factor—some of us recognize ourselves in it, whereas some of us recognize other people in it.

Poker was Berne's favorite game because people play it to win. He had little patience with losers and believed that players should play to win if they were going to play. Berne believed losers spent a lot of time explaining why they lost. In the final years of his life, Berne shifted his emphasis from games to life scripts.

Berne published eight books and sixty-four articles in psychiatric and other periodicals; he also edited the *Transactional Analysis Bulletin*. In an article in the *New York Times* magazine in 1966, Berne renounced the therapeutic value of shock treatment, hypnosis, and medication in favor of his easy-to-understand approach to psychotherapy. TA is a social psychology that has applications to counseling, psychotherapy, education, and organizational development.

THE NATURE OF PEOPLE AND THEORY OF COUNSELING

The nature of people and the theory of counseling are covered together in this section because the TA theory of counseling is basically a statement describing the human personality.

Berne had a positive view of the nature of people. He believed children were born princes and princesses, but shortly thereafter their parents and the environment turned them into frogs. He believed that people had the potential to regain their royal status, providing they learned and applied the lessons of TA to their personal lives. Berne believed that the early childhood years were critical to personal development. During these early years, before children enter school, they form their basic life script and develop a sense of being either "OK" or "not OK." They also arrive at conclusions about other people's "OK-ness." In Berne's view, life is very simple to live. However, people upset themselves to the point that they invent religions, pastimes, and games. These same people complain about how complicated life is, while persisting in making life even harder. Life is a series of decisions to be made and problems to be solved, and Berne believed that people have the rationality and freedom to make decisions and solve their own problems.

Shahin (1995), taking a dim view of human nature and the "I'm OK, you're OK" model, writes that the model best reflecting society is: "I'm a jerk, you're a jerk, and that's OK." He expresses dismay with a society that defines bullies as just people with low self-esteem, mean people as misunderstood, and liars as insecure and acting out. To him, these people are jerks.

The TA theory of human nature and human relationships derives from data collected through four types of analysis:

1. Structural analysis, in which an individual's personality is analyzed
2. TA, which is concerned with what people do and say to each other
3. Script analysis, which deals with the specific life dramas people compulsively enjoy
4. Game analysis, in which ulterior transactions leading to a payoff are analyzed

STRUCTURAL ANALYSIS

In explaining the TA view of human nature and the difficulties people encounter in their lives, the first step is to begin with the structural analysis of personality. Each individual's personality is divided into three separate and distinct sources of behavior, the three ego states: Parent, Adult, and Child (or P, A, and C). The ego states represent real people who now exist or once existed and had their own identities. Therefore, the conflicts among them often cause inconsistencies, as well as flexibility, in people.

The Parent, Adult, and Child ego states Berne proposed are not concepts like the superego, ego, and id of Freud, but rather phenomena based on actual realities. They each represent skeletomuscular and verbal patterns of behavior and feeling based on emotions and experiences perceived by people in their early years. The Parent, Adult, and Child are all located in the conscious area of functioning and, as such, are readily available for use in our day-to-day living. In Freud's model, only the superego and ego are available to the conscious, with the id buried in the unconscious.

PARENT   The Parent aspect of personality contains instructions, attitudes, and behaviors handed down mostly by parents and significant authority figures. It resembles a recording of all the admonitions, orders, punishments, encouragement, reinforcement, and caring experienced in the first years of life. The Parent ego state can take two different attitudes, depending on the situation: (1) Nurturing Parent manifests itself in nurturing or helping behavior, and (2) Critical Parent provides criticism, control, and punishment. The Parent feels and behaves as the one who reared you did—both critical and nurturing. The Parent admonishes, "you should" or "you should not," "you can't win," "boys will be boys," or "a woman's place is in the home."

The Parent, wanting to be in control and to be right, acts with superiority and authority, but the Parent is also responsible for giving love, nurturance, and respect to the Child in you.

ADULT   The Adult ego state operates logically and unemotionally, providing objective information by using reality testing and a computer-like approach to life. Your Adult uses facts as a computer does to make decisions without emotion. The Adult says, "This is how this works" with mature, objective, logical, and rational thinking based on reality. The Adult ego state is not related to age. A child is also capable of dealing with reality by gathering facts and computing objectively. In fact, it is incumbent on the counselor to ensure that counseling sessions are conducted in an adult-to-adult format. Clients often work hard to shift communication to a parent-to-child format, where the counselor takes the parent role and tells the client what should be done. Counselors can deflect client attempts to shift the interview from adult to adult by using any of the counseling responses presented in this text. Active listening is effective, as is reality therapy and the other counseling responses, to return the interaction to adult–adult.

CHILD   All the childlike impulses common to everyone are in the Child state. The Child is an important part of personality because it contributes joy, creativity, spontaneity, intuition, pleasure, and enjoyment. The Child has two parts: (1) Adaptive Child emerges as a result of demands from significant authority figures and is marked by passivity; and (2) Natural or Free Child represents the impulsive, untrained, self-loving, pleasure-seeking part of the Child.

The Child part of us is an accumulation of impulses that come naturally to a young person and recorded internal events or responses to what is seen and heard. It has an element of immaturity but also deep feeling, affection, adaptation, expression, and fun. Figure 10-1 presents the ego states and their divisions in graphic form.

The well-adjusted person allows the situation to determine which ego state is in control, striking an even balance among the three. A common problem is allowing one ego state to assume predominant control. For example, the Constant Parent is seen as dictatorial or prejudiced; the Constant Adult is an analytical bore; and the Constant Child is immature or over-reactive. No age is implied by any of these states, because even the young child has Adult and Parent states, and older adults can evince a Child response. In fact, whenever you are having fun or jumping up and down cheering at a ball game, you are in your Child ego state. Berne believed you could diagnose the strength of a marriage relationship by how well a couple enjoyed playing together. Couples who play well together are likely to enjoy a wonderful love life together. Making love is a form of playing, and it is an appropriate time for the couple to be in their child ego states. To coin a phrase: "The couple who plays well together stays together."

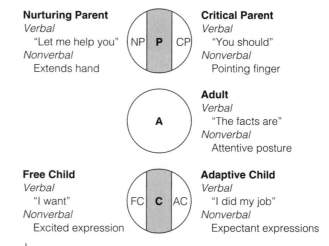

Nurturing Parent
Verbal
  "Let me help you"
Nonverbal
  Extends hand

Critical Parent
Verbal
  "You should"
Nonverbal
  Pointing finger

Adult
Verbal
  "The facts are"
Nonverbal
  Attentive posture

Free Child
Verbal
  "I want"
Nonverbal
  Excited expression

Adaptive Child
Verbal
  "I did my job"
Nonverbal
  Expectant expressions

FIGURE 10-1 | EGO STATES

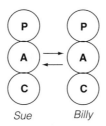

Sue   Billy

FIGURE 10-2 | COMPLEMENTARY TRANSACTION

TRANSACTIONAL ANALYSIS

The second type of analysis—the study of the transaction—is the heart of TA. Whenever a person acknowledges the presence of another person, either verbally or physically, a transaction has taken place. A *transaction* often is defined as a unit of human communication or as a stimulus–response connection between two people's ego states.

Transactions are grouped into three categories:

1. Complementary transactions, which Berne described as the natural communication of healthy human relationships, occur when a response comes from the ego state to which it was addressed (Figure 10-2).

  SUE: Billy, have you seen my bike?

  BILLY: Yes, it is in the backyard.

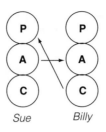

FIGURE 10-3 | CROSSED TRANSACTION

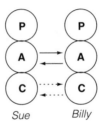

FIGURE 10-4 | COVERT TRANSACTION

2. Crossed transactions break communications. They occur when a response comes from an ego state *not* addressed (Figure 10-3).

SUE: Billy, would you help me find my bike?

BILLY: Can't you see I'm watching my favorite program?

3. Covert, or ulterior, transactions involve more than one ego state of each person and are basically dishonest. On the surface, the transaction looks and sounds like number 1 or 2, but the actual message sent is not spoken (Figure 10-4). For example, the ulterior message being sent in number 1 could be on a social or overt level.

SUE: Billy, why don't you help me find my bike so we can go riding?

BILLY: Okay, it's a good day for a ride!

Or the ulterior message could be on a psychological, covert, or ulterior level:

SUE: I wish you would be my boyfriend.

BILLY: I hope you like me better than the other boys.

FIGURE 10-5 │ LIFE SCRIPT: INJUNCTIONS

SCRIPT ANALYSIS

The nature of people can be further described by script analysis. A psychological script is a person's ongoing program for a life drama; it dictates where people are going with their lives and the paths that will lead there. The individual, consciously or unconsciously, acts compulsively according to that program. As mentioned earlier, people are born basically "OK"; their difficulties come from bad scripts they learned during their childhood.

Berne (1961) developed the theory of scripts as part of TA theory from its inception. A life script is that life plan your Child selected in your early years, based mostly on messages you received from the Child in your parents. For example, at the request of her mother, a little girl takes it upon herself to save her alcoholic father. The same script may emerge once again later in life as she tries to save an alcoholic husband in an attempt to regain some of the payoffs from the original experience. Although the Parent and Adult of your mother and father may have told you sensible things such as "Be successful," the unspoken injunction from the Child in your parents may communicate the message "You can't make it" (Figure 10-5). Injunctions are prohibitions and negative commands usually delivered from the parent of the opposite sex. Injunctions are seldom discussed or verbalized aloud. Values we hold as guidelines for living may have come from injunctions. These injunctions determine how we think and feel about sex, work, money, marriage, family, play, and people. For example, "Do not waste your time and money."

The best way to learn about scripts is to examine how we spend our time and how we relate (transactions) with others. Scripts have main themes, such as martyring, procrastinating, succeeding, failing, blaming, distracting, placating, and computing; scripts also have three basic types: winner, loser, and nonwinner. A small percentage of people seem to be natural winners; everything they touch turns to gold. Conversely, a slightly larger percentage of people seem to be natural losers; everything turns out badly for them. The majority, perhaps 80 or 85 percent, follow the nonwinners' script. Nonwinners are identified by a phrase they often use: "but at least . . ." (for example, "I went to school and made poor grades, *but at least* I did not flunk out.").

TA borrows heavily from fairy tales for its terminology and metaphors. For example, the Cinderella script is not an especially healthy plan because a prince or prize does not come to one who sits around waiting. Even martyr-dom, as Cinderella did for her stepmother and stepsisters, does not help. The Santa Claus script is based on a similar myth. LeGuernic (2004) points out that many fairy tales, like the warm fuzzy story, provide children with different, positive relationship models and social roles that can lead to personal growth and autonomy. Because life scripts are formed in early childhood, selecting children's stories requires considerable care.

In summary, Berne believed that scripts have five components: (1) directions from parents, (2) a corresponding personality development, (3) a confirming childhood decision about oneself and life, (4) a penchant for either success or failure, and (5) a pattern for behavior. Toth (2004) notes that script theories help teachers understand why students do what they do and how self-limiting behaviors such as fear of failure may be corrected.

GAME ANALYSIS

Unfortunately, most people, in following their scripts, learn how to use ulterior transactions; that is, they play games. A game is an ongoing series of complementary, ulterior transactions progressing to a well-defined, predictable outcome. Like every ulterior transaction, all games are basically dishonest, and they are by no means fun. One of the first games a child learns is, "Mine is better than yours." Its relatively benign outcome could range, in later years, to considerably more serious games. Three roles are played in games: persecutor, victim, and rescuer. There are no winners in these games; every player loses. *Games People Play* (Berne, 1964) offers a vastly entertaining, chilling overview of what might happen to a "not-OK" child.

Berne (1964) believed that the general advantages of a game are its stabilizing (homeostatic) functions. He defined *homeostasis* as the tendency of an individual to maintain internal psychological equilibrium by regulating his or her own intrapsychic processes. Change is difficult for people who automatically accept only what reinforces or confirms their personal prejudices, values, and views, and many people are not open to new data. Game playing functions to maintain homeostasis in one's life much like defense mechanisms do.

In reference to counseling, clients are ready to terminate counseling when their self-esteem is in order and they are able to exchange games for honest strokes from an "I'm OK, you're OK" view of human nature. In addition, fully functioning clients do confront and master the appropriate development tasks for age and stage. The ease with which children can understand TA concepts makes it a valuable approach for problem prevention.

In summary, games undermine the stability of relationships. Strokes are the motivation for games, and the need for strokes often turns an honest transaction into a game. Rackets are described as ego-state switches within the intrapsychic structure of an individual. Game analysis deals with transactions between two people. A racket could be the procrastination racket of "I'll do it tomorrow," in which the child masquerades as the adult. An example of a game is, "Why don't you; Yes, but," in which a person says, "Help me"; the helper gives advice, and the helpee says, "Yes, but that won't work."

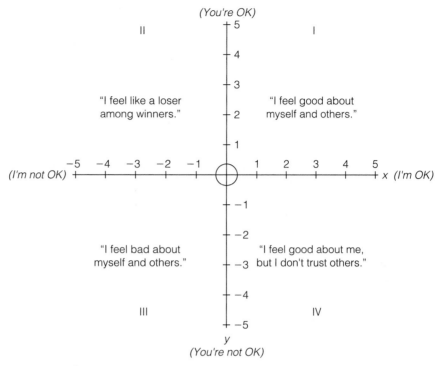

FIGURE 10-6 | LIFE POSITIONS

LIFE POSITIONS

On the basis of the transactions and scripts, children develop life positions that summarize their concepts of self-worth and the worth of others. The four life positions are as follows:

1. "I'm OK, you're OK": This position of mentally healthy people (mature independence) enables them to possess realistic expectations, have good human relationships, and solve problems constructively. It is a "winner's" position, defined as that of an authentic being. The extreme of this position is represented by +5 on both the x- and y-axes in Quadrant I of Figure 10-6. Marriages, business partnerships, and friendships work best when both people hold to the "I'm OK, you're OK" orientation to life.

2. "I'm not OK, you're OK": The universal position of childhood (total dependence) represents the introjective position of those who feel powerless. Adults in this position often experience withdrawal and depression. The extremes of this position are represented by a −5 on the x-axis and +5 on the y-axis in Quadrant II of Figure 10-6. Those who like to parent their partners will choose one from the "I'm not OK, you're OK" orientation.

3. "I'm not OK, you're not OK": This life position is the arrival point of the child who cannot depend on parents for positive stroking (see discussion later in this chapter). Already not OK, the child perceives Mom and Dad as not OK too. Adults in this category are losers who go through a series of helpless, disappointing experiences and may even become suicidal or homicidal. The extreme of this position is represented by a -5 on both the x- and y-axes in Quadrant III of Figure 10-6. Partners from this category are dangerous to your health and theirs.

4. "I'm OK, you're not OK": The individual feels victimized in this position. The brutalized, battered child ends up here. The position of the criminal and the psychopath is, "Whatever happens is someone else's fault." The extreme of this position is a $+5$ on the x-axis and a -5 on the y-axis in Quadrant IV of Figure 10-6. If you would like to be with a blamer, potential criminal, or sociopath, here is your person.

GAMES CLIENTS PLAY

Among the many games Berne identified, following is list of those especially to be avoided in the counseling interview:

1. *"Why don't you; Yes, but . . ."* The counselor's Adult is tricked into working for the client's Child as the Parent when the counselor gives advice.

   COUNSELOR: Why don't you ask your teacher to give you some extra help with math?

   CLIENT: Yes, but what if she says she doesn't have time?

   The payoff comes to the client in spreading bad feelings, as in the misery-loves-company game: "I am not okay, and you aren't either because you can't help me solve my problem."

   Summerton (2000) writes that Berne began his study of game analysis with the "Why don't you; Yes, but . . ." game. The overt communication appears to be adult to adult, but the covert communication is actually a one-upmanship move by the Child ego state trying to hook the Parent ego state of the "helper" into giving advice on what the "helpee" needs to do to solve a particular problem. However, in the game, the advice is always rejected as inadequate in an attempt to make the "helper" feel bad for not having the wisdom to be helpful. Woods (2000) distinguishes between the act of recognizing and confronting game playing and true game analysis. Recognition and confrontation of game playing is done to end the games. True game-playing analysis is done to explore how the client uses games as a defense and how games often communicate unconscious messages. Woods (2000) believes that people internalize the scenario of an early interpersonal relationship and unconsciously use it later as a template for further interpersonal interactions. One example is given of a client's father who always had a "Yes, but" statement for every self-assertive "I should" statement the client would make. In adulthood, the client projected his father's role onto others by rejecting all feedback, suggestions, and advice in the "Why don't you; Yes, but" game.

2. *"I'm only trying to help you."* Counselors sometimes play this game with their clients. The message to the client is, "You are not okay, and I know what is good for you." The payoff is for the counselor, who holds the faulty belief that "If I straighten my client out, then maybe I can get my own life in order." A truly helpful counselor offers help when it is requested, but believes that help can be accepted or rejected. When help fails or is rejected, the helpful counselor does not respond derogatorily, "Well, I was only trying to help you."

3. *Courtroom.* The courtroom game puts the counselor in the position of judge and jury if two clients can manipulate the counselor into placing blame. The payoff is bad feelings for all—persecutor, victim, and rescuer—because the rescuer (counselor) usually ends up being victimized by the other two players.

4. *Kick me and NIGYYSOB.* Counselors may find that some clients enjoy playing "kick me" with the counselor, just as they do with their bosses, colleagues, and spouses. They seem to enjoy being victimized and work at getting themselves rejected. They even work at getting themselves terminated from counseling before any gains have been made. Kick-me players manipulate others into playing NIGYYSOB (now I've got you, you son of a bitch) when they react to the bids for negative attention the kick-me players make. The NIGYYSOB game is played by itself if a person tries to trap others in a double bind: damned if you do and damned if you don't.

MOTHER: Johnny, do you love me?

JOHNNY: Yes, I do.

MOTHER: How many times have I told you not to talk with your mouth full!

5. *Gossiping.* Gossiping refers to talking about people who are not present. In a counseling interview, the counselor may wish to have clients role-play dialogue between themselves and a missing person, as suggested in Chapter 7. For example, a student complaining about a teacher could role-play a conversation between the two of them, with the student playing the role of the teacher and then responding as the student would in the classroom. The technique uses an empty chair to represent the missing person. Role-playing and role-reversal methods have a way of limiting gossip while creating greater awareness of the problem situations and proper assignment of responsibility for the problem.

6. *Wooden leg.* The wooden-leg game is a display of the inadequacy pattern described in Chapter 11. Clients playing wooden-leg games work to increase their disabilities as a way of avoiding responsibility for taking care of themselves. These clients are experts at making people give up on them. Children are adept at convincing parents and teachers that they cannot handle certain chores and school subjects. Paradoxical strategies, which are at times effective with these clients, focus on harnessing their rebellion into productive activity. The counselor might say, for example, "Frank, you've got me convinced that you really can't make it." The rebellious client, Frank, often rises to the occasion to show that the counselor is a

total idiot and begins to succeed in the face of the prediction that he could not. For clients who are really defeated and not rebellious, we recommend large doses of unconditional encouragement. Counselors of welfare and rehabilitation clients often find themselves in the wooden-leg game. The payoff goes to the clients, who justify not getting better, or even getting worse, as a way of increasing their benefits.

7. *If it weren't for you.* Related to the wooden leg, this game is another way of avoiding the assumption of responsibility for life and its unsolved problems. The client says, for example, "If it weren't for you and your good cooking, I could lose ten pounds." Using a paradoxical counseling method, the counselor may want to examine with the client the payoffs of being overweight and even develop a rationale of how being fat may be the preferred and "best" lifestyle for the client.

8. *Red Cross.* Red Cross happens when a person (the persecutor) pushes you (the victim) off a dock into deep water and then rescues you. This puts you (the victim) in debt to the rescuer. In this case, all three roles in the game are played by two people, with the persecutor and rescuer role played by the same person. Red Cross happens when people get other people in trouble and then "jump in" to "rescue" them from peril.

9. *Make someone sad.* One member of a couple decides to get more attention from the other person by making him or her jealous. The game works for a while until the victim discovers that the game can be played both ways. The result is that both people in the partnership end up hurting each other.

THE PURSUIT OF STROKES

Human beings need recognition; to obtain it, they exchange what Berne called *strokes.* A stroke is any act implying recognition of another person's presence. In acknowledging the presence of another person, people give a stroke, which can be either positive or negative; which is which usually is obvious, except in the case of ulterior transactions. Young children receive positive or negative physical strokes when they are cuddled or spanked, whereas adults obtain primarily symbolic strokes in conversations or transactions with others. Positive strokes, such as compliments, handshakes, open affection, or uninterrupted listening, are the most desirable, but negative strokes, such as hatred or disagreement, are better than no recognition at all. A middle ground is maintenance strokes, which keep transactions going by giving recognition to the speaker but neither positive nor negative feedback. All these strokes can be either conditional or unconditional—that is, given as a result of some specific action or given just for being yourself. Unconditional regard—"I like you"—has more positive stroke value than conditional acceptance—"I like you when you are nice to me" (Figure 10-7).

The pattern of giving and receiving strokes an individual uses most is determined by the person's life position, as explained in the section on life positions. How people view themselves and others controls their ability to give and receive conditional and unconditional positive and negative strokes. People

	CONDITIONAL	UNCONDITIONAL
POSITIVE	2-Positive for doing something	1-Positive for being you
NEGATIVE	3-Negative for doing something	4-Negative for being you

FIGURE 10-7 | TYPES OF STROKES

engage in transactions to exchange strokes. According to Berne (1964), people have an inherent psychological hunger for stimulation through human interactions and stroking, and any act implying recognition of another's presence is a means of satisfying these hungers. Failure to fulfill these needs may cause a failure to thrive in infants and feelings of abandonment and "not-OK-ness" in both children and adults. Satisfied hunger yields feelings of "OK-ness" and release of creative energy. Awareness of psychological hungers and the satisfaction of them are important.

Negative strokes, such as lack of attention, shin kicking, and hatred, send "You're not OK" messages. Diminishing, humiliating, and ridiculing strokes all treat people as though they are insignificant.

Positive strokes usually are complementary transactions. They may be verbal expressions of affection and appreciation, or they may give compliments or positive feedback; they may be physical, such as a touch, or they may be silent gestures or looks. Listening is one of the finest strokes one person can give another. All yield reinforcement to the "I'm OK, you're OK" position. Maintenance strokes, although lacking meaningful content, at least serve to give recognition and keep communication open.

STRUCTURING TIME   People have six options for structuring their time in pursuit of strokes:

1. *Withdrawing*—time alone in which no transaction takes place. It involves few risks, and no stroking occurs.
2. *Rituals*—involve prescribed social transactions such as "Hello," "Have a nice day," and "How are you?" These transactions are fairly impersonal.
3. *Pastimes*—provide mutually acceptable stroking. Pastimes are a means of self-expression but often involve only superficial transactions or conversations. Examples are conversations about baseball, automobiles, shopping, or other safe topics of conversation.

4. *Activities*—time is structured around some task or career. Activities are a way to deal with external reality and may involve more in-depth interaction with others.
5. *Games*—the need for strokes is met in dishonest or phony ways. Intense stroking often is received, but it may be unpleasant. Games are considered destructive transactions.
6. *Intimacy*—provides unconditional stroking. It is free of games, exploitation, and phony communication.

Obviously, some of these ways of structuring time are healthy and some are unhealthy, depending on the time and energy given to each. One of the goals of TA therapy is to help people learn productive ways of structuring their time.

Withdrawing may be the Adult's decision to relax or be alone, the Parent's way of coping with conflict, or the Child's adaptation for protection from pain or conflict. It is fairly harmless unless it happens all the time or when a person needs to pay attention. Withdrawing into fantasy may allow one to experience good stroking when the present setting does not appear to hold any.

A ritual is a socially programmed use of time in which everybody agrees to do the same thing. Brief encounters, worship rituals, greeting rituals, cocktail party rituals, and bedroom rituals may allow maintenance strokes without commitment or involvement. The outcome is predictable and pleasant, but most people need more intense stroking.

Pastimes are, as they imply, ways to pass time. They are superficial exchanges without involvement that people use to size up one another. Conversations concerning relative gas mileage, the weather, or potty training may yield minimal stroking at the maintenance level but allow one to decide whether to risk a more intimate relationship.

Doing work or activities with others is time spent dealing with the realities of the world. It is getting something done that one may want to do, need to do, or have to do. Activities allow for positive strokes befitting a winner.

Berne (1964) defined games as an ongoing series of complementary, ulterior transactions progressing to a well-defined, predictable outcome. A person who sends an ulterior message to another person, for some hidden purpose, is playing a game. The Adult is unaware that the Child or Parent has a secret reason for playing or wanting to play. Harris (1969) believes all games derive from the Child's "mine is better than yours" attempt to ease the "not-OK" feeling; that is, to feel superior while the other feels put down. Games are differentiated from rituals and pastimes in two ways: (1) their ulterior quality and (2) the payoff. Games also are a way of passing time for people who cannot bear the stroking starvation of withdrawal, and yet whose "not-OK" position makes the ultimate form of relatedness—intimacy—impossible (Berne, 1964; Harris, 1969).

Intimacy is a deep human encounter stemming from genuine caring. Steiner (1974) views intimacy as the way of structuring time so there are no withdrawals, no rituals, no games, no pastimes, and no work. Conditions favorable for intimacy include a commitment to the "I'm OK, you're OK" position and a satisfying of psychological hungers through positive strokes. The traditional view of how people structure their time to meet their needs for emotional space between themselves and others has been unidimensional, with intimacy and self-definition on opposite ends of the same continuum. The healthy position is viewed as holding the middle ground between the two extremes of total withdrawal from people versus being totally enmeshed in intimate relationships. Kaplan (2001), taking issue with the traditional view, suggests that the needs for self-definition (withdrawal) and intimacy exist on different dimensions, with their own continuums of high and low needs for each dimension. This bidimensional model, plotted on x- and y-axes, permits us to examine four lifestyles: (1) high needs for self-definition and intimacy, (2) high needs for intimacy and low needs for self-definition, (3) low needs for both self-definition and intimacy, and (4) high needs for self-definition and low needs for intimacy. The four-dimensional scale permits expansion of the two-scale model of high need for attachment versus fear of attachment to need for and fear of individuation and need for and fear of attachment. In other words, needs for intimacy and withdrawal are not opposite ends of the same continuum on the need to affiliate with people.

RACKETS

Some people find themselves involved in what is known in TA theory as a "stamp-collecting enterprise"; they save up archaic bad feelings until they have enough to cash in for some psychological prize. The bad-feelings racket, or stamp collecting, works in much the same way that the former supermarket stamp-collecting enterprise once worked. People save brown stamps for all the bad things others have caused them to suffer and gold stamps for all the favors others owe them. Gray stamps refer to lowered self-esteem, red stamps symbolize anger, blue stamps mean depression, and white stamps connote purity (James & Jongeward, 1971). The filled-up, bad-feelings stamp books may be cashed in for such things as a free divorce, custody of children, nervous breakdown, blowup, drunken binge, bout of depression, tantrum, runaway attempt, or love affair. Good-feelings stamps are used to justify playtime, relaxation, and breaks from work. Stamp collecting is a racket learned from parents. The collector uses the stamps as excuses for behavior and feelings, and the suppliers may not even be aware they are giving them out. "I'm OK, you're OK" people do not need stamps because they need no excuses for their behavior, which is honest, open, and ethical.

COUNSELING METHOD

TA is the ideal system for those who view the counseling process as teaching. As conveyed in this chapter, TA abounds with terms, diagrams, and models. Clients are taught the TA vocabulary so they can become proficient in identifying ego states, transactions, and scripts. The counselor's role includes teaching and providing a nurturing, supportive environment in which clients feel free to lift or eliminate restricting injunctions, attempt new behaviors, rewrite scripts, and move toward the "I'm OK, you're OK" life position. Contracting between counselor and client is a large part of the TA process. Guy (2003) and Poda (2003) write that TA with children and adolescents promotes the developmental assistance needed to foster a healthy balance between attachment and autonomy, while providing these clients with a reassuring awareness of their potential.

TA practitioners teach the principles of TA to participants and then let them use these principles to analyze and improve their own behavior. TA concepts have been taught to people of all ages and ability levels, from the very young to the very old and from mentally retarded children to gifted children. The following TA points are most useful in counseling children and adolescents:

1. Definition and explanation of ego states
2. Analysis of transactions between ego states
3. Positive and negative stroking (or "warm fuzzies" and "cold pricklies")
4. I'm OK, you're OK
5. Games and rackets
6. Scripts

In simple terms, the primary goal in TA is to help the person achieve the "I'm OK, you're OK" life position. Various methods and techniques can accomplish this aim. Because children can easily learn and understand the terms and concepts of TA, the approach has become popular in helping school-age children.

The "I'm OK, you're OK" life position is one the child chooses to take. The other three positions more or less evolve of themselves; the child feels no sense of free choice in the matter. According to Harris (1969), the first three positions are based on feelings, and the fourth position—"I'm OK, you're OK"—is based on thought, faith, and initiation of action. The first three have to do with "why"; the fourth has to do with "why not." No one drifts into a new position; it is a decision a person makes. Figure 10-6 provides a guide to plotting a person's progress in moving from one quadrant to another, providing each step on the number axis is defined in operational terms. The x-axis refers to gains and losses in self-esteem; the y-axis indicates the same for relationships with others.

Ideally, the role of a transactional analyst is teacher. TA concepts have been taught successfully to children, preadolescents, and adolescents (see Alvyn Freed's books *TA for Tots: And Other Prinzes* [1973/1998] and *TA for Teens and Other Important People* [1992] and Alvyn and Margaret Freed's book *TA for Kids: And Grown Ups Too* [1971/1998]). We recommend that counselors begin teaching the PAC model by showing children that all of us have these three parts that tell us what to do in certain situations. For example, our *Parent* tells us what we should do, our *Adult* tells us how to figure things out, and our *Child* tells us what to do for fun.

Once children have been taught how to speak the language of TA, the counselor can help them analyze their own transactions and see how their behavior affects others and vice versa. Children learn to identify the source of the reasoning that goes into their decisions; that is, they learn how to use their Adult in dealing with the demands of their Parent and Child.

Children can then be taught about the differences between the nurturing and critical parts of the Parent part of their personality. The Critical Parent sounds a lot like our real parents, because it tells us the right thing to do. The nurturing parent tells us that we are all right and takes care of us in a loving way.

The Adult is compared with a computer. It helps us think for ourselves, solve problems, and learn new things. The Adult can be contaminated by the Child. For example, when you are studying for a test using your Adult, your Child might say, "Take time out for snack and watch some TV." Children can be taught to organize their study periods into shorter, concentrated periods with frequent breaks for snacks and bathroom. In fact, more learning occurs at the beginning and ending points in a study period; this augurs well for shorter study periods with more starting and stopping points.

Sometimes the Child part of our personality is divided into three parts: the adapted child, the little professor, and the free child. The adapted child is the part of you that might be the rebel who refuses to do what PICs (People In Charge—parents, teachers) want us to do. The adapted child seems to come alive at about age 2 and enjoys a rebirth during the adolescent years. However, the adapted child reaction is a natural reaction to any person, such as a peer or friend, who acts too bossy. The little professor is that part of the child that does the creative and clever planning to help the Child get what he or she wants. The little professor does the daydreaming that stimulates the make-believe games that often lead to future careers and hobbies. The free (or natural) child is the part of the child that engages in spontaneous fun. When we are playing in a fun game, we are in our natural child. The free child is also free to feel and express any emotion and feeling that may arise, including the negative feelings of hate and anger. Our free child does the playing, has the fun, and is often impulsive. However, it also needs to be monitored by our Adult and Parent to keep our behavior within the limits of responsible behavior.

The key to understanding PAC is to know which part of our personality is in charge at any particular moment and whether that is the appropriate one for the situation. We know which ego state is in charge by how we talk, how we act, how others react to us, and how we feel. The Parent says things such as "Shame on you," "That's stupid," or "I love you very much and you are pretty sharp." The Adult says things such as "I can figure it out," "I'm going to do my homework," and "The answer is 64." The Child says things such as "Cool," "I want," and "That sucks!"

After they understand how the PAC model works, children are ready to learn how positive and negative strokes are transacted between people. Positive strokes are identified as warm fuzzies (symbolized with soft balls of wool yarn) that include pats on the back, hugs, compliments, and handshakes that make you feel warm and fuzzy all over when you get them. Strokes can be earned by doing good work, but the best strokes are the freebies you get just for being you. Negative strokes are taught by using hard, spiny plastic objects called cold pricklies that are not fun to hold in your hand. Cold pricklies are criticisms, punishments, and insults, as well as name calling, hitting, and kicking you might get from somebody.

Children are taught they were born as Prinzes (prince or princess), and later on, when they get some cold pricklies, they may begin to think they have turned into Frozzes (girl and boy frogs). If we get too many cold pricklies about how we are "not OK" and everybody else is, we develop an "I'm not OK and you're OK" attitude, which could lead to developing and following a loser life script. The only cure for the "I'm not OK" position is to receive an abundance of unconditional, positive strokes and love from our parents and plenty of positive strokes (warm fuzzies) from our friends.

Stamp collecting is taught as a racket in which we save up incidents that hurt our feelings or made us angry and then trade these stamps in later for a guilt-free tantrum or blowup. As mentioned earlier, sometimes people use different colors to label the different bad feelings they collect, such as red for anger and blue for fear. However, brown stamps are now used to symbolize all bad feelings. The Adult has the task of acting rationally on these bad feelings to prevent them from being stored and saved for a later irrational act. These brown stamps can be saved or thrown away. In fact, our Adult can refuse to let us even print them.

These brown stamps can be avoided if you track them down. Children are taught to act as soon as they begin to feel uncomfortable because someone annoys them or hurts their feelings. The tracking down of brown stamps takes 30 seconds and consists of answering the following seven questions:

1. How do I hurt?—anger, fear, or pain
2. Which part of me hurts?—P, A, or C (usually it is the Child)
3. Who did it?
4. With what?—P, A, or C
5. Why did he or she do it?
6. What can I do now?
7. What can I do differently next time?

Children can be taught the three types of transactions: complementary, crossed, and double (or hidden). Complementary transactions are parallel transactions where the arrows between your PAC and the other person's PAC do not cross. For example, the Adult question, "What was our math assignment?" is answered by the Adult response, "Page 104."

The transaction becomes crossed when the response to the Adult question comes from the Critical Parent: "You should have paid more attention in class." Another example of a crossed transaction might come from the Free Child, "Forget math, let's shoot some hoops." Crossed transactions often lead to arguments, fights, and other bad feeling activities. Double transactions have a hidden, unspoken meaning. For example, the Adult might appear to be saying to another Adult, "Let's play some ball." The Hidden Child to Child message might be, "Let's not do that math assignment for tomorrow."

Children are taught that TA games are not the same as fun games. TA games are played to get strokes, but they are crooked ways of getting them because the transactions are not open and honest. The first game children play is "mine is better than yours." Children play this game in an attempt to get rewarded with strokes when they do not believe they get strokes just for being themselves. "Tattletale" often becomes the next game, when children realize they can get strokes from PICs by telling on their siblings or classmates. Both of these games are indications that children need to be reassured they are all right. PICs also can give strokes when children are trying to earn them by doing the right things and are not trying to earn them at the expense of others.

Rackets are taught as activities that can lead to games. Rackets are ways of trying to control others by making them responsible for the bad feelings you have that never seem to go away. An example PICs might use to get children to do what they want is: "You really make me worried and nervous when you leave the house and go off with your friends," or "You know I have this heart condition and how upset I get when you don't make A's and B's."

Scripts are taught to children as what they are going to be when they grow up, but they are not written in stone. They can be changed (and often are) as we find out what we like to do and what we can do well. People can move from a loser's or nonwinner's script to a winner's script by being persistent in the pursuit of realistic, challenging goals that fall within their interest and ability levels. For children, the task involves moving from a failure identity to a success identity of "I am lovable and capable"—lovable because I have people in my life who care about me and whom I care about, and capable because I can do things such as succeed in school and other activities. In short, "I am OK."

Children can be taught to inoculate themselves against people poisons, that is, "put-down" remarks designed to make them feel bad. Freed and Freed (1971, 1998) recommend using parent shrinkers, actually critical parent shrinkers, to move the communication from the Critical Parent to the Adult. Some of these include:

1. Say, "You're right. What can we do about it now?"
2. Ask, "What did you say before you said that?"
3. Change the subject.
4. Say, "When you call me a name, I feel angry. So I wish you wouldn't do that."

Finally, children are taught about making and keeping contracts to make changes in their daily behavior. People do well when they keep their promises and hold to their contracts with friends and PICs. People who have difficulty in making and keeping their commitments to others get themselves in trouble. The way out of trouble is to commit to helpful behaviors they can and will do.

Probably the most important concept to remember when dealing with children is that everyone grows up feeling "not OK." Children function on the basis of the "OK-ness" they see in their parents. If Mommy frequently responds to the child with *her* "not-OK" Child, the stage is set for the establishment of the "I'm not OK, you're not OK" position. In the case of the severely abused child, the extreme "I'm OK, you're not OK" position is a real possibility. One of the best ways for youngsters to develop strong Adult ego states is to observe their parents use their Adults in handling inappropriate responses from the demanding Parent or Child.

Posters, pictures, humorous role-playing, and stories are useful in teaching TA principles to children, such as how to be "prinzes" instead of "frozzes." Children also learn how to give and get warm fuzzies (positive strokes) and how to avoid giving and getting cold pricklies (negative strokes). Of course, in getting strokes, one must not play games.

As mentioned earlier, the goal of TA counseling with children is to help them learn to control their responses with their Adult, thereby achieving the "I'm OK, you're OK" life position. However, strengthening a child's Adult causes his or her family role to shift. The child becomes less active in playing the destructive games that dominate many families. Other family members' roles of necessity also shift. For this reason, the child's parents must be included in the counseling process to achieve lasting results.

Children can learn all about warm fuzzies and cold pricklies, but because of the tremendous influence of their parents, it is next to impossible, without effective intervention, for them to reverse a "loser" life script if their parents have given it to them. Everything parents do and say to children tells them they are "OK" or "not OK," depending on what life position the parents themselves occupy. People attract not what they want, but rather what they are. People also rear not the children they want, but rather children who resemble their parents.

Positive stroking and respect are two things everyone needs to build a winner's script. The child needs positive strokes, both conditional ("We'll have some ice cream after you put away your toys.") and unconditional ("I love you no matter what."). Children come to see themselves as "OK" because their parents treat them that way. As a positive stroke, respect is hard to beat. The conclusion a child reaches is this: "If my OK parents think I'm OK, then I really must be OK."

Another useful TA principle for both teachers and parents is to teach "do" and *not* "don't." Parents' and other adults' attempts to teach appropriate behavior by catching children in *inappropriate* behavior baffle children. Because Mommy is "OK," a child thinks, "It must be all my fault, and I must be not OK."

A slightly different aspect of the same idea is that children who are counseled and taught to "do more" or "do better" must also know *what* to do. The Parent in everyone admonishes us to "do better"; the Adult supplies the "do *what* better."

As children and their families become better acquainted with the why's of their relationships, they learn to avoid undesirable ways of structuring time. Again, the goal of TA is to help the individual learn to lead a full, game-free life, and everyone has that choice. The usefulness of the PAC model is in creating awareness of how the Parent, Adult, and Child function in the decision-making process.

As mentioned earlier, several techniques can teach TA to children. The concepts of positive and negative stroking have been taught with smiling and frowning faces, as well as with fuzzy yarn balls and sharp, prickly plastic objects to connote warm fuzzies and cold pricklies, respectively. The following warm fuzzy, cold prickly fairy tale (Steiner, 1975) was written for the Child in everyone.

There once existed a town where people shared their warm fuzzies without fear of running out of their supply of fuzzies. One day a wicked witch appeared and planted the idea that people should hoard their fuzzies in case there happened to be a shortage of fuzzies. When the townspeople did this, their backbones began to shrivel up. The witch cured the shriveling backbones by giving everybody a bag of cold pricklies to share. The sharing of cold pricklies continued until a good witch arrived and put the townspeople back on the right track—sharing their warm fuzzies.

Counselors and teachers can follow the story by bringing a bowl of sugar-free candy to class and telling the children that they can have a piece of candy only if someone gives them a piece. The counselor or teacher serves as a model in the exercise to make sure that each child receives a piece of candy, symbolizing a warm fuzzy or a positive stroke. The best way to get warm fuzzies is to give them.

Posters can be made with representations of the various ideas of TA (stroking, ego states, "I'm OK, you're OK," lists of games with appropriate illustrations, lists of scripting phrases, and so on). Puppets, dolls, and make-believe stories can be successful with younger children who cannot yet read.

A three-step process is effective in teaching TA to any child. First, explain the principle by using a story, a poster, puppets, or other age-appropriate methods. Second, ask the children to "read" back what they understand of the TA principle (correcting them as they go along). Third, ask the children to give examples of the principle from their own experience ("What positive strokes have you received today?") or to identify examples of the principle from the explanation ("'You must always go to bed early' comes from which ego state?").

Teach new stroking patterns to children who are having interpersonal conflicts. They first need to analyze the other person's behavior. What response does parent, teacher, or friend give to the child's positive or negative strokes? What strokes does the other person like? Teach children new ways of stroking from among the following categories:

1. Self-strokes: doing nice things for yourself
2. Physical strokes: hugs, kisses, pats, back rubs, handshakes, "high fives" (be sure to distinguish between good and bad touching)
3. Silent strokes: winks, nods, waves, smiles
4. Verbal strokes: "I like you," "Good job," "Thanks"
5. Rewards or privileges: letting younger siblings go with you, playing with them, doing something for your parents

Young children (up to 7 years) may not be able to symbolize stroking and ego states as well as older children; thus, less technical language may be necessary. Young children can understand "warm fuzzy" if a stroke feels good and "cold prickly" if it feels bad after someone says or does something to them. They may need permission to ask for a warm fuzzy instead of manipulating for a cold prickly when they feel bad. Likewise, small children can understand

Key:

P The Parent refers to a person's values, beliefs, and morals.

   CP The Critical Parent finds fault, directs, orders, sets limits, makes rules, and enforces one's value system. Too much CP results in dictatorial or bossy behavior.

   NP The Nurturing Parent is empathic and promotes growth. The NP is warm and kind, but too much NP becomes smothering, and children will not be able to learn how to take care of themselves.

A The Adult acts like a computer. It takes in, stores, retrieves, and processes information. The A is a storehouse of facts and helps you think when you solve problems, but too much Adult is boring.

C The Child can be fun, expressive, and spontaneous, and sometimes it can be compliant and a follower of rules.

   FC The Free Child is the fun and spontaneous part of the child. When you cheer at a ballgame, you are in the Free Child part of your personality. However, too much FC might mean that you have lost control of yourself.

   AC The Adapting Child is the conforming, easy-to-get-along-with part of your personality. Too much AC results in guilt feelings, depression, other bad feelings, and robotlike behavior.

FIGURE 10-8 | EGO-GRAM

"my bossy part," "my thinking part," "my angry part," or "my happy part" rather than the ego states, which they sometime confuse with actual people.

Ego-grams are bar graphs showing children "how much" of each ego state they use (Figure 10-8). An ego-gram can indicate what changes might be made. A child who wants to make a change can work on strengthening low ego states by practicing appropriate behaviors. Determine whether the child thinks the ego-gram differs in various situations—at home, at school, playing with friends.

Once children understand ego states, they can learn to distinguish complementary, crossed, and ulterior transactions. If they bring in a situation that illustrates one of these, have them diagram it. In the case of crossed or ulterior transactions, encourage children to use their Adult to figure out ways to obtain a more successful result.

Some other methods for teaching the various TA techniques are as follows:

1. Talk about the feelings and behaviors that go with each ego state. Have children identify their own and others' ego states by relating the ego states to what children say about their experiences.

    CHILD: My brother always tells me what to do. He's not my father.

    COUNSELOR: You feel rebellious when your brother acts like a bossy parent.

As children become aware of their ego states and can discriminate between them, their Adult can gain control of which ego state is expressed and give them permission to replace destructive ideas with constructive ones.

2. The OK Corral diagram is useful in helping children identify how they feel and think about themselves and other people. Children are able to discuss what "OK-ness" and "not-OK-ness" mean to them in terms of specific behaviors.

3. Games intrigue children. Once they have the concept, they can readily pick up on games in themselves and others and describe them. Any time children describe a pattern of games or recognize that "this always happens to me," the counselor can introduce the concept of games as a way of getting negative strokes to replace the positive strokes children think they cannot get. For example, "You seem to mess up a lot. How do you manage that?" "What does this mean about you?" "How did it feel after it happened?" "What do you really want? How could you get it better?" "What 'bad' (scary) thing does this game prevent?" Children can also identify the three game roles of persecutor, rescuer, and victim and learn to stay out of them. The persecutor role can be demonstrated by having the child try to "put someone down" by pressing straight down on his or her shoulders. Putting people down this way is difficult unless they lean over or bend their knees. You can demonstrate the rescuer role by trying to pick up a limp person (of about the same size). Holding up a person who does not want to stand is also difficult. The victim role is demonstrated in relation to the other two by the partner's "giving in," lying down, and staying limp.

4. Racket feelings can be discussed in terms of stamp collecting. Children can usually identify the bad feelings they save up and the prize they get. Hypothetical situations such as the following create bad feelings: "Did you ever have a rotten day? Your mom yells at you at breakfast, your teacher catches you talking, the other guys play keep-away with your hat, and you drop your books in the mud when your dog jumps on you because he's so glad to see you home. All day long you have felt mistreated and hurt, and that is the last straw. So you pick a fight with your little sister." Talk about how cashing in stamps feels and how getting dumped on feels. As small people, children are often the target when stamps are cashed in. Awareness can help children stop collecting stamps (child abuse is the worst form of stamp cashing) by learning to talk about bad feelings with someone they can trust and by asking for and receiving the positive strokes they need.

5. For counselors working with script issues, useful questions for figuring out a child's script include many of the same questions used in the Adlerian lifestyle interview (Chapter 11):

> What are the "hurt" points in your family? (G)
>
> Who is in your family? (BP)
>
> What are the people in your family like? (BP)

Has anyone else ever lived with you? (BP) What were they like? (BP)

Who is boss in your family? (PI, P)

What is your mother's (or father's) favorite saying? (PI, CI)

Describe yourself in three words. (BP, D)

What words would other people in your family use to describe you? (PI, CI, BP)

What bad feeling do you have a lot of the time? (R)

What good feeling do you have a lot of the time? (BP)

Who is your mother's favorite? (PI, CI)

Who is your father's favorite? (PI, CI)

The preceding questions are coded to fit parts of the life script:

BP—Basic life position regarding how I feel about myself and others

PI—Parental injunction (message from parent's Child): "Don't do as I do"

CI—Counterinjunction (message from parent's Parent): "Do at least try"

G—Games (getting strokes at others' expense)

R—Racket (bad feelings)

D—Decision (how I have chosen to live my life)

P—Program (how to obey injunctions)

6. At some time during their lives, most people have kept a diary or journal in which they have recorded their innermost feelings, thoughts, and other events. Children and adolescents respond well to a homework assignment of keeping a diary. The diary provides the counselor and client with a record of feelings, thoughts, and life script to be explored. Keeping a journal or diary may also provide the child with a feeling of closeness to the counselor between sessions.

7. What *not* to do: The counselor who is not in a position to protect a child from negative consequences should not interfere with script behavior that still serves a purpose in the family. Do not ask children to give up their games or rackets before they learn more appropriate ways to get strokes. Do not decide for children what they "should" do. Do not encourage children to play TA counselor with people who have power over them and may not appreciate their comments. However, scripts are not written in stone and can be modified or rewritten to help children and adults find better ways to meet their needs. All the preceding exercises can be used in group and family counseling, as well as in individual counseling. Role-playing and acting-out games are effective group techniques. Families in TA counseling come to recognize where their transactions become crossed, how and when scripting occurs, and how stroking behavior can change family feelings.

Case Studies

Transcript I

Jimmy, age 5, is being seen by the school counselor because he has recently begun fighting with other children in his kindergarten class.

COUNSELOR: Jimmy, remember when I came to your class and read the story about the warm fuzzies and the cold pricklies? [He nods.] Well, everybody, kids and grown-ups, needs to get some of these to live. Sometimes people do things to get cold pricklies like slaps or frowns, or being yelled at. Would you like to find out how to give yourself and other people nice warm fuzzies like smiles and hugs, and get them back from others?

JIMMY: Yes. Everybody doesn't like me now.

COUNSELOR: What do you do to get hugs and smiles from your mommy?

JIMMY: I don't do anything, she just gives them to me. Or sometimes I hug her first or say "I love you."

COUNSELOR: Sometimes mommies are busy. What do you do to get her attention then?

JIMMY: Well, I get a hug from Grandma. But if I can't get one, I make my little sister yell. Then somebody comes to see what's happening.

COUNSELOR: If you can't get a warm fuzzy, you get them to give you a cold prickly?

JIMMY: Yeah.

COUNSELOR: What do kids in your class have to do to get a hug?

JIMMY: They hug you if you fall down. But I don't fall down, so nobody hugs me.

COUNSELOR: If you can't get a hug or other warm fuzzy when you want one, what do you do to get attention?

JIMMY: I make one of the other kids yell.

COUNSELOR: Sometimes getting yelled at is better than nothing, huh?

JIMMY: Yeah.

COUNSELOR: Do you think any of your teachers would give you a warm fuzzy?

JIMMY: Miss Sally has a nice face.

COUNSELOR: So when you feel bad inside and need a warm fuzzy, you could get one from Miss Sally?

JIMMY: Yeah, like when I miss my mommy. I could tell Miss Sally that and ask her to hug me.

COUNSELOR: That sounds like a good plan, Jimmy. And if you feel bad, or sad, or lonely, or angry, and need to talk about it, you can come here and talk to me about it.

JIMMY: Okay.

COUNSELOR: [gives Jimmy a hug] I give warm fuzzies too.

Counselor feedback to Jimmy's teacher should include talking about giving Jimmy some strokes when he is being good and not making a bid for attention in the form of negative feedback.

Transcript II

The child in this interview is a 10-year-old boy.

COUNSELOR: Christopher, you've read the Freeds' book about stroking. Can you explain to me what they mean by strokes?

CHRISTOPHER: Stroking is when somebody does some type of action, physical or verbal, that makes you feel either good or not so good.

COUNSELOR: I think that's a very good definition. Can you give me some examples of a positive stroke?

CHRISTOPHER: Patting somebody, or hugging them, or saying something nice.

COUNSELOR: Like what?

CHRISTOPHER: "You really did well today."

COUNSELOR: Can you think of a positive stroke you've given someone today?

CHRISTOPHER: Not really.

COUNSELOR: How about when I came in, and you looked up and smiled?

CHRISTOPHER: I guess. I smiled at most everybody in the class today.

COUNSELOR: You have to remember that they don't have to be words; just a smile is a positive stroke. Can you think of any negative strokes you've given anyone today?

CHRISTOPHER: No.

COUNSELOR: That's good. Of course, the same holds true for negative strokes; if, without realizing it, you looked at someone and gave them a hard frown or something, that could be a negative stroke that you didn't realize you gave.

CHRISTOPHER: I don't see why I would have given any, even by accident. There wasn't any reason to give any.

COUNSELOR: Well, good. Can you think of any positive strokes anyone gave you today?

CHRISTOPHER: When I got 100 on our test today, Mrs. Kincaid said that that was very good.

COUNSELOR: I'm glad. Any negative strokes?

CHRISTOPHER: No.

COUNSELOR: Well, I told you your hands and face were dirty and I didn't like you coming around like that, right? You think you've got the idea about how positive and negative strokes work?

CHRISTOPHER:	Yes.
COUNSELOR:	How would you use stroking?
CHRISTOPHER:	Well, whenever I thought somebody did a good job on something, I could tell them.
COUNSELOR:	You know, there's such a thing as giving strokes that are not asked for, strokes that you just offer freely. Can you give an example of one of those, maybe?
CHRISTOPHER:	Just saying something nice when they don't even really need it . . . well, they do need it. Just saying it, but just saying it even if they haven't done anything.
COUNSELOR:	Be more specific.
CHRISTOPHER:	Well, if you meet somebody, you can say, "I like your shoes," or "Your hair looks nice," or something like that.
COUNSELOR:	Yes, those would be nice to hear. Can you tell me how you might use nonverbal positive strokes?
CHRISTOPHER:	By patting somebody, or smiling at them, or giving them a hug.
COUNSELOR:	How do you think you would feel if you started giving more positive strokes and getting more positive strokes?
CHRISTOPHER:	All covered over with strokes.

CROSS-CULTURAL APPLICATIONS OF TRANSACTIONAL ANALYSIS

Eric Berne believed that the concepts used in TA were universal. That is, all people possess Parent, Adult, and Child functions in their personality, and all people transact their business with others through communicating from each of the three ego states. The user-friendly nature of TA is an advantage for transcending cultural barriers. Cultures and individuals within all cultures who prefer a direct, straightforward, educational approach to personal development over a healing approach to mental illness will find TA comfortable. TA practitioners offer the opportunity to learn new skills in both group and individual settings. As noted in Chapter 15, African Americans and Latinos have preferences for a psychoeducational context in which clients can learn useful skills. Asian Americans and Asians will find the emphasis on thinking an attractive feature of TA. Considerable thought is required to analyze transactions and communication patterns between people. Analysis of scripts, games, and rackets puts a premium on cognitive processes. However, the focus on feelings is not disregarded, especially in dealing with the giving and receiving of positive and negative strokes. Setting goals, role-playing, and modeling, which can be used in TA, have been recommended as effective interventions for African Americans. Once again, we want to emphasize the point that vast, individual differences exist within each culture regarding preferences for counseling theory and practice.

In using TA across cultures, there is little variation in the method. Clients will learn the basic terminology and make contracts. TA has been used successfully in several different cultures. Mazzetti (1997) recommends TA for treating antisocial behavior by children of immigrant families in Italy. Robinson (1998) describes a TA program for treating seriously disturbed clients in a small, residential therapeutic community in England. Guimaraes (1997) uses TA to teach student doctors to communicate and work more effectively with patients from lower socioeconomic levels in Brazil. Beslija (1997) reports success with TA in working with the psychological problems of refugees from the former Yugoslavia.

TRANSACTIONAL ANALYSIS, ACCOUNTABILITY, AND MANAGED HEALTH CARE

Managed care organizations (MCOs) favor the group counseling format that TA practitioners often use. As noted in Chapter 2, the psychoeducational approach used by TA practitioners also finds favor in the managed care environment. Considerable work and progress toward counseling goals can be done in ten group sessions, giving TA some advantage points for brief treatment and a goal-attainment focus. Cost for TA treatments is low, and client satisfaction is generally high as people practice the new skills learned in group sessions. Setting goals may involve writing a new life script to replace the old script, which was not helping clients meet their needs. In fact, old ineffective scripts are generally written out and destroyed in a "public" burning during a group session. Rewriting one's life script also involves reviewing the messages one received from one's father and mother about such topics as education, work, fun, religion, marriage, family, sex, money, politics, love, and power. Messages that do not work for you are discarded in favor of those values that do work for you in your present life.

TA is viewed by some as being a versatile and integrative approach to counseling (Nabrady, 2005). However, we believe TA practitioners use a variety of interventions that belong uniquely to the TA approach. Some examples include script analysis, group feedback on how one's communication style impacts others, structuring one's time, and clarification/evaluation of personal values. Hargaden & Sills (2002) refer to TA as a relational approach in much the same way the Rogers's person-centered counseling is described. Our view is that all counseling approaches need a significant relational component for interventions to be effective. TA practiced in groups does have a relationship focus offering clients the opportunity to see themselves as others see them, which may result in clients altering their behavior to improve their relationships.

Psychoanalytic therapists, in attempting to move their practice into the managed care era, have attached themselves to TA and identified themselves as transactional psychoanalysts (Novellino, 2005; Woods, 2005). Steiner and Novellino (2005) debate the merits of such a union. Novellino, supporting an integration of TA and psychoanalysis, practices transactional psychoanalysis that includes the standard psychoanalytic practice of analyzing transreference, countertransference, and unconscious phenomena. Stiener, a veteran TA practitioner, makes the stronger case for TA being a radical departure from psychoanalysis as Berne intended it to be.

TA enjoys some other advantages regarding MCO guidelines. It is a self-help psychology—people can be helped by reading about it because the concepts are easy to understand. In addition, people do not feel threatened by TA. It deals with observable behavior, the present, and the conscious area of functioning. The TA focus is on how people can change whatever they want to change; these changes often happen immediately as people learn how to communicate more effectively and develop contracts for behavior change. In summary, TA can be packaged in a format MCOs find attractive and worthy of support.

SUMMARY

The practitioners of TA continue to enjoy wide popularity for improving relationship and communication skills between individuals and within groups of various types. TA training is useful in conducting group guidance classes or group counseling sessions with students in the 5 to 17 age range. However, TA training can be modified for use with any age group; the TA concepts are more user-friendly than the language of traditional psychotherapy. TA material is extremely well received in parent education groups, where the focus is on the positive things parents have been doing and how to increase the frequency of such helpful, positive parent behaviors. The TA focus is on re-education rather than healing and, as such, is not based on the assumption that people are sick and need to be healed. Participants in TA groups appreciate their roles as learners over that of being patients. TA instruction helps people to become aware of what they do and how this affects other people in their families and in their circles of friends and acquaintances. This information supports decisions to make changes in behavior.

WEBSITES FOR TRANSACTIONAL ANALYSIS

Internet addresses frequently change. To find the sites listed here, visit www.thomsonedu.com/counseling/thompson for an updated list of Internet addresses and direct links to relevant sites.

International Transactional Analysis Association (ITAA) home page
Transactional Analysis Psychotherapy Counseling

REFERENCES

Berne, E. (1947). *The mind in action.* New York: Simon & Schuster.
Berne, E. (1949). The nature of intuition. *Psychiatric Quarterly, 23,* 203–226.
Berne, E. (1961). *Transactional analysis in psychotherapy.* New York: Grove.
Berne, E. (1964). *Games people play.* New York: Grove.

Beslija, A. (1997). Psychotherapy with refugees from Bosnia-Herzegovina. *Transactional Analysis Journal, 27,* 49–54.

Freed, A. (1992). *TA for teens and other important people* (Rev. ed.). Rolling Hills Estates, CA: Jalmar.

Freed, A. (1998). *TA for tots: And other prinzes.* Rolling Hills Estates, CA: Jalmar. (Original work published 1973).

Freed, A., & Freed, M. (1998). *TA for kids: and grown ups too.* Rolling Hills Estates, CA: Jalmar. (Original work published 1971).

Guimaraes, B. (1997). Medical omnipotence and transactional analysis: A pedagogical proposal. *Transactional Analysis Journal, 27,* 272–277.

Guy, R. (2003). A theoretical-educational approach of developing positive self-esteem in children by implementing the theories of transactional analysis in the context of the family. *Dissertation-Abstracts, 64*(4-A), 1138.

Hargaden, H., & Sills, C. (2002). *Transactional Analysis: A relational approach.* Philadelphia: Brunner-Routledge.

Harris, T. (1969). *I'm OK—You're OK.* New York: Harper & Row.

James, M., & Jongeward, D. (1971). *Born to win.* Reading, MA: Addison-Wesley.

Kaplan, K. (2001). TILT and structural pathology. *Transactional Analysis Journal Internet, 4.* Retrieved September 2, 2002, from www.tajnet.org/articles/kaplan tilt.html.

LeGuernic, A. (2004). Fairy tales and psychological life plans. *Transactional Analysis Journal, 34,* 216–222.

Mazzetti, M. (1997). A transactional analysis approach to adjustment problems of adolescents from immigrant families. *Transactional Analysis Journal, 27,* 220–227.

Nabrady, M. (2005). Emotion theories and transactional analysis emotion theory: A comparison. *Transactional Analysis Journal, 35,* 68–77.

Novellino, M. (2005). Transactional psychoanalysis: Epistemological foundations. *Transactional Analysis Journal 35,* 157–172.

Poda, D. (2003). A letter to parents about child therapy. *Transactional Analysis Journal, 33,* 89–93.

Robinson, J. (1998). Reparenting in a therapeutic community. *Transactional Analysis Journal, 28,* 88–94.

Shahin, J. (1995). Hey, ya jerk. *American Way, 28,* 32,37–38.

Steiner, C. (1974). *Scripts people live.* New York: Grove.

Steiner, C. (1975). *Readings in radical psychiatry.* New York: Grove.

Steiner, C., & Novellino, M. (2005). TAJ theoretical diversity: A debate about transactional analysis and psychoanalysis. *Transactional Analysis Journal, 35,* 110–118.

Summerton, O. (2000). The development of game analysis. *Transactional Analysis Journal, 30,* 207–218.

Toth, M. (2004). Dealing with fear of failure: Working with script concepts in the classroom. *Transactional Analysis Journal, 34,* 209–215.

Woods, K. (2000). The defensive function of the game scenario. *Transactional Analysis Journal, 30,* 94–97.

Woods, K. (2005). Correlations between psychoanalysis and transactional analysis. *Transactional Analysis Journal, 35,* 205–210.

Individual Psychology

Half of the harm that is done in this world is due to people who want to feel important. They don't mean to do harm. But the harm does not interest them.

—T. S. Eliot

It isn't that they can't see the solution. It's that they can't see the problem.

—G. K. Chesterton

Alfred Adler, the founder of individual psychology, was born in Vienna on February 7, 1870; he was the second of six children. When Adler was 10 years old, he was such a poor math student that his teachers suggested he be removed from school and assigned as an apprentice to a cobbler. As often happens with paradoxical counseling strategies, the boy became angry, studied harder, and placed first in his class. As a child, Adler suffered from rickets, pneumonia, and several accidents. The resulting frequent contact with doctors influenced Adler to study medicine.

Adler spent his entire youth in Vienna and received his medical degree from the University of Vienna in 1895. In addition to medicine, Adler was also knowledgeable in psychology, philosophy, the Bible, and Shakespeare. Two years after his graduation, Adler married

**Alfred Adler
(1870–1937)**

We owe appreciation to Harold Mosak, Ph.D., of the Adler School of Professional Psychology in Chicago, for his contributions and his review of the fifth edition of this chapter.

Raisa Timofeyeuna Epstein, an intellectual and friend of Freud's who had moved from Russia to study at the University of Vienna (Alexander, Eisenstein, & Grotjahn, 1966).

In the Fall of 1902, Adler joined Sigmund Freud's discussion group, which was to become the first psychoanalytic society. Adler was not a proponent of Freud's psychosexual theory, and his writings about "feelings of inferiority" in 1910 and 1911 initiated a disagreement with Freud. In 1910, in an attempt to reconcile the gap between himself and the Adlerians, Freud named Adler president of the Viennese Analytic Society and coeditor of a journal that Freud published. Nevertheless, Adler continued to disagree with Freud's psychosexual theory. Adler was the first psychoanalyst to emphasize human nature as being fundamentally social. On Freud's demand that his entire staff accept his theory without any conditions, Adler resigned, together with seven others, and founded the Society for Free Psychoanalytic Research. In 1912, Adler changed the name to the Society for Individual Psychology.

After World War I broke out, Adler served for 2 years as a military doctor and later was appointed to head a large hospital for the wounded and those suffering from shell shock. In 1926, Adler accepted a visiting professorship at Columbia University in New York; and in 1935, he moved his family to the United States. His children, one son and one daughter, became psychiatrists and worked with the principles of individual psychology. On May 28, 1937, while giving a series of lectures in Scotland, Adler suddenly collapsed on the street and died of heart failure.

Adler's achievements included founding *Zeitschrift für Individualpsychologie* (1912), introducing the term *inferiority feelings,* and developing a flexible, supportive psychotherapy to direct those emotionally disabled by inferiority feelings toward maturity, common sense, and social usefulness. Individual psychology originated from the German word *Individualpsychologie,* meaning "psychology of the whole that cannot be divided." Basically, it is a psychology that is concerned both with individuals as they are in themselves and in their relationships with others.

In 1919, Adler originated the network of child guidance clinics called *Erziehungsberatungsstellen,* which means literally "places to come for questions about education," or parent-education centers. Their staffs included physicians, psychologists, and social workers. Because of his idea of group discussions with families, many people believe Adler to have been 50 years ahead of his time; the current emphasis on group counseling, parent education, and full-service schools supports this claim.

Parent education had been a significant part of Adler's system from the beginning. Several Adlerian parent-education packages have been published and used successfully over the past several years. In addition, Adlerian parent groups meet regularly around the country. Adler favored efforts directed toward prevention of mental illness through parent-education programs. He recognized the difficulty of undoing in adulthood the wrongs done to individuals in their childhood.

Rudolf Dreikurs contributed perhaps the most helpful adaptations and development of Adler's work. A leading proponent of individual psychology until his death in 1972, Dreikurs was a pioneer in music therapy and group psychotherapy, which he introduced into private psychiatric practice in 1929. His most significant contribution to counseling children was his ability to translate theory into practice. Dreikurs developed many of Adler's complex ideas into a relatively simple applied method for understanding and working with the behavior of children in both family and school settings.

THE NATURE OF PEOPLE

If Freud had done nothing more than stimulate thinking and reactions in other theorists, he would have made a significant contribution to counseling and psychotherapy. Like many others, Adler reacted against Freud's ideas and developed a new theory. Freud attempted to interpret all behaviors and problems as extensions of sex, pleasure, and the death instinct; Adler believed that all people develop some sense of inferiority because they are born completely helpless and remain that way for a rather long childhood. Such feelings of inferiority may be exaggerated by body or organ defects (real or imaginary), by having older and more powerful siblings, or by parent neglect, rejection, or pampering. One way to cope with feelings of inferiority is compensation or gaining power to handle the sense of weakness. The effects of organ inferiority are reduced through development of skills, behaviors, traits, and strengths that replace or compensate for these thoughts of weakness and powerlessness. Mosak (personal communication, July 21, 1992) points out that Adler introduced the theory of organ inferiority in 1907, when Adler was a Freudian, and that Freud complimented Adler on a major addition to Freudian theory. Although it is not a part of Adlerian theory today, Adlerians and others have observed that some people with organ inferiorities do compensate for them.

Adler viewed human behavior as falling on a continuum between his concepts of masculinity, representing strength and power, and femininity, symbolizing weakness and inferiority. What he called *masculine protest*—a striving for power—was common to both sexes, particularly women. Adler replaced Freud's concept of sexual pleasure as the prime motivator of behavior with the search for power.

According to Adler, personality development progresses along a road paved with evidence of either personal superiority or inferiority. As infants—small, helpless, inexperienced—we are especially subject to others' whims and vulnerable to feelings of inferiority. As we grow older, both family and society emphasize the advantages of size, beauty, and strength. Therefore, our wishes and dreams for superiority, our attempts to achieve it, and the social realities that make us feel inferior are in continual conflict. This striving for power (masculine protest) occupies a place in his theory similar to that of the Oedipus situation in Freudian theory. A person develops into a normal, neurotic, or psychotic adult as the result of this struggle between the masculine protest and social reality.

Freud believed that love and work were the two important indexes of mental health in that a person's mental health depends on how well these two areas are progressing. In a similar vein, Adler believed that problems brought to therapy reside in the areas of career (occupation), love relationships (intimacy), and friendships.

The following points summarize the Adlerian view on the nature of people:

- Beginning in childhood, people develop feelings of inferiority stemming from being totally dependent on their parents. Life becomes a process of believing in ways to become less inferior and more independent. People behave in ways to give themselves feelings of perfection or superiority.

- The future determines the present as people behave in ways to become the fictionalized ideal person they have established as a goal in their future. All parts of the person are directed toward achieving the goal of becoming the ideal self: cognitive, affective, behavioral, conscious, and unconscious. Psychological goals are often unknown and have to be identified and explained to clients by their counselors as they examine the purposes of their clients' behaviors.
- Individual perceptions of events and relationships are governed by one's own unique view of the world and its people. Understanding one's relationship to others is a first step to understanding oneself.
- People need to be educated to value and exhibit social interest. Children and adults make contributions to social interest when they make their neighborhood (and world) a better place to live.
- Unsolved problems of an individual may become problems for society if they are not treated before they become too difficult to solve.

The Need for Success

Adler was struck by the importance of the hunger for success in human life— that is, the ways people seek power and prestige and strive for goals associated with social approval. He was concerned with the problems of competition, blocked ambition, feelings of resentment and hostility, and impulses to struggle and resist or to surrender and give in. Adler shifted his clinical attention from a primary focus on clients' psychosexual history to an examination of their success/failure pattern, or style of life. Adler's term *style of life* emphasizes the direction in which the individual is moving. Style-of-life analysis involves an assessment of children and adolescents for their habitual responses to frustration, to assumption of responsibility, and to situations that require exercising initiative.

Goals of Behavior

Adler's individual psychology emphasizes the purposive nature of human strivings. All behavior, including emotions, is goal directed (Carlson & Glasser, 2004). According to Adlerian theory, the issue is not the cause of the behavior but determining what children want to accomplish, either in the real world or in their own minds. Behaviors do not continue over time unless they "work" for children. By looking at the consequences of children's behaviors, adults can determine their goals. Adler's conception was that people are guided by a striving for ideal masculinity. Adler described what Horney (1950) termed the *neurotic search for glory*: Neurotics are characterized by an unrealistic goal of masculinity and mastery that they strive to overcome or attain. He also anticipated later psychoanalytic groupings in his emphasis on the social and constitutional determinants of one's style of life. To Adler, the term **individual psychology** emphasized the unity of personality as opposed to Freud's emphasis on instincts common to all people. An individual builds a style of life from interactions between heredity and environment; these lifestyle building blocks fit a person into life as that person perceives it.

LIFESTYLE

Adler believed that a person's behavior must be studied from a holistic viewpoint. Usually by the age of 4 or 5, children have drawn general conclusions about life and the "best" way to meet the problems life offers. They base these conclusions on their biased perceptions of the events and interactions that go on around them and form the basis for their lifestyle. The style of life, unique for each individual, is the pattern of behavior that will predominate throughout that person's life. Only rarely does a person's lifestyle change without outside intervention. Understanding their lifestyle—that is, the basic beliefs they developed at an early age to help organize, understand, predict, and control their world—is important for adults, but children who have not reached the formal stage of cognitive development are incapable of understanding their lifestyles. Therefore, in working with children, Adlerians focus on the immediate behavioral goals rather than on long-term goals. Socratic questioning methods help children learn their current lifestyle and goals through self-discovery.

Stiles and Wilborn (1992) developed a lifestyle instrument for children that describes those who responsibly cope with and solve problems and those who engage in social interest activities that help others. Based on Adler's four lifestyle types, the scale reflected six lifestyle themes: *pleasing, rebelling, getting, controlling, being inadequate,* and *being socially useful.* They found that boys (age 8–11) scored higher than girls of the same age on rebelling; girls scored higher on pleasing.

SOCIAL INTEREST

A person's amount of social interest is, according to Adler (1938/1964), a good barometer of mental health. Social interest is a feeling for and cooperation with people—that is, a sense of belonging and participating with others for the common good. Ansbacher (1992) has described how social interest and community feeling differ. He defined *social interest* as the more active of the two terms because it relates to how the individual handles the life tasks of love, friendship, and work in the social context. Social interest is the more concrete, workable term, whereas *community feeling* deals with the spiritual, universal order of a person's life.

Everyone has a need to belong to a group. Although social interest is inborn, it does not appear spontaneously, but rather must be encouraged and trained, beginning with the relationship between the newborn infant and his or her mother. Children who feel they are part of a group do useful things that contribute to the well-being of that group; those who feel left out—and therefore inferior—do useless things to prove their own worth by gaining attention. From this concept comes the idea that misbehaving children are discouraged children—that is, children who think that they can be known only in useless ways. Because children behave within the social context, their behavior cannot be studied in isolation. The study of human interaction is basic to individual psychology.

Many of life's problems center around conflicts with others. Solutions for these problems involve cooperating with people in the interest of making society a better place to live. A strong point in Adler's theory is his understanding of the implications of the social structure of life. Because every individual depends on other people for birth and growth; for food, shelter, and protection; and for love and companionship, a great web of interdependence exists among people. Thus, the individual, Adler pointed out, owes a constant debt to society. Each person is responsible to the group, and those who do not learn to cooperate are destroyed. Adler thought social interest was exhibited through such qualities as friendliness, cooperation, and empathy. He believed that a person cannot violate the love and logic that bind people together without dire consequences for the health of one's personality. Pronounced egocentricity (the opposite of social interest) leads to neurosis, and the individual becomes healthy again only when this egocentricity is renounced in favor of a greater interest in the well-being of the total group. Critics of Adlerian theory who hold a less positive view of human nature point out that people know they should cooperate but ordinarily do not do so until forced. Cross-cultural research evidence supports this view.

Three environmental factors affect the development of a child's personality: family constellation, family atmosphere, and the prevalent methods of training. Through the family atmosphere, children learn about values and customs and try to fit themselves into the standards their parents set. Children also learn about relationships by watching how their family members interact and about sex roles by seeing the patterns adopted by their parents. The family constellation is important in that children formulate personalities based on how they interpret their positions in the family relative to other siblings. The firstborn child dethroned by a new baby tries very hard to maintain the position of supremacy and seeks recognition by whatever means possible. The second child feels inadequate because someone is always ahead and seeks a place by becoming what the older child is not; this child may feel squeezed out by a third child and adopt the position that life is unfair. The youngest child may take advantage of being the youngest and become outstanding in some respect, good or bad, even by becoming openly rebellious or helpless.

In summary, Adler believed that the principal human motive, a striving for perfection, could become a striving for superiority, and thus overcompensation for a feeling of inferiority. Children are self-determining people able to create a style of life in the context of their family constellation. By trial and error and by observation, children form their own conclusions about life and their place in it.

The Family Constellation

One goal of counseling is to construct a picture of the family dynamics and the child's place in the family constellation. *Ordinal position* (the exact order in which the child was born, e.g., second or fourth) in the family constellation is a key to the lifestyle pattern being developed by the child, and it may have a significant effect on how that child perceives reality. Although certain characteristics are associated with each child's *birth order* (one of the Adlerian birth positions: first, second, middle, youngest, and only), there are many exceptions; thus, not all firstborns are alike. Mosak (Shulman & Mosak, 1977) has pointed out that the study of birth order and ordinal position has limited value because of the confounding variables of family size and number of children; for example, the second-born child is the youngest in a two-child family and the middle child in a three-child family.

However, in an effort to find their special place in the family, children tend to select different roles, behaviors, and interests. In general, some stereotypical behaviors based on birth order have been cataloged by Adlerians over the past century. The following sections summarize some of these generalizations.

ONLY CHILDREN   The only child enjoys some intellectual advantages by not having to share his or her mother and father with any siblings. Language development usually is accelerated because the child learns adult language patterns. However, the reverse is sometimes true in an extremely child-centered home where everyone talks baby talk. Only children may experience difficulties outside the home when peers and teachers do not pamper them, and only children may be skillful in getting along with adults, but not in making friends with their peers. They enjoy being the center of attention. Observing how they gain the approval and attention to maintain their center-stage position can help a counselor understand these children. Have they developed skills? Do they elicit sympathy by being helpless? Or, do they act shyly? Only children are more likely to have problems with the egocentrism block. They usually are interested only in themselves and may resort to tantrums and uncooperative behavior if their requests are not granted. They may depend too much on adults because they have not learned to do things on their own. Exceptions to the rule are those only children who learn to play ball and other games by themselves when they have not had an opportunity to be around friends. Shulman (Shulman & Mosak, 1977) wrote that only children never have rivals and that peers tend to be curiosities rather than rivals. Only children may not have learned how to share, compromise, and collaborate.

FIRSTBORN CHILDREN   Often considered the special child by the family, especially if a male child, firstborns enjoy their number-one ranking but often fear dethronement by the birth of a second child. Firstborns work hard at pleasing their parents. They are likely to be conforming achievers, defenders of the faith, introverted, and well behaved. Twenty-three of the first twenty-five astronauts were firstborn men. The National Aeronautics and Space Administration

(NASA) was interested in recruiting high-achieving followers for the space program; it had no need for "creative astronauts" who might decide to take the scenic route home. Firstborns often find themselves functioning as substitute parents in larger families. Shulman (Shulman & Mosak, 1977) believes that first-born children, having had it all at one time, still prefer to be first and foremost.

SECOND-BORN CHILDREN   Second-born children may be those extroverted, creative, free-thinking spirits that NASA was trying to avoid. More often than not, second-born children look at what is left over in the way of roles and behavior patterns that the firstborn child has shunned; picking another role is easier than competing with an older sibling who has a head start. Second-born children may get lower grades in school, even if they are brighter than their older sibling. Parents are often easier on second-born children and show less concern with rules. In fact, second-born children may be the family rebels— with or without a cause! In any case, a second-born is usually the opposite of the first child. Second-born children are easily discouraged by trying to compete with successful, older, and bigger firstborns. The more successful first-borns are, the more likely second-borns are to feel unsure of themselves and their abilities. They may even feel squeezed out, neglected, unloved, and abused when the third child arrives.

MIDDLE CHILDREN   Some of the idiosyncrasies common to the middle-child position may affect second-born children. Middle children are surrounded by competitors for their parents' attention. They have the pace-setting standard-bearers in front and the pursuers in the rear. Middle children often label themselves as squeezed children. However, many younger children increase their skills in academic, athletic, and other pursuits through competition with older siblings.

YOUNGEST CHILDREN   Often referred to as Prince or Princess Charming, the youngest child could find a permanent lifestyle of being the baby in the family. Youngest children often get a lot of service from all the other family members. They may become dependent or spoiled and lag in development. Youngest children readily develop real feelings of inferiority because they are smaller, less able to take care of themselves, and often not taken seriously. The really successful charmers may learn how to boss subtly or to manipulate the entire family. They decide either to challenge their elder siblings or to evade any direct struggles for superiority. Then again, the path is marked and the trail is broken for the youngest child. Family guidelines are clear, and the youngest children always retain their position. Perhaps the downside is the child's perception that a lot of catching up is necessary to ever find a place in the family.

When a 5-year difference exists between two children in a family, the situation changes. With this large a gap, the next-born child often assumes the characteristics of a firstborn; apparently, the 5 years remove the competitive barriers found between children who are closer in age.

Extreme behavior patterns often are observed in children who find themselves the only boy or girl among siblings of the opposite sex. They may tend to develop toward extremes in either masculinity or femininity. Sex roles children assume often depend on roles perceived as most favored in our culture.

Large families appear to offer some advantages in child-rearing by making it tough for parents to overparent each child. Children in large families frequently learn how to solve their own problems, take care of themselves, and handle their conflicts because their parents cannot give personal service and attention to each and every problem. Large families are probably good training grounds for learning how to be independent.

The following factors influence the perceptions children have of their particular roles in their family:

1.   The parents may have a favorite child.
2.   The family may move.
3.   Parents become more experienced and easygoing as they grow older.
4.   Some homes are single-parent homes.
5.   The children may have a step-parent living in the home.
6.   The family climate changes with each addition to the family.
7.   Chronic illnesses or handicaps may be a problem in the family.
8.   A grandparent may live in the home.
9.   Some families are blended families.

In summary, too much emphasis on birth order and ordinal position works in opposition to the Adlerian principle of free choice. People with the same birth order may share some commonalities, but they are not predestined to turn out the same. The key question for counselors is not birth order, but rather how each child finds his or her place in the family.

THE FAMILY ATMOSPHERE

Adlerians stress the importance of the family atmosphere in the development of the child. Whereas the family constellation is a description of how family members interact, the family atmosphere is the style of coping with life that the family has modeled for the child.

The following twelve family atmosphere profiles are indications of how a negative family atmosphere can adversely affect children:

1.   *Authoritarian.*   The authoritarian home requires unquestioned obedience from the children. Children have little or no voice in family decisions. Although these children are often well behaved and mannerly, they also tend to be more anxious and outer directed. Who was once a shy child may turn into a rebel with a cause in later life.

2.   *Suppressive.* In tune with the authoritarian home is the suppressive family atmosphere, in which children are not permitted to express their thoughts and feelings. Expression of opinion is limited to what the

parents want to hear. Frequently, children from such a family cannot express their feelings when they are allowed to in situations outside the home, such as counseling. This type of family atmosphere does not encourage close relationships.

3. *Rejective.* Children feel unloved and unaccepted in this family atmosphere. Some parents do not know how to show love and frequently cannot separate the deed from the doer. Children and parents need to know and understand that love can be unconditional and not tied to unacceptable behavior; for example, "I love you, but I am still angered by your irresponsibility." A child can easily become extremely discouraged in the rejective family.

4. *Disparaging.* A child criticized by everyone else in the family often turns out to be the "bad egg" everyone predicted. Too much criticism generally leads to cynicism and inability to form good interpersonal relationships.

5. *High standards.* Children living in the high-standards atmosphere may think such things as "I am not loved unless I make all A's." Fear of failure leads to the considerable distress perfectionist people experience. The tension and stress these children have often prevent them from performing as well as they are able.

6. *Inharmonious.* In homes with considerable quarreling and fighting, children learn the importance of trying to control other people and keeping others from controlling them. Power becomes a prime goal for these children. Discipline may be inconsistent in these homes and depend on the mood of the parents.

7. *Inconsistent.* Inconsistent methods of discipline and home routines are often sources of confusion and disharmony in the home. Lack of self-control, low motivation, self-centeredness, instability, and poor interpersonal relationships are often attributed to inconsistency in parenting practices.

8. *Materialistic.* In the materialistic type of home, children learn that feelings of self-worth depend on possessions and on comparisons with what peers own. Interpersonal relationships take a back seat to accumulating wealth.

9. *Overprotective.* Overprotective homes often prevent children from growing up because parents do too much for them. They protect the children from the consequences of their behavior and, in doing so, deny the reality of the situation. This parental overindulgence leads to a child who feels helpless and dependent. Dependent children fall into the class of outer-directed people who rely on others for approval.

10. *Pitying.* Like overprotectiveness, pitying also prevents children from developing and using the resources they have for solving their problems. Such may be especially the case with handicapped children, who may be encouraged to feel sorry for themselves and to expect favors from others to make up for their misfortunes.

11. *Hopeless.* Discouraged and "unsuccessful" parents often pass on these attitudes to their children, who make hopelessness a part of their lifestyle.

A pessimistic home atmosphere may be due to economic factors, especially if the breadwinners lack financial resources.

12. *Martyr.* People experiencing low self-esteem, hopelessness, and discouragement may have another pessimistic viewpoint, martyrdom. Once again, children may learn that life is unfair and that people should treat them better; martyrdom is a breeding ground for dependency.

Remember that atmosphere is not the total cause of behavior. Behavior is most influenced by the child's biased perceptions of the family climate.

THEORY OF COUNSELING

Adler (1938/1964) held that four ties create reality and meaning in people's lives:

1. People are on earth to ensure the continuance of the human species.
2. Our survival depends on our need to cooperate with our fellow human beings.
3. Human beings have a masculine and a feminine side of their personalities.
4. Human problems can be grouped into three categories: relationships, work life, and love life.

Adler viewed the counselor's job as helping the child substitute realistic goals for unrealistic life goals and instilling social interest and concern for others.

As with most approaches to counseling, the goal of establishing a positive sense of self-esteem is primary. To achieve this feeling of self-esteem, children need to feel good about finding a place in life and about their progress in overcoming the unpleasant sense of inferiority associated with the dependence, smallness, and vulnerability introduced in early childhood. In the Adlerian view (and we do not know where he found this child), the ideal or well-adjusted child exhibits the following qualities:

1. Respect for the rights of others
2. Tolerance of others
3. Interest in others
4. Cooperation with others
5. Encouragement of others
6. Courteousness
7. Strong, positive self-concept
8. Feeling of belonging
9. Socially acceptable goals
10. Exertion of genuine effort
11. Willingness to share with others
12. Concern with how much "we" can get rather than how much "I" can get

In response to the specific pattern of inferiority feelings experienced by a child in a specific home situation, one unitary way of coping with the problem is discovered, one fundamental attitude is developed, and one mode of compensation is achieved. Thus, a person forms a style of life early in child-hood—a style that is unitary, dependable, and predictable.

Adler recognized two fundamental styles of life: direct and indirect approaches to the good things, through strength and power or through weakness. A person usually tries power first; if power is blocked, a person chooses another road to the goal. The second road is paved with gentleness and bids for sympathy. If both roads fail, secondary feelings of inferiority arise. These secondary inferiority feelings, which Adler considered more serious than the primary, universal inferiority feelings, are ego problems, which can be the most burning problems of all. The focus of counseling, therefore, is harnessing this drive to compensate for weakness so that positive, constructive behavior results. Freud held that the backbone of civilization was sublimation. Adler thought that talent and capabilities arise from the stimulus of inadequacy. Adlerians believe that people are pulled by their goals and priorities. Knowledge of these goals is a major key to understanding behavior. For example, four priorities relate to the need to belong:

1. *To please others:* The main objective of pleasing others is to avoid rejection. Although other people may find a "me last" person quite easy to accept, the price for this behavior may be the rejection the person is trying to avoid. The "me last" position may also limit a person's growth and opportunities for learning, personal development, and general success in life. The pleasing attitude is supported by the faulty belief that "My meaningfulness and survival depend on whether I am loved by all," or that "Life is good when my approval rating is high and bad when it is not."

2. *To be superior:* The main objective of trying to be superior is to avoid meaninglessness. Such an attitude of superiority tends to make others feel inadequate. The price for superiority may be an overloaded lifestyle. Children may become overly responsible and perfectionistic, with all the resulting worry and anxiety when things are not perfect. People holding superiority as their number-one priority attempt to avoid insignificance by influencing others through high achievement, leadership, and martyrdom. The superiority priority is supported by the faulty belief that "I am meaningful and therefore can survive only if I am better, am wiser, or know more than others."

3. *To control:* The main objective of trying to control oneself, others, and the environment is to avoid unexpected humiliation. Controlling others tends to make them feel challenged, with the resulting price of increased social distance. Too much self-control results in an extremely structured life with little spontaneity. Control people are best described as uptight, and their faulty belief is that "I am meaningful and therefore can survive only if I can control my life and the events and people who are part of my life."

4. *To be comfortable:* Avoidance of stress and pressure is the main objective of those holding comfort as their number-one priority. At their extreme, comfort seekers specialize in unfinished business and unresolved problems and conflicts. They adopt a reactive rather than proactive stance toward life.

Delayed gratification is not one of their strengths; they often give way to the self-indulgent attitude of "I want what I want now." The comfort-seeking priority is supported by the faulty beliefs that "I am meaningful and therefore can survive only if I am left alone, unpressured, and free to move" and "Life is bad when I am uncomfortable."

Each priority has a price. As is done in the practice of reality therapy, the counselor can confront children and adults with a cost analysis of their chosen priorities. Because people are often reluctant to give up their number-one priority, counseling may focus on cost reduction by exploring how clients can manage their priorities in more cost-efficient ways. As is done in the practice of rational-emotive-behavioral therapy, the counselor can ask clients to modify their faulty beliefs that meaningfulness and survival rest solely on the total and constant fulfillment of their number-one priority.

GOALS OF MISBEHAVIOR

As children grow and interact with their environment, they gradually develop methods for achieving their basic goal: belonging. Several factors, including the child's place in the family, the quality of the parents' interaction with the child, and the child's creative reaction to the family atmosphere, are critical in the development of coherent patterns of behaviors and attitudes.

Dreikurs and Soltz (1964) make an especially insightful and useful analysis of the immediate goals by which children attempt to achieve their basic goal of belonging. Children with no pattern of misbehavior have an immediate goal of cooperation and constructive collaboration. They find their place and feel good about themselves through constructive cooperation. They generally approach life with the goal of collaborating, and their usual behavior is socially and personally effective. By contrast, discouraged children with a pattern of misbehavior are usually pursuing one of four mistaken goals: attention, power, revenge, and inadequacy or withdrawal. Understanding the goal for which a misbehaving child is striving helps put the behavior in perspective and provides a basis for corrective action.

ATTENTION   All children seek attention, especially those of preschool age. However, excessive attention-getting behavior should diminish in the primary school years before it becomes a problem to teachers, parents, and peers. The child's goal is to keep an adult busy, and the natural reaction is to feel annoyed and provide the service and attention the child seeks. Attention-getting behavior appears in four forms:

1. *Active constructive.* This child may be the model child, but with the goal to elevate self, not to cooperate. This is the successful student whose industrious and reliable performance is for attention only.

2. *Passive constructive.* This charming child is not as vigorous as the active-constructive child about getting attention. This child is a conscientious performer and a prime candidate for teacher's pet.
3. *Active destructive.* This nuisance child is the prime candidate for the child most likely to ruin a teacher's day—the class clown, show-off, and mischief-maker.
4. *Passive destructive.* This lazy child gets a teacher's attention through demands for service and help. This child often lacks the ability and motivation to complete work.

POWER　Some children have an exaggerated need to exercise power and superiority. They take every situation, debate, or issue as a personal challenge from which they must emerge the winner; otherwise, these children think they have failed. The child's goal is to be the boss. A teacher's reaction ranges from anger to feeling threatened or defeated. The child acts in a stubborn, argumentative way and may even throw tantrums; this child leads the league in disobedience. The power struggle takes two forms:

1. *Active destructive.* This child is the rebel who has the potential of leading a group rebellion.
2. *Passive destructive.* This child is stubborn and forgetful and also could be the lazy one in the group.

REVENGE　Some children feel hurt and mistreated by life. Their goal is to get even by hurting others. They achieve social recognition, although they usually make themselves unpopular with most other children. The child's goal, then, is to even the score, and the adult's reaction is usually to feel hurt. Revenge has two forms:

1. *Active destructive.* This child is violent and resorts to stealing, vandalism, and physical abuse to extract revenge. This child is a candidate to become a gang leader.
2. *Passive destructive.* This child is violent, but in a passive way, that is, quiet, sullen, or defiant. Both revenge types believe their only hope for alleviating hurt feelings lies in getting even.

INADEQUACY OR WITHDRAWAL　Many children often feel inferior and think they are incapable of handling life's problems. Their deficiencies may be real or imagined. By giving up, they hope to hide their inferiority and to prevent others from making demands on them. The child's goal is to be left alone, and the adult's reaction is helplessness and giving up. Inadequacy has only one form: passive destructive. These children usually are described as hopeless. They often put on an act of being stupid just to discourage the teacher from asking them to recite and do work. They may have an unwritten contract with their teachers that says, in effect, "I'll leave you alone if you leave me alone."

Manly (1986) has adapted the four goal questions into an informal inventory for use with students who have been referred to her for behavior or attitude problems. Manly tells her students that the goals inventory will help her know them better and know what they think. The goals inventory may be taken as a pencil-and-paper checklist or as an interview between counselor and client. Students are asked to indicate which of the following sentences are true for them:

ATTENTION

__ I want people to notice me.

__ I want people to do more for me.

__ I want to be special.

__ I want some attention.

POWER

__ I want to be in charge.

__ I want people to do what I want to do.

__ I want people to stop telling me what to do.

__ I want power.

REVENGE

__ I think I have been treated unfairly.

__ I want to get even.

__ I want people to see what it is like to feel hurt.

__ I want people to feel sorry for what they have done.

DISPLAY OF INADEQUACY

__ I want people to stop asking me to do things.

__ I want people to feel sorry for me.

__ I want to be left alone. I can't do it anyway.

__ I know I'll mess up, so there's no point in trying.

The questions may be intermixed or administered in these groupings. The four goal labels are not included on the inventory.

Adolescents often are confused in searching for their place in the world. Most teenagers move successfully through high school to become productive adults. However, some teens choose deviant behavior as a way to find their place in the world. The experiences children encounter and their interpretation of them lead to a life plan. The first social encounter is in the family. Children reared in democratic families are more likely to understand how to meet life's challenges in meeting their needs for love, productive work, and friendship. Children reared in autocratic families often search for ways to fulfill their needs through attaining goals of misbehavior based on faulty reasoning (Ballou, 2002).

As mentioned earlier, the four mistaken goals of misbehavior are pursued by students who are having difficulty finding their place in their peer group by doing appropriate behaviors. All four goals are referred to as mistaken goals because they are based on faulty logic by students who resort to them to get what they want, whether it is attention, power, revenge, or avoidance of failure (withdrawal and giving up). Most misbehavior by children will be directed toward one or more of the four goals. However, adolescents begin to develop their capacity to incorporate more examples of faulty logic into their belief systems. Hence, each new faulty belief can result in a new goal of misbehavior. For example, the irrational idea "I must be perfect" could lead a student to engage in several types of perfectionistic behavior that make life miserable for the student. Most irrational messages produce failure because they lead to unattainable goals. Therefore, when counseling adolescent students, it is important to help them examine the faulty logic behind their behavior, as well as the goal of the misbehavior. According to Ellis (1997), changing the word *must* to *it would be nice if* appears to help adolescents put irrational messages in a better perspective. For example, "It would be nice if I were perfect, but since I'm human and humans make mistakes, it is okay to make mistakes, and I'm okay when I do."

COUNSELING METHOD

Adler based the counseling methods he pioneered on his experience and philosophy about the nature of people. Later Adlerians, including Rudolf Dreikurs, Heinz Ansbacher, Harold Mosak, and Don Dinkmeyer, have used and modified many of Adler's original ideas.

Adlerian counseling makes no distinction between conscious and unconscious material. The counselor uses dreams, for example, to discover the lifestyle of adult clients—that is, the type of defense used to establish superiority. Many counselors use questions similar to adult lifestyle interviews with children as a means of assessing how well things are going for them. Although organ inferiority is not a part of current Adlerian theory, counselors frequently analyze the inferiority feelings that stem from real or fancied personal deficiencies, particularly so-called organ deficiencies (such as defective vision) or organic inferiority (weak heart), some form of which everyone is assumed to possess. Next, the counselor proceeds to examine the client's academic, extracurricular, and social adjustments to see how the client has maintained or achieved superiority in each of these major areas of life and to examine the inferiority feelings that may plague the client. A primary goal of Adlerian counseling is to point out to the client the overcompensation and defensive patterns the client is using to solve problems and to find more successful ways of solving problems related to school, play, and other social concerns.

The establishment of the counselor–client relationship is the key step in the process. The counselor's job is to re-educate children who have developed mistaken ideas about some concepts of their lives. The counseling relationship assumes that the counselor and child are equal partners in the process, and that the child is a responsible person who can learn better ways to meet personal needs. The positive view of human nature is indicated through the counselor's faith, hope, and caring attitude toward the child.

Adlerians believe that lives are holistic. Dinkmeyer, Pew, and Dinkmeyer, Jr. (1979) refer to *teleoanalytic holistic theory,* which regards any troubled or troublesome behavior as a reflection of one indivisible, unified, whole organism moving toward self-created goals. The foremost task of Adlerian counselors is to prove this unity in people, specifically in their thinking, feeling, and behavior—in fact, in every expression of their personality (Ansbacher & Ansbacher, 1956). Adlerians believe that children are the artists of their own personalities and are constantly moving purposefully toward self-consistent goals. An information interview based on questions used in the adult lifestyle analysis helps to reveal the pictures children have painted of their lives and their current personality development. The information interview consists of present and past (early) recollections of the children themselves and their families, how they fit into the family constellation, and how they perceive siblings and parents in relation to themselves. Questions often used include those in the following structured, interview guide:

INFORMATION INTERVIEW GUIDE

1. What type of concern or problem would you like to discuss, and how did this problem develop?
2. On a five-point scale (1 or 2 = great; 3 or 4 = medium; 5 = poor), how are things going for you?

   In school? _____

   With your friends? _____

   With your hobbies? _____

   With your parents? _____

   With your brothers and sisters? _____

   With your fun times? _____

3. Can you tell me about your mother and father? (Separate the answers for mother and father or for any other parental figures living at home with the child.)

   What do they do?

   What do they want you to do?

   How do you get along with them?

   How are you like your parents?

   How are you different from your parents?

4. What things in your family would you like to be better?

5. Can you tell me about your brothers and sisters? (Make a list of children in the family, from eldest to youngest, with their ages.) Of all your brothers and sisters, who is:

Most like you? How?

Most different from you? How?

6. What kind of child are you?
7. What kind of child did you used to be?
8. What scares you most?
9. What used to scare you most?
10. Have any of your brothers or sisters been sick or hurt?
11. What do each of the children in your family do best?

Who is the smartest?

Best athlete?

Mother's favorite?

Father's favorite?

Hardest worker?

Best behaved?

Funniest?

Most spoiled?

Best in mathematics?

Best in spelling?

Best in penmanship?

Most stubborn?

Best looking?

Friendliest?

Strongest?

Healthiest?

Best musician?

Best with tools?

The counselor uses these and other questions initially to explore the pictures children have painted of their lives. The information also is helpful in assessing how children are developing their lifestyles. The interview also can help older adolescents and adults understand their lifestyles. For example, Adlerian counselors hold that children and adolescents who have difficulty with mathematics also may have difficulty in solving their personal problems. They believe problem solving in mathematics and problem solving in life have some common elements. Therefore, when students report difficulties with mathematics, Adlerians check to see how well they are solving their personal problems. In a similar matter, Adlerians believe poor spelling and penmanship are symptomatic of the client's desire to rebel against authority and to break rules with a low-response cost. Poor penmanship and spelling are fairly safe ways to rebel. Adlerians also believe that the sibling most different from you has the greatest impact on your lifestyle development.

Terner and Pew (1978) recommend examining the client's personality structure (the lifestyle). They divided the counseling process into the following four phases:

Phase I: The first phase includes an examination of the formative years of the person in his or her family constellation. For younger children, this phase is an ongoing or current event; it is an early recollection (ER) of an older adolescent or an adult.

Phase II: The second phase focuses on collecting ERs from the client's past, which are detailed in the next section.

Phase III: The objective of the third phase is to illustrate for clients what they are doing in their lives and the principles under which they are operating. Clients are confronted with the goals they are attempting to reach.

Phase IV: The fourth phase is reorientation toward living through an encouragement process designed to build clients' self-confidence. The counselor assesses strengths within clients in lieu of the problems that need to be solved and attends to how clients make themselves sick and what they need to recover. The counselor identifies discouragement—that is, the loss of self-confidence—as the root of all deficiencies.

EARLY RECOLLECTIONS

Counselors use ERs to understand the child's earliest impressions of life and how the child felt about them. They ask children to remember as far back as they can, particularly recollections of specific incidents, with as many details as possible, including the child's reaction at the time. "If we took a snapshot when that happened, what would we see? How did you feel?" Three to six of those ERs help to show a pattern in the lifestyle. These recollections tend to reflect a prototype that is apparent in the lifestyle analysis. Although the occurrences children relate may not be factually accurate, they are true insofar as they reflect the children's memories and feelings. The counselor then has a clearer idea of the child's basic view of life and how some attitudes may have mistakenly crystallized. Examples of themes that may appear in these recollections and the child's accompanying mistaken beliefs include the following:

1. *Early Dangers.* Be aware of the many hostile aspects of life.
2. *Happy Times with Adults Around.* Life is great as long as many people praise and serve me.
3. *Misdeeds Recalled.* Be careful that they do not happen again.
4. *Pleasure versus Pain.* The easy way is best.
5. *Cheerful versus Depressed.* It does not pay to be happy.
6. *Pampered versus Mistreated.* I need someone to take care of me.
7. *Secure versus Jeopardized.* People cannot be trusted.

8. *Reward versus Punishment.* Life is good only when I get my way.
9. *Benevolent versus Hostile.* Doing the right thing does not pay.
10. *Obedient versus Defiant.* Stay out of trouble.
11. *Participant versus Observer.* When in doubt, do something; or when in doubt, do nothing.
12. *Praise versus Blame.* It is never my fault.
13. *Confident versus Inferior.* I will never be good at anything.
14. *We versus I.* I should be able to do it by myself.
15. *Active versus Passive.* It is always better to wait and see.
16. *Success versus Failure.* Nothing ever works out well for me and never will.

Myer and James (1991) present useful guidelines on ERs as an assessment technique to discern children's behavior patterns. A nonverbal child can produce ERs as drawings and in other types of play media. Counselors can make ERs a memory game or a "make up a story about when you were small" game. Modeling what the child is to do may be helpful. At least three ERs are needed to find a child's pattern of behaviors. The process should not be rushed. The counselor's job is to help the child teach the counselor about his or her situation by summarizing content and feelings. Open-ended statements are good if the counselor is not leading the child into one of the counselor's own ERs. Myer and James recommend paying attention to context (for example, a child alone may indicate isolation), content (for example, recurring topics such as food, water, animals, and wearing boots have special significance for the child), people (for example, family members left in and out of the story), movement (for example, passivity and compliance may indicate discouragement), and feelings (for example, hot and cold feeling words tell much about the child's outlook on life). The counselor must be careful to avoid overinterpreting or underinterpreting ERs in planning interventions for children.

UNDERSTANDING

Counselors must be understanding with children. No matter what children are doing, they are probably doing the best they can at the moment. Ways of relieving some anxiety and conflict include helping them interpret what is happening and giving the problem, child, or action a "handle." Use encouragement. Change negative situations to positive ones by telling fables where appropriate; for example, "The Miller and the Donkey" helps children understand they can never please everyone, even by absurdly attempting the impossible like trying to carry the donkey. "The Frogs in the Milk" tells about two frogs who jumped into a barrel of milk and simply paddled until they made butter; they were then able to jump out easily.

CONFRONTATION

When children are unable to change the mistaken ideas behind their behavior, confrontation is necessary (Myer & James, 1986). A counselor can confront children with educated guesses about the goals they are trying to achieve at others' expense. Be aware also of the child who sees the counselor as an obstacle and is using depreciation. Typically, the child is unwilling to move in a direction indicated by the counselor and attempts avoidance or wastes time. Counselors are advised to stay out of these power struggles.

STAGES

Actual changes in children's perspectives occur in stages. First, children are limited to afterthoughts of insight: They can clearly see what they are doing to cause mistaken ideas or unhappiness to persist, but only after they have misbehaved. In the second stage, children become able to catch themselves in the act of misbehaving. Added awareness enables them to sensitize themselves to inappropriate behavior. In the next stage, children have developed a heightened sense of awareness that enables them to anticipate the situation and plan a more appropriate behavior or response. These three stages match the preconventional, conventional, and postconventional stages in Piaget's theory of moral development. Stage 3 may not occur to about age 11, if it occurs at all.

INTERVENTIONS FOR THE FOUR GOALS OF MISBEHAVIOR

The four goals of misbehavior are intended to help parents, teachers, and counselors understand that how they feel about what the child is doing most clearly explains the child's mistaken goal (Dreikurs & Soltz, 1964). Analysis and description of the four mistaken goals (attention, power, revenge, and withdrawal), the ways of identifying them, and the methods of correction have resulted in an impressive array of guidance and counseling approaches to help discouraged children and their discouraged families. The steps outlined for determining a child's mistaken goals—learning the adult's corrective response to misbehavior and the child's reaction to the correction—are both penetrating and simple. The counselor who understands the child's goal can, through counseling the child and parents, help the child develop a constructive goal and appropriate behavior.

In describing and analyzing specific immediate goals, Dreikurs and his colleagues (Dreikurs & Grey, 1968; Dreikurs & Soltz, 1964) focus primarily on preadolescents. Dreikurs and his co-authors note that, in early childhood, the children's status depends on the impression they make on adults. Later, they may develop different goals to gain social significance in their peer group and, later still, in adult society. These original goals can still be observed in people of every age. However, they are not all-inclusive; teenagers and adults have additional goals of misbehavior based on irrational self-messages (see Chapter 8). Dreikurs reminds us that people often can achieve status and prestige more easily through useless and destructive means than through accomplishment.

Dreikurs advocates modifying the motivation rather than the behavior itself. When the motivation changes, more constructive behavior follows automatically.

The "four-goal technique" requires the following steps:

1. Observe the child's behavior in detail.
2. Be psychologically sensitive to one's own reaction.

3. Confront the child with the goal of the behavior.
4. Note the recognition reflex.
5. Apply appropriate corrective procedures.

Remember that misbehaving children are discouraged children trying to find their place; they are acting on the faulty logic that their misbehavior will give them the social acceptance that they desire. The first goal, attention getting, is a manifestation of minor discouragement; the fourth goal, display of inadequacy, is a manifestation of deep discouragement. Sometimes a child switches from one kind of misbehavior to another, which is often a signal that the discouragement is growing worse.

To identify a young child's goals, the counselor's own immediate response to the child's behavior is most helpful; it is in line with their expectations. The following four examples of behaviors show how the adult may feel, what the child may be thinking, what alternate behaviors exist, and what questions may come to mind about the child's behavior.

ATTENTION

You are annoyed; you begin coaxing, reminding.

Charlie thinks he belongs only when he is noticed, or life is only good when he is the center of attention.

You can (1) attend to the child when he is behaving appropriately or (2) ignore misbehavior (scolding reinforces attention-getting behavior).

You can ask: Could it be that you want me to notice you and the only way you know how to do this is to interrupt me without permission?

POWER

You are angry, provoked, and threatened.

Linda thinks she belongs only when she is in control or the boss, or life is good only when she gets her own way.

You can withdraw or "take your sail out of her wind" by leaving the room.

You can ask: (1) Could it be that you want to be the boss? (2) Could it be that you want me to do what you want and the way you do this is to break our rules?

REVENGE

You are deeply hurt and want to get even.

Sally thinks her only hope is to get even, or the best way to handle hurt feelings is to hurt somebody back.

You can (1) use group and individual encouragement and (2) try to convince her that she is liked by building a positive relationship with her.

You can ask: Could it be that you want to hurt me because I or someone else has hurt you, and the only way to handle hurt feelings is to hurt back?

INADEQUACY

You are feeling helpless, hopeless, and do not know what to do.

Tom thinks he is unable to do anything and that he belongs only when people expect nothing of him, or life is only good when adults do not require him to recite or do difficult work.

You can show genuine faith in the child and use encouragement to help Tom begin having success in class every day.

You can ask: Could it be that you don't feel very smart and don't want people to know, and the way to hide this is to never do any work at all?

SEQUENCE OF THE "COULD IT BE . . .?" QUESTIONS   A counseling interview that uses the four "Could it be?" questions might go as follows:

COUNSELOR: Alice, do you know what you were trying to get when you did (the misbehavior)?

ALICE: No. [This may be an honest response.]

COUNSELOR: Would you like to work with me so that we can find out? I have some ideas that might help us explain what you are trying to get when you do _____. Will you help me figure this out?

ALICE: Okay.

COUNSELOR: [using one question at a time, in a nonjudgmental, unemotional tone of voice]:

1. Could it be that you want Mr. Jones to notice you more and give you some special attention?
2. Could it be that you would like to be boss and have things your own way in Mr. Jones's class?
3. Could it be that you have been hurt and you want to get even by hurting Mr. Jones and others in the class?
4. Could it be that you want Mr. Jones to leave you alone and to stop asking you all those hard questions in math?

The counselor always asks all four of these questions sequentially, regardless of the child's answers or reflexes, because the child may be operating on more than one goal at a time. The counselor observes the body language and listens carefully for the response to catch the "recognition reflex." An accurate disclosure of the child's present intentions produces a recognition reflex such as a "guilty" facial expression, which is a reliable indication of his or her goal, even though the child may say nothing or even "no." Sometimes the confrontation itself helps the child change. Another indication of the child's goal is the child's response to correction. Children who are seeking attention and get it from the teacher stop the misbehavior temporarily and then repeat it or do something similar. Children who seek power refuse to stop the disturbance or even increase it. Those who seek revenge respond to the teacher's efforts to get them to stop by switching to some more violent action. Instead of cooperating, a child acting out the fourth goal remains entirely passive and inactive.

Once the counselor suspects the goal of the child's misbehavior, confronting the child is most important. The purpose of this confrontation is to disclose and confirm the mistaken goal of the child. The emphasis is on "for what purpose," not "why."

The next step after identifying the goal of misbehavior is to choose and use appropriate corrective procedures, which may range from encouragement to logical consequences.

ENCOURAGEMENT   Mosak and Maniacci (1998) have written that Adler and his followers considered encouragement a crucial aspect of living, as well as a crucial part of the counseling process. Encouragement is the key to developing positive expectations in the people we counsel, which help clients to engage in wider varieties of adaptive behaviors with less stress and discomfort. Conversely, according to Mosak and Maniacci (1998), maladaptive, pathological behavior is viewed as a reflection of discouragement, which leads to a lack of confidence. Lacking confidence, clients are likely to cling to their old, unhelpful attitudes and behaviors that give them a false sense of security but get them into trouble. Encouragement becomes an important key in breaking the vicious cycle of discouragement, which causes the client to cling to unhelpful attitudes and behaviors that, in turn, perpetuate more discouragement and a repetition of maladaptive behaviors.

Dreikurs and Soltz (1964) have written that encouragement implies faith in and respect for children as they are. One should not discourage children by having extremely high standards and ambitions for them. Children misbehave only when they are discouraged and believe they cannot succeed by other means. In fact, one evaluation of counseling is how far the child has moved from feeling discouraged toward feeling encouraged. Children need encouragement as plants need water and sunshine. Telling children they can be better implies they are not good enough as they are.

Problems with these ideas on encouragement arise when parents ask how they are supposed *not* to expect children performing below their ability levels to do better. The answer seems to be in loving children unconditionally despite their behavior and performance. However, one does not have to love or pretend to love the child's misbehavior.

Encouragement is advocated in place of praise and reinforcement, but bribery is strongly discouraged. Adlerians see praise as a message that tells children that, under conditions determined by the adult, they are all right. Praise focuses on the product. Encouragement, however, accepts children as they are; it focuses on the process. Encouragement occurs *before* the child completes a task or even starts it. For example:

- "I am proud of you."
- "That's a rough one, but I think you have what it takes to work it out."
- "I know you can do it; let me help you get started."

PRAISE   Praise (reinforcement) occurs *after* the child performs a behavior or completes a task. For example:

- "You certainly did a good job."
- "That was great work you did in math."
- "I like the way you handled that."
- "You played a good game."

BRIBERY   Bribery often occurs *during* the child's misbehavior. For example:

- "If you quiet down, I'll give you a candy bar."
- "I'll buy you a surprise if you stop fighting."
- "If you stop bothering me, you won't have to help with the dishes."

Adlerian counselors believe that extrinsic reward and illogical punishment have detrimental effects on the development of the child, particularly in the democratic atmosphere that prevails today. Only in an autocratic society are these reward-and-punishment systems an effective and necessary means of obtaining conformity; they presuppose a certain person is endowed with superior authority. Children may see rewards as one of their rights and soon demand a reward for everything they do if they are conditioned under this system. Adlerians agree with Kohn (1999), who writes in *Punished by Rewards* that an extrinsic reward system robs the child or adult of the intrinsic reward of simply engaging in an activity for its own enjoyment. Children rewarded for practicing the piano will begin to view playing the piano as work that nobody would do without pay. Children may interpret punishment as their right to punish others. In fact, children often are hurt more by their retaliation than by the punishment. They are experts in knowing how to hurt their parents, whether by getting into trouble or by earning low grades. Therefore, Adlerians reject reward-and-punishment methods that focus on extrinsic reinforcement in favor of encouragement, intrinsic reinforcement, and logical consequences.

NATURAL AND LOGICAL CONSEQUENCES

Natural and logical consequences are Adlerian techniques favored over reward and punishment because they allow children to experience the actual consequences of their behavior.

NATURAL CONSEQUENCES   Natural consequences are a direct result of a child's behavior. Careless children who touch the hot stove get burned and become more careful of stoves in the future. Natural consequences of irresponsible behavior are unfavorable outcomes that occur naturally without any prearranged plan or program. For example, if Sue leaves her baseball glove outside and it is ruined in a rainstorm, she has experienced a natural consequence. If I am late in making my airline reservation, I may find I cannot take the flight I want. Natural consequences to irresponsible behavior happen on their own, or naturally, without being planned and administered by others.

LOGICAL CONSEQUENCES   Logical consequences, established through rules and family policy, are fair, direct, consistent, and logical results of a child's behavior. For example, if Frank comes home late for dinner, his family has assumed that he would have been home on time to eat or would have called if he had been hungry. Therefore, they removed his plate from the table. He is allowed to fix any food he can as long as he cleans up after himself. Another example of a logical consequence is, if Mary breaks someone's window, she is asked to repair the damage or pay to have the damage repaired. If Mary does not have the cash or skill required to repair the damage, she can work off her debt by performing other jobs. In school, if John interferes with someone else's right to learn, he is moved to a place where he cannot continue to do so (some form of isolation). In other words, the consequence fits the misbehavior; it is a logical consequence. Punishment, as defined by Adlerians, is any illogical consequence for irresponsible behavior. For example, if Frank is late for dinner, he gets paddled and sent to bed. The punishment or consequence does not match the crime, but it teaches children that bigger people get to overpower smaller people. Children reared under a punishment-by-power system become very impressed with power and use it whenever they can to get what they want.

Both natural and logical consequences allow children to experience the results of their behavior instead of arbitrary punishment exercised through the parent's personal authority. These two techniques direct children's motivation toward proper behavior through personal experience with the social order in which they live. We are not recommending, however, that adults *not* protect children in dangerous situations, for example, teaching children about the dangers of street traffic through personal experience!

Natural and logical consequences focus on the Adlerian belief that people are responsible and capable of leading full, happy lives. Consequences allow the child to understand an inner message that is more likely to be remembered than punishment, which can harm the relationship with a child.

Natural and logical consequences give children the message that they are capable of making their own decisions. They have an opportunity for growth through weighing alternatives and arriving at a decision. Given overly severe limits, however, the child is deprived of making decisions that foster self-respect and responsibility. Children and adolescents need to do for themselves what they are capable of doing.

CASE STUDY

Identification of the Problem

J.B., a 9-year-old boy in the fourth grade at Spoonbill Elementary School, was referred to our group by the teacher because of his classroom behavior. J.B. repeatedly leaves his seat and does not complete his work.

Individual and Background Information

Academic. According to J.B.'s teacher, J.B. does less than average work. Most of his grades are U's. He does not usually complete his assignments; when he does, he hurries and commits many errors. His teacher believes that he is not working up to his potential in many areas. His test scores support the teacher's view that J.B. is an underachiever, and J.B. loves to read. His teacher reported that J.B.'s behavior sometimes annoyed her and at other times made her angry. She mentioned that she was discouraged about his schoolwork.

Family. J.B. is the youngest son of an older father and stepmother. The sibling closest to his age is 19. He came to live with his father last year after spending time in a home for boys because of his abusive mother. Recently, his stepmother threatened to send him back to the home for boys if he did not behave in school.

Social. J.B. has a friendly personality and seems to relate well with his peers.

Counseling Method

The counselor used the Adlerian counseling method to help J.B. identify the goals of his behavior and how well he was meeting his goals. They spent considerable time on helping J.B. understand what he did to get himself in trouble at school and what he could do to make his life more pleasant at school and at home. They looked at ways J.B. could meet his goals without getting into trouble.

Transcript

COUNSELOR: Well, J.B., it is good to see you again. We need to check up on how things are going with you in Ms. Johnson's room.

J.B.: Did she tell you I have been bad?

COUNSELOR: She feels discouraged about your schoolwork.

J.B.: Sometimes it is just too hard.

COUNSELOR: So sometimes you feel discouraged too.

J.B.: Yeah, I sure do.

COUNSELOR: It is sort of like sometimes you don't get the help you need.

J.B.: She won't look at me when I raise my hand to get her to help.

COUNSELOR: That must be frustrating to you. Do you know what I mean by frustrating?

J.B.: Yeah, I get mad and go up by her desk, and she tells me to get back in my seat.

COUNSELOR: So a lot of bad things seem to happen, one right after another one, and you just keep getting angrier.

J.B.: That's right!

COUNSELOR: Well, J.B., we've got some work to do. We need to figure out what you are trying to get and if you are getting what you want.

J.B.: What do you mean?

COUNSELOR: If we can find out what goals you are trying to reach, we will be able to figure out what you need to do to get what you want without getting into trouble.

J.B.: I'm not trying to get anything.

COUNSELOR:	Could be; let's check it out.
J.B.:	Okay, I guess.
COUNSELOR:	J.B., could it be when you do your work poorly or don't do it at all, you want to get Ms. Johnson to leave you alone?
J.B.:	What do you mean?
COUNSELOR:	Maybe if you convince her you can't do the work, she and your parents will get off your back about making better grades.
J.B.:	Sometimes I really do try to do it all.
COUNSELOR:	So, you really haven't given up on making better grades.
J.B.:	Oh, no, I haven't.
COUNSELOR:	Well, could it be you would like to have Ms. Johnson pay more attention to you, and the way to do that is break rules about talking out of turn and leaving your seat?
J.B.:	Yeah, sometimes she really loses it and everybody laughs.
COUNSELOR:	So, you end up getting a lot of attention, some good and some bad.
J.B.:	Yeah, but it's worth it.
COUNSELOR:	You seemed pleased with having the attention and don't mind the consequences or bad stuff that happens to you.
J.B.:	Well, I do wish I could move back to my old seat. I don't like sitting right in front of the teacher's desk.
COUNSELOR:	So attention is important to you, but sitting close to the teacher is not what you want.
J.B.:	You got that right! Can you get me moved?
COUNSELOR:	You and I can work on it. We might be able to figure out how.
J.B.:	Let's go for it!
COUNSELOR:	We have to figure out how to convince Ms. Johnson that you can be trusted to follow the class rules and do your work when you are sitting away from her desk.
J.B.:	How?
COUNSELOR:	Well, J.B., you know her a whole lot better than I do. I would like to know what you think would work.
J.B.:	Maybe I can make a deal. She likes deals.
COUNSELOR:	How would that work?
J.B.:	Well, I could ask her if I stay out of trouble and turn in all of my work for a whole week, could I move to my old seat?
COUNSELOR:	I wonder what she will say about how well your work needs to be done.
J.B.:	I could tell her that I will make at least a B in everything.
COUNSELOR:	Well, I guess you could try that. I wonder what she should do if you go back to your old seat and the old behavior comes back.

J.B.:	I guess I would have to go back to the front row.
COUNSELOR:	Could be. Tell you what. If Ms. Johnson agrees to your plan, would you come by the office each day on your way home and give me the word on how your day went?
J.B.:	Sure.
COUNSELOR:	If it doesn't work out, come back tomorrow, and we'll try to write a plan that will work.
J.B.:	See you.
COUNSELOR:	Let's shake hands on this deal. Hope it works out. See you tomorrow.

As noted in the interview transcript, the Adlerian counseling method works well in concert with many of the other counseling approaches discussed in this chapter. Encouragement, group discussions, and logical consequences often are used with shaping (positive reinforcement and extinction) and reframing to bring about positive behavioral change.

ADLERIAN PLAY THERAPY

Kottman (1997) explains that a counselor using Adlerian play therapy begins by assuming that the children who have been referred are discouraged children. Discouraged children have negative convictions about themselves and the world. Their self-defeating goals, behaviors, and attitudes reflect those negative convictions. The goal of Adlerian play therapy is the reduction of this discouragement. Therefore, the counselor chooses play techniques to provide encouragement.

This type of play therapy has four phases. The first phase involves establishing a democratic, empathic relationship. The counselor then explores the child's lifestyle, highlighting the child's beliefs, attitudes, goals, emotions, and motives. The counselor's goal in the third phase is to interpret the lifestyle, faulty convictions, and self-defeating goals and behaviors. During the final phase, the counselor's objective is to help the child use the insight and convert it into action such as behavioral and attitudinal changes. Kottman (1997) cautions the play therapist to recognize small shifts in attitude and behavior.

Kottman and Johnson (1993) discuss strategies to be used during the four phases of Adlerian play therapy. The counselor can use several approaches when establishing a relationship with the child. The counselor may choose to track the behavior of the child by giving a running account of what is being done and said. The counselor may also restate the content and reflect feelings so that the child knows that emotions, behaviors, and attempts to communicate are important to the counselor. The counselor also encourages the child by conveying respect for the child's strengths, faith in the child's abilities, and recognition of the child's attempts and improvement. During the first phase of Adlerian play therapy, the counselor sets limits to protect the child and others, to prevent toys or other things from being damaged, and to deter destructive behavior. In the second phase, the counselor explores the lifestyle of the child, examining the goals of the child's behavior. Considerations of the family atmosphere, family constellation, and the ERs of the child also are important in this phase. Based on this information, the counselor begins to form a hypothesis about the child's beliefs and shares this understanding with the child. The third phase includes a deepening insight into the child's lifestyle. The counselor shares hypotheses and interpretations with the child and may use therapeutic metaphors. During the fourth phase—reorientation and reeducation—the counselor helps the child develop alternative behaviors that are practiced and encouraged. The counselor also consults with the adults in the child's life.

The Family Art Assessment Technique is a method of gathering information about a family. This three-part drawing activity starts with the family divided into teams that work on separate pieces of paper. The family is then united to work as a team on one sheet of paper. DeOrnellas, Kottman, and Millican (1997) describe a case in which the family viewed the process as positive and enjoyable, and the therapists gathered helpful information about the family.

Brack, Hill, Edwards, Grootboom, & Lassiter (2003) recommend using Adlerian group work in the classroom much like what is done in Glasser's (1969) classroom meetings. They would use contracts to help students improve their behavior and academic performance. Guidelines for the group meetings would include respect for all opinions, active participation, sharing good news, and regular meeting times. Students would focus on learning to listen and to respond to other group members by encouraging positive behaviors. LaFountain, Garner, and Miedema (2003) go a step further in building students' confidence in their abilities. They found significant increases in student achievement and motivation when teachers matched their teaching styles to fit the learning styles, strengths, and interests of their students.

ADLERIAN FAMILY COUNSELING

Adlerian methods are well suited for counseling the entire family. The following interview guide is suggested:

1. Interview the parents on the following topics (while their children are observed in a playroom situation):
   a. Describe your children—their respective ordinal positions, schoolwork, hobbies, athletics, and so on.
   b. How does each child find his or her place in the family?
   c. What problems revolve around getting up? Mealtime? TV? Homework? Chores? Bedtime?
   d. Does something in your family need to be better?
   e. Would you like to make a change? (Before the counselor gives suggestions, it is preferable that the parents admit they are bankrupt in child-rearing ideas; that is, nothing has worked in improving the particular family concern.)

2. Interview the children on the following topics with the parents not present. (Use "Could it be?" questions when appropriate. Ask who is in charge of discipline.)

   a. Do you know why you are here today?
   b. Does anything bother you in the family that you would like to change?
   c. How can we make things better at home?
   d. Who is the good child?
   e. Who is Father's favorite?
   f. Who is Mother's favorite?
   g. Who is best in sports?
   h. What do each of you do best?
   i. Which are your best school subjects?
   j. Which are your worst school subjects?

3. Interview the entire family. Summarize plans for the coming week, clarifying roles, behaviors, and expectations. Recommendations for each family generally include the following:

   a. Provide individual parent time for each child, each day.
   b. Have one family conference per week. Use collaboration and/or compromise to reach family consensus in making decisions. *No voting.* Three-to-two votes split the family, with the losing voters dragging their heels and not being enthusiastic supporters of the issue supported by the "winning" side.
   c. Do one family activity per week.
   d. Each family member does chores.

Dinkmeyer (1988) bases "marathon family counseling" on Adlerian psychology. The process, completed in one 8-hour day, focuses on family constellation, mutual respect, encouragement, and taking responsibility for one's behavior. Dinkmeyer describes the following four stages:

STAGE I: ORIENTATION AND ORGANIZATION

1. Determine if this type of counseling is suitable for the family.
2. Obtain family background information.
3. Arrange for family members to participate.

STAGE II: EXPLORATION

1. Give overview and summary of Stage I.
2. Obtain an overview of the family's life circumstances.
3. Explore problems in more depth.

STAGE III: ACTION

1. Encourage family members to commit to doing something to improve the family situation.
2. Confront family members who are reluctant to change.
3. Encourage family members to take responsibility for their own behavior.

STAGE IV: TERMINATION

1. Have family members talk about their commitments to change and how they will accomplish their goals.
2. Thank family members for participating in the session.
3. Talk individually with family members who want more counseling.

Pew (1989) outlines a different approach for conducting brief marriage therapy, following an Adlerian style, that may extend over several sessions.

1. The counselor and couple discuss why the couple is seeking counseling.
2. The counselor and couple discuss the couple's goals for counseling.
3. The counselor shares expectations.
4. The counselor draws a family constellation for each person and uses this and ERs to construct a lifestyle form for each client.
5. The couple works on the basic marriage skills of conflict resolution, communication, and doing fun things together.
6. The couple uses the paradoxical strategies of practicing at home those things that annoy each partner.
7. The couple keeps daily journal entries of feelings, thoughts, and behaviors.

CROSS-CULTURAL APPLICATIONS OF INDIVIDUAL PSYCHOLOGY

Individual psychology by title alone would seem to suggest a focus on the individual above the family, group, or society in general. Such is far from the truth, however. Social interest development and the need to feel part of a group have always been main pillars supporting the practice of individual or Adlerian psychology (Sakin-Wolf, 2003). Therefore, as mentioned in Chapter 15, cultural groups favoring a family, group, and/or community emphasis in counseling will find individual psychology to be a comfortable and compatible way to examine their lives and behavioral patterns for possible change.

Hispanic, Native American, Italian, and Middle Eastern cultures are among those favoring the family and community social interest approach offered by the Adlerians. In fact, social interest development is equated with one's mental health and level of personal development in the Adlerian system. The practice of Adlerian counseling does not require clients and families to share information that would infringe on the families' self-disclosure comfort level and breach the boundaries accorded to the level of respect shown to the family elders. Adlerian concepts traditionally have been more on the culture-free side than not. Birth order, goals of behavior, ERs, lifestyles, and faulty reasoning problems transcend most cultures, and the client is never asked to fit a certain model described by the counselor (Carlson & Carlson, 2000).

Asian, African, and American clients will enjoy the pragmatic aspects of Adlerian psychology. The opportunity to learn new skills and practical information is readily available in the educational approach Adlerians use. Learning is conducted in several modes, dividing the counseling time among listening, information gathering, telling, demonstrating, and practicing. As such, most clients find one of the instructional modes compatible with their particular learning style. Again, we emphasize the differences within cultures and realize that any one counseling style will not be universally accepted by an entire cultural group. We do know that people in some cultures accept the idea of receiving counseling much more readily than others. For example, a colleague once shared the following observation from his practice in a culturally diverse neighborhood. He said when he gets a call from a Jewish mother about coming in for counseling, he treats it more matter-of-factly. However, if he gets a call from an Irish mother, he becomes quite alarmed, treats the call as an emergency, and has her come to the office right away.

Among African American and Latino families, it is typical to find that parenting is often shared among a variety of individuals, including grandparents, aunts, uncles, neighbors, friends, and siblings. Flanagan and Miranda (1995) report that this is especially true in times of family stress, and that African Americans, Latinos, and Native Americans may select spiritual types of interventions over the services of a professional counselor. In addition to members of these three cultures, members of Appalachian cultures have more hesitancy in divulging familial or personal issues to professionals. Mosely-Howard (1995) reports that Appalachians are more likely to seek help from extended family or clergy. However, other Americans with European backgrounds are more likely to seek help from professional counselors.

Flanagan and Miranda (1995) report that Asian fathers are publicly perceived as the figurehead and ruler of the family, whereas privately it is often the mother who decides the important child-rearing issues. Mosely-Howard (1995) notes that Filipinos and Japanese are much more protective of their children than are American families. Conversely, physical punishment is more acceptable among Appalachians, African Americans, and Samoans. Cultural awareness should help counselors work with the law requiring them to report anything resembling child abuse.

Compounding cultural differences is the changing nature of the family structure that was present when Rudolf Dreikurs was restructuring Adlerian theory to include his intervention strategies for families. Today, there are more blended families and more families headed by single parents of either sex. The change in family structure presents unique difficulties for Adlerian counselors. Carlson (1995) has found that in mother-headed, single-parent homes, problems causing unrest in the family were related to the mother's perceived or real inability to maintain the dual roles of parent–household manager and sole wage earner. These overburdened mothers were found to be more likely to suffer from depression, diminished parenting, and lack of social support from others. Male single parents are more likely to lack knowledge of child development and gender differences in development and to lack the ability to nurture as well as discipline children. The fathers, also lacking in social support, were found to minimize their thoughts and feelings about their parenting problems and were less likely to seek outside professional help. Again, counselors would do well to re-establish the Adlerian groups that were once more prominent. Carlson (1995) has found the added stresses of single parenting to result in overpermissiveness or, in low-income, single, father-headed homes, high rates of violence. In addition, higher school dropout rates have been reported for daughters of single fathers and sons of single mothers. Clearly, stress reduction should be one focus of today's family counselors. We recommend involving churches and schools in providing meeting space and child care for parent-education groups led by trained counselors. The Adlerian parent-education model has proved to be one of the most useful ways to help ineffective parents become better parents.

INDIVIDUAL PSYCHOLOGY, ACCOUNTABILITY, AND MANAGED HEALTH CARE

Practitioners of individual psychology should find managed care guidelines easier to meet than practitioners of the longer, insight-oriented psychotherapies (see the managed care section in Chapter 2). Granted, some insight is used in the practice of individual psychology, but such methods are directed toward helping children and their parents understand the goals the children are trying to reach with their misbehavior. Individual psychology has always been one of the briefer approaches to helping people find interventions to bring about symptom relief and solutions to problems. Wingett and Milliren (2004) propose a brief form of Adlerian counseling quite similar to solution-focused counseling. Clients are asked to: (1) describe the problem, (2) describe a time when they encountered a similar problem, (3) identify successful components of the past problem-solving strategy, and (4) apply their previously effective methods to the current problem. Their cornerstone or "miracle" question for clients is, "What would you do if I cured you immediately?" The counseling agenda can be built from their answers to this question.

Adlerian counselors have a 100-year history of supporting a preventive approach to treating mental health problems. Adler himself created parent-education groups that met regularly to discuss managing family problems regarding child-rearing practices and interventions. Problem prevention, group counseling, and educational skill building, which Adlerian or individual psychology practitioners use in their work, are favored by managed care companies.

Adlerians typically can accomplish their goals in a relatively short time and have considerable follow-up success if families join a local parent group to reinforce what they have learned about child rearing. Professional and school counselors may want to work together in re-establishing these Adlerian parent groups. Counseling goals are behaviorally stated and can be tracked on a weekly basis to termination of counseling. Client satisfaction typically runs high with recipients of Adlerian counseling because parents are largely bankrupt on what they should do about disciplining their children. They generally practice the ineffective interventions passed down through the generations to their own parents.

Adlerian, or individual, psychology has a lot to offer individuals who have presenting problems other than family issues. Lifestyle analysis is especially effective in helping people analyze their lives in light of how well their current behaviors are helping them get what they want. The Adlerians use a cognitive approach to help their clients identify the faulty logic underlying behavioral goals that get them into trouble. Clients also receive some insight on how they got to be the way they are and what they need to do to break the cycle of their ineffective or self-defeating behavioral patterns. Couples seeking counseling will find individual psychology useful in problem diagnosis and remediation. Individual psychology also is recommended for couples seeking a developmental approach to marriage enrichment.

Introduction to Individual Psychology

To gain a more in-depth understanding of the concepts in this chapter, visit www.thomsonedu.com/counseling/thompson to view a short clip of an actual therapist-client session demonstrating individual psychology.

Websites for Individual Psychology

Internet addresses frequently change. To find the sites listed here, visit www.thomsonedu.com/counseling/thompson for an updated list of Internet addresses and direct links to relevant sites.

Adler

Classical Adlerian Psychology: Alfred Adler Institutes

References

Adler, A. (1964). *Social interest: A challenge to mankind.* New York: Capricorn. (Original work published 1938.)

Alexander, F., Eisenstein, S., & Grotjahn, M. (1966). *Psychoanalytic pioneers.* New York: Basic Books.

Ansbacher, H. (1992). Alfred Adler's concepts of community feeling and social interest and the relevance of community feeling for old age. *Individual Psychology: The Journal of Adlerian Theory, Research, and Practice, 48,* 402–412.

Ansbacher, H., & Ansbacher, R. (1956). *The individual psychology of Alfred Adler: A systematic presentation in selections from his writings.* New York: Basic Books.

Ballou, R. (2002). Adlerian-based responses for the mental health counselor to the challenging behaviors of teens. *Journal of Mental Health Counseling, 24,* 154–165.

Brack, G., Hill, M.B., Edwards, D., Grootboom, N., & Lassiter, P. (2003). Adler and *ubuntu*: Using Adlerian principles in the New South Africa. *Journal of Individual Psychology, 59*(3), 316–326.

Carlson, C. (1995). Best practices in working with single-parent and step family systems. In A. Thomas & J. Grimes (Eds.), *Best practices in school psychology.* Washington, DC: National Association of School Psychologists.

Carlson, M., & Carlson, J. (2000). The application of Adlerian psychotherapy with Asian American clients. *Journal of Individual Psychology, 56,* 214–225.

Carlson, J., & Glasser, W. (2004). Adler and Glasser: A demonstration and dialogue. *The Journal of Individual Psychology, 60*(3), 308–324.

DeOrnellas, K., Kottman, T., & Millican, V. (1997). Drawing a family: Family art assessment in Adlerian therapy. *Individual Psychology: Journal of Adlerian Theory, Research & Practice, 53,* 451–460.

Dinkmeyer, D. (1988). Marathon family counseling. *Individual Psychology: The Journal of Adlerian Theory, Research, and Practice, 44,* 210–215.

Dinkmeyer, D., Pew, W., & Dinkmeyer, D., Jr. (1979). *Adlerian counseling and psychotherapy.* Monterey, CA: Brooks/Cole.

Dreikurs, R., & Grey, L. (1968). *A new approach to discipline: Logical consequences.* New York: Hawthorn.

Dreikurs, R., & Soltz, V. (1964). *Children: The challenge.* New York: Hawthorn/ Dutton.

Ellis, A. (1997). Must musterbation and demandingness lead to emotional disorders? *Psychotherapy, 34,* 95–98.

Flanagan, D., & Miranda, A. (1995). Best practices in working with culturally different families. In A. Thomas & J. Grimes (Eds.), *Best practices in school psychology.* Washington, DC: National Association of School Psychologists.

Glasser, W. (1969). *Schools without failure.* New York: Harper & Row.

Horney, K. (1950). *Neurosis and human growth.* New York: Norton.

Kohn, A. (1999). *Punished by rewards: The trouble with gold stars, incentive plans, A's, praise, and other bribes.* Boston: Houghton Mifflin Company.

Kottman, T. (1997). Adlerian play therapy. In K. O'Connor & L. M. Braverman (Eds.), *Play therapy theory and practice: A comparative presentation* (pp. 310–340). New York: Wiley.

Kottman, T., & Johnson, V. (1993). Adlerian play therapy: A tool for school counselors. *Elementary School Guidance and Counseling, 28,* 42–51.

LaFountain, R., Garner, N., & Miedema, P. (2003). Adler's contributions to learning styles and multiple intelligences theories. *Journal of Individual Psychology, 59*(2), 213–222.

Manly, L. (1986). Goals of misbehavior inventory. *Elementary School Guidance and Counseling, 21,* 160–161.

Mosak, H., & Maniacci, M. (1998). *Tactics in counseling and psychotherapy.* Itasca, IL: F. E. Peacock.

Mosely-Howard, G. (1995). Best practices in considering the role of culture. In A. Thomas & J. Grimes (Eds.), *Best practices in school psychology.* Washington, DC: National Association of School Psychologists.

Myer, R., & James, R. (1986, February). *Confrontation: A strategy for counseling.* Paper presented at the Tennessee Association for Counseling and Development state conference, Gatlinburg, TN.

Myer, R., & James, R. (1991). Using early recollections as an assessment technique with children. *Elementary School Guidance and Counseling, 25,* 228–232.

Pew, M. (1989). Brief marriage therapy. *Individual Psychology: The Journal of Adlerian Theory, Research, and Practice, 45,* 191–200.

Sakin-Wolf, S. (2003). Adler: East, West, and beyond. *The Journal of Individual Psychology, 59*(1), 72–83.

Shulman, B. & Mosak, M. (1977). Birth order and ordinal position: Two Adlerian views. *Individual Psychology, 33,* 114–121.

Stiles, K., & Wilborn, B. (1992). A lifestyle instrument for children. *Individual Psychology, 48,* 96–105.

Terner, J., & Pew, W. (1978). *The courage to be imperfect: The life and work of Rudolf Dreikurs.* New York: Hawthorn.

Wingett, W., & Milliren, A. (2004). "Lost? Or Stuck?" An Adlerian technique for understanding the individual's psychological movement. *Journal of Experimental Psychology, 60*(3), 265–276.

FAMILY COUNSELING

CHAPTER 12

Inappropriate helpfulness fosters helplessness.

—Murray Bowen

Life is interrelated. We are caught in an inescapable network of mutuality; tied in the single garment of destiny. Whatever affects one directly, affects all indirectly.

—Martin Luther King Jr.

It's surprising how many persons go through life without ever recognizing that their feelings toward people are largely determined by their feelings toward themselves, and if you're not comfortable within yourself, you can't be comfortable with others.

—Sydney J. Harris

HOW DOES FAMILY COUNSELING DIFFER FROM INDIVIDUAL COUNSELING?

The principal difference between family and individual counseling is that family counseling focuses on the family and its members' interactions and relations. Often, individual counseling tends to separate individuals and their problems from the family setting. Family counseling or family therapy, by contrast, almost always involves interventions to alter the way an entire family system operates. The family counseling and therapy label covers a wide variety of arrangements: It may be individual, husband and wife, parent and child, or the entire family, including all who live in the home.

Another key difference between individual and family counseling is problem diagnosis. Family therapists use a circular causality diagnosis, whereas individual therapists tend to rely on linear causality. For example, a linear causality diagnosis might be as follows: Alice fails to turn in homework to her teacher, and therefore earns a lower grade. A circular causality diagnosis might include how the teacher's reaction to Alice then influences how Alice reacts to her teacher, as well as to her parents. Mom nags Alice about not doing her homework; Alice, in turn, gets the attention, albeit negative, that she wants. The teacher sends home a failing note to Alice's parents, who, in turn, both start to nag Alice, who resists homework even more than before. In other words, a circular causality diagnosis involves the roles each family member plays. In fairness to the theories discussed in previous chapters, all have been effective in working with families.

Diamond and Josephson (2005), in a 10-year review of family therapy, have found it to be effective in treating substance abuse and conduct disorders in children and adolescents. Family therapy also was found to be effective in reducing behavioral problems associated with attention-deficit/hyperactivity disorder (ADHD) and showed promise in treating depression and anxiety. Parent management training, focused on teaching parents how to use positive reinforcement, was found to be effective in treating conduct disorders over a period of 14 years. Behavioral family therapy, similar to parent management training but including methods to reduce family factors such as stress in the parents' lives or the child's personality, also was found to be effective in reducing disruptive behavior in children and adolescents. Campbell and Palm (2004) concur about the benefits of parent education in helping parents understand how their behavior and child-rearing practices affect their children.

WHAT DEFINES A FAMILY?

Culture refers to "the sum total of the ways of living (values, traditions, idiosyncrasies) built up by a group of human beings and transmitted from one generation to another" (Turner, Weiling, & Allen, 2004, p. 260). Cultures embody communities consisting of substructures we define as families.

Definitions of *family* range from the nuclear family of breadwinner father, homemaker mother, and two children to multiple families living together. Between these extremes are at least eight types of families: extended, blended, common-law, single-parent, communal, serial, polygamous, and cohabitational. Families also are defined by their organizational structure, characterized by degrees of cohesiveness, love, loyalty, and purpose. High levels of shared values, interests, activities, and attention to the needs of its members serve to distinguish the functional family group from other organizational groups and teams.

Perhaps the most all-inclusive definition of family can be found in *Merriam-Webster's Collegiate Dictionary* (Mish, 2003), where *family* is defined as a group of people: "(1) bound together by philosophical, religious, or other convictions; (2) with a common ancestry; and (3) living together under the same roof" (p. 452). Another definition listed in Webster's defines *family* as "the basic biosocial unit in society having as its nucleus two or more adults living together and cooperating in the care and rearing of their own or adopted children."

How Does General Systems Theory Relate to Families?

Systems are organized whole elements or units made up of several interdependent and interacting parts. The whole unit is greater than the sum of its parts, and change in any part affects all other parts. Any family member's graduation from high school or hospital admission has effects on all other family members. Family therapists choose to view the family as a system in which each member has a significant influence on all other members. For significant positive change in an identified client, therefore, family members have to change the way they interact. Most family therapists work with present family relationships rather than with past family relationships and conflicts.

A key point of interest to all family therapists is the balance families maintain between the several sets of bipolar extremes that characterize dysfunctional families. For example, families may struggle to find a healthy balance between overinvolvement in each others' lives *(enmeshment)* and too much detachment from each other *(disengagement)*. A family could be viewed as a canoe full of people heading into the current of a river. Some canoes are balanced and stable, but maintaining this balance requires each family member to assume a uncomfortable position; a shift by one person necessitates a shift by everyone else for the canoe to remain upright. Other families are paddling balanced canoes while sitting comfortably, allowing them to adapt to the changes all families face as they go through the stages of family development; still other canoes capsize, with family members hanging on to the side just trying to survive. Family therapists see their job as righting capsized canoes and making family members comfortable in their canoe-paddling roles. Staying with the canoe metaphor, family therapists see an obvious advantage in working with the whole crew as a group rather than focusing on the identified problem member of the family.

SYSTEMS APPROACH TO FAMILY THERAPY

Murray Bowen (1913–1990)

Family therapy roots reach back to the turn of the twentieth century, beginning with Alfred Adler's parent groups and developing through various parent, family, and couple education groups within each decade until the 1950s, when family therapy as we know it today was born. Murray Bowen, an early theorist on family relationships, focused on how family members could maintain a healthy balance between being enmeshed and being disengaged. He believed each family member should develop an individual identity and independence separate from family identity, whereas also maintaining a sense of closeness and a feeling of togetherness with their families. The task for Bowen was to help people integrate the opposing forces of seeking independence from the family and maintaining a sense of family membership and closeness (Bowen, 1976, 1978).

Murray Bowen was born and grew up in Waverly, Tennessee, in 1913. He was the firstborn of five children in a cohesive and loving family. Waverly, a small town of 1000 people in 1913, is located in Humphreys County in middle Tennessee, 60 miles west of Nashville. Bowen completed his bachelor's degree at the University of Tennessee in 1934 and his M.D. degree from the University of Tennessee Medical School in Memphis in 1937. He served 5 years of active duty in the army during World War II from 1941 to 1946. Bowen's war experiences influenced his decision to turn down a fellowship in surgery at the Mayo Clinic and instead begin psychiatric training at the Menninger Foundation in Topeka, Kansas, in 1946. He spent the next 8 years researching symbiotic relationships of mothers and their schizophrenic children at Menninger, where he developed the concepts of anxious and functional attachment involved in the mother–child relationship. From 1954 to 1959, Bowen served as the first director of the Family Division at the National Institute of Mental Health, where he broadened his research on family attachment to include fathers. In 1959, Bowen joined the Department of Psychiatry at Georgetown University Medical Center, where he directed family programs. He founded and directed the Georgetown Family Center in 1975, where he remained until his death in 1990. Among his many honors, he received the Distinguished Alumnus Award from the University of Tennessee in 1986.

Bowen used process questions designed to help family members shift from reacting emotionally about the negative aspects of other family members to thinking rationally about how they personally contribute to the family's dysfunction and what they can do to improve the situation. Bowen assumed the role of coach or educator, whose job was to create an environment in which the family can function at its best. To accomplish this, counselors need to be aware of the emotional processes working in the family while personally remaining neutral (Dattilio & Bevilacqua, 2000). Bowen focused on the following qualities: (1) relationship between the spouses, (2) differentiation of self, (3) triangles, (4) nuclear family emotional process, (5) family projection process, (6) multigenerational transmission process, (7) sibling position, (8) emotional cutoffs, and (9) emotional process in society.

The Spousal Relationship

Bowen and his followers gave attention to defining and clarifying the relationship between couples: How well do they move in and out of the various roles healthy couples play? Do they care for and nurture each other? Do they solve problems and make decisions well? Do they play well together? Do they work well together? Do they parent well together? Are they able to differentiate themselves as individuals apart from the couple? Do they enjoy time alone?

Do they maintain individual relationships and friendships outside the marital dyad? Do they pursue individual goals, interests, and careers? Most important, how well do individuals handle differentiation within themselves and between other family members?

DIFFERENTIATION OF SELF

Differentiation within oneself refers to the ability to separate feelings from thoughts. For example, in crises, does the person put rational thinking on hold and react emotionally to the situation? Lack of differentiation between individuals refers to the degree to which people introject the thoughts and feelings of others or do the opposite by automatically reacting against these thoughts and feelings. Differentiation is our struggle to develop a sense of personal identity while still remaining a part of the family. This process is similar to being able to distinguish between thoughts and feelings. Bowen rated his patients' ability to differentiate on a scale of 0 to 100, with 0 being low. Those on the bottom end of the scale were regarded as undifferentiated, and their behavior, guided by their feelings, often left them with chronic anxiety resulting in relationship problems. Because they were undifferentiated from the family, their anxiety spilled over onto other family members. Highly differentiated people handle stress and anxiety better, because they are able to apply rational thought to the problem at hand. They are able to maintain a healthy balance between thinking and feeling. Bowen believed that marriage partners seek spouses with the same level of differentiation. Hence, the trait is passed down through several generations. Bowen believed that schizophrenia in children resulted from generations of undifferentiated individuals marrying each other. Thus, a primary goal for Bowen was to help people attain higher levels of differentiation from enmeshment in one's family. Differentiation enables people to enjoy meaningful relationships with family members while remaining autonomous and rational without falling back into unhealthy enmeshment with family patterns. Increased differentiation by one family member is likely to lead other family members to become more differentiated. Faber (2004), noting the divorce rate among remarried couples exceeds that of first marriages, cites low levels of the ability to differentiate between rational thoughts and feeling emotions as a principal cause of multiple divorces. Knauth and Skowron (2004) have found a significant correlation between adolescents' higher levels of differentiation with lower levels of anxiety and less symptoms of anxiety-related side effects.

Self-differentiation was Bowen's principal goal of family therapy. He believed that progress toward self-differentiation had to be self-motivated rather than directed by the therapist. Serving in the role of educator, the therapist's job was to move clients toward an intellectual processing of the couple's family system, rather than falling into the trap of responding to the emotional tone of the content brought to counseling. Also, Bowen observed that in providing too much "help," therapists could make the family situation worse. Bowen (1976) stated that "inappropriate helpfulness fosters helplessness."

DETRIANGULATION OF SELF FROM THE FAMILY EMOTIONAL SYSTEM

Triangulation, another important concept in Bowen's theory, refers to the practice of two family members bringing a third family member into conflictual situations. Therapists attend to the extent a husband or wife involves one of their children in a problem situation that the two of them should handle. Another example of triangulation is involvement of a person outside the marital dyad, such as a lover, to fulfill unmet needs in the marriage. Chapter 10 discusses a form of triangulation in reference to games and the roles people play in them; for example, one family member may take the role of prosecutor, another the victim, and the third a rescuer. All three roles are needed to maintain the game, and a shift in role by any one of the three alters the roles of the other two. Many of these dysfunctional interactions are similar to dances, where it takes two people to keep the dance going and one to stop it. Bowen believed there was no such thing as a two-person system because a third party is always drawn in when there is increased anxiety. As mentioned previously, third parties can be from inside or outside the family and even can be the memory of a departed loved one. The shifting set of alliances and reactive behaviors that occur with third parties makes it more difficult to resolve the conflict between the original two parties.

NUCLEAR FAMILY EMOTIONAL PROCESS

The nuclear family emotional process refers to how the family system operates to handle anxiety and stress in times of crisis. Several symptoms are indicators of how the system works. Emotional distance, when one family member avoids or gives the silent treatment to another, is an early symptom of family trouble. A second symptom could be transfer of a family problem to a child when a mother displaces her anxiety on the child by becoming worried and overly concerned about how the child is doing. A third symptom occurs when two family members become blamers, pointing their fingers at each other as the cause of the problem. Finally, a fourth symptom surfaces when one partner develops a disability or becomes dysfunctional. The second partner is forced to adapt to the dysfunctional partner by taking more control, making decisions, and handling responsibilities for the "dysfunctional" partner. Over time, the increased workload may be resented by the partner in charge as the dysfunctional partner becomes even more dependent and develops more symptoms. Such situations are generally headed toward major blowups.

FAMILY PROJECTION PROCESS

The family projection process refers to how parents pass good and bad things on to their children. In one example mentioned earlier, undifferentiated parents distract themselves from solving their conflicts by focusing intently on a child and the child's situation to the point that the child becomes more undifferentiated and dependent, thus blocking normal development toward becoming an autonomous person.

MULTIGENERATIONAL TRANSMISSION PROCESS

Multigenerational transmission process refers to how a family passes its good and bad baggage from one generation to another. The bad baggage is the tendency of families to become less differentiated as this trait is handed down. Families become more vulnerable to stress, anxiety, and problems as they become less differentiated; this became the point where Bowen directed his method of family therapy for changing the way family members respond to each other in times of crisis.

SIBLING POSITION

Bowen took the Adlerian position that birth order is a significant factor in how we develop our lifestyles. (See Chapter 11 for a detailed discussion of birth order traits.) Bowen held that birth order traits and behaviors carried to an extreme could lead to dysfunction in children. For example, a controlling firstborn may lead to a younger sibling's overly dependent behavior. As the younger child gets more service from the older child, dependence on the older child is increased, and developmental progress toward independence is blocked. Bowen also was concerned that trouble might arise when people of the same birth order married and each tried to maintain such respective birth order behaviors as leaders or followers.

EMOTIONAL CUTOFF

As mentioned earlier, when a marriage partner's method for handling anxiety and stress is to distance himself or herself from others, problems do not get solved. Emotional cutoffs (sometimes referred to as pouting) are thought to be ways of dealing with unresolved attachment to parents. Whatever the cause, emotional distancing can achieve the ultimate distancing goal of divorce.

EMOTIONAL PROCESS IN SOCIETY

Bowen saw parallels in how family members react within the family and within society. Undifferentiated people typically react emotionally rather than rationally in times of conflict, stress, crisis, and general anxiety. They do this within the family and carry forth their emotionality when they react in society. Unfortunately, the evidence in present society is that emotionality appears to trump rationality as the people's choice in solving the problems of the day.

In teaching clients about family systems and the intergenerational transmission process, Bowen used genograms and questions to move his clients to the intellectual level in discussing how their own family system had been influenced by material and baggage inherited from prior generations of the family. The genogram provides a generational map of the family including dates of marriages, births, and deaths; cultural and ethnic origins; socioeconomic status; work life; education; hobbies; religious affiliations; politics; and family

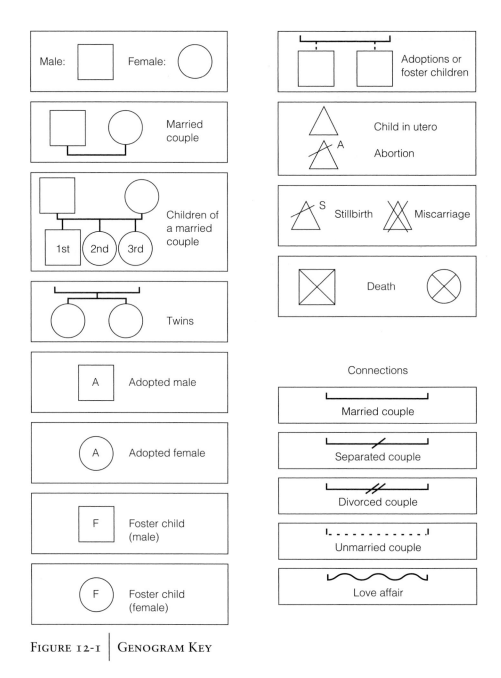

FIGURE 12-1 | GENOGRAM KEY

relationships. In short, the genogram describes *who* makes up your family, *how* they got to be family (birth, marriage, adoption), *when* they arrived (birth date, birth order, marriage dates), *what* they did (work, hobbies), *what* they valued (religion, politics), and *when* they left the family (death, divorce, or separation) (Figures 12-1 and 12-2).

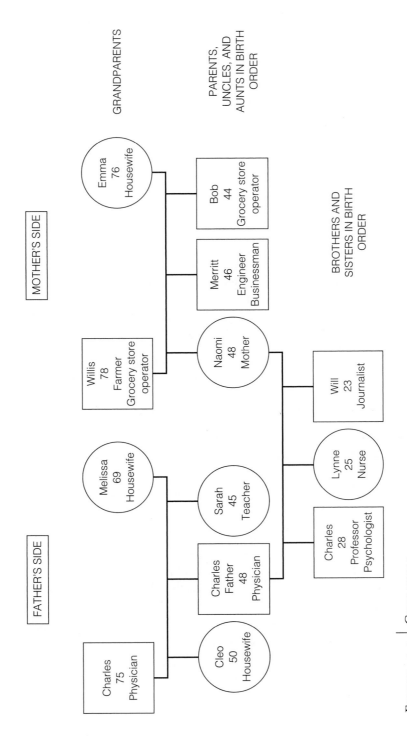

FIGURE 12-2 | GENOGRAM

343

Bowen (1980) included data from at least three generations in his genograms. He began by gathering as much information as he could (during the first interview) from the couple he was counseling. All family names and ages from at least three generations are listed on the genogram with the dates of marriages, births, deaths, and other significant life events. Notes explaining the significant events are added to the genogram. Completing the missing data can become a homework assignment for the couple to complete before the second session.

Thomas (1992) suggests the following questions that might be used in a genogram interview:

1. Can you tell me the names of the family members for at least three generations on both sides of the family?
2. When were these individuals born, married, separated, or divorced?
3. Which family members have died? When? Of what?
4. What jobs did the family members hold?
5. What were the family members' educational levels?
6. What were the ethnic/cultural, religious, and political values of the family members? How were these traditions passed on in the family?
7. Where did the family members live (city and state)? When, where, and why did they move?
8. How did people get along in the family? Who was close to whom? Did anyone not speak to another family member? What happened in these cases?
9. Which family members were very successful at what they did?
10. Which family members used alcohol or drugs, were arrested, had mental problems, committed suicide, or had other serious problems?
11. What illnesses are found in the family? How did family members cope with them?
12. Can you tell me any special life events that happened—positive, neutral, and negative?
13. Tell me about the stories that have been passed down through the generations of your family.
14. Tell me about the family themes that seem to repeat in your family. If your family had a motto, what would it be?
15. If you were an elder in the family, what advice would you give to a younger member of the family?

Thomas (1992) offers the following ten questions to aid the family counselor in writing a genogram analysis:

1. *Health:* How healthy were the family members? What were the most common health problems? What was done to prevent or treat these health problems?
2. *Structure:* What types of family structures were repeated in the genogram (single parent, nuclear, extended, blended)?
3. *Themes:* What family themes have been carried through the generations?
4. *Occupations:* Which occupations occur most frequently in your family?

5. *Stages:* What stages in the life cycle have been easier for your family to handle? What stages have been the most difficult?
6. *Events:* Which life events have affected family functions throughout generations of your family?
7. *Triangles:* Where are the triangles present in the genogram? Which relationships are close, distant, conflicted, or fused? Where are the emotional cutoffs?
8. *Patterns:* What patterns are repeated, such as educational or work success, religious commitment, political activity, alcohol or drug use, or other behaviors?
9. *Size:* How large are the families in the genogram? Which families stand out as larger or smaller than the genogram norm? What stresses might have occurred due to the family size or family imbalance?
10. *Contract:* What values and behaviors passed on to you by your family have worked so well for you that you plan to keep them and even pass them on to your children? What family values and behaviors have not worked well for you, and what do you plan to do with them? Are there some family patterns that bother you? If so, what could you do to change them?

EMOTIONAL SYSTEMS OF THE FAMILY

Understanding family emotional systems and how they work is also central to Bowen's theory. Once again, failure to achieve differentiation between family members results in unhealthy family relationships that recycle from one generation to the next unless some helpful intervention interrupts the cycle. Bowen might well have envisioned himself as a cycle breaker, which is not a bad role for a counselor to take. In fact, Bowen often assumed the role of educator in teaching people about family emotional systems. Once again, when the family of origin lacks differentiation, children have either totally absorbed their parents' feelings and emotions or have totally detached themselves. These children often seek out mates who are also undifferentiated, thus providing fertile ground for future family conflict and discord. Undifferentiated people typically do not develop close, lasting relationships. They do not solve problems or resolve conflicts, and they often develop psychosomatic symptoms in an attempt to meet their needs. In addition, undifferentiated people tend not to take responsibility for their behavior. Many of these consequences are in concert with what Glasser (see Chapter 4) has written about people who have not developed or have not had healthy and caring relationships in their lives.

MODELING DIFFERENTIATION

Bowen favored modeling for teaching differentiation to his patients. He did this by using "I" statements and taking ownership of his own thoughts, feelings, and behaviors; for example, he'd say, "I think the best thing for me to do is to confront my colleague about his behavior, but thinking about doing it gives me an uneasy feeling." In addition to owning one's thoughts and feelings, this statement lends some help for separating feelings and thoughts.

STRUCTURAL FAMILY THERAPY

Structural family therapy is closely related to Bowen's family systems theory. Structural family therapists also operate on the assumption that the individual client should be treated within the context of the family system. The therapist does not see the client as a sufficient source of information about the problems brought to counseling or as the only source of causes of the problem. Changes resulting from individual counseling are not stable enough to stand against the pressures a dysfunctional family brings to bear. Therefore, the overall goal of structural family therapists is to alter the family structure to empower the dysfunctional family to move toward functional ways of conducting or transacting family business and family communications.

Structural family therapy also is based on the assumption that families are evolving, hierarchical organizations with rules and behavioral patterns for interacting across and within the family subsystems. Families get into trouble when their members become either overly enmeshed in each other's business or totally disengaged. Family members should feel a sense of belonging to the family that does not destroy their sense of being unique individuals within and outside the family context. In other words, functional families are characterized by each member's success in finding the healthy balance between belonging to a family and maintaining a separate identity.

One way to find the balance between family and individual identity is to define and clarify the boundaries between the subsystems; for example, a family may have a spousal subsystem, a sibling subsystem, and a parent–child subsystem. Each subsystem contains its own subject matter that is private and should remain within that subsystem. Spouses have matters they need to discuss that do not belong in the context of the parent–child and child–child subsystems. Such topics might include their sex life, financial concerns, and interpersonal conflicts. Dysfunctional families often discuss and play out these topics in an open family forum. Boundaries between subsystems range from rigid to diffuse. Private subject matter from one subsystem that leaks out to other subsystems indicates diffuse, poorly established boundaries. Diffuse boundaries can lead to family members becoming overly enmeshed in the private business of other family members; rigid boundaries allow too little interaction between family members, resulting in disengagement from the family. Once again, the secret to developing functional families is finding the right boundary balance between too rigid and too diffuse; boundaries need to be clearly defined. For example, parents need to provide enough love and support but also enough room for children to develop independence. A parent–child subsystem and a sibling subsystem also have communications and subject matter that belong to and are unique to those subsystems. Families who understand and respect differences between healthy and unhealthy subsystem boundaries and rules function successfully; families who do not understand and respect these differences find themselves in a dysfunctional state of conflict, either disengaged from or enmeshed in the family business. Structural family therapy is directed toward changing the family organizational structure as a way of resolving the presenting problem or changing a family member's behavioral patterns. For example, in a particular session, Dad might be asked to give up being in charge of the children's homework assignments. The structural therapist actively directs the session and participates as a family member. The therapist may even take over the family ruler role as a way of sidetracking the dominant family member.

SALVADOR MINUCHIN'S CONTRIBUTIONS TO STRUCTURAL FAMILY THERAPY

Salvador Minuchin is considered the founder of structural family therapy as it is currently practiced. He was born in 1921 to Russian Jewish parents in a small Argentinian town. According to Simon (1984), Minuchin benefited from a multicultural childhood and became an activist early in life. As a university student, he joined a Zionist organization and was arrested for taking part in a protest against Juan Perón in 1943. After spending 3 months in jail, Minuchin was expelled from the university and then studied in Uruguay for a time. Later, he completed his medical degree in Argentina. Next for Minuchin came a residency in child psychiatry and an 18-month tour of duty as a doctor in the 1948 Israeli war. Minuchin came to the United States with the intention of working with Bruno Bettelheim in Chicago's Orthogenic School; however, he met Nathan Ackerman in New York and eventually decided to work in Ackerman's child-development center. Minuchin sandwiched in 3 years of work with African and Asian immigrant children in Israel before receiving more analytic training and becoming director of family research at the Wiltwyck School for Boys in New York.

Minuchin's best training did not come from books and classes. As so many therapists have noticed, traditional psychoanalytic methods often do not work with populations such as delinquent boys. The recidivism rate seemed to be close to 100%, with the young men repeating their delinquent behaviors on their release. Noticing that some families produced several delinquent children, Minuchin concluded that families must be making a significant contribution to the problem. Therefore, he began to develop an approach for working with families who did not have the verbal skills for traditional psychotherapy, instead focusing on the nonverbal communication, a standard practice in individual, group, and family therapy.

Much of what Minuchin learned about families was by observation through a one-way glass and in collaboration with his colleagues at the school. In a method similar to the Adlerian method for working with families, Minuchin and his colleagues developed a three-step approach: Two counselors met with the entire family; then one counselor met with the parents, and the other with the children. The process culminated in a final stage in which everyone gathered to share information and plans for change. Further observation and study led to a language for describing family structure and a system of interventions designed to change unhelpful and even harmful patterns of family organization. Just as Glasser wrote his first successful book based on his experience at the Ventura School for Girls, Minuchin wrote *Families of the Slums* (1967) based on his experiences at Wiltwyck.

Minuchin's next project was transforming the Philadelphia Child Guidance Clinic into a model family therapy center. He had a flair for the dramatic and was highly critical of seminar case presentations that did not meet his standards. As a practicing family therapist, he set the family scene, assigned roles, started and stopped the action, and took a leading or supporting role himself.

Working with Jay Haley, Minuchin developed the clinic's family orientation and the Institute for Family Counseling, which was designed to train paraprofessionals. Perhaps his most notable accomplishment during this period was the treatment he developed for psychosomatic families, particularly those of anorexics. He wrote *Families and Family Therapy* (1974) during his 10 years as director of the clinic. After stepping down as director, Minuchin served as head of the training center until 1981. His next book, *Psychosomatic Families,* was published in 1978. Since then, Minuchin has continued family research with "normal" families, written several plays, and written a book for the lay public, *Family Kaleidoscope* (1984).

Minuchin has been praised for rescuing family therapy from intellectuality and mystery. His pragmatic approach contributed both to understanding how families function and to productive interventions for correcting malfunctions in them. Minuchin worked with children and families written off by the psychiatric community as unsuitable for treatment. His achievements are rooted in his philosophy of putting clients first and in his total commitment to their cases.

Once Minuchin diagnosed a flaw in the family system, he appeared willing to go to any length to bring about a needed change. His techniques ranged from gentle persuasion to outright provocation and confrontation. He viewed psychosomatic illness as a symptom brought on and maintained by the family and successfully treated eating disorders, asthma, and uncontrolled diabetes. As mentioned earlier, Minuchin's structural family therapy approach is directed toward changing the family structure or organization as a way of modifying family members' behavior. The counselor makes interventions by becoming an active "family" member.

Minuchin described traditional psychotherapy as a magnifying glass and structural family therapy as a zoom lens that can focus on the entire family or zoom in for a close-up of any family member. The structural therapist works with the family belief system to effect behavior changes between people. Rule changes may be the immediate goal as the family explores three questions: (1) How do family members relate to one another? (2) Who is allied with whom against whom? and (3) What is the nature of the parental dyad? The idea is to change the immediate context of the family situation and thereby change the family members' positions. The cognitive dissonance principle operates much the same way.

For example, Minuchin (1978) described the case of a 12-year-old girl with psychosomatically triggered asthma. She had a history of heavy medication, missed school, and several trips to the emergency department. During the first family interview, the counselor directed the family's attention to the eldest sister's weight problem, and the family's concern then shifted to the newly identified patient. The result for the asthmatic was fewer symptoms, less medication, and no lost school time.

Minuchin referred to the preceding case as the foundation of family therapy. The family structure had changed from two parents protectively concerned with one child's asthma to two parents concerned with one child's asthma and one child's obesity. The asthmatic child's position in the family changed, and that changed her experience.

As with all counseling approaches, the counselor's first step is to establish a trusting relationship with the family. Minuchin recommended three ways to establish trust: (1) *tracking,* or demonstrating interest in the family by asking a series of questions about the topics they bring up; (2) *mimicry,* or adapting the counselor's communication style to fit the family's; and (3) *support,* which includes the first two ways, plus acceptance of the problem as presented by the client.

Minuchin's style was to get the family to talk briefly until he identified a central theme of concern and the leading and supporting roles in it. At this point, he operated like a play director or group dynamics consultant in determining the roles being played, what was interrupting the flow, what was silencing communication, and what diverting maneuvers were blocking family interaction.

Next, the counselor examines boundaries or family rules, which define (1) who participates in what and how, (2) areas of responsibility, (3) decision making, and (4) privacy. When rules have been broken, the family works on them with the help of "stage directions." The counselor may ask a family member to observe the family interaction but not interfere. Minuchin paced the family by adopting their mood and tempo and gradually changing it as the interview proceeded. He asked questions in the enactive mode; that is, not "Why doesn't your mother talk to you?" but "See if you can get your mother to talk to you."

The counselor might assign tasks related to the manipulation of space, such as ask a child to move his chair so he cannot see his mother's signals or ask a husband to sit next to his wife and hold her hand when she is anxious. Assigned tasks can dramatize family transactions and suggest change.

Minuchin (1974) shared a case about an anorexic girl and her family to illustrate how he conducts family therapy. Once again, like a play director, he set the stage. The family of six and Minuchin sat down at the table to have lunch.

Minuchin began to develop the crisis in the family by announcing that Sally must eat or soon die. He assigned her father the task of helping her eat. The father tried bribery with ice cream and a soft drink, to no avail, and was "rewarded" by Sally with a minor tantrum.

Next, having received the assignment to help Sally eat, the mother tried pleas, guilt inducements, and lectures that went unheeded except for more tantrum behavior in the corner of the room (including slapping the mother).

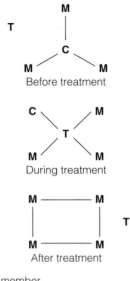

FIGURE 12-3 | STAGES OF STRUCTURAL FAMILY THERAPY

Minuchin began a new stage in the process by standing up and ordering Sally to sit at the table. At this point, the family is exhausted and searching for a way to solve the problem. The reality therapy philosophy that no one stops any behavior until thorough disgust sets in may come into play at this stage.

The therapist offered a way out of the trap: a negotiation model that allowed Sally to negotiate with a pediatric resident, who presented several choices from all the required food groups from which Sally was to select her daily meals. The therapist blocked any attempt by the parents to intervene in the process and developed a separation between Sally and her parents and a therapeutic dyad between Sally and the therapist. The one rule of the game remained: Sally must eat. The strategy of offering alternatives empowered Sally with control over her life that she had attempted to achieve through not eating. In 1 month, she returned to her normal weight. Krautter & Lock (2004) report success with a method similar to Minuchin's in working with anorexic adolescents.

In summary, Minuchin's approach to structural family therapy was both active and directive. The first task is to shift the family focus from the identified client to the therapist, which allows the identified client to begin the process of rejoining the family as a regular family member. The shift in focus to the therapist occurs when the therapist joins the family and becomes part of the family system. When treatment is complete, the therapist moves outside the family structure and leaves the family intact and connected without the loss of individual family member identities (see Figure 12-3).

STRATEGIC FAMILY THERAPY

Following the popularity of structural family therapy in the 1970s, strategic family therapy dominated the 1980s, led by Milton Erickson, Jay Haley, and Cloé Madanes. The popularity of the solution-focused and paradoxical counseling methods for families has continued into the first decade of the new millennium.

Strategic family therapy is based on the assumption that family member behavior, which is ongoing and repetitive, can be understood only in the family context. The family's ineffective problem solving develops and maintains symptoms. The counselor's role is to design a strategy for solving the presenting problem. Haley (1973) defines *strategic family therapy* as any therapy in which the therapist initiates what happens in therapy and designs a plan for solving each problem. It is characterized by its brief duration, generally no more than ten sessions. The therapist takes on a very high activity level by giving specific directives for behavioral change that are carried out as homework assignments. Many of the therapists' directives are paradoxical interventions and solution-focused brief counseling methods (see discussion in Chapter 5).

Paradoxical Interventions

Paradoxical interventions harness the strong resistance clients have to change and to taking directives from the therapist. Rather than working against the client's resistance, the therapist uses it to bring about the changes in behavior needed to correct the problem and repair the family system. The client is in the double-bind position of either obeying the therapist, which the client does not want to do, or stopping the problematic, "uncontrollable" behavior. The client soon discovers that the behavior is controllable and stops the undesirable behavior. For example, the counselor tells an insomniac to see how long the person can go without sleep, maybe even enter a stay-awake contest or go for the world's record, or tells a tantrum-throwing child to have more tantrums and the child's parents to provide a private room for the tantrums. The counselor also might tell children who lose their tempers and commit aggressive acts to do so between 4 P.M. and 5 P.M. daily in a room equipped with a punching bag and tell their parents to remind the children when it is time to vent anger.

In another paradoxical intervention, the counselor takes a "one-down" position, encouraging the client not to do too much too soon. Clients often play the wooden-leg game (see description in Chapter 10), which highlights the client's disabilities and the reasons why the client cannot function properly. In the one-down position, the counselor emphasizes all that the client is already doing despite problems and suggests that the client must have great inner strength even to show up for counseling.

Clients who handicap themselves through anticipatory anxiety over activities such as making speeches, taking tests, or meeting new people are directed to practice all the symptoms they fear, such as blushing, speaking in a trembling voice, stuttering, passing out, or completely failing the test. They often tell test-anxious people to take practice tests and fail each one.

Madanes (1981) often asked children to pretend doing the symptom the family was trying to prevent. The other family members were directed to play along and encourage the child to act out the symptoms. Counselors often treat displays of inadequacy and learned helplessness with directives to the child to act more helpless more often and with directives to other family members to overhelp by providing too much service.

Although strategic or brief therapy is directed toward symptom removal, counselors distinguish between first- and second-order changes. First-order change occurs when the symptom is temporarily removed, only to reappear later because the family system has not been changed. Haley (1976) points out that the behaviors of family members do not occur in isolation. Rather, family behaviors occur in a sequence in which one member's behavior is both the result of and the catalyst for other members' behaviors. Fixing the symptom while failing to fix the system does not fix the family. First-order change is typical for dysfunctional families who work hard to maintain the status quo.

Second-order change occurs when the symptom *and* the system are repaired and the need for the symptom does not reappear. For example, Mom and Dad quarrel, the children start a fight, Mom and Dad stop their quarrel to deal with their children, and a period of family peace is achieved. Until Mom and Dad find a better way to resolve conflicts, the sequence repeats frequently and the peace is only temporary. Healthy families with an adaptive facility for repairing the family system when it is broken engage in second-order change.

Contributions of Milton Erickson, Jay Haley, and Cloé Madanes to Strategic Family Therapy

Jay Haley, director of the Family Therapy Institute of Washington, DC, was a longtime colleague and student of Milton Erickson. He described Erickson as his mentor and major source of ideas about therapy. Since Erickson's death in 1980, Haley perhaps has been his best interpreter. Haley also worked closely with Salvador Minuchin at the Philadelphia Child Guidance Clinic. For the past several years, Haley's work has been shared with that of his wife, Cloé Madanes. They founded the Family Therapy Institute and currently conduct lectures and workshops on strategic family therapy.

To strategic family therapists, the term *strategic* refers to the development of a specific strategy, planned in advance by the therapist, to resolve the presenting problem as quickly and efficiently as possible. Erickson promoted the idea that insight, awareness, and emotional release are not necessary for change. Rather, people need to solve their immediate problems and eliminate bothersome symptoms to move ahead with their lives. Followers of Erickson's approach do not have the client's personal growth and development as a primary therapeutic goal. Problem solving through minimal intervention is the key goal for the strategic group. It is important to note that strategic interventions often foster changes in the family structure when structural interventions fail.

Erickson's approach incorporated three principles in addition to discounting the importance of achieving insight: (1) the therapist uses the client's reality rather than attempting to fit the client to the views of others in the world such as parents or colleagues, or even to those of the therapist; (2) both the therapist and client play active roles in the action-oriented process; and (3) minimal change must occur in one or more areas of the client's life for change in the family system to result. Eclecticism is alive and well in family therapy practice as the therapist works to construct strategies to implement the needed changes.

A typical example of an Erickson case concerned a mother and her 61-pound anorexic daughter, Barbie, who was limiting her daily diet to one oyster cracker and a glass of ginger ale. Initial treatment began with routine questions for Barbie, which her mother answered. Erickson allowed the mother's behavior to continue for 2 days as a way of building rapport and establishing a pattern before initiating an intervention. The next stage began with Erickson's scolding the mother in front of Barbie for answering all of Barbie's questions. Barbie developed a new perspective on her mother. The next step was to punish Barbie for keeping her mother awake at night with her whimpering. The punishment was forcing Barbie to eat scrambled eggs; this was acceptable to her because she viewed eating as punishment. In the next stage, Erickson used storytelling as a way of indirectly replacing Barbie's maladaptive behavioral patterns with good associations of food in various social settings. He altered her role as victim by placing herself in other roles in the stories, such as rescuer or persecutor. Barbie's treatment was successful and remained so during a lengthy follow-up period (Erickson & Zeig, 1985).

In a similar treatment approach for anorexia nervosa, the therapist viewed the illness as originating from an overprotective family, leading to suppression of autonomy in the adolescent, Cathy, and surfacing in the form of an illness rather than outward rebellion. The therapist used two interventions: (1) Cathy's refusal to eat was termed "disobedient behavior" and was dealt with as unacceptable by the parents, and (2) parental intervention in her eating habits was prevented. Cathy's defiance of the parental rules surfaced in her eating habits. She controlled the family by manipulating her eating behavior. Therapy with the entire family focused on discussing, negotiating, and resolving difficult family issues. The children gained more autonomy and responsibility for their decisions, and the parents spent more time with each other. Any weight gain Cathy showed was reinforced by allowing her more autonomy. Weight loss was punished by loss of new privileges. In other words, Cathy's eating behavior now controlled only her own autonomy and the number of privileges available to her.

Haley (1976) combined a strategic and structural approach to treat a young boy's fear of dogs. A problem of family dynamics was that the boy was close to his mother but disengaged from his father. Haley's first step was to get father and son to interact by having them talk about the dangers of dogs in the neighborhood. When the mother tried to interrupt, Haley neutralized her by explaining that this was Dad's area of expertise. The second step was to get a

dog into the home to help in three areas: (1) to continue the father–son interaction, (2) to achieve systematic desensitization of the dog phobia, and (3) to
stimulate change in the family dynamics. Haley accomplished Step 2 by asking
the boy to pick out a dog that was afraid and to work with his father on teaching the dog not to be afraid.

The preceding case illustrates a common malfunction in a child-centered
family structure. Generally, one or more overinvolved dyads exist, one of which
usually includes the "problem" child. Haley (1973) describes three ways to
handle the overinvolved dyad: (1) act on the relationship between the child and
the mother (neutralize mother); (2) modify the relationship between father and
child (interact about the dog); and (3) change the relationship between spouses
(bring the dog into the home for the son to care for and teach with the father's
help). Haley (1984), in another application of the same three steps, describes
an intervention for misbehaving children as "ordeal therapy." When all else
fails, the counselor might present the father of a teenage son with the following directive:

> When Bill misbehaves at school, he will be sent to me with a note of explanation.
> I will call you, Dad, at your office to pick up Bill, take him home, and supervise his
> digging of a 3- by 3- by 3-foot hole in your flower bed. On completion of the dig-
> ging, Bill is to place one of his CDs in it, fill the hole, tramp it down, clean the
> shovel, and return the shovel to the garage. You will then return Bill to me, and I
> will return him to his class. At the end of the day, you, Dad, are to speak with your
> wife about Bill's behavior for that day.

Dysfunctional symptoms in a family system might be evidenced in several
ways. Intensive criticism between children and parents in families highly resistant to change could result in anything in children from suicidal depression to
refusal to attend school. Strategic family counselors often fix both problems by
prescribing more criticism and putting the family in the double bind of having
to choose between obeying the counselor or disobeying by doing the "right"
thing of stopping the criticism. Family resistance against counseling and the
counselor is harnessed to work for the good of the family as they refuse to criticize each other.

DeShazer and Molnar (1984) have described a useful team approach for
prescribing four common interventions in their practice of solution-focused
brief family therapy. The therapy hour is divided as follows: (1) a 40-minute
interview with the family, (2) a 10-minute consultation with the team, and (3) a
10-minute delivery of the intervention message and closing of the session. The
first intervention, designed for families who focus on the perceived stability of
their problem pattern, requires family members to observe one another
between sessions so that "you can tell us next time what happens in your family
that you want to continue to have happen." The second intervention is for
families who are bankrupt of ideas about how to solve the problem. The therapist requests that they "do something different." The third intervention is for
clients who believe their problem is out of their control. The therapist asks
them to "pay attention to what you do when you overcome the temptation or

urge to _____." The fourth intervention works well for clients who are convinced they are doing the only logical thing. The therapist responds, "A lot of people in your situation would have _____." All four interventions are designed to help clients experience change.

Chasin, Roth, and Bograd (1989), in an article on action methods in strategic therapy, present another solution-focused brief family counseling method. In an approach to therapy that involves de-emphasizing the problems, their main focus was on looking for clients' strengths and using various action strategies to open up new perspectives and discussions. The authors provide a five-step outline:

1. Therapists and clients contract to promote safe, voluntary participation. The clients have the right to disclose at the level they choose and can refuse to answer any question or participate in any activity.
2. Each participant is invited to list his or her individual strengths and the strengths of the relationship.
3. Participants enact three dramatizations. First, the couple enacts what would happen if the goals for the relationship were reached. Second, each client enacts a painful past experience. Third, each client enacts the painful past experience "as it should have been." The partner's roles in this enactment are preventive, protective, and/or resolving.
4. Each participant states what he or she perceives to be the problem in the relationship.
5. The therapist recommends the next step (homework, follow-up appointment, and so on) based on what happened during the session.

A final example of strategic family therapy is the use of metaphor in bringing about rapid change. Parents bring an 8-year-old girl to family counseling with the problem that she is spoiled, stubborn, argumentative, and whiny. Although the parents obviously view this behavior as bad, their daughter does not. The counselor asks her age, and the child says she is 8. The counselor looks incredulously at the mother and father, shakes his head, and says to the parents, "This can't be, for this girl is 8, and this behavior you described is the behavior of a 6-year-old." With a puzzled look, the counselor asks the girl how old she was on her last birthday and how old she will be on her next birthday. The counselor notes that the behavior she is exhibiting during the session is that of an 8-year-old, and he asks the parents to keep a log of the child's behavior for 1 week. The direct challenge of age appeals to children's desire to look their age or older.

In summary, the job of the strategic family therapist is fourfold. First, the hierarchical structure of the family must be identified. "Who is in charge of whom and what?" and "What role does each family member play?" are the critical questions to be answered. Confusion about who is in charge and about role identity is characteristic of dysfunctional families. Second, the sequence of behaviors that causes and maintains the problem symptom needs to be identified. For example, what is the presenting problem, and what family conditions create and maintain the problem? Third, the therapist develops an intervention plan to serve as a directive for how family members are to change certain behaviors. Fourth, the therapist and family evaluate the plan's effectiveness in removing the symptom and repairing the family system. Haley (1976) distinguishes between advice and directives. Giving advice is telling people what they ought to do, what job to take, or what person to marry. Giving a directive is like assigning behavior homework or writing a behavior prescription designed to alter family interaction sequences.

Haley (1976) describes four stages of a typical first interview applying strategic therapy:

1. Stage 1, the *social stage,* accomplishes three tasks: building rapport, observing family communication patterns and alliances, and forming tentative hypotheses about how the family functions.
2. In Stage 2, the *problem stage,* the main task is obtaining a clear statement of the problem that meets with each family member's agreement. Haley suggests involving reluctant participants first in the problem discussion and the identified client last, a procedure followed in most family therapies to bring everybody into the discussion without focusing on the identified client as the scapegoat for the family's dysfunction.
3. Stage 3, the *interaction stage,* accomplishes two tasks: Everybody should discuss the problem, and everybody should interact with all other family members. During Stage 3, the therapist does not become personally involved in the family interaction because the family interaction patterns require full attention. The therapist directs the family to discuss their disagreements and to role-play or act out a typical family problem such as deciding who does what family chores. We prefer to observe how a typical family meeting might operate, even if the family is not accustomed to holding them. All these interactions provide valuable information about problem sequences, communication patterns, and the lines of authority in the family hierarchy.
4. In Stage 4, *goal setting,* the obvious task is to define the goal for therapy in concise, observable, behavioral terms. For example, in a family that does not discuss family conflicts, an acceptable goal might be weekly 30-minute family meetings to clear the air of conflicts. The therapist could add a paradoxical directive encouraging the family not to resolve any of the conflicts during the meetings. Again, complete clarity and agreement on the goals are necessary if the family is to have ownership in the therapy process and the resulting cooperation and commitment to make therapy work. Todd (2000) describes a similar, successful adaptation of strategic family therapy as it was applied to a parent-education class for rearing challenging teens.

Selekman (2002) uses what he refers to as reversal questions to tap adolescents' wisdom about what their parents can do differently to gain their cooperation on the conflicts that frequently occur between parents and teenagers, including following family rules, doing homework, maintaining good grades, and completing chores. Reversal questions, by putting teenagers in the expert role, help build the relationship between counselor and client. Examples of reversal questions include:

Do you have any advice for your parents about how they can get you to do those things they always ask you about school and grades?

What do you think your parents could do to reduce the number of arguments between you?

What is the first thing your parents could do differently that would help all of you get along better?

THE COMMUNICATIONS APPROACH TO FAMILY THERAPY

Our discussions of systems, structural, and strategic approaches to family therapy have highlighted several commonalities and overlap between methods, as well as specific differences. Perhaps the common thread that unites the field of family therapy is the focus on how family members communicate. Communication is the heart of the two methods presented next in our discussion: John Gottman's behavioral family therapy and Virginia Satir's conjoint family therapy.

JOHN GOTTMAN'S BEHAVIORAL INTERVIEW METHOD

Gottman's behavioral family therapy (1979, 1990) has much more in common with traditional family therapy than it does with the behavioral counseling and therapy discussed in Chapter 9. The therapist in Gottman's system functions more as an educator than as a healer, as is true for most of the practitioners of the theories and systems presented in this book.

Family therapists following a communications approach to family therapy naturally hold the view that accurate communication is the key to solving family problems. All families are faced with problems; however, some families solve more of their problems than other families. Families that are good at problem solving hold several traits in common. They communicate in an open and honest manner rather than relying on phony or manipulative roles when trying to meet their needs or resolve family crises. In addition, these family members match the intent and impact of their communication. For example, a wife might want more cooperation from her husband on household chores. She stated her request in clear terms and listened empathically to her husband's response about his needs; the intent of her communication achieved the desired impact. Had she been sarcastic, the impact of her message might have resulted in less cooperation from her husband. Dysfunctional families have low success rates in matching the impact with the intent of their communications.

Gottman built his approach around matching the intent and impact of communication (Gottman, 1979, 1994; Gottman, Notarius, Gonzo, & Markman, 1976). He designed his behavioral interviewing method to teach people about what they are doing that is not working and to help them correct the situation by learning how to get the impact they want from their communication.

In Stage I, how a couple or family made the decision to seek therapy is explored. The therapist also determines the level of commitment to therapy and who, if anyone, might be a reluctant client. The dynamics give the therapist an opportunity to view the family interaction pattern firsthand. Areas of family or couple agreement and disagreement surface during this stage.

In Stage II, the goals each person has for therapy, some of the fears they have about coming to therapy, and fears about what could go wrong are identified. The therapist asks clients what their situation would be like if all their goals were attained; that is, how would they be behaving differently, and how would an observer know they had met their goals? More specifically, what would their typical day be like if they achieved their goals? Couples in counseling often state their goals (for treatment) in terms of what they want for each other; a better focus would be the goals the couple wants for the partnership. The therapist can facilitate goal setting by presenting each client with a list of possible goals—improve communication, have more fun, do more things together, become more of a team, become better parents, end fighting, manage finances better, improve love-making, cooperate more on household jobs—and instructing them to select just one goal each. The clients then elaborate on their choices and explain why the goal is important to them. The second task in Stage II is to identify any fears or inhibitions the couple might have about counseling. A good introduction to the subject is asking the couple the worst possible thing that could happen from counseling. The therapist can use this opportunity to explain how treatment is conducted and the roles of the therapist and clients. If the couple is having a problem with finances, for example, the therapist's role is not to solve the money problem per se; rather, the therapist focuses on the couple's communications. Better and more effective communication should provide the means to solve problems more efficiently, including handling finances better.

In Stage III, the counselor asks the couple to articulate their perceptions of their marital issues or problems. Again, the couple completes a checklist of several marital issues and rates each issue for its severity on a scale of 0 to 10, with 10 being most severe. The typical list of issues approximates the goals list used in Stage II—for example, house and yard chores, fighting, finances, sex, in-laws, communication, cooperation, parenting, time together, and addictions. Again, the couple's discussion of their marital issues affords the therapist another opportunity to observe the couple's communication pattern.

In Stage IV, the therapist asks the couple to select one issue to discuss, just as they might try to resolve it at home, and then observes the free interaction to note whether the intent of each communication attempt is getting the desired impact.

In Stage V, a play-by-play analysis of the couple's interaction focuses on miscommunications in which the intent of the speaker's message did not get the desired impact. In fact, the miscommunication often gets an effect opposite the intended meaning. The intent might be to get a partner to help out around the house more, but the result is that the other partner is helping even less than before. After pointing out the differences between intent and impact for a series of communications, the therapist might ask one partner to assume the role of a play director to describe how the other partner could have responded better to the statement just made. Then the couple compares the desired response with the one actually made. As in reality therapy, the couple can decide whether what they are doing is getting the desired response, and they can stop or change what they are doing. The receiver of the message can validate the impact of the sender's message, and the sender then analyzes the receiver's return message for intent and impact. Step V might require the therapist to lecture on the intent and impact equation: *Good communication occurs when intent equals impact.* The therapist explains that choice of words, nonverbal communications, and the sender's and receiver's value filters can distort the intent of the message and lead to an undesired impact. Restating and clarifying the sender's message before reacting often can help. In other words, the couple may have to pass the message back and forth before the receiver understands it the way it was intended. Even with a clear message, the sender may not get the intended impact of the message and need to alter it to get the desired response. The receiving partner can help by stating how he or she wishes to be approached on the presenting issue.

In Stage VI, the therapist concludes the session by negotiating a contract with the couple on what goal(s) they will try to achieve and the method of treatment they will use. The clients' job is to decide on the objective, and the therapist's job is to supply the process. Again, as is true with most counseling approaches, the principal goal is to teach people a communication process that enables them to solve more of their own problems.

Virginia Satir's Conjoint Family Therapy

When Virginia Satir (1916–1988) was 5 years old, she decided to become a detective to help children figure out parents. She was not sure what she would be looking for, but even at that age she knew that more strange things were going on in families than met the eye. More than half a century later, after working with thousands of families, Satir reported that she still found a lot of puzzles in families.

Satir viewed family life as an iceberg. Most people are aware of only one tenth of what is happening in the family—the tenth that they can see and hear. Like the ship that depends on the captain's awareness of the total iceberg, the family must depend on the total awareness of the family structure to survive. Satir referred to the hidden 90% as the family's needs, motives, and communication patterns. In four books, *Conjoint Family Therapy* (1967), *Peoplemaking* (1972), *Helping Families to Change* (Satir, Stachowiak, & Taschman, 1975), and *Step by Step* (Satir & Baldwin, 1983), Satir shared some of the answers she found to some family puzzles. According to Satir, she embellished some of the early concepts in *Conjoint Family Therapy* as a result of her work with the Gestalt concepts presented by Fritz Perls and the body-awareness work of Bernard Gunther.

Virginia Satir earned excellent qualifications as a parent detective: formal academic training in psychological social work at the University of Chicago and work as a teacher, consultant, and practitioner in psychiatric clinics, mental hospitals, family service centers, growth centers, and private practice. In 1959, she joined with two psychiatrists to form the initial staff of the Mental Research Institute in Palo Alto, California. She also served as the first director of training at the Esalen Institute in Big Sur, California, and lectured in most parts of the world. She was a visiting professor to at least ten universities and a consultant to the Veterans Administration and to several other agencies and schools. As is true about many theorists presented in this book, she was more effective demonstrating her methods than lecturing about them.

Satir cited several contributors to the development of her system—including Harry Stack Sullivan's interpersonal theory of the 1920s (an individual's behavior is influenced by his or her interaction with another) and the growth of group therapy, also during the 1920s, the major contributors of which were J. L. Moreno and S. R. Slavson. Gregory Bateson and Murray Bowen began to look at families to discover why individuals became "schizophrenic." They believed that one person could represent the family situation.

Bateson, who conducted research at the Mental Research Institute, contributed the idea of double-bind communications that occur when one person sends a conflicting, double message to another person; for example, Mom says, "Jane, if you really loved me, you would make better grades at school."

Much of Satir's theory has roots not only in classic theories of clinical psychology and psychiatry but also in her past research at the Mental Research Institute and the National Institute of Mental Health. Satir synthesized older with newer theories and added original techniques.

THE NATURE OF PEOPLE   Satir had a positive view of human nature. After studying 12,000 families in depth, she was convinced that, at any time, whatever people are doing represents the best they are aware of and the best they can do. She believed that people are rational and have the freedom and ability to make choices in their lives. Although Satir viewed people as basically free, she considered the extent of their knowledge as the biggest limitation on personal freedom. People can learn what they do not know and change their ways of interacting with others. People can also make themselves healthier by freeing themselves from the past. Like Maslow, Satir believed that people are geared toward surviving, growing, and developing close relationships with others. Although some behaviors may be labeled psychotic, sick, or bad, Satir saw these behaviors as attempts to reach out for help.

Self-esteem plays a prominent role in Satir's system. She believed that self-esteem and effective communication beget one another. Conversely, low self-esteem and dysfunctional communication are also correlated. Satir saw self-esteem—the degree to which people accept both their good and their bad points—as the basic human drive. Self-esteem is a changing variable that fluctuates within a healthy range, depending on the amount of stress one is experiencing. It is related to one's participation in the family interaction. When individual family members experience stress, their ability to communicate openly, give and receive feedback, and solve problems depends on the collective self-esteem of the family. Family members may try to block communication to protect their own self-esteem under stress or in crises. Family members with low self-esteem are likely to create disturbances to make the others feel as bad as they do. For example, parents guilty of child abuse often have low self-esteem and may unconsciously internalize their feelings; for example, they may think, "One way to punish myself for my wasteful ways is to punish that same behavior in one of my children."

Behavior, according to Satir, is directly related to one's family position and view of it. Good or bad feelings about ourselves are probably communicated to others. Satir viewed people as mature and functional when they behave in acceptable and helpful ways and take responsibility for their actions. Satir (as well as Adler and Glasser) saw irresponsibility and poor communication as symptoms of low self-esteem.

Satir made the point that a person needs a high degree of self-esteem to qualify as a good marriage partner. People with healthy self-concepts view their partners as enhancing their own self-esteem. However, people who have low self-esteem look to their partners as extensions of themselves. A marital relationship is dysfunctional if one partner looks to the other to supply what is missing in themselves. In this dysfunctional couple relationship, a person sees the marriage or partnership as a place for getting and not giving. For example, someone may marry as a type of therapy for strengthening an inadequate personality. However, the general outcome of a "taking" relationship is disappointment and an even lower sense of self-esteem.

By the same token, parents with low self-esteem may compensate for feelings of inferiority by having a child. The child may be used to demonstrate the parents' worth to the community and their self-worth as parents, as well as an extension of themselves. Unconsciously, they appear to be thinking, "If I did not fulfill many of my life's aspirations, perhaps I can relive them through my child." In such situations, parents never see children as individuals with separate worth, value, and identities. Children of parents deficient in self-esteem have a heavy, difficult burden to bear: to live out their parents' fantasies. They see success and failure from the vantage point of the parent. Children who show individuality and different points of view may be accused of not loving their parents through comments such as "After all I have done for you, how could you do this to me?" or "If you loved me, you would practice the piano more."

Satir (1967) held that children are the third angle of the family triangle. As such, their position may be intolerable, similar to the persecutor-victim-rescuer triangle described in transactional analysis (see Chapter 10). Parents in conflict consider any direction the child turns as a turn for or against one of the parents. Given this state of affairs, Satir wrote that children who seem to side with one parent run the risk for seeming not to love the other parent. Because children need both parents, making such a choice inevitably hurts them. Both parents have interlocking roles to play in the process of educating children emotionally, and the failure of one angle of the family triangle (one parent) disturbs the entire system; frequently, the result is disturbed children.

A further complication in the triangle is that the child has already established an identity with the same-sex parent, and the hurt of taking sides is further compounded by the stunted or stifled psychosexual development that may occur. Children need the opposite-sex parent to admire, respect, and love, and they need the same-sex parent as a good role model. When the parents are divided, arguing and fighting, children cannot achieve these identity and interpersonal goals. In a family with no parental coalition—that is, cooperation between father and mother to fulfill their respective roles as man and woman and husband and wife—the child may need counseling to fulfill unsatisfied wishes. Satir conceptualized this child as the *identified client*, even though the entire family is counseled.

Satir did not believe in the concept of triangular relationships; that is, she believed there is no such thing as a relationship among three people, but rather only shifting two-person relationships, with the third member in the role of observer. The building blocks of Satir's system are two-person, interacting relationships. The key to success or failure in this system is the relationship between husband and wife. If the system is dysfunctional and they are not acting in a parental coalition, then both mates may look to the child to satisfy their unmet needs.

According to Satir, children who are triangulated into a marital situation in the role of *ersatz mate*—an ally who is wooed seductively by the parent of the opposite sex—are not happy. The child has loyalties to and needs for both parents. Although a child may appear closer to one parent, such an alliance is illusory. Children cannot unambivalently side with either parent.

Satir wrote that people develop self-esteem in the early childhood years. Beyond the obvious physical needs, children need a warm, ongoing, predictable mastery over their world and validation of themselves as distinct and worthwhile people. They also require a sense of what it is to be male or female and to accept this role. If parents consistently show that they consider their children masterful, sexual people and demonstrate a gratifying, functional male–female relationship, their children acquire self-esteem and become increasingly independent. In every way, self-esteem, independence, and individuality go together.

Satir viewed mature people as those who are fully in charge of their feelings and who make choices based on accurate perceptions of themselves and others. The mature person takes full responsibility for choices that have been made. In summary, Satir regarded mature people as: (1) being in touch with their feelings, (2) communicating clearly and effectively, and (3) accepting differences in others as a chance to learn.

THEORY OF COUNSELING   Satir believed that four components in a family situation are subject to change and correction: the members' feelings of self-worth, the family's communication abilities, the system, and the rules of the family. The rules are the way things are accomplished in the family. They are the most difficult component to uncover during therapy sessions because they usually are not verbalized or are consciously known to all members of the family. Satir wanted all members of a family to understand the rules that govern their emotional interchanges, including (1) freedom to comment, (2) freedom to express what one is seeing or hearing, (3) freedom to agree or disapprove, and (4) freedom to ask questions when one does not understand. The family unit becomes dysfunctional when members do not understand the unwritten rules. Satir told families who were having problems with a member that families have no bad members who cause pain, only bad rules. She believed that what goes on at a given moment is the natural consequence of the experience of one's own life; consequently, anything can change. However, Satir believed that change is not a "have to," but rather one possibility among several. She believed in taking risks, controlling the counseling process, and leaving the outcome to the family.

In family systems theory, the main idea is that the family functions as a unit, with certain rules, expectations, and emotions. Members of the family unit are interdependent; therefore, stress applied to one part of the system or to one family member is felt throughout the system by all members in varying degrees. The family system has both the potential to share and deal with the stress in a healthy, open, and productive way and the potential to close the communication process by focusing blame for the stress on one family member (the identified client).

Analyzing the interaction processes between the family members and the family system is as important as analyzing the communications content to bring about changes in a family's functioning. Questions of who is right and who is wrong border on value judgments that have no place in the process of family growth and further development. The focus is on discovering how individuals can adjust to the various events within the family to achieve satisfaction and to avoid withdrawing and other harmful roles.

Satir emphasized the necessity of developing trust before any meaningful change process can begin. Given willingness to take a risk, trust can be assumed. The second step is developing awareness, or knowing what one is doing. With awareness comes understanding and applying this new understanding to effective decision making. At this point, the new decision-making behavior can be put to use. The underlying theme is the development of self-worth and the freedom to comment.

Satir believed that whether a family grows is primarily the responsibility of counselors and their input. They must be able to put clients in touch with themselves at a feeling level. The counselor assumes the role of teacher to reeducate the family to new ways of thinking, feeling, and communicating.

Communication, the most important factor in Satir's system, is the main determinant of the kinds of relationships people have with one another and of how people adjust to their environment, as well as being the tie that binds the family together. When a family is operating smoothly, communication among family members is open, authentic, assertive, and received. Conversely, when a family system is in trouble, communication is blocked or distorted in a futile attempt to ward off anxiety and tension.

Fear of rejection is a common source of anxiety. Because people fear rejection, they resort to one response pattern or to a combination of patterns to communicate with others. These universal response roles are the placater, the blamer, the computer, the distractor, and the leveler. The last response, leveling, helps people develop healthy personalities; the other four responses hide real feelings for fear of rejection. In such situations, people feel and react to the threat of rejection, do not want to reveal "weakness," and attempt to conceal it. Satir (1971) agreed with Gestalt theory on nonverbal behavior: The body expresses your whole integration. Each response pattern is accompanied by a unique body posture and nonverbal behaviors, and each has its own way of dealing or not dealing with the context (or subject matter of the situation), the needs of the other family members, and the personal or self needs of the person playing the particular role.

Placater   Placaters placate so others do not get angry. Their motto is "peace at any price." They talk in ingratiating ways to try to please, or they apologize. They never disagree and even take on the air of a "yes person." They have low self-esteem. They cannot negotiate solutions of mutual benefit because the process is too threatening. In other words, placaters negate self in the interest of serving others and staying within the context of the situation. Nonverbal behaviors of the placater send the message that "Whatever you want is okay with me; I am just here to make you happy."

Blamer   Blamers are the faultfinders, directors, and bosses. They also do not feel good about themselves. They may feel lonely and unsuccessful and attempt to compensate by trying to coerce others into obeying them so they can feel that they amount to something. Blaming also is a good way to create distance and prevent others from getting too close. The blamers are good guilt inducers; for example, they may say, "After all I have done for you, how could you do this to me?" Blamers negate others while focusing on the context of the situation and on themselves. Nonverbal behaviors from the blamer send the message that "You never do anything right. What is the matter with you?"

Computer   Computers are calm and correct, show no feelings, and speak like a recording. They pretend there is no conflict when there is. Computers are the super-reasonable people. Their bodies reflect their rigid personalities. They negate the context of the situation and others to concentrate on getting what they want. They cover up their vulnerability with big words to establish self-worth. Nonverbal behaviors from the "computer" send messages that "I am cool, calm, and collected." They also may take the position of "See it my way" at the expense of others and of the context of the situation.

Distractor   Distractors make completely irrelevant statements. They change the subject and never respond honestly. Their strong point is evading the issue. They may even resort to withdrawing from the situation to avoid a crisis or conflict. Distractors negate all three elements of reality: self, others, and the context

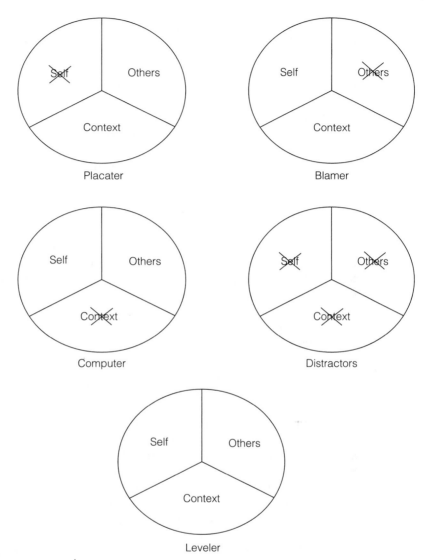

FIGURE 12-4 | SATIR'S FIVE COMMUNICATION STYLES

of the situation. Nonverbal behaviors from distractors send messages that "Maybe if I do this long enough the problem will really go away." Distracting, doing and saying irrelevant things, withdrawing from family interaction, or a combination of these behaviors function to prevent the family from discussing painful, unresolved issues that should be faced in open and honest discussion.

Leveler Levelers communicate their honest thoughts and feelings in a straightforward manner that addresses self, others, and the context of the situation (Figure 12-4). Their verbal messages and nonverbal body posture are consistent. Leveling occurs when all aspects of communication are congruent: body, vocal tone, context, and facial expression. Levelers do not cover up or put other people down in the name of being open and honest. They are not phonies. Levelers tell the truth about what they are thinking, feeling, and doing, and they allow others to do the same. Their relationships are free and honest, with few threats to self-esteem. The leveling response is the truthful message for a particular person at a given time. It is direct and to the point, with no hidden agenda. There is openness and a feeling of trust in interactions with a person who is leveling. This response allows people to live as complete persons in touch with their behavior, thinking, and feelings. Being a leveler allows a person to have integrity, commitment, honesty, intimacy, competency, creativity, and the ability to solve real problems. The other four forms of communicating result in doubtful integrity, commitment by bargain, dishonesty, loneliness, incompetence, strangulation by tradition (inability to change traditional patterns), and destructive ways of dealing with fantasy problems.

Our society does not encourage leveling responses. Although people would like to be honest, they are afraid and instead play games. Satir outlined a variety of experiences to help family members become aware that they can choose to change their responses and understand how they can do so. Levelers can choose one of the other four response patterns if they are willing to accept the consequences; but for them, such responses would not be the automatic response of people locked into a particular pattern. Levelers can choose to placate, blame, compute, or distract; the difference is that they know what they are doing and are prepared to accept the result of their behavior.

The message of the leveler is consistent. If a leveler says, "I like you," the voice is warm and the eye contact and body speak the same message. If the leveler is angry, the voice is harsh, the face is tight, and the words are clear: "I am angry about what you have done!"

Satir pointed out that every person she has seen with a behavior or coping problem was a member of a family in which all significant communication was double level—that is, phony or hidden (Satir et al., 1975). If people learn to recognize harmful communication patterns and level with their family members, then the family has a chance to make its members' lives better and to solve problems more efficiently. As mentioned earlier, Satir's system is based on two-person, interacting relationships. However, every couple has three parts: you, me, and us. For the relationship to continue and for love to grow, each part has to be recognized and not dominated by the other two. Although love as a feeling begins a marriage, the process makes it work. The process is the "how," which is what Satir taught her clients.

Satir divided all families into two types: nurturing and troubled. Each type has varying degrees. Her main objective for her clients was recognition of their type, and then change from either troubled to nurturing or from nurturing to more nurturing. The nurturing family helps its members develop feelings of self-worth, whereas the troubled family diminishes these feelings. In every family, factors to be considered include feelings of self-worth, communication, rules, and links to society.

According to Satir (1972), aliveness, honesty, genuineness, and love mark nurturing families. These families have the following characteristics:

1. People are listened to and interested in listening to others.
2. People are not afraid to take risks because the family understands that mistakes are bound to happen when taking risks.
3. People's bodies are graceful, and their facial expressions are relaxed.
4. People look at one another and not through one another or at the floor.
5. The children are friendly and open, and the rest of the family treats them as people.
6. People seem comfortable about touching one another and showing their affection.
7. People show love by talking and listening with concern and by being straightforward and real with one another.
8. Family members feel free to tell one another how they feel and what they think.
9. Anything can be discussed—fears, anger, hurt, criticism, joys, achievements.
10. Family members plan, but if something does not work out, they can adjust.
11. Human life and feelings are more important than anything else.
12. Parents see themselves as leaders and not as bosses. They acknowledge to their children their poor judgment, as well as their good judgment, and their hurt, anger, or disappointment, as well as their joy. Their behavior matches their teaching.
13. When nurturing, parents need to correct their children. They rely on listening, touching, understanding, and careful timing and are aware of children's feelings and their natural wish to learn.
14. Nurturing parents understand that children learn only when they are valued, so they do not respond in a way that makes the child feel devalued.

COUNSELING METHOD   The counseling method of conjoint family therapy involves the entire family and is based on communication, interaction, and general information. The approach Satir taught to families was both physical and emotional. Counselors who prefer to work less with emotions and more with behavior find the Adlerian method more comfortable.

Satir's goals for family counseling were to establish the proper environment and to assist family members in clarifying what they want or hope for themselves and for the family. She wanted them to explore the present state of the family, including who plays which roles. She sought to build each member's self-esteem. Satir also worked to help families operationalize their definitions of words such as *respect* and *love*. For example, she asked clients, "What would be happening that would let us know you were getting the respect and love you desire?" or "What must be done for you to make you feel respected and loved?" Satir also used reframing to turn negatives into positives, thus allowing clients to view difficult situations in a better light and see possibilities for cooperation, conflict resolution, and change.

Satir led the family in role-playing both family situations and each other's actions and reactions to the happenings in a typical day. She used some Gestalt techniques of "sculpting" a family argument or interaction; she believed that the body is often a more honest reflection than the verbal message. Satir used videotape replay to teach communication, and her role-play dramas used various props, such as ropes and stepladders, to demonstrate and analyze the types of family interactions. She staged these dramas to help family members learn how to level with each other, express their emotions, and use honest, direct language. Satir examined the family history by drawing family trees to look at how past and immediate family styles are passed on from parent to child. She used ropes to demonstrate the complicated process of communication between parents and children.

Even with a multitude of techniques, Satir proposed no formula for therapy because therapy involves human feelings and the ability to respond on a human level. Satir viewed the family as a "people-making factory" in which people are made by a process that is crude at best and destructive at worst. Loeschen (1998) points out that Satir viewed parents as children themselves who have learned "the rules" from their own families and brought those rules forward to their current families.

An Example of Satir's Method   A 40-year-old woman sits in a fetal position on the floor, hiding behind a sofa. Her husband, sitting in a chair, points an accusing finger at her from across the room. One daughter, with arms outstretched, tries to make peace. Two children sit with their backs to the group, and a fourth child rubs his mother's back. Satir breaks the silent role-play, rests her hand on the father's shoulder, and asks how he feels right now. She has asked the family to act out silently how each feels during a family argument. This sculpting method is excellent in creating awareness of personal feelings, as well as awareness of the feelings of other family members.

Satir reported research data indicating blood pressure, galvanic skin response, and electroencephalographs were significantly affected when people changed their stance and body posture and held them for at least 10 seconds during role-play demonstrations with double-level, verbal, and nonverbal communication. For example, assuming the blamer posture caused a physiological response, as well as an emotional response, after 10 seconds. In other words, people engaging in harmful role behavior over a given time period have the potential to make themselves physically ill.

The Importance of Including Children   Including children is imperative for family counseling success in Satir's system. Satir advocated inclusion of all the children, not just the child who has a problem, because all are part of the family homeostasis—a process by which the family balances forces within itself to achieve unity and working order. Satir operated from the assumption that all members feel dysfunction within the family in some way. Therefore, the counselor works with all members of the family to help them redefine their relationships. Family members have their own perceptions of what is going on in the family, and each member's input is vital in building a functional family. The counselor works with the family's interpersonal relationships to discover how the members interact so they can strengthen their bonding.

Satir suggested meeting with the marital pair before bringing in the children. She made the couple aware of themselves as individuals, as well as mates and parents. She also suggested preparing the parents in the initial interview for bringing the children into the counseling sessions. After the parents agreed that the children's role in family counseling was important, the children were included.

Working with children means the counselor needs to be fully aware of the children's capabilities and potential. The counselor can plan the length of sessions according to the children's ages. Children have short attention spans, and the counseling process must hold their interest. Counselors confronted with these obstacles can work within them and make the counseling process beneficial, productive, and enjoyable for all.

The counselor should begin by recognizing all the children and repeating their names, ages, and birth order to let the children know they are being heard. The counselor also sets rules for the sessions; for example, no one may destroy property within the room, no one may speak for anyone else, all must speak so they can be heard, and everyone must enable others to be heard. When the ground rules have been established, in-depth discussion can begin.

The counselor should set the mood by asking questions in a warm, specific, matter-of-fact way. The setting should encourage people to take the risk of looking clearly and objectively at themselves and their actions. Satir suggested many questions, emphasizing they must be those the children are able to answer. During this time, the counselor must be sure the children understand what is happening and what the family is striving to gain. The children need to feel comfortable and be aware of themselves as individuals who are different from one another. They need to know the importance of communicating with one another—for example, to feel free to agree or disagree with other family members, to say what they think, and to bring disagreements out in the open. Children need to know that the counselor will treat them as people with perceptions and feelings.

The counselor should demonstrate individuality by speaking to each child separately, differentiating each child, and restating and summarizing what each child says. Counselors need to convey their sincerity by honoring all questions from each child and demonstrating that questions are not troublemaking and illegitimate, and that all family members should ask questions about what they do not know or are unsure about. Counselors who convey their expectations of the children increase the likelihood that the children will rise to meet them. Children listen, are interested, and contribute to the discussions.

The counselor must ask the children their ideas about why they are in counseling and then repeat what each child says to make sure the child's meaning is understood. The counselor may proceed by asking the children where they got their ideas about why they are there, who told them, and what was said. From this exchange, the counselor can gain insight into communication within the family. The counselor encourages the children to talk about themselves and their feelings in relation to each family member. The counselor also helps the children express frustration and anger and has the children ask their family members for answers to any questions they may have. The counselor may use confronting questions to provoke thought in the child. As the counseling sessions advance, questions concerning family rules and roles arise. After establishing good rapport and a comfortable atmosphere, the counselor may begin to bring out underlying feelings and confront people concerning the family's dysfunction. The basis for further probing and confronting must be established between counselor and parent; counselor and child; parent and child; and counselor, parent, and child in the initial interviews. From the initial interviews, the counselor must gain the child's confidence to move forward.

The counselor wants to see each child's place in the family unit. In the beginning, to build the children's self-esteem, the counselor focuses on them—not ignoring the parents, but having the parents respond intermittently. Counselors help children understand their parents as parents and people and themselves as children and people (Johnsen, Sundet, & Torsteinsson, 2004). Lurn, Smith, and Ferris (2002) describe a youth suicide intervention model based on the principles of Satir's model listed earlier. They point out a suicide could have been averted had the adolescent had the benefit of family counseling with Satir's orientation.

THREE KEYS TO SATIR'S SYSTEM   Satir's approach to family counseling focused on three key ingredients:

1. Increase the self-esteem of all family members by facilitating their understanding of the family system and teaching them to implement changes toward open systems and nurturing attitudes and behaviors.
2. Help family members better understand and analyze their encounters with each other and learn the leveling response so that they can improve and open communication patterns.
3. Use experiential learning techniques in the counseling setting to help the family understand present interactions and encourage family members to take personal responsibility for their own actions and feelings.

Satir viewed the counselor as a facilitator, a change agent who assists in the process of moving toward a more open family system and a more nurturing family. The counselor is not the expert, but rather one who helps family members become the experts on their family's problems and growth.

SATIR'S TECHNIQUE   Family therapists use a variety of techniques to assist the family in self-discovery. Satir's method was designed to help family members discover what patterns do not work and how to better understand and express their feelings in an open, level manner. Rather than have them rehash past hurts, Satir had the family analyze its "systems" in a present interaction in the counseling setting. Among the many ways to accomplish this analysis are the following:

1. The counselor asks the family to describe a situation that causes the difficulties that have brought them to counseling or asks them to describe a typical situation from their recent experience that usually results in the problem. Family members enact the situation.

2. The counselor has the family sit in chairs in a circle to simulate their family decision-making process, such as deciding where to go on their next vacation.

3. The family participates in a family sculpture, as in the example presented earlier. The counselor asks someone to describe a typical family argument and then has that person "sculpt" the argument by placing each family member in appropriate positions—complete with gestures, facial expressions, and touching. The counselor might then ask each of the other members how he or she would change it and allow each to make the changes. Discussion aimed at leveling and participation by each family member follows.

4. Each family member takes some long ropes, one for each of the others in the family, and ties all of them around his or her waist. Next, the counselor instructs each of them to tie one rope to each of the other family members. Discussion of the resulting tension and mass of ropes can help the family better understand its complex relationships and crossed transactions.

5. Role-playing and reverse role-playing stimulate family discussion.

6. Videotaped family sessions and discussions help family members achieve a better understanding of all members' reactions and responses.

7. Games include: (a) the simulated family game, (b) the systems game, and (c) communication games.

Satir's games, which are used for counselor training, as well as family therapy, are based on her definition of a *growth model,* which assumes that an individual's behavior changes as a process that is represented by transactions with other people. People function fully when they are removed from the maladaptive system or when the system is changed to promote growth. This model differs greatly from the *sick model,* which proposes that a client's thinking, values, and attitudes are wrong and therefore must be changed, and from the *medical model,* which purports that the cause of the problem is an illness located in the patient.

Satir developed games to deal with the family's behavior when family members operate within these three models. All family members are present during the family counseling process, including the games.

Simulated Family Game   In the simulated family game, various family members simulate each other's behavior; for example, the son plays the mother. The therapist may also ask family members to pretend that they are a different family. After this enactment, the counselor and family members discuss how they differ from or identify with the roles.

Systems Games   Systems games are based on either open or closed family systems; learning and insight can be obtained from both family types. Satir believed that emotional and behavioral disturbances result directly from a member being caught in a closed family system. The closed system does not allow an individual the right to honest self-expression. The family views differences as dangerous, and the overriding "rule" is to have the same values, feelings, and opinions. In the open-system family, honest expression and differences are received as natural occurrences, and open negotiation resolves such differences by "compromising," "agreeing to disagree," "taking turns," or finding win–win solutions.

One set of games entails having family members take roles revolving around the five interactional patterns of behavior discussed earlier: (1) the placater, (2) the blamer, (3) the distractor, (4) the computer, and (5) the leveler. Various games have been constructed from these interactional patterns, including:

1. *Rescue game.* Behaviors 1, 2, 3, and 4 are played. Who plays each role is variable, but each member must remain in this role throughout the session.
2. *Coalition game.* Behaviors 1 and 2 are played. Two people always disagree and gang up on a third person.
3. *Lethal game.* Behavior 1 is used. Everyone agrees.
4. *Growth vitality game.* Each person includes himself or herself and others by honest expression and by permitting others to express themselves (leveling).

These techniques can be broadened beyond the initial family triad by incorporating all family members into a prescribed family situation and assigning various roles to each member. These sessions are vital for younger children who have been ruled by the adage "Children should be seen but not heard." The games aid families in understanding the nature of their own family system. They also allow family members to experience new interactional patterns through identification of their current behavior and insight into possible alternatives. By using the growth vitality game and the leveling role, families can experience movement from a pathological system of interaction to a growth-producing one.

COMMUNICATION GAMES Communication games are aimed at establishing communication skills. Satir believed that an insincere or phony message is almost impossible to deliver if the communicator has skin contact, steady eye contact, or both forms of contact with the listener. One communication game involves having two members sit back to back while they talk. Then they are turned around and instructed to stare into each other's eyes without talking or touching. Satir (1967) reported that this type of interaction leads to many insights concerning the assumptions that each makes about the other's thoughts and feelings. Next, the participants continue to stare and then touch each other without talking. This process continues in steps until each partner is talking, touching, and "eyeballing" the other. Assuming these positions, they are asked to disagree, which Satir found was nearly impossible. People either enjoy the effort or are forced to pull back physically and divert their eyes to get angry.

The counselor's role is an important part of these games. Throughout and after each session, the counselor intervenes and discusses each member's responses, feelings, and gut reactions to himself or herself and to other family members.

THE COUNSELOR'S ROLE In Satir's approach to family counseling, the counselor is a facilitator who gives total commitment and attention to the process and the interactions. The counselor does not take charge and must be careful not to manipulate the participants' reactions and verbalizations. By careful and sensitive attention to each family member's interactions, transactions, and responses (or lack of responses), the counselor can intervene at certain points to ask whether the messages are clear and correct and how a particular person is feeling. Each person thus has a chance to interact or make corrections. For example, the counselor might interrupt the dialogue when one person makes a statement about how another feels or thinks by asking the second person if the statement is accurate and how he or she feels at that moment.

In summary, the counselor intervenes to assist leveling and taking responsibility for one's own actions and feelings. The counselor also intervenes to give quieter family members permission to talk and be heard. Analyzing a present interaction in the counseling setting should help family members understand past hurts and problems. Understanding what patterns produced the trouble also helps family members. With experience in openness and leveling, family members can change their communication style and growth can occur. The family then is better able to continue the discussions, come to new insights, and implement appropriate changes.

CASE STUDIES

People's ability to assume other roles in the family group situation supports the idea that people can change their response roles and families can change their ways of interacting and solving problems. Family members need to learn to share both positive and negative feedback in ways that do not hurt or belittle others. Following is a family role-play transcript in which the leveling response is omitted:

DON: [Father/husband, blaming] Why isn't our dinner ready?

SANDY: [Mother/wife, blaming] What are you yelling about? You've got as much time as I have.

BILL: [Son, blaming] Aw, shut up. You two are always yelling. I don't want any dinner, anyway.

DON: [Blaming] You keep your trap shut. I'm the one who makes the rules around here *because* I'm the one who pays the bills.

SANDY: [Blaming] Says who? Besides, young man, keep your nose out of this.

DON: [Placating] Maybe you'd like to go out to dinner for a change?

SANDY: [Computer] According to the last issue of *Woman's Day*, they say eating out is cheaper than cooking the same things at home.

DON: [Placating] Whatever you would like to do, dear.

BILL: [Placating] You always have good ideas, Mother.

SANDY: [Computer] That's right. I have a list of the restaurants offering specials this week.

Perhaps one good leveling response by any of the family members could have helped these short exchanges. Perhaps Sandy could have said that she needed a rest from a long, hard day and would like to have dinner out. Don could have made a statement rather than asking a phony question. Perhaps a leveling remark by Don might have informed Sandy that he was wondering what she wanted to do about dinner. Bill could have changed his remark to "I really worry when we argue and fight in this family, and I would like this to stop." The counselor's job is to rehearse these leveling responses until the problem is solved in the role-playing setting, and then make plans to try the leveling response in real life.

In a second family session with the counselor present, the Frazier family is seated clockwise around the counselor: Jody, 43-year-old the wife/mother; Frank, 11-year-old son; Larry, 44-year-old husband/father; Joyce, 14-year-old daughter; and Kathy, 16-year-old daughter.

KATHY: Mom, just say yes or no. Am I going to be allowed to go out on weekdays or not?

JODY: Why don't you do what you want? You always do anyway.

COUNSELOR: [To Kathy] How does this make you feel?

KATHY: Angry. I'd like to be able to do what the rest of the kids are doing, but I know Mom and Dad don't approve.

COUNSELOR: That sounds funny because I heard your mom say it was up to you. [To Jody] Is that what you said? Maybe it was the expression on your face and the way you spoke your message to Kathy that made her think you didn't really mean "Do what you want to do."

KATHY: Yes, her stern face said "no."

COUNSELOR: What did she do with her face to tip you off?

KATHY: Well, she squinted her eyes and wrinkled up her nose.

COUNSELOR: It's hard to read your mom's mind, but I am guessing that she thinks nobody listens to her very much. We can check this with her later. But I'm wondering if you have ever felt this way.

KATHY: Sometimes.

COUNSELOR: [To Jody] Do you ever have this feeling?

JODY: I think maybe we've hit on something new.

COUNSELOR: Do you think no one listens to you?

JODY: I have a rough day just keeping house for this family. Larry comes home from work too tired to talk, and all I ever talk to the children about are their fights and arguments. I have to handle all the family problems.

LARRY: Well, my job is all I can handle.

JODY: See, no one listens to my side of the story.

COUNSELOR: [To Larry] Were you aware of what Jody was saying when she said that? What did it feel like, Larry?

LARRY:	It irritates me that everybody thinks it's my fault that things don't go better in our family.
COUNSELOR:	Hold it one minute. Frank is doing something over here.
LARRY:	[To Frank] Settle down over there and shape up.
COUNSELOR:	Let's take some time out and find out what's going on with Frank. I haven't been paying much attention to Frank and Joyce. [To Frank] How did you feel about what was going on over here?
FRANK:	Well, I, uh . . .
JOYCE:	[Blaming Frank] You weren't even paying attention.
KATHY:	Frank, if you move over here with me, we can get along better.
JODY:	[To Larry] Can't you do anything to make him mind me? It's all your fault he acts like he does.
COUNSELOR:	[To Kathy and Larry] An interesting thing happened before Frank started acting up. I was wondering, Kathy, how you felt when your father said to your mother, "It's all my fault that things don't go better in our family."

In this short segment, the counselor attempts to look at present communication patterns and the feelings these patterns conceal. After achieving awareness of the communication blocks, the family can begin to practice leveling as an alternative way of communicating.

Virginia Satir's method could fit well into a systems, structural, or communications approach for counseling families. She focused on developing better family communication by making family members aware of how others in the family react to their communication styles. Satir saw improved communication skills as leading to better family conflict resolution and problem solving.

Shortly before her death, Satir contributed to an article on family reconstruction and sculpting in group counseling (Satir, Bittner, & Krestensen, 1988). The therapists created a drama around each group member, with members starring in their own dramas. Scripts for each drama were developed from family maps, family life fact chronologies, and the family wheel of influence. Core moments of each member's family drama were re-enacted in a psychodrama with group members as family players in the drama. Role-players enacted verbal and nonverbal behaviors of the members in each person's family.

PLAY THERAPY WITH FAMILIES

Play therapy has the advantage of helping children communicate their story to the therapist. Engaging the family in play therapy activities offers a rich observational field for evaluating the family system in action. A principal therapeutic effect from play therapy is the opportunity to help children move from dysfunctional enmeshment with a parent to functional individualization.

Likewise, overly rigid family boundaries might be relaxed to allow for a healthy sense of family cohesion. Similar breakthroughs in family therapy with children have been reported for storytelling, art therapy, and outdoor adventure programs.

Interventions combining family and play therapy have been used in prevention programs in elementary schools (McDonald & Morgan, 1997) and in working with the difficulties of alcoholism (Carmichael & Lane, 1997). Gladding (1993) encourages families to play, but in a manner that is fair, tolerant, and trusting. His admonition was to set up cooperative play environments where everyone shares and wins. Several theorists have provided models for promoting that type of play therapy with families.

Dynamic Family Play Therapy

Harvey (1997) has explained dynamic family play therapy. This type of play therapy engages family members in creative activity by using natural play. The counselor's goal is to help the family develop and increase spontaneity. Creating metaphors about the difficulties in relationships is another goal. In this style of family play therapy, a counselor uses art, drama, movement, and video making to encourage family play. As family members engage in creative play moments, the counselor guides them into initiating interactive play in which metaphors emerge. The metaphors help them experience a mutual catharsis, understanding, and sense of mastery in their experiences with each other.

By helping family members engage in play, counselors help families develop or restart their own natural play with each other. Over the progression of therapy, painful and conflicting issues emerge through play. Counselors can guide family members to generate the naturally creative playful spirit that will produce trust and affiliation. Then counselors can focus on the content of play to help family members reconstruct their relationships. The counselor begins by issuing directive activities such as tug-of-war, scribble war, or follow the leader. The counselor remains alert to avoidance, interference, and resistance. The family members' actions evolve into more elaborate and flexible interactions, and eventually they develop their own unique style of play episodes (Harvey, 1997).

Filial Therapy

Filial therapy is a play therapy method in which the parents are directly involved. Filial therapy is based on the principles of child-centered therapy. Guerney (1997) believes that children's adjustment problems are caused by parents' failing to learn how to understand their children. She defines these problems as learning problems and reasons that teaching parents to conduct child-centered play sessions may overcome parental shortcomings. Parents are so important to their children that she believes acceptance from them would be extremely meaningful for their children.

The goals of filial therapy are to reduce the children's problem behaviors, to help parents gain the skills of the child-centered play therapists to use when relating to their children, and to improve the parent–child relationship. The training proceeds using learning theory and behavioral therapy for the parent training principles by completing the following steps:

1. Introduce parents to methods for conducting client-centered play therapy.
2. Consider the other demands of parents' lives, and assure them they are expected to practice these skills only in the play sessions.
3. Model the behaviors as complete tasks. Wachtel (2001) sees the counselor's role as coaching and modeling helpful parent interactions and behaviors with the child. For example, having parents say, "I am noticing how you are helping yourself not to be scared," rather than "You were brave" promotes more positive self-esteem in the child.
4. Reduce each task to small, separate components and practice each component.
5. Reassemble the complete tasks and role-play without children.
6. Encourage parents to conduct sessions observed by the counselor or held at home and reported to the counselor.
7. Gradually increase the length of the sessions and have home play weekly.

As in child-centered play therapy, the child is encouraged to express his or her needs, thoughts, and feelings. Optimally, during the process, children and parents perceive each other in a more positive light as they learn how to play and talk together more effectively.

STRATEGIC FAMILY PLAY THERAPY

Ariel (1997) explains strategic family play therapy as a form of counseling in which all family members and the counselor play. The play is free, imaginative, and make-believe. Toys, costumes, and props may or may not be used. Ariel reports that strategic family play therapy has been practiced successfully with a wide range of problems and is applicable to families of various cultural and social backgrounds.

Ariel (1997) continues by describing the integrated theory that is based on information processing and the theory of signs. The hypothesis is that the processing of information is aided if the information is associated with the person's central emotions. The information related to the central emotion will be overrepresented in make-believe play, allowing the counselor and player an arena for addressing the themes of the intense emotions. Make-believe play is a moderator, helping family members conduct their transactions and conflicts in a nonthreatening way. The family initiates its play themes, and the counselor then watches and tries to identify unhealthy interactions. Next, the counselor begins play moves, weaving into the family's play but gently steering the activity in well-chosen directions. Those choices are based on the curative properties of play, or what Ariel calls "bug-busters," because they remove or weaken the difficulties in the family's programs.

THERAPLAY

Theraplay is a treatment method modeled after the healthy parent–child inter-action. Koller and Booth (1997) explain this intensive, short-term approach as a therapy in which parents are involved as observers and then as cotherapists. Jernberg (1993) distinguishes theraplay from other approaches by noting it is playful, requiring no toys and few props. The person using this approach avoids questions and focuses on health. The adult structures the sessions, and physical contact is encouraged. The agenda of the sessions is designed to meet the child's needs, encouraging regression and enhancing the parent–child attachment. Theraplay integrates the elements of structure, challenge, intru-sion/engagement, and nurture. Theraplay uses activities that require building trust between children and their parents through physical touch and caring (Crain, 2004; Johnsen, Sundet, & Torsteinsson, 2004). Some examples are holding hands with the child and looking into the child's eyes, having the child jump off a chair into the parent's arms, and trust falls, which require children to fall backward, trusting the parents will be there to catch them. Other activ-ities could include playing patty-cake and stacking hands (putting one hand on top of the other, alternating between the parent's and child's hands). The adult enforces structure by clearly stating safety rules.

CROSS-CULTURAL APPLICATIONS OF FAMILY COUNSELING

Sue and Sue (2003) point out that many different cultures are represented in the United States, and that counselors are finding people from many various cultures coming to their offices for family counseling. Therefore, in addition to understanding psychopathology, counselors need to familiarize themselves with the customs, styles, symbols, and standards of behavior of these diverse groups. Family counselors are not expected to become experts on all cultures, but rather, as mentioned in Chapter 15, they can be open to understanding the uniqueness of every family they counsel, how that family's behavior matches its culture, and how it adapts to U.S. culture (Weitan & Lloyd, 2003).

Yaccarino (1993) has presented some helpful guidelines for adapting struc-tural family therapy to families from different cultures. Using Italian American families as an example, he has detailed several points defining family norms for this culture. For example, individuality is secondary to family obligations; family roles are clearly defined, with the husband/father earning the money, wife/mother maintaining the home, and children working to help with the family finances; and acceptance by the family is a measure of one's accom-plishment. He describes Italian American families as tending toward enmesh-ment, which could support unhealthy symptoms within the family system.

As with any counseling method, family therapists must have thorough knowl-edge of cultural family norms and communication patterns to be effective in their assessment and treatment of families from unfamiliar cultures (Cox, 2003). Tamura and Lau (1992) make many of these same points in their research of Japanese families, as do Szapocznik, Kurtines, Santisteban, and Rio (1990) with

Hispanic families, Soto-Fulp and Delcampo (1994) with Mexican American families, and Becvar and Becvar (2000) with African American families. Jen Der Pan (2000) has found Satir's model used in group counseling to be effective in working with Taiwanese college students who were experiencing family problems.

Richeport-Haley (1998) suggests two models available to family counselors for adapting treatment to multicultural differences. The first model is the directive family approach developed by Jay Haley and based on the work of his mentor, Milton H. Erickson. The directive approach minimizes ethnicity as a factor for change in therapy by focusing on the structural changes within the family. The directive approach encourages behaviors that help the family to become mainstream with their new culture within the context of their cultural belief system. The example given was a couple new to the United States from a culture where the husband is the breadwinner of the home. The wife finds a better job than the husband, which causes conflict between the two. The family counselor's role is to know how to intervene to resolve the conflict. The key is to reframe the situation with respect to the clients' roots and solve the problem without molding the couple to behave like the dominant culture.

Richeport-Haley's (1998) second model is a culture-focused approach in which counselors train in cultural sensitivity. Having completed the training, the counselor has four options when faced with clients holding an alternative belief system. The first option is to minimize the alternative belief system. If a couple moves to the United States from a country where wife beatings are the norm, the legal system can be involved to stop the violence. New and legal behaviors can be practiced during counseling without using the alternative belief system. The second option is to use parts of the alternative belief system. One East Indian couple believed they were being followed by an evil spirit. Working with the couple's belief in spirits, the counselor was able to change the meaning of the spirit from evil to good. The third option is the referral of the client to a recognized healer. The fourth option is collaborating with the healer to bring about needed change.

Perhaps the cultural training combined with the directive model offers the best option available to counselors for meeting the cross-cultural challenge.

FAMILY COUNSELING, ACCOUNTABILITY, AND MANAGED HEALTH CARE

Practitioners of family counseling will do well under managed care if they use approaches that meet the managed care guidelines listed in Chapter 2. Short-term family counseling will find favor with managed care organizations (MCOs) if it helps clients reach specific, measurable goals in ten to fifteen sessions. Goal attainment at termination and maintenance of goal attainment at follow-up sessions are important criteria, as well as client satisfaction and low cost of treatment (Anderson, 2000).

Lee (1997) and Nichols and Schwartz (1998) have observed that the limited mental health coverage under managed care has resulted in the rush to short-term therapy. They favored solution-focused brief family therapy because, as mentioned in Chapter 5, the focus is on finding solutions and gives minimal attention to defining or understanding threatening problems. The goal is to help clients do something different by changing their interactive behaviors or their interpretations of behaviors and situations to develop a solution. The paradoxical strategies mentioned in Chapter 5, as well as reality therapy, rational-emotive-behavioral therapy, cognitive-behavioral therapy, and behavioral methods, could be used in family counseling and meet managed care guidelines.

In general, MCOs favor working with the entire family to remediate causes of problems and to prevent future problems. Remediation and prevention limit future costs. In cases where the MCO covers only individual counseling, it is recommended that the counselor treat the identified client whereas using the rest of the family members as consultants.

SUMMARY

Although this chapter focuses on differences between the schools and proponents of the various family therapies, similarities do exist. First, all agree that families are like engines with interdependent parts. When one part malfunctions, the total engine is adversely affected; that is, one malfunction may cause other parts to break down as well. For lasting behavioral change, therefore, the entire family may need to change. Second (to change the analogy), the family is like a canoe floating downstream; that is, maintaining its balance only because one member of the family is leaning way out over the right side and two other members are tilted slightly to the left. In other words, the canoe is balanced, but uncomfortably so. The goal of family therapy is to relieve the pain by finding a more comfortable balance without upsetting the canoe. Families often say, "Stabilize us, but do not change anything." Third, to bring about successful change, the counselor may need to tip the canoe; however, the counselor's job is to ensure that the emergency process is a safe one. Fourth, all family therapy approaches borrow heavily from the material discussed in the previous chapters, as well as from sources outside this book. Once again, as with other theories, eclectic and integrative themes continue in the current literature on family therapy. Family therapy has branched out to include more nontraditional problems, including delinquency, anxiety disorders, schizophrenia, mood disorders, family violence, family abuse, and addictive disorders. Traditionally, family therapists had been mainly concerned with marital, sexual, and child concerns. Storytelling helps the family members talk about the painful topics that are disrupting the continuation of the larger family story. Loss of a family member through death or divorce is a painful event that is difficult to talk about, yet talking is an effective healing method.

Storytelling can provide the means to speak the unspeakable. Many therapists use storytelling to assess the family system before and after treatment; people think in metaphors and in storytelling formats, and, as we all know, people listen better to stories than to lectures. Riley (1993) makes some of the same points for art therapy as a means of illustrating the family story. From a social constructivist position, art therapy can be used to obtain each family member's invented reality of the family and the world. Art therapy can be a method of assessment, treatment, and evaluation. It provides an opening into unspoken thoughts, feelings, and perceptions and can be a bridge across cultural and perceptual boundaries.

An appropriate concluding statement for this chapter on family counseling is Satir's view of the family and the nature of people. Satir believed everyone has untapped potential and a need for growth and change. Families, viewed as incubators for people, can either block or facilitate the growth of their members.

INTRODUCTION TO FAMILY COUNSELING

To gain a more in-depth understanding of the concepts in this chapter, visit www.thomsonedu.com/counseling/thompson to view a short clip of an actual therapist–client session demonstrating family counseling.

WEBSITES FOR FAMILY COUNSELING

Internet addresses frequently change. To find the sites listed here, visit www.thomsonedu.com/counseling/thompson for an updated list of Internet addresses and direct links to relevant sites.

Family Therapy

Allyn & Bacon, Family Therapy, Bowen

Family Re-Union

Psychwatch

Parenting

Father's World—resource for single fathers

Single Rose—resource for single mothers

Stepfamily Foundation—information on successful step-parenting

REFERENCES

Anderson, C. (2000). Dealing constructively with managed care: Suggestions from an insider. *Journal of Mental Health Counseling, 22,* 343–353.

Ariel, S. (1997). Strategic family play therapy. In K. O'Connor & L. M. Braverman (Eds.), *Play therapy theory and practice: A comparative presentation* (pp. 358–395). New York: Wiley.

Becvar, D., & Becvar, R. (2000). *Family therapy: A systemic integration.* Needham Heights, MA: Allyn and Bacon.

Bowen, M. (1976). Theory in the practice of psychotherapy. In P. J. Guerin, Jr. (Ed.), *Family therapy: Theory and practice* (pp. 42–89). New York: Gardner.

Bowen, M. (1978). *Family therapy in clinical practice.* New York: Aronson.

Bowen, M. (1980). Preface. In E. A. Carter & M. Goldrick (Eds.), *A framework for family therapy* (p. xiii). New York: Gardner.

Campbell, D., & Palm, G. (2004). *Group parent education*. Thousand Oaks, CA: Sage.

Carmichael, K. D., & Lane, K. S. (1997). Play therapy with children of alcoholics. *Alcoholism Treatment Quarterly, 15,* 43–52.

Chasin, R., Roth, S., & Bograd, M. (1989). Action methods in systemic therapy: Dramatizing ideal futures and reformed pasts with couples. *Family Process, 28,* 121–136.

Crain, W. (2004). *Theories of development: Concepts and applications* (5th ed.). Upper Saddle River, NJ: Prentice Hall.

Cox, R. (2003). *Health related counseling with families of diverse cultures: Family, health, and cultural competencies*. Westport, CT: Greenwood Press.

Dattilio, F., & Bevilacqua, L. (2000). *Comparative treatments for relationship dysfunction*. New York: Springer.

DeShazer, S., & Molnar, A. (1984). Four useful interventions in brief family therapy. *Journal of Marital and Family Therapy, 10,* 297–304.

Diamond, G., & Josephson, A. (2005). Family-based treatment research: A 10-year update. *Journal of the American Academy of Child & Adolescent Psychiatry, 44,* 872–888.

Erickson, M., & Zeig, J. (1985). The case of Barbie: An Erickson approach to the treatment of anorexia nervosa. *Transactional Analysis Journal, 15,* 85–92.

Faber, A. (2004). Examining remarried couples through a Bowenian family systems lens. *Journal of Divorce and Remarriage, 40,* 121–133.

Gladding, S. T. (1993). The therapeutic use of play in counseling: An overview. *Journal of Humanistic Education and Development, 31,* 106–115.

Gottman, J. (1979). *Marital interaction: Experimental investigations*. New York: Academic Press.

Gottman, J. (1990). Finding the laws of close personal relationships. *Methods of Family Research, 1,* 249–263.

Gottman, J. (1994). *What predicts divorce?* Hillsdale, NJ: Lawrence Erlbaum.

Gottman, J., Notarius, C., Gonzo, J., & Markman, H. (1976). *A couple's guide to communication*. Champaign, IL: Research Press.

Guerney, L. (1997). Filial therapy. In K. O'Connor & L. M. Braverman (Eds.), *Play therapy theory and practice: A comparative presentation* (pp. 131–159). New York: Wiley.

Haley, J. (1973). *Uncommon therapy*. New York: Norton.

Haley, J. (1976). *Problem-solving therapy*. New York: Harper & Row.

Haley, J. (1984). *Ordeal therapy: Unusual ways to change behavior*. San Francisco: Jossey-Bass.

Harvey, S. (1997). Dynamic family play therapy: A creative arts approach. In K. O'Connor & L. M. Braverman (Eds.), *Play therapy theory and practice: A comparative presentation* (pp. 341–367). New York: Wiley.

Jen Der Pan, P. (2000). The effectiveness of structured and semistructured Satir model groups on family relationships with college students in Taiwan. *Journal for Specialists in Group Work, 25,* 305–318.

Jernberg, A. (1993). Attachment formation. In C. E. Schaefer (Ed.), *The therapeutic powers of play* (pp. 241–265). Northvale, NJ: Jason Aronson.

Johnsen, A., Sundet, R., & Torsteinsson, V. (2004). *Self in relationship: Perspectives on family therapy from developmental psychology*. London: Karnac.

Knauth, D., & Skowron, E. (2004). Psychometric evaluation of the differentiation of self inventory for adolescents. *Nursing Research, 53*(3), 163–171.

Koller, T. J., & Booth, P. (1997). Fostering attachment through family theraplay. In K. O'Connor & L. M. Braverman (Eds.), *Play therapy theory and practice: A comparative presentation* (pp. 204–233). New York: Wiley.

Krautter, T., & Lock, J. (2004). Is manualized family-based treatment for adolescent anorexia nervosa acceptable to patients? Patient satisfaction at the end of treatment. *Journal of Family Therapy, 26,* 66–82.

Lee, M. (1997). A study of solution-focused brief family therapy: Outcomes and issues. *American Journal of Family Therapy, 26,* 77–90.

Loeschen, S. (1998). *Systematic training in the skills of Virginia Satir.* Pacific Grove, CA: Brooks/Cole.

Lurn, W., Smith, J., & Ferris, J. (2002). Youth suicide intervention using the Satir model. *Contemporary Family Therapy, 10,* 139–159.

Madanes, C. (1981). *Strategic family therapy.* San Francisco: Jossey-Bass.

McDonald, L., & Morgan, A. (1997). Families and schools together (FAST): Integrating community development with clinical strategies. *Families in Society, 78,* 140–156.

Minuchin, S. (1967). *Families of the slums.* New York: Basic Books.

Minuchin, S. (1974). *Families and family therapy.* Cambridge, MA: Harvard University Press.

Minuchin, S. (1978). *Psychosomatic families.* Cambridge, MA: Harvard University Press.

Minuchin, S. (1984). *Family kaleidoscope.* Cambridge, MA: Harvard University Press.

Mish, F. C. (Ed.). (2003). *Merriam-Webster's Collegiate Dictionary,* (11th Ed.). Springfield, MA: Merriam-Webster, Inc.

Nichols, M., & Schwartz, R. (1998). *Family therapy: Concepts and methods* (4th ed.). New York: Allyn & Bacon.

Richeport-Haley, M. (1998). Ethnicity in family therapy: A comparison of brief strategic therapy and culture-focused therapy. *American Journal of Family Therapy, 26,* 77–90.

Riley, R. (1993). Illustrating the family story: Art therapy, a lens for viewing the family's reality. *Arts in Psychotherapy, 20,* 253–264.

Satir, V. (1967). *Conjoint family therapy: A guide to theory and technique* (Rev. ed.). Palo Alto, CA: Science and Behavior Books.

Satir, V. (1971, January). Conjoint family therapy. In G. Gazda (Ed.), *Proceedings of a symposium on family counseling and therapy* (pp. 1–14). Athens, GA: University of Georgia.

Satir, V. (1972). *Peoplemaking.* Palo Alto, CA: Science and Behavior Books.

Satir, V., & Baldwin, M. (1983). *Step by step.* Palo Alto, CA: Science and Behavior Books.

Satir, V., Bittner, J., & Krestensen, K. (1988). Family reconstruction: The family within—a group experience. *Journal for Specialists in Group Work, 13,* 200–208.

Satir, V., Stachowiak, J., & Taschman, H. (1975). *Helping families to change.* New York: Tiffany.

Selekman, M. (2002). *Living on the razor's edge.* New York: W.W. Norton & Company.

Simon, R. (1984, November-December). Stranger in a strange land. *Family Networker,* 21–31, 66–68.

Soto-Fulp, S., & Delcampo, R. (1994). Structural family therapy with Mexican-American family systems. *Contemporary Family Therapy, 16,* 349–361.

Sue, D. & Sue, D. (2003). *Counseling the culturally different: Theory and practice* (4th ed.). New York: Wiley.

Szapocznik, J., Kurtines, W., Santisteban, D., & Rio, A. (1990). Interplay of advances between theory, research, and application in treatment interventions aimed at behavior problem children and adolescents. *Journal of Consulting and Clinical Psychology, 58,* 696–703.

Tamura, T., & Lau, A. (1992). Connectedness versus separateness: Applicability of family therapy to Japanese families. *Family Process, 31,* 319–338.

Thomas, M. (1992). *An introduction to marital and family therapy.* New York: Merrill (Macmillan).

Todd, T. (2000). Solution-focused strategic parenting of challenging teens: A class for parents. *Family Relations, 49,* 165–168.

Turner, W., Weiling, E., & Allen, W. (2004). Developing culturally effective family-based research programs: Implications for family therapists. *Journal of Marital & Family Therapy, 30,* 257–270.

Wachtel, E. (2001). *Fostering resiliency through child-in-family therapy.* Retrieved September 8, 2002, from www.athealth.com/practitioner/newsletter/fpn_4_3l.html

Weiten, W., & Lloyd, M. (2003). *Psychology applied to modern life: Adjustment in the 21st century* (7th ed.). Belmont, CA: Wadsworth/Thomson Learning.

Yaccarino, M. (1993). Using Minuchin's structural family therapy techniques with Italian-American families. *Contemporary Family Therapy, 15,* 459–466.

Personality Types

CHAPTER 13

Zelma Lansford

We should spend less time ranking children and more time helping them to identify their natural competencies and gifts and cultivate these. There are hundreds and hundreds of ways to succeed and many, many different abilities that will help you get there.

—Howard Gardner

Carl Jung was born in a small village in Switzerland. The oldest surviving son of a Swiss Reform pastor and a mother who suffered from "nervous disorders," Jung described himself as a solitary child. Possibly because of his parents' marital problems, young Carl and his father shared a bedroom. As an adult, Jung recalled being frightened by strange, mysterious noises coming from his mother's bedroom during the night. These sounds probably led to his having nightmares, and might have contributed to his interest in understanding dreams as a part of his study in later years.

From the age of 11 until he completed medical school, the Jung family lived in Basel. With diverse interests and a solid background in Latin and the classics, young Carl completed his third year of medical school pursuing interests in surgery and internal medicine. When making a decision for specialization, limited finances and a couple of occult experiences piqued his interests in psychopathology. Jung's professors were disappointed in his decision to jeopardize his potential as a physician in favor of what they believed was the absurd field of psychiatry. Despite a lack of professional respect for the domain at that time, Jung accepted his first professional appointment as an assistant at Europe's famous Burgholzi Mental Hospital in Zurich. Jung never worked in general medicine. Instead, he taught at the University of Zurich, and later developed an extensive private psychiatric practice.

For a number of years, Jung enjoyed a close personal relationship with Sigmund Freud. After Jung's 1906 publication of *The Psychology of Dementia*

**Carl Jung
(1875–1961)**

Praecox (schizophrenia), Freud invited Jung and his wife to visit him in Vienna. This visit led to several years of collegial exchange between the two. In one of his frequent letters to Jung, Freud referred to Jung as his adopted son and indicated that he wanted Jung to be his successor to carry on the devotion to his theories. Freud insisted that Jung take the leadership role of the International Psychoanalytic Association and become its first president. Jung, however, became increasingly frustrated by Freud's insistence on the central importance of infantile sexuality. Whereas Freud held that neurosis was rooted in early childhood, as a result of incestuous fantasies and desires connected with the Oedipus complex, Jung thought that the cause of neurosis usually lay in the present. He indicated that the infantile fantasies that Freud detected were secondary phenomena.

The publication of Jung's *Symbols of Transformation,* in which he publicly disagreed with Freud, led to a heated debate during the Fourth Psychoanalytical Congress in Munich in 1912. Freud insisted that the symbol was a distorted expression of inner, unconscious thoughts and was created out of the experience and environment of the individual, whereas Jung believed that the symbol was the psyche's mechanism for transporting information. Although this disagreement contributed to their conflict, Jung's growing dissatisfaction with making "dogma" of childhood sexuality against Freud's insistence on complete obedience was probably the root of their dispute. Accounts of Jung's observations of the relationship between Freud and his wife and Freud and his wife's sister could lead to speculation that Freud's obsession with sex might have been influenced by his "very intimate" relationship with his sister-in-law (Campbell, 1976). In any event, Jung was not a "yes-man" who could be content as a passive advocate for someone else's ideas. Instead, he was flexible, open-minded, and a source of new ideas.

Jung made Zurich his home for most of his adult life. He married in 1903 and lived in a Zurich suburb. Later, he built a country retreat at Bollingen, at the far end of Lake Zurich, where he sometimes saw patients, but more often retreated to contemplate and write. Jung's use of his wife's money, his lifestyle, and his inference of the role of inherited characteristics have been criticized; however, he was a prolific writer and made numerous contributions to the field of psychology. He worked in the United States, lecturing and delving into Native Americans' religious stories and activities. He also traveled to Africa in pursuit of an understanding of the native spirituality and myths. He spent many years attempting to improve methods of psychoanalysis, exploring humans' inner world, and advocating an improved quality of life through self-understanding.

Perhaps because his writing style is not easily read, or because of his interest in mysticism, Jung's work was not totally appreciated during his lifetime. In the 1980s's and 1990s's, partly because of the work of Isabel Myers, Katharine Briggs, Joseph Campbell, and others, there was a resurgence of interest in Jung's ideas and his concepts of how personality is defined by preferences and type.

THE NATURE OF PEOPLE

Jung's view of the nature of people is reflected in his statement, ". . . the sole purpose of human existence is to kindle a light in the darkness of mere being" (Jung, 1961/1989, p. 326). Jung's expansion of Freud's concepts indicated a more positive view of humankind. Freud was a proponent of the scientific concept of *causality*—the idea that everything has a cause. Freud's attempt to point to the cause of a person's present difficulty in childhood trauma was not rejected by Jung, but he expanded the idea with an orientation of *teleology*—meaning that present behavior is determined by future goals, as well as past events. Although Jung respected the person's past, his reason for not relying on the causal component alone might be found in his reluctance to leave the person with feelings of despair and a sense of being a prisoner of past traumas. He suggested that this concept of teleology can stabilize the present by helping the person to gain hope in a future that he or she can create, free of the past. He indicated, "I am neither spurred on by excessive optimism nor in love with high ideals, but am merely concerned with the fate of the individual human being—that infinitesimal unit on whom a world depends, and in whom, if we read the meaning of the Christian message aright, even God seeks his goal" (Jung, 1958, p. 125).

THEORY OF COUNSELING

After an original association with the Freudian school of psychoanalysis, Jung developed his own system of psychoanalysis, calling it *analytical psychology,* using a variety of theories and methods. It is for this reason that there is no standard approach to Jungian therapy. Instead, Jung indicated that, "The more deeply we penetrate the nature of the psyche, the more the conviction grows upon us that the diversity, the multidimensionality of human nature, requires the greatest variety of standpoints and methods in order to satisfy the variety of psychic dispositions" (Jung, 1967, p. 9). One of Jung's major contributions to psychology was through the introduction of new concepts and variations on earlier used terms that led to increased understanding. The following topics outline the major components of Jungian theory.

PSYCHE

Jung used the term *psyche* to describe the part of the personality that embodies thoughts, feelings, and behaviors—both conscious and unconscious. He did not accept the idea that personality is acquired piece by piece and that one's quest must be to attain wholeness. Instead, Jung believed that humans are born whole but that circumstances sometimes cause an erosion of that whole. He believed that the work of the psychoanalyst was to help the patient recover lost wholeness, strengthen the psyche, and enable the person to face future problems without any threat to loss of the whole.

PSYCHIC ENERGY

Jung differed from Freud's belief regarding the libido as representing only sexual drive. He expanded the concept to include the *energy* through which the work of the personality is performed. Storr (1983) described Jung's view of the libido as follows:

When the natural course of a man's development through life was held up, either by misfortune or by his failure to face life's obligations, his libido became turned in upon himself and reactivated the attitudes and feelings of childhood that would normally have been left behind. (p. 17)

Although he could not prove it, Jung indicated strong suspicion about a reciprocal action between physical and psychic energies. He thought that it is possible for psychic energy to become physical energy and vice versa. As with many of his theories, others have explored and substantiated his observations. Jung laid the groundwork for such contemporary ideas as *flow,* the concept described by Csikszentimihalyi (2003) in which an optimal joy, engagement, and fulfillment so occupy the person through high challenge, skills, and effectiveness that time and normal distractions have no meaning as one is propelled by a harmonious rush of energy. As the quality of psychic existence grows, the physical energy for continued productivity *flows.* A similar example is "runners' high" in which athletes describe a sense of euphoria that accompanies strong physical performance. While research continues on the exact physiology, scientists suspect the release of brain chemicals that act as neurotransmitters. Dietrich's (2004) research at Georgia Institute of Technology suggests that anandamide, a lipid molecule, produces the sensation. Perhaps future science will confirm the exact physical relationship between physical and psychic energy.

Consciousness

Consciousness refers to that part of the psyche that is known to the person. Jung developed the concept of four mental functions within the consciousness that he called *thinking, feeling, sensing,* and *intuiting.* In addition, he developed the idea that there are two attitudes that determine orientation of the consciousness, *extraversion* and *introversion.* Although Jung believed that all people use these functions and attitudes, the levels to which they use them consciously lead to what he called *individuation,* a process by which uniqueness is attained. He believed that the goal of individuation should be to know oneself as completely as possible. Jung concluded that the process of achieving individuation through the conscious led to a new element—the *ego.*

The Personal Unconscious

Jung believed that experiences that did not gain recognition by the ego do not disappear from the psyche but are stored in an adjoining level of the mind—the unconscious. They are available to the consciousness when the ego allows them to pass into greater awareness. This idea emphasizes Jung's concept of the ego as the gatekeeper or the manager of the personality.

The Ego

A refinement from Freud, Jung used the term *ego* to describe the *organization of information, feelings, memories, and perceptions.* Jung determined that the ego acts as a gatekeeper to the consciousness, and unless the ego acknowledges the approach of a new idea, thought, feeling, memory, or perception, it cannot be brought into consciousness. It is probably for this reason that some people are described as being not really "open to new ideas." Their egos become very selective gatekeepers, not allowing many new ideas to pass into their consciousness. According to Jung, the ego provides identity to the personality through the selection and elimination of any material that is not consistent with the personality and that might be overwhelming or objectionable.

Jung believed that the dominant function (thinking, feeling, sensing, or intuition) is a major determinanter of what the ego gatekeeper will allow to penetrate the consciousness. In essence, if the person has a dominant function for sensing, when facts are presented at the gate, the ego is more likely to allow them into the consciousness, especially if they are from a strong experience. Thus, the ego gate gatekeeper for the sensing preference is likely to be more open to facts, details, and concrete data than for concepts or big picture ideas. For example, when a social studies teacher is presenting material about the American colonists' decision to separate from England, he or she will capture the attention of the sensing types by showing the children a copy of the Declaration of Independence and what the colonists were saying. The teacher will point to the signatures and talk about the bravery of the men who signed the document. A picture of Thomas Jefferson and information about his role, followed by a photograph of Independence Hall in Philadelphia and a review of the activities that led up to the Declaration on July 4, 1776, will help to captivate the interests of the sensing types. The teacher will then emphasize the effect that this document had on the English people, their reaction to it, and its impact on the rest of the world. At this point, the instructor has also achieved comprehension for the intuitive types. Their preference for understanding the whole or the context may mean that their gatekeeper is not fully open to this new information until it can be put into the setting of the world in 1776. The facts of "life, liberty, and the pursuit of happiness" enter through the gate when they fit the whole.

The youthful ego seems to be a gatekeeper who enjoys swinging on the gate to welcome new information, feelings, and perceptions into consideration. If at first the ego does not allow new information to enter, it is also capable of reversing its decision and re-evaluating the situation. This is an enormous opportunity for parents, teachers, counselors, and other adults to encourage openness to new learning in the young child. By ensuring psychological safety and security, adults can increase the child's ego strength in managing the personality and widen the child's view to new learning and new experiences.

THE EGO GATEKEEPER

Jung also believed that anxiety can increase the ego's intensity, thereby decreasing the ego's openness. In popular parlance, the term *ego* is often used to describe someone whose anxiety or lack of individuation keeps ideas and experiences away by limiting the amount of new material from the consciousness. This protects and allows the person to cling to a preferred or overly important image of the self. Obviously, in order to persuade the ego gatekeeper to be open to a new idea or action, it is essential to avoid confronting the ego with any-thing that might cause anxiety or be threatening to the image that it is protect-ing. Sometimes in interactions, it is easy to see that another person is becoming defensive about what is being said. This defensiveness arises from the ego's attempt to "defend" the gatekeeping position and resist letting any informa-tion through that might not fit with the concepts and ideas that are already imbedded in the consciousness. This filtering to "save face" can result in denial of information and lead to faulty decision making, as demonstrated in the investigation of the 1986 explosion of the space shuttle, *Challenger*. Despite considerable indications that the launch was risky, several of the engineers involved had ego gatekeepers that denied the validity of the information regarding a possible weather-related malfunction of an O-ring. For them, the ego gatekeeper attempted to avoid humiliation and put a good face on NASA's need to launch. When delving into numerous historical events, it is obvious how the role of the ego gatekeeper keeper prevented certain realities from entering the consciousness. It was unthinkable to King George that the American colonists should not comply with the rules for every British Colony.

Some diplomacy may be required to avoid evoking defensiveness. Usually, carefully chosen words are necessary to induce sufficient openness to achieve the purpose. With children, it is essential to help them avoid denial, and, instead, develop confidence that allows the ego gatekeeper to become a wise and informed decision maker.

At times, the ego gatekeeper is more intent upon consistency than on effec-tiveness. The gatekeeper ushers in only the facts and information that are con-sistent with what is already there, whereas sound decision making requires consideration of a wide range of facts and information to ensure that effective decisions are made. The exclusion of any information that does not fit what already resides in the consciousness can result in a mistaken conclusion. Without any disagreeing facts or pertinent data, the easy conclusion is, "This is correct." The results leave one being right but not effective! For example, when a man says to a woman, "That dress is ugly," it may be a factual statement; the observer may be right, but the communication is not effective." When the eighth grader storms out of class saying, "Mr. Smith is boring!" the student may be correct, but the action results in time in detention. Mr. Smith may be a compe-tent teacher, but his gatekeeper keeper has led him to the erroneous conclusion that the current students are the same as in previous years. He may not have rec-ognized the need to be effective in challenging a very bright student who seeks more advanced learning activities. The student may be correct in his assessment of Mr. Smith's teaching method but ineffective in his response. If the ego gate-keeper only allows in information that is consistent with the data already there, one may be like the driver of a small sports car who sees a green light and assumes that he has the right-of-way of way. He proceeds across the intersec-tion, despite the fact that a large truck is ignoring the red light. The driver of the sports car has the right-of-way, and the driver is *right,* but the driver may also be *dead right*. Situations arise in the classroom almost daily in which one's ego gatekeeper can enable one to be *right,* but not *effective*.

COMPLEXES

Complexes described Jung's concept of a large group of ideas or common experiences stored within the unconscious. Jung (1961/1989) indicated that they "interfere with the intentions of the will and disturb the conscious performance; they produce disturbances of memory and blockages in the flow of associations" (p. 393). For example, if the child is bombarded over a period of time with numerous experiences and messages indicating incompetence, then anxiety will probably cause the ego to be protective and not allow information to enter the consciousness. Because the information is repressed in the conscious, it is moved to the unconscious. Although the child may be unaware of the information of "inferiority," its presence in the unconscious may hinder the child's normal life and may be observable in the child's actions. The child's lack of self-esteem may result in lower classroom performance and hesitance to try new experiences. Jung's view was that psychoanalysis could bring the information of the complexes into the conscious and dissolve it, freeing the person from the dysfunctional grip of this *inferiority complex*.

INDIVIDUATION

Jung used the metaphor of a plant to describe the growth of the individual psyche and how each person becomes unique. The seed represents a "whole" that is capable of becoming balanced parts of the plant, adapted to specific needs: roots, stems, or leaves. He believed that each person is a whole with balance and unity. Jung's primary developmental concept was *individuation*, a process by which the person becomes a psychological individual, developing specific functions but remaining a balanced whole. This process of individuation takes place through expanding consciousness by knowing and understanding oneself as completely as possible. Jung believed that the purpose of psychotherapy was to help the person find balance and restore "wholeness" through increased self-knowledge.

To expand the plant metaphor, the highly individuated person could be compared with a highly complex plant. This person might be represented by a seed, or an acorn. The acorn's potential is there but undeveloped. The acorn is a whole but lacks individuation within the whole. The oak's potential is realized as its complex systems are developed. The person's potential is unleashed when maturity and growth allow the complexity and uniqueness to flower.

DREAMS

Jung called dreams the "product of psychic activity occuring during sleep (Jung, 1958/1991, p. 59). He believed dreams to be the clearest path to the unconscious mind, because they are not under the influence of the will or consciousness. Although Freud analyzed specific dreams, Jung saw value in considering recurring themes or dreams in series. He did not believe in using a "dream dictionary" or a defined set of symbols to interpret dreams, but rather preferred to consider the individual circumstances and the condition of the dreamer.

Jung believed that when people encountered difficulty in relationships with others, it would be reflected in their psyche; therefore, it could also be reflected in their dreams. By helping people to uncover their internal disharmony, he hoped that it could lead them toward improved external relationships. In children, the occurrence of frequent nightmares or frightening dreams may be an indication of abuse, trauma, or excessive fears—real or imagined.

PROGRESSION AND REGRESSION

Using the term *progression* to refer to a person's psychological adaptation to daily experiences, Jung (1973, p. 39) believed that *regression* describes the backward movement of the libido. He saw that withdrawing into oneself and into earlier periods, one could possibly activate unconscious material and use it to resolve current issues.

THE COLLECTIVE UNCONSCIOUS

Although his descriptions were somewhat limited by the science and technology of his time, Jung regarded the brain as an evolutionary product of many generations of mutations. He saw the result as an increase in humans' chances of survival on the planet. Jung pioneered the idea that the mind is not solely the product of environmental experiences but also contained cumulative psychological predispositions.

ARCHETYPES

Jung devoted much of the last part of his career to the study of archetypes. He was fascinated by the common, recurring themes in myths and stories from varied cultures throughout history. He believed that they spring from unconscious images of instinctual behavioral patterns. Birth, rebirth, death, power, the hero, the child, the trickster, the demons, the wise old man, the earth mother, mountains, rivers, fire, and other objects are endless repetitions that have engraved experiences into the psyche as forms without content. They are not visual images in the mind, but prototypes that represent the possibility of a certain type of perception or action. Jung believed that such archetypes are universal, with everyone inheriting the same basic images, while at the same time, parental and environmental influences determine the variations. He believed that the following four archetypes of the self, anima and animus, shadow, and persona are a part of every human person.

THE SELF   A central focus of Jungian psychology is the concept of a total personality or psyche. It was regarded by Jung as the central archetype in the collective unconscious. He did not believe that the self can become evident until middle age or when the personality is fully developed. Perhaps self-knowledge is the means to self-realization. A person cannot fulfill oneself without fully knowing and understanding oneself.

THE ANIMA AND ANIMUS   Jung called the *anima* the inward feminine side of the male psyche and the *animus* the inward masculine side of the female psyche. These terms were used to describe the traits in both sexes that are not associated with gender. "Since the image is unconscious, it is always unconsciously projected upon the person of the beloved, and is one of the chief reasons for passionate attraction or aversion" (Jung, 1961/1989, p. 391). Jung noted that Western civilization has placed value on behavior that is consistent with gender. His emphasis appeared to be, not so much on the particular behavior, as on the conflict that is produced by the expectation of conformity.

THE SHADOW   An archetype of the same sex, the *shadow* includes everything in the psyche outside consciousness and contains more of a person's basic animal instincts than any other archetype. For Jung, the shadow represents the hidden, repressed, guilt-laden part of the personality that resides in the unconscious.

THE PERSONA   From the idea of a mask worn by an actor in a drama, Jung used the term *persona* to describe the display of a public facade for the purpose of gaining acceptance in society and sometimes referred to it as the "conformity" archetype. The Persona is a major asset in helping the individual to interact with others. Difficulty arises, however, when the individual identifies more with the Persona (mask) than with the whole self. The ego's identification with the persona is called *inflation;* thus, the common expression, "inflated ego" is used to describe one who has an exaggerated sense of self-importance as a facade.

References to an inflated ego have evolved into common usage and are often used to describe objectionable behaviors. The term *confident* generally describes one who knows and understands the potential and the limits of his or her abilities and skills. The term *inflated ego* implies an exaggerated sense of self-importance that is not based on a real estimation of abilities and skills. The inference is that the facade connotes a fear of inferiority. It could be compared with a Hollywood set that appears to the movie camera to be a row of buildings, but is really only a front with nothing behind the doors. Perhaps the facade, with its inflated ego, is an attempt to protect others from discovering that there is something lacking behind this "front." In its inflated state, the ego can never back up and admit a mistake. It is this inflated front that allows very little penetration of new information, only that which fits the fantasized picture of the self—the facade. Real achievement builds genuine confidence and does not appear to inflate the ego.

Fear of failure, sense of inadequacy, insecurity, and/or abuse can cause the facade to be so inflated that the "ego gatekeeper" becomes a barrier to allowing any new information, ideas, or perceptions to go through the gate and into the conscious. When dealing with people with an inflated ego, it helps to make any new information or ideas fit with what is already there. This technique lessens the threat and allows the inflated ego to keep the facade in intact and not become defensive. In dealing with someone who has an inflated ego, it helps to see the goal as being effective with that person, getting what is needed, and not worrying about the encounter.

When teachers or counselors have an inflated ego, they hide behind their facade of "knowing all of the answers." This can impede the learning and impact appropriate relationships with children. Another hazard of the inflated ego is that it is more difficult to develop trust among people if there is an inflated ego in the group. Others seem always to suspect the facade. Trust is usually only invested in people who appear to be real and genuine. Because it is difficult to trust someone without really knowing that person, the facade can become a barrier that prevents people from believing that they know and understand the real person. Obviously, a counselor's inflated ego would inhibit the bond that needs to be developed with the child for the counseling to be effective.

Self-doubt, fear of humiliation, and insecurity appear to be ego inflators in children. The inflated ego in the child is often an indication of trauma or fear of inadequacy and should be explored by the astute counselor. Indicators of an inflated ego may be fanciful stories, exaggerated accounts of accomplishment, or attempts to conceal the child's real circumstances.

Word Association

Sir Francis Galton (1822–1911) had attempted to establish an intelligence test based upon verbal response speed. The subject would be told to respond to each of a series of words with the first word that came into his or her head. Of course, the test was of little use in determining intellectual capacity, but Jung found that a small adaptation could lend new usefulness. Jung conducted the test in a similar manner, but noted response times and any delays. Often, the subjects were unaware of delays. Jung's probing demonstrated that the word had evoked an emotional response. Later, he studied the expression of emotion and changes in pulse rate, breathing, and in the electrical conductivity of the skin. Jung's work served as a forerunner of the development of the modern polygraph test.

Psychological Types

Much of the early work of Freud and others in the field of psychology came through their experiences in mental hospitals and with abnormal patients with abnormal behaviors. This was also true of Jung's early work. His ideas about *type,* however, were initiated by his studies of people beyond those with abnormal behaviors and formed the basis for later work that would distinguish the concept of *type* and make it an especially useful concept for the general public. Jung (1961/1989) described the origin of his ideas for writing *Psychological Types*, published in 1921, in his autobiographical work, *Memories, Dreams, Reflections:*

> This work sprang originally from my need to define the ways in which my outlook differed from Freud and Adler's. In attempting to answer this question, I came across the problem of types; for it is one's psychological type which from the outset determines and limits a person's judgment. . . . The book on types yielded the insight that every judgment made by an individual is conditioned by his personality type and that every point of view is necessarily relative. (p. 209)

In trying to understand his differences with Freud and Adler, Jung attempted to analyze the conflict between Adler and Freud in order to learn something to apply to his own break with Freud. He realized that his conflict with Freud, as well as Adler's with Freud, was not a simple matter of a difference of opinion. Instead, he recognized that both were fundamentally different approaches; therefore, he decided to demonstrate how both Freud's and Adler's theories could be applied to actual cases. He conducted his comparative study in great detail over a considerable period. This led to Jung's deduction that Adler's approach was largely internal—the attempt to overcome the childhood feelings of inferiority with feelings of power and superiority. In contrast, he saw Freud's approach as external in the child's response to the Oedipus complex, the child's attitude toward the parent of the opposite sex, coupled with a desire to displace the parent of the same sex. Jung saw these two approaches as the result of an orientation:

> Freud, the *extravert*, was focused on the outer world and responses to it.
>
> Adler, the *introvert*, was focused on the inner world and its responses and reflections.

Some experts have disagreed with Jung and have made a strong case for Freud's having beening an introvert. As indicated earlier, perhaps Freud's greatest contribution to psychology is his stimulation of others. His actual preference for introversion or extraversion is less important than the concept that his behavior inspired Jung to formulate.

As Jung thought about himself, he recognized that he was also an *introvert*; however, this concerned Jung as he realized how different he was from Adler. Musing on these differences led Jung to the realization that there are also two pairs of mental processes: *sensing* and *intuiting*, which relate to taking in and using information, along with *thinking* and *feeling*, which relate to drawing conclusions and making decisions. He realized that these are the "tools" for specific mental objectives. He indicated that these preferences are innate and become evident even in the very young child (Jung, 1921/1990). Jung continued to work on the development of these concepts for several years through observations of countless patients and other people. He refined and elaborated on these conclusions, also developing the idea of *dominant* and *auxiliary* functions in which there is greater reliance on one function over the others.

Energizing

Extravert (E) _____|_____ Introvert (I)

Gathering Information and Attending

Sensing (S) _____|_____ Intuition (N)

Deciding

Thinking (T) _____|_____ Feeling (F)

Living

Judging (J) _____|_____ Perceiving (P)

Although Jung's attempt to understand his differences with Freud was the catalyst for developing the concept, psychological types are a part of his larger theory that described the progress of consciousness and how people have different pathways to development. Jung continued his analysis and research on type during the course of his work with patients. It is an incredibly complex theory that is merely summarized in this chapter. Jung's ideas about type were only partially accepted by several decades of psychologists. It was not until two women developed an application for Jung's complexity, that his ideas could be implemented and become a tool for establishing individual preferences and encouraging effective utilization of the diversity among people.

In 1942, a 44-year-old housewife, encouraged by her mother's interests in writing, began the development of an instrument that would become the key to applying Jung's concept that apparently random behavior is not really random, but rather the result of inborn *preferences*. Because Isabel Briggs Myers wanted to pursue *everyday* behavior, she used *everyday* language, thus creating a very simple approach to a highly complex theory. Although lacking the formal training needed for such research, Myers was a brilliant scholar who pursued relentlessly the knowledge necessary for her project. She had absorbed her father's scientific approach and her mother's devotion to Jung. Isabel had accompanied her mother, Katherine Briggs, to a meeting with Jung in New York in 1937 when he was giving lectures at Yale University. She also attempted a conference with Jung during a 1950 family trip to Switzerland. Unfortunately, Jung was ill at the time, and other subjects had supplanted his interest in type, but he wrote a kind letter to her, complimenting the *Type Indicator* and her work. First published by Educational Testing Service (ETS) and then, Consulting Psychologists Press (CPP), the *Myers Briggs Type Indicator*® (MBTI®) (1998) is available only to users who have been qualified through special training or who hold graduate degrees in psychology and related areas. This control is reflective of Myers's fear that the instrument might be misused, as when she saw a bank terminate all of its employees who indicated a preference for *intuition,* viewing them as troublemakers. Myers and Briggs' intent was that the MBTI® become a positive tool for helping people to understand themselves and to make better choices, thus improving their decisions. Myers also saw the potential for people to be more understanding and accepting, thus enhancing interpersonal interactions (Saunders, 1991). Although attempts to classify personality date back to ancient Greece, interest in Jung's original concepts and perhaps the success of the MBTI® have led to additional typology attempts. Because these aspects are something basic in the personality, it is not surprising that other authors have become alert to preferences and type. Although some offer intriguing insights and useful information, even comparing personalities to colors, the decades of research and solid validity of the MBT® make it the first choice for applying Jung's concepts to adults. It is helpful to consider this key to Jung in working with parents, teachers, and one's own type. (The key to using Jung with children is discussed later in this chapter.)

MYERS BRIGGS TYPE INDICATOR (MBTI®)

What mother and daughter were able to achieve was an application for Jung's idea that apparently "chance variation in human behavior is not due to chance; it is in fact the logical result of a few basic, observable *preferences*" (Myers, McCaulley, Quenk, & Hammer, (1999, p. 11). The MBTI® is an inventory based on several assumptions, one of which is that people can give an indication of their *preferences that combine to form type,* directly or indirectly, on a self-report inventory. The questions in the MBTI® have no intrinsic good or bad, right or wrong answers. The descriptions of *type* focus on *what is right with people.* This emphasis on *normal* and valuable differences makes the instrument especially useful in all kinds of situations, from counseling to education and business, because it gives the respondents a sense of worth and dignity concerning their own qualities. Many psychological instruments are constructed for the purpose of giving the counselor information about the client—intelligence, psychopathology, or career interests. Whereas most instruments give information back to the person through a qualified professional, the MBTI® information is intended for the person using the instrument and complete results are given to the user. The MBTI® is available at most career, college, and counseling centers, as well as in many business organizations. Websites listed at the end of this chapter are available for qualified sources for using the MBTI® and obtaining feedback. Myers, et al. (1999) indicated the objective of the instrument as the identification of four basic preferences. "The indices EI, SN, TF, and JP are designed to point in one direction or the other. They are not scales for measurement of traits or behaviors. While letters indicate the *direction* of the preference, the numerical score indicates the *strength* of the preference" (p. 3). Myers liked to compare these preferences to the preference that most humans have for using one hand more than the other. People typically use both sides of each preference, although not with equal liking. Myers was adamant that there is no one best preference and no perfect score on the MBTI®.

Jung, together with Myers and Briggs, gave special meaning to some words in their classifications. They are as follows: *energizing, attending, deciding, and living.*

Energizing   The attitude that determines how a person gets renewed psychic energy.

Extravert (E): The preference for interaction and drawing energy from people, activities, and the environment.

Introvert (I): The preference for drawing energy from within, from internal concepts and ideas.

Extravert does not mean "talkative," and Introvert does not mean "shy." Rather, this preference is an attitude that relates to gaining psychic energy or "re-energizing" from an external or internal world. It is observable in the individual's preference to "talk things out" (E) or "think things through before speaking" (I). The focus for re-energizing, it may influence the way in which people prefer to socialize, but neither preference ensures nor degrades one's ability to enjoy and be effective with people. For example, an Introvert and an Extravert can go to a lively party and interact with many people, having an equally good experience. The Introvert will go home and prefer to go straight to bed, being exhausted from interacting with so many people. In contrast, the Extravert will go home and need to "unwind," feeling energized by all of the interactions with people. The same is true of children. John, an Introvert, is a handsome 8-year-old, the son of an engineer and an artist. At school, John is reserved but talks about his science projects with excitement and animation. When he arrives at home, however, John prefers time in his room to tinker with models or to wander through the wooded area in the backyard before dinner. With the family, he happily takes his turn describing his day. The conversation follows the solitude that John needs to re-energize after he has used energy in the many interactions of the school day. John's mother understands his need for some quiet time and does not bombard him with questions or attempt extensive conversation when he first arrives from the school bus. Conversely, Jo, who is an Extravert, needs her mom's attention as soon as she opens the car door. She is eager to tell her parent all about her social studies lesson and about the argument that she had on the playground. At home, she engages neighborhood friends for impromptu soccer and play. After dinner, she spends time alone reading, but only after some lively conversation with her parent and sibling. Introverts and Extraverts re-energize differently.

Attending   The function of finding-out, gathering, and taking-information:

Sensing (S): The preference for taking-information through the senses—sight, touch, and hearing, leading to a focus on facts, the concrete, and the present.

Intuition (N): The preference for using the facts to make a bigger picture of what is visible beyond the information from the senses to see connections and possibilities.

A major influence on how people learn, accept new ideas, and take actions, the *Sensing* (S) and *Intuition* (N) preferences impact the ego in its gatekeeper role. How the information is presented impacts how readily the gate swings open or remains closed. This function is especially relevant in such situations as the classroom. Sensing types need details and specific facts, whereas those with a preference for Intuition want to see the big picture and how the issue or event fits into the larger concept. To be effective, people need both the facts and details (S), together with the big picture (N). The attending function is not an "either/or" process. Instead, it determines which is considered first and on which greater reliance may be placed.

In the United States, Sensing types are in the majority and learn best when material is concrete and proceeds step-by-step with examples and hands-on experiences. Specific facts come easier than the connections between facts and their interpretation. It is easier for Sensing types to learn about what is real than to learn symbolic concepts. Intuitive types score somewhat higher on reading tests and appear to read more books. They are in the majority in programs for the "gifted."

This preference for how one takes in information may have a significant influence on success in school. Because many educational institutions must be designed for facilitating the learning of large groups, rather than for individuals, the learning preference of each student may or may not be accommodated. It is unfortunate that some children grow into adulthood with a self-concept that is based on their belief that they are not very smart. In reality, they may be very capable, but they may have had preferences for learning that were not accommodated by their schools. The Sensing types may be successful in a fact-based high school course where the concrete is emphasized—dates, places, and specific facts—but may be have to work harder in a university course that emphasizes context analysis.

When it is possible to match one's preferred means of taking in information to an area of study, it is possible to enhance success. Terry knew that he needed a minimum grade of B in history to maintain his college scholarship. He carefully researched the history professors who taught the course and obtained their syllabi. Recognizing that one professor required knowledge of facts such as, "When did Columbus discover America, and what were the routes of each voyage?" The other professor required comprehension of significance, such as, "What effect did Columbus's voyage have upon Spain, and how did this period of discovery impact Western Europe?" Knowing that he was an INTP, Terry chose the latter professor and placed himself in the best learning environment. Conversely, when such a choice is not possible, it can be reaffirming to understand why one must work harder. When Jamie, an ESTJ, took an art course in sculpture because he thought that he would find the construction and mechanical aspects interesting, he struggled and had to seek assistance with the design aspects. Although he was superb with the logical, detailed composition, he had difficulty seeing the possibilities for the larger designs. Understanding his type kept him from wasting energy or feeling stupid and allowed him to be very open to seeking the teacher's coaching with the design aspects.

Deciding The function that is a preference for decision making:

Thinking (T): The preference for analytical, logical, objective, "tough-minded" decisions.

Feeling (F): The preference for value-based, person-centered, empathetic decisions.

It is important not to regard Feeling types as "emotional" and Thinking types as "cold." Rather, they are part of the functions that Jung described and are paths through which people come to conclusions and reach decisions. Both preferences are important for effective decision making. Thinking types contribute by providing logical, rational, analysis and focus on the tasks. Feeling types provide personal involvement and seek harmony, focusing on the effect that the decision will have on people. These people may be especially reactive to insensitivity and cynicism.

Significantly more women prefer Feeling and more men prefer Thinking as their first consideration for deciding. Probably because this preference also appears to be a part of the gender expectation in many parts of the world, males who have a preference for Feeling and females for Thinking may not seem typical and may experience frustration in school interactions. Joel, a large, handsome 10-year-old boy with strong preferences for Feeling, felt rejected in many situations because he was constantly told, verbally and through inference, that he needed to keep his emotions under control. As might be expected, he was taunted as being a "sissy" because he became teary eyed at sad situations and overly expressive when excited. It was not until Joel became a soloist with the local boys' choir that he was able to become comfortable using his enthusiasm and passion as an asset. Joel became a student leader in high school. After college, he was recruited by a large sales organization where he ultimately became vice president. Again, he found a situation in which his preference for Feeling was an asset. Conversely, Tina, a small sixth grader who excelled in math and science was constantly told by her peers that she was not "soft" enough and that the boys would not like her. As an adolescent, Tina dressed in a very feminine style to soften her appearance as she learned to understand her preference and continued to pursue her interest in becoming a physician.

Effective decision making is not achieved by using one preference alone. Instead, this preference is about what is considered first. Mature decision makers consider both preferences, but they understand where they begin and on what they rely.

Living   A preference for the person's orientation to the outer world:

Judging (J): A preference for external order, organization, schedules, systems, planning, and achieving closure.

Perceiving (P): A preference for flexibility, spontaneity, adaptability, and options, with less need for external order.

People with a preference for Judging (J) are decisive (but are not necessarily *judgmental*) and like reaching closure about how they want to be in the world. They like to live in a systematic, sequential, precise, well-planned environment. They love checklists and timetables. It is as if they have an agenda, and anything that comes into their world, must be put on that agenda that often seems "carved in stone." Kroeger and Thuesen (2002) assert that "moan time" is necessary before those with a preference for Judging can insert new data into their agenda. Perhaps that is why Mason whines, "Do I have to do the math now?" He likes math, but he is resisting the change in schedule. Judging types may not necessarily object to a new idea or information, but they may resist adding anything to their already set agenda. The world of education, and much of the world of business fit the Judging concept. Systems, schedules, order, and follow-through abound. People with a preference for Judging usually find this comfortable and are often drawn to such an environment.

In contrast, people with a preference for Perceiving (P) are not necessarily "perceptive," but they like to live with spontaneity, adaptability, and a flexibility that allows them to keep their options open. They have less need for order and schedules and seem to perform most comfortably in less structured environments. They are often curious children who have a much clearer idea of what they do not like than what they actually like. The Perceiving types can be found in the creative corner, less structured activities, and last coming in from the playground.

Perhaps one of the easier preferences to observe, it can be an issue in interpersonal friction and an impediment to parent and child or teacher and student relationships as different choices for order collide. The Judging parent may attempt to force a Perceiving child to be neat and decisive. Unfortunately, this puts the child in a world that is not comfortable. The child may prefer to keep options open, but the parent insists on decisions, saying, "Make up your mind now and let's move on!" For the Perceiving child, this restricts options and seems too final. The Judging parent likes "a place for everything and everything in its place," but for the Perceiving child, "out of sight is out of mind," so the child wants everything stacked on the desk and toys readily accessible. The reverse conflicts take place when Judging child is seen by the Perceiving parent as rigid or obsessive. The Judging child is cajoled to relax and be less of a "neatnick." The same kinds of conflicts can take place in the classroom.

It is important to note that the Judging or Perceiving preferences are not necessarily about neatness. Judging types can be sloppy and Perceiving types can be neat. Rather, it is about the preference for one's orientation to the world. Neither Judging nor Perceiving types are good or bad, but it is tragic when children are forced to be different from their preference. This results in the falsification and disrespect of uniquenesses that Jung and Myers cautioned against. In analyzing the Judging and Perceiving preferences, Myers extended Jung's model by making explicit one aspect of type theory that was implied but not developed in Jung's work.

To understand his theory, one must comprehend Jung's uses of the terms *judgment* and *perception*. For Jung, perception includes the many ways of becoming aware of things. He considered that *sensing* and *intuition* are the two categories of perception. Jung believed that judging is about all the ways of coming to conclusions about what has been perceived and that *thinking* and *feeling* are the two kinds of judgment. Every waking activity is concerned with *perceiving* and *judging*. Thus, type differences appear in a very wide range of human activities, including learning, communicating, and working.

The Type Table™

Obviously, the four pairs of preferences of the MBTI® can be combined in 16 different ways. Isabel Myers devised a grid in which she arranged the 16 types according to a clever rationale and included a short sketch of each of the types. It is a visual means for people to gain an understanding of Jung's overall concept in the interplay among the various combinations of preferences. A complete profile of each of the 16 types is found in *Introduction to Type®* (Myers, Kirby, & Myers, 1970/1998). A more detailed description may be found in Myers and Myers' *Gifts Differing* (1980/1995), and in several other publications on type.

Dominance

The incredible complexity of Jung's theory becomes evident in the concept of dominance. For each type, Jung observed that there is a preferred ranking that reflects a specific attitude. People use their favorite or dominant function most in the world in which they are energized. For example, the Extraverts (E) use their dominant function in the outer world of people and experiences, whereas Introverts (I) use their dominant function in the inner world of thoughts and ideas. The third and fourth are assumed to be less developed and may be the focus of growth in maturity.

Temperament

Building on the work of Myers and Briggs, David Kieirsey (1998) included the ancient concept of temperament and somewhat similar interpretation by placing major importance on the preferences of *sensation* and *intuition*. Although considering extraversion and introversion to be important, they were regarded as minor when compared with the ways that people think. By linking the preferred information-gathering function to the deciding function for *intuitives* and to the living and ordering function for *sensors,* Kiersey achieved a synthesis that he called *temperaments*.

NF	NT	SJ	SP
Intuitive/Feeling	Intuitive/Thinking	Sensing/Judging	Sensing/Perceiving

With no acknowledgment of dominant or auxiliary functions, and little importance placed on extraversion/introversion, this model reduces Jung's concepts considerably. Although there is an inventory based on the temperament model, it does not have the same statistical validity and reliability as the MBTI®. As a concept, however, temperaments can be useful as a shortcut to behavioral insights. One useful application is how these four temperaments may prefer the learning environment to be structured. Because counseling is often called a process in learning, these considerations are especially useful in structuring the child's counseling environment, regardless of the counseling theory that is used.

PREFERENCES IN LEARNING

Different types may like learning in similar ways or become bored by the same things *but for different reasons*. For example, the ENFP and the ISTJ may enjoy "hands-on" manipulatives, but the attraction for the ENFP comes from the interaction and experience, whereas being able to discover the facts and control the action appeals to the ISTJ.

Extroverts generally like to "talk it out," to verbalize ideas, brainstorm, and discuss. Because extroverts often "do not know what they think until they say it," talking about the subject can help them to process and remember. Conversely, introverts like to contemplate and think about what they are learning before discussing it. They may prefer writing about the subject more than talking and discussing. Different learning styles appeal to different temperaments.

NF	NT	SJ	SP
Who	Why	What	When
Experience	Experiment	Find the facts	Here and now
Interact	Design	Construct	Act
Context/big picture	Conceptualize	Specific details	Realism
Create	Discover	Read/listen	Craft it/fix it
Inspire	Challenge	Observe	Show and share
Explore possibilities	Change	Make rules	Make practical
Please the teacher	Debate	Diagram	Draw/illustrate
Help people	Research	Order/categorize	Live it
Make it fun	Make it original	Independent study	Just get it done

Traditional educational settings often have more appeal to the SJ type because the classic classroom environment is better structured for their needs than for some other types. Unfortunately, SPs, which comprise a considerable portion of the population, seem to struggle with traditional teaching models. They may appear hyper or unfocused because they simply learn differently. NTs may be impatient with redundancy or repetition. SJs will comply with an authority figure, but NTs usually need a better reason than power or authority. NFs have a strong need to please and have a relationship with authority figures.

It is very confirming when the child's preferred path of learning is accommodated. This makes it possible for the ESFP child, who is not fond of reading, to talk about, touch, and learn through experience. Concomitantly, it is possible for the INTJ child to read about, imagine, and experiment as he or she learns.

Even classroom discipline can be enhanced by considering the child's type. For example, "time out" or isolation may be less punishing to an introvert, whereas it can have considerable impact to the talkative extravert who lives to interact. Appealing to the SJ's natural sense of duty and need for order can be effective. Counselors must be careful not to trigger the Feeling type's need to please in ways that cause the child to focus more on winning immediate approval than making effective behavioral changes. Making the child's type a part of the discipline consideration can assist the teacher and counselor in facilitating self-discipline and achieving effective discipline systems.

Student type distributions vary widely among schools, and sometimes from class to class in the same school. This fact is important for predicting needs for materials, curricula, and activities.

PSYCHOLOGICAL DIVERSITY IN CHILDREN

One means of enhancing any child's sense of well-being comes from learning about the diversity of type and competencies among his or her peers. As the ESTJ child watches the INTP's approach to solving a puzzle, he or she may become discouraged. When the ENTP child visits the ISFJ's home and sees the collection of insects neatly arranged and labeled, it may generate feelings of inadequacy. When children study type differences, they quickly realize that some of their peers are better at some things, and some are not as good at other things as they are. In an appropriate environment, the child figures out how to learn from those who are better and share with those who need help. The child also becomes aware of his or her own experiences of ease and struggles. In recognizing the vast diversity of abilities, it is possible for the child to learn that some tasks may require more effort and some require less effort, and that the situation differs for each person. As this awareness grows, the child has greater power over his or her learning and understands how to manipulate the learning environment in order to improve the learning. Ideally, parents and educators support the learning environment through intervention with preferred learning styles when the child experiences difficulty.

Savvy parents recognize type in children from an early age. They notice one child's being very expressive and engaging, while at the same time, another child is reserved and observant. Because parents and teachers are the primary people in children's lives, it is essential that the differences in psychological type in children be recognized and honored both at home and at school. Type differences appear to have a profound effect on early learning, as well as almost every area of the child's life. With information as to how each child best perceives and processes information and how each child prefers to interact with the world, parents, educators, and counselors can provide stimulating and effective environments for learning.

One of the most empowering aspects of helping any child to learn about psychological type is the confirmation and validation that come from the description of type. When the ISTJ child from a family in which everyone else is extroverted and perceiving has the opportunity to see that his or her need for structure and quiet is all right, the child experiences enormous growth in self-esteem and confidence. When the ENFP adolescent girl understands that if she is standing on the soccer field with 100 classmates, there will probably only be five to seven other ENFPs there, she begins to grasp why she often feels different. At a time when the teen needs to "be like everyone else," she can feel all right and learn to value who she is. Simply knowing about her innate needs to be loved and avoid rejection can be liberating for her. This is especially useful in helping the teen understand the difference between her need to be loved and a boyfriend's pursuit of sex.

Children need to feel psychological safety. When parents, teachers, and counselors adjust their approach to accommodate the child's type, the child's feelings of confidence, safety, and well-being can be increased.

Usefulness in Counseling

With regard to counseling, Myers, et al (1998) indicated that "people often come to counseling because of a long period of disconfirmation by others. When they see a road toward excellence and happiness which they can travel by discovering and following their own intrinsically valuable preferences, they often become hopeful" (p. 63). Even though the MBTI® was not developed on the basis of *abnormalities*, but on observations and experiences with a large cross section of *normal* people, some encounter the MBTI® in a counseling situation in the counselor's attempt to understand the person's *type* and most preferred path to reaching the goals of the counseling need. The nonthreatening implications of the instrument appear to appeal to people who are receiving the feedback from the Indicator. As they learn about their type, they notice that each of the descriptions has positives and aspects that are not positive. It is useful to compare the positives and negative aspects to the person's height. The tall person has no difficulty reaching objects on high shelves but may need to be alert for low hanging objects or doorways. The person who is not tall has no problem with low hanging objects but may need a step stool for retrieving objects from high shelves. Each condition has advantages and obstacles for which to be aware. This same aspect, however, is a part of the MBTI® that is disliked by a few critics. There appears to be a fear that a positive confirmation of the person's type, rather than going straight to the essence of the counseling problem, is a waste of time.

THEORY OF TYPE DEVELOPMENT

Some people may encounter the MBTI® in church or in the workplace as organizations attempt to facilitate a better understanding among people for the purpose of enhancing interactions. The benefit is gained through appreciation of the gifts of other types. Regardless of the source of introduction, it is essential that people have the opportunity and resources for learning about type and the tremendous growth that it can provide, and not just receive the label for their preferences. If people emerge from MBTI® sessions with only the type label, and without the recognition that this is merely the beginning of a scenic road toward human understanding, there may be little retention.

Much of the formal training that uses the MBTI® appears to be intended for the purpose of *identification* of the preferred type. The emphasis is on distinguishing and verifying one's preferences. Jung's theory and the MBTI®, however, are capable of yielding a much greater depth of information and resources for growth and development. *Type development* is a life-long process, involving more accurate perceptions and more effective decision making. It is fostered in many applications of the MBTI®.

In observing people who are learning about their type, occasionally it is possible to see a defensiveness arise when the situation includes something other than their preferences. Many people avoid dealing with anything other than what is very comfortable for them. Some people tend to confuse areas of strength with their preferences, probably because they see success when they are operating within the realm of their type. Conversely, they see areas of the opposite type as areas of personal weakness. When this happens, some people can get into denial and defensiveness. Both Jung and Myers emphasized repeatedly that the preferences are a core, not an end. Instead of identifying with strengths and weaknesses, Lansford (2006) has found that it is conducive to pursue an understanding of areas of preference that are developed and areas that are not as developed as needed. Being able to recognize and understand one's preferences is a tremendous nucleus of authenticity for both children and adults.

An additional tool for development is the MBTI®Step II™, that provides an individualized type report, reflecting the distinctive ways of expressing preferences. Research continues on the work that Isabel Myers was doing at the time of her death, an analysis that will help people to better utilize their natural types. When published, the MBTI® Step III™ will be yet another tool to enhance the quality of existence and effectiveness.

COUNSELING METHOD

As noted earlier, there is no standard Jungian method of therapy. While using an individualized approach, Jungian analysts apply his concepts to enhance the self-healing potential of the psyche. Two major areas for applications of Jung's theories with children are in play therapy (see Chapter 14) and in the use of type.

Jung's conceptual system for describing certain individual differences is extremely complex and can consume a lifetime of study; however, Isabel Myers, with her mother's inspiration, developed an instrument for adults that can be used to unlock the preferences and value diversity. Murphy and Meisgeier (1987) developed an instrument for identifying type in children. The *Murphy-Meisgeier Type Indicator for Children*® (MMTIC®) may be used appropriately used from grades two through eight. Like the MBTI®, the MMTIC® is a series of questions with two possible choices and measures the same four preference scales. It uses a second-grade reading level and may be read aloud to younger children or to those who have reading or test-taking difficulties.

Although it is useful for the child to complete the MMTIC® and be given the feedback and materials, it is possible to use Jung's concepts in observing for type and responding appropriately. Thus, one of the most effective applications of Jung's work is the study and utilization of Myers's work by the adults in the child's life—counselors, teachers, and parents. As the adults understand their own type, they begin to honor differences in the children. The following case study provides an example of applying Jung type theory to children and using the MMTIC®.

Case Study

Identification of the Problem

Andrea was an 8-year-old girl who was referred by her teacher to the counselor at the end of second grade because she seemed depressed.

Individual and Background Information

Academic. Andrea's standardized test scores were at the 99th percentile. School records indicated that she had demonstrated excellent performance in kindergarten and had straight A's in first grade and for the first quarter of second grade. The subsequent grading periods showed a steady deterioration in grades, primarily because many assignments were either incomplete or late. An IQ score of 142 indicated that Andrea was very capable of academic performance.

Family. Andrea was the only child of an ophthalmologist and a registered nurse who was working on a graduate degree. They lived in an upper socioeconomic neighborhood, appeared to have a very stable relationship, and provided a nurturing environment for the child.

Social. Observations and an interview with her teacher indicated that Andrea was frequently sought as a playmate by her peers, was helpful to others, and appeared to enjoy many friends. Her interactions in play groups and on the playground seemed to be age appropriate. She rarely had conflicts, and when she did, she seemed to generate alternatives and achieve resolution without intervention.

Counseling Method

The Jungian objectives are to stabilize the present and gain hope in a future that the child can create. The basic steps are to: (1) establish a relationship, (2) analyze the present situation, (3) increase the client's awareness of the present situation, and (4) help the client gain awareness that will enable her to effectively manage future situations. The following transcript illustrates the Jungian objectives:

COUNSELOR: Good morning, Andrea. I enjoyed watching you paint yesterday when I visited your classroom.

ANDREA: I like to paint, but we don't get to do it often enough.

COUNSELOR: Painting is fun, and you'd like to do it every day.

ANDREA: [smiling] Yeah, every day.

COUNSELOR: What else do you enjoy as much as painting?

ANDREA: Not much. I like the playground, free time, the puppets, and I used to like writing.

COUNSELOR: And what do you like to do on the playground?

ANDREA: I like to play tag and play in the sand with my friends Katie and Madison.

COUNSELOR: That must be fun. Tell me about the writing and when you used to like it.

ANDREA: Well, Ms. Brown, my teacher last year, used to let us use puppets to tell stories. Then she would help us write what we wanted, draw pictures about it, and she would help us make it into a book and we could take it home.

COUNSELOR: And it was fun to share your stories and your drawings with Mom and Daddy.

ANDREA: Yeah, and I liked showing them what I had done.

COUNSELOR: Talk about what you write in second grade.

ANDREA: Well, we don't write stories. No, we just write. See, we have to write sentences and practice our cursive letters, so we don't write stories, we just write. Ms. Jones doesn't have time to do stories very much, so we just write sentences, do math, work in our books—and sometimes, we get to paint.

COUNSELOR: And you miss making up your own stories and sharing what you're thinking.

ANDREA: Yeah, how did you know that?

COUNSELOR: Well, Andrea, do you remember when you came here on Tuesday, and you did an activity with me where I asked you to answer some questions about what you like—about how you feel and think about things? Let's look at how your answers came out.

ANDREA: Did I make a bad grade? Are you gonna be upset with me like Ms. Jones?

COUNSELOR: No, Andrea. There are no good or bad grades on this activity. It just tells about what you prefer, and something about you. [The counselor shows Andrea the child's *MMTIC® Results Form,* 1999]

Your answers to the questions described someone with the description in this box (ENFP).

Would you like for me to read it to you?

ANDREA: [Andrea eagerly takes the form.] No, I can read it! "Friendly, ready to help anyone with a problem. Have good imaginations. Can do almost anything that they are interested in." [with an enthusiastic smile] Yep, that's me! [Continuing] "Often wait till the last minute to do things. Have lots of new ideas. Want to do new things." That's me too! "Enjoy talking." Wow! How did you know this about me and put all of that in this paper?

COUNSELOR: Andrea, I didn't do this. You gave this description of yourself by the way that you answered the questions. You see, this is an instrument that helps us understand ourselves and how we are different from each other.

ANDREA: That part about the talking, that's what gets me into so much trouble with Ms. Jones. She expects me to do my work and sit quietly, but I forget, and I want to tell Jason about what I've read. Then, I get points.

COUNSELOR: And that makes you feel as if Ms. Jones doesn't like you.

ANDREA: Right! She doesn't like me.

COUNSELOR: Actually, Andrea, Ms. Jones likes you very much. She just becomes concerned when you don't do your assignments.

ANDREA: Are you sure? Do you think Ms. Jones really likes me?

COUNSELOR: I'm certain of it, Andrea. And now that you understand Ms. Jones's concerns, let's look at what you can do to complete your assignments.

ANDREA: OK, but what?

COUNSELOR: We can look at the kinds of things that are easy for you and that you like to do. Then, we can look at the things that are not so easy and find ways to make them more fun.

ANDREA: And not so boring.

COUNSELOR: Sure, Andrea, you like making everything fun. It sounds as if you really prefer creating your own ideas and pictures more than doing the assignments that your teacher gives you. What happens when you're supposed to do the cursive assignment?

ANDREA: Mostly, I don't do it. I just sit there and think about stories, or playing with Chris, or going to the park with Daddy.

COUNSELOR: And when you're thinking about those other things, you don't do the assignment, you're not practicing the cursive writing, and you don't get A's like you used to.

ANDREA: Uh-huh.

COUNSELOR: Well, Andrea, I understand that you like to make up stories and draw pictures. And you know, writing in cursive could help you write more stories because you could actually write faster. Let's try something, you practice the cursive writing, do your assignment in class, and when you are at home, ask Mom to help you write some stories like you used to, but use the cursive writing.

ANDREA: I guess I could try.

COUNSELOR: And let's try something else. Would you like to participate in the summer computer classes here at the school?

ANDREA: You mean not get out of school in two weeks?

COUNSELOR: Not exactly. You'll still have the summer holiday, but you'll come for a special class that Ms. Smith will be teaching each morning in June from 10:00 o'clock to noon. You'll learn how to use the computer to write stories. And you can write even more stories.

ANDREA: [excited] My mom has a computer, and sometimes she lets me play games on it. But you mean I could use it for my stories?

COUNSELOR: Ms. Smith will show you how to do that by helping you develop what we call keyboard skills—how to use your fingers to type the letters instead of a pencil.

ANDREA: (moving her fingers as if on a keyboard) I would like that.

COUNSELOR: When you come to see me next week, we'll talk more about this. Today, I'm going to send these papers (Meisgeier, *Parents Guide to Type*, 1989) to your mom and dad so that they can know about the activity that you did. If it's okay with you, I can also talk with Ms. Jones about it.

ANDREA: Sure, I'm glad she likes me.

COUNSELOR: And Andrea, I like you, too.

ANDREA: See you next week. [She skips down the hall.]

Case Summary

Although Andrea's sad face, falling grades, and lack of participation might have been signals of depression in children, the problem was actually a lack of intellectual challenge, boredom with the curriculum, and a lack of understanding of the teacher's (ISFJ) type. The counselor recognized that, for the ENFP, anything that disrupts the relationship threatens the child's learning.

The counselor arranged a session with the teacher to help her understand Andrea's type and her classroom needs. Together, they recommended that Andrea be assigned to a third grade classroom that used an individualized program and a less structured classroom environment, along with enrichment classes for the gifted. In addition, the counselor arranged a session with the parents to provide understanding of Andrea's needs. Subsequently, the parents completed the MBTI® to understand how their type influenced their parenting style. They also joined a parents' support group for gifted children.

CROSS-CULTURAL APPLICATIONS OF JUNG

Jung was intrigued by the human attributes and myths that transcend culture. One of his easiest concepts to apply to different cultures is that of *type*. The tool for identifying and applying type is the MBTI®. It has been used by millions of people and has been translated into different languages around the globe. It has also has been a part of several thousand books, articles, theses, dissertations, and studies. It has been used in research from numerous perspectives, from the way people pray and learn to the ways they choose work or fall in love. New forms of the original instrument are developed by the publisher in order to maintain relevance to current society and reflect ongoing research into the original work. Much of the structure and approach of therapy can be applied to children from various cultures, especially when there is no language barrier between the counselor and the child.

SUMMARY

Although largely overlooked during the middle part of the twentieth century, Carl Jung developed some new terms and ideas that, unlike much of the psychology of his time, were not focused on abnormalities. A resurgent interest in Jung may be attributed to the recognition of the validity and usefulness of several of his concepts. Jungian Institutes are located around the world, even in some small cities. It is possible to see similarities in the work of later psychologists, such as the related themes of Myers' ISTJ type to Berne's *parent* (see Chapter 10). One can also find corresponding ideas in some work done on communication styles, such as in connecting extraversion and introversion to gender, as the talkative wife, and the silent husband (Tannen, 2001; Gray, 2002). Jung also left a considerable legacy of ideas for the current positive psychology movement.

Jung's work is highly complex, as complicated as the task of developing a system of understanding human personality. Myers and Briggs provided normal laypeople with the usefulness of Jung's ideas. Because of their lifelong pursuit of *type,* today, many people smile and understand situations that, without MBTI® learning, could have caused frustration and emotional injury. Further utilization of the MMTIC®*Murphy Meisgeier Type Indicator for Children* and classroom use of types will afford children the same understanding and opportunities to build their confidence. Perhaps the greatest implication for education is in the utilization of type in accommodating varied learning styles in order to increase individual development and enhance each child's self self-concept. Future developments will probably lead to greater understanding of Jung's work and of the human psyche.

WEBSITES FOR JUNGIAN COUNSELING

Internet addresses frequently change. To find the sites listed here, visit www.thomsonedu.com/counseling/thompson for an updated list of Internet addresses and direct links to relevant sites.

Association for Psychological Type

Center for Applications of Psychological Type

Consulting Psychologists Press

International Association for Analytical Psychology

REFERENCES

Campbell, J. (Ed.). (1976). *The portable Jung*. New York: Penguin.

Csikszentimihalyi, M. (2003). *Good business: Leadership, flow, and the making of meaning*. New York: Penguin Books.

Dietrich, A. (2004). *Research locates source of runner's high experienced by athletes*. Atlanta, GA: Georgia Institute of Technology News Room.

Gray, J. (2002). *Men, women, and relationships*. New York: Harper Paperbacks.

Jung, C. G. (1958). *The undiscovered self*. New York: Mentor.

Jung, C. G. (1967) *Collected works: Vol. 16. The practice of psychotherapy*. Princeton, NJ: Princeton University Press.

Jung, C. G. (1989). *Memories, dreams, reflections*. New York: Random House. (Original work published 1961)

Jung, C. G. (1990). *Psychological types*. Princeton, NJ: Princeton University Press. (Original work published 1921)

Keirsey, D. (1998). *Please understand me II: Temperament, character, intelligence*. Del Mar, CA: Prometheus Nemesis Books.

Kroeger, O., & Thuesen, J. M. (2002). *Type talk at work*. New York: Doubleday.

Lansford, Z. (2006). *Psychology for normal people*. Unpublished manuscript.

Meisgeier, C. (1989). *Parent's guide to type*. Gainesville, FL: Center for Applications of Psychological Type, Inc.

Murphy, E., & Meisgeier, C. (1987). *Murphy-Meisgeier Type Indicator for Children®*. Gainesville, FL: Center for Applications of Psychological Type, Inc.

Myers, I., & Briggs, K. (1998). *Myers-Briggs Type Indicator®*. Palo Alto, CA: Consulting Psychologists Press. (Original work published 1975)

Myers, I., Kirby, L., & Myers, K. (1998). *Introduction to type®*. Palo Alto, CA: Consulting Psychologists Press. (Original work published 1970)

Myers, I., McCaulley, M., Quenk, N., & Hammer, A. (1998). *MBTI® Manual: A guide to the development and use of the Myers-Briggs Type Indicator®*. Palo Alto, CA: Consulting Psychologists Press, Inc.

Myers, I., & Myers, P. (1995). *Gifts differing: Understanding personality type*. Palo Alto, CA: Davies Black Publishing. (Original work published 1980)

Saunders, F. W. (1991). *Katharine and Isabel: Mother's light, daughter's journey*. Palo Alto, CA: CPP, Inc.

Storr, A. (1983). *The essential Jung*. Princeton, NJ: Princeton University Press.

Tannen, D. (2001). *You just don't understand: Women and Men in Conversation*. New York: Quill.

COUNSELING WITH
CHILDREN: SPECIAL TOPICS

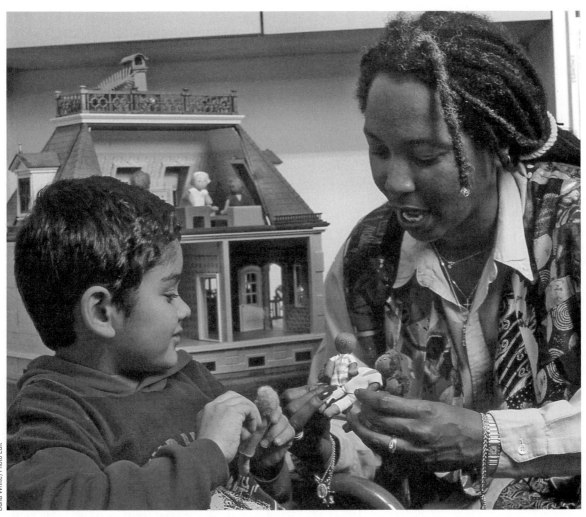

14 CHAPTER | PLAY THERAPY

Juleen K. Buser

You can discover more about a person in an hour of play than in a year of conversation.

—Plato

Rather than Freud's "talking cure" as a descriptor of therapy, Kaduson, Cangelosi, and Schaefer (1997a) propose "playing cure" as more appropriate to describe therapy with children. Play is "the child's natural medium of self expression" according to Virginia Axline (1947, p. 9) in her classic book *Play Therapy: The Inner Dynamics of Childhood.* Others concur with her premise (Landreth, 1991; Moustakas, 1981; Schaefer, 1993). Landreth (1993) explains that play is children's symbolic language and provides a way for them to express their experiences and emotions in a natural, self-healing process. "A child's play is his talk and toys are his words," proposed Ginott (1994, p. 33). Orton (1997) states that play assists in establishing a relationship with a child, helps the child state his or her concerns, aids in the assessment process, and promotes healing and growth. In this chapter, we review definitions of play therapy, procedures of play in therapy, and evidence of the effectiveness of play therapy. We also provide some example activities of play therapy.

DEFINING PLAY THERAPY

Schaefer (1993) has identified common characteristics of play. He states that play is pleasurable and, therefore, intrinsically motivating. During play the child is more concerned with the play itself than with the end result, and the child is often deeply engrossed in the play activity. Play is not literal—it has a make-believe quality. Play is flexible. It has the power to enhance normal development and alleviate abnormal behavior. The child feels comfortable when playing. Play is a natural way for children to express themselves, to act out sensitive material, to gain security, and to increase their self-confidence (Bradley & Gould, 1993). Another significant attribute of play is that it is free from evaluation and judgment by adults so that children are safe to make mistakes (Sweeney, 1997).

ADVANTAGES OF PLAY THERAPY

Albon (1996) states that facilitating play into therapy "powerfully facilitates development" even with minimal verbal interactions. Besides this general benefit, incorporating play into counseling has several other advantages:

- The child is given freedom to make choices.
- Play evokes fantasies and unconscious feelings.
- Play offers familiar tools for children to use.
- The only limits required are to keep the child and others safe from harm.
- Play therapy allows the child a safe place to act out feelings, to gain understanding, and to change (Bradley & Gould, 1993, p. 86).

Kottman (2001) has explained the advantages of play therapy for counselors. Play helps counselors establish rapport with children, as well as understand the children, the way they interact, and their relationships. Play also allows the teaching of social skills.

The Association for Play Therapy (1997) defines play therapy as the "systematic use of a theoretical model to establish an interpersonal process in which trained play therapists use the therapeutic powers of play to help clients prevent or resolve psychosocial difficulties and achieve optimal growth and development." Schaefer (1993) outlines fourteen therapeutic powers of play and the beneficial outcome of each, which Sweeney (1997) and Kottman (2001) have interpreted. These powers are as follows:

1. *Overcoming resistance:* Play draws children into a working alliance with the counselor. Many children do not make the choice to enter counseling, thus play provides a way to establish a working alliance with them.
2. *Communication:* Play provides a natural medium of self-expression. Counselors convey their respect by being willing to "speak" in the child's language. Watching the child's activity and choices provides the counselor with a quick and smooth understanding.
3. *Competence:* Play satisfies the need to explore and master, thereby building self-esteem. Counselors build confidence by pointing out that the child is working hard and making progress.
4. *Creative thinking:* Problem-solving skills are encouraged so that innovative solutions to dilemmas can occur. Play provides opportunities for creativity and imaginative solutions.
5. *Catharsis:* Children can release strong emotions they have had difficulty confronting. The sense of relief can be an experience that leads to growth for the child.

6. *Abreaction:* In play, children can process and adjust to difficulties by symbolically reliving them with appropriate emotional expression. Play gives children a place to re-enact and gain a sense of mastery over the negative experience.

7. *Role-play:* Children can practice new behaviors and develop empathy for others.

8. *Fantasy:* Children use their imagination to make sense of painful reality. They can also experiment with the possibility of changing their lives, a process that instills hope.

9. *Metaphoric teaching:* Children gain insight by facing their conflicts and fears through the metaphors generated in play. Stories, playing, and artwork can be used to look at situations differently.

10. *Attachment formation:* Children develop a bond with the counselor and learn to increase their connections with others.

11. *Relationship enhancement:* Play enhances the positive therapeutic relationship, allowing children to move toward self-actualization and to grow closer to others. The children begin to believe they are worthy of love and positive attention.

12. *Positive emotion:* Children enjoy playing. They can laugh and have a good time in an accepting place.

13. *Mastering developmental fears:* Repeated play activities help reduce anxiety and fear. By working with toys, art supplies, and other play media, children can recognize their skills for coping with fear and for taking care of themselves.

14. *Game play:* Games help children socialize and develop ego strength. They have opportunities to expand their interaction skills.

The therapeutic factors of play therapy have been supported in counselors' work with children who have these and other difficulties: abuse (Costas & Landreth, 1999; Doyle & Stoop, 1999; Pelcovitz, 1999; Tyndall-Lind, 1999), aggression (Fischetti, 2001; Johnson & Clark, 2001), attachment disorder (Jernberg & Booth, 1999), depression (Briesmeister, 1997), divorce (Cangelosi, 1997; Robinson, 1999), fear (Kottman, 2002; Knell, 2000), and family violence (Tyndall-Lind, Landreth, & Giordano, 2001). Kaduson (1997) recognizes the therapeutic factors in working with children with attention-deficit/hyperactivity disorder (ADHD). Henniger (1995) proposes that play could serve as an antidote to childhood stress, and Albon (1996) recognizes that play allows children to expose and explore troublesome emotions. Fall (1999) has investigated client-centered interventions in the school setting with children with poor coping skills for learning. She found support for the use of six sessions of play therapy as increasing support for the children. Bratton and Ray (2000) summarize further support in their review of the case study research in this field. They have summarized eighty-two studies and presented the effectiveness of play therapy with several specific issues and populations. The following sections provide more specific information related to the effectiveness of play therapy.

EMPIRICAL SUPPORT FOR PLAY THERAPY

The field of play therapy is gaining momentum, as empirical validation of its interventions and comprehensive research reviews of outcomes emerge. Researchers have previously drawn attention to the serious shortage of empirical evidence in play therapy and have highlighted the need for more specialized outcome studies that are associated with particular child populations and childhood struggles (White & Allers, 1994; Phillips, 1985; Ogawa, 2004).

Several studies concentrate on measuring the effectiveness of play therapy and determine general outcomes for play techniques. Leblanc and Ritchie (1999) have conducted a meta-analysis and underscored two conditions as being valuable for successful therapy outcomes. The active participation and involvement of parents in therapy contributed to efficacious play sessions. In addition, the length of the treatment promoted successful outcomes, as the authors note that a length of thirty to thirty-five sessions was a common factor in beneficial play interventions. These conclusions were verified in a later meta-analysis, which also asserted the facility of play therapy with emotionally troubled children and stated that play interventions work comparably to nonplay interventions (Leblanc & Ritchie, 2001).

Ray, Bratton, Rhine, and Jones (2001) have conducted a meta-analysis of play therapy, reviewing ninety-four efficacy studies from 1940 to 2000. Their results support the previous meta-analyses finding that play therapy is effective for a variety of problems, populations, in numerous settings, and with a multitude of clinical orientations. Again supporting earlier studies, Ray et al. have discovered that parental involvement and therapy duration of thirty-five to forty-five sessions were common elements of effective play interventions (p. 94).

A case study research review conducted by Bratton and Ray (2002) pinpoints several childhood disorders for which play therapy is noted to be particularly effective. These authors document the usefulness of play interventions with social maladjustment, conduct disorder, problem school behavior, emotional maladjustment, anxiety/fear, poor self-concept, and physical, mental, or learning disabilities. In line with this case study review, Kottman (2001), drawing from anecdotal evidence and empirical research studies, has outlined groupings of childhood problems that are impacted positively through the interventions of play therapy. Kottman distinguishes among different degrees of play therapy effectiveness, asserting (1) when play therapy of any orientation would be the chosen treatment for a disorder or struggle, (2) when a specific play therapy technique has benefited children with certain problems, (3) when a combination of play therapy and another intervention is most useful, and (4) when play therapy would not be the chosen intervention. Table 14-1 summarizes Kottman's conclusions on the use of play therapy with childhood problems.

Yet the case studies and meta-analyses often do not connect specific play therapy interventions to particular childhood populations and troubles. Reddy, Files-Hall, and Schaefer (2005b) note, however, that this specific base of play therapy research does exist for some disorders; they state that "over the past

TABLE 14-1 | PLAY THERAPY

Play therapy (regardless of the approach) would be treatment of choice	Certain approaches to play therapy have been useful in treating these children	Play therapy can be an effective intervention when combined with other interventions	Play therapy would not be the treatment of choice for these children
Adjustment disorder	Attachment disorder (therapy and thematic play)	Attention deficit–hyperactivity disorder	Severe conduct disorder
Post-traumatic stress disorder		Major depressive disorder	Severe attachment disorder
Dissociative disorder	Selective mutism (cognitive-behavioral play therapy and client-centered play therapy)	Separation anxiety disorder	Manifest signs of psychosis
Depressive episodes			
Specific fears and phobias			
Aggressive, acting-out behavior		Enuresis or encopresis	
Anxiety and withdrawn behavior		Learning disabilities	
Abuse and/or neglect	Moderate to severe behavior problems (filial therapy, Adlerian play therapy, and ecosystematic play therapy)	Mental retardation	
Divorce of parents		Physical handicaps	
Family violence and other family problems			
Grief issues			
Adoption and foster care–related issues			
Severe trauma (e.g., earthquake, car wreck, war, or kidnaping)			
Hospitalization			
Chronic or terminal illness			

two decades, well-designed controlled play intervention studies have emerged" (p. 4). Reddy et al. have conducted a review of the literature, gathering outcome data on play therapy interventions with specific child populations. These authors provide clear research designs, practical suggestions for outcome study, and replication procedures for each therapy technique. The empirical studies document a range of play therapy interventions, settings, clinicians, and childhood problems (Files-Hall & Reddy, 2005). Reddy et al. (2005) provide compelling evidence for the effectiveness of play techniques; their synthesis of the research on play interventions for identified childhood populations and struggles reveals consistent and impressive outcomes.

Reddy et al. (2005) have studied children's developmental difficulties. They examined the following applications of play therapy: the Primary Mental Health Project (PMHP) with at-risk children in school; intensive individual and sibling group play therapy to intervene with children privy to domestic violence; the Children of Divorce Intervention Program (CODIP) with children of divorced parents; post-traumatic play techniques to address children experiencing post-traumatic stress disorder; guided fantasy with chronically ill children; child-centered, short-term play therapy with children in hospital care; the Child Attention Deficit Hyperactivity Multimodal Program (CAMP) program to treat children with ADHD; Parent-Child Interaction Therapy (PCIT) with behaviorally troubled children; a cooperative games intervention with aggressive children; the Denver model of play therapy to aid children with autism; and a range of filial therapy applications. The following section integrates a discussion of the theories of play therapy with this available outcome data. However, as Reddy and her colleagues assert, the empirical base is not yet wide enough. Numerous childhood struggles and play interventions still do not have the support of outcome studies. As evident in the following discussion, the field currently is challenged by an imbalance between play interventions that can draw on significant empirical evidence and those therapies that cannot yet make use of the power of outcome data.

CROSS-CULTURAL APPLICATIONS OF PLAY THERAPY

An additional benefit of play therapy is the applicability across cultural groups. Glover (2001), Kao and Landreth (2001), Kottman (2001), and others emphasize that counselors must be able to work with children from different cultures. Henderson and Gladding (1998) argue that using the creative arts could enhance multicultural counseling. Certainly the links between play therapy and creative arts are ample reasons to extend that hypothesis to multicultural counseling and play therapy. All children play. One of the barriers in multicultural counseling is language; play is a natural way to overcome that difficulty. Cochran (1996) proposes play and art therapy as methods to help students who are culturally diverse overcome barriers to school success, particularly through aiding communication and increasing self-esteem. For all these reasons, the use of play therapy with children of different cultures seems to be a promising practice. Coleman, Parmer, and Barker (1993) and Glover (2001) provide the following specifics for working with children from multicultural populations:

1. Respect the historical, psychological, sociological, and political aspects of the child's culture. The counselor may gather information about and gain an experience of the culture. Play materials should be chosen to express respect for cultural differences.
2. Investigate the role of play in diverse populations to avoid comments or interpretations that may violate the culture. Stock the play room with toys appropriate for the self-expression of a child in that particular group.
3. Become familiar with the values, beliefs, customs, and traditions of a child's culture, paying particular attention to language differences.

4. Recognize the ongoing process of becoming multiculturally competent.
5. Examine the appropriateness of the philosophical basis of the play therapy theory to determine whether there is a mismatch with cultural values.
6. Be aware of personal cultural biases, values, beliefs, and attitudes.
7. Interact with multicultural populations.

In addition to working with children from different cultures, counselors will want to include their parents. For examples, counselors will want to ask parents about their background, such as their traditions, celebrations, and religion. Gonzalez-Mena (1998) provides one way of understanding a home environment. This author explains two opposing goals of parenting styles: individualism versus connectedness. Parents who value individualism will work to help the child develop autonomy and self-help skills. The parent may encourage the idea of passion, making choices, and expression of feelings. Independence, self-assurance, competence, and a sense of being special may be emphasized with this type of parenting. Parenting to maintain connections, however, emphasizes interdependence as the greatest value. Parents may promote peace and harmony among family members rather than independence and autonomy. Humility and humbleness are valued. Worthiness is connected to fitting in, belonging, and putting others first. You may refer to the discussion on children of different cultures in Chapter 15 for more guidelines in working with children from diverse cultures.

Counselors who use play therapy must begin by considering their own personal characteristics that may be indicators of their suitability for that type of intervention. Then, by considering the varying theoretical approaches to play therapy, counselors can construct their understanding of that process. Awareness of the stages of play therapy, criteria for the selection of play materials, and examples of play therapy techniques will contribute to a foundation for integrating play into counseling practices.

PLAY THERAPY APPROACHES

APPLICATIONS OF PLAY THERAPY

Many of the theoretical approaches to counseling have been explained as modes of play therapy, and those discussions are included within the chapters on counseling theories. Some other practices of play therapy are outlined in the following sections.

GROUP PLAY THERAPY

Children age 2 to 12 with similar problems or experiences affecting their behavior may benefit from a play therapy group. Pedro-Carroll and Jones (2005) underscore the encouragement, connection, and reality-checking function present in groups of children. In addition, Landreth and Sweeney (2001) have identified many advantages to using group play therapy. Children will have an experience that helps them learn to function well, to explore their actions, to develop tolerance, and to find joy in working with others.

O'Connor (1991) underscores some fundamental requirements for a play therapy group, stating that the children should display a range of functioning both to avoid competition for attention and to provide models. He suggested no more than six children per adult in the group, and no more than ten children in a group with two adults. Children should be within a 3-year age span among members, come from similar socioeconomic status and ethnic background, and have no more than 15 IQ points separating them. The advisability of mixing boys and girls in one group depends on the age of the members, the type of group, and the group goals. Using play in group counseling is similar to using it with individuals, and the theoretical approaches should guide a counselor in those decisions.

Schaefer, Jacobsen, and Ghahramanlou (2000) have explained a play group for children with social skills deficits. They note the significance of social relationships in childhood and cite Hartup, who concluded that IQ, school grades, and classroom behavior were not predictors of adult success. Instead, the way a child gets along with others is the single best predictor of adult adaptation. The social skills training program includes ten sessions that focus on specific social skills for elementary children. Their book chapter includes the curriculum for that group activity.

Pedro-Carroll and Jones (2005) have explained a play therapy group for children experiencing the impact of parental divorce. The CODIP is a school-based play intervention that integrates prevention, developmental theory, and an emphasis on resiliency principles, distinguishing it from other prevalent interventions for children of divorce. Instead of focusing on the detrimental, troubling effects of divorce, the CODIP model emphasizes the protective factors that enable children to overcome the potentially disabling consequences of divorce. As Pedro-Carroll (1997) asserts: "If divorce is to provide a solution to a failed marriage, with opportunities for family members to thrive as well as survive, then our efforts must focus on the promotion of health, resilience, and psychological well-being" (p. 237).

Pedro-Carroll and Jones (2005) have identified a range of protective factors apparent in the research—that is, individual traits, family characteristics, and elements outside the family that contribute to a child's ability to overcome the negative effects of divorce. The essence of the CODIP intervention is to promote these protective factors to help children deal with the trauma associated with divorce and, at the same time, to support the personal competence and healthy growth of children in their developmental journey. Specifically, CODIP is a school-based group ideally co-led by a man and a woman. The length and content of these sessions are amended for four different age levels. Pedro-Carroll and Jones (2005) note that older children benefit from a weekly 1-hour group with 12-14 sessions, and younger children gain more from weekly 45-minute sessions, in smaller groups, that last for 12-16 sessions.

In general, CODIP accents two main objectives—the creation of a compassionate group setting and the fostering of children's ability to identify and productively communicate emotions. The sessions focus on gaining awareness about divorce and discrediting myths about divorce, helping children learn coping skills and personal mastery abilities, and augmenting both the self-concept of children and their views about family. Play techniques are an integral part of

CODIP. Pedro-Carroll and Jones (2005) suggest that younger children play games such as the feeling grab-bag, where they choose an emotion and act it out in silence for others to guess (p. 60). The Daring Dinosaurs board game is another play technique later in the CODIP sessions in which children pick premade questions about divorce, coping skills, and emotions and attempt to answer them or ask the group members or the group puppet for help (pp. 62–63). Older children, however, may benefit more from interventions such as creative writing (Pedro-Carroll & Jones, 2005, p. 56). Another play activity appropriate for older children in the 9- to 12-year-old range is a technique that creates a "panel of experts" out of certain group members who answer divorce-related questions from the remainder of the group, who serve as an audience (Pedro-Carroll, 1997, p. 225). This group play therapy model has had such impressive outcomes that Pedro-Carroll and Jones (2005) note that CODIP "has recently been designated a national 'Model Program' by SAMHSA (Substance Abuse and Mental Health Services Administration)" (p. 64).

Another model of group play therapy is a cooperative games intervention to address the aggressive behavior of preschool children. Although not a structured, segmented group as other models may be, this intervention uses the theories and benefits of group interaction in a cooperative game format. Bay-Hinitz and Wilson (2005) discuss the detrimental effects of competitive games and the impetus for aggression that is built into their very structure (p. 192). These authors also note, however, the benefits of cooperative games and activities and their natural promotion of collective, helpful behavior (Bay-Hinitz & Wilson, 2005). Bay-Hinitz, Peterson, and Quilitch (1994) have conducted a study with seventy preschool age children that exhibited the beneficial impact of cooperative games on aggressive behavior. Using observer ratings of cooperative and aggressive behavior, Bay-Hinitz et al. show that cooperative games increase supportive behavior, whereas competitive games enhance aggressive behavior. Notably, during free play time, the behavioral effects of the cooperative games endure. Bay-Hinitz et al. (1994) assert that "games are a central aspect of children's play" (p. 435), making a case for the apparent simplicity, and yet deep relevance of this play intervention. Bay-Hinitz and Wilson (2005) note the flexibility and adaptability of this intervention and the reality that almost any game can be modified into a cooperative structure to promote the sharing, helpful behaviors of children.

PRESCRIPTIVE PLAY THERAPY

Schaefer et al. (2000) explain that counselors who use prescriptive play therapy tailor their interventions for each child. To do this, they must have both a conceptual and practical knowledge base about the many theories of play therapy. That knowledge will allow the counselor to understand the child and the child's problems. Kaduson, Cangelosi, and Schaefer (1997a) have outlined the responsibilities of counselors who use prescriptive play therapy:

- Know every approach to play therapy, including the theory's philosophical foundations, constructs, and strategies.

- Have skill in applying the constructs and strategies.
- Understand the psychological and emotional issues related to childhood disorders.
- Be capable of identifying the short- and long-term needs of children with specific diagnoses to form treatment plans for those needs.
- Know the current outcome research to choose the most effective treatment for the specific problem.

Kaduson, Cangelosi, and Schaefer (1997a) provide details about this approach to play therapy in their book.

PLAY THERAPY WITH FAMILIES

Interventions combining family and play therapies have been used in prevention programs in elementary schools (McDonald & Morgan, 1997) and in working with the difficulties of alcoholism (Carmichael & Lane, 1997). Johnson, Franklin, Hall, and Prieto (2000) discuss the use of play therapy to work with a child who has attention difficulties. These authors coached parents on relationship-building techniques with a successful outcome for the child and parents. Gladding (1993) encourages families to play, but in a manner that is fair, tolerant, and trusting. His admonition was to set up cooperative play environments where everyone shares and wins. Rotter and Bush (2000) also emphasize the importance of families playing together in therapy. Several theorists have provided models for promoting play therapy with families (Ariel, 1992, 1997; Harvey, 1997; Jernberg, 1993; Koller and Booth, 1997). Two of these models—filial therapy and PCIT—have substantial outcome data as support for the effectiveness of the interventions.

FILIAL THERAPY   Bernard and Louise Guerney developed filial therapy, a play therapy method in which the parents are directly involved. Filial therapy is based on the principles of child-centered therapy. Guerney (1997) believes that adjustment problems experienced by children were caused by parents' failing to learn how to understand their children. She defined these problems as learning problems and thought that teaching parents to conduct child-centered play sessions might overcome parental shortcomings and help children feel accepted by their parents.

The goals of filial therapy are to reduce the children's problem behaviors, to help parents gain the skills of the child-centered play therapists to use when relating to their children, and to improve the parent–child relationship. Using learning theory and behavioral therapy for the parent training principles, the training proceeds by completing the following steps:

1. Introduce parents to methods for conducting client-centered play therapy.
2. Consider the other demands of parents' lives and assure them they are expected to practice these skills only in the play sessions.
3. Model the behaviors as complete tasks.
4. Reduce each task to small, separate components and practice each component.

5. Reassemble the complete tasks and role-play without children.
6. Encourage parents to conduct sessions observed by the counselor or held at home and reported to the counselor.
7. Gradually increase the length of the sessions and have home play weekly.

VanFleet (2000) suggests that a counselor needs specific skills to use filial therapy: structuring skills, empathic listening skills, imaginary play skills, and limit-setting skills. As in child-centered play therapy, the child is encouraged to express his or her needs, thoughts, and feelings. Optimally, during the process, children and parents change their perceptions of each other.

Johnson (1995) lists the benefits of filial therapy as providing a bridge between individual child treatment and family therapy, as empowering parents, and as a springboard to address many family issues. Filial therapy has been described as helpful with children who have tendencies toward perfection (VanFleet, 1997), with single parents (Bratton, 1994; Ray, Bratton, & Brandt, 2000), grandparents (Bratton, Ray, & Moffit, 1998), and with incarcerated fathers (Lobaugh, 1992). VanFleet, Ryan, and Smith (2005) have conducted a critical review of filial therapy studies and noted some rigorous outcome designs while studying the effects of filial therapy. Landreth and Lobaugh (1998) have examined the impact of filial therapy with incarcerated fathers and reported that, at the end of 10 weeks, fathers in the filial therapy group had higher scores on scales of parental acceptance of children, acceptance of children's feelings, acceptance of children's autonomy, and love of children than fathers in the control group. Parenting stress and child behavior issues also diminished in the filial therapy group. Applying the filial therapy model with incarcerated mothers, Harris and Landreth (1997) found an increase in the mother's acceptance of children's distinctive personalities, emotional expression, and autonomy. The researchers also found that the mothers showed enhanced empathy in their interactions with their children, and that the children exhibited fewer problem behaviors (Harris & Landreth, 1997).

Costas and Landreth (1999) used a 10-week filial therapy treatment with nonoffending parents of sexually abused children. At the end of therapy, parents in the filial therapy group gained compassion, empathy, and acceptance for their children and reported reductions in stress and the problem behaviors of their children. A control group of parents documented no such gains. Kale and Landreth (1999) investigated another population of children and demonstrated the effectiveness of filial therapy with children who have learning problems. This study reports a lessening of parental stress and a heightening of parental acceptance of children after the intervention. Bratton and Landreth (1995) have studied filial therapy with single parents and reported benefits for the children and the parents; the parents experienced less stress, interacted in more empathic ways with their children, and made gains in accepting their children; the children engaged in fewer problem behaviors and achieved more self-control.

Several studies also have been conducted that examine the cross-cultural application of filial therapy. Chau and Landreth (1997) have found that Chinese parents experienced a variety of benefits through filial therapy, as both their empathic behavior and their attitude of acceptance toward their children increased and their stress decreased. Native America parents and children of the Flathead Reservation in Montana also experienced advantages through taking part in filial therapy. Glover and Landreth (2000), using a 10-week filial therapy model with this Native American group, recorded the parent's gains in empathic interactions with their children and the children's enhanced play behavior. Jang (2000) underscores the effectiveness of filial therapy with Korean parents, as parents grew in empathic play interactions with their children, accepted their children's feelings and expression to a greater degree, reduced their stress level, and reported less problem behaviors with their children. Overall, the relationship dynamics among all family members seemed to be enhanced and improved through filial therapy (Jang, 2000).

A unique application of filial therapy was undertaken by Jones, Rhine, and Bratton (2002). These authors discuss a filial therapy model that used high school students as the therapy facilitators with elementary age children who were experiencing adjustment problems in school. As part of a Peer Assistance and Leadership (PALS) high school course, thirty-two high school students received ten filial therapy training sessions lasting 1.5 hours, were supervised in twenty play sessions lasting 20 minutes each, and received 20 minutes of individual supervision after every play session (Jones et al., 2002, p. 53). The outcomes of this study reported benefits for both the high school students and the elementary children. The internalizing behavior problems of the elementary children declined significantly, in addition to decreases in externalizing behavior difficulties. The high school students made a variety of gains, including increases in empathic play interactions, a greater ability to convey acceptance of children, patience in permitting the self-direction of children, and enhanced engagement in the play session.

PARENT-CHILD INTERACTION THERAPY   In addition to filial therapy, another family play intervention that has gained a solid empirical foundation is PCIT. This play therapy model was developed to treat children exhibiting externalizing behavioral problems such as resistance and aggression—behaviors that are part of the diagnostic conditions for conduct disorder (CD) and oppositional defiant disorder (ODD) (Herschell & McNeil, 2005). In treating these behaviors, PCIT focuses on the parent–child relationship and is based on developmental psychology and social learning theory. Those fields of knowledge have established a link between parent–child relationships, parenting styles, and the behavior of children. In fact, Herschell and McNeil (2005) asserted that programs with an emphasis comparable with PCIT are "currently considered the treatment of choice for child conduct problems" (p. 174).

PCIT takes place once a week in a 1-hour therapy session. The duration of treatment is from 10 to 14 weeks (Herschell & McNeil, 2005). Herschell and McNeil describe the two stages that make up the actual process of PCIT, both of which are centered on coaching parents on ways to use appropriate and advantageous methods of interaction with their child. PCIT relies heavily on in vivo coaching; for at least 30 minutes of each session, the therapist gives immediate feedback to the parent during his or her play session with the child, through the use of a one-way mirror and a bug in the ear. Modifications have been made when such a setting is not available, such as "in-room" coaching where the therapist sits behind the parent and provides feedback (Herschell & McNeil, 2005, p. 180). Before beginning each stage, parents receive a didactic session in which they not only have a lesson but also participate in role-plays. Counselors model the skills that parents will then display in an interaction with their child.

In the initial stage of PCIT, termed *child-directed interaction,* parents are coached to ignore the negative and disruptive behaviors of their child and to concentrate on the positive, suitable behavior that their child presents. In the second stage of *parent-directed interaction,* parents are coached on methods to gain and maintain the compliance of their child, such as learning to give understandable commands and to set up house rules (Herschell & McNeil, 2005). Parents also commit to interact and play with their child every day for 5 to 10 minutes outside the play therapy room. That interaction is an essential portion of PCIT (Herschell & McNeil, 2005). Ongoing assessments are also a vital portion of this therapy. Several instruments have been designed to measure PCIT goals, outcomes, and treatment progress according to these ongoing assessments. Brestan, Jacob, Rayfield, and Eyberg (1999) have documented the psychometric soundness of the Therapy Attitude Inventory, an instrument developed specifically for PCIT to evaluate the satisfaction of parents after the course of therapy.

The effectiveness of PCIT has been documented extensively in the literature. Measurable changes in children's behavior have been noted; specifically, the decline of disruptive behavior and the increase of compliant behavior have been reported consistently. The generalizability of PCIT gains to school behavior is also a striking trend throughout this evidence-based literature. Eyberg and Matarazzo (1980) have measured PCIT against parent group didactic training and found greater behavioral improvement for the PCIT approach than the didactic training approach. McNeil, Capage, Bahl, and Blanc (1999) compared a group of children receiving PCIT for disruptive behavior with a control group not receiving PCIT. After fourteen sessions of PCIT over 3.5 months, the participating children improved enough to be assessed as within the normal range of behavior. The wait-list control group, however, showed no gains or changes in behavior. McNeil, Eyberg, Eisenstadt, Newcomb, and Funderbunk (1991) have conducted a study of ten children, ages 2 through 7, who had a history of destructive behavior and met the criteria for a *Diagnostic and Statistical Manual of Mental Disorders (DSM)* diagnosis of CD, ODD, or ADHD. Even with no classroom training sessions, both parents and teachers reported behavioral improvements after the 14-week PCIT intervention. Similar results were found by Eisenstadt, Eyberg, McNeil, Newcomb, and Funderbunk (1993). In a compilation of research that explored the behavioral improvements of disruptive children receiving PCIT, Gallagher (2003) inspected the results of 17 studies involving preschool age children with disruptive-behavior disorder. She concluded that PCIT can be endorsed as an "evidence-based intervention" for "improving behavior outcomes in preschool age children with disruptive behavior disorder" (Gallagher, 2003, p. 7). Behavioral improvements consisted of lower parent and teacher ratings of problem behaviors, less unconstructive behaviors in clinic settings, and a decrease in *DSM* diagnoses for a disruptive behavior disorder (Gallagher, 2003, p. 6).

In addition, the effects of PCIT are maintained. Gallagher (2003), in her synthesis of 17 studies on PCIT, found that 75 percent of the long-term studies on PCIT showed that post-treatment improvements were maintained. For example, in an initial long-term follow-up of the study completed by Einsenstadt et al. (1993), Eyberg et al. (2001) found that, of the eleven families who reported clinically meaningful gains in behavioral issues at the end of therapy, nine families sustained this improvement 2 years later. Funderbunk et al. (1998) assessed the long-term maintenance of improvements after a fourteen-session PCIT intervention with preschool children with disruptive behavioral disorders and also found enduring effects, with the children being "indistinguishable from comparison children" at this point (p. 32). Boggs et al. (2004) documented the durability of treatment effects 10 to 30 months after a PCIT intervention; twenty-three families who engaged in PCIT reported less disruptive behavior and less parental stress in a follow-up study. Hood and Eyberg (2003) also added to this research base of long-term efficacy. Following up with 23 mothers who engaged in PCIT with their children 3 to 6 years earlier, Hood and Eyberg (2003) document that the mothers reported a preservation of and even gains in the behavioral improvements that were evident at the end of treatment years before. In addition, the confidence the mothers achieved in terms of being able to influence their child's behavior was an enduring impact of PCIT. Bagner and Eyberg (2003) have documented the disparity in follow-up reports from families participating in PCIT, depending on the involvement of the father. Although not making a marked difference immediately after treatment, the involvement of the father appeared to have a weighty impact on the maintenance of treatment gains.

PCIT, although used primarily for disruptive behavioral disorders in children, is also being used for other childhood problems. Several studies (Borrego, Urquiza, Rasmussen, & Zebell, 1999; Chaffin et al., 2004; Urquiza & McNeil, 1996) have focused on the use of PCIT for families in which physical abuse has occurred. In addition, Choate, Pincus, Eyberg, and Barlow (2005) have conducted a pilot study on the use of PCIT to treat separation anxiety disorder in children and reported a reduction in separation anxiety behaviors, and Eyberg and Matarazzo (1980) have examined the effectiveness of PCIT with children who had delays in speech and language.

PLAY THERAPY WITH SPECIFIC CHILD POPULATIONS AND PROBLEMS

CHILDREN EXPERIENCING ADJUSTMENT DIFFICULTIES IN SCHOOL

The PMHP is a school-based play intervention built on the humanistic and child-centered play theories of Axline's nondirective play therapy (Johnson, Pedro-Carroll, & Demanchick, 2005). The preventative value of child-centered play therapy has been documented by Post (1999). Cowen, Hightower, Pedro-Carroll, Work, Wyman, & Haffney (1996) have described the focus of PMHP as a secondary prevention. The program focuses on identifying elementary children who have a distinct risk for problems before the disruption becomes full-blown. Johnson et al. (2005) defines "five structural components" of PMHP integral to its success:

- Focus on young children
- Early screening and selection
- Use of paraprofessionals to provide direct services to children
- Role change of the school-based mental health professional
- Ongoing program evaluation. (p. 16)

This concrete structure has allowed for a host of PMHP programs to develop in schools across the United States and be subject to continual empirical reviews during the past five decades (Cowen et al., 1996). As discussed previously, the PMHP focuses on elementary age children for its play intervention and also carefully screens potential participants in this program to fit the criteria of secondary prevention. Children also are observed and scored by teachers on various measures and may be asked to self-report their behavior and emotions using instruments such as the Child Rating Scale, a socioemotional self-rating scale (Hightower et al., 1987). Assessment measures are also used to develop treatment goals and processes. Child associates (paraprofessionals), trained and supervised by mental health clinicians in the school, conduct the play sessions. Usually, the paraprofessional meets with a child once a week for 30 minutes. The overarching emphasis of this play intervention is on building a supportive, trusting, collaborative relationship between the child and child associate. As Johnson et al. (2005) explain, "because the Primary Mental Heath project is primarily driven by a theoretical grounding in child-centered play therapy, it is fundamental that the child is able to lead, uncover, and work with troubling thoughts and emotions as the process unfolds" (p. 21). However, the child associate is not a passive play partner, but rather actively engages in the play process and takes advantage of certain moments in the session to delve into relevant themes or to help the child develop needed abilities (Johnson et al., 2005).

Since its origin in 1957, PMHP has been the subject of research evaluations (Cowen et al., 1996). Johnson et al. (1996) note that the National Mental Heath Association honored PMHP as an exemplary prevention program, giving it the Lela Rowland Prevention Award (p. 23). Using a wait-controlled design, Nafpaktitis and Perlmutter (1998) measured the efficacy of PMHP on the school adjustment of first- through fourth-grade children identified as at-risk. For children receiving the child-centered play intervention, teacher ratings regarding school adjustment showed improvement. When compared with the wait-list groups, the children who began PMHP first made statistically significant gains in terms of their shy and anxious behavior, their ability to be appropriately assertive, their success in peer relationships, their frustration tolerance, and their studies (Nafpaktitis & Perlmutter, 1998). Winer-Elkin, Weissberg, and Cowen (1988) have compared at-risk students in a school delivering

Primary Project interventions and similarly at-risk children in a school without this program. According to teacher ratings one academic year later, students receiving the Primary Project intervention made gains in behavior and personal mastery, whereas the control group displayed no such progress. Chandler, Weissberg, Cowen, and Guare (1984) have evaluated the longer term impact of PMHP. Based on the investigation of the adjustment of sixty-one fourth-through sixth-grade students who received PMHP services 2 to 5 years previously, these authors discovered that these children maintained their original treatment effects and were markedly superior in adjustment health compared with demographically matched students currently identified as at-risk.

CHILDREN WITNESSING DOMESTIC VIOLENCE

Kot and Tyndall-Lind (2005) have developed an intensive play therapy technique. Claiming that a specific theory of play therapy is not a determining factor in the effectiveness of the intervention, the authors advocate instead for a brief duration of therapy, a compression of the time between therapy sessions, effective therapeutic space, and therapist preparation and training (p. 37). Kot and Tyndall-Lind (2005), using these four principles, designed an intervention to treat children residing in a shelter due to domestic violence. In 2 to 3 weeks, children received twelve play therapy sessions in rooms prepared with play materials and conducted by trained counselors. The researchers compared a group engaging in individual play therapy and a group receiving sibling play therapy. They established a similarity of treatment effects between the two groups. According to the Child Behavior Checklist and the Joseph Preschool and Primary Self-Concept Screening Test, children in both individual and sibling play therapies exhibited a reduction in externalizing and total behavioral problems, in addition to showing gains in self-concept. The authors note that sibling play therapy, however, may be more efficacious in reducing aggressive and anxious-depressed behaviors (Kot & Tyndall-Lind, 2005, p. 41).

CHILDREN FACING PERSISTENT ILLNESS AND CHILDREN IN THE HOSPITAL

Some children struggle with a host of painful issues and troubling losses, as illness and physical debilitation threaten to replace the joy, the freedom, and the *childhood* in their lives. Johnson and Kreimer (2005) have formulated a rationale for guided fantasy play with children who are chronically ill, citing the value of relaxation, lessening anxiety, diminishing pain, and the processing of loss and grief, in addition to the experience of enjoyment and satisfaction that is no longer available through physical activity. The instinctual, innate quality of play makes it also appropriate for children who, perhaps, have forgotten the carefree play of childhood. The process of guided fantasy, according to these authors, is relatively simple, with the therapist integrating the child's developmental level and interest into a guided fantasy play session where the main tool that is necessary is an imaginative construction of a make-believe world (Johnson & Kreimer, 2005, p. 109).

Guided imagery and related practices become techniques that the child can use to cope with the physical and emotional pain of chronic illness. For example, Jacknow, Tschann, Link, and Boyce (1994) taught self-hypnosis techniques to 20 children with cancer and reported that these children experienced reduced nausea and vomiting related to chemotherapy and decreased their use of antiemetic mediation. These self-hypnosis techniques were similar to the tenets of guided imagery; although progressive relaxation was taught to the older children, the younger children were simply asked to close their eyes and imagine a favorite place or activity (Jacknow et al., 1994, p. 260). Also citing the coping function of fantasy play techniques, Johnson, Whitt, and Martin (1987) report on the reduction in anxiety demonstrated in chronically ill children who received a guided fantasy intervention. As with any other intervention, counselors who choose to use guided imagery or to teach children self-hypnosis techniques should talk to the child and the parent about the procedure and secure permission from them before proceeding.

Other play interventions focus on a broader population of hospitalized children. Rae and Sullivan (2005) stress the unpredictable psychological impact of hospitalization and the role of play therapy in preparing children for this likely unnerving event in their lives (p. 124). The physical and psychological benefits gained through various play interventions in hospital settings is a striking subset of the play therapy literature. Rae, Worchel, Upchurch, Sanner, and Daniel (1989) have documented a diminishment of hospital fears in children receiving therapeutic play; in their self-reports, these children expressed fewer fears than children who experienced diversionary play, verbal support, and no treatment. Young and Fu (1988) assert the value of play in pain management, discussing a needle play intervention that reduced children's objective response to pain. Hewson-Bower and Drummond (2001) use guided imagery and relaxation exercises with children who experienced recurrent upper respiratory tract infections and found a reduction in duration of symptoms that was maintained 1 year later. Castes, Hagel, Palenque, Canelones, Corao, and Lynch (1999) also used guided imagery and relaxation techniques with 35 Venezuelan children who suffered from the dual effects of asthma and parasites. Immune system function improved, inhaler use decreased, and occurrences of asthma diminished after this play intervention. Gillis (1989) conducted a study using structured play activity with immobilized children in a hospital. This researcher discovered that, in comparison with a control group, immobilized children exposed to play experienced gains in self-concept and positive emotions, perhaps because play provides a child with the ability to be "the decision maker and master of control" (Gillis, 1989, p. 267).

Autistic Children

The Denver Model uses play to address autism in children. Initially, the working frame of the Denver Model was a therapeutic preschool setting with daily sessions for a 12-month period, but several variations on the duration and frequency of this original model have been used successfully (Rogers, 2005). Focusing on two types of play deficiencies in autistic children—affective play and symbolic play—this model has been evaluated in various research designs as a viable treatment option for children with autism. The Denver Model promotes affective play—the emotional and social interchanges between adult and infant—through setting up a play interaction and modeling the affective exchange of eye contact, body movement, and reciprocal interaction. Symbolic play—the cognitive aspect of play—is taught through encouraging autistic children to use play materials and thematic elements suitably and realistically (Rogers, 2005). Rogers and Lewis (1989) has replicated a study of the Denver Model. Thirty-one children with infantile autism and pervasive developmental disorder participated in this play intervention and made remarkable improvements 6 months later. Symbolic play improved, social interaction developed and became more appropriate for peer relationships, and autistic symptoms declined (Rogers & Lewis, 1989). Rogers and DiLalla (1991) performed a comparative study of the Denver Model and conducted a play intervention with two groups of preschool children—one group with autism-related disorders and another group with conduct-related disorders. Contrary to the researchers' initial hypothesis, the children with autistic disorders made comparable progress to the children without autism (Rogers & DiLalla, 1991, p. 29).

Related to this Denver Model, other play techniques focusing on one of the two types of play have been developed as credible treatment options. Two studies (Stahmer, 1995; Thorp, Stahmer, & Schriebman, 1995) emphasize symbolic play skills in their Pivotal Response Training; both studies report gains in cognitive tasks and play abilities by the end of treatment. In a study focusing on the affective elements of play, Dawson and Galpert (1990) instruct mothers in imitative play with their autistic children; after 2 weeks of daily imitative play, the researchers found that the affective play proficiency of the children was enhanced, as they gazed longer at their mother's face and made gains in creative toy play. In addition, the social elements of play have been studied by researchers. According to Hwang and Hughes (2000), in a review of sixteen studies, peer play interventions have been used in the treatment of autistic children and have improved language and communication skills in addition to increasing appropriate social behaviors such as eye contact and nonverbal cues. Other studies also have used peer play techniques: Wolfberg and Schuler (1993) have used integrated peer groups and report benefits of increased social play and corresponding enhancement in language and communication; Odom and Strain (1986) have documented the increased play responsiveness of autistic children when peers initiated the play session; and Coe, Matson, Fee, Manikam, and Linarello (1990) have reported on the success of teaching a play skill to three developmentally disabled children in a peer group setting.

Children Experiencing Post-Traumatic Stress Disorder

Shelby and Felix (2005) said, "It is unfortunate to note that advances in theory and methods for assessing child and adolescent trauma victims often lag 5 to 10 years behind similar advances made with adult populations," (p. 98). Post-traumatic Play Therapy is an emerging theory spearheaded by Shelby and

Felix. The authors synthesized available research on post-traumatic techniques and combined them into a framework for treating children experiencing PTSD. Constructing a paradigm where the therapist initially identifies the child's presenting symptom and foremost problem, the authors set up a system for the clinician to coordinate treatment with "a prescriptive chart" that categorizes interventions and readings according to the child's problem (Shelby & Felix, 2005, p. 85). Shelby and Felix categorized the main presenting symptoms of PTSD as intrusive re-experiencing, arousal, dissociation, loss of social competence, and traumatic grief. They then outlined directive or nondirective therapy techniques that the research shows to be most useful in PTSD treatment. Requirements for post-traumatic play therapy include consideration of the child's developmental level, the involvement of the parents in treatment, a therapist knowledgeable about diagnosis and trained in a variety of techniques, and flexibility in the length of treatment according to the child's needs (Shelby & Felix, 2005, pp. 87–88).

Other studies also have examined play therapy techniques for PTSD in children. Examining case study accounts, Ogawa (2004) noted that release play therapy and child-centered play therapy often are used with this population and have gained anecdotal support through case documentation. Release play therapy is encouraging the child to re-enact the traumatic event, with the therapist setting up appropriate toys or even setting up the scene. Child-centered play therapy, in contrast, does not have an explicit agenda for the content of play and focuses instead on the therapeutic value of the therapist–child relationship (Ogawa, 2004). In addition, in applying counseling for trauma to a school setting, Shen and Sink (2002) outlined a child-centered play intervention for elementary children dealing with traumatic life events. The authors propose various school-specific interventions, in addition to a case presentation of child-centered play with a first grader dealing with the aftermath of a disastrous earthquake. In a cross-cultural documentation of play therapy in the aftermath of trauma, Shen (2002) examined the impact of short-term, child-centered play therapy with Chinese elementary students in Taiwan dealing with the repercussions of a 1999 earthquake. Shen reported improvements in the children participating in play therapy when compared with a control group. Those changes included less anxiety, fewer fears, and diminished suicide risk. Shen also noted the cultural considerations to be aware of when beginning play intervention with this population. Because Chinese children often do not experience a high level of cultural permission to play, it may be difficult for some to "fully enjoy the intervention" (Shen, 2002, p. 55).

PLAY THERAPY IN COMBINATION WITH OTHER INTERVENTIONS

Some interventions do not rely solely on the therapeutic power of play, but rather incorporate other techniques into a multimodal program to treat a certain childhood problem. Reddy et al. (2005) have documented CAMP, an empirically valid early intervention for children who have been diagnosed with

ADHD. Designed for children up to 8.5 years of age, CAMP uses behavioral training with parents, children, and teachers, in addition to using techniques of play therapy. Children receive treatment in a separate therapy group. Parents participate in a separate training group. Parents and teachers receive behavioral consultation in their respective settings of home and school. Children and parents participate in CAMP once a week for 90 minutes, and the intervention usually lasts for 10 weeks (Reddy et al., 2005).

The Child Training Group is structured around three goals. This group works to enhance the social skills, self-control, and anger and stress coping skills of children with ADHD (Reddy et al., 2005). Behavioral principles, therapeutic games, and step-by-step skill training are used to aid children in attaining the goals of therapy. Reddy et al. discuss developmentally appropriate games as an integral element of the CAMP model. These games are "competency-based and enjoyable," and draw from the research completed by Bay-Hinitz et al. (1994), which established the positive behavioral impact of cooperate games and the negative effects of competitive games (Reddy et al., 2005, p. 148). The curriculum includes topics of sharing, emotional coping skills, and identification of feelings, anger management, handling stress, refusal skills, and social rules (Reddy et al., 2005). Throughout the sessions, developmentally appropriate games are used in the groups as the children engage in gross motor games that stress cooperation, initiative, and interaction across ability levels.

The Parent Training Group instructs parents in efficacious methods of interacting with their child and supporting their child's unique requirements at home and at school (Reddy et al., 2005). The group format brings universality to the parents' experience, and discussion as well as lectures, handouts, and homework are part of the group times (Reddy et al., 2005). The third element of the CAMP model is the behavioral consultation conducted with parents and teachers in individual sessions.

Reddy et al. (2005) document the impact of the CAMP model with this summary: this intervention has been found effective in reducing aggressive and other externalizing behaviors, diminishing internalizing behaviors, and decreasing parental stress; it has also proven useful in enhancing parental competence and improving children's social ability.

CONSIDERATIONS IN PLAY THERAPY

THERAPIST

Some authors such as Barnes (1996), Landreth (1991), Schaefer and Greenberg (1997), and Kottman (2001) identify the personal characteristics and personality of the counselor as key elements in the play therapy process. According to Kottman (2001), the effective play therapist will most likely be a person who has the following qualities:

- Appreciation of children, treating them with a respectful, kind manner
- A sense of humor and willingness to laugh at oneself

- Playful and fun-loving attitude
- Self-confidence and self-reliance
- Openness and honesty
- Acceptance
- Willingness to use play and metaphors as communication tools
- Flexibility and ability to deal with ambiguity
- Comfort with children and experience interacting with them
- Ability to set limits and maintain personal boundaries
- Self-awareness (pp. 12–13)

Cattanach (1994) has commented on the various ways to be a play therapist. The counselor needs to understand the developmental processes of the child and to learn to play in ways to stimulate the child's participation in the therapeutic relationship. The counselor's style of interacting depends on the children with whom he or she works, his or her personality and skills, and the level of his or her training. Whatever theoretical choice a counselor makes, however, keeping the child safe in the play therapy process is the top priority. Cattanach recognizes that because the counselor is responsible for the process, he or she should seek training and continuing supervision. The importance of training in play therapy was also highlighted by Ray, Armstrong, Warren, and Balkin (2005), who investigated play practices among elementary school counselors. Overall, the largest impediment to carrying out play therapy sessions in the school was a lack of training among the school counselors.

Harris and Landreth (2001) have identified the principles that guide a client-centered play therapist—principles that appear to be applicable across several theoretical approaches. These guidelines include the therapist being interested in the child, as well as being warm, caring, and accepting. In addition, the therapist creates an environment of safety and allows the child opportunities to express himself or herself freely. The therapist attends to the child's feelings, trusts the child's inner directions, and respects the child's capacity to act responsibly.

APPROPRIATE CLIENTS

Kottman (2001) identifies most play therapy clients as children between 3 and 11 years of age, although some younger (as young as 2) and older children (12–15 years old) may participate. He suggests that counselors ask the children whether they would rather sit and talk or play with toys.

Anderson and Richards (1995) direct counselors to begin by assessing the following capabilities of the potential child client:

1. The ability to tolerate/build/use a relationship with an adult
2. The ability to tolerate/accept a protective environment
3. The capacity to learn new ways of coping
4. The potential to gain new insight and the motivation to try
5. The attention span and cognitive organization to participate

These authors also admonish counselors to consider whether play therapy is an effective way to address this particular child's concern and whether conditions in the child's environment will impede the play therapy process. A child's limited ability in the five capabilities mentioned above or a negative answer to the other considerations would imply that play therapy would not be the appropriate choice for that child.

PLAY STAGES

Gumaer (1984) states that the use of play media by a counselor must be attended by purposeful interaction to allow maximum effectiveness. Orton (1997) presents an integrated approach to the therapeutic play process that moves through five stages: (1) relationship, (2) release, (3) re-creation, (4) re-experiencing, and (5) resolving. Through this process, a strong relationship is built in which the child feels accepted and understood. The child uses play to express feelings and to ease tension through cathartic release. As the relationship grows, the child begins to explore significant events or relationships that trigger uncomfortable thoughts and feelings. Children begin to understand the links between past events and to connect that knowledge with current thoughts, behaviors, and feelings. The final stage is reached when children are able to act on their understanding and to experiment with various solutions.

Bradley and Gould (1993) discuss a three-stage process. Stage one is relationship building. The counselor focuses on emotions evident in the child's playing and responds to them. At the same time, the counselor develops hypotheses about the child's problems or needs. In the second stage, the relationship is well established and the counselor becomes more assertive in directing the child's play. While reviewing the hypotheses and determining one that appears to be the most crucial, the counselor encourages play with specific toys or in specific ways that are likely to evoke feelings and behaviors related to the hypothesis. The counselor may initiate deeper exploration of the feelings and behavior that the child demonstrates during play. If the hypothesis seems incorrect, the counselor should redirect the play to another area. During the third stage, the counselor is more active and engages the child in structured play sequences that encourage the child to confront the problem area.

Rasmussen and Cunningham (1995) describe a similar model that integrates focused play and nondirective play. As in the stages discussed by Orton (1997), these authors suggest that play therapy proceed from nondirective to more directive play. Across all the sessions, the counselor should respond to feelings, clarify behavior, and use open-ended questions to encourage the child to talk. Fall (1997) has examined the transcripts of 186 play therapy sessions with elementary students. She reports four descriptive categories of children's play. During the sessions all the children at some time exhibited play that was characterized as "connected" and "safe play." The other two categories were "unsafe play" and "resolution." Those categories of play have direct implications to counselors who may use them to help in monitoring the progress through the stages proposed earlier. Cattanach (1995) suggests that children exhibit sensory play, projective play, and dramatic play, and that the most satisfying play contains elements of all types.

Gumaer (1984) defines the play therapy process as being controlled by the counselor and being related to specific factors. One aspect central to the play therapy process involves the counselor's ability to build a helpful relationship with the child. A second feature concerns the goals of counseling, which include the counselor's ability to understand the child's problem. Another critical factor relates to the counselor's planning skills and use of play material. The counselor's facilitative responding skills influence the play therapy process, as well as the time available to spend with the child. In summary, these experts suggest that the stages of play therapy begin with building a relationship with the child and allowing free play to become more focused play in which the child can explore his or her difficulties and move toward a resolution. Other factors that Gumaer outlines also influence the play therapy process.

PLAY THERAPY AND MANAGED HEALTH CARE

Barnes (1991) has suggested criteria for assessing progress toward goals of play therapy:

1. The child comes to the sessions looking more hopeful and relaxed.
2. The child appears to have increased confidence.
3. The child can summarize what has happened and what has been learned.
4. The child's interactions with parents appear more relaxed.
5. Play patterns, interactions, and/or body language have changed.
6. The child openly raises a problem or concern.

These criteria could be used to help formulate outcomes for the goals of play therapy, allowing counselors to document the effectiveness of play therapy for themselves, for their clients, and for managed care purposes. The previous discussion of managed care in Chapter 2 offers further guidelines on this type of documentation.

PLAY THERAPY MEDIA AND STRATEGIES

The materials and props a counselor may use in these sessions are play media. These tools help capture children's interest, provide children with a way to express themselves, and can aid the counselor in assessing a child's difficulty. For example, Ashby, Kottman, and Martin (2004) examined perfectionism in children and found that the ways in which a child manipulated the play media could provide a window into whether the child's perfectionism was an adaptive and potentially helpful trait or a maladaptive and harmful characteristic. The authors found that adaptively perfectionist children placed high standards on their play behavior and performance, but did not revert into global, self-deprecating remarks or total desertion of the activity if they, for example, do not construct a block structure in the exact way that they desired. Maladaptively perfectionist children, however, gave up easily when they made a mistake with play media and quickly moved into comments about total failure if their performance did not meet their expectations (Ashby et al., 2004).

The counselor should consider the complexities, the nuances, and the vital role of play material in therapy sessions as they make choices about play media. The materials should be chosen based on the following criteria:

1. Facilitating the relationship between the counselor and child
2. Encouraging the child's expression of thoughts and feelings
3. Helping the counselor gain insight into the child's world
4. Providing the child with an opportunity to test reality
5. Providing the child with an acceptable means for expressing unacceptable thoughts and feelings

The material should be selected carefully rather than merely accumulated (Landreth, 1993). Barlow, Strother, and Landreth (1985) provide three categories of play media that could be helpful in collecting materials: real-life toys, acting-out and aggressive-release toys, and creative expression and emotional-release toys. Bradley and Gould (1993) suggest the following specific examples for each of those categories:

> *Real-life toys:* doll house and furniture, dolls, doll clothes, doll buggy, bendable doll family, rag doll, household items (iron, ironing board, play kitchen, dishes), telephone, cars, farm animals and buildings, medical kit, school kit, play money, plastic fruit, purse, jewelry
>
> *Acting-out and aggressive-release toys:* handcuffs, balls, dart gun and suction darts, dart board, suction throwing darts, pounding bench and hammer, drum, blocks, toy soldiers and military equipment, rubber knife, toy gun, masks, inflatable punching toy
>
> *Creative expression and emotional-release toys:* colored chalk and eraser, sandbox and sand pencils, paints and brushes, felt-tip pens, white and colored paper, easel, crayons, tape, paste, blunt scissors, Play-Doh clay or plasticine, pipe cleaners, hats and costumes, rags or old towels, hand puppets (p. 87)

Neil and Landreth (2001) list items for a portable play bag used by a traveling play therapist in a school. Gil (1991) emphasizes the use of sunglasses in her work with abused children, noting that children believe they are invisible when they put on sunglasses. She also underscores the use of therapeutic stories in her therapy. Kottman (2001) includes toys for older children such as craft supplies, carpentry tools, office supplies and equipment, and more sophisticated games.

The strategies a counselor uses with play media will depend on the theoretical approach that is being followed. Rasmussen and Cunningham (1995) state that both directive and nondirective techniques have advantages. They suggest that in choosing strategies, the counselor should consider: (1) the characteristics of the child, (2) the child's problem(s) and needs, and (3) the stage of the counseling process. Certainly the therapeutic goals must be considered as well.

As an example of the use of different media, Fall (1994) incorporates the use of clay, puppets, and beanbag chairs in a school counseling practice. Some common techniques and media useful in communicating with children are art, puppets, and sand play. The next section further explores these props as examples of play therapy techniques. Counselors and children engaging in play therapy have many other possibilities from which to choose. The books *101 Favorite Play Therapy Techniques* (Kaduson, Cangelosi, & Schaefer, 1997b) and *Windows to our Children* (Oaklander, 1988), as well as many others, contain valuable examples of the use of storytelling, drama, poetry, games, and other techniques.

BASIC SKILLS OF PLAY THERAPY

Kottman (2001, 2004) explains the basic skills used by all play therapists. He identifies and explains the generic skills of tracking, restating content, reflecting feelings, returning responsibility to the child, using the child's metaphor, and limiting.

Counselors use tracking to describe what the child is doing. The counselor avoids labeling objects by keeping descriptions vague. Counselors use pronouns such as "this" or "it" and phrases such as "moving back and forth" or "looking up and down." An example of tracking would be the response "You are picking that up" as the counselor sees a child lift a doll off the shelf.

Restating content refers to paraphrasing what the child has said to convey concern and understanding. Counselors use their own words to relay the content, but choose vocabulary appropriate to the child's level of understanding. An illustration of restating occurs in the following interchange. A child says, "My mom likes for me to practice piano, but I hate it," and the counselor replies "Your mom and you have different ideas about playing the piano."

Counselors reflect children's feelings to deepen the relationship and to help the child understand emotions, learn more about being with others, and expand their affective vocabulary. Counselors use phrases such as "You seem happy today" or "You're scared when the puppet yells."

Kottman (2001), Landreth (1991), and Muro and Kottman (1995) explain that the strategy of returning responsibility to the child builds self-reliance, self-confidence, and self-responsibility. The practice can also help with decision making, a sense of accomplishment, and feelings of mastery and control. Counselors allow children to take action ("I think you know how to close the play chest.") or to make decisions ("It can be whatever you want it to be.")

Using the child's metaphor means that the counselor maintains the child's story without imposing the counselor's interpretation of the meaning. Kottman (2004) explains this as the counselor being careful to restrain and "avoid 'breaking' the metaphor by going outside the story to the 'real' world" (p. 122).

Finally, the skill of setting limits in the play area keeps the child safe, increases a sense of self-control, and enhances self-responsibility. Appropriate limits include those intended to (1) protect the child from hurting self or others, (2) keep the child from damaging the play setting, (3) maintain the toys and play media in the play setting, and (4) stay in the session for the scheduled amount of time.

Counselors who use these basic skills may find the following strategies helpful in conducting play therapy sessions.

ART

Counselors may choose the use of art in therapy for many reasons. Gladding (2005) notes that visual arts offer five benefits for counselors. One benefit is the access to the unconscious. A second advantage is the symbolizing of emotions in tangible ways. A third benefit is that visual arts help people become more self-aware. Fourth, the visual arts are a nonthreatening method and are open to self-interpretation. Finally, they can easily be combined with other play methods. Orton (1997) states that art helps establish a relationship, helps children express and resolve their conflicts, and promotes self-expression, problem solving, and confidence.

Kramer (1971) focuses on the healing power of the act of creating. She explains that process and product are ways of releasing conflict, re-experiencing and rechanneling it, and resolving it. Art is soothing and can serve as a lubricant for communicating thoughts and feelings (Rubin, 1988). Children should have their choice of medium, and counselors can be directive or nondirective about leading them to a certain subject. Landgarten (1981) suggests giving themes for children to address in their artwork such as emotions, wishes, dreams, plans, self-image, fantasies, families, and situations. Time at the end of the counseling session should be devoted to a discussion of the children's work (Nader & Pynoos, 1991).

Art materials can include crayons, finger paint, felt-tip markers, paints, clay and Play-Doh, paper, scissors, paste, glue, and glitter. Gladding (2005) also suggests using published pictures and photography. Campbell (1993a,b) suggests a school counselor might keep an easel with paper, paint, and brushes available for children to use while talking with the counselor.

For counselors to use the "magic art" technique, they need to have a range of colors of construction paper and assorted colors of liquid tempera paint with small openings in the tops. The child is allowed to select a piece of paper and at least three colors of paint to make a magic picture. The counselor tells the children to draw lines, dots, or any figure they like. After the picture is finished, the child is asked to fold the paper lengthwise. The counselor says, "magic picture, what will (child's name) draw today?" Then the child unfolds the paper to reveal the new "picture." The counselor asks the child to describe what she or he sees in the picture and is questioned about what makes it look like that (Walker, 1998). Another strategy for counselors is to use yarn to create drawings. Leben (1997) states that this alternative to paper-and-pencil drawing is more appealing to children with low self-esteem.

Berger and Tyler (1994) have practiced a model called the "color-emotive brain." Children illustrate their brain, visualizing their level of emotion, then move to a deeper level of disclosure and increased motivation to reach their goals. Shelby (1997) describes extensive use of visual arts in her work with children who had survived a disaster. Steinhardt (1995) reports the use of art with a boy who was diagnosed with a borderline disorder. This case study includes the child's response to drawing, masks, and clay. The author notes the effectiveness of providing an environment in which the child discovered his suppressed emotions while playing.

Clay is an art medium that can be used in play therapy. Some activities using clay can be connected to therapeutic goals. Children can roll clay into a ball and then smash it down. They could also squeeze the clay through their fingers with varying degrees of pressure. To use clay as an activity for self-awareness, children can create a personal mobile. They may use different amounts of clay to represent the value they place on decision points. Clay also can be used to help children clarify goals, build communication skills, and develop time-management strategies.

A final example of the use of art as therapy is provided by Hanes (1997), who presented a case study of a child with aggressive behavior, uncontrollable tantrums, and other behavioral problems. The child produced "messy mixtures" with art materials as she progressed through therapy, eventually improving enough to be released from the hospital.

Puppets

Axline (1947, 1969) suggests that puppets provide opportunities for children to play out their feelings, to re-enact events that produced anxiety, and to try out new behaviors. Puppets also allow children to develop communication skills, overcome isolation, build self-esteem, release emotions, and make decisions (Jewel, 1989). Children can use puppets to tell stories and play out their fantasies. They can act out feelings and deal with their thoughts through puppetry. The child can create a separate person who communicates things too difficult for the child to express directly. Finally, the puppet may be the target of the child's strong emotions—an object of displacement so that anger can be expressed in a healthy way (Bromfield, 1995; Orton, 1997). Gil (1991) identifies a benefit of puppet play as the child creating a story anonymously, using characters to enact hidden concerns. Puppet play is also an effective activity for large or small groups of children.

Puppets can be bought or handmade. Carter and Mason (1998) have explained some practical guidelines for selecting puppets. Some of the guidelines are also useful in selecting dolls. Counselors should determine how they intend to use the puppets and should have a variety for the children's choice. The puppets should be chosen to represent a range of emotions such as aggression, friendship, and neutrality. Puppets should also be representative of family and cultural groups. Other categories for puppets are occupations, symbolic types (witch, pirate), and wild and tame animals. The collection of puppets should relate symbolically to the problems of children. James and Myer (1987) list these other important selection considerations:

- Ease of manipulation
- Lack of universal symbolism (not Santa Claus)

- Ability to fit both children's and adult's hands
- Unless ventriloquist's dummies or marionettes, soft and cuddly rather than firm and rigid
- Washable

The final selection consideration is whether the puppet has a "personality" to which the counselor responds with an engaged imagination (Carter & Mason, 1998).

The counselor who plans to use puppets does not have to be a ventriloquist. Basic skills are developing a voice for the puppet's personality, keeping the puppet active enough to engage and hold the child's attention, and knowing when to talk to the child and when to talk to the puppet. To use puppets successfully, counselors must become transparent, real, and courageous. The puppet should look up and out. Only the lower jaw of the puppet should move. Counselors should practice creating emotional expressions and other "moves" in front of a mirror to achieve a realistic presentation (Bradley & Gould, 1993; Carter & Mason, 1998; James & Myer, 1987).

Irwin (1991) uses puppets in the following process. First, the child is offered a selection of puppets and invited to tell a story using them as characters. The child chooses the puppets and creates the story as the counselor observes the child's coping skills in dealing with this experience. The child introduces the puppets as "characters" in the show and "enacts" the story. After the play, the counselor asks the puppets about the plot and themes of the story, extending the make-believe story. For the final step, the child is invited to discuss the story and the experience with the counselor. Gil (1991) suggests allowing the child to sit behind a sheet so that the play can be conducted with the child hidden.

The use of puppets with certain groups of children has been examined. Herring and Meggert (1994) discuss using puppets in working with Native American children. The authors report that puppetry is beneficial because of the Native American children's love of humor, the importance of clownlike figures in their folklore, and their love of storytelling. Aiello (1988) provides information about the puppet program "Kids on the Block." The puppets in this program represent children who are disabled, as well as those who are not disabled. The goal of the program is to aid in understanding and appreciating differences.

SAND

Bradley and Gould (1993) consider sand play to be a self-healing process for the child. Kalff (1981) identifies the counselor's role in sand play as being a respectful witness. Gil (1991) suggests that children enjoy the experience of touching, molding, and shaping sand, as well as letting it run through their fingers. She concludes that some children feel nurtured, calmed, or soothed by sand play. Other children use sand play to "make a world," as first discussed by Lowenfeld (1935/1991) as "the World Technique." Kalff (1981) states that the child resolves conflicts and traumas by externalizing and developing a sense of mastery and control when using sand play. Vinturella and James (1987) believe that sand play is more beneficial than other approaches because no skill is required.

The sand tray is a container with the general dimensions of 20 × 30 × 3 inches. Some counselors use two trays, one for dry sand and one for wet sand; others use only a dry tray. The interior of the tray is painted blue to simulate water. Carmichael (1994) suggests a transparent plastic storage container with a blue top that can be placed under the tray to provide the blue color. Some dry materials that can be substituted for sand are cornmeal, dried beans or peas, rice, popcorn, and aquarium gravel. The child is offered a choice of miniatures in the following categories:

Buildings: houses, schools, churches, castles

People: domestic, military, fantasy, mythological

Animals: domestic, wild, zoo, prehistoric, marine

Vehicles: land, air, water, space, war machines

Vegetation: trees, bushes, shrubs, plants, vegetables

Structures: bridges, fences, gates, doorways, corrals

Natural objects: shells, driftwood, stones, bones

Symbolic objects: wishing well, treasure chests, jewelry (Allan, 1988, p. 231; Stermback, 1991).

In addition to these miniatures, Allan (1988) indicates that families of items be included—for example, three dinosaurs, four snakes, or a doll family.

The process begins with an invitation to create a miniature world. The counselor provides unconditional positive regard, empathy, warmth, and genuineness (Allan & Berry, 1987; Carmichael, 1994; Landreth, 1993; Stermback, 1991). Allan and Berry describe "the sand as the process, the sand tray as the medium, and the world as the product" (p. 301). DeDomenico (1988) states that the session should progress without adult interference. The counselor is an attentive observer in the process (Carmichael, 1994).

According to Allan and Berry (1987), three stages occur in sand play: chaos, struggle, and resolution. In the chaos stage, the child imposes no order on the toys or sand. During the struggle phase, battles are waged. At the beginning, no winner emerges. As the sessions progress, the fighting may become more intense and organized and struggles may become more balanced. A hero emerges, who wins the fight against the dark side. The child who demonstrates resolution restores order and balance in the sand play. The toy figures are in place, and completion and wholeness are apparent (Allan & Berry, 1987; Kalff, 1981).

Mulherin (2001) provides a case study using the sand tray with a mother and child. She discusses the processes of separation, individuation, rapprochement, and recovery that occurred during the stage of treatment. She provides pictures to illustrate how the child represented his emotional states. Vaz (2000) also presents pictures to chronicle the process of sand play. Vaz surveys other therapists who use sand play. She concludes that most therapists consider the sand play process complete when the images used in the tray reflect the client's return to a more effective approach to life.

Sand trays were used as a nonviolent method of helping children deal with emotional distress (Wheat, 1995). Each child in an early childhood group was allowed 30 to 60 minutes a week with the sand trays. Teachers who observed the process commented that the children worked through feelings of sadness, anger, and disappointment, returning to the classroom group in a more relaxed state. The teachers were supportive of the sand play.

This brief overview of using art, puppets, and sand trays serves as an example of the possibilities of play media. Counselors are encouraged to investigate others ways, as well as to create their own ways of incorporating play materials into their counseling practice. The following case study illustrates one additional method.

Case Study[1]

Identification of the Problem

Amos is a sixth-grade student in a rural middle school. His teacher referred him to the school counselor because his grades had dropped since the beginning of the school year and he was frequently distracted in class.

Individual and Background Information

Academic. School records indicate that Amos's ability is in the average range. He received good grades in elementary school, and teachers noted his positive disposition and quiet nature. End-of-grade tests indicate that his math skills are much stronger than his verbal skills.

Family. Amos lives with his mother and stepfather. He has an older half brother who is in eighth grade at the same school and a younger brother in the third grade at a nearby elementary school. Although Amos has not told the counselor, she knows his older brother was in a serious accident during the past summer and recently has had an operation. The brother has not returned to school.

Social. According to teachers' reports, Amos is well liked and easily forms friendships. He is involved with several school sports teams and clubs. He enjoys interacting with his classmates.

Counseling Method

After the initial meeting with Amos to assess the problem, the counselor decided he might benefit from an alternative method of counseling rather than verbal interactions only. She decided to use a nondirected play therapy approach.

---

[1]Margery Peskin contributed the case of Amos.

Transcript

COUNSELOR: Hi, Amos! How are you doing today?

AMOS: Fine.

COUNSELOR: Last time we met you mentioned you had a basketball game that night. How did it go?

AMOS: Okay.

COUNSELOR: How did you think the game went?

AMOS: Pretty good.

COUNSELOR: That sounds positive. Today I thought we could try something a little different than what we've been doing. I laid out on the table here some supplies. You can see I've got colored paper, markers, crayons, glue, yarn, scissors, clay, and watercolors.

AMOS: I love clay. I work with clay at home all the time.

COUNSELOR: Great. It sounds like you've had some experience with some of these materials. Here's what I'd like you to do. Using any combination of the materials here, create something that shows me what you have been thinking about the most over the past few days. You can use just one kind of material or as many as you want. Also, I want you to understand that there is not a "right" or "wrong" way to do this; create anything you want. Remember that our relationship is confidential, so I'm not going to show what you've made to anyone else unless you ask me to. Any questions?

AMOS: No.

COUNSELOR: Okay.

After some time has passed:

AMOS: I'm done.

COUNSELOR: I wonder if you'd tell me what you've made.

AMOS: Well, the two clay figures are my parents. See my mom has long blond hair, so this one has yellow string on the top, and my dad has short blond hair, so this one has a short yellow string. This rectangle of paper on the table is a hospital bed, and this clay is my brother because he's been really sick and had an operation on his neck.

COUNSELOR: It must be hard that your brother is so sick. One thing I notice is that you're not in this scene.

AMOS: Well, I would have made myself, but there wasn't enough clay.

COUNSELOR: You're feeling left out.

AMOS: Lots of the time I think they have forgotten me.

COUNSELOR: So it sounds like your parents are spending a lot of time with your brother in the hospital.

AMOS: Yeah, they go there every afternoon, so when I get home from school no one is at home.

COUNSELOR: That must be pretty difficult because you are worried about your brother but feel lonely too.

AMOS: Yeah, sometimes.

COUNSELOR: I'm wondering if you ever feel guilty because you wish your parents weren't spending so much time with your brother so they might have more time to spend with you.

AMOS: Exactly. But I feel really bad about that.

COUNSELOR: It sounds like there are a lot of different things for you to be worried about that might be making it hard to concentrate in school.

AMOS: Usually I like school, but right now I'm sad all the time. I keep wondering if the doctors have found out anything about my brother, and then I wonder if my mom or dad will be home after school, and then I feel bad because my brother needs them too.

COUNSELOR: You have lots of different things fighting for your attention. Maybe we can figure out some ways to help you relax a bit. Let's meet again on Wednesday to see what we can try.

AMOS: That sounds good.

SUMMARY

The field of play therapy is simultaneously amending a deficit and gaining authority as an outcome-based intervention for specific childhood problems and populations as the empirical research base of effectiveness grows (Reddy et al., 2005). Researchers may now move to focus on additional therapeutic approaches and childhood difficulties (Files-Hall & Reddy, 2005). Play is integral and natural to the world of a child; it is an innate tendency and an essential language. Establishing the base of measurable outcomes, the value of play as a therapeutic intervention can gain a credible and extensive application.

Lowenfeld (1935/1991) and her staff at the Institute of Child Psychology in London recorded and classified the play of 229 children between the years 1928 and 1934. Her book documented the classification of the children's play as bodily activity, repetition of experience, demonstration of fantasies, realization of the environment, and preparation for life. She concluded that play served the following four purposes for children:

- Play is children's means for making contact with the environment in a way similar to the social aspect of work in an adult's life.
- Play helps children bridge consciousness and emotional experiences as conversation, introspection, philosophy, and religion do for adults.

- Play represents to the child the overt expression of his or her emotional life as art does for an adult.
- Play serves the child as relaxation and amusement. (Lowenfeld, 1935/1991, p. 232).

Lowenfeld argued that play is an essential function of moving from immaturity to emotional maturity. With the instinctive, innate quality of play and its unique attributes and additions to the world of children, play can hold a pivotal position in helping children through a variety of problems, traumas, and obstacles. Counselors strive to enhance the development of children, and play therapy can be used as a significant way of influencing that growth.

INTRODUCTION TO PLAY THERAPY

To gain a more in-depth understanding of the concepts in this chapter, visit www.thomsonedu.com/counseling/thompson to view a short clip of an actual therapist-client session demonstrating play therapy.

WEBSITES FOR PLAY THERAPY

Internet addresses frequently change. To find the sites listed here, visit www.thomsonedu. com/counseling/thompson for an updated list of Internet addresses and direct links to relevant sites.

Association for Play Therapy, Inc.

Canadian Play Therapy Institute

REFERENCES

Aiello, B. (1988). The Kids on the Block and attitude change: A 10-year perspective. In H. E. Yucker (Ed.), *Attitudes toward persons with disabilities* (pp. 223–229). New York: Springer.

Albon, S. L. (1996). The therapeutic action of play. *Journal of American Academy of Child Adolescent Psychiatry, 35*(4), 545–547.

Allan, J. (1988). *Inscapes of the child's world: Jungian counseling in schools and clinics.* Dallas, TX: Spring.

Allan, J., & Berry, P. (1987). Sand play. *Elementary School Guidance & Counseling, 21,* 300–306.

Anderson, J., & Richards, N. (1995, October). *Play therapy in the real world: Coping with managed care, challenging children, skeptical colleagues, time and space constraints.* Paper presented at the First Annual Conference of the Iowa Association of Play Therapy, Iowa City, IA.

Ariel, S. (1992). *Strategic family play therapy.* New York: Wiley & Sons.

Ariel, S. (1997). Strategic family play therapy. In K. O'Connor & L. M. Braverman (Eds.), *Play therapy theory and practice: A comparative presentation* (pp. 358–395). New York: Wiley & Sons.

Ashby, J., Kottman, T., & Martin, J. (2004). Play therapy with young perfectionists. *International Journal of Play Therapy, 13*(1), 35–55.

Association for Play Therapy. (1997). Play therapy definition. *Association for Play Therapy Newsletter, 16*(2), 4.

Axline, V. (1947). *Play therapy: The inner dynamics of childhood.* Boston: Houghton Mifflin.

Axline, V. (1969). *Dibs: In search of self.* Boston: Houghton Mifflin.

Bagner, D., & Eyberg, S. (2003). Father involvement in parent training: When does it matter? *Journal of Clinical Child and Adolescent Psychology, 32*(4), 599–605.

Barlow, K., Strother, J., & Landreth, G. (1985). Child-centered play therapy: Nancy from baldness to curls. *The School Counselor, 32,* 347–356.

Barnes, M. (1991). *The magic of play therapy: A workshop on specialized therapeutic skills with children.* London, Ontario, Canada: Mandala Therapeutic Services.

Barnes, M. (1996). *The healing path with children: An exploration for parents and professional.* Kingston, Ontario, Canada: Viktoria, Fermoyle & Berrigan.

Bay-Hinitz, A., Peterson, R., & Quilitch, H. (1994). Cooperative games: A way to modify aggressive and cooperative behaviors in young children. *Journal of Applied Behavior Analysis, 27,* 435–446.

Bay-Hinitz., A., & Wilson, G. (2005). A cooperative games intervention for aggressive preschool children. In L. A. Reddy, T. M. Files-Hall, & C. E. Schaefer (Eds.), *Empirically based play interventions for children* (pp. 191–211). Washington, DC: American Psychological Association.

Berger, S. N., & Tyler, J. L. (1994). The color-emotive brain: Gone a long journey. *International Journal of Play Therapy, 33*(1), 57–70.

Boggs, S., Eyberg, S., Edwards, D., Rayfield, A., Jacobs, J., Bagner, D., & Hood, K. (2004). Outcomes of Parent-Child Interaction Therapy: A comparison of treatment completers and study dropouts one to three years later. *Child & Family Behavior Therapy, 26*(4), 1–22.

Borrego, J., Urquiza, A., Rasmussen, R., & Zebell, N. (1999). Parent-child interaction therapy with a family at high risk for physical abuse. *Child Maltreatment, 4*(4), 331–342.

Bradley, L. J., & Gould, L. J. (1993). Individual counseling: Creative interventions. In A. Vernon (Ed.), *Counseling children and adolescents* (pp. 84–117). Denver, CO: Love Publishing.

Bratton, S. C. (1994). *Filial therapy with single parents* (DAI-A 54/08). Unpublished doctoral dissertation, University of North Texas, Denton, TX.

Bratton, S., & Landreth, G. (1995). Filial therapy with single parents: Effects on parental acceptance, empathy, and stress. *International Journal of Play Therapy, 4*(1), 61–80.

Bratton, S., & Ray, D. (2000). What the research shows about play therapy. *International Journal of Play Therapy, 9*(1), 47–88.

Bratton, S., & Ray, D., & Moffit, K. (1998). Filial/family play therapy: An intervention for custodial grandparents and their grandchildren. *Educational Gerontology, 24,* 391–407.

Brestan, E., Jacobs, J., Rayfield, A., & Eyberg, S. (1999). A consumer satisfaction measure for parent-child treatments and its relations for measures of child behavior change. *Behavior Therapy, 30,* 17–30.

Briesmeister, J. M. (1997). Play therapy with depressed children. In H. G. Kaduson, D. Cangelosi, & C. E. Schaefer (Eds.), *The playing cure: Individualized play therapy for specific childhood problems* (pp. 3–28). Northvale, NJ: Jason Aronson.

Bromfield, R. (1995). The use of puppets in play therapy. *Child and Adolescent Social Work Journal, 12*(6), 435–444.

Campbell, C. A. (1993a). Interview with Violet Oaklander, author of *Windows to our Children. Elementary School Guidance & Counseling, 28*(1), 52–61.

Campbell, C. A. (1993b). Play, the fabric of elementary school counseling programs. *Elementary School Guidance & Counseling, 28*(1), 10–16.

Cangelosi, D. M. (1997). Play therapy for children from divorced and separated families. In H. G. Kaduson, D. Cangelosi, & C. E. Schaefer (Eds.), *The playing cure: individualized play therapy for specific childhood problems* (pp. 119–142). Northvale, NJ: Jason Aronson.

Carmichael, K. D. (1994). Sand play as an elementary school strategy. *Elementary School Guidance & Counseling, 28*, 302–307.

Carmichael, K. D., & Lane, K. S. (1997). Play therapy with children of alcoholics. *Alcoholism Treatment Quarterly, 15*(1), 43–52.

Carter, R. B., & Mason, P. S. (1998). The selection and use of puppets in counseling. *Professional School Counseling, 1*(5), 50–53.

Castes, M., Hagel, I., Palenque, M., Canelones, P., Corao, A., & Lynch, N. (1999). Immunological changes associated with clinical improvement of asthmatic children subjected to psychosocial intervention. *Brain, Behavior, and Immunity, 13,* 1–13.

Cattanach, A. (1994). *Play therapy: Where the sky meets the underworld.* Bristol, PA: Jessica Kingsley Publishers.

Cattanach, A. (1995). Drama and play therapy with young children. *The Arts in Psychotherapy, 22*(3), 223–228.

Chaffin, M., Silvosky, J., Funderbunk, B., Valle, L., Brestan, E., Balachova, T., Jackson, S., Lensgraf, J., & Bonner, B. (2004). Parent-child interaction therapy with physically abusive parents: Efficacy for reducing future abuse reports. *Journal of Consulting and Clinical Psychology, 72*(3), 500–510.

Chandler, C., Weissberg, R., Cowen, E., & Guare, J. (1984). Long-term effects of a school-based secondary prevention program for young maladapting children. *Journal of Consulting and Clinical Psychology, 52*(2), 165–170.

Chau, I., & Landreth, G. (1997). Filial therapy with Chinese parents: Effects on parental empathic interactions, parental acceptance of child and parental stress. *International Journal of Play Therapy, 6*(2), 75–92.

Choate, M., Pincus, D., Eyberg, S., & Barlow, D. (2005). Parent-child interaction therapy for the treatment of separation anxiety disorder in young children: A pilot study. *Cognitive and Behavioral Practice, 12,* 126–135.

Cochran, J. L. (1996). Using play and art therapy to help culturally diverse students overcome barriers to school success. *The School Counselor, 43*(4), 287–298.

Coe, D., Matson, J., Fee, V., Manikam, R., & Linarello, C. (1990). Training nonverbal and verbal play skills to mentally retarded and autistic children. *Journal of Autism and Developmental Disorders, 20,* 177–187.

Coleman, V., Parmer, T., & Barker, S. (1993). Play therapy for a multicultural population: Guidelines for mental health professionals. *International Journal of Play Therapy, 2*(1), 63–74.

Costas, M., & Landreth, G. (1999). Filial therapy with non-offending parents of children who have been sexually abused. *International Journal of Play Therapy, 8*(1), 43–66.

Cowen, E., Hightower, A., Pedro-Carroll, J., Work, W., Wyman, P., & Haffney, W. (1996). *School-based prevention for children at risk: The Primary Mental Health Project.* Washington, DC: American Psychological Association.

Dawson, G., & Galpert, L. (1990). Mothers' use of imitative play for facilitating social responsiveness and toy play in young autistic children. *Development and Psychopathology, 2,* 151–162.

DeDomenico, G. (1988). *Sand tray world play: A comprehensive guide to the use of the sand tray in psychotherapeutic and transformational settings.* San Francisco, CA: San Francisco State University.

Doyle, J., & Stoop, D. (1999). Witness and victim of multiple abuses: Case of Randy, age 10, in a residential treatment center, and follow-up at age 19 in prison. In N. V. Webb (Ed.), *Play therapy with children in crisis* (2nd ed., pp. 131–163). New York: Guilford.

Eisenstadt, T., Eyberg, S., McNeil, C., Newcomb, K., & Funderbunk, B. (1993). Parent-child interaction therapy with behavior problem children: Relative effectiveness of two stages and overall treatment outcomes. *Journal of Clinical Child Psychology, 22*(1), 42–51.

Elkin, J. I. W., Weissberg, R., & Cowen, E. (1988). Evaluation of a planned short-term intervention for schoolchildren with focal adjustment problems. *Journal of Clinical Child Psychology, 17*(2), 106–115.

Eyberg, S., Funderbunk, B., Hembree-Kigin, T., McNeil, C., Querido, J., & Hood, K. (2001). Parent-child interaction therapy with behavior problem children: One and two year maintenance of treatment effects in the family. *Child & Family Behavior Therapy, 23*(4), 1–20.

Eyberg, S., & Matarazzo, R. (1980). Training parents as therapists: A comparison between individual parent-child interaction training and parent group didactic training. *Journal of Clinical Psychology, 36*(2), 492–499.

Fall, M. (1994). Physical and emotional expression: A combination approach for working with children in the small areas of a school counselor's office. *The School Counselor, 42,* 73–77.

Fall, M. (1997). From stages to categories: A study of children's play in play therapy. *International Journal of Play Therapy, 6*(1), 1–21.

Fall, M. (1999). A play therapy intervention and its relationship to self-efficacy and learning behaviors. *Professional School Counseling, 2,* 194–205.

Files-Hall, T., & Reddy, L. (2005). Present status and future directions for empirically based play interventions for children. In L. A. Reddy, T. M. Files-Hall, & C. E. Schaefer (Eds.), *Empirically based play interventions for children* (pp. 267–279). Washington, DC: American Psychological Association.

Fischetti, B. (2001). Use of play therapy for anger management in the school setting. In A. Drewes, L. Carey, & C. Schaefer (Eds.), *School-based play therapy* (pp. 238–256). New York: John Wiley & Sons.

Funderbunk, B., Eyberg, S., Newcomb, K., McNeil, C., Hembree-Kigin, T., & Capage, L. (1998). Parent-child interaction therapy with behavior problem children: Maintenance of treatment effects in the school setting. *Child & Family Behavior Therapy, 20*(2), 17–38.

Gallagher, N. (2003). Effects of parent-child interaction therapy on young children with disruptive behavior disorders. *Bridges: Practice-Based Research Synthesis, 4*(1), 1–17. Retrieved September 15, 2005, from http://www.evidencebasedpractices. org/bridges/bridges_vol1_no4.pdf

Gil, E. (1991). *The healing power of play: Working with abused children.* New York: The Guilford Press (p. 33).

Gillis, A. (1989). The effect of play on immobilized children in hospital. *International Journal of Nursing Studies, 26*(3), 261–269.

Ginott, H. G. (1994). In C. E. Schaefer & H. Kaduson (Eds.), *The quotable play therapist: 238 of the all-time best quotes on play and play therapy.* Northvale, NJ: Jason Aronson.

Gladding, S. T. (1993). The therapeutic use of play in counseling: An overview. *Journal of Humanistic Education and Development, 31,* 106–115.

Gladding, S. T. (2005). *Counseling as an art: The creative arts in counseling* (3rd ed.). Alexandria, VA: American Counseling Association.

Glover, C.J. (2001). Cultural considerations in play therapy. In G.L. Landreth's (Ed.), *Innovations in play therapy: Issues, process, and special populations* (pp. 31–42). Philadelphia: Brunner-Routledge.

Glover, G., & Landreth, G. L. (2000). Filial therapy with Native Americans on the Flathead Reservation. *International Journal of Play Therapy, 9*(2), 57–80.

Gonzalez-Mena, J. (1998). *The child in the family and the community* (2nd ed.). Upper Saddle River, NJ: Merrill.

Guerney, L. (1997). Filial therapy. In K. O'Connor & L. M. Braverman (Eds.), *Play therapy theory and practice: A comparative presentation* (pp. 131–159). New York: Wiley & Sons.

Gumaer, J. (1984). *Counseling and therapy for children.* New York: Free Press.

Hanes, M. (1997). Producing messy mixtures in art therapy. *American Journal of Art Therapy, 35*(3), 70–73.

Harris, T. E., & Landreth, G. L. (2001). Essential personality characteristics of effective play therapists. In G. L. Landreth's (Ed.), *Innovations in play therapy: Issues, process and special populations* (pp. 23–31). Philadelphia: Brunner-Routledge.

Harris, Z. L., & Landreth, G. L. (1997). Filial therapy with incarcerated mothers: A five week model. *International Journal of Play Therapy, 6*(2), 53–73.

Harvey, S. (1997). Dynamic family play therapy: A creative arts approach. In K. O'Connor & L. M. Braverman (Eds.), *Play therapy theory and practice: A comparative presentation* (pp. 341–367). New York: Wiley & Sons.

Henderson, D. A., & Gladding, S. T. (1998). The creative arts in counseling: A multicultural perspective. *The Arts in Psychotherapy, 25*(3), 183–187.

Henniger, M. L. (1995). Play: Antidote for childhood stress. *Early Child Development and Care, 105,* 7–12.

Herring, R. D., & Meggert, S. S. (1994). The use of humor as a counselor strategy with Native American Indian children. *Elementary School Guidance & Counseling 29,* 67–75.

Herschell, A., & McNeil, C. (2005). Parent-child interaction therapy for children experiencing externalizing behavior problems. In L. A. Reddy, T. M. Files-Hall, & C. E. Schaefer (Eds.), *Empirically based play interventions for children* (pp. 169–190). Washington, DC: American Psychological Association.

Hewson-Bower, B., & Drummond, P. (2001). Psychological treatment for recurrent symptoms of colds and flu in children. *Journal of Psychosomatic Research, 51,* 369–377.

Hightower, A., Cowen, E., Spinell, A., Lotyczewski, B., Guare, J., Rohrbeck, C., & Brown, L. (1987). The child rating scale: The development of a socioemotional self-rating scale for elementary school children. *School Psychology Review, 16*(2), 239–255.

Hood, K., & Eyberg, S. (2003). Outcomes of parent-child interaction therapy: Mothers' reports of maintenance three to six years after treatment. *Journal of Clinical Child and Adolescent Psychology, 32*(3), 419–429.

Hwang, B., & Hughes, C. (2000). The effects of social interactive training on early social communicative skills of children with autism. *Journal of Autism and Developmental Disorders, 30*(4), 331–343.

Irwin, E. C. (1991). The use of a puppet interview to understand children. In C. E. Schaefer, K. Gitlin, and A. Sandgrund (Eds.), *Play diagnosis and assessment* (pp. 617–642). New York: John Wiley & Sons.

Jacknow, D., Tschann, J., Link M., & Boyce, W. (1994). Hypnosis in the prevention of chemotherapy-related nausea and vomiting in children: A prospective study. *Developmental and Behavioral Pediatrics, 15*(4), 258–264.

James, R. K., & Myer, R. (1987). Puppets: The elementary school counselors' right or left arm. *Elementary School Guidance and Counseling 21,* 262–265.

Jang, M. (2000). Effectiveness of filial therapy for Korean parents. *International Journal of Play Therapy, 9*(2), 39–56.

Jernberg, A. (1993). Attachment formation. In C. E. Schaefer (Ed.), *The therapeutic powers of play* (pp. 241–265). Northvale, NJ: Jason Aronson.

Jernberg, A., & Booth, P. (1999). *Theraplay* (2nd ed.). San Francisco: Jossey-Bass.

Jewel, D. L. (1989). *Confronting child abuse through recreation.* Springfield, IL: Charles C. Thomas.

Johnson, B., Franklin, L. C., Hall, K., & Prieto, L. R. (2000). Parent training through play: Parent-child interaction therapy with a hyperactive child. *Family Journal, 8,* 180–187.

Johnson, D., Pedro-Carroll, J., & Demanchick, S. (2005). The Primary Mental Health Project: A play intervention for school-age children. In L. A. Reddy, T. M. Files-Hall, & C. E. Schaefer (Eds.), *Empirically based play interventions for children* (pp. 13–30). Washington, DC: American Psychological Association.

Johnson, L. (1995). Filial therapy: A bridge between individual child therapy and family therapy. *Journal of Family Psychotherapy, 6*(3), 55–70.

Johnson, M., & Kreimer, J. (2005). Guided fantasy play for chronically ill children: A critical review. In L. A. Reddy, T. M. Files-Hall, & C. E. Schaefer (Eds.), *Empirically based play interventions for children* (pp. 105–122). Washington, DC: American Psychological Association.

Johnson, M., Whitt, J., & Martin, B. (1987). The effect of fantasy facilitation of anxiety in chronically ill and healthy children. *Journal of Pediatric Psychology, 12*(2), 273–284.

Johnson, S., & Clark, P. (2001). Play therapy with aggressive acting-out children. In G. Landreth (Ed.). *Innovations in play therapy: Issues, process, and special populations* (pp. 323–333). Philadelphia: Taylor & Francis.

Jones, L., Rhine, T., & Bratton, S. (2002). High school students as therapeutic agents with young children experiencing school adjustment difficulties: The effectives of a filial therapy training model. *International Journal of Play Therapy, 11*(2), 43–62.

Kaduson, H. G. (1997). Play therapy for children with attention-deficit hyperactivity disorder. In H. G. Kaduson, D. Cangelosi, & C. E. Schaefer (Eds.), *The playing cure: Individualized play therapy for specific childhood problems* (pp. 197–228). Northvale, NJ: Jason Aronson.

Kaduson, H. G., Cangelosi, D., & Schaefer, C. E. (1997a). *The playing cure: Individualized play therapy for specific childhood problems.* Northvale, NJ: Jason Aronson.

Kaduson, H., Cangelosi, D., & Schaefer, C. (Eds.). (1997b). *101 favorite play therapy techniques.* Northvale, NJ: Jason Aronson.

Kale, A., & Landreth, G. L. (1999). Filial therapy with parents of children experiencing learning difficulties. *International Journal of Play Therapy, 8*(2), 35–56.

Kalff, D. M. (1981). *Sand play: A psychotherapeutic approach to the psyche.* Boston: Sigo Press.

Kao, S., & Landreth, G. (2001). Play therapy with Chinese children. In G. Landreth (Ed.), *Innovations in play therapy: Issues, process, and special populations* (pp. 43–49). Philadelphia: Taylor & Francis.

Knell, S. (2000). Cognitive-behavioral play therapy for childhood fears and phobias. In H. Kaduson & C. Schaefer (Eds.), *Short-term play therapy for children* (pp. 79–99). New York: Guilford.

Koller, T. J., & Booth, P. (1997). Fostering attachment through family theraplay. In K. O'Connor & L. M. Braverman (Eds.), *Play therapy theory and practice: A comparative presentation* (pp. 204–233). New York: Wiley & Sons.

Kot, S., & Tyndall-Lind, A. (2005). Intensive play therapy with child witnesses of domestic violence. In L. A. Reddy, T. M. Files-Hall, & C. E. Schaefer (Eds.), *Empirically based play interventions for children* (pp. 31–49). Washington, DC: American Psychological Association.

Kottman, T. (2001). *Play therapy: Basics and beyond.* Alexandria, VA: American Counseling Association.

Kottman, T. (2002). Billy, the teddy bear boy. In L. Golden (Ed.), *Case studies in child and adolescent counseling* (3rd ed., pp. 8–20). Columbus, OH: Merrill Prentice Hall.

Kottman, T. (2004). Play therapy. In A. Vernon (Ed.), *Counseling children and adolescents* (3rd ed., pp. 111–136). Denver, CO: Love Publishing.

Kramer, E. (1971). *Art as therapy with children.* New York: Schocken.

Landgarten, H. B. (1981). *Clinical art therapy: A comprehensive guide.* New York: Brunner/Mazel.

Landreth, G. L. (1991). *Play therapy: The art of the relationship.* Bristol, PA: Accelerated Development.

Landreth, G. L. (1993). Child-centered play therapy. *Elementary School Guidance & Counseling, 28*(1), 17–29.

Landreth, G. L., & Lobaugh, A. F. (1998). Filial therapy with incarcerated fathers: Effects on parental acceptance of child, parental stress, and child adjustment. *Journal of Counseling & Development, 76,* 157–165.

Landreth, G. L., & Sweeney, D. S. (2001). Child-centered group play therapy. In G. L. Landreth (Ed.), *Innovations in play therapy: Issues, process, and special populations* (pp. 181–202). Philadelphia: Brunner-Routledge.

Leben, N. Y. (1997). The yarn drawing game. In H. Kaduson & C. Schaefer (Eds.), *101 favorite play therapy techniques* (pp. 61–63). Northvale, NJ: Jason Aronson.

Leblanc, M., & Ritchie, M. (1999). Predictors of play therapy outcomes. *International Journal of Play Therapy, 8*(2), 19–34.

Leblanc, M., & Ritchie, M. (2001). A meta-analysis of play therapy outcomes. *Counseling Psychology Quarterly, 14,* 149–164.

Lobaugh, F. A. (1992). *Filial therapy with incarcerated parents* (DAI-B 53/04). Unpublished doctoral dissertation, University of North Texas, Denton, TX.

Lowenfeld, M. (1991). *Play in childhood.* London: MacKeith Press. (Original work published 1935)

McDonald, L., & Morgan, A. (1997). Families and schools together (FAST): Integrating community development with clinical strategies. *Families in Society, 78*(92), 140–156.

McNeil, C., Capage, L., Bahl, A., & Blanc, H. (1999). Importance of early intervention for disruptive behavior problems: Comparison of treatment and waitlist-control groups. *Early Education & Development, 10*(4), 445–454.

McNeil, C., Eyberg, S., Eisenstadt, T., Newcomb, K., & Funderbunk, B. (1991). Parent-child interaction therapy with behavior problem children: Generalization of treatment effects to the school setting. *Journal of Clinical Child Psychology, 20*(2), 140–151.

Moustakas, C. (1981). *Rituals, rhythms and relationship.* Detroit: Center for Humanities Studies.

Mulherin, M. A. (2001). The Masterson approach with play therapy: A parallel process between mother and child. *American Journal of Psychotherapy, 55,* 251–272.

Muro, J., & Kottman, T. (1995). *Guidance and counseling in the elementary and middle schools: A practical approach.* Dubuque, IA: Brown and Benchmark.

Nader, K., & Pynoos, R. S. (1991). Play and drawing techniques as tools for interviewing traumatized children. In C. E. Schaefer, K. Gitlin, & A. Sandgrund (Eds.), *Play diagnosis and assessment* (pp. 375–389). New York: John Wiley & Sons.

Nafpaktitis, M., & Perlmutter, B. (1998). School-based early mental health intervention with at-risk students. *School Psychology Review, 27*(3), 420–433.

Neil, B., & Landreth, G. L. (2001). Have toys-will travel: A traveling play therapist in the school setting. In G. L. Landreth (Ed.), *Innovations in play therapy: Issues, process, and special populations.* Philadelphia: Brunner-Routledge.

Oaklander, V. (1988). *Windows to our children: A gestalt therapy approach to children and adolescents.* Highland, NY: The Center for Gestalt Development.

O'Connor, K. (1991). The practice of group play therapy. *The play therapy primer: An integration of theories and techniques* (pp. 143–156). Northvale, NJ: Jason Aronson.

Odom, S., & Strain, P. (1986). A comparison of peer-initiation and teacher-antecedent intervention for promoting reciprocal social interaction of autistic preschoolers. *Journal of Applied Behavior Analysis, 19,* 59–71.

Ogawa, Y. (2004). Childhood trauma and play therapy intervention for traumatized children. *Journal of Professional Counseling and Practice, Theory, & Research, 32*(1), 19–29.

Orton, G. L. (1997). *Strategies for counseling with children and their parents.* Pacific Grove, CA: Brooks/Cole.

Pedro-Carroll, J. (1997). The Children of Divorce Intervention Program: Fostering resilient outcomes for school-age children. In G.W. Albee & T. Gullotta (Eds.), *Primary prevention works* (pp. 213–238). Thousand Oaks, CA: Sage.

Pedro-Carroll, J., & Jones, S. (2005). A preventive play intervention to foster children's resilience in the aftermath of divorce. In L. A. Reddy, T. M. Files-Hall, & C. E. Schaefer (Eds.), *Empirically based play interventions for children* (pp. 51–75). Washington, DC: American Psychological Association.

Pelcovitz, D. (1999). Betrayed by a trusted adult: Structured time-limited group therapy with elementary school children abused by a school employee. In N.B. Webb (Ed.), *Play therapy with children in crisis* (2nd ed., pp. 183–202). New York: Guilford.

Phillips, R. D. (1985). Whistling in the dark?: A review of play therapy research. *Psychotherapy, 22,* 752–760.

Post, P. (1999). Impact of child-centered play therapy on the self-esteem, locus of control, and anxiety of at-risk 4th, 5th, and 6th grade students. *International Journal of Play Therapy, 8*(2), 1–18.

Rae, W., & Sullivan, J. (2005). A review of play interventions for hospitalized children. In L. A. Reddy, T. M. Files-Hall, & C. E. Schaefer (Eds.), *Empirically based play interventions for children* (pp. 123–142). Washington, DC: American Psychological Association.

Rae, W., Worchel, F., Upchurch, J., Sanner, J., & Daniel, C. (1989). The psychosocial impact of play on hospitalized children. *Journal of Pediatric Psychology, 14*(4), 617–627.

Rasmussen, L. A., & Cunningham, C. (1995). Focused play therapy and nondirective play therapy: Can they be integrated? *Journal of Child Sexual Abuse, 4*(1), 1–20.

Ray, D., Armstrong, S., Warren, E., & Balkin, R. (2005). Play therapy practices among elementary school counselors. *Professional School Counseling, 8*(4), 360–365.

Ray, D., Bratton, S. C., Brandt, M. A. (2000). Filial/family play therapy for single parents of young children attending community colleges. *Community College Journal of Research & Practice, 24*, 469–487.

Ray, D., Bratton, S., Rhine, T., & Jones, L. (2001). The effectiveness of play therapy: Responding to the critics. *International Journal of Play Therapy, 10*(1), 85–108.

Reddy, L., Files-Hall, T., & Schaefer, C. (2005a). Announcing empirically based play interventions for children. In L. A. Reddy, T. M. Files-Hall, & C. E. Schaefer (Eds.), *Empirically based play interventions for children* (pp. 3–10). Washington, DC: American Psychological Association.

Reddy, L., Springer, C., Files-Hall, T., Schmelzer Benisz, E., Hauch, Y., Braunstein, D., & Atamanoff, T. (2005b). Child ADHD multimodal program: An empirically supported intervention for young children with ADHD. In L. A. Reddy, T. M. Files-Hall, & C. E. Schaefer (Eds.), *Empirically based play interventions for children* (pp. 145–167). Washington, DC: American Psychological Association.

Robinson, H. (1999). Unresolved conflicts in a divorced family: Case of Charlie, age 10. In N. B. Webb (Ed.), *Play therapy with children in crisis* (2nd ed., pp. 272–293). New York: Guilford.

Rogers, S. (2005). Play interventions for young children with autism spectrum disorders. In L. A. Reddy, T. M. Files-Hall, & C. E. Schaefer (Eds.), *Empirically based play interventions for children* (pp. 215–239). Washington, DC: American Psychological Association.

Rogers, S., & DiLalla, D. (1991). A comparative study of the effects of a developmentally based instructional model on young children with autism and young children with other disorders of behavior and development. *Topics in Early Childhood Special Education, 11*(2), 29–44.

Rogers, S., & Lewis, H. (1989). An effective day treatment model for young children with pervasive developmental disorders. *Journal of the American Academy of Child and Adolescent Psychiatry, 28*, 207–214.

Rotter, J. C., & Bush, M. V. (2000). Play and family therapy. *Family Journal, 8*, 172–177.

Rubin, J. A. (1988). Art counseling: An alternative. *Elementary School Guidance and Counseling, 22*, 180–185.

Schaefer, C. (Ed.). (1993). *The therapeutic power of play*. Northvale, NJ: Jason Aronson.

Schaefer, C., & Greenberg, R. (1997). Measurement of playfulness: A neglected therapist variable. *International Journal of Play Therapy, 6*(2), 21–32.

Schaefer, C. E., Jacobsen, H. E., & Ghahramanlou, M. (2000). Play group therapy for social skills deficits in children. In H. G. Kaduson & C. E. Schaefer's (Eds.), *Short-term play therapy for children* (pp. 296–344). New York: The Guilford Press.

Shelby, J. S. (1997). Rubble, disruption, and tears: Helping young survivors of natural disaster. In H. G. Kaduson, D. Cangelosi, & C. E. Schaefer (Eds.), *The playing cure: Individualized play therapy for specific childhood problems* (pp. 143–170). Northvale, NJ: Jason Aronson.

Shelby, J., & Felix, E. (2005). Posttraumatic play therapy: The need for an integrated model of directive and nondirective approaches. In L. A. Reddy, T. M. Files-Hall, & C. E. Schaefer (Eds.), *Empirically based play interventions for children* (pp. 79–103). Washington, DC: American Psychological Association.

Shen, Y.-J. (2002). Short-term group play therapy with Chinese earthquake victims: Effects on anxiety, depression, and adjustment. *International Journal of Play Therapy, 11*(1), 43–63.

Shen, Y.-J., & Sink, C. (2002). Helping elementary age children cope with disasters. *Professional School Counseling, 5*(5), 322–330.

Stahmer, A. (1995) Teaching symbolic play skills to children with autism using pivotal response training. *Journal of Autism and Developmental Disorders, 25*(2), 123–141.

Steinhardt, L. (1995). Longterm creative therapy with a borderline psychotic boy. *American Journal of Art Therapy, 34*(2), 43–50.

Stermback, S. (Ed.). (1991). *Sand play studies.* Boston, MA: Sigo Press.

Sweeney, D. S. (1997). *Counseling children through the world of play.* Wheaton, IL: Tyndale House Publishers.

Thorp, D., Stahmer, A., & Schriebman, L. (1995). Effects of sociodramatic play training on children with autism. *Journal of Autism and Developmental Disorders, 25*(3), 265–282.

Tyndall-Lind, A. (1999). Revictimization of children from violent families: Child-centered theoretical formulation and play therapy treatment implication. *International Journal of Play Therapy, 8*(1), 9–25.

Tyndall-Lind, A., Landreth, G., & Giordano, M. (2001). Intensive group play therapy with child witnesses of domestic violence. *International Journal of Play Therapy, 10*(1), 53–84.

Urquiza, A., & McNeil, C. (1996). Parent-child interaction therapy: An intensive dyadic intervention for physically abusive families. *Child Maltreatment, 1*(2), 134–144.

VanFleet, R. (1997). Play and perfectionism: Putting fun back into families. In H. G. Kaduson, D. Cangelosi, & C. E. Schaefer (Eds.), *The playing cure: Individualized play therapy for specific childhood problems* (pp. 61–82). Northvale, NJ: Jason Aronson.

VanFleet, R. (2000). *A parent's handbook of filial therapy: Building strong families with play.* Boiling Springs, PA: Play Therapy Press.

VanFleet, R., Ryan, S., & Smith, S. (2005). Filial therapy: A critical review. In L. A. Reddy, T. M. Files-Hall, & C. E. Schaefer (Eds.), *Empirically based play interventions for children* (pp. 241–264). Washington, DC: American Psychological Association.

Vaz, K. M. (2000). When is a sandplay psychotherapy process completed? *International Journal of Action Methods: Psychodrama, Skill Training, and Role Playing, 53,* 66–81.

Vinturella, L., & James, R. (1987). Sand play: A therapeutic medium with children. *Elementary School Guidance and Counseling, 21*(3), 229–238.

Walker, R. (1998). Magic art. In H. Kaduson & C. Schaefer (Eds.), *101 favorite play therapy techniques* (pp. 61–63). Northvale, NJ: Jason Aronson.

Wheat, R. (1995). Help children work through emotional difficulties—sand trays are great! *Young Children, 51,* 82–83.

White, J., & Allers, C. T. (1994). Play therapy with abused children: A review of the literature. *Journal of Counseling and Development, 72*(4), 390–394.

Wolfberg, P., & Schuler, A. (1993). Integrated play groups: A model for promoting the social and cognitive dimensions of play in children with autism. *Journal of Autism and Developmental Disorders, 23*(3), 467–489.

Young, M., & Fu, V. (1988). Influence of play and temperament on the young child's response to pain. *Children's Health Care, 16*(3), 209–215.

CULTURAL FACTORS IN COUNSELING CHILDREN

To have one's individuality completely ignored is like being pushed quite out of life. Like being blown out as one blows out a light.

—Evelyn Scott

Culture can be defined as the shared meanings, norms, and values of a large social group. More specifically, we can understand the scope of the concept of culture from the following definition provided by Vontross (1995; as cited in Pedersen, Draguns, Lonner, & Trimble, 2002):

> (Culture is) a way of life of the totality of the individual artifacts, behaviors, and mental concepts transmitted from one generation to the next in a society. It is visible and invisible, cognitive and affective, conscious and unconscious, internal and external, rational and irrational, and coercive and permissive at the same time. This conception of culture implies that it is generally out of sight and out of mind. People do not think about it. They take it for granted. (p. ix)

Culture is transmitted by caregivers (Cole, Bruschi, & Tamang, 2002; Hays, 2001), as well as by peers, institutions, and the media. Some of the dimensions that may be used to define cultural groups are race, ethnicity, socioeconomic status (SES), gender, religious affiliation, and sexual orientation. Ethnic group identification refers to ancestry and generally a place of origin. Marsella and Yamada (2000) explain that ethnocultural identity refers to the patterns of behavior, values, feeling of belonging, and traditions of the ethnic group. Race may be used as a cultural marker, as well as demographic characteristics such as age, gender, and SES. In the diverse United States, the cultural identity of most individuals involves many dimensions rather than one single feature (Shapiro, Friedberg, & Bardenstein, 2006). The concept of multidimensionality (Brown & Trusty, 2005; Richardson & Jacob, 2002; Robinson, 1993) refers to the importance of seeing people for the many aspects of their identities. As noted by Brown and Trusty (2005), race, ethnicity, social class, age and developmental level, gender, religion and spirituality, nationality, disability status, family characteristics, and other factors influence people's cultures, values, and experiences in ways that interact.

Counselors will always have opportunities to work with children who may have cultural practices and beliefs that the counselors may not know. Baruth and Manning (2003) list the following challenges counselors may face in those situations:

- Communication difficulties
- Misunderstanding the culture and the impact of the culture on the process of counseling
- Mistaken assumptions about cultural assimilation
- Different social class values and orientations
- Stereotypical generalizations
- An assumption of cultural bias
- Inability to understand the worldview of the client (p. 20)

Pedersen (1997) includes other cautions: cultural beliefs influence diagnosis and treatment; diagnoses differ across cultures; clients express symptoms differently across cultures; diagnoses may vary according to categories found most often in the majority populations; and finally, most counselors are members of the majority population, whereas most clients are members of the minority population.

Counselors who are members of the dominant culture, which currently in North American culture is white European American, must begin by becoming aware of their own racial identity. The goals of that growing awareness are the development of a healthy white racial identity and the elimination of intentional or unintentional racism and other biases. Helms (1990) considers this process one of exploring how being white influences one's development. She proposes the White Racial Identity Development Model (Helms, 1990, 1995); this model contains six stages. The stage of *contact* is one of unawareness of racial identification with minimal acknowledgment of the benefits that one's ethnicity has granted him or her. In the *disintegration* stage, people begin to challenge earlier beliefs but also deny the existence of racism. As people move to the *reintegration* phase, they either overtly or covertly express white superiority. *Pseudoindependence* incorporates an intellectual acceptance of racism but not acceptance of responsibility. If they reach the *immersion/emersion* stage, people learn about being white and develop a positive racial identity; and in the *autonomy* phase, they welcome relationships with many ethnic groups and are committed to continuing growth as an ethnic person. Understanding and engaging in this process will help white counselors work with others from different backgrounds.

All counselors in some ways work with culturally diverse people. Rather than be daunted by the challenges, we recommend counselors make a commitment to continuous renewal and vigilance to increasing their awareness of self, as well as a refinement and deepening of the knowledge and skills needed to be an effective counselor in an increasingly pluralistic world. This chapter is intended only as an overview of some considerations necessary in counseling across cultures. We use the terms *diversity, cross-cultural, multicultural,* and *pluralistic* as synonyms for the concept of working with someone who has a cultural heritage different from the counselor.

COMPETENCE

Pedersen (2002) explains that training in multicultural competence has focused on three areas. A beginning part involves increasing one's awareness of culturally learned attitudes, beliefs, and values. A second component focuses on knowledge of culturally relevant facts. The third part of the sequence concentrates on developing skills for interventions that are culturally appropriate. Ponterotto and Casas (1987) propose that multicultural competence has been achieved when a counselor has the necessary skills to work with people from different cultural backgrounds. According to Holcomb-McCoy (2003), that means that counselors with multicultural competence know that child–counselor cultural differences and similarities are important variables in the counseling relationship. In contrast, counselors with low multicultural competence ignore those critical variables.

The areas of awareness, knowledge, and skills have been identified as the main areas of multicultural counseling competence (Sue, Arredondo, & McDavis, 1992). Awareness refers to the understanding of personal worldviews, including that of the counselor. Knowledge relates to the importance of understanding the worldview of the culturally different clients. The skills dimension includes the process of developing and practicing strategies for working with culturally different people. Let us now consider more detailed information about counseling competencies and working with selected groups.

MULTICULTURAL COUNSELING COMPETENCIES

Multicultural counseling competencies, based on this model of knowledge, awareness, and skills, have been articulated by Arredondo and her colleagues (1996). They clearly outline the attitudes and beliefs, knowledge and skills that counselors should develop in becoming aware of their own cultural values and biases, their clients' worldviews, and appropriate intervention strategies. The competencies deserve intense study and ongoing practice. Lee (2001) suggests that counselors who succeed with clients from a variety of ethnic backgrounds use a perspective that "acknowledges human differences and celebrates human similarities" (p. 583). Multicultural counseling competencies guide counselors in achieving that perspective and the resulting skills.

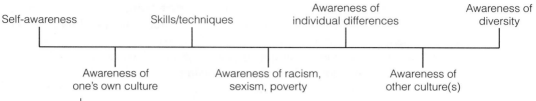

FIGURE 15-1 | CROSS-CULTURAL AWARENESS CONTINUUM

Pedersen & Carey, *Multicultural Counseling in Schools: A Practical Handbook,* Second Edition. Published by Allyn and Bacon, Boston, MA. Copyright © 2003 by Pearson Education. Reprinted by permission of the publisher.

AWARENESS

Self-awareness involves gaining an understanding of the specific things that influence one's psychological, emotional, and cultural attributes. Baruth and Manning (2003) and Lee (2001) suggest that counselors investigate their own cultural background and the impact it has on their beliefs, attitudes, and values. Washington (1994) outlines a three-step process to clarify cultural knowledge. His outline includes questions and a process that may be adapted for a cultural inventory both for the counselor and for those with whom a counselor works.

As well as knowledge of self, counselors must develop extensive awareness of racism, sexism, and poverty; individual differences; other culture(s); and diversity (Locke & Parker, 1994). Building an understanding of how culture influences educational opportunities, cognitive development, and the interpretation of history (Arredondo et al., 1996) is another desired outcome of the awareness process. Locke (2003) proposes a cross-cultural awareness continuum, a linear illustration that has levels of awareness building on previous levels. He explains that competence in cross-cultural relationships must be a life-long process of growing self-awareness and developing cultural skills (Figure 15-1). The process of awareness is flexible with absolute mastery elusive. Nevertheless, counselors must undertake the challenge to be helpful in cross-cultural interactions. Locke states that counselors must begin with self-understanding that includes intrapersonal and interpersonal dynamics. Counselors must explore their own culture, and they must understand the effects of racism, sexism, and poverty on themselves and others. Locke continues by explaining that people must be recognized as both individuals and members of their particular cultural group. Those four levels form the foundation for exploring other cultural groups.

Based on his research of cultural difference in forty countries, Hofstede (1980) proposes four ways that cultural groups differ: power distance, uncertainty avoidance, individualism/collectivism, and masculinity/femininity. Locke (2003) explains five other components of culture:

1. *Activity*—How important are goals in life? Who make decisions? How are problems solved?

2. *Social relations*—How are roles defined? What are relationships with people of different status? How are sex roles determined? What does friendship mean?

3. *Motivation*—What is the achievement orientation? What is emphasized, cooperation or competitiveness?

4. *Perception of the world*—What is the predominant worldview, view on human nature, nature of truth? How is time defined? What is the nature of property?

5. *Perception of the individual*—How is self defined? Where is a person's identity formed? What is the nature of the individual? What kinds of individuals are valued and respected? (p. 174).

The questionnaire contained in Table 15-1 could be seen as a self-check on awareness, knowledge, and skills needed to work with a multicultural population.

KNOWLEDGE

Pedersen (2002) explains that "all behaviors are learned and displayed within cultural contexts" (p. 3). He states that a counselor who considers the cultural context will be able to measure behavior more accurately, to define personal identity more clearly, to understand problems more fully, and to counsel more meaningfully. Baruth and Manning (2003) point out that culture should not be considered as fixed but as fluid. As stated earlier, we must recognize the impact of the world in which a child lives as we build and maintain a helpful counseling relationship.

Lee (2001) proposes various knowledge bases needed for planning, delivering, and evaluating counseling services. Counselors should understand the impact of economic, social, and political systems on ethnic groups. Counselors should accumulate information about the history, customs, and values of various groups in an effort to understand the intersection of ethnic contexts with the person. He suggests counselors use media, the Internet, and personal experiences with diverse groups to gain the knowledge needed.

Among some of the important terms in the field of cross-cultural counseling that counselors need to understand are *race, ethnic, ethnicity, worldview, ethnic identity development,* and *acculturation.* The following paragraphs provide explanations for some of these terms.

Hernandez (1989) explains that *race* refers to a concept from anthropology used for classifications of people according to physical characteristics. Mio, Trimble, Arredondo, Cheatham, and Sue (1999) define race as a classification system based on "hair texture, skin color, eye color, and facial features" that is used to categorize people into four groups: Asian, black, white, or American Indian. They contend that these racial classifications are scientifically meaningless.

An *ethnic* group refers to a population with members that have a collective identity and heritage. Ethnic, according to Mio and colleagues (1999),

TABLE 15-1 | CRITERIA FOR COUNSELING WITH ETHNIC MINORITY CHILDREN

Skills	Yes	No	Needs improvement
Do you constantly assess your values, attitudes, and beliefs and refrain from imposing them on children?			
Do you frequently attend training or skill sessions for working with a culturally diverse population?			
Are you familiar with the strategies that promote equity in a pluralistic society?			
Are you able to recognize the child's reality, including the effect of racism and poverty?			
Do you have an awareness and understanding of both verbal and nonverbal language patterns of different ethnic groups?			
Are you able to discuss openly racial/ethnic differences and issues?			
Do you have high expectations for all and help them gather resources and opportunities necessary for success?			
Do you have the ability to understand the child's help-seeking, including the child's idea of the problem and solution?			
Do you consider the links between the systemic problems and the child's individual concerns?			
Can you consider the implications of a suggested solution in relation to the child's cultural reality?			
Are you able to determine and select from three goal categories: Situational stress (isolation, poverty); Cultural transition (conflictual family–school practice); Transcultural patterns (developmental difficulties)?			
Can you help the child form a goal that is problem or growth oriented, structured, realistic, concrete, practical, and achievable?			
Do you have the skills to apply new strategies consistent with the needs and problem of the child, the degree of acculturation, and the motivation for change?			

NOTE: Adapted from Greenberg, J. M., and Shaffer, S. (1991). *Elements of equity: Criteria for equitable schools.* The Mid-Atlantic Equity Consortium, http://www.maec.org/counsel.html. And Ho, M. K. (1990). *Minority children and adolescents in therapy.* Newbury Park, CA: Sage Publications (pp. 28–29).

refers to the various situations in which a group has lived and acted together, one's values, and a shared style of life. Using these definitions, Lee (2001) states that the "personality characteristics among people that become reinforced through association over time. . . these long-standing dynamics of thinking, feeling, and behaving that form the cultural basis of **ethnicity** or an **ethnic group**" (p. 582). He suggests using terminology that captures the realities of ethnic group membership such as Irish American, Korean American, Lakota, and Jamaican American.

Worldview, according to Sodowsky and Johnson (1994), consists of an individual's experiences and the social, moral, religious, educational, economic, or political influences of one's group. Lonner and Ibrahim (2002) contend that worldview constitutes the source of personal values, beliefs, and assumptions, or one's dominant cognitive framework (Baruth & Manning, 2003). Some authors (Grieger & Ponterotto, 1995; Ibrahim, Roysircar-Sodowsky, & Ohnishi, 2001) assert that worldview is the most important variable in multicultural counseling.

Sue, Ivey, and Pedersen (1996) suggest that "multicultural psychologists have also noted that theories of counseling and psychotherapy represent a variety of worldviews, each with its own values, biases, and assumptions about human behavior" (p. 7). They list several definitions of the term *worldview,* with most of the definitions focusing on one's perception of his or her relationship with the world and the way one understands the world, including individual attitudes, values, opinions, and concepts that influence how a person thinks, makes decisions, and behaves. They point out that our present counseling theories represent different worldviews; thus, it is possible that a counselor's theoretical orientation could clash with a client from a different culture. Sue, Ivey, and Pedersen propose a theory (metatheory) of multicultural counseling and therapy with a number of propositions and corollaries with which they describe its implications for practice, training, and research.

Trevino (1996) has drawn on the works of Sue and Ibrahim regarding the worldview of counseling to develop her model of the change process in cross-cultural counseling. She contends that "worldviews are formed out of personal experience through interaction with members of an individual's culture" (p. 200). These experiences can be shared or common to all members, or they can be unique, particular to one's personal and family history. Trevino (1996) believes that these worldviews are organized into general views or basic understandings of the world, and that specific views represent particular perceptions (for example, specific views of marriage, illness, companionship). She writes that "without an understanding of how their clients are perceiving and understanding the world, counselors would be unable to understand and assess client problems, establish a therapeutic alliance, or formulate effective strategies for intervention" (p. 199). The counselor's role is to work with the client to find a better way of understanding and interacting with the world through cognitive, behavioral, or affective techniques. Trevino postulates that both congruency and discrepancy facilitate change—congruency enhances understanding and the relationship, whereas discrepancy facilitates change. According to Trevino (1996), her model, although needing further research, is a "powerful way of understanding and operationalizing the process of seeing the world through the eyes of another human being" (p. 212).

Fischer, Jome, and Atkinson (1998), however, suggest that there are common factors in counseling that can bridge the gap between "culturally-specific" counseling and "universal approaches." They contend these common factors, combined with a thorough knowledge of the client's culture, can serve as a framework for understanding multicultural literature on counseling, can have empirical support, and may be useful in serving as a guide for future research, training, and practice. Fischer, et al. propose four common factors as essential to the success of all, including multicultural, counseling:

- The therapeutic relationship—a positive trusting and healing relationship between the counselor and client is supported by Western integrationists and transcultural literature
- A shared worldview—a common framework from which counselor and client conduct their work together
- Client expectations—based on a shared worldview that increases the client's positive expectations that counseling will be helpful
- Rituals or interventions—effective techniques are believed by both client and counselor to be appropriate for positive outcomes

ETHNIC IDENTITY DEVELOPMENT   Ho (1992) explains the difference between ethnicity and ethnic identity. Ethnicity refers to the person's sense of membership in a group and the associated thoughts, feelings, and behavior; that is, ethnicity denotes group patterns. Ethnic identity refers to the person's incorporation of those patterns and the acceptance of the beliefs, feelings, and actions as one's own. Ethnic identity would shape beliefs about mental health and illness, styles, coping, and help seeking. Lee (2001) calls this the "interior vision," a foundation of social pratices and personality dimensions.

Ethnic identity development has been described as a series of stages (Atkinson, Morten, & Sue, 1993; Cross, 1995) and as personality statuses (Helms, 1995). Identity development models have been proposed for biracial individuals (Henriksen & Trusty, 2002), Asian Americans (Sodowsky, et al., 1995), Latinos (Casas & Pytluk, 1995), Native Americans (Choney, Berryhill-Paapke, & Robbins, 1995), African Americans (Cross, 1995), and whites (Helms, 1995). The Minority Identity Development Model (Atkinson, et al., 1993) and the Model of Ethnic Identity Development (Phinney, 1993) are more generic explanations of the concept. Readers are encouraged to investigate those models for more specific details about ethnic identity development.

Phinney (1993) states three influential factors that affect the personal and social development of people from ethnic groups: cultural values associated with belonging to that group, the subjective sense of identity with the group, and the associated experiences such as discrimination and powerlessness. Atkinson, et al (1993) suggest that people move from a stage of *conformity*, in which the dominant group is considered superior to the ethnic group, to a stage of *dissonance,* in which people begin to question their previous beliefs, struggle with discrimination experiences, and have more positive perceptions of their own ethnic group. In the *resistance* and *immersion* stage, people have developed an appreciation for their own ethnic group and a diminished valuing of the dominant group. Stage 4 of the identity development model, *introspection,* refers to more flexibility with both the birth and the dominant culture that leads to the *integrative awareness* stage. That fifth stage represents the time in which individuals realize that both their birth culture and the dominant culture have positive and negative aspects.

Helms (2003) proposes three interacting components that influence a person's ethnic identity: personal, affiliative, and reference group. The personal component relates to self-concept, "Who am I?" The affiliative component relates to the degree to which the person believes that he or she shares whatever happens to other members of his or her ethnic group. The reference group component includes the person's level of conforming to the norms of the group. Helms explains that young children probably reflect the identity climate of their home. During the school years their understandings become more complex and they may struggle with exclusion in their schools and communities. To help meet these challenges, Washington et al. (2003) have detailed a developmental group process that helps young people recognize their cultural identity group and develop confidence and pride.

Yasuri, Dorham, and Dishion (2004) and Zaff, Blount, Phillips, and Cohen (2002) have studied ethnic identity as a protective factor for young people. They conclude that high levels of ethnic identity predict positive social and emotional adjustment in adolescents. Greig (2003) explains that teens with secure ethnic identity have higher self-esteem and better mental health. Brown and Trusty (2005) suggest that counselors who work with children can use identity development models to understand a child's perceptions of self and others and to conceptualize the process of counseling. These authors recommend using a two-dimensional model of acculturation (see discussion below) to support children living in the dominant culture, as well as their own culture. Counselors should also work with families and help students develop healthy identities.

ACCULTURATION   Acculturation is the process of becoming like another culture. Ramirez (1999) explains that when children are born into a culture different from the dominant culture, they acquire, at some degree, the second culture. One way of understanding that concept is to think of a continuum with strong connections to the birth culture at one end and strong connections to the dominant culture on the other end (Phinney, 1990). This bipolar acculturation model suggests that connecting with one culture excludes a connection with another. A bicultural model, however, is based on the idea that people can connect with two cultures, only one culture, or neither culture (Brown & Trusty, 2005).

Garrett (1995) describes levels of acculturation. In the *traditional* level, a person embraces traditional beliefs and values. A person in the *transition* level holds on to the traditional mores and those of the dominant culture. This person may not accept all of either culture. At the *bicultural* level, the person accepts and is accepted by both the dominant and the traditional cultures. The fourth type of acculturation is *assimilation*—that is, accepting only the dominant cultural beliefs and values. Ho (1992) suggests that group counseling is most appropriate for minority children who are experiencing difficulties related to acculturation, ethnic identity, and/or bicultural skills.

One way to investigate whether culture is an important factor to a young person is to determine the level of acculturation. Burnam, Hough, Karno, Escobar, and Telles (1987) have a five-question scale that contains questions about language, leisure, and identity. Barona and Miller (1994) have prepared the *Short Acculturation Scale for Hispanic Youth*. Other instruments developed to assess acculturation are as follows: *The Asian Values Scale* (Kim, Atkinson, & Yang, 1999), *A Scale to Assess African American Acculturation* (Snowden & Hines, 1999), and *Rosebud Personal Opinion Survey* (Hoffman, Dana, & Bolton, 1985).

Hughes (2003) studied parents' messages about racial socialization. Their study focuses on cultural socialization and messages about ethnic pride, history, and heritage, and also concentrates on preparation for bias and messages about discrimination and racial bias. The authors conclude that communications from parents to children about ethnicity and race have important consequences for children's identity and well-being. Those in-group and out-group attitudes may be identified with preschool-aged children (Kowalski, 2003).

SKILLS

Counseling involves the ability to aid people in resolving problems or in making decisions. Culturally competent counselors have skills to accomplish this in a way that is consistent with their clients' cultures. Counselors begin by acknowledging the reality of cultural influences rather than ignoring that aspect of the client. Counselors recognize differences as differences, not as deficiencies. Third, counselors avoid stereotypes and an ethnocentric perspective. They affirm individuals within a multidimensional context. Counselors develop a repertoire of helping approaches to incorporate diverse views and practices. Through those approaches the counselor respects the following concepts: kinship influences, language preferences, sex-role socialization, religious/spiritual influences, and help-seeking attitudes and behaviors (Lee, 2001).

Kincade and Evans (1996) have looked more closely at the process of selecting appropriate counseling interventions in a multicultural counseling context. They point out that when a counseling relationship begins, boundaries are established between the counselor and client, which may differ with clients from different cultures. As an example, the amount of physical space between counselor and client may need to vary, depending on the culture. In the United States, three feet is usually considered comfortable; however, Latinos prefer about half that distance for conversation. Latin American and

Arab individuals are less comfortable with variation in distance than closeness, whereas clients from the United States are more comfortable with distance. Kincade and Evans suggest discussing with clients how comfortable they are with the room arrangement.

Kincade and Evans (1996) also caution that emotional boundaries—distance and closeness in relationships—are present in multicultural counseling contexts and are more difficult to observe. For example, Indo-Chinese individuals discuss problems only with family members; therefore, the relationship with the counselor must be redefined. The authors point out that the client may ask the counselor personal questions or give the counselor small presents to make the relationship more similar to a family.

Kinship terms may not mean the same thing in all cultures, according to Kincade and Evans (1996). For example, in Asian and African American cultures, terms such as *Aunt* or *Uncle* may be honorary rather than indicate actual family relationships.

One important point that Kincade and Evans (1996) emphasize is related to the client's hierarchy of needs. The writers point out that clients worried about fulfilling their needs of hunger or safety will not be receptive to counseling techniques that do not consider these issues. Issues of daily survival may be especially important and overwhelming to children from low-income homes.

Trust is the last issue that Kincade and Evans (1996) address. Many children have been taught not to trust others, especially those who are members of oppressed groups. Thus, Kincade and Evans encourage counselors to openly and honestly address differences in cultures to be truly genuine and build trust.

General guidelines for multicultural counselors that Kincade and Evans (1996) suggest include the following:

- Make no assumptions—gather information and re-evaluate your biases often.
- Learn about your client's culture from sources other than the client; that is, the library, tapes, brochures, novels, poems, other literature
- Admit your ignorance about your client's culture—be willing to ask questions and learn
- Look for similarities in order to connect—find common ground to share.
- Be sensitive to client expectations and needs—together define what counseling is and is not

Holcomb-McCoy (2004) has prepared a checklist for school counselors to use in assessing their multicultural competence. She includes specific competencies for counseling, consultation, assessment, and family counseling. She also earmarks the need to understand racism and resistance, racial and ethnic identity development, social advocacy, cross-cultural interactions, and development of partnerships within the community. Her document would be helpful for counselors to use in targeting their needed areas of study and practice. This forgoing overview of the components of multicultural counseling competencies also provides some guidance for practicing with clients from a cultural different than the counselor. The following sections contain information more specific to working with children from different cultures.

CHILDREN

Children who have ethnic or social class backgrounds different from those of the majority population may face challenges related to not being accepted, receiving unfair treatment, being ridiculed, and being subjected to lower expectations. The SES of a family contributes sometimes favorably and sometimes unfavorably to the activities, friends, educational attainment, lifestyle, occupational aspirations, and social roles of the family members. All of those variables may also create stressors for children.

Blum (1998) has examined the school experience of children from ethnic groups and concludes it may be punctuated by stresses of several types. The students may experience difficulties in combining the roles and values of their specific culture with those of the dominant culture. Children may incorporate roles and values from another culture more quickly than other family members, thereby creating clashes at home. They may also contend with more limited opportunities to succeed. The adolescent struggle for identity will include another variable as teens struggle with defining self and meaning. Children and adolescents may be subjected to verbal rejection, discrimination, and perhaps even physical attacks. They may suffer social isolation and derisive labels. Children of different ethnic groups may face these and other possible stresses.

Gibbs and Huang (1989) have suggested three perspectives to use in examining the influence of ethnicity on children. A developmental perspective helps counselors consider the role an ethnic group has had on a child's growth. The ecological perspective provides counselors with a means to investigate the interaction of systems such as family, school, government, social and economic policies, and the impact on available risks and opportunities for the child. Finally, the cross-cultural perspective compares the child's culture of origin and dominant culture.

Bernal, Knight, Garza, Ocampo, and Cota (1993) have explained a model of children's ethnic identity development. Although the five components were discussed in terms of Hispanic children, the model can be used to help understand the process as it occurs with other children.

1. *Ethnic self-identification:* Children categorize themselves as members of an ethnic group.
2. *Ethnic constancy:* Children develop knowledge that their ethnic characteristics are constant across time and place.
3. *Ethnic role behavior:* Children take part in behaviors that reflect cultural values, customs, and language.
4. *Ethnic knowledge:* Children understand that some role behaviors, traits, styles, traditions, and language are relevant to their ethnic group.

5. *Ethnic feelings and preferences:* This represents children's emotional response to their ethnic group.

In agreement with other researchers we have discussed earlier, Garrett (1999) emphasizes the importance of assessing cultural identity and level of acculturation before deciding on interventions. He states the client's cultural frame of reference and mode of communication are essential considerations in working with ethnic children.

Ho (1992) has written about working with ethnic minority children. He suggests individual counseling when the child's problem is related to stresses of immigration and acculturation, of developmental tasks, of past traumatic reactions, of self-identity, and of serious behavioral issues. The goals of the individual therapy would involve strengthening the child's self-image, helping the child acquire coping skills in a bicultural world, improving the child's interpersonal relationships, and modifying inappropriate behavioral patterns. He recommends short-term supportive therapy, cognitive-behavioral therapy, music therapy, and play therapy for intervention choices. Ho states that group therapy would be beneficial for minority youth who are struggling with the acculturation process, their ethnic identity, bicultural socialization skills, and feelings of isolation. More specific information about the counseling process with selected ethnic groups follows.

Fascoli (1999) and Kottman (2001) recommend that counselors who work with children investigate the following facts for the child and family:

1. What is the country of origin and cultural identity of the child and his or her family?
2. Which generation of family emigrated?
3. What languages are spoken? Where are the languages spoken?
4. What English knowledge do the parents have? Can they understand the written word? Spoken word? How adequately can they express themselves in English?
5. What are the sleeping and eating patterns at home?
6. What are the expectations for children in the culture?
7. What is the level of acculturation?
8. Which holidays, celebrations, and cultural responsibilities are important?
9. What is the attitude of the family about play?
10. Who are playmates of the child at home and in the community?
11. With what materials does the child play? What are the child's play activities?
12. What are family members' attitudes toward discipline?
13. What are the patterns of discipline?
14. What responsibilities and expectations does the child have at home?

A disadvantage in discussing specific ethnic groups is the tendency to stereotype all members of the group with the same characteristics and to ignore the individual personalities and changes in the culture (Clemente, 2004). We want to emphasize that stereotypes may interfere with a counselor's perspective of other-culture clients. Counselors need to strive to avoid being influenced or biased by overly generalized descriptions of individuals and groups. Children who have been reared in American cultures have a great deal in common with one another and with other cultures; however, counselors should not overlook possible differences between cultures and should work to understand both the similarities and the differences, the multidimensionality of the world in which we and our child clients exist.

AFRICAN AMERICAN CHILDREN

African American children represent 15 percent of the population in the United States (Child Trends, 2005). That percent is expected to remain relatively steady into 2020. Their heritage may be from Africa, the Caribbean, or other countries. Many are descendants of slaves. The effects of slavery and the scars and attitudes that have been suffered because of it remain central to this population (Clemente, 2004). African American children are over-represented in the foster care and child welfare system, constituting about 45 percent of all children in foster care and more than half of the children awaiting adoption (Surgeon General, 2002).

Baruth and Manning (2003) suggest that African American children may experience problems that warrant counseling interventions. Failing to develop a strong cultural identity, being subjected to the adverse effects of racism and inappropriate value judgments, and being unable to overcome the perception of being "problem children" may cause these children difficulties. Interpersonal relations, autonomy, academic performance, and future plans may also be concerns African American young people bring to counselors. Fusick and Bordeau (2004) remind us to focus also on the strengths and potential of African American children.

Jones, Forehand, Brody, and Armistead (2002) have investigated different models of assessing the impact of risk factors on African American children in families with single mothers. They suggest looking at the multiplicity of risk factors as predictors of difficult adjustment in children and note a possible "trigger point" that occurs between three and four risks. Another way to consider risk factors is offered by Vontross (1995), who emphasizes the many ways young black boys and men may be overwhelmed by the world they inhabit and the unhelpful habits they may develop to survive. He instructs counselors to reconsider their role and lists several recommendations. Counselors should use group and individual sessions to help the young men understand themselves better and relate more effectively with others. Recognizing the impact of racism on the lives of African Americans, counselors refrain from denying its existence, but work on modifying any system that maintains the barriers. For example, African American students may be struggling with institutional racism and stereotyping that is either undetected or ignored by the school staff (Sue & Sue, 2003).

Fusick and Bordeau (2004) add that counselors must be aware of the healthy paranoia or wariness these children may have toward counseling. Sue and Sue (2003) point out that many people of color are reluctant to seek counseling because they see it as a sociopolitical force. African American families sometimes are required to go for counseling as a consequence of encounters with the law or their interactions with other community agencies. Counseling may be perceived as a punishment rather than as a helpful process. According to Allen and Majidi-Ahi (1989), the traditional clinical or medical model, which focuses on a person's weaknesses or deficits, is not appropriate for working with African American children because many of them adjust well despite poverty, prejudice, and other barriers to their development. Allen and Majidi-Ahi prefer a socioecological approach, with an emphasis on understanding how economic status, education, health care, housing, racism, and other ecological factors affect the child.

Clemente (2004), Lee and Bailey (1997), and Locke (1989) identify the following traits as specific guidelines for counselors working with African American children:

- Counselors should be open and honest.
- Counselors should demonstrate respect and appreciation of cultural differences.
- Counselors should participate in activities of the community.
- Counselors reject prejudice and racism.
- Counselors question the child about his or her culture.
- Counselors hold high expectations for the child.
- Counselors are developmental in nature.
- Competent adult African American resources are identified for the young person.
- Counselors should incorporate the strengths of the family and the culture into the counseling process.
- If the young person has been referred against his or her will, counselors should explore feelings about the counseling process.
- If the counselor is not African American, the issue of the lack of a racial match should be addressed.
- Talk about role models who are inspirational and the young person's strengths.
- After goals have been established, work with a solution-focused and problem-solving approach.

Locke (1995) recommends the following steps to building an understanding of an African American young people. First, encourage the young people to talk about themselves, their families, and their experiences. The counselor should focus on the strengths evident in these stories. Counselors should ask about social class status rather than make assumptions about it. Asking young clients to describe holiday celebrations, kinship networks, and the role of religion in their lives helps counselors appreciate those aspects. Counselors should solicit the concerns of the young people. Using music and dance as areas of special interest will also help the counseling process, according to Locke (1995).

Bradley (2001) summarizes a six-session group for African American adolescent boys. The group moves from an introduction to understanding prejudice and racism. The young men learn about challenges within the educational system and then develop survival skills. Bradley concludes that the group sessions help the participants to clarify concerns about race and to successfully navigate some challenges in the environment and school.

Some authors (Vontross, 1995; Belgrave, Chase-Vaughn, Gray, Addison, & Cherry, 2000) support gender- and culture-specific interventions for adolescents. Belgrave and her colleagues (2000) have worked with adolescent African American girls, and they conclude that a group intervention designed around Afrocentric values, gender, and ethnic identity benefited the participants. Richardson (1991) writes that counseling professionals must recognize nontraditional means for providing services to their clients. He suggests that the African American church can be helpful in bolstering the self-esteem of its members who have been negatively affected by racism and oppression. The church provides means for self-expression, gaining of self-respect and community recognition, and achievement through holding of church officers, titles, and responsibilities. Richardson provides guidelines for counselors as they attempt to develop relationships with African American churches for the benefit of their clients.

Parham (1996) argues that traditional psychology has been oppressive to different cultures and has ignored the influence of African ideas on Western civilization, citing research that suggests that psychiatry and psychology have increased oppression among African Americans as indicated by higher rates of mental illness, misdiagnosis of psychological conditions, and mistreatment in the mental health system. Parham (1996) cautions that multicultural counselors "must avoid dancing around the issues of environmental oppression and call them what they are: Racism! Sexism! Classism!" (p. 187). He writes that multicultural counseling cannot be relevant to African Americans if it does not teach clients, families, and children to confront and understand racism. He urges that the African personality must be defined, including its spiritual aspect, and the appropriate human functioning must be redefined in terms of a "culturally centered frame of reference." Finally, he calls for specific interventions that will help African Americans achieve a greater congruency with their cultural essence.

In their summary of issues and strategies for counseling African American students, Fusick and Bordeau (2004) identify the following barriers to effective counseling: counselor bias, ignorance, rescuing, or oversympathizing; cultural conflict between the client and the counselor; client resistance, mistrust, ignorance of counseling process, or bias. These authors suggest combining peer group, individual, and family counseling and providing early intervention. Identity development, peer support groups, career exploration and development, peer mediation, and goal-setting activities are some of their other recommendations for working with African American young people.

American Indian and Alaskan Native Children

Within American Indians and Alaska Natives the Bureau of Indian Affairs recognizes 561 tribes (Surgeon General, 2002) with more than 252 different languages (Garrett, 1999). These children comprise about 1 percent of the U.S. population (Child Trends, 2005). Although these children comprise a small proportion of the total population, their problems are significant. The suicide rate for Native Americans is 1.5 times the national rate. It is estimated that 8 percent of Americans who are homeless are American Indians. Also, the rate of violent victimization in these cultures is more than twice the national average.

Baruth and Manning (2003) recommend that counselors acknowledge the diversity in American Indian children and the differences among the many tribes. One way of achieving that understanding has been researched. Salzman (2000) describes a cross-cultural mentorship project that allows educators to better serve the needs of Native Americans. The expanded understanding of the European Americans contributed to their increased effectiveness.

Lazarus (1982) suggests that counselors working with Native American children be aware of their particular values to prepare them for the difficulties of growing up in the present-day world. Each Native American tribe is different, but Lazarus lists general guidelines for understanding values:

1. Children are respected to the same degree as adults.
2. Cooperation and harmony are valued.
3. Generosity and sharing are important, and individuals are judged on their contributions.
4. Competition is encouraged if it does not hurt anyone.
5. Native Americans live in the present, with little concern for planning for tomorrow.
6. The school culture for children is strange; some behaviors are considered ill-mannered (loud talking and reprimands).
7. Older people are respected for their wisdom and knowledge.
8. Ancient legends and cultural traditions are important.
9. Peace and politeness are essential; confrontation is rude (p. 84).

Native Americans traditionally hold a worldview that is more spiritual, holistic, harmonious, and collective. Wellness is seen as harmony and lack of wellness as disharmony in spirit, mind, and body (LaFromboise & Jackson, 1996).

Herring (1991) reminds readers that the history of Native Americans is characterized by military defeat, ethnic demoralization, and forced displacement—forces that negatively influence Native American youth. The Native American family is often faced with overwhelming poverty and unemployment, family dissolution due, in part, to federal government policies, and educational failure.

LaFromboise and Jackson (1996) state that knowledge of and respect for the Native American worldview is essential for counseling Native American clients, especially an understanding of the culture, social contexts, and roles that healers play. A client's world must be considered in the light of the community, because an individual's problem becomes a problem of the community. All members of the community try to understand the client and find ways to integrate him or her back into the group.

Herring (1997) outlines recommendations for building a counseling environment for Native American youth. These recommendations are as follows:

- The counselor demonstrates sensitivity and openness by openly addressing the issue of ethnic dissimilarity. Dufrene and Coleman (1992) have identified the frank discussion of distrust as a key to their success.
- The counselor considers ethnic identity and degree of acculturation of the young person. Dress, daily activities, family involvement, body language, participation in tribal functions, friendship patterns, and eye contact provide information about these.
- The counselor should allow flexibility in the schedule as American Indians may prefer open-ended sessions free from time constraints.
- Counselors may want to include family members and tribal elders in the counseling process and perhaps hold sessions in the home. Johnson and Johnson (1998) also recommend the involvement of kin.
- Creative arts such as art, dance, and music are suggested interventions. Other recommendations include humor (Herring, 1994), storytelling, story reading, puppetry, and games (Herring & Meggert, 1994).
- Counselors should include natural healing practices into individual treatment. Herring (1997) suggests four circles, talking circle, and sweat lodge ceremonies (pp. 61–62).

LaFromboise and Jackson (1996) also suggest that cognitive behavioral interventions may be more appropriate than other theories such as psychodynamic or client-centered theories because they can (and should) be adapted to the culture and community. The authors believe that one of the most important goals for a counselor of Native American clients is to facilitate *conscientizacao*—that is, helping clients see themselves in relation to the familial and cultural influences on development—and to help them see their many strengths, their uniqueness, and their resources. They caution that conventional Western theories alone cannot prepare counselors to understand the cultural world of Native Americans and work effectively with them. Given the collective identity of Native Americans, it is suggested that respected community leaders, traditional leaders, extended family, elders, and other supportive groups be included in the helping process.

One other caveat was noted by Herring (1991), who cautions that young clients evaluate the counselor from the first moment—his or her manner of greeting, appearance, communication style, and knowledge of the Native American culture. Herring also suggests that community and tribal leaders can be a valuable source of help in counseling Native American youth, as can bias-free media resources that show realistic, accurate portrayals of Native American culture.

ASIAN AMERICAN CHILDREN

Asian Americans and Pacific Islanders include 43 ethnic groups with more than 100 languages and dialects (Surgeon General, 2002). Around 35 percent live in households of limited English proficiency. Asian and Pacific Islander children represent 4 percent of the population in 2001 and are predicted to increase to 5 percent by 2020 (Child Trends, 2005). Asian Americans may have roots in China, Japan, Korea, Vietnam, Cambodia, or elsewhere. Although Asian Americans come from different countries, Lee and Richardson (1991) believe all of these groups are influenced by old religious traditions that are passed down through the generations, including issues related to moderation of behavior, self-discipline, patience, humility, honor, and respect.

However, Leong (1996) emphasizes strongly that the phrase *Asian American* represents a diverse set of ethnic groups and cautions counselors to avoid stereotypes and to be aware of between-group differences, as well as within-group variations. He urges counselors to determine the degree of cultural identity and assess the depth of acculturation as they work with clients. Stereotypes of Asian American culture would have us believe that all adults are hardworking and successful and all children are high achieving (Sue & Sue, 2003); however, some Asian American families live in poverty and feel the stresses of discrimination (Huang & Ying, 1989). To visit a counselor for help with problems may be viewed as shameful and embarrassing and produce a sense of failure; therefore, the number of clients in treatment is low, and research on effective therapeutic interventions is limited.

Counselor credibility can be an issue with Chinese American children because it is often based not only on therapeutic skills but also on cultural roles related to age and gender. Counselors must communicate thoroughly with Chinese American families about what is going on in counseling to enlist their support (Huang & Ying, 1989). Sue and Sue (2003) advise counselors that "issues such as independence, the necessity of eliciting emotional reactions, and the equality of family members must be seen from a cultural perspective and not as a given" (p. 89).

Much of the Japanese culture evolved from the philosophies of Confucianism and Buddhism. These teachings continue to influence the lives of Japanese Americans and are factors that must be recognized in counseling (Tomine, 1991):

- The family is more important than the individual.
- The family roles and rules for behavior are formalized, and adherence to these roles and rules is expected to avoid shame and loss of face.
- The father is the leader and authority; the mother is the nurturing parent.
- Communication is usually indirect, and confrontation is avoided.
- Problems are kept within the family, and all problems are solved within the family unit.

In addition to possible acculturation concerns and problems of coping with prejudices, Japanese American children may be dealing with lingering anger over World War II internment issues in the family. They may also feel the impact of other political and economic decisions that affect American–Japanese relationships (Nagata, 1989). Tomine (1991) cautions counselors to attend carefully to the personal, cultural, and defensive factors that influence the coping mechanisms of Japanese Americans.

Some authors (Chandras, Eddy, & Spaulding, 1999; Clemente, 2004; Hartman & Askounis, 1989; Omizo & Omizo, 1989) provide several recommendations for working with Asian American children:

- Counselors need to ascertain individual strengths and weaknesses.
- Counselors should determine degree of acculturation.
- Counselors should recognize the difficulty in self-disclosure and the meaning of restraint as an attribute of emotional maturity. They need to acknowledge the belief that having problems may be seen as shaming the entire family. Mercado (2000) has adapted family systems theory for working with young people who are substance abusers and their families.
- Questions should be relevant to the problem, and counselors should refrain from asking too many personal questions.
- Confrontational, emotionally intense counseling approaches may be inappropriate. Active and direct counseling is recommended. Competition should be minimized.
- Counselors may explore the role of interdependence from the Asian perspective and independence from the American perspective in the young person's life.
- Counselors should emphasize the importance of confidentiality.
- Therapy should be limited in time and focused on resolutions.
- Yeh (2001) admonishes counselors to learn to recognize common concerns of Asian American children because of their reluctance to reveal emotional difficulties.
- Counselors are encouraged to ask about the culture of the client.
- Counselors can assume an active role, but must allow the young person to evaluate options and make decisions.
- Counselors should focus on the present time.
- Counselors work to gain an understanding of nonverbal skills.

Berg and Miller (1992) have outlined other techniques to use with Asian American clients. Counselors can ask the client to talk about exceptions to the problem. Counselors may use relationship questions to discover information about social interactions. Asking a client to describe a miracle that would solve the problem helps generate goals and solutions. Probing for coping strategies can help the counselor and the client highlight strengths. Certainly, the counselor needs a wide range of skills to adapt to the client's needs. Counselors deal carefully with expression of feelings by encouraging children to express only a little more than their comfort zone allows. Because of the strong family orientation, family members may serve as a nontraditional means of providing counseling, but the family may also hinder the process by preferring to solve problems within the nuclear structure.

Lee and Cynn (1991) contend that Korean Americans have cultural values similar to those of Chinese Americans and Japanese Americans. The primary adjustment problems of children from this group may be due to the rate of acculturation. Young persons adopt American values and behaviors more quickly than parents who have only recently immigrated. Lee and Cynn call on counselors to recognize this problem and the expectations both the old and new cultures place on children. Calling adjustment problems a normal part of the acculturation process can save face for the family and enable them to continue counseling with a positive attitude. Counseling strategies must be consistent in degree of acculturation and stage of ethnic identity development.

Leong (1996) recommends that counselors learn about culture-specific variables in their clients' lives; for example, the importance of harmony in interpersonal relationships, the need to avoid loss of face, preferences for more subtle forms of communication, and individualism versus collectivism. These values may negatively affect the counselor–client relationship, especially if they are misunderstood and confuse or frustrate the client.

LATINO CHILDREN

In 2004, Latino children represented 19 percent of the U.S. child population, and this percentage is expected to increase to 24 percent by 2020 (Child Trends, 2005). Mexican Americans represent about two thirds of the Latino population, with the remaining third being of Puerto Rican, Cuban, South American, Central American, Dominican, and Spanish roots (Surgeon General, 2002). According to Baron (1991), labels have psychological meaning for groups. He uses the terms *Chicano* and *Mexican American* interchangeably in his writings. Arredondo (1996) writes:

> Latina(o)s in the United States are of African, Asian, European, and Indian heritage, of many shades of skin color and phenotype. . . various levels of acculturation, urban and rural lifestyles, many educational and economic backgrounds, and varied English/Spanish language proficiency. Most government institutions use the label **Hispanic** to try to easily categorize multiple nationalities that have roots in Latin-American countries and Spain." (p. 220)

Latino young people experience more anxiety-related and delinquency behaviors, depression, and drug use than non-Hispanic white youth. In 1997, the Latino youth reported more suicidal ideation and attempts than other young people (Surgeon General, 2002).

Gloria and Rodriguez (2000) list the following questions to use with Latino clients:

- How do you identify yourself (Hispanic, Chicano, Latino American)?
- What does that word(s) mean to you?
- How hard has it been for you to maintain your cultural values here?
- What is your primary language?
- Who are your friends?
- What holidays and traditions do you celebrate?

- What does your family expect from you?
- Who helps you at home?

Baruth and Manning (1992) contend that Hispanic American children may be less competitive to avoid standing out in their group. They usually adhere to different male and female gender roles. Attributes such as warmth, dignity, masculine pride, and respect for authority are important in their lives. These children tend to stand close to others and like to touch, but avoid eye contact. Counselors must also understand family behaviors of Hispanic American homes, including a strong family commitment, parental styles that emphasize obedience, and the assumption of important family responsibilities early in the child's life. Because of the Hispanic American emphasis on the family, family counseling can be an effective tool. Arredondo (1996) adds that loyalty to family comes first; authority figures such as teachers (and counselors) are highly respected and not questioned; pride and dignity are strongly promoted; gender roles are clearly defined, with *machismo* being valued, but there is a reverence for motherhood. Religion, mainly Roman Catholic, and spirituality strongly influence the beliefs of Latinos; according to Arredondo (1996), they believe that moral character is related to one's health or lack of it. Illness may also be caused by environmental or supernatural causes. These beliefs will also influence the types of interventions believed by the client to be effective.

Arredondo (1996) also points out that most Latin American countries have a history of political struggle with the United States, and this perceived oppression may influence the counseling relationship. Latinos are also the most economically disadvantaged group in the United States and tend to underuse health and mental health services. Poverty, feelings of oppression, and lack of care all combine to make Latinos a high-risk group for dropping out of school and other risky behavior. Arredondo urges that counseling theories and practices focus on "inclusion, value, self-definition, strengths (not just deficits), differences balanced with commonalities, and history to inform the present and the future" (p. 233).

Arredondo (1996) recommends that the counselor make every effort to understand the client's belief system, as well as symptoms; determine the degree of acculturation and experiences; and learn more about the roles of economics and institutional racism, language differences, or other discriminatory factors on the client's beliefs and behaviors.

Clemente (2004) provides some general guidelines for working with Latino young people:

- With less acculturated Latino youth, counselors should use a formal stance. For example, use last names and a title such as Mr. or Ms.
- Counselors may want to provide a tentative solution to the problem and explain the counseling process and expectations.
- Counselors should be respectful of the child's worldview and sensitive to religious issues that may be misidentified as fantasies or hallucinations.
- Counselors should ask about including family members in the sessions.
- Counselors should understand the person from a systemic perspective and consider the environmental impacts that may be influencing the young

person's mental health and behavior (for example, poor nutrition or neighborhood violence).

- Counselors should reassure the youth that sessions are confidential and that information will not be released to government agencies such as the Immigration and Naturalization Service.

Multiracial Children

According to Lee and Bean (2004), one in forty people identifies themselves as multiracial. Currently, 4 percent of the child population has two or more races (Child Trends, 2005), and about 13 percent of U.S. marriages involve partners of different races. Obviously, those interracial marriages contribute to the increase in multiracial identifications. The stresses of an interracial marriage may be severe, and the pressure on children of these marriages to understand and adapt to the history and culture of each parent may increase confusion and stress in their lives. In addition to having unusual characteristics and the potential for problems because of their dual ancestry, Gibbs (1989) notes that multiracial children may have identity problems related to their ambiguous ethnicity. They may encounter problems with family approval, acceptance in the community, discrimination, and isolation. Gibbs enumerates their conflicts as the following:

- *Racial-ethnic identity*—Who am I?
- *Social marginality*— Where do I fit?
- *Sexuality*—What is my sexual role? (with regard to orientation, gender identity, and sexual activity)
- *Autonomy*—Parents may have attempted to protect or isolate children from reality.
- *Educational and occupational aspirations*—Where am I going? Also, clients may desire to determine whether their expectations are realistic in light of prejudices and discrimination.

Gibbs encourages counselors to assist children in exploring their ancestry and recognizing the impact of their heritage on themselves. Qian (2004) cites the influences of the ethnicity of the minority parent, the characteristics of the couple, and the composition of the neighborhood on the children's ethnic identities.

Herring (1992) also states that biracial children may have issues in the development of self-identity. First, they must integrate two racial and cultural backgrounds while developing their own self-identity. In addition, during adolescence, they must deal with the task of developing peer relations and deciding their gender roles and preferences. Difficulties with racial identity may lead the child to experience conflicts over separation from parents and to have concerns about career choices. However, Bracey, Bamaca, and Umana-Taylor (2004) have studied self-esteem and ethnic identity in biracial adolescents and have discovered a significant and positive relationship.

Herring (1992) advises counselors to: (1) develop a positive, trusting relationship with the child; (2) understand that the child's presenting problem may cover a deeper ethnic identity concern; (3) be aware that biracial children usually identify with the minority culture, believing that the white culture is not willing to accept them; (4) become familiar with the customs of all their students to serve them better; (5) permit the children to vent their feelings about their identity and its meaning in society; (6) assist in building the children's self-esteem through supportive techniques; (7) see the link between their confusion over ethnic and cultural background and other developmental concerns; and (8) involve the entire family to promote individual and family growth.

SUMMARY

Liu and Clay (2002) suggest a decision-making model to use when working with children from diverse backgrounds. They advise counselors first to evaluate which, if any, cultural variables are relevant. Counselors must decide the level of skills and knowledge needed for them to provide competent treatment. The helping professional must assess how much, when, and how to pull in cultural issues. Counselors should always examine the cultural implications of all possible treatments and choose strategies that focus on cultural strengths.

This section has provided an overview of the awareness, knowledge, and skills needed for multicultural counseling. The characteristics and needs of some of the many cultures that professionals may encounter when they work with children have been discussed. Research on the counseling needs of culturally different clients is limited. Counselor-education training programs have only begun to prepare more culturally aware professionals. Materials and resources are limited, although books, media, and special programs are beginning to appear. The number of minority group members living in the United States will continue to grow in the twenty-first century. Counselors must be prepared to bridge cultural gaps and adopt techniques and procedures to meet the needs of many different children and families.

WEBSITES FOR CULTURAL FACTORS IN COUNSELING CHILDREN

Internet addresses frequently change. To find the sites listed here, visit www.thomsonedu.com/ counseling/thompson for an updated list of Internet addresses and direct links to relevantsites.

The Committee for Hispanic Children and Families

Coalition for Asian American Children and Families

National Center for Children in Poverty

National Indian Child Welfare Association

Southern Poverty Law Center

REFERENCES

Allen, L., & Majidi-Ahi, S. (1989). Black American children. In J. Gibbs & L. Huang (Eds.), *Children of color: Psychological interventions with minority youth* (pp. 148–178). San Francisco: Jossey-Bass.

Arredondo, P. (1996). MCT theory and Latina (o)-American populations. In D. W. Sue, A. Ivey, & P. Pedersen (Eds.), *A theory of multicultural counseling and therapy* (pp. 217–235). Pacific Grove, CA: Brooks/Cole.

Arredondo, P., Toporek, R., Brown, S. P., Jones, J., Locke, D. C., Sanchez, J., & Stadler, H. (1996). Operationalization of the multicultural counseling competencies. *Journal of Multicultural Counseling and Development, 24*(1), 42–78.

Atkinson, D. R., Morten, G., & Sue, D. W. (1993). *Counseling American minorities: A cross-cultural perspective* (4th ed.). Madison, WI: Brown & Benchmark.

Baron, A. (1991). Counseling Chicano college students. In C. Lee & B. Richardson (Eds.), *Multicultural issues in counseling: New approaches to diversity* (pp. 171–184). Alexandria, VA: American Association for Counseling and Development.

Barona, A., & Miller, J. A. (1994). Short Acculturation Scale for Hispanic Youths (9SASH-Y): A preliminary report. *Hispanic Journal of Behavioral Sciences, 16,* 155–162.

Baruth, L., & Manning, M. (1992). Understanding and counseling Hispanic American children. *Elementary School Guidance and Counseling, 27,* 113–122.

Baruth, L. G., & Manning, M. L. (2003). *Multicultural counseling and psychotherapy: A lifespan perspective* (3rd ed.). Upper Saddle River, NJ: Merrill.

Belgrave, F. Z., Chase-Vaughn, G., Gray, F., Addison, J. D., & Cherry, V. R. (2000). The effectiveness of culture-and gender-specific intervention for increasing resiliency among Afro-American preadolescent females. *Journal of Black Psychology, 26*(2), 133–147.

Berg, I. K., & Miller, S. (1992). Working with Asian American clients: One person at a time. *Families in Society, 73,* 356–363.

Bernal, M. E., Knight, G., Garza, C., Ocampo, K., & Cota, M. K. (1993). *Ethnic identity: Formation and transmission among Hispanics and other minorities.* Albany, NY: State University of New York Press.

Blum, D. J. (1998). *The school counselors' book of lists.* West Nyack, NY: The Center for Applied Research in Education.

Bracey, J. R., Bamaca, M. Y., & Umana-Taylor, A. J. (2004). Examining ethnic identity and self-esteem among biracial and monoracial adolescents. *Journal of Youth and Adolescence, 33,* 123–132.

Bradley, C. (2001). A counseling group for African-American males. *Professional School Counseling, 4,* 370–373.

Brown, D., & Trusty, J. (2005). *Designing and leading comprehensive school counseling programs: Promoting student competence and meeting student needs.* Belmont, CA: Thomson Brooks/Cole.

Burnam, M. A., Hough, R. L., Karno, M., Escobar, J. I., & Telles, C. A. (1987). Acculturation and lifetime prevalence of psychiatric disorders among Mexican Americans in Los Angeles. *Journal of Health and Social Behavior, 28,* 89–102.

Casas, J. M., & Pytluk, S. D. (1995). Hispanic identity development: Implications for research and practice. In J. G. Ponterotto, J. M. Casas, L. A. Suzuki, & C. M. Alexander (Eds.), *Handbook of multicultural counseling* (pp. 155–180). Thousand Oaks, CA: Sage.

Chandras, K. V., Eddy, J. P., & Spaulding, D. J. (1999). Counseling Asian Americans: Implications for training. *Education, 99,* 239–247.

Child Trends. (2005). Child trends data bank: Racial and ethnic composition of the child population. Retrieved November 15, 2005, from http://databank.childtrends.org/indicators/60RaceandEthnicComposition.cfm

Choney, S. K., Berryhill-Paapke, E., & Robbins, R. R. (1995). The acculturation of American Indians. In J. G. Ponterotto, J. M. Casas, L. A. Suzuki, & C. M. Alexander (Eds.), *Handbook of multicultural counseling* (pp. 73–92). Thousand Oaks, CA: Sage.

Clemente, R. (2004). Counseling culturally and ethnically diverse youth. In A. Vernon (Ed). *Counseling children and adolescents* (3rd ed., pp. 227–256). Denver, CO: Love.

Cole, P. M., Bruschi, C. J., & Tamang, B. L. (2002). Cultural differences in children's emotional reactions to difficult situations. *Child Development, 73,* 983–996.

Cross. W. E. (1995). The psychology of Nigrescence: Revisiting the Cross model. In J. G. Ponterotto, J. M. Casas, L. A. Suzuki, & C. M. Alexander (Eds.), *Handbook of multicultural counseling* (pp. 93–122). Thousand Oaks, CA: Sage.

Das, K. D. (1995). Rethinking multicultural counseling: Implications for counselor education. *Journal of Counseling and Development, 74,* 45–52.

Dufrene, P., & Coleman, V. (1992). Art and healing for Native American Indians. *Journal of Multicultural Counseling and Development, 22,* 145–152.

Fascoli, L. (1999). Developmentally appropriate play and turtle hunting. In E. Dau (Ed.), *Child's play: Revisiting play in early childhood* (pp. 53–59). Sydney, Australia: Maclennan & Petty.

Fischer, A., Jome, L., & Atkinson, D. (1998). Reconceptualizing multicultural counseling: Universal and healing conditions in a culturally specific context. *The Counseling Psychologist, 26*(4), 525–588.

Fusick, L., & Bordeau, L. C. (2004). Counseling at-risk Afro-American youth. *Professional School Counseling, 8,* 102–115.

Garrett, M. W. (1995). Between two worlds: Cultural discontinuity in the dropout of Native American youth. *The School Counselor, 42,* 186–195.

Garrett, M. T. (1999). Soaring on the wings of the eagle: Wellness of Native American high school students. *Professional School Counseling, 3,* 57–64.

Gibbs, J. (1989). Biracial adolescents. In J. Gibbs & L. Huang (Eds.), *Children of color: Psychological interventions with minority youth* (pp. 322–350). San Francisco: Jossey-Bass.

Gibbs, J. T., & Huang, L. N. (1989). A conceptual framework for assessing and treating minority youth. In J. T. Gibbs & L. N. Huang (Eds.), *Children of color: Psychological interventions with minority youth* (pp. 10–29). San Francisco: Jossey-Bass.

Gloria, A. M., & Rodriguez, E. R. (2000). Counseling Latino university students: Psychosocial issues for consideration. *Journal of Counseling and Development, 78,* 145–154.

Greig, R. (2003). Ethnic identity development: Implications for mental health in African-American and Hispanic adolescents. *Issues in Mental Health Nursing, 24,* 317–331.

Grieger, I., & Ponterotto, J. G. (1995). A framework for assessment in multicultural counseling. In J. G. Ponterotto, J. M. Casas, L. A. Suzuki, & C. M. Alexander (Eds.), *Handbook of multicultural counseling* (2nd ed., pp. 357–374). Thousand Oaks, CA: Sage.

Hartman, J. S., & Askounis, A. C. (1989). Asian American students: Are they really a "model minority"? *School Counselor, 37,* 109–111.

Hays, P. A. (2001). *Addressing cultural complexities in practice: A framework for clinicians and counselors.* Washington, DC: American Psychological Association.

Helms, J. E., (Ed.). (1990). *Black and white racial identity: Theory, research, and practice.* Westport, CT: Greenwood.

Helms, J. E. (1995). An update of Helms's White and People of Color racial identity models. In J. G. Ponterotto, J. M. Casas, L. A. Suzuki, & C. M. Alexander (Eds.), *Handbook of multicultural counseling* (pp. 181–198). Thousand Oaks, CA: Sage.

Helms, J. E. (2003). Racial identity in the social environment. In P. B. Pedersen, & J. C. Carey (Eds.). *Multicultural counseling in schools: A practical handbook* (2nd ed., pp. 44–58). Boston: Allyn & Bacon.

Henriksen, R. C., & Trusty, J. (2002). Racial, ethnic, and cultural identity development models. In J. Trusty, E. J. Looby, & D. S. Sandhu (Eds.), *Multicultural counseling: Context, theory and practice, and competence* (pp. 55–104). New York: Nova Science.

Hernandez, H. (1989). *Multicultural education: A teacher's guide to content and practice.* Upper Saddle River, NJ: Merrill.

Herring, R. (1991). Counseling Native American youth. In C. Lee & B. Richardson (Eds.), *Multicultural issues in counseling: New approaches to diversity* (pp. 37–47). Alexandria, VA: American Association for Counseling and Development.

Herring, R. (1992). Biracial children: An increasing concern for elementary and middle school counselors. *Elementary School Guidance and Counseling, 27,* 123–130.

Herring, R. D. (1994). The clown or contrary figure as a counseling intervention strategy with Native American Indian clients. *Journal of Multicultural Counseling and Development, 22,* 153–164.

Herring, R. D. (1997). Counseling indigenous American youth. In C. C. Lee (Ed.), *Multicultural issues in counseling: New approaches to diversity* (2nd ed., pp. 53–70). Alexandria, VA: American Counseling Association.

Herring, R. D., & Meggert, S. S. (1994). The use of humor as a counselor strategy with Native American Indian children. *Elementary School Guidance and Counseling, 29,* 67–76.

Ho, M. K. (1992). *Minority children and adolescents in therapy.* Thousand Oaks, CA: Sage.

Hoffmann, T., Dana, R., & Bolton, B. (1985). Measured acculturation and MMPI-168 performance of Native Americans. *Journal of Cross-Cultural Psychology, 16,* 243–256.

Hofstede, G. (1980). Motivation, leadership and organization: Do American theories apply abroad? *Organizational Dynamics, 2,* 19–25.

Holcomb-McCoy, C. (2003). Multicultural competence. In B. Erford (Ed.), *Transforming the school counseling profession* (pp. 317–330). Upper Saddle River, NJ: Pearson.

Holcomb-McCoy, C. (2004). Assessing the multicultural competence of school counselors: A checklist. *Professional School Counseling, 7,* 178–186.

Huang, L., & Ying, Y. (1989). Chinese American children and adolescents. In J. Gibbs & L. Huang (Eds.), *Children of color: Psychological interventions with minority youth* (pp. 30–66). San Francisco: Jossey-Bass.

Hughes, D. (2003). Correlates of African American and Latino parents' messages to children about ethnicity and race: A comparative study of racial socialization. *American Journal of Community Psychology, 31,* 15–33.

Ibrahim, F.A., Roysircar-Sodowsky, G., & Ohnishi, H. (2001). Worldview: Recent developments and needed directions. In J. G. Ponterotto, J. M. Casas, L. A. Suzuki, & C. M. Alexander (Eds.), *Handbook of multicultural counseling* (2nd ed., pp. 425–456). Thousand Oaks, CA: Sage.

Johnson, C., & Johnson, D. (1998). Working with Native American families. *New Directions for Mental Health Services, 77,* 89–96.

Jones, D. J., Forehand, R., Brody, G., & Armistead, L. (2002). Psychosocial adjustment of Afro-American children in single-mother families: A test of three risk factors. *Journal of Marriage and Family, 64,* 105–116.

Kim, B. S. K., Atkinson, D. R., & Yang, P. H. (1999). The Asian Values Scale: Development, factor analysis, validation, and reliability. *Journal of Counseling Psychology, 46,* 342–352.

Kincade, E., & Evans, K. (1996). Counseling theories, process and intervention in a multicultural context. *Multicultural counseling competencies: Implications for training and practice.* Alexandria, VA: Association for Counselor Education and Supervision.

Kottman, T. (2001). *Play therapy: Basics and beyond.* Alexandria, VA: American Counseling Association.

Kowalski, K. (2003). The emergence of ethnic and racial attitudes in preschool-aged children. *The Journal of Social Psychology, 143,* 677–690.

LaFromboise, T., & Jackson, M. (1996). MCT theory and Native American populations. In D. W. Sue, A. Ivey, & P. Pedersen (Eds.), *A theory of multicultural counseling and therapy* (pp. 192–203). Pacific Grove, CA: Brooks/Cole.

Lazarus, P. J. (1982). Counseling the Native American child: A question of values. *Elementary School Guidance and Counseling, 17,* 83–88.

Lee, C. C. (2001). Defining and responding to racial and ethnic diversity. In D. C. Locke, J. E. Myers, & E. L. Herr (Eds.), *The handbook of counseling* (pp. 581–588). Thousand Oaks, CA: Sage.

Lee, C. C., & Bailey, D. F. (1997). Counseling Afro-American male youth and men. In C. C. Lee (Ed.), *Multicultural issues in counseling: New approaches to diversity* (2nd ed., pp. 123–154). Alexandria, VA: American Counseling Association.

Lee, C. C., & Richardson, B. (Eds.). (1991). *Multicultural issues in counseling: New approaches to diversity.* Alexandria, VA: American Association for Counseling and Development.

Lee, J., & Bean, F. D. (2004). America's changing color lines: Immigration, race/ethnicity, and multiracial identification. *Annual Review of Sociology, 30,* 221–242.

Lee, J., & Cynn, V. (1991). Issues in counseling 1.5 generation Korean Americans. In C. Lee & B. Richardson (Eds.), *Multicultural issues in counseling: New approaches to diversity* (pp. 127–140). Alexandria, VA: American Association for Counseling and Development.

Leong, F. (1996). MCT theory and Asian-American populations. In D. W. Sue, A. Ivey, & P. Pedersen (Eds.), *A theory of multicultural counseling and therapy* (pp. 204–216). Pacific Grove, CA: Brooks/Cole.

Liu, W. M., & Clay, D. L. (2002). Multicultural counseling competencies: Guidelines in working with children and adolescents. *Journal of Mental Health Counseling, 24,* 177–187.

Locke, D. C. (1989). Fostering the self-esteem of Afro-American children. *Elementary School Guidance and Counseling, 23,* 254–259.

Locke, D. C. (1995). Counseling interventions with Afro-American youth. In C.C. Lee (Ed.), *Counseling for diversity: A guide for school counselors and related professionals* (pp. 21–40). Boston: Allyn & Bacon.

Locke, D. C. (2003). Improving the multicultural competence of educators. In P. B. Pedersen & J. C. Carey (Eds.), *Multicultural counseling in schools: A practical handbook* (2nd ed., pp. 171–189). Boston: Allyn & Bacon.

Locke, D. C., & Parker, L. D. (1994). Improving the multicultural competence of educators. In P. Pedersen & J. C. Carey (Eds.), *Multicultural counseling in schools: A practical handbook* (pp. 39–58). Boston: Allyn & Bacon.

Lonner, W. J., & Ibrahim, F. A. (2002). Appraisal and assessment. In P. B. Pedersen, J. G. Draguns, W. J. Lonner, & J. E. Trimble (Eds.), *Counseling across cultures* (5th ed., pp. 355–380). Thousand Oaks, CA: Sage.

Marsella, A. J., & Yamada, A. M. (2000). Culture and mental health: An introduction and overview of foundations, concepts, and issues. In I. Cuellar & F. A. Paniagua (Eds.), *Handbook of multicultural mental health* (pp. 3–24). San Diego: Academic Press.

Mercado, M. M. (2000). The invisible family: Counseling Asian American substance abusers and their families. *Family Journal, 8,* 267–272.

Mio, J. S., Trimble, J. E., Arredondo, P., Cheatham, H. E., & Sue, D. (1999). *Key words in multicultural interventions: A dictionary.* Westport, CT: Greenwood.

Nagata, D. (1989). Japanese American children and adolescents. In J. Gibbs & L. Huang (Eds.), *Children of color: Psychological interventions with minority youth* (pp. 67–113). San Francisco: Jossey-Bass.

Omizo, M. M., & Omizo, S. A. (1989). Counseling Hawaiian children. *Elementary School Guidance and Counseling, 23,* 282–288.

Parham, T. (1996). MCT theory and African-American populations. In D. W. Sue, A. Ivey, & P. Pedersen (Eds.), *A theory of multicultural counseling and therapy* (pp. 177–191). Pacific Grove, CA: Brooks/Cole.

Pedersen, P. B. (1997). The cultural context of the American Counseling Association code of Ethics. *Journal of Counseling and Development, 76*(1), 23–28.

Pedersen, P. B. (2002). Ethics, competence, and other professional issues in culture-centered counseling. In P. B. Pedersen, J. G. Draguns, W. J. Lonner, & J. E. Trimble (Eds.), *Counseling across cultures* (5th ed., pp. 3–28). Thousand Oaks, CA: Sage.

Pedersen, P. V., Draguns, J. G., Lonner, W. J., & Trimble, J. E. (2002). *Counseling across cultures* (5th ed.). Thousand Oaks, CA: Sage.

Phinney, J. S. (1990). Ethnic identity in adolescents and adults: Review of research. *Psychological Bulletin, 108,* 499–514.

Phinney, J. S. (1993). A three-stage model of ethnic identity development in adolescence. In M. Bernal & G. Knight (Eds.), *Ethnic identity: Formation and transmission among Hispanics and other minorities* (pp. 61–79). Albany, NY: State University of New York Press.

Ponterotto, J. G., & Casas, J. M. (1987). In search of multicultural competence within counselor education programs. *Journal of Counseling and Development, 65,* 430–434.

Qian, Z. (2004). Options: Racial/ethnic identification of children of intermarried couples. *Social Science Quarterly, 85,* 746–766.

Ramirez, M., III (1999). *Multicultural psychotherapy: An approach to individual and cultural differences* (2nd Ed.) Boston, MA: Allyn & Bacon.

Richardson, B. (1991). Utilizing the resources of the Afro-American church: Strategies for counseling professionals. In C. Lee & B. Richardson (Eds.), *Multicultural issues in counseling: New approaches to diversity* (pp. 65–75). Alexandria, VA: American Association for Counseling and Development.

Richardson, T. Q., & Jacob, E. J. (2002). Contemporary issues in multicultural counseling: Training competent counselors. In J. Trusty, E. J. Looby, & D. S. Sandhu (Eds.), *Multicultural counseling: Context, theory and practice, and competence* (pp. 31–53). New York: Nova Science.

Robinson, T. (1993). The intersections of gender, class, race, and culture: On seeing clients whole. *Journal of Multicultural Counseling and Development, 21,* 50–58.

Salzman, M. (2000). Promoting multicultural competence: A cross-cultural mentorship project. *Journal of Multicultural Counseling & Development, 28,* 119–123.

Shapiro, J. P., Friedberg, R. D., & Bardenstein, K. K. (2006). *Child and adolescent therapy: Science and art.* Hoboken, NJ: John Wiley & Sons.

Snowden, L. R., & Hines, A. M. (1999). A scale to assess African American acculturation. *Journal of Black Psychology, 25,* 36–47.

Sodowsky, G. R., & Johnson, P. (1994). Worldviews: Culturally learned assumptions and values. In P. Pedersen & J. C. Carey (Eds.), *Multicultural counseling in schools: A practical handbook* (pp. 59–79). Boston: Allyn & Bacon.

Sodowsky, G. R., Kwan, K. K., & Pannu, R. (1995). Ethnic identity of Asians in the United States. In J. G. Ponterotto, J. M. Casas, L. A. Suzuki, & C. M. Alexander (Eds.), *Handbook of multicultural counseling* (pp. 123–154). Thousand Oaks, CA: Sage.

Sue, D. W., Arredondo, P., & McDavis, R. J. (1992). Multicultural counseling competencies and standards: A call to the profession. *Journal of Counseling and Development, 70,* 477–486.

Sue, D., & Sue, D. W. (2003). *Counseling the culturally different: Theory and practice* (4th ed.). New York: Wiley.

Sue, D. W., Ivey, A., & Pedersen, P. (1996). *A theory of multicultural counseling and therapy.* Pacific Grove, CA: Brooks/Cole.

Surgeon General. (2002). Mental health: Culture, race, ethnicity. Retrieved August 9, 2002, from www.surgeongeneral.gov

Tomine, S. (1991). Counseling Japanese Americans: From internment to reparation. In C. Lee & B. Richardson (Eds.), *Multicultural issues in counseling: New approaches to diversity* (pp. 91–105). Alexandria, VA: American Association for Counseling and Development.

Trevino, J. (1996). Worldview and change in cross-cultural counseling. *The Counseling Psychologist, 24*(2), 198–215.

Vontross, C. (1995). The breakdown of authority: Implications for counseling young Afro-American males. In J. G. Ponterotto, J. M. Casas, L. A. Suzuki, & C. M. Alexander (Eds.), *Handbook of multicultural counseling.* Thousand Oaks, CA: Sage.

Washington, E. D. (1994). Three steps to cultural awareness: A Wittgensteinian approach. In P. Pedersen & J. C. Carey (Eds.), *Multicultural counseling in schools: A practical handbook* (pp. 81–102). Boston: Allyn & Bacon.

Washington, E. D., Crosby, T., Hernandez, M., Vernon-Jones, R., Medley, R., Nishamura, B., & Torres, D. (2003). Cultural identity groups and cultural maps: Meaning making in groups. In P. B. Pedersen & J. C. Carey (Eds.), *Multicultural counseling in schools: A practical handbook* (pp. 26–43). Boston: Allyn & Bacon.

Yasuri, M., Dorham, C. L., & Dishion, T. J. (2004). Ethnic identity and psychological adjustment: A validity analysis for European American and African American adolescents. *Journal of Adolescent Research, 19,* 807–825.

Yeh, C. J. (2001). An exploratory study of school counselors' experiences with and perceptions of Asian-American students. *Professional School Counseling, 4,* 349–357.

Zaff, J. F., Blount, R. L., Phillips, L., & Cohen, L. (2002). The role of ethnic identity and self-construal in coping among African American and Caucasian American seventh graders: An exploratory analysis of within-group variance. *Adolescence, 37,* 751–773.

CONSULTATION AND COLLABORATION

CHAPTER 16

You must be the change you wish to see in the world.
—Mahatma Ghandi

Counselors may expand their opportunities to improve children's lives by engaging in cooperative relationships with other adults. The processes of consultation and collaboration, as well as collaborative teamwork, provide ways to build those types of working relationships. These related kinds of interactions allow counselors to serve children indirectly. Dettmer, Dyck, and Thurston (1999) explain that consultation, collaboration, and teamwork have these common characteristics:

- Addressing a problem
- Interacting
- Using specialized information to achieve goals
- Sharing resources
- Stimulating change or improvement

For purposes of our discussion, we use some arbitrary parameters to differentiate consultation and collaboration. Consultation will be considered as a method of sharing expertise. Collaboration will be used as a term for an interactive relationship of conferring and collective problem solving. The type of collaboration focusing on teams refers to a group that works together for the good of the whole in which each person contributes a specific effort to a plan of action. The following more specialized definitions, models, and examples will allow counselors to determine ways to incorporate each of these methods in working with children. That discussion is followed by examples of some specific consultation interventions.

CONSULTATION

Consultation is a process in which the consultant (counselor) works with the consultee (parent, teacher, other adult) with the goal of bringing about a positive change in the client (child). Kurpius and Fuqua (1993) summarize consultation as: "In general, consultants help consultees to think of their immediate problem as part of the larger system, and not only to understand how problems are solved but also to understand how they were developed, maintained, or avoided" (p. 598).

Brown, Pryzwansky, and Schulte (2006) offer a definition for consultation that identifies it as a voluntary problem-solving process aimed at helping consultees develop attitudes and skills that will allow them to work more effectively with a client, which can be an individual, group, or organization. According to these authors, the twofold goals of consultation are enhanced services and improved functioning.

Dougherty (2005) further reports that human service professionals may be asked to consult with adults who work and live with children, and the young people are ultimately the beneficiaries of the services. He suggests that consultants work with principals to discuss the concerns of students. Consultants may be asked to consult about a particular school program, or they may be involved in organization development. Consultants also work with teachers to enhance professional skills in areas such as effective parenting, enhancing children's self-concepts, choosing instructional materials, or conflict resolution. Consultants may meet with parents to help them understand more about children's growth and development or behavior, although they do not engage parents as frequently as might be expected or as may prove beneficial. Dougherty suggests that the range of roles in which a consultant may practice include that of advocate, expert, trainer/educator, collaborator, fact finder, process specialist, or other less common roles. Keys, Green, Lockhart, and Luongo (2003) echo those possibilities.

According to Glosoff and Koprowicz (1990), consultation directed primarily toward children typically involves the following:

- Conducting professional development workshops and discussions with teachers and other school personnel on subjects such as substance abuse or child abuse
- Assisting teachers in working with individual students or groups of students
- Providing relevant materials and resources to teachers, especially relating to classroom guidance curriculum
- Helping to identify and develop programs for students with special needs
- Participating in school committees that address substance abuse, human growth and development, school climate, and other guidance-related areas
- Designing and conducting parent education classes
- Interpreting student information, such as results of standardized tests, for students and team members
- Consulting regularly with other specialists such as social workers, psychologists, and other representatives from community agencies

Brown and Trusty (2005) suggest that consultation might be considered an information function or a problem-solving function that focuses on children's immediate needs and is often not a stand-alone activity when working in the child's interest.

MODELS OF CONSULTATION

MENTAL HEALTH CONSULTATION   Mental health consultation focuses on primary prevention and involves helping professionals and nonprofessionals. Caplan and Caplan (1993) explain mental health consultation as a "process of interaction between two professionals—the consultant, who is a specialist, and the consultee, who invokes the consultant's help in a current work problem that he believes is within the consultant's area of specialized competence" (p. 11). In this model, the consultant, considered an expert, diagnoses a problem and provides a solution. However, the consultant has no responsibility for carrying out the changes that have been recommended.

The model proposed by Caplan and Caplan (1993) consists of four ways of approaching the consultation relationship. In *client-centered case consultation,* the consultant helps the consultee with a client. The consultant assesses the problem and recommends a plan for the consultee to implement. The consultant's responsibilities include performing an accurate diagnosis and suggesting an effective intervention that focuses on the client. In *consultee-centered case consultation,* the consultant helps the consultee gain the knowledge, skills, self-confidence, and/or objectivity needed to work with a particular client. By focusing on the consultee's behavior and attitude, the consultant facilitates change. A consultant using *program-centered administrative consultation* focuses on the area of planning and administration such as the development of a program or the improvement of an existing project. The consultant collects information about the organization and suggests solutions with the goal of prescribing an effective course of action. Finally, *consultee-centered administrative consultation* focuses on remedying difficulties among consultees that interfere with their abilities to perform their work. These problems may be the individual difficulties noted in consultee-centered case consultation or may be the result of poor leadership, authority difficulties, communication blocks, and other group problems. Table 16-1 provides a comparison of these four types of consultation.

PROCESS CONSULTATION   Edward Schein (1999) has proposed a model of consultation he labels *process consultation.* He considers this approach to consultation as a skill. He emphasizes the interest in how things happen between people rather than what is actually done. More specifically, he defines process consultation as a "set of activities on the part of the consultant which help the (consultee) to perceive, understand, and act upon process events which occur in the (consultee's) environment" (Schein, 1988, p. 11). This type of consultation focuses on how problems are solved and on the system in which the problems occur. The consultant and consultee examine six different areas: (1) communication patterns, (2) group member roles, (3) group problem

TABLE 16-1 | MENTAL HEALTH CONSULTATION

	Client-centered case consultation	Consultee-centered case consultation	Program-centered administrative consultation	Consultee-centered administrative consultation
Focus	Focuses on developing a plan that will help a specific client.	Focuses on improvement of the consultee's professional functioning in relation to specific cases.	Focuses on improvement of programs or policies.	Focuses on improvement of consultee's professional functioning in relation to specific programs or policies.
Goal	To advise the consultee regarding client treatment.	To educate consultee using his or her problems with the client as a lever.	To help develop a new program or policy or improve an existing one.	To help consultee improve problem-solving skills in dealing with current organizational problems.
Example	School psychologist called in to diagnose a student's reding problem.	School counselor asks for help in dealing with students' drug-related problems.	Nursing home director requests help in developing staff orientation program.	Police chief asks for help in developing ongoing program to deal with interpersonal problems between veteran and new officers.
Consultant's Role and Responsibilities	Usually meets with consultee's client to help diagnose problem. Is responsible for assessing problem and prescribing course of action.	Never, or rarely, meets with consultee's client. Must be able to recognize source of consultee's difficulties and deal with them indirectly.	Meets with groups and individuals in an attempt to accurately assess problems. Is responsible for correctly assessing problem and providing a plan for administrative action.	Meets with groups and individuals in an attempt to help them develop their problem-solving skills. Must be able to recognize source of organizational difficulty and serve as catalyst for action by adminitrators.

NOTE: Reprinted from Duane Brown, Walter B. Pryzwansky and Ann C. Schulte (2001). *Psychological Consultation: Introduction to Theory and Practice*, 5e. Published by Allyn and Bacon, Boston, MA. Copyright © 2001 by Pearson Education. Reprinted by permission of the publisher.

solving and decision making, (4) group norms and growth, (5) leadership and authority, and (6) intergroup cooperation and competition (Keys, Bemak, Carpenter, & King-Sears, 1998). The consultant may operate as a catalyst in helping the consultee find a solution or as a facilitator who aids the consultee through a problem-solving process (Dougherty, 2005).

Harrison (2004) explains three strategic goals of process consultation. The first is to encourage a situation in which the client will ask for help. The next is to diagnose or create a situation so that information will surface and people understand better what is happening. The third goal is to build a team or create an environment in which the client will take responsibility for the problem and the solution. To accomplish these broad goals, Schein (1999) outlines these principles that can guide any consultation approach:

1. Constantly try to be helpful.
2. Stay in touch with reality by being alert to what is going on with you, with the situation, and in the consultee and client system.
3. Remain open to information and monitor your own ignorance particularly around racial, ethnic, and gender differences.
4. Remember that everything done is an intervention.
5. The client owns the problem and the solution.
6. Go with the sense of flow that emerges from the process.
7. Timing is critical in everything but particularly in shifting focus or method.
8. Find and build on existing motivation and cultural strengths.
9. Errors are inevitable.
10. When in doubt, share the problem (summarized in Harrison, 2004, pp. 228–232).

BEHAVIORAL CONSULTATION   For school or mental health counselors interested in a more structured model of consultation, behavioral consultation may be appealing. Bergan and Kratochwill (1990) outline behavioral consultation and therapy as the application of systems theory and principles of learning a problem-solving process. The consultant gathers information from the consultee and then defines the problem in concrete terms, as well as identifying the environmental conditions that maintain it (Brack, Jones, Smith, White, & Brack, 1993). The consultant tries to help the consultee solve the problem by changing either the client's or consultee's behavior or the system in which the client and the consultee exist. Dougherty (2005) outlines the sequence of behavioral consultation as follows:

1. *Problem identification:* After a detailed analysis is performed, the problem is formulated in succinct, behavioral terms.
2. *Problem analysis:* A functional analysis of the problem is studied within its framework; antecedents and consequences are identified as well as task demands (cognitive, time, educational, and others).
3. *Selection of a target behavior:* The focus of the consultation is chosen.

4. *Behavior objectives:* Specific goals of the intervention are generated.
5. *Plan design and implementation:* A behavioral plan is developed and applied.
6. *Evaluation of the behavioral change program:* Measurement of behavioral outcomes in relation to goals established occurs (pp. 272–273).

This model emphasizes operant conditioning—reinforcement, punishment, and shaping of behavior. Other behavioral techniques, such as those described by social learning theory and cognitive behavioral theory, also can be applied in the consultative setting (see Chapters 8 and 9). Most models of behavioral consultation rely on a problem-solving process that describes the client's problem in behavioral terms, looks at the antecedents and consequences, selects a target behavior to change, generates behavioral objects, implements a behavioral plan for change, and evaluates outcomes (Dougherty, 2005). MacLeod, Jones, Somers, and Havey (2001) have investigated the effectiveness of school-based behavioral consultation. Their findings support the importance of consultant skills and the quality of consultation in generating successful outcomes.

Brown, Pryzwansky, and Schulte (2001) have developed general interview guidelines for behavioral noncrisis and crisis consulting. The consultant in a noncrisis situation (developmental interview) focuses on the following tasks:

1. Establishing clear general objectives
2. Reaching agreement with the consultee in the relationship between general objectives and more specific ones
3. Generating clearly defined, prioritized performance objectives with the consultee
4. Deciding how accomplishment of performance objectives will be assessed and recorded
5. Deciding on follow-up meetings

In a crisis or problem-centered interview, the outline focuses on the following tasks:

1. Identifying and describing problematic behavior(s) by collecting data from several sources concerning the nature of the problem
2. Determining the conditions under which these behaviors occur, their antecedents, and their consequences; the consultant and consultee analyze either the setting or interpersonal factors that contribute to the problem or the client's skill deficits
3. Deciding on assessment procedures; the consultant and consultee design a plan to deal with the problem by identifying objectives, selecting behavioral interventions, considering barriers to overcome, and evaluating progress
4. Scheduling future meetings (Brown, et al. 2001, pp. 52–53)

MacLeod, et al. (2001) conclude that intervention planning was positively correlated to student outcome. Teachers reported that a step-by-step plan, adhering to the treatment plan, and the comparison of baseline and treatment data related to student behavioral change.

Keys, et al. (1998) state that school counselors who consult with parents and teachers typically use the models of client- or consultee-centered mental health consultation (Caplan & Caplan, 1993) or behavioral consultation (Bergan & Kratochwill, 1990). Counselors may choose the process consultation model (Schein, 1988, 1999), the program-centered administrative process, or the consultee-centered administrative process to work for systemic change.

CROSS-CULTURAL CONSULTATION   Sheridan (2000) has identified considerations of multiculturalism to the behavioral consultation process. She recommends particular attention to the awareness and sensitivity of the consultant, that is, the ability to consider various perspectives and procedures to include those qualities into the process. She also discusses factors that may enhance the multicultural consultative relationship, such as trust, acknowledgment of diversity, avoiding technical jargon, and considering the effect of interpreters. Although specific to behavioral consultation, her suggestions are also applicable to other models.

Ingraham (2000) offers a summary of her ideas of multicultural consultation. She emphasizes methods for supporting consultee and client success that a consultant should consider using. Consultants should value multiple perspectives and create emotional safety and support. That support should be balanced between new learning and interventions based on principles of mastery. Systems that support learning and development should be part of a consultant's strategy. Those strategies would include cross-cultural learning, bridging methods matched to the consultee's style, building confidence and self-efficacy, and working to increase knowledge, skill, and objectivity. For the consultant's development, Ingraham (2000) suggests continuing to learn, engaging in professional development, seeking feedback, and finding cultural teachers.

Ramirez, et al. (1998) have reviewed cross-cultural issues in school-based consultation. They discuss ways that culture may affect consultation and how consultants may adapt during each stage of the process to be more responsive to cultural differences.

Brown, Pryzwansky, and Schulte (2006) caution that cross-cultural consultation has many complexities. They emphasize that the cultural beliefs of the consultee should influence verbal and nonverbal communication, the consultation model, the hierarchy in the relationship, and the nature of the intervention. They recommend asking the following questions or making these statements before making decisions about the consulting process:

- *To help determine the hierarchy*: I'm used to people calling me by my first name, but some people prefer something more formal. What do you prefer?
- *To assess who should be involved*: Based on the situation, what people other than you and me should be included in the consulting process?
- *To determine what leads to use*: Some people are uneasy talking about their emotions. We can focus only on behavior. Which is your preference?
- *Allowing the right not to participate*: Any time our discussion makes you uncomfortable, just tell me that you would rather not answer (p. 168).

CONSULTING PROCESS

Kurpius, Fuqua, and Rozecki (1993) contended that consultation takes place in the following six stages, whether the process is a short-term individual consultation or a long-term organizational consultation. Dougherty (2005) suggests four stages. Following is a summary of the sequence, tasks, and goals of the consulting process and the steps suggested by those authors.

The first step is *pre-entry*. Consultants look at themselves to see whether they are right for the task and what services they can provide. Consultants may consider these questions: As a consultant, how do you view humans? Are you more attracted to some than others? How do you listen and respond to leaders at the top of the organization as compared with workers at the bottom? What do you think and feel when consultees disagree with you and confront you or your ideas? What about your espoused theories versus your theories-in-use (Kurpius, et al. 1993, p. 601)? Dougherty (2005) states that effective consultants must posses a personal and professional growth orientation, knowledge of consultation, and human behavior and consultation skills. How do you rate yourself on those requirements?

Lippitt and Lippitt (1986) suggest four questions that help consultants focus on their competence: (1) What can I do given this situation? (2) What is the right thing to do in this situation? (3) Do I have the ability to do the right things? and (4) What is the right thing to do that is in the best interests of the consultee and the organization?

The second step is *entry, problem exploration, and contracting*. During the initial contact, the consultant needs to learn about the presenting problem, the people involved, what interventions have been tried, and the expectations of the person or organization seeking consultative services. At this point, the consultant must decide whether he or she can be helpful and establish a contract. Kurpius, et al. (1993) recommended for any work other than individual consultation a written contract describing the purposes, objectives, ground rules, expectations, resources needed, and time lines for consultation; individual consultation, such as between a counselor and a classroom teacher or another helping professional, should have a brief written agreement, even if it is only a memorandum of understanding. Dougherty (2005) summarizes these steps of the entry stage as exploring the needs of the organization, contracting, then physically and psychologically entering the system.

The third step is *information gathering, problem confirmation, and goal setting*. Kurpius, et al. (1993) encourage consultants to spend enough time gathering valid and reliable data, both qualitative and quantitative, to ensure delivery of high-quality services. Accurate data are important for defining the problem and attributing ownership—all essential steps to establishing the problem as a goal to be reached. Without agreement about the ownership of the problem (the teacher, parent, child, other child or adult), interventions the consultant suggests are not effective because no one takes responsibility for implementing the plan. According to Dougherty (2005), the diagnosis stage includes gathering information, defining the problem, setting goals, and generating possible interventions.

Wagner (2000) has identified four processes that consultants use in their conversations to promote change. One thing the consultant does is help externalize the problem so that the person sees the difficulty in a different way. The consultant also allows the consultee to gain a larger, more detached view of the problem. According to Wagner, that process allows a paradigm shift, where there is recognition of the complex patterns between the focus and features of the situation, as well as the possibilities of change. Finally, Wagner remarks that the process of consultation encourages consultees to engage in self-reflection, recognizing their own roles and avoiding the dynamics of blame.

In the fourth step, *solution searching and intervention selection,* consultants must avoid seeing all problems in the light of their favorite paradigm or counseling theory. Pointing out that human service organizations tend to see human factors as causing most problems and that industry and business most often see their problems as coming from structural causes, Kurpius, et al. (1993) suggest that consultants carefully consider both the human and structural factors (the school or other systems in the child's life) as possible causes of the problem and areas for intervention. Therefore, this implementation stage includes choosing an intervention, developing and implementing the plan, and then evaluating the success of the intervention (Dougherty, 2005).

Kahn (2000) proposes a model of Solution-Focused Consultation that shifts the consultation emphasis to solutions and strengths. The model rests on the assumptions of a future orientation and the helper being seen as a facilitator or coach, among other roles. Little time is spent exploring the problem before a goal is set. The goal is stated in positive language. The helper and the helpee explore exceptions to the problem, choose the best solutions, and create a plan to implement these solutions. The helper also encourages trying something different to change the problem. Kahn encourages school counselors to consider her propositions.

The fifth step is *evaluation.* As with any counseling task, evaluation ensures professional effectiveness. Kurpius, et al. (1993) suggest asking certain questions to evaluate the outcomes of consulting services. For example, have the consulting goals been achieved and to what degree? How well have interventions worked? Were there unexpected outcomes, and have they been addressed effectively? Evaluation should give the consultant information about how each step in the process worked. Outcomes may include the changes in the client or in the system in which the client exists. Dougherty (2005) concludes that three ways to evaluate a plan's outcome are individual goal-attainment measures (see Chapter 2 for examples), standardized outcome assessment devices, and consumer satisfaction surveys. Sladeczek, Elliott, Kratochwill, Robertson-Mjaanes, and Stoiber (2001) use goal-attainment scaling not only to evaluate but also to facilitate a behavioral consultation case. Hughes, Hasbrouck, Serdahl, Heidgerken, and McHaney (2001) have tested an instrument, the Consultant Evaluation Rating Form (CERF), that also could be used.

During the sixth step, *termination,* when the consultant and consultee agree that the process should be terminated, the consultant should review with the consultee each step in the process, describing what was successful or not successful. If the work was successful, this review process provides an opportunity for clarification, recognition of successes, and reflection on how the process brought about improvements. If the consultation process was not successful, the session helps all members understand the reasons for the failure. Brown, et al. (2006) provide several instruments that can be used to assess all aspects of the consultation process.

COMBINATIONS

Myrick (2003) has explained a model of consultation that may also serve as framework for the processes of collaborating and teamwork. His systematic facilitative approach for practice involves the following steps:

1. Identify the problem clearly after careful discussion and listening.
2. Continue to clarify the situation by determining:

   a. The emotional and value components
   b. The specific behaviors involved
   c. The expectations of the people involved
   d. What has been done previously
   e. The strengths of the people, systems, or both
   f. The resources available

3. Determine the desired goal or outcome in specific (preferably behavioral) terms.
4. Gather any needed information for further clarity.
5. Develop a plan of action and determine the responsibilities for implementing it.
6. Evaluate and revise as needed and discuss the next steps.

Persi (1997) proposes a set of questions to encourage discussion in a consulting relationship. His questions mirror Myrick's consultation model. These questions are:

1. How have these problems affected you?
2. What has worked well for you with these problems?
3. What has not worked?
4. What type of support do you need?
5. Is there anything I can do for you?
6. Have we left anything out?
7. May I come back for a follow-up visit? (p. 347)

The tasks of consultation that Kurpius, et al. (1993) describe are, in summary, assessing one's own competency, collecting data, defining the problem, setting a goal, selecting interventions, evaluating results, and terminating the relationship—all activities with which counselors are familiar. To ensure high-quality consultative services, however, counselors inexperienced in consulting should work with a colleague or seek supervision as they begin their consultative work, and all counselor-consultants should periodically evaluate the effectiveness of their professional services.

CONSULTATION INTERVENTIONS

Consulting can help counselors reach more children by teaching adults (parents, teachers, and other significant people in the children's lives) to behave in more helpful ways. Providing indirect services to children through consultation can be an important part of the counselor's role; unfortunately, few counselors use their skills in this area. Next are techniques counselors may wish to try in their consultative efforts with the adults in the child's world. Not every technique works with every child. Each child's uniqueness and specific needs must be considered before one selects any counseling or consulting procedure.

ROLE SHIFT   Simply changing one's own behavior may elicit a behavioral change in another person. Adults who change their responses to children's behaviors may cease to reinforce them or present children with an unexpected response that causes change.

Counselors might want to ask adults to list *everything* they have tried with the child that has been effective and ineffective. The counselor then asks them to commit themselves to dropping those ineffective techniques with this child. The list should be kept as a reminder of what not to do with the child, as well as what responses work.

When the child has behaved inappropriately, adults can stop and ask themselves, "What response does this child expect?" Does the child expect the adult to be shocked, outraged, or angry? For instance, Glen reacted to his mother's scolding by drawing grotesque pictures of her and placing them around the house. He took great delight in watching her reactions when she found the pictures.

Glen's mother decided that Glen enjoyed her outrage. The next time she found a picture, she calmly commented to him, "I must have really made you angry when I scolded you for you to draw me like this." She left the picture up and went on with her work. Glen quietly removed his pictures later that day. This technique appears to work best when the child expects to get attention, elicit shock (as with curse words or dirty language), cause frustration or anger, or get revenge.

LISTING OF BEHAVIORS   A technique similar to the descriptive discussion is listing behaviors. For instance, Mr. Jones told the counselor that Sherry was a crybaby who cried at *everything* that did not go her way. The counselor asked Mr. Jones to keep an exact count of the times that Sherry cried during the next week. The next week Mr. Jones admitted that, according to his count, Sherry had cried only three times that week—once when she fell, once when she was told to go to bed, and once when she was refused a request. Mr. Jones began to change his perception of Sherry as a crybaby.

Listing the number of times a behavior occurs also can provide a baseline count to determine whether an intervention has reduced an inappropriate behavior or increased an appropriate one.

LOGICAL CONSEQUENCES   Proponents of Adler's individual psychology advocate allowing children to experience the natural or logical consequences of their behavior, rather than punishment, as the preferred form of discipline (see Chapter 11). They suggest that adults who punish children become authority figures and lose the friendship of the child. They also point out that natural or logical consequences are reality oriented and teach the child the rules of society, whereas punishment may teach unwanted lessons such as "power is authority." Obviously, adults cannot allow children to experience the consequences of all their behaviors; for example, children cannot learn that busy streets are dangerous by playing in them. However, a thoughtful adult can find ways for children to see the consequences of inappropriate behavior. When Peter colors on the walls instead of on paper, for instance, he is responsible for using the sponge and cleanser to remove the coloring. The natural consequence of being late is to miss an event or a meal. The logical consequence of damaging someone's property is to earn enough money to replace it. The logical consequence of behaving inappropriately in a group is usually rejection by the group or isolation. Discipline with logical consequences quickly teaches children the order and rules of society.

ISOLATION TECHNIQUES   At times, children's behaviors become so unacceptable that they must be removed from the group (the classroom, family, or peer group). For many years, parents sent children to their rooms when they acted out. Our society isolates adults who behave inappropriately by ostracism and, in extreme cases, by imprisonment. Isolation techniques are a form of logical consequences (see Chapter 11).

Children with minor problems of maintaining attention can go to a seat away from the group, in a quiet place but not out of sight. Children who are not attending to the task of the group may be quietly reminded that their present seat is for working on science, participating in a group discussion, and the like. If they choose to continue their nonattentive behavior, they must go to their quiet corner and can return when they want to participate in the group's task.

The second step of isolation is the quiet corner. Some children are highly distractible and highly distracting to their peers. They must be completely screened from the group to accomplish their work. A quiet corner can be made with screens, study carrels, bookshelves (books facing outward), or large, decorated furniture cartons. The quiet corner should contain a desk, a chair, books, puzzles, or other quiet materials and no windows or doors. When a child misbehaves, the adult quietly signals the child that his or her behavior is not appropriate and asks the child to go to the quiet corner. Children choose to return to the group when they are ready to participate demonstrating a more acceptable behavior. The adult may have to impose a short time limit of 10 to 15 minutes before allowing children this choice.

Counselors can suggest a time-out room for more severe problems when children need to be completely away from the group. Time-out should be used not as a punishment, but rather as a cooling-off time. The adult can instruct the child to make a plan while in the time-out room for avoiding trouble in the future.

When children's problem behaviors are so severe that the first three isolation procedures have not worked, the adult can quietly ask the child to leave the premises (school, church, club, recreational center) and come back tomorrow to try again. Children should be aware of what behaviors are acceptable and unacceptable and of the conditions for remaining in the group. Because this procedure often requires the assistance of parents, school personnel, or other community workers, a written agreement must be established among all parties. Many schools use in-house suspension to provide a place where children who cannot remain in the group can go for supervised study. Other community resources that provide youth services may cooperate in arranging for supervision.

Followers and students of Adlerian psychology have suggested that parents who find themselves as referees in children's conflicts with others take a time-out in the bathroom. Their contention was that children try to involve adults in their conflicts to get attention, that children learn to settle their differences (and learn the consequences) more effectively without relying on adults, and that only danger of physical harm or property damage requires adult intervention. Dinkmeyer and Carlson (2001) provide specific consultation procedures to help adults implement these and other Adlerian interventions with children.

Isolation techniques teach children the logical consequences of their behavior. Acceptable and unacceptable behaviors should be clearly defined for children. When using the procedures, adults should not nag, lecture, or scold. Isolation techniques should be viewed as a positive method of discipline rather than as punishment.

COLLABORATION

Friend and Cook (2000) define collaboration as "a style for direct interaction between at least two coequal parties voluntarily engaged in shared decision making as they work toward a common goal" (p. 6). They note this definition conveys how the process occurs—as a partnership. These authors identify defining characteristics of collaboration to clarify their definition. First, they emphasize that collaboration is voluntary. Collaboration requires parity among participants. That is, each participant has a voice equal to any other participant, and all contributions are valued equitably. The parties involved in collaboration base their work on mutual goals and they share responsibility for the process and the outcomes. They also share their resources and decision making. O'Loony (1996) defines collaboration as an informal process that involves sharing goals, values, ideas, and joint activity.

Harrison (2004) explains that the goals of collaboration are centered on the relationship and the treatment. The primary goal focuses on developing a working relationship with all the members of the collaboration. The second goal refers to the treatment, arriving at the best possible solution for the client. Collaborations need to be effective decision-making processes.

Porter, Epp, and Bryant (2000) state that collaboration among school professionals is a necessity. Collaboration is a process of connecting schools, families, and communities (Taylor & Adelman, 2000). Niebuhr, Niebuhr, and Cleveland (1999) present a rationale for collaboration between principals and counselors, and Shoffner and Williamson (2000) discuss a preservice seminar devoted to that type of collaboration. Geroski, Rodgers, and Breen (1997) list examples of ways school counselors may work on a collaborative service delivery team. School counselors may be alert for the typical problem behaviors of young people, provide interventions and support services, and provide referrals to other services as appropriate. Becicka (2000) discusses collaborating with teachers to promote the social and emotional competence of students. Sink (2000) urges school counselors to model collaboration for both the school and the larger community.

Keys, et al. (1998) believe that a collaborative consultation model can result in a "more comprehensive and integrated program" to address the complex problems of youth and families (p. 123). They point to the increasing number of youths and families facing serious problems such as poverty, family instability, substance abuse, physical and sexual abuse, violence, and other societal issues, and conclude that new ways of helping require service integration through collaboration. According to these authors, "Collaborative consultation is a model that actively involves parents, educators, youths, and counselors as equal participants and experts in problem solving a specific issue . . . it is the sharing and transferring of knowledge and information between and among all team members that enables the group to determine and carry out a more comprehensive plan" (p. 127). Their five stages of problem solving for collaborative consultation involve the following:

1. Coming together—establishing a commitment among all participants to collaborate on a certain issue
2. Defining a shared vision—sharing knowledge and information; building trust; and defining vision, goals, and objectives
3. Developing a strategic plan to accomplish goals and objectives
4. Taking action on the plan
5. Evaluating progress by determining if specific objectives are accomplished

The authors called for school and community mental health counselors to redefine their roles and to see themselves as a part of the broader community.

Some authors (Taylor & Adelman, 2000; Porter, et al. 2000) suggest that collaborative efforts may involve nurturing relationships to increase resources, to enhance effectiveness, to decrease fragmentation, and to be cost-efficient. Their ideas of "school-community" collaboration include agencies; organizations that provide services and programs, such as health and human services, juvenile justice, and economic development; institutions that share facilities such as schools, parks, and libraries; and other entities such as young people, families, religious groups, civic groups, and businesses. Porter, et al. (2000) argue that collaboration among school mental health professionals must occur and provide examples of collaborative programs that have been implemented successfully.

Bemak (2000) calls for counselors to collaborate with school personnel, communities, and families. Within the school, collaborators work with school administrators to collect and share data on school performance, to develop programs to overcome barriers, to design strategies for school problems, and to emphasize a healthy school climate. Collaborators work with teachers to improve classroom performance, to understand cultural learning styles, and to develop group skills and conflict resolution strategies. Otwell and Mullis (1997) outline a staff development model to accomplish those goals. Bemak (2000) further suggests that, with community agencies, collaborators can help with coordination of services and with outreach. Working with families would revolve around linking schools and homes and building cooperative relationships.

Lusky and Hayes (2001) describe collaborative consultation for program evaluation. The collaborator used action research to implement a needs-assessment process. They presented the method for developing instruments to be used for determining the effectiveness of programs. Their case example provides details to recreate the process.

Dougherty (2005) suggests guidelines to help in determining whether consultation or collaboration should be chosen. First, one should determine how the two services are viewed by the consumer. Next, consultants should reflect on their personal reactions to the two services and their comfort with the assumptions of each. Dougherty suggests that collaboration may be the method to choose if the parameters of consultation cannot be met. The consultant's skill level and the consultee's (or collaborator's) skill level also influence the decision. Fundamental to the choice are the nature of the problem, the context in which it occurs, and the skills of everyone involved.

Harrison (2004) lists prerequisites for collaborative efforts. First, the participants need to understand the language of each discipline that is involved. All team members should be trusted and respected. The shared responsibilities should be acknowledged. Cultural differences should be recognized and understood. Collaborators should create models, goals, and strategies that promote children and families. Open communication must be maintained. Finally, collaborators must accept that each professional will have different outcome orientations.

Some activities have been proposed by Dettmer, Dyck, and Thurston (1999) to advance collaborative discussions and to build interactive formats. Three activities are as follows:

Jigsaw. The group decides on an issue and several subtopics. The large group divides into smaller groups. Each small group researches one of the subtopics and shares what is learned by teaching it to the others.

Compare-and-Contrast. A small group identifies terms and phrases that represent different perspectives on an issue. The group's work is combined with all the work in the larger group to result in a broad list of ways of thinking about an issue.

Circle response. A small group sits in a circle. A leader begins by introducing or by repeating a topic. Moving clockwise, each person takes a turn responding to the issue or by saying "I pass." At the end of the time the ideas are summarized and integrated into the larger group.

TEAMING

Collaboration also can take place in specialized groups called teams that have a specialized work purpose. Teams have shared goals and are interdependent. Basham, Appleton, and Lambarth (1998) have identified the characteristics of effective teams. They note that team members are committed to building and maintaining constructive relationships among themselves. Effective teams have goals and identified roles. Each person on the team is aware of the focus of the team, the responsibilities of the members, and the plan for accomplishing the task of the team. Gladding (2003) suggests that effective teams emphasize continuous improvement on interpersonal, process, and product levels. Teams in schools include grade-level teams, school-based special needs teams, and referral teams (Brigman, Mullis, Webb, & White, 2005). Counselors who are interested in developing team expertise in educational settings may find the monograph by Basham, Appleton, and Dykeman (2004) a roadmap for team building.

ASSESSMENT AS A CONSULTING AND COUNSELING INTERVENTION

In their attempts to understand children's developmental and other critical problems, counselors often use a variety of tools such as self-report surveys, interviews, tests, case histories, and behavioral observations. Sattler (1998) has created a comprehensive volume that outlines procedures, forms, and issues related to interviewing children and families. Counselors also need to be familiar with standardized tests, understand their results, and use them effectively in counseling and in consulting with other professionals. Some of the more commonly used assessment tools are discussed in the following section.

THE INTERVIEW   Counselors usually are comfortable with interviewing their child clients and can obtain much information through this procedure. Counselors are adept not only in listening to what is being said but also in noting how it is said and the accompanying behaviors. Typically, the interviewer seeks to learn something about the child (name, age, family information) and the presenting problem. While interviewing the child, the counselor has an opportunity to observe whether the child can make good eye contact, is outgoing or shy, attentive or distracted, overactive or lethargic, talkative or reluctant to speak, confused or thinking clearly, anxious or depressed. Some counselors prefer structured interviews; others allow clients to reveal themselves at their own pace. Some counselors will use self-report surveys that ask children open-ended questions (my best friend . . .; I like it when my mother . . .). Counselors can learn much through observation of appearance, behaviors, affect, and verbal and nonverbal communications of children.

One interview, the Mental Status Examination (MSE), may be used to provide an inventory of the person's behavior. Hohenshil and Getz (2001) outline the following types of observations to be included:

General appearance, behavior, and attitude: Counselors note whether the child's appearance and dress are appropriate to the situation. Observations may also include posture, odd mannerisms, activity level, and facial expression. Whether the client is cooperative, sullen, assertive, impulsive, dependent, evasive, or friendly may also be noted.

Speech characteristics and thought process: Hohenshil and Getz (2001) note that speech indicates thought processes. Characteristics of verbal activity such as the pattern of speech, the amount of detail, the goal of speech, fragmented ideas, loosely connected phrases, and silences are included.

Emotional status and reactions: What the person says and how he or she behaves provide evidence of emotional status. The counselor observes facial expressions, whether he or she is flushed and whether the affect is appropriate to the situation.

Content of thought: This involves a determination of whether the client's thought patterns are within normal limits. Delusional thinking, rigidly held false beliefs, and obsessions are examples of thoughts beyond the normal range.

Orientation and awareness: The counselor ascertains whether the client is oriented to time, place, and person. This is a critical element of a mental status examination and may be chosen to begin the interview. The counselor may ask the client the setting, his or her name, and the day, month, and year. This may need to be modified to the cognitive ability of the child.

Memory: The counselor may ask the person to talk about the previous day, a birthday, or some past life experience.

General intellectual functioning: A child may be asked to demonstrate an academic skill relevant to his or her grade level to assess general knowledge. Judgment and reasoning might include something like "What would you do if you saw a fire?" or "How are a cat and dog alike?"

Insight: The counselor tries to determine how much the client understands about the current problem situation.

MSE summary: The counselor summarizes the observations and may include recommendations for further assessment (Hohenshil and Getz, 2001, pp. 272–273).

CASE HISTORIES   A case history gives professionals complete biographical information about the child client. Interviewing the child and his or her parents and other family members and reviewing school records and the records of other professionals working with the child (doctors, speech therapists, special teachers, and others) provide data for the case history.

BEHAVIORAL OBSERVATIONS   In certain cases, the counselor will need to observe children in their work and play situations to understand more about their functioning and their relationships with others. Personal observation can tell the counselor whether a child's behavior is appropriate, any circumstances that stimulated certain responses, and how others around the child respond. Counselors may use published checklists or develop their own methods for recording behavioral observations.

FORMAL PSYCHOLOGICAL AND EDUCATIONAL TESTS

Children referred for learning and behavioral problems often take a battery of tests to help professionals understand more about their level of functioning. Psychologists working with the child usually decide the tests to be included in the battery.

INTELLIGENCE TESTS   Intelligence is a difficult concept to define, but most agree that it is related to a person's general mental ability. Tests for children usually include some measure of knowledge, concept formation, and reasoning. Many tests tap both verbal and nonverbal abilities. Some of the more popular tests for measuring children's intelligence are the Stanford-Binet Intelligence Scale, 4th edition; the Wechsler Intelligence Scale for Children–Revised (WISC-III); the Wechsler Preschool and Primary Scale of Intelligence (WPPSI-R); the Otis-Lennon School Ability Test; and the California Test of Mental Maturity. The Stanford-Binet and Wechsler scales must be administered individually by a trained professional; the Otis-Lennon and California tests can be administered in the classroom to groups in grades 1 through 12. The tests yield a numerical intelligence quotient, the IQ score, with 100 being the mean or average and a 15- to 16-point standard deviation to indicate how far above or below the mean the child scores.

For special groups of children, counselors may wish to consider alternative assessments such as Multiple Assessment for Multiple Intelligences designed by David Lazear. A quick estimate of intelligence can be obtained with the Peabody Picture Vocabulary Test–Revised (PPVT-R). Children respond by pointing to the picture that best describes the word read by the administrator. The test taps only one area of the child's ability, and therefore is not considered to be a measure of general intelligence. A newer test of intelligence and achievement is the Kaufman Assessment Battery for Children (K-ABC). The developers of the K-ABC define *intelligence* in terms of a child's information-processing skills and problem-solving abilities. The test has been a helpful diagnostic tool for both normal and exceptional children. Individuals using either the PPVT-R or the K-ABC need training and supervision in the administration and interpretation of these instruments. Children often are labeled or classified by intelligence test results, and extreme care is needed to avoid harming any child through the misuse of assessment measures. Hohenshil and Getz (2001) caution counselors in interpreting results for ethnic and cultural groups.

PROJECTIVE TECHNIQUES   Professionals sometimes ask children to respond to an unstructured stimulus, a picture, or a story to learn more about their thoughts and feelings. One projective technique, the Children's Apperception Test (CAT), uses animals as stimuli for children aged 3 to 10. An alternative form, the CAT-H, uses human figures. The administrator asks the children what they see when they are shown each card.

Trained professionals can use Machover's Draw-A-Person and the Kinetic Family Drawing tests to learn more about the child's psychological functioning. They ask children to draw a person or their family on a blank sheet of paper, and these pictures reveal how children feel about themselves and the relationships among their family members.

Counselors do not ordinarily administer, score, and interpret projective instruments; however, counselors may need to be familiar with the tests to consult effectively with other professionals about their clients and their families.

ACHIEVEMENT TESTS   Achievement tests are educational assessments that measure the accomplishment of learning. These tests focus on the level of knowledge, skill, or accomplishment in a particular area—what the person currently knows or can do (Hohenshil & Getz, 2001). A battery of achievement tests covers more than one academic area (reading, mathematics, language, and others). Some of the more popular group tests used in kindergarten through grade 12 include the California Achievement Test, Metropolitan Achievement Test, SRA Achievement Test, Comprehensive Test of Basic Skills, Iowa Tests of Basic Skills, Wide Range Achievement Test, and Stanford Achievement Test Series (Aiken, 1997). The Peabody Individual Achievement Test (PIAT) is administered individually. The results of achievement tests can be used for placement of children or to determine educational areas of strengths and weaknesses.

APTITUDE TESTS   Amplitude tests are similar to achievement tests but are given to predict learning or behavior, for example, school or reading readiness. The Metropolitan Readiness Test (MRT) measures children's school readiness in reading and mathematics. The System of Multi-Cultural Assessment (SOMPA) was designed to be a measurement of aptitude that would be culturally fair; however, the test has been controversial, and many critics have attacked its validity.

OTHER TESTS   Counselors may want to administer other tests, surveys, or scales to learn more about a child's interests, values, study habits, social acceptance by peers, or the age appropriateness of their behaviors. Follow-up diagnostic testing in mathematics or reading may be helpful after the results of an initial intelligence or achievement test have been obtained. Special tests are available for children with exceptional conditions—the learning disabled, the hearing or visually challenged, the mentally challenged, and others. The *Murphy-Meisgeier Type Indicator for Children*® and the *Myers-Briggs*[1] *Type Indicator*®, both self-report instruments, may help students with self-awareness and self-acceptance. The tests selected depend on the nature of the child's problem and the counseling objectives to be accomplished.

Before selecting any test for administration—and before accepting the results of any test—the user of assessment data should know whether the test is a good measure. At least two concepts give counselors an indication of the "goodness" of a particular instrument: validity and reliability. *Validity* is the extent to which a test measures what it is supposed to measure—intelligence, interests, achievement, or aptitude. A test that measures the child's current level of achievement in grade 2 is not a measure of the child's aptitude or intelligence; the test is valid only for measuring achievement. The *reliability* of a test indicates the consistency with which the test provides accurate measurements. Are the results of an intelligence test similar when the test is administered to the same child 2 days, 2 weeks, or 2 months apart? Correlation coefficients indicate the degree to which tests are valid and reliable. Counselors also need to know the type of population used in the process to determine the "normal" values. A test with normative data for children younger than 5 years is not appropriate for administration to a 6-year-old child. Complete information on validity and reliability, as well as a description of the norm group, can be found in the technical manuals that accompany tests, or the counselor can consult other references such as catalogs, journal reviews, *Tests in Print*, or *The Mental Measurement Yearbook*.

Counselors must be cautious in working in the area of assessment. Most are trained in interviewing, developing case histories, and behavioral observation. However, their training in assessment procedures varies, and counselors should administer and interpret only those tests for which they have received instruction. In addition, counselors can consult books such as Sattler's *Assessment of Children: Revised and Updated* (1998) and other literature on assessment to keep current about new and revised instruments. Professionals can refer to their appropriate professional code of ethics to determine their roles in assessment and appraisal.

SUMMARY

Although problems exist with theoretical foundations and evaluative research on consultation, we should not overlook the technique as a possible means for helping children in need. Helping techniques presented to significant people in children's lives through small groups, psychological education, outreach

---

[1]Myers-Briggs Type Indicator is a trademark or registered trademark of the Myers-Briggs Type Indicator Trust in the United States and other countries.

programs, and preventive education may reach children to whom a lone counselor's direct services would not be available. For our purposes, consultation refers to the one-to-one interaction between the counselor and a significant adult in the child's life or to a counselor-led group of significant adults, with the purpose of finding ways to assist children in functioning more effectively. Counselors will also have opportunities to work collaboratively with other health services and educational professionals, as well as other people who influence a child's life. In addition, the use of teamwork allows counselors to contribute to cooperative efforts on the behalf of young people.

WEBSITES FOR CONSULTATION AND COLLABORATION

Internet addresses frequently change. To find the sites listed here, visit www.thomsonedu. com/counseling/thompson for an updated list of Internet addresses and direct links to relevant sites.

Association for Supervision and Curriculum Development

Georgetown University Center for Child and Human Development

American Educational Research Association

Association for Assessment in Counseling and Education

REFERENCES

Aiken, L. R. (1997). *Psychological testing and assessment.* Boston: Allyn & Bacon.

Basham, A., Appleton, V., Lambarth, C. (1998). The school counselor's role in organizational team building. In C. Dykeman (Ed.), *Maximizing school guidance program effectiveness: A guide for school administrators & program directors* (pp. 51–58). Greensboro, NC: ERIC/CASS Publications.

Basham, A., Appleton, V., & Dykeman, C. (2004). Team building in educational settings. *Counseling and Human Development, 36,* 1–8.

Becicka, C. (2000). Promoting social and emotional competence through teacher/counselor collaboration. *Education, 120,* 668–675.

Bemak, F. (2000). Transforming the role of the counselor to provide leadership in educational reform through collaboration. *Professional School Counseling, 3,* 323–331.

Bergan, J. R., & Kratochwill, T. R. (1990). *Behavioral consultation and therapy.* New York: Plenum.

Brack, G., Jones, E., Smith, R., White, J., & Brack, C. (1993). A primer on consultation theory: Building a flexible worldview. *Journal of Counseling & Development, 70,* 487–498.

Brigman, G., Mullis, R., Webb, L., & White, J. (2005). *School counselor consultation: Developing skills for working effectively with parents, teachers, and other school personnel.* Hoboken, NJ: Wiley & Sons.

Brown, D., Pryzwansky, W. B., & Schulte, A. C. (2001). *Psychological consultation: Introduction to theory and practice* (5th ed.). Boston: Allyn & Bacon.

Brown, D., Pryzwansky, W. B., & Schulte, A. C. (2006). *Psychological consultation: Introduction to theory and practice* (6th ed.). Boston: Allyn & Bacon.

Brown, D., & Trusty, J. (2005). *Designing and leading comprehensive school counseling programs: Promoting student competence and meeting student needs.* Belmont, CA: Brooks/Cole.

Caplan, G., & Caplan, R. B. (1993). *Mental health consultation and collaboration.* San Francisco: Jossey-Bass.

Dettmer, P. A., Dyck, N. T., & Thurston, L. P. (1999). *Consultation, collaboration and teamwork for students with special needs* (3rd ed.). Boston: Allyn & Bacon.

Dinkmeyer, D., Jr., & Carlson, J. (2001). *Consultation: Creating school-based interventions* (2nd ed.). Philadelphia: Brunner-Routledge.

Dougherty, A. M. (2005). *Psychological consultation and collaboration in school and community settings* (4th ed.). Pacific Grove, CA: Brooks/Cole.

Friend, M., & Cook, L. (2000). *Interactions: Collaboration skills for school professionals* (3rd ed.). New York: Longman.

Geroski, A. M., Rodgers, K. A., & Breen, D. T. (1997). Using the DSM-IV to enhance collaboration among school counselors, clinical counselors, and primary care physicians. *Journal of Counseling and Development, 75,* 231–239.

Gladding, S. T. (2003). *Group work: A counseling specialty* (4th ed.). Upper Saddle River, NJ: Merrill.

Glosoff, H., & Koprowicz, C. (1990). *Children achieving potential: An introduction to elementary school counseling and state-level policies.* Washington, DC: National Conference of State Legislatures and American Association for Counseling and Development.

Harrison, T. C. (2004). *Consultation for contemporary helping professionals.* Boston: Pearson.

Hohenshil, T. H., & Getz, H. (2001). Assessment, diagnosis, and treatment planning in counseling. In D. C. Locke, J. E. Myers, & E. I. Herr (Eds.), *The handbook of counseling* (pp. 269–285). Thousand Oaks, CA: Sage.

Hughes, J. N., Hasbrouck, J. E., Serdahl, E., Heidgerken, A., & McHaney, L. (2001). Responsive systems consultation: A preliminary evaluation of implementation and outcomes. *Journal of Educational and Psychological consultation, 12,* 179–201.

Ingraham, C. L. (2000). Consultation through a multicultural lens: Multicultural and cross-cultural consultation in schools. *School Psychology Review, 29,* 320–343.

Kahn, B. B. (2000). A model of solution-focused consultation for school counselors. *Professional School Counseling, 3,* 248–255.

Keys, S. G., Bemak, F., Carpenter, A., & King-Sears, M. (1998). Collaborative consultant: A new role for counselors serving at-risk youths. *Journal of Counseling and Development, 76,* 123–133.

Keys, S. G., Bemak, F., & Lockhart, E. J. (1998). Transforming school counseling to serve the mental health needs of at-risk youth. *Journal of Counseling and Development, 76,* 381–388.

Keys, S. G., Green, A., Lockhart, E., & Luongo, P. F. (2003). Consultation and collaboration. In B. T. Erford (Ed.), *Transforming the school counseling profession* (pp. 171–190). Upper Saddle River, NJ: Merrill.

Kurpius, D., & Fuqua, D. (1993). Fundamental issues in defining consultation. *Journal of Counseling and Development, 70,* 598–600.

Kurpius, D., Fuqua, D., & Rozecki, T. (1993). The consulting process: A multidimensional approach. *Journal of Counseling and Development, 7,* 601–606.

Lippitt, G., & Lippitt, R. (1986). *The consulting process in action* (2nd ed.). La Jolla, CA: University Associates.

Lusky, M. B., & Hayes, R. L. (2001). Collaborative consultation and program evaluation. *Journal of Counseling and Development, 79,* 26–38.

MacLeod, I. R., Jones, K. M., Somers, C. L., & Havey, J. M. (2001). An evaluation of the effectiveness of school-based behavioral consultation. *Journal of Educational and Psychological Consultation, 12*, 203–216.

Myrick, R. D. (2003). *Developmental guidance and counseling: A practical approach* (4th ed.). Minneapolis, MN: Educational Media Corporation.

Niebuhr, K. E., Niebuhr, R. E., & Cleveland, W. T. (1999). Principal and counselor collaboration. *Education, 119*, 674–679.

O'Loony, J. (1996). *Redesigning the work of human services.* Westport, CT: Quorum.

Otwell, P. S., & Mullis, F. (1997). Counselor-led staff development: An efficient approach to teacher consultation. *Professional School Counseling, 1*, 25–30.

Persi, J. (1997). When emotionally troubled teachers refer emotionally troubled students. *The School Counselor, 44*, 344–352.

Porter, G., Epp, L., & Bryant, S. (2000). Collaboration among school mental health professionals: A necessity, not a luxury. *Professional School Counseling, 3*, 315–322.

Ramirez, S. A., Lepage, K. M., Kratochwill, T. R., & Duffy, J. L. (1998). Multicultural issues in school-based consultation: Conceptual and research considerations. *Journal of School Psychology, 36*, 479–509.

Sattler, J. M. (1998). *Clinical and forensic interviewing of children and families: Guidelines for the mental health, education, pediatric and child maltreatment fields.* San Diego, CA: Jerome M. Sattler Publisher.

Schein, E. (1988). *Process consultation: Vol. 1. Its role in organization development* (2nd ed.). Reading, MA: Addison-Wesley.

Schein, E. (1999). *Process consultation revisited: Building the helping relationship.* Menlo Part, CA: Addison-Wesley.

Sheridan, S. M. (2000). Considerations of multiculturalism and diversity in behavior consultation with parents and teachers. *School Psychology Review, 29*, 344–353.

Shoffner, M. F., & Williamson, R. D. (2000). Engaging preservice school counselors and principals in dialogue and collaboration. *Counselor Education and Supervision, 40*, 128–140.

Sink, C. A. (2000). Modeling collaboration through caring communities of learners. *Professional School Counseling, 3*, ii–iii.

Sladeczek, I. E., Elliott, S. N., Kratochwill, T. R., Robertson-Mjaanes, S., & Stoiber, K. C. (2001). Application of goal attainment scaling to a conjoint behavioral consultation case. *Journal of Educational and Psychological Consultation, 12*, 45–58.

Taylor, L., & Adelman, H. S. (2000). Connecting schools, families, and communities. *Professional School Counseling, 3*, 298–307.

Wagner, P. (2000). Consultation: Developing a comprehensive approach to service delivery. *Educational Psychology in Practice, 16*, 9–18.

17 CHAPTER | GROUP COUNSELING WITH CHILDREN

Many counselors find that working with groups is more natural than individual counseling. Children and adults function as members of groups in their daily activities—in the classroom, the work setting, or with a group of colleagues. Our beliefs about ourselves and about other people evolve from the feedback of significant people in groups who are important to us—especially our family, friends, and peers. Psychologists such as Alfred Adler emphasized that people are social and their development is influenced significantly by the groups around them; therefore, group counseling contains a reality orientation, what Corey and Corey (2006) considered a "natural laboratory." For children who have difficulties forming or maintaining relationships, being included in group counseling would give them opportunities to improve those relationship skills. In groups, young people can improve their awareness of their own and other people's values and priorities. They can develop an appreciation for different views. More importantly, groups provide a place where children can unlearn inappropriate behaviors and learn new ways of relating through interaction and feedback in a safe practice situation with their peers. Goodnough and Lee (2004) agree and state that children learn best when they learn from each other.

Bergin (2004) explains that the interactive process of groups influences children in several ways. As group members express caring, acceptance, and support for each other, participants learn to trust and share. In addition, the group's reality and emphasis on conscious thought allow participants to explore their thoughts, feelings, and actions as well and to express those genuinely. Finally, Bergin explains that as group members show understanding to each other, they grow in tolerance and an accepting attitude. He encourages the participation of all group members in helping each other make education choices about their personal behaviors.

Many authors support the effectiveness of group counseling (Burlingame, et al. 2004a; Markus & King, 2003; Piper & Ogrodniczuk,

2004; Robinson & Jones, 1996). The process and outcome variables that contribute to that effectiveness have been reviewed (Burlingame, et al. 2004b; DeLucia-Waack, 1997; Shechtman, 2002), as well as the components of effective group leadership (DeLucia-Waack, & Bridbord, 2004; Riva, et al. 2004). Hoag and Burlingame (1997) conducted a meta-analysis of group treatment for children and adolescents. They have found that group treatments produced significantly better effects than wait-list or placebo control group. Clearly, these positive outcomes suggest that counselors will want to include groups in their practice.

Counselors who are prepared to conduct groups will have completed coursework and supervised practicum to help them develop skills in this area. This chapter presents an overview of working with children in groups, with suggestions for those who already possess the knowledge and skills to conduct groups or for those who intend to pursue further training.

DEFINITION OF GROUP

Gladding (2003) defines a group as "a collection of two or more individuals who meet in face-to-face interaction, interdependently, with the awareness that each belongs to the group and for the purpose of achieving mutually agreed-on goals" (p. 497). His definition captures the concepts Johnson and Johnson (2000) identified related to several definitions of groups: goals, interdependence, interpersonal interactions, participants' perception of membership, structured relationships, mutual influence, and motivation. These characteristics allow members in groups to deal with their own concerns, as well as to help other participants develop.

Dye (2002) has identified assumptions basic to group work. One assumption maintains that social behavior is learned; therefore, new experiences can produce new understandings. Another foundation is that people have reasons for their actions. Bringing about a change of behavior is the goal of counseling, a learning experience. The elements of group counseling consist of expressed goals, membership criteria, roles of members and leader(s), counseling methods and techniques, and interactions among the participants.

TYPES OF GROUPS

Groups function in many ways depending on the goal. The main goal of group work consists of creating opportunities for children to increase the knowledge and skills to help them make and accomplish their choices (Bergin, 2004). Explanations of some common types of groups allow a counselor to determine which might be most appropriate to the situation and population with which they are working. Even though these descriptions may appear to indicate clear distinctions across types of groups, considering the types along a continuum would be more accurate. Jacobs and Schimmel (2005) remind us that group leaders must be clear about the type and purpose of the group.

Psychoeducational groups emphasize using educational methods to obtain information and develop meaning and skills (Brown, 1997, p.1). In these groups, children often learn to strengthen their coping skills, as well as their self-esteem (Conyne, 1996). This growth occurs through their new knowledge. The groups may focus on such topics as attitudes, beliefs, working together, communicating, and building friendship skills. Bergin (2004) suggests that psychoeducational groups could be planned to help children investigate their identity concerns, developmental transitions, academic matters, and career planning. According to Boutwell and Myrick (1992), the social interaction in the group helps the members gain a sense of well-being that can lead to preventing future problems. When young people encounter others in the group who are facing similar concerns, they have opportunities to master more than the targeted skills, as well as gain an understanding of different types of coping.

Some psychoeducational groups occur as classroom guidance activities in schools. Furr (2000) provides a format for designing a psychoeducational group. This format includes stating the purpose, establishing goals, identifying objectives, determining content, choosing exercises, and conducting evaluation. The design she proposes contains three components: giving information, practicing skills, and talking about the process. Her outline and examples would help counselors plan and deliver these groups. Akos, et al. (2004) provide another useful resource in planning groups. These authors recommend that when planning groups, leaders consider the developmental level of group participants, multicultural issues, school climate, and the overall mission of the program.

Stoiber and Kratochwill (1998) believe that schools are in a strategic position to respond to mental health and health care needs, and that they have special opportunities for both prevention and intervention. These authors suggest that children and families are more likely to take advantage of school-based services because there is less stigma attached. In addition, Stoiber and Kratochwill write that the dramatic changes in the United States' economic, social, and demographic structures have created an urgent need for community-based services to address individual, community, and environmental issues relevant to mental health. They conclude that the schools and community must collaborate to address the complexity and multitude of problems that exist for children and families. Bemak and Keys (2000) agree with these points and provide specific skills for working with violent and aggressive young people.

Counseling groups are also growth oriented. Each person's behavior and development is the focus. The members of counseling groups are generally normal people who are experiencing some stress in their lives. The interaction with other in the groups may revolve around concerns with interpersonal relationship, social skills, study skills, values, problem solving, or making decisions (Dansby, 1996). Arman (2000) suggests that counseling groups help children reduce their sense of social isolation and negative emotions. The groups may also be designed for children who are facing transitions in their lives such as divorce of parents, a death, or school problems. Children with behavioral problems may also benefit from counseling groups. Orton (1997) lists the benefits of the group as trust, caring, understanding, and support. In groups, children can help not only themselves but also others. Counseling groups may be held in schools, institutions, or mental health agencies.

Group therapy deals with unconscious motivations with the goal of personality change for the group members. These groups are held for the remediation and treatment of people who are severely disturbed, are suffering from deep psychological problems, or are exhibiting socially deviant behavior. Those groups most often occur in mental health agencies and institutions.

THEORETICALLY ORIENTED GROUP COUNSELING

The number of group counseling methods almost equals the number of counseling theories, most of which can be adapted to a group counseling setting. *Adlerian counselors* used group work in their child guidance center in the early 1900s for group discussions involving parents (see Chapter 11). Adlerians believe that people are essentially social and need to belong to a community or group; consequently, they see group counseling as a natural environment for helping children see the reality of the situation and meet their needs through social interactions in the group. As in individual counseling, Adlerian group counselors rely on investigation and interpretation of the child's life by establishing the relationship, exploring the dynamics operating in the child's life, communicating back to the child an understanding of self, and reorienting the child's behavior in new directions (Corey, 2000).

Adlerian groups emphasize the interpretation of a person's early history so that group members recognize and understand the ways they have created their own lifestyles. Adlerian groups also include the practice of having individual, interpersonal, and group process goals throughout the duration of the group. Gladding (2003) explains that individual goals involve developing insight, interpersonal goals revolve around becoming socially oriented and involved, and group process goals entail promoting and experiencing a cooperative group environment. Adlerian group leaders focus on understanding the current patterns of behavior of group members and challenging them to modify those patterns. When working with children in groups, the leaders may use encouragement to imply their faith in the child's ability to change. They may also emphasize natural consequences of behavior. Wick, et al. (1997) have used Adlerian adventure therapy with a group of elementary school children. The group was given unfamiliar, noncompetitive, and cooperative tasks to teach social interest and responsibility to the participants.

Reality therapy (see Chapter 4) originally was used in groups more extensively than with individuals. The principles adapt effectively to group work because the group is a microcosm of the real world. The psychological needs of belonging, power, freedom, and fun can all be met by group members in that setting. Also, the members provide feedback about the reality of their behavior and plans for change. They reinforce one another in their commitments and check on the completion of homework assignments. The group leader focuses on helping the group members take responsibility for what they do, find better ways to have their needs met, and change their inappropriate or destructive behaviors (Glasser & Breggin, 2001). Reality therapy has been a popular method for helping groups of children and adolescents in schools, those confined to correctional institutions, substance abusers, and those with handicaps.

The principles of *behavioral counseling* (see Chapter 9) are also used in groups when the clients' goals are similar or members can help one another by providing feedback, support, or reinforcement to alter maladaptive behaviors, learn new behaviors, or prevent problems. Relaxation training, assertion training, modeling techniques, and self-management programs to control overeating or other negative behaviors are examples of behavioral techniques that can be used effectively in group settings. Corey (2000) points out that because behavioral group counseling is a type of education, leaders must assume an active, directive role in the group, applying their knowledge and skills to the resolution of problems. Leaders emphasize current experiences, learning, and defining goals specifically. Leaders choose group procedures that are adapted to member's needs and that are scientifically verified. Gladding (2003) notes the prevalence of the use of positive reinforcement, extinction, desensitization, and modeling in behavioral group counseling.

Rational-emotive-behavioral therapy (REBT) (see Chapter 8) attempts to teach people to think rationally about events and to assume responsibility for their feelings. The techniques of this theory can be applied effectively in groups. Members are encouraged to recognize and confront their irrational thoughts and feelings, take risks, try new behaviors, and use others' feedback to learn new social skills. Members are taught to apply REBT principles to one another. REBT leaders provide information, discuss problem-solving strategies, and may use many cognitive and/or emotive techniques. The group leader should be a role model for responsible and reality-oriented behavior, show care and respect, and teach participants to evaluate their present behaviors, as well as those planned. Sommers-Flanagan, Barrett-Hakanson, Clarke, and Sommers-Flanagan (2000) have discussed a school group designed to improve social and coping skills of middle school students. Based on cognitive-behavioral theory, the groups included interventions to help students understand moods, identify pleasant events, reduce tension and increase strength, and solve problems.

Transactional analysis (TA; see Chapter 10) is an ideal counseling method for groups; in fact, most counselors adhering to the principles of TA prefer treatment in groups. This method focuses on analysis of life scripts, games, and interactions among people, and the ideal setting for this teaching and learning is within a group that simulates life's interactions. Group members facilitate the counseling process by representing other individuals with whom past and present transactions can be analyzed.

Gestalt therapy (see Chapter 7) focuses on the here and now and on maintaining personal awareness. Some Gestalt counselors ask for volunteers and focus on one client at a time within the group; for example, the hot seat technique requires the counselor to work with one person in the presence of the other group members. Structured interaction between other group members may be encouraged at certain times. Gestalt group leaders must be skillful enough to find the appropriate technique to help children gain awareness.

Other counseling methods have their place in group work but do not adapt to it as readily as those already mentioned. The relationship skills set forth by *person-centered* counselors are appropriate in an individual or group setting. The therapeutic relationship is an essential ingredient for all clients to feel free enough to explore their world and make changes.

GROUP LEADERSHIP SKILLS

In groups for children and adolescents, counselors primarily work as facilitators of the group process. Counselors will complete the following tasks: assess the needs for a group, define the purposes of the group, select participants, arrange permission for participants, organize the schedule, plan the activities, and arrange for materials and space to meet. According to the Association for Specialists in Group Work (1991), to create effective groups, leaders must apply the following 16 skills:

1. Encourage the participation of group members.
2. Observe and identify group process events.
3. Pay attention to and acknowledge the behavior of group members.
4. Clarify and summarize statements.
5. Begin and end group sessions.
6. Give information when needed.
7. Model effective behavior.
8. Engage in appropriate self-disclosure.
9. Receive and deliver feedback.
10. Ask open-ended questions.
11. Empathize with members.
12. Confront group members' behavior.
13. Help members recognize the meaning of an experience.
14. Help group members integrate and apply what they learn.
15. Demonstrate ethical and professional standards.
16. Keep the group focused on accomplishing its goals (p. 14).

Corey (2000) contends that the group leadership's personal characteristics and skills cannot be separated from techniques used. He believes that "leaders bring to every group their personal qualities, values, and life experiences. . . the most effective group direction is found in the kind of life the group members see the leader demonstrating and not in the words they hear the leader saying" (p. 53). He suggests the following personal characteristics as essential to a group leader:

- *Presence*—genuine caring in "being there" for clients
- *Personal power*—self-confidence and awareness of one's power
- *Courage*—ability to take risks and be vulnerable
- *Willingness to confront oneself*—being honest and aware of self
- *Sincerity and authenticity*—sincere interest in well-being of others; behaving without pretense
- *Sense of identity*—knowing one's values, strengths, and limitations
- *Belief and enthusiasm for the group process*
- *Inventiveness and creativity*—open to new ideas and experiences

The professional skills needed by group leaders, as identified by Corey (2000), include: active listening, restating, clarifying, summarizing, questioning, interpreting, confronting, reflecting feeling, supporting, empathizing, facilitating communication, initiating direction, setting goals, evaluating, giving feedback, suggesting, protecting, self-disclosure, modeling, linking (looking for themes), blocking (stopping counterproductive behaviors by confronting it), and terminating. (See Chapter 2 for a detailed discussion of these counseling skills.) Gladding (2003) explains that three specific skills are significantly different in group counseling. He states that leaders in groups facilitate by helping group members communicate among themselves. Group leaders protect members by barring unnecessary attacks from others in the group, a skill unnecessary in individual counseling. A related skill, blocking, entails a group leader intervening in a group activity to stop counterproductive behavior. Group leaders also encourage participation, keep the group on task, and move the group in the direction of the stated objectives (Greenberg, 2003).

In summary, Jacobs and Schimmel (2005) have identified the knowledge and skills needed by group counselors. Group leaders need to be clear about the purpose of the group and must know the theory from which they are working. Group leaders should be familiar with the topics being covered and should be creative. Finally, the authors recommend that group leaders understand and accommodate students from diverse cultures.

GETTING STARTED

GROUP FOCUS

Counselors determine the logistics of a group based on the type of group being held. Some groups may include materials that relate to a wide range of individuals. Others may be for focused on specific areas such as divorce or grief. In addition, resources chosen for a group may be predicated on the age of the participants. The counselor could identify a topic by his or her perception of what is needed, from the results of a needs assessment, or by the special needs of the school and/or community (Greenberg, 2003). The topics will vary according to the children's ages and the settings in which the groups are to be held.

Gazda, et al. (2001) recommend that children younger than 12 should take part in groups that include play and action with counselors using techniques such as sociodrama, child drama, and psychodrama. Ginott (1968; as cited in Gladding, 2003) recommends the use of water colors, finger paints, clay, and sand for children younger than 9. Therefore, groups for children and young adolescents may be more action oriented than those for teenagers. Carroll, et al. (1997) suggest that structured exercises may help individuals in adolescent groups form trust and cohesion and become more open in their communication. Theme-oriented groups may also help adolescent groups. Gladding (2003) suggests having young people check off a list of interests and/or problems to determine a theme for a group.

Bergin (2004) notes some elements basic to all groups. Groups must have purposes that are defined and reflected in the goals and objectives prepared before group participants are selected. The goals direct the group process, and the objectives clarify that focus by outlining anticipated outcomes for group members. The objectives also help the counselor determine the activities and discussion procedure to use, as well as how to determine whether the purpose(s) has been attained. He continues by noting that all groups must have requirements for membership. Finally, he states that counselors incorporate structured activities to stimulate group interaction and self-reflection.

Greenberg (2003) classifies groups as remedial, support, or preventive groups. Remedial groups concentrate on the problems faced by most students such as study skills, listening skills, and overcoming test anxiety. Support groups deal with more personal problems and allow children to realize that others face similar challenges. Examples include groups about parental divorce, stopping a habit, or being new to the school. Preventive groups focus on avoiding difficulties. Problem-solving, anger management, and handling stress could be topics of preventive groups. Wilson and Owens (2001) explain that prevention groups have focused on preventing psychological disorders, difficulties in relationships, failure in roles, failure in work groups, and physical distress. Kulic, et al. (2001) outline concepts and methods for counselors who use prevention groups with children and adolescents.

Some examples of Bergin's classifications follow. The developmental groups that Bergin (2004) describes involve helping young people meet their challenges in the process of growing. Examples of these challenges include personal identity, relationships, emotional and behavioral development, academic achievement, and career planning. The groups are oriented to growth and to the development of behaviors and skills to enhance a person's ability to be independent and responsible. Activities in these groups may incorporate videos, books, games, worksheets, simulations, and role plays. The Life Skills Training program incorporates activities related to self-identity, problem solving, decision making, social skills, and physical health (Shechtman, 2004). Bergin (2004) and Corey and Corey (2006) suggest the following topics for children:

- Listening and other communication skills
- Recognizing and dealing with emotions

- Social skills and friendship
- Academic achievement
- Self-concept
- Career awareness
- Problem solving and/or decision making
- Loss and grief
- Feeling isolated, lonely, or incompetent
- Homelessness

They suggest the following topics for adolescents:

- Communication
- Assertiveness training
- Managing stress
- Social skills and making friends
- Personal identity
- Career exploration and planning
- Problem solving and/or decision making
- Depression and anxiety
- Substance abuse
- Truancy

According to Bergin (2004), problem-centered groups are more open ended, with topics determined by the concern of the group participants at the time of the meeting. These groups focus on the here-and-now experience. Members have the opportunity to engage every other member in exploring their problems, examining potential alternatives and the consequences of those possibilities, and deciding on a course of action. These groups may be more appropriate for older children who have the ability to state their concerns and to attend to others. Some topics that may concern elementary students include relationships with family and friends, conflicts with authority figures, relationships with peer groups, and moving into middle school. Adolescents may be troubled by relationships, dating, sexual matters, teachers, homework and school, balancing commitments, and planning for the future. Two successful group formats that may be used in problem-solving groups are Shure's (1992) *I Can Problem Solve* and Goldstein and McGinnis's (1997) Skillstreaming Curriculum. Both focus on improving the social competence of children and adolescents.

Topic-specific groups focus on the needs of young people who have a situational difficulty that is causing negative feelings and stress (Bergin, 2004). The group members share some serious, immediate concerns. The group setting allows members to understand the issue in depth, to explore feelings, and to find coping strategies. This type group may arise from a crisis event such as a death. In that case, the group purpose is to provide support in dealing with the crisis. The following concerns may be addressed by topic-specific groups: physical abuse, grief and loss, sexual abuse, aggressive behavior, divorce and separation, fear and stress, children of alcoholics, suicide, and teen parenting. The Children of Divorce Intervention Program (Pedro-Carroll & Cowen, 1985) is an example of a multimodal group developed to support children in sharing their divorce-related feelings and in building their competence.

The topic of groups will determine the criteria for selecting members to participate. Some general guidelines for that process are included in this section.

SELECTING GROUP MEMBERS

Shechtman (2004) states the most relevant variables in forming groups are age, sex, problem, and size of group. Some counselors, such as Adlerians, hold that anyone who wishes to participate in a group should be allowed to do so, given similar, age-related levels of interest and intellectual abilities. Other counselors attempt to select members for either heterogeneity or homogeneity. Some counselors prefer a balance of boys and girls in the same group unless the presence of the opposite sex would hinder discussion (on some sex education topics, for example). Other counselors prefer to eliminate tension by holding same-sex groups.

Homogeneity may be desirable for common-problems groups, such as children whose parents are divorced. However, a homogeneous group of underachievers or drug users probably would be counterproductive because no peer model and peer reinforcement for improved behaviors would be present. Riva and Haub (2004) also caution that a group format may increase the likelihood of early adolescents learning deviant behaviors unless more socially adept young people are also included in the groups. Parents and adult caregivers should also be part of that type of treatment. For children who act out or withdraw, a heterogeneous group provides active discussion and role models.

The counselor should seriously consider the possible consequences of including children with highly dissimilar interests or maturity levels and extremely dominating, manipulative, gifted, or mentally retarded children. Children with extreme behaviors may be better candidates for individual counseling, especially during the initial stages of therapy. Riva and Haub (2004) suggest that extremely shy or anxious young people may find the group format too stressful.

FORMING A GROUP

Counselors may begin by recruiting members for groups. Ritchie and Huss (2000) suggest that counselors avoid labeling groups with names that imply a diagnosis or dysfunction. Children may be identified by offering adults behavioral checklists, having children volunteer, or from responses to needs assessments. Corey and Corey (2006) remind counselors that some children are not ready to be members of groups. Counselors need to establish clear criteria for all group participants.

Some reports of people being verbally attacked and hurt in groups that use extreme methods may leave parents or children with reservations about participating in a group. Counselors should explain fully the purpose of the group and the experiences planned to allay fears and clarify possible misconceptions. By providing this information to children before starting the group, the counselor can inform the children of their roles and what is expected of them and explain the role and expectations of the counselor as well. Explaining the process provides the structure needed to facilitate interaction once the group is begun. Following is an example of an informative statement:

> We are forming a group made up of young people about your age to talk about things that bother or upset us. Many of us have similar concerns, and it is often helpful to share these worries and help each other try to find ways of solving them. Each member will be expected to talk about what bothers him or her and try to figure out what can be done about these situations. In addition, members will be expected to listen carefully to each other and to try to understand the other members' worries and help them solve their problems. The counselor, too, tries to understand what all the members are saying or feeling, to help them explain and clarify their thoughts and feelings and to find solutions to their concerns.
>
> Most group members learn they can trust the others in the group and feel free to discuss things that worry them. Members are free to talk about anything or anyone that bothers or upsets them. However, the group will not be a gripe session, a gossip session, or a chatting session. We will be working together to find solutions to what is upsetting you. There may be very personal information or feelings that you would prefer not to discuss in the group. You should not feel pressured to disclose these feelings or thoughts to the group. Whatever is said in the group cannot be discussed with anyone except the counselor. If there is anyone you would rather not have in a group with you, discuss this with the counselor.

SCREENING INTERVIEW

Many group leaders prefer to hold an individual conference or intake interview with prospective members before forming the group. Other group leaders think that anyone should be eligible to join a group and that the intake interview is unnecessary. An intake interview allows the leader an opportunity to talk privately with prospective members, to learn a little about them and their concerns, and to define some possible goals. The leader also has an opportunity to determine whether the child will benefit from a group experience or whether individual counseling would be more helpful. The group leader would begin by identifying the characteristics of the group members that would be beneficial to the process, as well as criteria that would signify the person should be excluded (Ritchie and Huss, 2000). Children who are overly aggressive and who are overly sensitive to criticism would probably not benefit from group counseling. Overly angry, hyperactive, self-centered, unstable children should also be helped with other types of interventions (Ritchie & Huss, 2000; Shaffer, et al. 1998; Shechtman, 2004).

During the screening interview the counselor can check the young person's willingness to engage in self-improvement, the desire to help others, the commitment to group progress, and compatibility with other group members (Bergin, 2004). Greenberg (2003) states other criteria for group members. The child should have the language skills to communicate with other group members and should be willing to participate in group interactions. The young people should be prepared to share their individual feelings and experiences. They should accept and abide by group rules and be committed to the group members. Greenberg suggests that counselors ask potential group participants about each of these areas.

Holcomb-McCoy (2003) emphasizes the importance of counselors being attuned to cultural beliefs and how culture affects the child's concerns. She suggests asking potential group members to discuss their perceptions of counseling and their expectations of the group. Group activities and structure could be modified accordingly. Ritchie and Huss (2000) list the following as possible screening questions:

How does this concern affect you at school, at home, at play?

Do you spend time worrying about this concern?

Would you like to talk with someone about this issue?

Do you feel comfortable talking about your feelings in a group? (p. 150)

Size of Group

The number of children in the group depends on age, maturity, and attention span. Children ages 5 and 6 years have very short attention spans and are unable to give much attention to others' concerns. Counselors may want to limit group size at this age to three or four and to work with the children for only short time periods at frequent intervals—for example, 20 minutes twice a week. Counselors can work with a larger number of older, more mature children for longer periods—for example, six children, ages 10 and 11, for 30 minutes twice a week. The maximum number of children in a group that functions effectively seems to be eight.

Group Setting

A room away from noise and traffic is the best setting. In addition, children should not fear being overheard if they are expected to talk openly about their concerns. Groups should be conducted with all members sitting in a circle so that everyone can see everyone else's face. Some counselors prefer to have the children sit around a circular table; others think tables are a barrier to interaction. Many counselors prefer to have groups of children sit in a circle on a carpeted floor, which provides easy access for counselors to move the group into play therapy.

GROUP STAGES

The interactions in groups change as participants continue to meet. Several authors have explained these different group stages and most include a movement through stages of beginning, transition, working, and leaving.

Gladding (2003) and Corey (2000) have identified four stages of group counseling. The initial stage—orientation and exploration—is one of getting acquainted, determining the structure of the group, and exploring the members' expectations. Group leaders focus on creating a safe environment for the participants. Members are somewhat tentative and reserved at this point; therefore, the leader should focus on making sure they feel included and on developing trust. The leader and the group establish ground rules and group procedure. In almost all groups, the leader should clarify the purpose of the group and the responsibilities of the group members. The leader should emphasize the need for confidentiality and other crucial guidelines. Some common procedures for groups with children include having only one person speak at a time, listening to the speaker, taking turns, and not making fun of each other. During the beginning of the group, the goal is for members to build rapport and to learn to participate in the group. In summary, the early stage of group process involves getting acquainted, warming up to other members, learning about expectations, and building trust. Jacobs and Schimmel (2005) recommend that group leaders pay attention to the ways group members relate to each other, as well as their connection with the purpose and content of the group in this and all other stages of the group.

The transition phase of the group involves members testing each other. They experiment with the new relationships and with the process of the group to determine who and how much to trust. Corey (2000) characterizes this phase as one of dealing with resistance, in which feelings of anxiety may increase and the group leader may be challenged. The members will test the leader to determine whether the counselor can be trusted and decide whether to get involved. The leader structures the group, clarifies the purpose, and models trust.

As the members begin to accept each other, they move to the working stage. This is the stage of cohesion and productivity. During this stage the members focus on identifying their goals and concerns, and they are willing to work both in the group and outside to address these concerns. As they focus on the issues on which they are working, they explore and clarify the concerns, set goals, and practice new behaviors.

The last stage of group work includes the members evaluating what has been accomplished and then exiting the group experience. The final stage—consolidation and termination—is extremely important, according to Corey (2000), because consolidation of learning takes place and members must be able to transfer what they have learned to other situations outside the group. There may be some anxiety and reluctance to terminate; therefore, the leader must deal with these feelings and any other unfinished business, and then prepare members to use their new skills in their daily lives. The leader should make arrangements for some follow-up and evaluation of the group process to determine the effectiveness of the group and its effects on the member. A final group session, an individual session, or a questionnaire may be used for this purpose.

Jones and Robinson (2000) have created a model for choosing topics and exercises appropriate for the different group stages. Their framework involves generating activities appropriate for the group theme, and then matching the activities to the goals and stages of the group. They discuss intensity, creating a climate of work, and building relationships through all the phases of group work.

GROUP COUNSELING PROCESS

THE FIRST SESSION

Early sessions should include introductions, discussion of the group purpose, and explanations about confidentiality. The members learn how the group functions, define their goals and expectations, and find their place in the group. Part of the first group counseling session will be devoted to establishing ground rules and agreeing on some guidelines for the group. The group or the leader determines the frequency of the meetings, the length of each meeting, the setting, and the duration of the group. Members also need to discuss confidentiality and what might be done if confidentiality is broken by a member, what to do about members who do not attend regularly, and whether to allow new members should a member drop out.

Confidentiality is an important concept to discuss with children. They often do not understand the necessity for "keeping what is discussed in our group" and not talking to others about what happens. The leader can provide specific instances of other children asking about their group and have participants role-play their responses.

The group leader also has to remind members to listen carefully to each other, to try to understand each other's feelings and thoughts, and to help one another explore possible solutions to problems. The children can be encouraged to wait until members appear to have explored and discussed their concerns thoroughly before changing the subject. The group leader can provide the role model for listening and reflecting feelings and content, and then reinforce these behaviors in group members.

By establishing ground rules and structuring the group during the initial session, the group leader defines expected behaviors. When inappropriate behaviors occur, the leader can ask the group, "What was the ground rule?" or present the problem to the group for discussion and resolution.

Group members may be reluctant to begin by bringing up concerns or worries for discussion, especially if the participants are not acquainted. The leader can reflect their feeling of reluctance and, if appropriate, try an icebreaker counseling technique; for example, the leader might ask members to introduce themselves and describe themselves with three adjectives, or members might be asked to introduce themselves and complete a statement such as "If I had three wishes, I would wish _____." Another icebreaker is to complete the statement "I am a _____, but I would like to be a _____," using animals, vegetables, automobiles, flowers, or other nonhuman categories; for instance, "I am a dandelion, but I'd like to be a long-stemmed rose." These activities can be done in the entire group or in dyads; either method eases the tension of the first session and promotes interaction.

Building cohesiveness and trust is important for counselors. Children have had little experience listening to one another and trying to help one another solve problems. Unless these behaviors are taught, the group experience can become little more than unstructured play and chatter.

Guidelines for the Remaining Sessions

Before the second group session, the counselor reviews thoroughly the content of the first meeting (names, behaviors, concerns, other personal information) and develops a plan for guiding the second meeting. At this point, the counselor should have tentative goals in mind for each member, based on the initial interview, and should be aware of who in the group will facilitate the group process—a good listener, encourager, or problem solver—and who will distract—dominating, too talkative, silly, or confrontational. The counselor may want to develop plans for dealing with distracting behaviors, should they occur.

Corey and Corey (2006) advise counselors that providing structure is particularly important in groups with children. One way to accomplish that is to use a standard format. Gilbert (2003) recommends that group leaders begin each meeting with a routine that may include welcomes, reviews of rules and previous sessions, focus on current topic, an exercise related to the topic, discussion about the exercise, and a closing activity in which participants talk about what they have learned or experienced.

The second session opens with a brief summary of the initial meeting. If homework was assigned, the results should be shared. The group is then ready to address a member's concerns, either one that was identified earlier or a situation that occurred between meetings that may be concerning a member. If no one volunteers to discuss a problem or concern, those identified in the pregroup interviews can be suggested by the counselor: "When we talked in our interview before the first meeting of the group, some of you shared with me that you were worried because you are going to high school next year. Who would like to start by telling the group about what frightens you about that change?"

Just as in individual counseling, a group leader establishes a therapeutic counseling atmosphere by demonstrating the facilitative skills of empathetic understanding, genuineness, and respect for group members. Counselors can demonstrate their caring by being nonjudgmental and accepting and by providing encouragement, support, and guidance. Counselors need to be adept at identifying, labeling, clarifying, and reflecting group members' feelings and thoughts. This process becomes difficult as the group size increases. The counselor-facilitator must be concerned about and aware of the reactions of each child in the group. As the leader models facilitative behaviors, group members begin to participate in the helping process and become more effective helpers for one another.

The group counseling process closely follows the format for individual counseling:

1. Establishing a therapeutic relationship
2. Defining the problems of the member or members
3. Exploring what has been tried and whether it has hurt or helped
4. Deciding what could be done and looking at the alternatives
5. Making a plan—goal setting
6. Trying new behaviors by implementing the plan
7. Assigning homework
8. Reporting and evaluating the results

Also, as in individual counseling, the counselor-facilitator is responsible for helping children identify and define their problems and the accompanying feelings and thoughts. The process of defining what is happening in the child's life and looking at alternatives for solving the conflict is enhanced in the group setting because of the other group members. Ideally, the child has several counselors to listen, understand, and help search for solutions, whereas enjoying the acceptance, encouragement, support, and feedback of a number of helpers. The counselor must be skilled in facilitating these interactions and suggesting appropriate interventions. The counselor must also possess information about group dynamics and counseling skills to intervene and facilitate progress through the various steps of the counseling process.

IMPLICATIONS FOR DIFFERENT AGES

The role of group counselors varies with different aged children. For instance, elementary school counselors work with children who are in their formative years. Group counseling can help these children acquire social skills and shape a positive attitude toward school. Littrell and Peterson (2002) discuss a case study of establishing group work in an elementary school. Gilbert (2003) suggests topics that should be routinely offered to this age group. These topics include children dealing with divorcing parents, children with attention-deficit/hyperactivity disorder, friendship, loss, academic achievement, and single-parent homes. She provides outlines for these groups. Kizner and Kizner (1999) have outlined a group counseling process for adopted children to help them with their questions and concerns. Groups for elementary students have been used to help children build skills in empathy (Akos, 2000), reduce aggression (Shechtman, 2001), deal with divorcing parents (DeLucia-Waack, 2001), and live with a cancer patient (Stanko & Taub, 2002).

Drucker (2003) reminds counselors that young people during their preadolescent years are unsettled in many areas. Group counseling could support them. She lists some fundamental group topics for these children as getting along with family, dealing with peer pressure, anger management, and others. Rainey, et al. (1997) provide a procedure for delivering a support group for elementary and middle school students. Their writing contains session outlines and materials. Portman and Portman (2002) present a group intervention to develop social justice awareness, knowledge, and advocacy skills in middle school students. Their eight-session group format ends with the students completing a social justice project. Shechtman, et al. (2002) outline group counseling processes to build friendships in adolescents. Wilson (2003) suggests those topics for high school students, as well as making choices, stress, and aggression. Ripley and Goodnough (2001) outline the steps for planning and implementing groups in high schools. The escalating problem of eating disorders was addressed in school group counseling interventions (Daigneault, 2000; Van Lone, et al. 2002) that resulted in improved attitudes and expanded understandings of the participants. Zinck and Littrell (2000) have had similar success with at-risk adolescent girls and incarcerated juvenile offenders in improving their behavior (Claypoole, et al. 2000).

Brantley, et al. (1996) have paired counselor interns with children in impoverished public school districts in Michigan. Each group consisted of five to six students and two interns. Each group had no more than three acting out children, two model children, and one child who behaved "normally." The sample was divided into structured groups, unstructured groups, and a control group. The experimental groups met weekly for 45 to 50 minutes for approximately 8 weeks. Teachers were asked to complete a behavior checklist after each group. Analysis on those students classified as acting out showed that they learned positive behavior skills, positive interactions with adults, and conflict resolution skills. Those in the structured group received slightly more positive ratings. Both counseling interns and students found the project to be profitable, as well as enjoyable.

Reeder, et al. (1997) have used small-group counseling techniques to improve racial relationships among second-grade students. The students were chosen because they tended to be overly sensitive to race issues, had difficulty getting along with peers of a different race, and did not appear to have the skills necessary to interact with peers of another race. The groups consisted of five boys—two African American, two white, and one Hispanic student. The group met for 1 hour for 8 weeks. The teachers and counselors noted a change in racial attitudes and behavior after the group sessions, and positive results were obtained on a racial relations survey administered as a pretest and post-test.

Garrett and Crutchfield (1997) believe that the "Unity Model" is effective as a comprehensive approach to helping children to develop the dimensions of self-esteem, self-determination, body awareness, and self-concept. The Unity Model is based on an idea from the Native American culture, which emphasizes that the whole is greater than the sum of its parts. In other words, individuals are not separate in their dimensions of mind, body, heart, and other parts, and we need to find balance among all parts of our world. The Medicine Wheel represents this inter-relationship: east represents self-esteem or how the child feels about self and his or her ability to grow; south represents self-determination or one's ability to explore and develop potentials; west represents body awareness or how one experiences one's physical presence; and

north represents the self-concept or what one thinks about self and one's potential. The "talking circle" models this inter-relationship and is a reminder that it
is all right to express one's thoughts and feelings in an atmosphere of acceptance. The "talking stick" represents truth and understanding. Group members
may speak only when they have the stick. The authors describe a seven-session
plan addressing the four inter-related areas, which has worked effectively for
them in group counseling with children.

EVALUATION OF GROUPS

The effectiveness of group work can be measured in many ways. Questions
that can guide these decisions and their purpose are discussed in the following
paragraphs.

What did we set out to accomplish? As stated earlier, the purpose of the
group determines the type of group being led. During the planning process the
goal of the group is identified, as well as the means for determining whether the
goal was met. For example, in a friendship group, the goal may be for each
member to initiate a conversation with a stranger. For an educational group,
an assessment of the change in the participants' knowledge about the subject
would be an evaluation possibility.

How did the participants respond? Feedback from the group members
helps the leader monitor the progress and adapt the procedures as needed.
Participants can respond to open-ended questions, rating scales, and summary
statements to sum up their reflections and reactions.

What behaviors changed outside the group setting? The group leader may
involve other adults in assessing changes in children who participated in
groups. Teachers and parents may be asked to complete behavioral observations before, during, and after the group. They may be given a rating sheet
about the behaviors that have been targeted. The group leader can interview
the adults and ask for observations about the child's behavior.

How effective was the leader? One way to assess the group leader's effectiveness is to consider the answers to the previous three questions. Observations by colleagues, self-reflections, and input from the group members on
rating scales or other instruments can also provide useful data. Bruckner and
Thompson (1987) provide a model for evaluating weekly group counseling
sessions with children in elementary school that could be adapted for use
with group counseling programs in any setting. They developed an instrument containing the following six incomplete statements and two forced-
choice items:

1. I think coming to the group room is _____.
2. Some things I have enjoyed talking about in the group room are _____.
3. Some things I would like to talk about that we have not talked about
   are _____.
4. I think the counselor is _____.
5. The counselor could be better if _____.

6. Some things I have learned from coming to the group room are _____.
7. If I had a choice, I (would) (would not) come to the group room with my class.
8. Have you ever talked with your parents about things that were discussed in the group? (yes) (no)

Some of these items may be used as a needs survey for future group sessions. The results of the survey are checked by someone other than the group leader. Two independent people rate student responses on a five-point scale, ranging from 5 for statements showing an outright positive, accepting attitude toward the item to a rating of 1 for statements showing an outright rejecting, negative attitude toward the item. A rating of 3 is awarded to neutral, ambivalent, or evasive responses. Limited positive and negative responses receive ratings of 4 and 2, respectively. Raters should reach 85 percent levels of agreement and generally experience little difficulty in obtaining agreement on the remaining 15 percent.

GROUP COUNSELING EXAMPLE

The process and techniques used in individual counseling (such as role-playing, role rehearsal, play therapy, homework assignments, and contracting) are just as appropriate for group counseling. In fact, individual counseling often is conducted in groups, as the following example shows. Karen, Susan, Peggy, Mark, Ken, and Mike are 11-year-old children in their fourth session in a counseling group. Following is an excerpt from this session:

COUNSELOR: Last time we met, Susan told us about the misunderstanding she was having with her neighbor, Mrs. Jackson. As I remember, Susan, you were going to offer to use your allowance to replace the storm window you broke playing baseball or offer to babysit free of charge for her until the bill was paid. Can you bring us up to date on what's happened?

SUSAN: Well, she decided she would rather have me babysit for her to pay for the window. I babysat one hour last week. We are keeping a list of the times I sit and how much will go toward the cost of the window.

COUNSELOR: It sounds as though you and Mrs. Jackson have worked things out to the satisfaction of both of you.

SUSAN: Yeah, she really liked the idea of my babysitting to pay for the window.

COUNSELOR: Good. Is there anyone else who has something they would like to discuss today?

ALL SIX CHILDREN: Mr. Havens!

COUNSELOR: You all sound pretty angry at Mr. Havens. Could one of you tell me what's happened?

KEN: We were all going on a trip to the ice-skating rink next week. Yesterday, somebody broke some equipment that belonged to Mr. Havens. No one would tell who did it, so he is punishing us all by not letting us go ice-skating.

COUNSELOR: You think Mr. Havens is being unfair to punish everyone because of something one person did. You'd like to find out who broke the equipment.

KAREN:	That's right. We didn't break his equipment, so why should we have to miss the trip?
COUNSELOR:	Have you thought of anything you could do to work this out?
MIKE:	Yeah, break the rest of his old equipment!
COUNSELOR:	How would that help you get to go skating?
MARK:	It wouldn't. It would just make him madder.
PEGGY:	[timidly] We could tell him who did it.
OTHER FIVE CHILDREN:	You know who did it? Who?
PEGGY:	[very upset] If I tell, I'll be called a tattler, and no one will like me. Besides, I don't want to get anyone in trouble.
COUNSELOR:	Peggy, it sounds as though you are really feeling torn apart by this. You just don't know what to do. If you don't tell, the whole group will miss the skating outing. If you do tell, you'll get someone in trouble, and your friends might think you're a tattler and not want you around.
PEGGY:	Yeah, I don't know what to do!
COUNSELOR:	What do you think you could do?
PEGGY:	Well, I could tell who did it.
COUNSELOR:	What would happen if you told? [Silence.] Let's help Peggy think of all the things that could happen if she told who broke Mr. Havens' equipment. [The group thinks of all the possible positive and negative results of Peggy telling who broke the equipment: the group might still get to go skating, the person might beat up Peggy or try to get back at her in some other way, she might not be believed, the person could deny it and say Peggy broke the equipment, and so on.]
COUNSELOR:	We've listed all the things that could happen if Peggy told. What will happen if Peggy does *not* reveal who broke the equipment?
KAREN:	We won't get to go skating, and the person will get away with it! [Other possibilities— such as Mr. Havens's distrust of the whole group or the person thinking he or she "can get away with anything"—are discussed.]
COUNSELOR:	Can anyone think of any alternatives to solve this other than Peggy telling or not telling Mr. Havens?
KEN:	She could write him an anonymous letter telling him who did it.
COUNSELOR:	What would happen if she did?
MIKE:	He probably wouldn't believe an anonymous letter.
COUNSELOR:	What do the rest of you think about that? [They all agree by nodding their heads that Mike is probably right.]
COUNSELOR:	Is there anything else you could do to straighten this out?

SUSAN: Peggy could tell you [the counselor], and you could tell Mr. Havens.

COUNSELOR: How would my telling Mr. Havens help you all solve your problem?

MARK: Mr. Havens would believe you, and we'd get to go skating!

COUNSELOR: I would have to tell Mr. Havens how I knew and give him some details to assure him that I was right. I really think this is the group's problem. What can you do to work it out?

KAREN: Seems like it's up to Peggy, then.

COUNSELOR: You all think it's up to Peggy to decide whether to tell. [The group agrees it is Peggy's decision.]

COUNSELOR: Peggy, we have looked at the consequences of your telling on the other person and not telling, and we've tried to think of other alternatives. Have you made any decision about what to do?

PEGGY: No, I still don't know.

COUNSELOR: So far, it seems that we have come up with two possible alternatives—to tell on the person or not to tell. I wonder if you can think of any other alternatives that might help Peggy. [Silence.] Well, our time is about up for today, but this topic is really important. Let's meet together tomorrow and try to help Peggy come to some decision at that time. Peggy, I wonder if you would go over the list of alternatives and think about them before tomorrow. [Peggy agrees.] How would the rest of you feel about trying to put yourselves in Peggy's place and think of what you would do if you knew who broke Mr. Havens's equipment? Also, you might think about how you would feel if you were the person who broke the equipment. What would you want Peggy to do? [The group agrees and adjourns.]

The counselor checked on the results of the last homework assignment for the group, listened, and reflected the group members' angry feelings that Mr. Havens was being unfair. The counselor then helped them clarify and define the problem, look at possible alternatives, and consider the consequences of these alternatives. No decision has been reached, but the group has agreed to a homework assignment of thinking further about the problem. Possibly, the next session will bring new ideas and a resolution.

CLASSROOM MEETINGS

School counselors may want to show teachers ways to use group meetings in their class. Glasser (1969) discusses three types of meetings. Educational-diagnostic classroom meetings are used to determine how much students know about a topic before a new unit is begun or at the conclusion of a unit of study. Social-problem-solving meetings are designed to help the classroom group solve their concerns. Teachers help students consider how their behaviors are helpful, not helpful, or perhaps harmful to themselves and/or to others. Classroom members in the problem-solving meetings follow the reality therapy questions to determine action to resolve the difficulty. Open-ended classroom meetings allow students opportunities to introduce and discuss thought-provoking questions related to their lives. Teachers can use the following guidelines to lead those meetings.

GUIDELINES FOR LEADING CLASSROOM MEETINGS

1. Identify the topic clearly:
    a. The topic for today is _____.
    b. Would someone restate what we will discuss today?
    c. Today we can discuss _____ or _____. Which will it be?
2. Ask for definitions:
    a. What do you mean by _____?
    b. What is _____?
3. Ask for specifics:
    a. What else do you need to know about _____?
    b. Tell me more about _____?
4. Ask for personal examples:
    a. Who do you know who has _____?
    b. Have you ever _____?
    c. How does _____ relate to your life?
5. Ask for agreements and disagreements:
    a. Who agrees with you?
    b. Who disagrees with you?
    c. Why?
6. Challenge the group:
    a. How can you find out more about that?
    b. What would you like to learn more about that idea?
7. Present hypothetical situations involving the topic:
    a. What would happen if we did not have _____?
8. Withhold personal judgment of right and wrong in students' answers and opinions. Help them arrive at their own evaluation of their thinking and behaving.
9. Refrain from asking any embarrassing questions or questions the person asking would be unwilling to answer. Each person always has the right to pass on responding to any question.
10. Uphold the right to state an opinion without being ridiculed.
11. Use the reality therapy problem-solving model to reach a resolution to a specific concern.

GROUP CRISIS INTERVENTION

Two classmates are killed in a fiery car wreck.

A 12-year-old puts a gun to his head and commits suicide.

The mother of a 9-year-old dies of cancer.

The father of a 7-year-old is murdered.

War breaks out, and the television shows bombings on 24-hour newscasts.

Economic recession hits, and many parents lose their jobs.

Reports of an earthquake forecast send feelings of fear and panic throughout the population.

A hurricane devastates an entire section of the state.

In recent years, professionals have been asked to provide crisis counseling to children in schools, churches, and clubs. Incidents such as these stimulate fear, helplessness, loss, sadness, and shock. Children worry about the loss of their parents (their security), their friends ("Could it happen to me? Why did it happen?"), and their security ("Where will I go if I lose my home?"). In some cases, their parents may be coping with their own loss or grief and be unable to help the children. In other cases, the situation may be related to the school, church, or an organizational group, and children may feel that their parents do not really understand the situation. Some parents may not realize their children are worried; some children are not able to verbalize their pain.

Those who work with children recognize that young people cannot learn or perform their daily activities with these fears and concerns. They become irritable and restless, moody, or agitated. They have difficulty concentrating and sleeping. They may experience physical symptoms such as nausea or diarrhea. Someone has to help them cope, which is usually effected through group discussion and group counseling.

James and Gilliland (2005) propose six steps for crisis counseling that are similar to the reality therapy model described in previous chapters of this book. These steps include: (1) defining the problem; (2) ensuring the client's physical and psychological safety; (3) providing support through verbal and nonverbal means; (4) examining alternatives; (5) making plans—definite action steps; and (6) obtaining the client's commitment to take positive action. They urge counselors to evaluate the severity of the crisis in the clients' eyes; appraise clients' thinking, feelings, and behaviors; determine the danger and the length of time in a crisis mode; look for contributing factors; and evaluate resources, coping mechanisms, and support systems. James and Gilliland (2005) suggest that counselors may want to begin sessions with a nondirective approach, but shift to more directive counseling as the need arises. Crisis counseling is short term, and counselors should carefully consider some children's need for referrals or other arrangements to ensure that each client successfully copes with the crisis in the days and weeks to follow.

Graham (1990) presents a plan for helping children after a trauma, such as a hurricane or plane crash. Incorporating ideas presented by Graham with those of James and Gilliland (2005), we suggest the following outline for group crisis counseling:

I.   Introductory phase
A.   Ask members to introduce themselves and tell why they are in the group.
B.   Help members clarify their goals regarding what they would like to accomplish in the meeting.
C.   Discuss confidentiality—what group members talk about stays in the group. Get a commitment from all members to maintain confidentiality.
D.   Discuss basic rules:

1. Take a bathroom break first because no one can leave the room after the group begins.
2. Encourage group members to stay the entire time. The group generally runs for 2 hours; the time depends on the ages of the children.
3. Elect or appoint a co-leader or a peer leader to keep the gate (that is, not let people in or out).
4. Remind the group that no group member holds rank over any other group member and that everyone's participation is valued equally.

II. Fact phase
A. Focus on discussing what happened.
B. Encourage everyone to participate.

III. Feeling phase
A. Ask "What happened then?"
B. Ask "What are you experiencing now?"

IV. Clients' symptoms

A. Ask "How is this affecting you?" (Is the member having trouble sleeping or studying, or is the member worrying too much?)
B. Ask "How is this affecting your grades, your studies, your health?"

V. Teaching phase
A. Explore the common responses to this incident.
B. Brainstorm about how people have been responding to the incident.
C. Discuss how each response is helpful or not helpful to people.

VI. Summary phase
A. Raise questions and provide answers.
B. Summarize what has been learned and shared.
C. Develop action plans for individuals and/or the group, if needed.
D. Provide support for group members to ensure their physical, emotional, and psychological safety. An action plan should be made to protect any group member needing protection.
E. Conduct a follow-up meeting in 3 to 5 days to see how well the group members are coping.
F. Arrange individual counseling sessions for group members who need further assistance.

SUMMARY

In conclusion, group counseling can be a highly effective method for changing children's lives or, better still, preventing excess stress and conflict in their lives. Finding their place in a group and helping one another are rewarding accomplishments for children. Watching the children grow and develop into caring, functioning group members is rewarding for the group counselor. Group counseling is an effective, efficient intervention to improve children's worlds.

WEBSITES FOR GROUP COUNSELING WITH CHILDREN

Internet addresses frequently change. To find the sites listed here, visit www.thomsonedu.com/counseling/thompson for an updated list of Internet addresses and direct links to relevant sites.

Association for Specialists in Group Work

National Center for PTSD

REFERENCES

Akos, P. (2000). Building empathic skills in elementary school children through group work. *Journal for Specialists in Group Work, 25,* 214–223.

Akos, P., Goodnough, G. E., & Milsom, A. S. (2004). Preparing school counselors for group work. *Journal for Specialists in Group Work, 29,* 127–136.

Arman, J. F. (2000). In the wake of tragedy at Columbine High School. *Professional School Counseling, 3,* 218–220.

Association for Specialists in Group Work. (1991). *Professional standards for the training of group workers.* Alexandria, VA: Author.

Bemak, F., & Keys, S. (2000). *Violent and aggressive youth: Intervention and prevention strategies for changing times.* Thousand Oaks, CA: Corwin Press.

Bergin, J. J. (2004). Small-group counseling. In A. Vernon (Ed.), *Counseling children and adolescents* (3rd ed., pp. 355–390). Denver, CO: Love Publishing.

Boutwell, D. A., & Myrick, R. D. (1992). The go for it club. *Elementary School Guidance and Counseling, 27,* 65–72.

Brantley, L., Brantley, P., & Baer-Barkley, K. (1996). Transforming acting-out behavior: A group counseling program for inner city elementary school pupils. *Elementary School Guidance and Counseling, 31,* 96–104.

Brown, B. M. (1997, March). Psychoeducational group work. *Counseling and Human Development, 29,* 1–16.

Bruckner, S., & Thompson, C. (1987). Guidance program evaluation: An example. *Elementary School Guidance and Counseling, 21,* 193–196.

Burlingame, G. M., Fuhriman, A. J., & Johnson, J. (2004a). Current status and future directions of group therapy research. In J. L. DeLucia-Waack, D. Gerrity, C. R. Kalodner, & M. T. Riva (Eds.), *Handbook of group counseling and psychotherapy* (pp. 651–660). Thousand Oaks, CA: Sage.

Burlingame, G. M., Fuhriman, A. J., & Johnson, J. (2004b). Process and outcome in group counseling and psychotherapy: A perspective. In J. L. DeLucia-Waack, D. Gerrity, C. R. Kalodner, & M. T. Riva (Eds.), *Handbook of group counseling and psychotherapy* (pp. 49–61). Thousand Oaks, CA: Sage.

Carroll, M., Bates, M., & Johnson, D. (1997). *Group leadership* (3rd ed.). Denver, CO: Love Publishing.

Claypoole, S. D., Moody, E. E., Jr., & Peace, S. D. (2000). Moral dilemma discussions: An effective group intervention for juvenile offenders. *Journal for Specialists in Group Work, 25,* 394–411.

Conyne, R. K. (1996). The Association for Specialists in Group Work Training Standards: Some considerations and suggestions for training. *Journal for Specialists in Group work, 21,* 155–162.

Corey, G. (2000). *Theory and practice of group counseling* (5th ed.). Pacific Grove, CA: Brooks/Cole.

Corey, M. S., & Corey, G. (2006). *Groups: Process and practice* (7th ed.). Pacific Grove, CA: Brooks/Cole.

Daigneault, S. D. (2000). Body talk: A school-based group intervention for working with disordered eating behaviors. *Journal for Specialists in Group Work, 25,* 191–213.

Dansby, V. S. (1996). Group work within the school system: Survey of implementation and leadership role issues. *Journal for Specialists in Group Work, 21,* 232–242.

DeLucia-Waack, J. L. (1997). Measuring the effectiveness of group work: A review and analysis of process and outcome measures. *Journal for Specialists in Group Work, 22,* 277–293.

DeLucia-Waack, J. L. (2001). *Using music in children of divorce groups: A session-by-session manual for counselors.* Alexandria, VA: American Counseling Association.

DeLucia-Waack, J. L., & Bridbord, K. H. (2004). Measures of group process, dynamics, climate, leadership behaviors, and therapeutic factors: A review. In J. L. DeLucia-Waack, D. Gerrity, C. R. Kalodner, & M. T. Riva (Eds.), *Handbook of group counseling and psychotherapy* (pp. 126–135). Thousand Oaks, CA: Sage.

Drucker, C. (2003). Group counseling in the middle and junior high school. In K. R. Greenberg (Ed.), *Group counseling in K-12 schools: A handbook for school counselors* (pp. 81–96). Boston: Allyn & Bacon.

Dye, A. (2002). Designing a counseling group. *Group Work Practice Ideas, 7,* 9–12.

Furr, S. R. (2000). Structuring the group experience: A format for designing psychoeducational groups. *Journal for Specialists in Group Work, 25,* 29–49.

Garrett, M., & Crutchfield, L. (1997). Moving full circle: A unity model of group work with children. *Journal for Specialists in Group Work, 22,* 175–188.

Gazda, G. M., Ginter, E. J., & Horne, A. M. (2001). *Group counseling and group psychotherapy: Theory and applications.* Boston: Allyn & Bacon.

Gilbert, A. (2003). Group counseling in an elementary school. In K. R. Greenberg (Ed.), *Group counseling in K-12 schools: A handbook for school counselors* (pp. 56–80). Boston: Allyn & Bacon.

Ginott, H. (1968). Group therapy with children. *Group work: A counseling specialty* (4th ed.). Upper Saddle River, NJ: Merrill.

Gladding, S. T. (2003). *Group work: A counseling specialty* (4th ed.). Upper Saddle River, NJ: Merrill.

Glasser, W. (1969). *Schools without failure.* New York: Harper & Row.

Glasser, W., & Breggin, P. R. (2001). *Counseling with choice theory.* New York: HarperCollins.

Goldstein, A. P., & McGinnis, E. (1997). *Skillstreaming the adolescent: New Strategies and perspectives for teaching prosocial skills.* Champaign, IL: Research Press.

Goodnough, G. E., & Lee, V. V. (2004). Group counseling in schools. In B. T. Erford (Ed.), *Professional school counseling: A handbook of theories, programs and practices* (pp. 173–182). Austin, TX: ProEd.

Graham, C. (1990, November). *A normal response to an abnormal situation: The crisis debriefing.* Paper presented at the meeting of the Southern Association for Counselor Education and Supervision, Norfolk, VA.

Greenberg, K. R. (2003). *Group counseling in K-12 schools.* Boston: Allyn & Bacon.

Hoag, M. J., & Burlingame, G. M. (1997). Evaluating the effectiveness of child and adolescent group treatment: A meta-analysis review. *Journal of Clinical Child Psychology, 26,* 234–246.

Holcomb-McCoy, C. C. (2003). Multicultural group counseling in the school setting. In K. R. Greenberg (Ed.), *Group counseling in K-12 schools: A handbook for school counselors* (pp. 150–164). Boston: Allyn & Bacon.

Jacobs, E., & Schimmel, C. (2005). Small group counseling. In C. Sink (Ed.), *Contemporary school counseling: theory, research, and practice* (pp. 82–115). Boston: Lahaska Press.

James, R. K., & Gillilard, B.E. (2005). *Crisis intervention strategies* (5th ed.). Pacific Grove, CA: Brooks/Cole.

Johnson, D. W., & Johnson, F. P. (2000). *Joining together: Group theory and group skills* (7th ed.). Boston: Allyn & Bacon.

Jones, K. D., & Robinson, E. H., III. (2000). Psychoeducational groups: A model for choosing topics and exercises appropriate to group stage. *Journal for Specialists in Group Work, 25,* 356–365.

Kizner, L. R., Kizner, S. R. (1999). Small group counseling with adopted children. *Professional School Counseling, 2,* 226–229.

Kulic, K. R., Dagley, J. C., & Horne, A. M. (2001). Prevention groups with children and adolescents. *Journal for Specialists in Group Work, 26,* 211–218.

Littrell, J. M., & Peterson, J. S. (2002). Establishing a comprehensive group work program in an elementary school: An in-depth case study. *Journal for Specialists in Group Work, 27,* 161–172.

Markus, H. E., & King, D. A. (2003). A survey of group psychotherapy training during predoctoral psychology internship. *Professional Psychology: Research and Practice, 34,* 203–209.

Orton, G. L. (1997). *Strategies for counseling with children and their parents.* Pacific Grove, CA: Brooks/Cole.

Pedro-Carroll, J. L, & Cowen, E. L. (1985). The children of divorce intervention program: An investigation of the efficacy of a school-based prevention program. *Journal of Consulting and Clinical Psychology, 53,* 603–611.

Piper, W. E., & Ogrodniczuk, J. S. (2004). Brief group therapy. In J. L. DeLucia-Waack, D. Gerrity, C. R. Kalodner, & M. T. Riva (Eds.), *Handbook of group counseling and psychotherapy* (pp. 641–650). Thousand Oaks, CA: Sage.

Portman, T. A. A., & Portman, G. L. (2002). Empowering students for social justice. *Journal for Specialists in Group Work, 27,* 16–31.

Rainey, L. M., Hensley, F. A., & Crutchfield, L. B. (1997). Implementation of support groups in elementary and middle school student assistance programs. *Professional School Counseling, 1,* 36–40.

Reeder, J., Douzenis, C., & Bergin, J. J. (1997). The effects of small group counseling on the racial attitudes of second grade students. *Professional School Counseling, 1,* 15–19.

Ripley, V. V., & Goodnough, G. E. (2001). Planning and implementing group counseling in a high school. *Professional School Counseling, 5,* 62–65.

Ritchie, M. H., & Huss, S. N. (2000). Recruitment and screening of minors for group counseling. *Journal for Specialists in Group Work, 25,* 146–156.

Riva, M. T., & Haub, A. L. (2004). Group counseling in schools. In J. L. DeLucia-Waack, D. Gerrity, C. R. Kalodner, & M. T. Riva (Eds.), *Handbook of group counseling and psychotherapy* (pp. 309–321). Thousand Oaks, CA: Sage.

Riva, M. T., Wachtel, M., & Lasky, G. B. (2004). Effective leadership in group counseling and psychotherapy: Research and practice. In J. L. DeLucia-Waack, D. Gerrity, C. R. Kalodner, & M. T. Riva (Eds.), *Handbook of group counseling and psychotherapy* (pp. 37–48). Thousand Oaks, CA: Sage.

Robinson, F. F., & Jones, E. N. (1996). Research on the preparation of group counselors. *Journal for Specialists in Group Work, 21,* 172–178.

Shaffer, J., Brown, L. L., & McWhirter, J. J. (1998). Survivors of child sexual abuse and dissociative coping: Relearning in a group context. *Journal for Specialists in Group Work, 23,* 74–94.

Shechtman, Z. (2001). Prevention groups for angry and aggressive children. *Journal for Specialists in Group Work, 26,* 228–236.

Shechtman, Z. (2002). Child group psychotherapy in the school at the threshold of a new millennium. *Journal of Counseling and Development, 80,* 293–299.

Shechtman, Z. (2004). Group counseling and psychotherapy with children and adolescents: Current practice and research. In J. L. DeLucia-Waack, D. Gerrity, C. R. Kalodner, & M. T. Riva (Eds.), *Handbook of group counseling and psychotherapy* (pp. 429–444). Thousand Oaks, CA: Sage.

Shechtman, Z., Freedman, Y., Kashti, Y., & Sharabani, R. (2002). Group counseling to enhance adolescents' close friendship. *International Journal of Group Psychotherapy, 52,* 537–554.

Shure, M. (1992). *I can problem solve (ICPS): An interpersonal cognitive problem solving program for children.* Champaign, IL: Research Press.

Sommers-Flanagan, R., Barrett-Hakanson, T., Clarke, C., & Sommers-Flanagan, J. (2000). A psychoeducational school-based coping and social skills group for depressed students. *Journal for Specialists in Group Work, 25,* 170–190.

Stanko, C. A., & Taub, D. J. (2002). A counseling group for children of cancer patients. *Journal for Specialists in Group Work, 27,* 43–58.

Stoiber, K., & Kratochwill, T. (1998). *Handbook of group intervention for children and families.* Boston: Allyn & Bacon.

Van Lone, J. S., Kalodner, C. R., & Coughlin, J. W. (2002). Using short stories to address eating disturbances in groups. *Journal for Specialists in Group Work, 27,* 59–77.

Wick, D. T., Wick, J. K., & Peterson, N. (1997). Improving self-esteem with Adlerian adventure therapy. *Professional School Counseling, 1,* 53–56.

Wilson, C. (2003). Group counseling in the high school. In K. R. Greenberg (Ed.), *Group counseling in K-12 schools: A handbook for school counselors* (pp. 97–111). Boston: Allyn & Bacon.

Wilson, F. R., & Owens, P. C. (2001). Group-based prevention programs for at-risk adolescents and adults. *Journal for Specialists in Group Work, 26,* 246–255.

Zinck, K., & Littrell, J. M. (2000). Action research shows group counseling effective with at-risk adolescent girls. *Professional School Counseling, 4,* 50–59.

COUNSELING CHILDREN WITH SPECIAL CONCERNS

I have found the paradox that if I love until it hurts, then there is no hurt, but only more love.

—Mother Teresa

In previous chapters we described some of the challenges inherent in our complex society—difficulties with which children must cope during their major years of growth and development. Counselors obviously cannot supply all the answers to these problems; however, several concerns of children are pressing, and children facing those challenges are seen frequently by counselors. This chapter suggests ways of working with children with these special needs and problems. The suggestions should be incorporated into a caring, accepting counseling atmosphere and modified to meet the unique needs of the child and the presenting concern. The reader may wish to refer to Appendices A and B for special procedures to handle the problem behaviors that may accompany these societal problems. This chapter examines the following problems: child maltreatment, substance abuse in the family, children who encounter death, depression and suicidal behaviors, family complications such as divorce and separation, homelessness, single-parent homes, stepfamilies, violence, and disabilities.

CHILD MALTREATMENT

Child maltreatment is a general term that includes several kinds of abuse. In 2003, an estimated 906,000 children were victims of abuse and neglect (Childhelp USA, 2005). In those cases, child neglect was most prevalent (60%), followed by physical abuse (20%), sexual abuse (10%), and psychological abuse and neglect (5%). Approximately 80 percent of the abusers are parents (Administration for Children and Families, 2003). Every day in the United States more than four children die as a result of child abuse. Of the fatalities, 89 percent were children 8 years or younger, and more than 40 percent were younger than 1 year. Surprisingly, most adults who were polled (nine in ten people) recognize child maltreatment as a serious problem, even though only one in three reported abuse when faced with an actual situation (Childhelp USA, 2005).

In the Child Abuse Prevention and Treatment Act (1996), or CAPTA (Public Law 93–247), the federal government provides minimum standards for definitions of child abuse and neglect required to be incorporated into state statutes (National Clearinghouse on Child Abuse and Neglect Information, 2005a). Other authors also present definitions of child maltreatment (Edgeworth & Carr, 2000; Miller-Perrin, 2001; Berk, 2001). For example:

Physical abuse: nonaccidental physical injury to the child; may include striking, kicking, burning, or biting the child or some other action that results in substantial risk for physical or emotional harm to the child. Johnson (1990) describes physical abuse as the use of an instrument on any part of the body, tissue damage beyond simple redness from a slap, and injury from heat, caustic substances, chemicals, or drugs.

Sexual abuse: the use of a child for sexual gratification. Sexual abuse may vary in intrusiveness (from viewing to oral/anal/genital penetration) and frequency (from a single incident to frequent abuse). The U.S. National Center on Child Abuse and Neglect has defined sexual abuse as an act perpetrated on a child by a significantly older person with the intent to stimulate the child sexually and satisfy the aggressor's sexual impulses (as cited in Moeller, et al. 1993).

Emotional abuse: actions, such as intentional and frequent rejection, criticism, punishment for minor infractions, belittling, and threatening, that damage the child cognitively, emotionally, or in their social interactions. Moeller, et al. (1993) provide six categories of emotional abuse: (1) chronic denigration of the child's qualities, capacities, desires, and emotional expressiveness; (2) isolation; (3) terrorization; (4) excessive age-inappropriate demands; (5) witnessing extreme parental violence (including excessive use of drugs and alcohol); and (6) not providing services for a seriously emotionally handicapped child.

Physical neglect: failing to provide a child's basic needs such as food, clothing, shelter, medical attention, supervision, and hygiene

Emotional neglect: failure to provide children's needs for affection and emotional support

All statistics underestimate the prevalence of child maltreatment. Those miscalculations are caused by variations in definitions of child abuse across the nation, as well as the fact that many incidents of child abuse are unreported or misreported. A growing menace in the maltreatment of children occurs with online relationships in which minors are enticed, invited, or persuaded to meet for sexual acts (National Center for Missing and Exploited Children, 2006). Predators may use e-mail, instant messages, bulletin boards, and chat rooms to gain the young person's confidence, and then to arrange a meeting. The federal government and all states have laws related to child pornography and other types of child sexual exploitation. Those statutes are summarized on the website of the National Center for Missing and Exploited Children (www.ncmec. org). Parents and other adults in protective roles should know the signs for children who may be at risk for online victimization.

Child abuse occurs at all levels of social, economic, and educational status. In a large number of cases, the offender is a male relative or friend of the family. The offender may use bribes, threats, guilt, or coercion to ensure secrecy. To protect the family and this relative or friend, the abuse may be ignored or hushed up in a variety of ways, the incidents are never reported or recorded, and the child and family never confront the issue or receive treatment.

Several hypotheses have been advanced to explain the causes of child abuse. Currently, the origins of child abuse are understood as the interacting variables of the child, the family, community, and culture (National Clearinghouse on Child Abuse and Neglect Information, 2004). Children are not responsible for the maltreatment inflicted on them. Yet, some child characteristics such as having disabilities significantly correlate with an increased risk for abuse or neglect. Younger children are more likely to be neglected and the risk for sexual abuse increases with age. Female children and adolescents are more likely than male children and adolescents to be subjected to sexual abuse.

Some family characteristics are linked to child maltreatment. Families with substance abuse problems have a higher risk for abuse (Child Welfare League of America, 2001). The families are often rigid, authoritarian, and isolated from one another and the outside world. They may be experiencing marital, financial, or parent–child relationship problems, but lack the resources and skills to cope with them. Poverty, unemployment, parents who were victims of abuse themselves, and stressful changes such as moving or marital separations are often associated with abuse. The community may be one of social isolation with few gathering places such as parks, child-care or recreational centers, and churches to serve as family supports. Societal factors such as the acceptance of domestic violence and corporal punishment may also contribute to the incidence of child abuse. The abused child is usually thought of in negative terms and may be isolated, rejected, ignored, or even terrorized.

The Family Support Network (2002) has discussed protective factors within children and families, as well as social and environmental factors that reduce the risks for child maltreatment. Good health, intelligence, creativity, humor, optimism, good peer and social skills, an easy temperament, a positive disposition, an active coping style, positive self-esteem, and a balance between seeking help and autonomy are protective child factors. In the family, protective factors include secure attachments, parental reconciliation with own history of abuse, household rules and monitoring of the child, extended family support, stable relationship with parents, family expectations of prosocial behavior, and high parental education. Social and environmental protection comes from adequate socioeconomic status, access to health care and social services, neighborhood stability, consistent parental employment, adequate housing, family participation in a religious faith, good school, and supportive adults beyond the family.

Counselors and others should work to create and augment protective factors as a response to the prevalence of child maltreatment. Counselors will need to understand the signs and symptoms of abuse and the ways to support the young person who has been victimized. Victims of child maltreatment demonstrate a variety of responses to the abuse. Table 18-1 presents Miller-Perrin's (2001) summary of the signs and symptoms associated with forms of maltreatment.

Counselors should be aware that the exact link between experiences of abuse and mental health outcomes has yet to be determined. The counselor may see constellations of symptoms that cross several areas of a child's functioning. Webb and Terr (1999) discuss two types of trauma: Type I, a traumatic, single event in an otherwise normal life, and Type II, prolonged and repeated trauma in which anticipated and actual pain, violence, and chaos occur. The coping mechanisms of denial, numbing, self-hypnosis, dissociation, and shifts between rage and passivity are developed (Webb & Terr, 1999). Gil (1996) explains that children will demonstrate the impact of abuse either with internal or external behaviors. Children who internalize the trauma cope with the pain alone. They avoid interaction and may seem depressed, without joy, full of fear, hypervigilant, and regressed. They may also have physical symptoms such as sleeping problems, headaches, and stomachaches. Severe cases may self-mutilate or become suicidal. Children who express their pain externally may be hostile, provocative, or violent. They may hurt animals, destroy property, and show sexualized behaviors.

The National Clearinghouse on Child Abuse and Neglect Information (2005b) summarizes the most common physical, psychological, and behavioral consequences of child maltreatment and acknowledges that the categories often overlap. Children's reactions to abuse are affected by their age and developmental status when the maltreatment occurred; the type of abuse; the frequency, duration, and severity of the abuse; and the relationship between the victim and the abuser (Chalk, et al. 2002).

PHYSICAL ABUSE AND NEGLECT

The *Harvard Mental Health Letter* ("Child Abuse, Parts I and II," 1993) concluded that the long-term effects of physical abuse are not fully understood; the effects of abuse and those of other familial or environmental effects are difficult to distinguish. However, it estimated that "at least 25% of physically abused children have serious psychiatric problems, including chronic anxiety and depression and sometimes neurological damage" (p. 3). Kelley, et al. (1997) report that abused children display an overwhelming set of problems in school, such as dropping out, teen pregnancy, institutionalization,

TABLE 18-1 | POTENTIAL SIGNS AND SYMPTOMS OF MALTREATMENT

	Sexual abuse		Child neglect	Physical abuse		Psychological maltreatment
	Children	Adolescents		Children	Adolescents	
Physical complications:	Genital bleeding, pain, odors; eating or sleep disturbances; somatic complaints; enuresis or encopresis	Somatic complaints, eating disturbance, sleep disturbance	Failure to thrive	Bruises; head, chest, and abdominal injuries; burns; fractures		
Affective-behavioral problems:	Anxiety and fears, nightmares, guilt, anger/hostility, depression, low self-esteem, sexualized behavior and preoccupation, aggression, regression/immaturity, hyperactivity	Anxiety, anger, depression, guilt, suicidal ideation, low self-esteem, social withdrawal, self-injurious behavior, sexualized behavior, delinquency, running away, substance abuse	Low self-esteem, aggression, anger, frustration, conduct problems	Aggression, hopelessness, depression, low self-esteem, fighting, noncompliance, defiance, property offenses, arrests		Aggression, self-abusive behavior, anxiety, shame, guilt, anger and hostility, pessimism, dependency

Cognitive deficits:	Learning difficulties, poor attention and concentration, declining grades	Learning difficulties, poor concentration and attention, declining grades	Language deficits, academic problems, intellectual delays, poor problem solving	Decreased intellectual and cognitive functioning; deficits in verbal faculty, memory, problem solving, perceptual-motor skills, and verbal abilities; decreased reading and math skills; poor school achievement; increase in special education services		Academic problems, deficits in cognitive abilty, poor problem solving
Social deficits:			Disturbed parent–child attachment and interactions, deficits in pro-social behavior, social withdrawal and isolation	Delayed play skills, infant attachment problems, poor social interaction skills, difficulty making friends, deficits in pro-social behaviors and deficits in social competence with peers, avoidance of adults	Violent interpersonal behavior, delinquency, violent offenses, substance abuse	Insecure attachments, poor social adjustment
Other:	Attention problems, depressed school performance, increased daily stress, low self-esteem					

low scores on standardized tests of language and math, and repeating one or more grades. They had lower educational aspirations and more behavioral problems in the classroom than other children. Academic failure was the most obvious factor among children classified as neglected; however, this group did not experience significant behavioral problems in class or display significant adjustment difficulties as do children who are physically abused.

Edgeworth and Carr (2000) have reviewed treatment studies and conclude that for physical abuse and neglect, residential treatment, therapeutic day care, and resilient peer therapy are effective interventions. Therapeutic day treatment often includes group activities, opportunities to interact with peers, and learning experiences to enhance development. Miller-Perrin (2001) note that prevention training in self-protection is an important component of treatment. Teaching children to identify harmful situations and move to a safer location are examples that may be included in that intervention. Other suggested techniques for working with abused children include empathic listening, clarification of the child's words and sentences ("What do you mean?"), discussions of "good" and "bad" touching, and emphasizing the child's right to say no to inappropriate touching, as well as to talk to a trusted adult about any incident that causes him or her to feel uncomfortable.

Parent-focused interventions that focus on physical abusive and neglectful parents have involved the following parts:

- Teaching parents about normal child development to correct unrealistic expectations
- Educating parents about appropriate discipline procedures and other child management strategies
- Practicing anger-control techniques and coping skills
- Discussing stress management techniques (Schellenbach, 1998)

CHILD SEXUAL ABUSE

Schoen and Davis (1998) report that results from a survey of adolescent boys documented that one in eight high school boys (13 percent) had been physically or sexually abused, or both. Most (66 percent) of those who reported the abuse on the survey said the abuse happened at home, and 68 percent stated the abuser was a family member. Almost half of the boys said they had told no one about their abuse. One in five high school girls reported abuse on the survey, with 53 percent stating it had happened at home and 20 percent reporting they had not told anyone of the abuse. According to Green (1993), reporting of sexual abuse cases in the United States substantially increased during the 1980s. Sexual abuse of girls is reported more often than abuse of boys. Boys are more likely to be approached by strangers, and girls are more likely to be victims of incest ("Child Abuse, Parts I and II," 1993). Children in frequent contact with their abusers have additional problems in maintaining the relationship, as well as coping with the trauma of the abuse.

Green (1993) concludes that no specific behavioral patterns in children indicate sexual abuse, and that some cases might show no symptoms; diagnosis must be based on a variety of data, including a history, assessment of the reliability of the child's disclosure, psychiatric evaluation, physical examination, evaluation of the child's prior psychological functioning, and assessment of the family's functioning.

GENERAL COUNSELING STRATEGIES FOR WORKING WITH CHILDREN WHO HAVE BEEN ABUSED

Counselors who work with abused children may find it helpful to consider this question: What does this child need to understand about the traumatic situation that he or she does not know right now? (Shapiro, et al. 2006). The answers to that query can guide an educational component of the treatment directed toward helping the abused child revise some of his or her misunderstandings about the victimization. As Shapiro, et al. explain, molestation violates our ideas about privacy, pleasure, adult–child relationships, and trust. To counter the self-blame children may be experiencing, the victims need to know that abuse has also happened to some other young people and that they are not alone in suffering with being maltreated. Those authors suggest some resources: *My Very Own Book about Me: A Personal Safety Book* (Dietzel, 2000); *Something Happened and I'm Scared to Tell: A Book for Young Victims of Abuse* (Kehoe & Deach, 1987); *It Happened to Me: A Teen's Guide to Overcoming Sexual Abuse* (Carter, 2002); *The Rainbow Game* (Rainbow House, 1989); and therapeutic stories by Davis and Sparks (1988).

Miller-Perrin (2001) has outlined some ways of intervening with children who have been victims of abuse. One goal suggested was to help the child learn to manage the negative cognitions and emotions associated with the incident(s). Emotions such as guilt, shame, anger, stress, stigma, and fear occur as a result of abuse. Relaxation training, anger management, problem-solving skills, positive coping statement, and the use of imagery are possible techniques. Cognitive-behavioral approaches are useful to help victims change their ideas about being different from other children, as well as feeling they are somehow responsible for the abuse. Group therapy to counter such beliefs and to confront secrecy is helpful to children who are able to discuss their abuse with peers who have also been abused.

James and Burch (1999) suggest some activities that can be conducted in schools:

1. Prepare school personnel by teaching about normal sexual development, symptoms of abuse, state law, school policy, and reporting procedures.
2. Deliver an abuse prevention program at school that educates children to danger signs, preventions skills, and the importance of telling adults about abuse.
3. Develop a network of professionals to build skills in assessment and knowledge base of ways to work with abused children. The network

should include child protection workers, other counselors, therapists, and agencies that diagnose and treat victims.

4. Have toys, books, and games in the counseling office to ease discussions of family, feelings, or trauma.
5. Have resources about testifying in court.
6. Keep accurate professional records that are clear and objective (p. 216).

Some specific ideas for working with abused children are as follows:

1. In counseling all abuse victims, counselors must be prepared to become totally involved with the child client, including the child's repeated testing of the counselors' caring.
2. Relaxation and visualization may help the child develop a more positive attitude toward self and life.
3. Play therapy may help abused children to communicate their thoughts and feelings.
4. Shapiro, et al. (2006) recommend cognitive-behavioral therapy as the core for working with children who have been abused.
5. Sexually abused children require extra consideration, understanding, and support from the counselor. Often, the children initially are unable to discuss the problem with the counselor because of intense feelings of guilt. They believe that somehow they provoked the attack or that they could have done something to prevent it. They may feel worthless and ashamed of having been abused in such a manner. They may be more affected by the questions and reactions that follow than by the act itself. And they often feel intense guilt at having gotten a parent or other adult in trouble, in jail, or barred from the home because the child "told." Empathetic listening and clarification of words and nonverbal expressions is essential.
6. Specific techniques such as bibliocounseling, role-playing, play therapy, or group counseling may be considered, depending on the child's maturity. Placing sexually abused children in groups requires caution, especially if the trauma is recent. The child may not be ready to share intense feelings.
7. Children may need information about what is appropriate and inappropriate touching or treatment and to be assured that certain parts of their bodies are private. They may need to be told that the adult's sexual or punishing behavior was inappropriate. Because of children's limited cognitive development and understanding, and to allay the anxiety surrounding the topic, most programs designed to teach children about child abuse use role-play, puppets, coloring books, filmstrips, movies, and so on. The vocabulary used is not explicit, but instead refers to *touching* and *private areas*. The programs are designed not for sex education, but to give children information and strategies for coping with abusive situations.
8. Children may need to learn how to say no or how to handle potentially abusive situations. The child needs help to determine the warning signs of abuse and to plan ways for coping with the situations (for example, calling

a special person when the father or mother begins to drink). Role-playing these strategies prepares children to handle such situations more effectively. Counselors need to do a careful assessment of the child's situation so that the new skills would not place the child at an increased risk.

9. Encourage children to tell someone right away when an abusive situation occurs. Adults who abuse children sexually often warn the children to keep "their secret." Children need help discerning when they should tell a secret and when information should be kept confidential, and also in deciding whom they should tell and what to do if the adult does not believe their story.

10. Counselors must deal with issues of trust at some point in work with abused children. Developmental theorists have emphasized that children must develop trust in people and their interactions to live effectively, yet children receive a multitude of daily messages, designed to protect them, that imply that the world and the people in it are dangerous.

Childhood abuse is a part of an overall pattern of abusive behavior, and the family network, as well as the personality of the abuser, must be considered. In addition, family reactions to the child who has been abused will enhance or interfere with counseling treatment and progress. Counselors should consider family therapy at an appropriate time in their treatment plans.

Counselors working with abused children must be prepared to provide understanding and support for all persons involved. The natural reaction is anger at anyone who hurts a child; however, these feelings must be recognized and resolved for the counselor to work effectively with the child and the family, particularly the abuser. Counselors who are overly sympathetic with abused children lose objectivity and their ability to help the child; counselors who are extremely angry and judgmental toward the family of an abused child (for allowing this to happen) or toward the abuser can never establish the relationship necessary to help these individuals. Before beginning counseling with victims of abuse, counselors may need to examine their own feelings and views about the case.

CHILDREN'S MEMORIES OF ABUSE

James and Burch (1999) caution counselors to avoid contamination of a child's story, such as leading questions, feeding information, providing details, asking many questions, or pressuring. Yapko (1993) lists guidelines for professionals working with the possibility of child abuse:

- Do not jump to conclusions.
- Do not ask leading questions.
- Get external corroboration when the situation is ambiguous.
- Be conservative in suggesting any method of limiting communication with the client's family.
- Do not rely on your own memory, especially if sensitive information is discussed.

James and Burch (1999) offer these suggestions for interviewing a child who may be abused:

1. Use statements and questions such as "Tell me about a time something happened to you that made you feel uncomfortable." "Tell me what happened to you." "Has anyone tried to touch your private parts?" (Counselors can define "private" as parts of the body covered by a bathing suit.)
2. Pay attention to the child's body language as the interview progresses. The child may tell more nonverbally than with words.
3. Let the child tell his or her own story.
4. Be empathic but neutral.
5. Use clarification and summary skills.
6. Use the child's terms when paraphrasing (p. 215).

Child maltreatment is a tremendous problem in our world. Children who have been victims need extra care and attention to overcome the effects of their trauma. Counselors can be instrumental in protecting the child's safety and providing helpful interventions for enhancing the child's life.

CHILDREN IN CHEMICALLY DEPENDENT FAMILIES

Children living in families affected by chemical dependency may have special needs. According to the Substance Abuse and Mental Health Services Administration (2002), alcoholism and drug addiction affects approximately 8.3 million children; about 11 percent of young people under the age of 18 live with someone who needs treatment for chemical dependency. They are often left out of an alcoholic parent's treatment even though the entire family is affected. Those children have significant risks for mental illness or emotional problems, physical health difficulties, and learning problems. Compared with other children, they are three times more likely to be abused and four times more likely to be neglected (Substance Abuse and Mental Health Services Administration, 2002).

Children of chemically dependent parents frequently do not have their physical or psychological needs met in the family. Money needed for food and shelter may be spent on alcohol or drugs; even if there is money, the parents may be too preoccupied with their chemical dependency to attend to the child's physical needs. Parents who have lost control of their lives and frequently dislike themselves cannot meet the child's need for love, belonging, and security. Children who live in homes where rules are consistently broken and with family members who cannot be relied on to provide love and nurturance cannot be expected to grow and develop into fully functioning, well-adjusted individuals.

Children in families that have chemical dependency issues frequently are the victims of abuse and neglect, have little structure in their lives, receive inconsistent discipline, and cope with constant conflict in the home. Households with alcoholic residents often are described as turbulent and lacking in parental warmth and affection (The NSDUH Report, 2005). Children adapt the roles they need to survive in this environment and often fail to learn the variety of roles children from homes with open communication and consistent lifestyles master (James & Gilliland, 2005). The adverse effects of conflicted home environments are seen in behavior such as school absenteeism, poor academic performance, isolation from peers, physical symptoms such as headaches and stomachaches, psychological symptoms (fears, moods, regressive behaviors), and "people-pleasing behaviors" (O'Rourke & Worzbyt, 1996, pp. 55–56). Sciarra (2004) summarizes seven problems that may occur for children in families with chemically dependent members: family conflict, abuse and neglect, inconsistent discipline and inadequate structure, disruption of family rituals, role reversal and parentification, distortion, and the denial of reality and isolation.

In addition, several writers (Black, 1981; Glover, 1994; Muro & Kottman, 1995; Sciarra, 2004) have outlined roles children of chemically dependent families may assume to cope with their parents' dependence: chief enabler (the addict's confidant and support); family hero (overly responsible, mature); scapegoat (one who is blamed for all problems); lost child (scared and isolated); placater ("people pleaser"); or mascot (the clown). In addition to these roles children assume, they also learn the family's unspoken rules. Those guidelines for surviving in an alcoholic family have been summarized by Doweiko (1999), Black (1981), and James and Gilliland (2005):

- *Don't talk/Don't have problems.* This stems from the denial of the problem of alcoholism, as well as the lack of recognition of the child's problem. Doweiko (1999) explains that the family will make clear no problem exists and you better not discuss it. Black (1981) further explains the belief that if one does talk, bad things will happen.
- *Don't trust.* Children cannot depend on the drinking parent and often cannot depend on the nondrinking partner who is so busy meeting the needs of the alcoholic (Black, 1981).
- *Don't feel.* Children learn that expressing fear, guilt, anger, sadness, or other feelings will bring more pain to the family.
- *Don't behave differently.* Shifting roles is not allowed.
- *Don't blame chemical dependency.* Blame typically is assigned to people, situations, or things outside the family. Denial of personal responsibility for actions is the norm.
- *Do behave as I want.* If a child does not comply with the wishes of the alcoholic, the threats of losing love or support, abuse, and increased drinking may occur.
- *Do be better and more responsible.* No matter what a family member does, it will never be enough to satisfy the alcoholic.
- *Don't have fun.* Broken promises, angry recriminations, embarrassment of the family situation, unpredictable outbursts, and exhaustion keep children from enjoying life.

Growing up in an alcoholic family has different effects on children, according to Jones and Houts (1992). They classify families of the subjects participating in their research as "regular problem drinking," "occasional problem drinking," "minor problem drinking," or "non–problem drinking." Young adults who grew up in homes where drinking was a regular problem said they received less positive regard and less attention to their feelings from their parents. The researchers did not find significant differences among the problem-drinking groups for the parents' level of criticism of the child or emotional support. They conclude that their findings support the idea that to understand the impact of growing up in an alcoholic family, it is important to describe specific characteristics of the family and conceptualize these characteristics as interacting with problem drinking to create a family environment that influences developmental processes. At the same time, the results suggest that it is inappropriate to assume that growing up in an alcoholic family has comprehensive and maladaptive outcomes for young adult children (Jones and Houts, 1992, p. 55). Ferquist (2000) hypothesizes that the chronic stress that occurs in families with chronic drinking could contribute to youth suicide.

INTERVENTIONS FOR CHILDREN FROM CHEMICALLY DEPENDENT FAMILIES

One method to screen children of alcoholics is the Children of Alcoholics Screening Test (CAST) (Jones, 1985). This thirty-item inventory measures negative life events associations with alcoholic families such as emotional distress, marital discord, attempts to control parental drinking, efforts to escape from alcoholism, exposure to drinking-related violence, and desire for help. CASTD (Pidcock, et al. 2000) is the shortened version of the instrument that has fourteen items and has been adapted to include other types of substance use. Family CAGE (Price & Emshoff, 1997) is also a useful diagnostic tool.

Brake (1988) states that children of alcoholics need a counselor to help them understand they can love their parents without liking their behavior, and that these children need help feeling worthwhile as individuals. She suggests group counseling preceded by an individual session. Films and books may be needed to encourage talking because these children have learned to avoid conflict by not talking. Time and patience are required to build trust. Wilson and Blocher (1990) suggest developmental support groups incorporating bibliotherapy, role-play of problem situations, rational-emotive-behavioral therapy techniques for assessing behavior and coping more effectively, Gestalt activities to express feelings, assertiveness to express needs and rights, and relaxation techniques to reduce stress.

O'Rourke (1990) provides an outline for a children's support group that includes attention to the preceding needs and provides information about alcoholism for young participants. These children also need activities to improve their self-esteem, assertiveness training to teach them to say no to drugs and alcohol, and help with developing problem-solving and decision-making skills.

Arman and McNair (2000) outline a nine-session group that also incorporates the identified needs of children from chemically dependent families. O'Rourke and Worzbyt (1996) caution that prevention programs should respect the conditions under which the children of alcoholics live and understand that they live in a world with limited choices. They encourage counselors to focus on strengthening self-esteem and building strengths, resources, and resiliencies.

James and Gililland (2005) summarize treatment goals for children from substance abusing families. In working with these children, counselors will want to accomplish the following goals:

- Give emotional support to the children.
- Provide accurate, nonjudgmental information about chemical dependency.
- Correct children's perceptions of being the cause of the parental problems and the attached guilt and shame.
- Help children focus on their own behavior to gain a sense of control, to make responsible choices, and perhaps to teach them to have fun.
- Help children learn to cope with possible situations that may occur because of the abuse.
- Reduce children's isolation (p. 312).

DEATH AND BEREAVEMENT

When asked about death or dying, most adults try to avoid the subject or excuse themselves by expressing their inadequacy to discuss such a subject with young people. Discussions about death may be accompanied by a great deal of adult discomfort, anxiety, vagueness, and avoidance behavior. Yet talking about death may help people accept it as a part of life and cope with the feelings that accompany it. Children often are affected by the death of pets or grandparents, if not by loss of parents, friends, or siblings. Counselors need to be prepared to help children accept the reality of death as a part of life. To work effectively with children on the issue of death, counselors must first examine their own attitudes toward death so that the helping professionals can be open to a child's grieving process.

Children have trouble understanding death for many reasons. As Piaget (1954) points out, children are limited in understanding by the stage of their cognitive development. Young children are unable to understand the finality and irreversibility of death; they feel they are immortal and have trouble understanding how others are not. As children grow, they begin to question death and its causes. They may recognize it as inevitable and final, but comprehending the process is still difficult for children. Children often believe that only old people die.

O'Rourke and Worzbyt (1996) write that "how children view loss and death is a matter of development, personal experiences, adult guidance, and innate abilities" (p. 303). They report that there is limited understanding of responses to death for children younger than 3, who do not understand the difference between dying and going away. Children from 3 to 5 years old consider death a temporary condition and may show little reaction to it or understanding of it. They may believe they caused the death. Sciarra (2004) suggests some important points to make to young children who have suffered a loss. They need to know someone will take care of them and that the death is not their fault. These young people need to be told that they have their own feelings that may be different than the feelings of people around them, and that they can have as much time as they need to figure things out; they do not need to rush or pretend to feel differently.

Children from 6 to 8 years old begin to understand the finality of death and become curious about the details, but it may not hold a personal meaning (O'Rourke & Worzbyt, 1996). James and Gililland (2005) explain that for children 6 or 7 years old, death is more specific, precise, and factual. Children want to know the details of the death and may ask many questions as they try to understand. Children in the concrete operational stage of cognitive development grasp the cause-and-effect aspect of death.

As they move into formal operational thought, children can grasp the idea that everyone eventually dies and that death is irreversible. That understanding may frighten them as they realize they, too, will die. If they experience a loss, children after the age of 11 or 12 may have trouble concentrating on their school work, may withdraw from friends and family, and may seem angry and sad, as well as being tired and drowsy (Sciarra, 2004). Adults should remember children are concerned about whether they caused the death, whether they will be cared for, and whether they will die soon. Sheller and Watts (1999) recommend that up to the age of 12 children have pictures, scrapbooks, videos, and other aids to anchor their memories of the deceased. They suggest a picture to help remind the child of the special relationship.

Adolescents may show more variations in their response to death. They are more cognitively capable of understanding the finality and inevitability of death. Teens may experience deep pain, fear, guilt, helplessness, and grief, but may not know how to express those emotions. Often, their peers help teenagers cope with death. Sheller and Watts (1999) note that adolescents may distract themselves from the loss by becoming intensely involved in sports or socializing or music that "tunes out" everything. Sciarra (2004) advises these books to help adolescents deal with loss: *Say Goodnight, Gracie* (Deaver, 1988), *Shira: A Legacy of Courage* (Grollman, 1988), *The Sunday Doll* (Shura, 1988), and *Tiger Eyes* (Blume, 1981). Sciarra cautions adults to be alert to teens who appear to be "perfectly fine" after the death of a family member or friend. Those adolescents may be hiding their grief as they attempt to appear mature and independent.

Many factors in the child's environment may encourage faulty concepts concerning death. The mass media often portray death violently. Children may also be exposed to a media figure dying one week and then appearing the next in another program. Adults in the child's life may react negatively to death. Often, they attempt to protect the child from death by refusing to discuss the subject and by hiding their own feelings. Understanding adult reactions may be difficult for children. They may think they caused or contributed to the death in some way or decide that death is a punishment for something bad they have done. Unfounded fears and anxieties arise out of these misunderstandings. Euphemistic explanations often cause misconceptions in children. If told that the person is "only asleep" or that "God has called her," children can learn to fear sleep or fear that God will call them away from their world. For the most part, children have difficulty learning effective ways of handling death, and the adults in their lives may not provide the answers needed or demonstrate appropriate behaviors.

Sciarra (2004) outlines the stages many who experience grief may encounter. First, shock and denial occur. People may then feel anger and resentment. As those emotions fade, those grieving may become more disorganized and may experience despair and depression. Finally, they may accept the loss and incorporate it into their world.

From her work with terminally ill patients, Kübler-Ross (1969) defines the stages that most patients and their families go through in facing death. The first reaction is denial: "This is not happening to me." Second, the patient and family experience anger over the situation: "Why did this have to happen to me and not to somebody else?" The next stage includes bargaining. People may try to make a bargain with God to be a better person if God will let them or their loved one live. When the inevitability of death must be faced and the pressures become a harsh reality, depression is common. Eventually, the patient comes to the realization of the inevitability of death and often a peaceful acceptance.

Freeman (2001) discusses the grief experience as a progression through ten stages. The person moves from shock, to an emotional release, to depression, and often to physical symptoms of distress. The bereaved shows anxiety, hostility, and then guilt and fear. The last two stages include healing through memories and acceptance of the death. He states that the tasks of mourning involve expressing the reality of the death, tolerating the suffering, and converting the relationship from the present to one of memory. The final tasks are developing a new identity of self without the deceased and finding some meaning in grief. Moore and Carr (2000) provide examples (Table 18-2) of the child's statements that might indicate these stages.

INTERVENTIONS FOR CHILDREN WHO ARE GRIEVING

Worden (1996) lists four tasks for grieving children to accomplish: (1) accepting the reality of the loss, (2) experiencing the pain or emotional aspects of the loss, (3) adjusting to an environment in which the significant one is missed, and (4) relocating the person within one's life while finding ways to memorialize the person.

Shapiro, et al. (2006) outline three immediate needs of children after a loss: having their emotions validated, being given accurate information, and reassurance about the future. First, children should be given permission to experience the emotions they have, not what they "should" have. That reaction helps the children know their emotions are valid responses to the loss.

TABLE 18-2	THEMES UNDERLYING CHILDREN'S GRIEF	
Grief process	Underlying theme	Behavioral expressions of grief processes
Shock	• I am stunned by the loss of this person	• Complete lack of affect and difficulty engaging emotionally with others • Poor concentration and poor school work
Denial	• The person is not dead	• Reporting seeing or hearing the deceased • Carrying on conversations with the deceased
Yearning and searching	• I must find the deceased	• Wandering or running away • Phoning relatives
Sadness	• I am sad, hopeless, and lonely because I have lost someone on whom I depended	• Persistent low mood, tearfulness, low energy, and lack of activity • Appetite and sleep disruption • Poor concentration and poor school work
Anger	• I am angry because the person I needed has abandoned me	• Aggression, tantrums, defiance, delinquency • Conflict with parents, siblings, teachers, and peers • Drug or alcohol abuse • Poor concentration and poor school work
Anxiety	• I am frightened that the deceased will punish me for causing their death or being angry at them. I am afraid that I too may die of an illness or fatal accident	• Separation anxiety, school refusal, regressed behavior, bedwetting • Somatic complaints, hypochondriasis, and agoraphobia associated with a fear of accidents • Poor concentration and poor school work
Guilt and bargaining	• It is my fault that the person died so I should die	• Suicidal behavior
Acceptance	• I loved and lost the person who died and now I must carry on without them while cherishing their memory	• Return to normal behavioral routines

NOTE: Reprinted from Moore, M., and Carr, A. (2001). Depression and grief. In A. Carr (Ed.) *What works with children and adolescents? A critical review of psychological interventions with children, adolescents, and their families.* Andover, UK: Routledge, p. 209. Reprinted with permission of Taylor & Francis.

Second, children should be given an age-appropriate explanation of death that is respectful of the family's religious beliefs. Finally, children's concerns about what the death will mean for their lives should be addressed. Adults should help children express their fears and reassure them about their future.

Some situations may point to a need for professional help for children who have suffered a loss. Some of those instances are as follows: consistent problems such as pain or withdrawing, intensification of symptoms over time, a dramatic or sudden behavioral change, an adult who cannot cope, and extremes in the child's behavior. Bereavement is often a family transition, and each member's grieving affects others (Shapiro, et al. 2006). Moore and Carr (2000) suggest a six-session family therapy that focuses on grief work for all family members to improve the child and parent adjustment. Webb (1993) lists several advantages of family counseling. The advantages are that the counselor has the opportunity to observe the child's role in the family and to assess the availability of other family members to the child, the reality of death is shared with other family members, and the family has the opportunity to understand the pace and form of the child's grieving process. The disadvantages include the possibility of the child not being focused on because of grieving adults in the family, and that the family may be so grief stricken they cannot empathize with the child.

In summary, counseling strategies for helping children who have experienced loss through death include the following:

1. Listen carefully to children's thoughts, feelings, and concerns, and respond clearly and objectively with statements at the child's level of understanding. Clarify children's questions or statements that may have a double meaning or suggest a hidden concern. Be aware of the child's cognitive level of development.

2. Allow children to express their grief, talk freely, and ask questions. Play therapy, the use of puppets, role-playing, creative artwork, bibliocounseling, a visit to a nursing home, videos on dealing with loss, family drawing, relaxation and imagery, letter writing to say good-bye, the open-chair technique, and individual or group discussions may be helpful counseling techniques for working with these children. Counselors can also recommend books, pamphlets, or other resources to adults who provide support for these children. Children experiencing a loss through death may feel abandoned or insecure and need extra amounts of time, energy, and reassurance.

3. Help the child learn more about death and dying by talking about the death of an animal or a plant (Costa & Holliday, 1994).

4. Children sometimes have trouble understanding concepts such as heaven and eternity. Counselors may want to consult with the family's clergy for assistance in dealing with this sensitive topic. Avoid half truths such as death is "sleeping."

5. Counselors are often asked if children should attend the funeral of someone who has died. The answer depends on the child's age, the kinship of

the deceased, and the child's reaction to the death. Children need to learn that death is part of the natural order of life. They need the opportunity to say good-bye to a close loved one. However, also consider the child's reaction to death and his or her concern about attending the funeral.

6.   Work to reduce stress in the child's life. Try to maintain as much familiar structure as possible. Be aware that the child may regress to behaviors of an earlier developmental stage or manifest physical symptoms of distress (Costa & Holliday, 1994). Family counseling may be indicated.

7.   Allow for individual differences in the grieving process.

8.   Watch for triggers of grief—birthdays, holidays, the anniversary of the death (Costa & Holliday, 1994).

More information is needed describing effective methods for counseling with children and their reactions to death and dying, especially empirical studies. Perhaps researchers avoid the subject, as do parents and other adults. The severity of pain associated with the death and dying of a loved one indicates a need for study of both the short-term and long-term effects of the trauma.

DEPRESSION AND SUICIDE

The Child Welfare League of America (2006) reports as many as one in eight adolescents and one in thirty-three children have clinical depression. In a recent survey, 29 percent of students in grades 9 through 12 reported feeling sad or hopeless almost every day for two or more weeks during the last year (ChildTrends, 2006). Persisting sadness and hopelessness are troubling predictors of clinical depression, which is significantly linked to suicidal behavior. Suicide is the third leading cause of death for 15- to 24-year-olds and the sixth leading cause of death for 5- to 14-year-olds. The prevalence of suicidal behavior may be even greater because some may be reported as accidental deaths. These figures do not reflect suicide attempts, which may outnumber deaths by at least eight to one and perhaps even more (Child Welfare League of America, 2003).

Signs of depression include sadness that persists, hopelessness, loss of interest in normal activities, changes in eating or sleeping habits, school absenteeism or poor performance, aches and pains that do not get better with treatment, and thoughts about death or suicide. The *Harvard Mental Health Letter* ("Depression in children—Part I," 2002) outlines symptoms for young children. Signs include being accident-prone and subject to phobias, extreme self-reproach, clinging behavior, avoiding new people and challenges, and excessive worry. Adolescents may appear to be angry rather than sad. McWhirter, et al. (2004) report that children and adolescents may have frequent physical complaints such as headaches, stomachaches, muscle aches, or fatigue. They may often be absent from school, may not be successful with academics, and may have outburst of anger, irritability, or crying. These troubled young people may have no interest in previously engaging activities, may abuse substances, and may have problems with their relationships.

Emslie (1997) identifies three common symptoms: irritable, oppositional, and negative behavior; excessive unexplained physical complaints such as headaches or stomachaches not related to clear causes; and hyperactivity/impulsivity with severe aggression accompanied by a denial that anything is wrong. The occurrence of these symptoms may be episodic. Emslie recommends multimodal treatment that could include individual counseling (cognitive-behavioral or interpersonal), family counseling, education, or pharmacological treatment.

Symptoms can vary in degree, intensity, and duration. Sciarra (2004) explains that the variations help in the identification of four different types of depression. Normal depression, the least severe type, occurs in everyone from time to time as a response to setbacks. Chronic depression is a more persistent feeling of sadness that may occur after an event or for no apparent reason. Crisis depression is a response to an external event and interferes with a person's life in a debilitating way. Finally, clinical depression is the most severe form, with extreme psychosocial impairment and thoughts of suicide occurring often. A three-part typology for depression outlines an affective type dominated by sadness and helplessness, a self-esteem type dominated by discouragement and negative self-esteem, and a guilt type dominated by guilt and self-destructive thoughts.

Some assessment instruments help screen for symptoms of depression. The Reynolds Adolescent Depression Scale (Reynolds, 1987) and the Reynolds Child Depression Scale (Reynolds, 1989), self-report measures, are both easy to administer and to take. The Beck Depression Inventory (Beck & Steer, 1993) and the Children's Depression Inventory (Kovacs, 1985) are two other possibilities.

INTERVENTIONS FOR DEPRESSION

Medication has been used for young people who are depressed even though the effectiveness of antidepressants for children and adolescents has not been established (Capuzzi & Gross, 2004). Counselors who work with depressed youth should ask them whether they are taking any medicines. Capuzzi and Gross have presented an excellent summary of pharmacological treatment of depression.

Some therapists (Mellin & Beamish, 2002; Mufson & Dorta, 2003) provide a treatment protocol using interpersonal theory for working with adolescents with depression. Others (Seligman, 1998) have linked depression to a model of learned helplessness, a response to failures to solve a problem or to improve a situation. According to that model, a person becomes convinced nothing attempted will make a difference. Therefore, the individual gives up and depression occurs. Some strategies for working with students who exhibit learned helpless follow. One recommendation is to give work in small steps so the child can develop a sense of mastery. Another strategy includes providing opportunities for selecting assignments or other choices. Giving feedback and explanations that help a child see cause-and-effect relationships may also help. Finally, encouraging depressed children to increase their sense of confidence by allowing them to identify their helpful behaviors and outcomes will support their overcoming learned helplessness (Sciarra, 2004). Cognitive models to treat depression (Capuzzi & Gross, 2004; Clarke, et al. 2003; Weersing & Brent, 2003; Weisz, et al. 2003) focus on replacing negative self-statements with positive self-talk and on developing other coping skills.

Counselors will want to teach life skills to any young person who is struggling. A life skills training program would include interpersonal communication skills, cognitive change strategies, and anxiety coping approaches. Interpersonal communication skills would include listening, reading social cues, and learning to say no. Cognitive change strategies involve problem solving, decision, making, self-control, and reframing thoughts. Relaxation, exercise, and imagery would be included in anxiety coping approaches. Counselors could help children improve in those areas by teaching, modeling, allowing the children to practice, giving feedback and reinforcement, and providing ways to practice the skills (Capuzzi & Gross, 2004).

SUICIDE

Why a child attempts suicide is a complex question. James and Gilliland (2005) offer two theories: Freud's theory of inward aggression and Durkheim's social integration approach. Those authors also outline some emergent theories such as biochemical malfunction, mental deficiencies, escape, and interactional explanations. Capuzzi and Gross (2004) add psychiatric disorders, poor self-efficacy, sexual or physical abuse, concerns over sexual identity, and other issues. Beautrais (2000) has reviewed risk factors for youth suicide in Australia and New Zealand. She identifies social and education disadvantage, childhood and family adversity, mental disorders, personal vulnerability, stressful life events and circumstances, and contextual factors as risks.

Some researchers believe that suicidal children are highly sensitive, have a low tolerance for frustration, and have feelings of depression, guilt, hostility, and anger that they are unable to express (Stefanowski-Harding, 1990). Popenhagen and Qualley (1998) contend that some young people "are just confused and do not know what to do" (p. 30). Nelson and Crawford (1990) ask counselors to indicate factors they thought contributed to suicidal attempts and completions in the group they saw. They rate family problems such as divorce, separation, and parental alcoholism as highly probable contributors. Peer pressure and pressure to achieve academically were ranked second and third, respectively. Drug abuse, physical handicap, and economic stress were ranked very low. Stefanowski-Harding (1990) also found several researchers who indicated that family problems related to death, divorce, separation, physical assault, rejection, or a suicidal parent were probably factors related to child suicide.

Sciarra (2004) summarizes behavioral and personality traits that may help identify children and adolescents at risk for suicide. He also incorporates suggestions for working with those students. Suicide may be seen as the only option for those who feel hopeless and helpless about improving their situation. Groups that focus on problem solving and building self-esteem may help these children. Students with a history of impulsive and aggressive behaviors may also be at great risk. Truancy, running away, and a lack of cooperation are warning signs of these problems, and groups that incorporate methods to control anger can help. Children who are isolated from peers and have no other support system are also a great risk. Small groups that include building relationship skills may be an important intervention for the alienated students. Low self-esteem is another trait that may indicate risk for suicide, with an obvious intervention being a self-esteem group. High stress and poor life skills are risk factors. A stress management group should be considered. The related trait of perfectionism also may indicate suicidal behavior with cognitive behavioral interventions aimed at changing the thoughts about having to be perfect. Students with cognitive deficits may have an increased risk for suicide. Finally, excessive, persuasive guilt is another risk factor, one that requires long-term counseling treatment.

In considering risk factors, Wise and Spengler (1997) and Capuzzi and Gross (2004) conclude that the single best predictor of suicide is persistent suicidal ideation. Suicide attempts also are a high-risk indicator. Capuzzi and Gross (2004) report that as many as 40 percent of people who have attempted suicide will make future attempts. Attempts that may be misclassified as accidents must also be considered. Parental suicide, depression, marital discord, family violence, child abuse and neglect, and poor academic performance were all identified as high-risk factors. Wise and Spengler (1997) recommend that evaluations include interviews with the child and family; observations of play looking for developmentally inappropriate activities, dangerous or reckless behaviors, or activities indicating death or violence fantasies; discussions about what the child is thinking and feeling; and perhaps psychological testing on instruments such as the Child Suicide Potential Scale.

Counselors who want to assess the risk for suicide may use a suicide interview. McWhirter, et al. (2004) state that interviews are the most effective way to assess suicide. With the young person counselors will probe for suicidal ideation (the frequency, duration, and intensity of thoughts of suicide), suicidal volition, a suicide plan, and the history of attempted suicide (Sciarra, 2004). Jacobsen, et al. (1994) suggest questions such as the following, among others, to interview children about suicidal ideation and behaviors:

- Did you ever feel so upset that you wished you were not alive or wanted to die?
- Did you ever do something that you knew was so dangerous that you could get hurt or killed?
- Did you tell anyone that you wanted to die or were thinking about killing yourself?
- What would happen if you died? What would that be like?

- How do you remember feeling when you were thinking about killing your-self or trying to kill yourself?
- Has anything happened recently that has been upsetting to you or your family?
- Have you had a problem with feeling sad, having trouble sleeping, not feeling hungry, losing your temper easily, or feeling tired all of the time recently? (p. 450)

Other interview protocols can be found in the guides of Holinger, Offer, Barter, and Bell (1994) and McWhirter (2002). The Adapted SAD PERSONS Scale (Juhnke, 1996), the Suicide Ideation Questionnaire (Reynolds, 1988), the Suicide Risk Screen (Thompson & Eggert, 1999), and the Scale of Suicide Ideation (Beck, et al. 1979) are other inventories. Although it is difficult to determine the factors associated with children's potential for suicide, guidelines such as these give counselors some basis for assessment of risks.

INTERVENTIONS FOR SUICIDE

Strategies for counselors working with suicidal children include those offered by Capuzzi (2002), Capuzzi and Gross (2004), James and Gililland (2005), McWhirter, et al. (2004), and Sciarra (2004):

1. Trust your suspicions if you think the young person may be self-destructive.
2. Never ignore threats, hints, and continued comments about destroying oneself, "leaving this world," "you're going to miss me," or "life is not worth living." These comments may be attention-getting, but children who use these techniques to get attention need help. Follow up the threat immediately with active listening in an attempt to discover the feelings or events that brought on the self-destructive feelings.
3. Tell the young person you are worried and listen to him or her in a non-judgmental and supportive way. Reinforce the youngster for seeking help.
4. Ask direct, specific questions about whether the child is considering suicide and whether there is a plan. Confront the child with your thoughts and feelings. You are not placing the thought in the child's mind, but you may provide an opening and opportunity for the child to discuss troublesome thoughts and feelings.
5. If suicidal children admit to self-destructive thoughts, ask about their plan. A well-thought-out plan is a significant danger signal.
6. Do not debate whether suicide is right or wrong.
7. Do not promise to keep the suicidal intentions a secret.
8. Do not leave the youngster alone if you think the threat of suicide is imminent. Ensure the safety of the child and that the appropriate adults who are responsible for the child have been notified.
9. You should remain actively involved with the youngster. Take an active, directive role to protect the youngster. In a crisis situation, do not attempt in-depth counseling until more stability is established. Monitor progress.

10. If you believe a child could be seriously contemplating suicide, suggest to the parents that they consult a doctor or psychiatrist. Hospitalization may be indicated for consistent care and monitoring. Inpatient treatment should be considered if the youngster is agitated, has not been eating, is overly tired or dehydrated, or has some other physical condition.

11. Use the resources that are available. Never hesitate to consult with someone thoroughly trained in suicide prevention—suicide-prevention centers, clinics, or psychiatrists—or refer suicidal children to them.

12. Assure the young person that something is being done, that the suicidal urges are serious, and that you are with them through this emergency. Tell them that survival is a step-by-step process, that help is available, and that asking for help directly is critical when the urges are strong.

13. Use techniques to enhance the self-concept of children who exhibit suicidal tendencies.

14. At a time of crisis, listen to the child carefully in a nonjudgmental manner. Have the child tell you everything that has happened during the previous few hours or days. You may gain some understanding or knowledge of factors contributing to the depression.

15. Suicidal children need permission to call, and the phone number of, a person (the counselor or another close and understanding friend) they feel they can talk with in times of distress.

16. The parents of a suicidal child should be made aware of the child's feelings and thoughts and helped to understand the situation without panic or guilt. Counsel with them about how to listen to and talk with the child. Consult with them concerning danger signals and make a plan for handling crises, should they arise.

17. Talk with suicidal children about what has happened in their lives recently. Losses of loved ones, pets, and other significant objects in the children's lives; feelings of personal failure; feelings of extreme shame or grief; and other traumatic events contribute to suicidal thoughts. Allow children to express their feelings without being judgmental, glossing over, or denying their right to these feelings.

18. Ask suicidal children to tell you about their fantasies or dreams. Ask them to draw a picture or write out their thoughts. These techniques often give the adult some insight into the child's thoughts and feelings.

19. Often, children do not understand death as final and irreversible; therefore, any child who is seriously disturbed or depressed needs careful attention.

20. The months after the threat also are crucial, and careful attention should continue until the conflict is completely resolved. A sudden recovery after severe depression may be a warning signal that the client has made a decision to end his or her life.

POSTSUICIDE INTERVENTIONS

Roberts (1995) has found that interventions made after a youth suicide can be preventive, as well as assist the grieving process. He recommends that a "psychological autopsy" be performed to try to understand all the factors that contributed to the child's decision to commit suicide, to determine why the death occurred at that particular time, to provide information to prevent other suicides, and to aid in the grieving process. Roberts urges schools to develop "postvention" plans to deal with a child's suicide during the school year and during vacation. McWhirter, et al. (2004) explain issues that should be addressed after a nonfatal suicide attempt.

Many writers in this area suggest psychological education and peer-group counseling as preventive measures. In addition to forming peer-counseling groups, Herring (1993) advocates psychological education as part of the middle school curriculum, that parents be involved in training sessions to help them understand the issue of suicide, and that counselors serve as consultants, providing information and knowledge about what to do and where to refer clients.

Siehl (1990) suggests that all schools should have a disaster plan to use in the event of a suicide, just as they have a plan for hurricanes, tornadoes, earthquakes, and other traumatic events. Some of Siehl's suggestions include:

1. Develop a team of resource people to handle the emotional crisis.
2. Present in-service training programs to the entire staff on the causes of suicide, warning signs, and sources of help for suicidal students.
3. Establish a network to inform all faculty members of the facts of the tragedy.
4. Designate special crisis centers for children needing additional help.
5. Develop a checklist of activities to be included in the classroom announcement.
6. Plan for cautions about the dangers in the days following a suicide.
7. Carry out home visits.
8. Develop guidelines for media coverage.
9. Develop procedures to continue alertness for several months.

Because helping professionals are aware that children may imitate other children who commit suicide, such a plan, together with psychological education and group counseling, is appropriate for counselors to consider.

FAMILY STRUCTURES

CHILDREN OF DIVORCE

The National Center for Health Statistics (2005) reports that almost 50 percent of all marriages in the United States end with divorce. That split may be devastating to the children involved who may feel confused, insecure, fearful, trapped, angry, unloved, and guilty (James & Gilliland, 2005). Counselors are often the support anchor the youngsters need in the midst of their changing world.

The lives and relationships of children in a divorcing family are profoundly affected—socially, economically, psychologically, and even legally. MacFarland and Tollerud (2004) suggest considering the stresses of divorce as a chain of events. It begins with the conflict before the divorce and continues with the aftermath that may involve relocations, loss of friends, changes in socioeconomic status, redefining relationships with both parents, and perhaps adjusting to the remarriage of one or both parents. Children must adjust to separation from one parent and formation of a new and different relationship with the other. A change in the family's economic status, possibly a change in the home and school environment, different parenting styles, custody battles, and sometimes a totally different lifestyle create feelings that may be positive or negative. Often, mothers who were totally involved in the care of children and home may have to go to work; many are unskilled and accept low-paying jobs. Children may be torn by conflicting loyalties or learn to manipulate the parents to get their own way. Children of divorced parents may be asked to assume the role of the absent parent and to fulfill physical or emotional responsibilities beyond their maturity level.

Wallerstein and Kelly (1996) identify these concerns of young people. The children are afraid. They may not understand who will provide food, housing, clothes, and protection. They may be concerned that if the marriage can fail, the parent–child relationship could also be terminated. The children may be sad; may have changes in sleeping, eating, and paying attention; and may have emotional swings. They may want more contact with the absent parent and may continue to hope for reconciliation. The children may be lonely, overlooked by parents who are preoccupied with the divorce. The youngsters may feel rejected and may have conflicting loyalties. Finally, they may be angry about all the changes in their lives.

Wallerstein and Kelly (1996) note that the "central hazard of divorce" is adverse effects on the child's development. Numerous studies suggest that the child's developmental level is related to the reaction that follows the separation. Wallerstein and Kelly (1996) and Wallerstein and Blakeslee (1989) suggest that infants respond mainly to the emotional reactions of their caretaker; for example, mothers or fathers under stress convey their feelings to the infant through their handling and verbal communication. Very young children appear to have many of their needs met regardless of the stress of the caretaker. Very young children are dependent and demand attention to their needs. Preschoolers (ages 3–5) have only a vague understanding of the family situation because of their limited cognitive development; thus, they often feel frightened and insecure, experience nightmares, and regress to more infantile behaviors. School-age children, who have more advanced cognitive and emotional development, see the situation more accurately. However, children ages 6 to 8 often believe the divorce was their fault ("If I had not been bad, Dad would not have left."), and children at this age often hold unrealistic hopes for a family reconciliation. They may feel loss, rejection, guilt, and loyalty conflicts. Ages 9 to 12 are a time when children are developing rapidly and rely on their parents for stability. They may become angry at the parent they blame for the divorce or may take a supportive role as they worry about their troubled parents. Because of their anxiety, they may develop somatic symptoms, engage in troublesome behaviors, or experience a decline in academic achievement. The parents' divorce during children's adolescent years brings a different set of developmental problems. Young people at this age are striving for independence and exploring their own sexuality. They need structure, limits, and guidance in dealing with their sexuality. They also may worry about their own relationships and the possibility of repeating their parents' mistakes.

Dacey and Kenny (1997) suggest that within 2 to 3 years after a divorce, parents and children have adjusted to their new life. Factors that affect that adjustment include the cumulative stress the youngsters experience after the divorce, the children's temperament and personality, and the children's ages. The results of research relating risk to age have been contradictory. In her 10-year follow-up, Wallerstein (1984) found that children who were very young at the time of the divorce seem to have suffered less—they remember less about that time in their lives. A multitude of factors other than developmental level may influence the effects of divorce on the child, including the amount of tension and conflict in the home, the length of time the child has lived with the conflict, the parents' reactions to the conflict, and the parents' personal adjustment to divorce and the resumption of parenting roles.

Wallerstein and Blakeslee (2003) describe "psychological tasks" that children of divorce must successfully resolve. These tasks are described in the following paragraphs.

Acknowledging the reality of the marriage breakup. Young children often experience terrifying fantasies, feel abandoned, and tend to deny the reality of the family situation. Because of their own stress, parents often fail to reassure children and help them understand the situation and their future. Older children also may experience some fantasies of disaster, reduced ability to think and cope, and even psychosomatic symptoms indicating their anxiety. Supportive counseling techniques, including listening, reflection, clarification, and problem solving, and perhaps stress-reduction techniques such as relaxation or guided imagery are appropriate for children working through this task. MacFarland and Tollerud (2004) propose writing a "Dear Abby" letter, creating a collage to illustrate the family situation, or holding support groups. Children should be given an opportunity to discuss, process, and resolve his or her feelings about the divorce to avoid being overwhelmed by negative feelings.

Wallerstein and Blakeslee (1989) state that the most critical factor in helping children through divorce is parental support. Both parents should talk with all the children together about the decision to divorce several days before one parent leaves the home. Children should be provided with a clear explanation about why their parents are divorcing, although they need not be told the details of an infidelity or other sexual problems. The parents should convey that, unfortunately, they have made a mistake in their marriage, but they remain committed to the family. According to the authors, understanding the divorce and its consequences is the first psychological task for children of divorcing families.

Disengaging from parental conflict and distress and resuming customary pursuits. The resolution of this task calls for the children to distance themselves from the crisis in their household and resume their normal learning tasks, outside activities, and friendships. Parents must work to help children keep their lives in order and not let the divorce overshadow all their activities by keeping familiar routines and encouraging participation in extracurricular activities. To maintain school work, group counseling and individual techniques directed toward improving academic achievement (for example, contingency contracting) are recommended.

Resolution of loss. Divorce brings not only loss of a parent but also often loss of familiar surroundings and possibly a different lifestyle. Wallerstein (1983) notes that the task of resolving these losses may be the most difficult: "At its core this task demands that the child overcome his or her profound sense of rejection, of humiliation, of unlovability, and of powerlessness which the one parent's departure so often engenders" (p. 237). Wallerstein and Blakeslee (1989) suggest that a consistent pattern of visitation by the absent parent and an emphasis on building a new and positive relationship can help children through this stage. Unfortunately, many children do not have this relationship with the absent parent and remain disappointed for years. They feel rejected by the absent parent and, thus, unlovable and unworthy. Role-playing, puppetry, writing, drawing, feelings, charades, and other techniques can encourage children to express their feelings.

Individual and group sessions focusing on building self-esteem may be helpful—for example, strengths testing, peer teaching, finding the child a "buddy," and the techniques of cognitive restructuring.

Resolving anger and self-blame. Because divorce is a voluntary decision by one or both parents, children tend to blame them for being selfish and unresponsive to their needs, or they may blame themselves for the breakup of the family. Intense anger at one or both parents is characteristic of children of divorce, especially older children. The researchers found that the child's ability to forgive himself or herself for the divorce or lack of reconciliation was a significant step toward forgiving the parents and reconciling the relationship. There are some excellent children's books that can help them understand the divorce process and the reality that they are not to blame for the divorce. Most of these books emphasize that sometimes adults just cannot live together or resolve their differences. Counselors can recommend specific books for the developmental level of their clients and discuss the books with the children. MacFarland and Tollerud (2004) have some recommendations.

The child's intense anger often results in acting-out behavior. A consistent, structured environment at home and at school provides some of the security the child needs during this period of turmoil and change. Group counseling that focuses on role-playing, play therapy, drawing, and writing can help children express their anger and feelings of guilt. Group problem-solving discussions help children find constructive ways of handling their feelings.

Accepting the permanence of divorce. Wallerstein (1983) points out that the fantasy of a reunited family persists tenaciously for children of divorce, even after the parents marry other partners. Whereas losing a parent through death has finality about it, the fact that both partners are alive contributes to the continuing fantasy of restoring the intact family. Reality therapy may help the child accept the permanence of divorce. Group counseling with other children who are going through divorce or who have experienced it may also help. Drawings of the family before the divorce and at the present time, good and bad family changes since the divorce, and filmstrips and books about divorce and other family lifestyles (the stepfamily or single-parent family) often stimulate excellent discussions.

Achieving realistic hope regarding relationships. During the adolescent years, the child of divorce must resolve issues surrounding relationships—learning to take a chance in relationships while knowing full well that they might not be fulfilling or that they might fail. Doing so requires that the child feel lovable and worthy. Children often feel rejected, unlovable, and unworthy because they feel guilty over the divorce or because they believe that one or both parents rejected them and cared little about their feelings and welfare. Wallerstein and Blakeslee (2003) note that some adolescents engage in acting-out behavior (promiscuity, alcohol or drug abuse, among other similar behaviors) that indicates low self-esteem. An important task for adolescents is realizing they can love and be loved. They must learn to be open in relationships while knowing that divorce or a loss is possible. According to Wallerstein and Blakeslee, effective resolution of this last psychological task of "taking a chance on love" leads to freedom from the psychological trauma of divorce and provides second chances for children of these families.

Wallerstein and Blakeslee (2003) conclude that the effects of divorce are much more pervasive and longer lasting than originally thought. In earlier research, Wallerstein and Kelly (1996) had reported that boys showed more signs of trauma from the divorce during their developmental years than girls did. Wallerstein and Blakeslee (1989) found a sleeper effect—the girls' problems became more apparent as they entered young adulthood. Twenty years after Wallerstein began her initial research, she found parents' continuing anger still a factor in their children's lives. Many of the sample of children, now adults, were underachievers or drank heavily; a few had been involved in serious crimes. One third of the girls had relationship problems.

McConnell and Sim (2000) report on a successful innovative counseling service offered to children of divorce or children and custodial parents. The authors emphasize thorough assessments to determine the most effective way to intervene. DeLucia-Waack and Gerrity (2001) provide a group counseling intervention for elementary school students. The group work includes normalizing the experiences and feelings of the children, creating a safe and supportive environment, and helping children express their feelings and develop new coping skills.

Counselors working with the parents of children involved in a divorce can be of assistance by providing consultative advice. In their comprehensive article attempting to link intervention to basic research on children of divorce, Grych and Fincham (1992) also suggest helping parents understand how their behavior affects their children's adjustment and assist them in minimizing the effect of the divorce on children. Parents and counselors need to remember that adjustment after a divorce takes time for a child and requires continuing understanding and reassurance. Parent group meetings can help parents understand the problems their children are experiencing, learn new methods for communicating with their children, try new methods of discipline, and resolve some of their own frustration. Some suggestions that counselors may want to offer parents are as follows:

1. Talk with the child about the divorce at his or her cognitive level (counselors may want to rehearse this with the parents). Explain what has happened at the child's level of understanding and try to relate the experience to one that the child may have had. Emphasize that the child is not at fault. Keep the lines of communication open so the child's misconceptions or fears are recognized immediately. Avoid blaming or criticizing the other parent and relating all the unpleasant details.
2. Plan for ways to make the child's life as stable and consistent as possible, even though changes may be necessary. Household routines, school schedules, and consistent discipline help children understand that their world is not completely wrecked. Involve teachers, counselors, ministers, grandparents, and other support systems.
3. Avoid using the children as go-betweens to carry messages ("The child support check is late!") or to find out about the other parent's life ("What does the apartment look like?"). Children love both parents and are already torn by conflicting loyalties.
4. Arrange for regular visits from the absent parent to assure the children that they are loved by both parents. Children are sometimes disappointed by absent parents who fail to call or come for a visit. Custodial parents need to provide a lot of love and reassurance at these times.
5. Talk with the children about the future. Involve them in the planning without overwhelming them with problems. They need to know what to expect.
6. Children experiencing a divorce in their family are still children at a particular developmental level. Avoid asking them to assume responsibilities beyond their capabilities—being the man of the family, babysitting younger children, or taking on excessive household chores.

Although many children of divorce do experience increased risks for social, emotional, and academic difficulties, others have successfully adjusted to the disruption and do not display significant signs of distress as a result of the experience. Gately and Schwebel (1992) have found some areas in which the children experienced favorable outcomes:

1. *Maturity,* because they tended to assume greater responsibility for chores
2. *Improved self-esteem,* because they coped effectively with their changing life's circumstances
3. *Empathy,* due to increased concern for family members
4. *Androgyny,* as a result of seeing models not confined by stereotypical sex roles

Positive factors in their lives that contributed to the development of these attributes were positive personality, supportive family environment, and supportive social environment (Gately & Schwebel, 1992).

CHILDREN IN STEPFAMILIES

Coleman, et al. (2000) say that one third of children will live in a stepfamily. This combination of adults and a child or children from a previous relationship may also be referred to as a blended family. Whatever the terminology used to describe the change, joining two families into one presents children with another set of unique problems with which to cope at a time when the effects of the biological parents' divorce may still be troublesome. Because the step-family is not considered a "normal" family, expectations and relationships are more ambiguous and complex. Not only are cultural and social guidelines unclear but children who are members of two households, moving in and out, also have ambiguous and complex home guidelines and schedules. Adults and children experience changes in roles, alliances, parenting arrangements, house-hold responsibilities, rules, expectations, and demands. For children who are attempting to regain stability after the first family breakup, this lack of struc-ture may bring additional stresses and strains.

MacFarland and Tollerud (2004) explain four categories of issues in blended families. In the early development of the new family, issues about loy-alty, loss, attachment, and fantasies of reconciliation may occur, as well as redefining roles and feelings of rejection. Developing family issues, a second category, includes discipline, family roles, sibling conflict, time with the non-custodial parent, and moving between families. A third category is feelings about self and others that may be influenced by negative images of stepfami-lies. Children may act out their stresses in school and may hide their emotions. If the new parents have a child of their own, stepchildren may feel less valued and other difficulties may arise. Adult issues that relate to the new family involve financial support and alimony, competition among parents, continuing conflicts, and different parenting styles in the blended family.

Papernow (1995) outlines the following stages of stepfamily development:

I. Early stage

   a. *Fantasy stage*—there is the dream the new family will be ideal and everyone will love each other
   b. *Immersion stage*—reality indicates that something in the family is different and may not be right
   c. *Awareness stage*—identifying new position in family structure and clarifying understanding of associated feelings

II. Middle stage

   a. *Mobilization*—more conflict may emerge as the new family begins to move toward a new structure
   b. Action stage—the new family reaches consensus on the family structure and operation

III. Later stages

   a. *Contact stage*—deeper stepfamily relationships are formed

 b. *Resolution stage*—step relationships become more intimate and solid; family norms and procedures are established

Families and individual members proceed through these stages at varying rates. Papernow (1995) believes counselors must assess the family and individual dynamics to really understand the developmental levels of members and the structure of the stepfamily.

Counselors need to help both parent and children in the stepfamily to find their appropriate roles and clearly define expectations of all members. Defining these new roles requires time and patience. Thoughts and feelings must be expressed and clarified, routines and expectations established, visitations with other parents planned, and discipline guidelines agreed on. Play therapy is especially helpful for counseling with younger children. Drawings, journals, bibliocounseling, and group counseling with other children in stepfamilies may assist older children in working through their feelings and concerns. Family counseling is encouraged to help the newly organized family increase awareness and acceptance of each other and individual differences, facilitate problem solving, and build support for each other.

Zeppa and Norem (1993) have tested the generally accepted conclusion that stepfamilies have more stress compared with first families. Although acknowledging their study's flaws, the authors conclude that significantly fewer differences divide first families and stepfamilies than had been thought. Their results showed that stepfamilies experience more stress, but they suggest that the idea that stepfamilies are different from first families and have more problems may be due to socioeconomic factors or bias against stepfamilies.

It has been a generally accepted conclusion that children in stepfamilies have more difficulties than children growing up in nuclear families, and they are often labeled delinquent or thought not to be well adjusted because of the crisis of divorce and development of the new family. Coleman and Ganong (1995) point out that stepfamilies must deal with cultural stereotypes that may interfere with the establishment of good relationships within the family. Step-parents often are perceived as unloving or abusive—the "wicked stepmother," for instance. *Stepchild* is a word often used to describe someone who is rejected or unwanted. Love and acceptance of a new father or mother, of brothers and sisters, does not occur instantly. The child may be angry at the "replacement" of a parent and the intrusion of other children into his or her life. The adjustment may be particularly difficult for adolescents, who are dealing with their own sexuality, growing maturity, need for independence, and search for identity. Visher and Visher (1995) recognize that stepfamilies often experience disorganization and dysfunction, but warn against "over-pathologizing" their needs.

Counselors need to give youngsters in blended families emotional support. The young people must come to terms with loss, their feelings of helplessness, role frustrations, and communication difficulties. Counselors may use creative arts to help children gain insight, consider relationships, and develop coping strategies. MacFarland and Tollerud (2004) recommend kinetic art, creative drama, role-play, bibliotherapy, and group counseling.

We have suggested that periodically counselors need to examine their own attitudes and beliefs about certain clients to maintain the highest levels of objectivity and efficiency. Because negative stereotypes of step-parents are common, people in the helping professions may sometimes unwittingly adopt stereotypical thinking and evaluate step-parents or stepchildren clients in light of these negative stereotypes.

In addition, schools need to evaluate their activities in light of their effects on stepfamilies—Do policies and activities allow step-parents' participation in the child's school life? Do special occasions such as Mother's Day and Father's Day include references to step-parents? Are living arrangements and name differences clearly indicated in records to avoid embarrassment? School may be the one place a child in a new step-parent home finds structure and familiarity. Counselors can help school personnel make the environment more comfortable and accepting for children in a changing world.

CHILDREN IN SINGLE-PARENT HOMES

Twenty-three percent of children in the United States are being raised in mother-only families (McWhirter, et al. (2004). Two-fifths of single mothers have never been married (Bianchi & Caspar, 2000). Single mothers are vulnerable economically because their earnings are usually low and many do not receive child support. Single motherhood appears to be strongly related to poverty, and never-married mothers are particularly apt to end up receiving welfare. Poverty, of course, has a strong correlation with children's low academic achievement, conduct disorders, and even juvenile crime.

Richards and Schmiege (1993) were concerned that most of the literature on single-parent homes focused on the negative effects for children experiencing divorce and not living in the ideal two-parent household. They studied 60 single-parent mothers and 11 single-parent fathers to learn more about the problems faced in the homes and the strengths identified by the parents. The single-parent mothers most often said that money was their biggest problem area, with role and task overload following. Social life and problems with their ex-spouses were rated third and fourth. Single-parent fathers rated role and task overload and problems with ex-spouses as first and second on their list of problems, with financial problems ranking last. Both single-parent mothers and single-parent fathers rated their parenting skills as their main strength. Family management (being organized, dependable, and able to coordinate schedules) was second for both groups, and good communication and personal growth were also rated as strengths by both groups.

The authors suggest that, given the likelihood of young people living in a single-parent household, a stronger emphasis on family education is necessary. They encourage their readers not to accept negative stereotypes and to acknowledge that single-parent homes do have strengths.

Downey (1994) compares the school performance of children from single-mother and single-father families with the performance of children living with both parents. The single fathers were better educated than single mothers in the sample, but the children of single fathers did not earn higher grades. Neither group performed as well in school as the children from two-parent families. Economic problems may be affecting the children in single-parent homes, especially single-mother households. The researchers suggest that single fathers spend less time talking to their children, and less parental involvement in the children's school and play activities may be a significant factor.

Counseling strategies to help children in single-parent homes are similar to many described for children of divorce and children in stepfamilies. The counselor must help the child deal with feelings of loss, whether the loss resulted from divorce, separation, or death. Emotions must be recognized and discussed. These children need stability, security, and consistency in their lives. Therefore, counselors may want to recommend to the child's parent and other family members that they join a support group to help the family reorganize effectively after the loss. Counselors in schools can provide group activities for children of single-parent homes to help them discuss their fears, concerns, and feelings about having only one parent in the home. Crosbie-Burnett and Pulvino (1990) describe a classroom guidance program for children in nontraditional families that focuses on eight aspects of nontraditional families and includes topics such as having less money, feelings of anger or sadness, questions friends ask, and time alone.

As stated earlier in this section, considerable research substantiates that children from single-parent homes have a higher rate of conduct disorders and other adjustment problems than children from intact homes. However, well-adjusted children live in single-parent homes. Counselors must be careful not to allow generalizations or personal bias to interfere with their objectivity in working with these children.

Homeless Children

Homelessness means a person's primary residence is a shelter, emergency housing, a hotel or motel, or another public space such as parks, cars, abandoned buildings, or aqueducts (National Coalition for the Homeless, 2005). Many communities have concerns about the increasing number of homeless families. McWhirter, et al. (2004) report from a conference of mayors who talked about requests for food assistance increasing by 19 percent and requests for shelter increasing by 22 percent. More than half of the emergency shelter requests could not be met. The mayors identified a lack of affordable housing as the primary cause cited for homelessness. Families wait an average of 16 months for public housing. Families with children are the fastest growing group of homeless people, representing 40 percent of that group. Children younger than 18 represent at least 39 percent of the homeless population (National Coalition for the Homeless, 2005).

Styron, et al. (2000) and the National Coalition for the Homeless (2005) describe homeless families. They are more likely to be families of color; to be young, with parents who probably were abused as children and battered as adults; and to have limited social networks. In a survey across 10 locations,

25 percent of the women who were homeless mothers reported having been physically abused during the past year. Domestic violence has been identified as a primary cause of homelessness (National Coalition for the Homeless, 2005).

According to Schmitz, et al. (1995), homelessness has a very negative impact on a child's physical, educational, and emotional development. The child's life lacks continuity, consistency, privacy, cleanliness, permanency, and belonging, which may result in unacceptable behaviors such as acting out, fighting, restlessness, depression, moodiness, and low frustration tolerance. Children of homeless parents often are prohibited from entering school because of requirements such as residency, proof of age, communication, and lack of school records. Other barriers include transportation and other enrollment requirements (Strawser, et al. 2000). The children often perform poorly in school and have erratic attendance (Office of Elementary and Secondary Education, 2000).

If the children do enter school, placement and support services may be inadequate. Remediation and tutoring in basic skills is the most frequently identified educational need of homeless children, according to Rafferty (1995). Congress passed a law in 1987 requiring that homeless children be admitted to schools and integrated into the present public educational system. Homeless children must also receive services comparable with those received by other children, that is, transportation, meals, and programs for the disabled or gifted (Rafferty, 1995). Counselors should also be aware of the need for day care, counseling, and nutritional and educational support for homeless children.

Daniels (1992) states that school can provide a "reprieve from the frightening realities of wandering the streets" (p. 104), as well as a sense of normalcy in a child's life. She suggests interventions based on Maslow's hierarchy of needs and the developmental guidelines of Erik Erikson (see Chapters 1 and 2). Daniels developed a six-session group counseling unit to increase self-esteem and address developmental concerns. The activities include an assessment of self-esteem; drawing a family portrait of those with whom the children lives, as well as where they live; drawings of feelings; sharing an accomplishment of which they are proud; identifying stress and worries in their lives; and, finally, drawing a group mural. These and other group activities can increase self-esteem and promote peer acceptance and appreciation. Strawser et al. (2000) have identified other direct and indirect ways school counselors can help homeless children.

Counselors can help by facilitating the child's entrance into school, helping the child and family find some kind of stability in their lives, assisting the child in overcoming excessive fears and distrust of people, and being alert to the possibility of abuse. Counselors need a variety of referral resources to help the child meet physical needs such as shelter, food, and medical care. Assessing the child's educational level and helping him or her develop social skills requires time, energy, and patience.

Masten, et al. (1993) compared 159 homeless children with 62 low-income children living in a home. As would be expected, the homeless children experienced more stress and disrupted schooling and friendships than did the low-income children in homes. The researchers conclude that homeless children's behavioral problems are related more to parental distress and adversity than to housing conditions or income.

Vostanis, et al. (2001) have investigated the mental health problems and social supports among homeless mothers and children. They emphasize the need for multiple levels of social support.

The counselor must avoid being influenced by generalizations about the homeless such as that they are mentally ill, are unmotivated, could find a job if they wanted to, or abuse alcohol or drugs. Education is the best method for overcoming the problems of the homeless, but it requires a broad spectrum of services within the school and community. The counselor may be called on to coordinate these services and act as an advocate for the child.

CHILDREN AND VIOLENCE

Antisocial behavior refers to behavior that conflicts with social norms. It may sometimes include criminal activity. McWhirter, et al. (2004) list the most common antisocial behaviors of young people as: (1) aggression and coercive misbehaviors in the family; (2) problems in school that often lead to a diagnosis of conduct disorder; (3) community and school problems such as fighting and property destruction; (4) minor criminal activity such as vandalism, substance use, and running away; (5) major criminal activity such as theft, robbery, and larceny; and (6) violence and gang membership. Information related to the incidence of juvenile arrests is provided by the U.S. Department of Justice (August 2005). Antisocial behavior, aggression, delinquency, and violence have common antecedents and consequences.

James and Gilliland (2005) ponder the reasons for violence in young people and list multiple causes: poor parenting, disenfranchised students, lack of role models, hate crimes, bullying, media violence, and other causes. Finn (2004) acknowledges that many factors contribute to youth violence. Finn defines violence as action or threat of action that would result in intimidation, coercion, physical harm, or personal injury (p. 353). The U.S. Department of Health and Human Services (2001) disseminated a report of the Surgeon General that included statistically relevant facts associated with youth violence, such as a history of criminal offenses, substance abuse, weak social connections, antisocial delinquent peers, and gang membership. The report also identified subcategories. Late-onset characteristics of violent young people occur after puberty. Those variables include all of those above, as well as risk-taking behaviors, criminal activities, and violence toward other people. Early-onset risk factors emerge before puberty. Factors such as poor parent–child relationships, little supervision or discipline, and having neglectful parents, as well as poor school performance and attitude relate to the incidence of youth who are violent. McWhirter, et al. (2004) summarize with a progressive model of aggression and violence that can be found in their volume.

Children may be the witnesses to violence or the perpetrators of that action. Chronic exposure to violence has significant detrimental effects on children (McWhirter, et al. 2004). Graves, et al. (1993) suggest that children need an opportunity to talk about the violence they witness, and that mental health professionals should obtain specialized training in treating children who witness violence and experience symptoms of stress. They also urge society to ensure a safe environment for children to grow and develop.

Osofsky (1995) surveyed children and mothers exposed to violence and found that there is an impact on young children even though they may not verbalize their feelings. Young children exposed to violence are more apt to exhibit nonverbal reactions such as behavioral or adjustment problems, which may be the result of witnessing violence or of parental fears of violence, which severely limit the child's activities.

School-age children exposed to violence often experience anxiety, have sleep disturbances, have difficulty paying attention and concentrating, and are less likely to explore and play freely. Soriano, et al. (1994) point out that the chances of children being a victim of violent crime are greater than being hurt in a traffic accident, and youth of color are at greater risk. According to Underwood (2003), homicide and suicide contribute to 25 percent of deaths for 10- to 25-year-old individuals. Soriano, Soriano, and Jimenez (1994) suggest that racism, classism, sexism, and racial privilege are related to school violence and are influenced by socioeconomic variables such as poverty, lack of affordable housing and health care, adult joblessness, overcrowded schools, racial stereotypes, and economic exclusion.

Stephans (1994) reports that many educational professionals believe that the increase in school violence is not due to the educational process, but rather reflects factors such as societal changes, the breakdown of the family unit, and role modeling of violence in the media. The 10 things perceived to be the most likely contributors to the increase in violence were lack of rules or family structure, lack of parental supervision and involvement, modeling parental acting-out behavior, drug/alcohol abuse, violence in movies, violence on television, student poor self-esteem or emotional disturbance, gang activities, violent games, and changes in the traditional family. However, Pietrzak, et al. (1998) found in their survey of elementary and middle school personnel that those responding not only feared students but also feared their parents. Thirty-two percent indicated they were worried about verbal threats and attacks from students' parents, and 21 percent were concerned or very concerned.

McRary (1998) interviewed Dr. Helen Smith, who at that time was writing a book entitled *Killer Kids: Why Kids Kill and What We Can Do to Stop It*. Dr. Smith indicated that youth who kill feel deeply alienated, believe no one cares about them, and feel that no one else has rights. Smith suggested that it is not because these young people have low self-esteem that they kill, but rather they kill because they have inflated self-esteem and blame everyone but themselves for their problems. Dr. Smith cautioned that warning signs show up as early as the preschool years and suggested looking for signs such as head banging and screaming uncontrollably, fire setting or a fascination with fire, and torturing or killing animals.

Fitzsimmons (1998) explains that aggressive children often misinterpret social cues and may judge a neutral situation as hostile. They have poor coping skills and low frustration for tolerance. Holmes and Holmes-Lonergan (2004) guess they may be attempting to get a high status at school to counteract the critical family environment. Girls may exhibit "social aggression" such as gossiping, spreading rumors, and excluding others (Underwood, 2003). Brown and Parsons (1998) provide a chart that can help with identifying aggressive behaviors, and Studer (1996) has developed an identification model for triggers to aggression.

All the above authors (Brown & Parsons, 1998; Fitzsimmons, 1998; Studer, 1996; Underwood, 2003) urge early, comprehensive interventions. Bay-Hinitz and Wilson (2005) suggest a group play therapy intervention for preschool children. The intervention involves cooperative games to reduce aggression and increase cooperation. PEACE is a school curriculum designed to increase empathy skills and to interpret social cues. Salmon (2003) provides further details. Aggression Replacement Training focuses on the strengths and potential of children to help them change (Roth & Striepling-Goldstein, 2003).

Dealing with violence as a result of societal change may require that the role of the school be re-examined, according to Pietrzak, et al. (1998). They suggest that the school may need to take a more central role in the socialization of many children, including parent education programs, parent involvement activities, before- and after-school programs, and use of the school as the center of community services for families and children. Finn (2004) recommends schools target bullying: coercive verbal comments, physical intimidation, or a combination of these. The impact of bullying on the victims is that of chronic, systematic terrorism. The bully also suffers negative consequences, and schools in which bullying is tolerated are hostile environments (Olweus, et al. 1999). The Bullying Prevention Program is designed to address bullying issues at the school, in the classroom, and with individuals, and it has had impressive outcomes (Finn, 2004).

Morrissey (1998) reports that schools often contact the National School Safety Center for assistance after a violent incident. The officials of this Center make the following recommendations, according to Morrissey (1998, p. 36):

- Establish clear behavioral standards.
- Provide adequate adult presence and supervision.
- Enforce the rules fairly and consistently.
- Supervise closely and sanction offenders consistently.
- Cultivate parental support.
- Control campus access.
- Create partnerships with outside agencies.
- Believe they can make a difference.

The Schools without Violence program developed by the International Alliance for Invitational Education and co-directed by William Purkey has reported success with its program focusing on the five "P's" that make up a school system—processes, programs, places, people, and policies. According to Purkey (as cited in Morrissey, 1998), the goal of the program is to make school a more exciting, satisfying, and enriching experience for all.

Osofsky (1995) offers public policy initiatives for dealing with children and violence. She recommends a national campaign to change attitudes toward violence and tolerance of violent behaviors that would require politicians and media leaders to cooperate in bringing about change. In addition, she recommends a family and community-centered approach to addressing violence prevention, and additional education about the negative effects of violence, as well as about the dangers of firearms.

In addition to treatment, children need the tools to resolve their difficulties without resorting to violent behavior. Children who learn problem-solving skills or conflict resolution are less impulsive and aggressive and tend to be more rational and patient. The basic principles of conflict resolution are similar to the problem-solving strategies described previously: Listen objectively to the other person, identify the problem, brainstorm for alternatives, agree on common grounds, and find a win-win solution. Most programs discuss the nature of the conflicts encountered by children, incorporate rules for attacking the problem (not the person) and treating others with respect, and emphasize accepting responsibility for one's behavior. Participants may also discuss issues related to diversity, power, and anger control. Role-plays, simulations, stories, and discussions provide practice for children learning the new skills required for conflict resolution.

Peer mediators are trained to facilitate the conflict resolution process. Lane and McWhirter (1992, 1996) describe a peer mediation model for elementary and middle school children with 19 steps for the mediation. Peer mediators learn specific actions concerning introductions, listening, ascertaining "wants," and finding solutions. Peer mediators are trained in the steps and must make a complete report of all interactions at the completion of the process.

Johnson and Johnson (1994) believe that all students should learn to negotiate and mediate and have the experience of serving as a mediator. They cite studies showing that conflict resolution and mediation training results in less student-to-student conflicts and increased student management of their conflicts without adult intervention.

Johnson and Johnson (1996) have conducted a comprehensive review of the literature describing conflict resolution and peer mediation programs in elementary and secondary school. They describe the types of programs found as those that train a small number of students or the total student body to be mediators; conflict resolution programs that are preventive and curriculum-based, designed to teach students alternatives to violent behavior; and conflict resolution and peer mediation programs that teach students interpersonal and small-group skills to resolve conflicts, or academically oriented programs that teach the cognitive skills necessary for conflict resolution, or structural change approaches that emphasize team building in the school. The most common types of conflicts addressed in these programs were verbal harassment, arguments, rumors and gossip, physical fights, and dating/relationship issues. Although they found methodological problems with the research reviewed, they conclude that "conflict resolution and peer mediation programs do seem to be effective in teaching students integrative negotiation and mediation procedures. After training, students tend to use these conflict strategies, and constructive outcomes tend to result" (p. 498). In fact, McWhirter, et al. (2004) discuss the ripple effects of peer mediation program implementation. They cite improved school climate, less playground problems, less referrals to the principal's office or to the nurse, and less conflict in homes as benefits.

Carruthers, et al. (1996) also have reviewed the literature on conflict resolution programs. They found reports that indicated higher levels of student academic performance associated with the integration of conflict resolution principles and practices into the curriculum, learned prosocial attitudes, and the generalization of skills in actual conflict situations. Although admitting there are theoretical and methodological problems with many studies, the writers encourage practitioners to continue to conduct limited studies. They conclude that many researchers sharing their results will yield useful information that can add to the understanding of the field.

Gangs[1]

The U.S. Department of Justice (June 2005) highlights national youth gang activity that is reported by law enforcement agencies. The summary concludes that most gangs, gang members, and gang-related homicides are concentrated in larger cities. The U.S. Department of Justice estimates there are more than 16,000 different gangs and more than 500,000 active gang members. In contrast, James and Gilliland (2005) and Burnham (2004) state that gangs are in all geographic locales, all socioeconomic environments, and all ethnicities. They describe five types of gangs. The homegrown copycats/wannabes constitute one type. Another type is the homegrown survivalist, Aryan nation, neo-Nazi, extreme right-wingers based on political and/or religious philosophies. Transients from a megagang are offshoots from large metropolitan groups who have relocated. Megagangs opening new territory may occur when the groups try to find new territory to sell their drugs or other wares. Finally, James and Gilliland discuss the small gangs started for a variety of reasons the authors call smorgasbord home boys.

Strong (1998) believes that there are critical socioeconomic factors encouraging the development of gangs: (1) the erosion of the family including growth in the number of teen parents, no family or social support systems available to the young person, and the development of values from the media; (2) community depersonalization or the loss of community attachment and sense of responsibility; (3) and economic malaise, resulting in poverty and hopelessness. McWhirter,

[1]Sincere appreciation is expressed to Donna Maxwell Casteel, The University of Tennessee, for her contribution to the material on gangs and gang membership.

et al. (2004) include low commitment to school, high levels of antisocial behavior, low commitment to positive peers, and friends who are using drugs. Strong (1998) contends that society must focus on risk factors predictive of gang involvement; encourage "protective factors" such as positive relationships with family, teachers, and other adults; and intervene early with multiple prevention and intervention strategies.

Scheidlinger (1994) has studied adolescent group violence since the 1960s and 1970s. He finds that adolescent peer groups differ today from the organized crime of the past in which group loyalty was common. Today, group identity is lacking due to what Scheidlinger attributes to de-individuation caused by a lack of self-awareness and a lack of self-inhibition. Scheidlinger contends that preventive intervention efforts may be difficult because of this de-individuation, as well as the other psychological factors present in these groups.

The Tennessee Law Enforcement Training Academy (1997) profiled the typical gang member, focusing on both individual and cultural characteristics. The Academy found that the average gang member came from a single-parent or unstable family structure, received no discipline or overly harsh discipline in the home, had poor relationships with parents and peers, could not express emotion appropriately, achieved poorly in school and in other endeavors, had a history of abuse, and was usually average or above average in intelligence.

Nawojczyk (1998) cautions parents that they should be concerned about their child's involvement with gangs if he or she:

- Buys or is obsessed with one particular color of clothing or shows a desire for a particular logo
- Wears sagging pants
- Wears excessive jewelry and distinctive designs and wears them only on the right or left side of the body
- Is obsessed with gangster-influenced music, videos, and movies, and imitates talk or lifestyle observed through media
- Withdraws from family with an accompanying attitude change
- Associates with undesirables and breaks curfew rules
- Develops an unusual desire for privacy and secrecy about peers
- Uses hand signs or there is evidence of peculiar drawings or language on school books, clothing, or the body
- Possesses unexplained cash or goods, that is, clothing and jewelry
- Exhibits possible use of alcohol and drugs with attitude change

Obviously, parents and teachers should look for these signs as part of an overall behavioral pattern. A student wearing baggy pants to school one day may means his pants were purchased a size too big or that he prefers that style, rather than that he is a gang member.

Parks (1995) reviewed the literature on school-related gangs and reported that gangs operate at every level of school, including at the elementary level. She found that a newly developed form of gang activity revolved around providing "protection" from threats or assaults—that is, giving "permission" to enter or leave the school or pass through an area or to use a certain school facility, which is extortion. Arthur and Erickson (1992) report that school gang activities include drug sales and use, graffiti to indicate "owned" territory, roaming of hallways, class disruptions, assaults (especially on female students), and possession of weapons.

Bender and Leone (1996) interviewed leaders and others who worked with youth and gangs. Among the opinions expressed about how street gangs can be controlled were to send a message to youth that violence never resolves issues and to the general society to unite against "thugs," eradicate poverty and despair by providing jobs and other opportunities, toughen laws on gangs whereas providing support for victims and protection for witnesses, utilize data tracking systems, intercede in schools and communities, and pass laws dealing with specific gang problems. Another person interviewed opposed toughening laws and advocated prosecuting the crime because of the broad and vague definition of gangs and suggested that a return to high principles and moral responsibility was necessary. Still another person interviewed made a strong argument for guiding and empowering youth to overcome their need to join a gang. The differing opinions found in these interviews underscore the conclusion that society does not know enough about gangs to be able to develop effective prevention and intervention programs. The best solution may be different for differing groups and may require a combination of techniques working together.

Suggestions for controlling gangs include creating a more culturally relevant structure and curriculum for students, encouraging in-school gang mediation programs, and offering after-school activities as alternatives to gang membership (Parks, 1995). Parks recommends obtaining community agreement about the nature of gang incidents and organizing external advisory groups from the community, including religious organizations. Parks also believes that parents, families, and teachers must be involved as reinforcing groups to change gang behavior. They need instruction in understanding, monitoring, and correcting violent behavior.

Burnham (2004) and Strong (1998) suggest similar procedures for addressing gang behavior. They recommend providing experiences to promote understanding of other cultures and values, developing conflict resolution and peer mediation procedures to handle conflict, providing training about gang issues for parents, encouraging involvement in the gang reduction program, developing re-entry programs for suspended students that provide structure and positive role models, and avoiding the use of fear or intimidation tactics with individuals in gangs.

Huesman (1994) concludes that comprehensive program planning is necessary to deal with the current problems, and that it must be individualized to meet specific needs. Active input from previous gang members was crucial to understanding the need for youth's involvement with gangs. James and Gilliland (2005) tout the SARA model (scanning, analysis, response, assessment). This program involves people such as parents, service clubs, businesses, churches, the justice system, and other community agencies and organizations. They trade information and work for change in the school and the community. They begin by identifying problems and publicizing their findings. The information is analyzed and presented in concrete, measurable terms. The response phase involves developing options based on the gathered information, then selecting and implementing a response. The phase of assessment gauges the effectiveness of the response. The comprehensive program may well lead to safer schools.

SUMMARY

Many children have special concerns, challenges that may create troubling situations in their lives. This chapter has highlighted a small portion of some of the more common difficulties some children may face. As with any young people, counselors begin by developing a knowledge base of relevant information and then listening to children to learn about their world and their needs. Counselors maintain a careful study of current practices and of valuable resources to be effective, efficient helping professionals. In the situations we have highlighted, many authors emphasize working with parents, teachers, and other people who touch the youngsters' lives. They also suggest building strong connections with the children as the counseling partnership develops. Children always need to receive respect and hope from their counselors, no matter how discouraging the world might be during difficult times.

Websites for Counseling Children with Special Concerns

Internet addresses frequently change. To find the sites listed here, visit www.thomsonedu.com/counseling/thompson for an updated list of Internet addresses and direct links to relevant sites.

Centers for Disease Control and Prevention

Substance Abuse and Mental Health Services Administration

National Institute of Mental Health

References

Administration for Children and Families. (2003). *Summary: Child maltreatment 2003*. Retrieved January 16, 2006, from www.acf.hhs.gov/programs/cb/pubs/cm03/summary.htm

Arman, J. F., & McNair, R. (2000). A small group model for working with elementary school children of alcoholics. *Professional School Counseling, 3,* 290–293.

Arthur, R., & Erickson, E. (1992). *Gangs and schools.* Holmes Beach, FL: Learning Publications.

Bay-Hinitz, A., & Wilson, G. (2005). A cooperative games intervention for aggressive preschool children. In L. A. Reddy, T. M. Files-Hall, & C. E. Schaefer (Eds.), *Empirically based play interventions for children* (pp. 191–211). Washington, DC: American Psychological Association.

Beautrais, A. L. (2000). Risk factors for suicide and attempted suicide among young people. *Australian and New Zealand Journal of Psychiatry, 34,* 420–436.

Beck, A. T., Kovacs, M., & Weissman, A. (1979). Assessment of suicidal intention: The scale for suicidal ideation. *Journal of Clinical and Consulting Psychology, 47,* 343–352.

Beck, A. T., & Steer, R. A. (1993). *Beck Depression Inventory.* San Antonio, TX: Psychological Corporation.

Bender, D., & Leone, B. (1996). How can street gangs be controlled? In C. Cozic (Ed.), *Gangs: Opposing viewpoints* (pp. 91–131). San Diego, CA: Greenhaven Press, Inc.

Berk, L. E. (2001). *Development through the lifespan* (2nd ed.). Boston: Allyn & Bacon.

Bianchi, S., & Caspar, L. (2000). American families. *Population Bulletin, 55,* 3–41.

Black, C. (1981). Innocent bystanders at risk: The children of alcoholics. In G. Lawson, J. Peterson, & A. Lawson (Eds.), *Alcoholism and the family.* Rockville, MD: Aspen.

Blume, J. (1981). *Tiger eyes.* Scarsdale, NY: Bradbury.

Brake, K. (1988). Counseling young children of alcoholics. *Elementary School Guidance and Counseling, 23,* 106–111.

Brown, K., & Parsons, R. (1998). Accurate identification of childhood aggression: A key to successful intervention. *Professional School Counseling, 2,* 135–140.

Burnham, S. C. (2004). "I am somebody": Gang membership. In D. Capuzzi & D. R. Gross (Eds.), *Youth at risk: A prevention resource for counselors, teachers, and parents* (4th ed., pp. 303–327). Alexandria, VA: American Counseling Association and Merrill Publishing.

Capuzzi, D. (2002). Legal and ethical challenges in counseling suicidal students. *The Professional School counselor, 6,* 36–45.

Capuzzi, D., & Gross, D. R. (2004). "I don't want to live": The adolescent at risk for suicidal behavior. In D. Capuzzi & D. R. Gross (Eds.), *Youth at risk: A prevention resource for counselors, teachers, and parents* (4th ed., pp. 275–302). Alexandria, VA: American Counseling Association and Merrill Publishing.

Carruthers, W., Sweeney, B., Kmitta, D., & Harris, G. (1996). Conflict resolution: An examination of the research literature and a model for program evaluation. *The School Counselor, 44*(1), 5–18.

Carter, W. L. (2002). *It happened to me: A teen's guide to overcoming sexual abuse.* Oakland, CA: New Harbinger.

Chalk, R., Gibbons, A., & Scarupa, H. J. (2002, May). The multiple dimensions of child abuse and neglect: New insights into an old problem. *Child Trends Research Brief.* Retrieved August 5, 2002, from www.childtrends.org

Child abuse, parts I and II. (1993, Special supplement). *Harvard Mental Health Letter,* 1–6.

Child Abuse Prevention and Treatment Act. (1996). Retrieved September 18, 2003 from http://www.acf.hhs.gov/programs/cb/laws.

Child Trends. (2006). *Childhood depression.* Retrieved January 18, 2006, from www.childtrendsdatabank.org/indicators/30FeelSadorHopeless.cfm

Child Welfare League of America. (2001). Alcohol, other drugs, & child welfare. 2001/0-87868-839-0#8390. Washington, DC: Author.

Child Welfare League of America. (2003). *The poison within.* Retrieved January 29, 2006, from www.cwla.org/articles/cv0311poison.htm

Child Welfare League of America. (2006). *Recognizing child and adolescent depression.* Retrieved January 15, 2006, from https://www.cwla.org/ programs/health/ healthtipschilddepression.htm

Childhelp USA. (2005). *National child abuse statistics.* Retrieved January 10, 2006, from http://www.acf.hhs.gov/programs/cb/pubs/cm04/chapterthree.htm

Clark, G. N., DeBar, L. L., & Lewinsohn, P. M. (2003). Cognitive-behavioral group treatment for adolescent depression. In A. E. Kazdin & J. R. Weisz (Eds.), *Evidence-based psychotherapies for children and adolescents* (pp. 120–134). New York: The Guilford Press.

Coleman, M., & Ganong, L. (1995). Insiders' and outsiders' beliefs about stepfamilies: Assessment and implications for practice. In Huntley, D. (Ed.), *Understanding stepfamilies: Implications for assessment and treatment. The family psychology and counseling series* (pp. 101–112) Alexandria, VA: American Counseling Association.

Coleman, M., Ganong, L., & Fine, M. (2000). Reinvestigating remarriage: Another decade of progress. *Journal of Marriage and the Family, 62,* 1288–1307.

Costa, L., & Holliday, D. (1994). Helping children cope with the death of a parent. *Elementary School Guidance and Counseling, 28,* 206–213.

Crosbie-Burnett, M., & Pulvino, C. (1990). Children in nontraditional families: A classroom guidance program. *School Counselor, 37,* 286–293.

Dacey, J., & Kenny, M. (1997). *Adolescent development.* Boston: McGraw & Hill.

Daniels, J. (1992). Empowering homeless children through school counseling. *Elementary School Guidance and Counseling, 27,* 104–112.

Davis, N., & Sparks, T. (1988). *Therapeutic stories to heal children* (Rev. ed.). Oxon Hill, MD: Psychological Associates.

Deaver, J. R. (1988). *Say goodnight, Grace.* New York: Harper & Row.

DeLucia-Waack, J. L., & Gerrity, D. (2001). Effective group work for elementary school-age children whose parents are divorcing. *The Family Journal: Counseling and Therapy for Couples and Families, 9,* 273–284.

Depression in children—Part I. (2002). *Harvard Mental Health Letter, 18,* 1–4.

Dietzel, M. (2000). *My very own book about me: A personal safety book* (7th ed.). Spokane, WA: ACT for Kids.

Doweiko, H. E. (1999). *Concepts of chemical dependency* (4th ed.). Pacific Grove, CA: Brooks/Cole.

Downey, D. (1994). The school performance of children from single mother and single father families: Economic or interpersonal deprivation? *Journal of Family Issues, 15,* 129–147.

Edgeworth, J., & Carr, A. (2000). Child abuse. In A. Carr (Ed.), *What works with children and adolescents? A critical review of psychological interventions with children, adolescents and their families* (pp. 17–48). Philadelphia: Brunner-Routledge.

Emslie, G. (1997). Children and depression. *Treatment Today, 9*(2), 10–11.

Family Support Network. (2002). *Child abuse and neglect.* Retrieved January 10, 2006, from www.familysupport.org/Abuse.cfm

Ferquist, R. M. (2000). Problem drinking in the family and youth suicide. *Adolescence, 35,* 551–559.

Finn, A. (2004). Death in the classroom: Violence in schools. In D. Capuzzi & D. R. Gross (Eds.). *Youth at risk: A prevention resource for counselors, teachers, and parents* (4th ed., pp. 353–372). Alexandria, VA: American Counseling Association and Merrill Publishing.

Fitzsimmons, M. (2000). *Violence and Aggression in children and Youth* (Report No. ED429419). Reston, VA: ERIC Clearinghouse on Disability and Gifted Education.

Freeman, S. J. (2001). Death and bereavement. In E. R. Welfel & R. E. Ingersoll (Eds.), *The mental health desk reference* (pp. 38–43). New York: John Wiley & Sons.

Gately, D., & Schwebel, A. (1992). Favorable outcomes in children after parental divorce. In *Divorce and the next generation.* Binghamton, NY: Haworth.

Gil, E. (1996). *Treating abused adolescents.* New York: Guilford Press.

Glover, J. (1994). The hero child in the alcoholic home: Recommendations for counselors. *The School Counselor, 41,* 185–190.

Goldstein, A. P. (1994). Delinquent gangs. In L.R. Huesmann (Ed.) *Aggressive behavior: Current Perspectives* (pp. 255–274). New York: Plenum Press.

Graves, B., Zuckerman, B., Marans, S., & Cohen, D. (1993). Silent victims: Children who witness violence (Commentary). *Journal of the American Medical Association 269,* 262–264.

Green, A. (1993). Child sexual abuse: Immediate and long-term effects and intervention. *Journal of the American Academy of Child and Adolescent Psychiatry, 32,* 890–902.

Grollman, E. A. (1988). *Shira: A legacy of courage.* New York: Doubleday.

Grych, J., & Fincham, F. (1992). Interventions for children of divorce: Toward greater integration of research and action. *Psychological Bulletin, 111,* 434–454.

Herring, R. (1993). Suicide in the middle school: Who said kids will not? *Elementary School Guidance and Counseling, 25,* 129–137.

Holinger, P. C., Offer, D., Barter, J. T., & Bell, C. C. (1994). *Suicide and homicide among adolescents.* New York: Guilford Press.

Holmes, J., & Holmes-Lonergan, H. (2004). The bully in the family: Family influences on bullying. In C. E. Sanders & G. D. Phye (Eds.), *Bullying: Implications for the Classroom* (pp. 111–135). New York: Elsevier Academic Press.

Jacobsen, I., Rabinowitz, I., Popper, M., Solomon, R., Sokol, M., & Pfeffer, C. (1994). Interviewing prepubertal children about suicidal ideation and behavior. *Journal of the American Academy of Child and Adolescent Psychiatry, 33,* 439–452.

James, R. K., & Gilliland, B. E. (2005). *Crisis intervention strategies* (5th ed.). Pacific Grove, CA: Brooks/Cole.

James, S. H., & Burch, K. M. (1999). School counselors' roles in cases of child sexual behavior. *Professional School Counseling, 2,* 211–217.

Johnson, C. (1990). Inflicted injury versus accidental injury. *Pediatric Clinics of North America, 37,* 791–814.

Johnson, D., & Johnson, R. (1994). Constructive conflict in the schools. *Journal of Social Issues, 50,* 117–137.

Johnson, D., & Johnson, R. (1996). Conflict resolution and peer mediation programs in elementary and secondary schools: A review of the research. *Review of Educational Research, 66(4),* 459–506.

Jones, D., & Houts, R. (1992). Parental drinking, parent-child communication and social skills in young adults. *Journal of Studies on Alcohol, 53,* 48–56.

Jones, J. W. (1985). *Children of alcoholics screening test.* Chicago: Camelot Unlimited.

Juhnke, G. A. (1996). The Adapted-SAD PERSONS: A suicide assessment scale designed for use with children. *Elementary School Guidance and Counseling, 30,* 252–258.

Kehoe, P., & Deach, C. (1987). *Something happened and I'm scared to tell: A book for young victims of abuse.* Seattle, WA: Parenting Press.

Kelley, B. T., Thornberry, T. P., & Smith, C. A. (1997). *In the wake of childhood maltreatment.* Washington, DC: National Institute of Justice.

Kovacs, M. (1985). The Children's Depression Inventory (CDI). *Psychopharmocology Bulletin, 21,* 995–1124.

Kübler-Ross, E. (1969). *On death and dying.* New York: Macmillan.

Lane, P. S., & McWhirter, J. J. (1992). A peer mediation model: Conflict resolution for elementary and middle school children. *Elementary School Guidance and Counseling, 27,* 15–24.

Lane, P. S., & McWhirter, J. J. (1996). Creating a peaceful school community: Reconciliation operationalized. *Catholic School Studies, 69,* 31–34.

MacFarland, W., & Tollerud, T. (2004). Counseling children and adolescents with special needs. In A. Vernon (Ed.), *Counseling children and adolescents* (pp. 257–309). Denver, CO: Love Publishing.

Masten, A., Miliotis, D., Graham-Bermann, S., Ramirez, M., & Neemann, J. (1993). Children in homeless families: Risks to mental health and development. *Journal of Consulting and Clinical Psychology, 61,* 335–341.

McConnell, A. R., & Sim, A. J. (2000). Evaluating an innovative counseling service for children of divorce. *British Journal of Guidance & Counselling, 28,* 75–87.

McRary, A. (1998, June 18). Kids who kill: Psychologist says watch for warning signs. *The Knoxville News-Sentinel,* pp. B1–B2.

McWhirter, E. H., Shepard, R. E., & Hunt-Morse, M. C. (2004). Counseling at-risk children and adolescents. In A. Vernon (Ed.), *Counseling children and adolescents* (pp. 311–354). Denver, CO: Love Publishing.

McWhirter, J. J. (2002). Will he choose life? In L. B. Golden (Ed.), *Case studies in child and adolescent counseling* (3rd ed., pp. 81–89). New York: Merrill/Prentice Hall.

McWhirter, J. J., McWhirter, B. T., McWhirter, E. H., & McWhirter, R. J. (2004). *At-risk youth: A comprehensive response* (3rd ed.). Belmont, CA: Brooks/Cole.

Mellin, E. A., & Beamish, P. M. (2002). Interpersonal theory and adolescents with depression: Clinical update. *Journal of Mental Health Counseling, 24,* 110–126.

Miller-Perrin, C. L. (2001). Child maltreatment: Treatment of child and adolescent victims. In E. R. Welfel & R. E. Ingersoll (Eds.), *The mental health desk reference* (pp. 169–176). New York: John Wiley & Sons.

Moeller, T., Bachmann, G., & Moeller, J. (1993). The combined effects of physical, sexual, and emotional abuse during childhood: Long-term health consequences for women. *Child Abuse and Neglect, 17,* 623–640.

Moore, M., & Carr, A. (2000). Depression and grief. In A. Carr (Ed.), *What works with children and adolescents? A critical review of psychological interventions with children, adolescents and their families* (pp. 203–232). Philadelphia: Brunner-Routledge.

Morrissey, M. (1998). Mitigating school violence requires a system-wide effort. *Counseling Today, 40*(12), 36–37.

Mufson, L., & Dorta, D. P. (2003). Interpersonal psychotherapy for depressed adolescents. In A. E. Kazdin & J. R. Weisz (Eds.), *Evidence-based psychotherapies for children and adolescents* (pp. 148–164). New York: The Guilford Press.

Muro, J., & Kottman, T. (1995). *Guidance and counseling in the elementary and middle school: A practical approach.* Dubuque, IA: Brown & Benchmark.

National Center for Health Statistics. (2005). *Divorce rates for 2004.* Retrieved January 19, 2006, from www.cdc.gov/nchs/fastats/divorce.htm

National Center for Missing and Exploited Children. (2006). *Laws concerning the sexual exploitation of children.* Retrieved January 16, 2006, from http://www.missingkids.com/missingkids/servlet/PageServlet?LanguageCountry=en_US&PageId=1481#2

National Clearinghouse on Child Abuse and Neglect Information. (2004). *Risk and protective factors for child abuse and neglect.* Retrieved January 10, 2006, from http://nccanch.acf.hhs.gov/topics/prevention/emerging/riskprotectivefactors.cfm

National Clearinghouse on Child Abuse and Neglect Information. (2005a). *Definitions of child abuse and neglect.* Retrieved January 10, 2006, from http://nccanch.acf.hhs.gov/general/legal/statutes/define.cfm

National Clearinghouse on Child Abuse and Neglect Information. (2005b). Long-term consequences of child abuse and neglect. Retrieved January 10, 2006, from http://nccanch.acf.hhs.gov/pubs/factsheets/long_term_consequences.cfm

National Coalition for the Homeless. (2005). *NCH fact sheet #3: Who is homeless?* Retrieved January 30, 2006, from www.nationalhomeless.org/publications/facts/Whois.pdf

Nawojczyk, S. (1998, Winter). Warning signs of possible gang involvement. *Help & hope: News for the at-risk professional* Retrieved on March 28, 2006 from http://www.gangwar.com/dynamics.htm

Nelson, R., & Crawford, B. (1990). Suicide among elementary school-aged children. *Elementary School Guidance and Counseling, 25,* 123–128.

The NSDUH Report. (2005). *Alcohol dependence or abuse among parents with children living in the home.* Retrieved January 9, 2006, from http://oas.samhsa.gov/2k4/ACOA/ACOA.htm

Office of Elementary and Secondary Education. (2000). *Education for homeless children and youth program* (EDD00014). Washington, DC: U.S. Government Printing Office.

Olweus, D., Limber, S., & Mihalic, S. F. (1999). *Blueprints for violence prevention: Book 9. Bullying prevention program.* Boulder, CO: Center for the Study and Prevention of Violence.

O'Rourke, K. (1990). Recapturing hope: Elementary school support groups for children of alcoholics. *Elementary School Guidance and Counseling, 25,* 107–115.

O'Rourke, K., & Worzbyt, J. (1996). *Support Groups for Children.* Washington, DC: Accelerated Development.

Osofsky, J. (1995). The effects of exposure to violence on young children. *American Psychologist, 50*(9), 782–788.

Papernow, P. (1995). What's going on here? Separating (and weaving together) step and clinical issues in remarried families. In Huntley, D. (Ed.), *Understanding stepfamilies: Implications for assessment and treatment. The family psychology and counseling series* (pp. 3–24). Alexandria, VA: American Counseling Association.

Parks, C. (1995). Gang behavior in the schools: Reality or myth? *Educational Psychology Review, 7*(1), 41–68.

Piaget, J. (1954). *The construction of reality in the child.* New York: Basic Books.

Pidcock, B., Fischer, J. L., Forthun, L. F., & West, S. (2000). Hispanic and Anglo college women's risk factors for substance use and eating disorders. *Addictive Behaviors: An International Journal 25,* 705–723.

Pietrzak, D., Petersen, G., & Speaker, K. (1998). Perceptions of school violence by elementary and middle school personnel. *Professional School Counseling, 1*(4), 23–29.

Popenhagen, M., & Qualley, R., (1998). Adolescent suicide: Detection, intervention, and prevention. *Professional School Counseling, 1*(4), 30–35.

Price, A. W., & Emshoff, J. G. (1997). Breaking the cycle of addiction: Prevention and intervention with children of alcoholics. *Alcohol Health and Research World, 21,* 241–246.

Rafferty, Y. (1995). The legal rights and educational problems of homeless children and youth. *Educational Evaluation and Policy Analysis, 17*(1), 39–61.

The Rainbow Game. (1989). Houston, TX: Rainbow House Children's Resource Center.

Reynolds, W. M. (1987). *RCDS manual.* Odessa, FL: Psychological Assessment Resources.

Reynolds, W. M. (1988). *The Suicide Ideation Questionnaire.* Odessa, FL: Psychological Assessment Resources.

Reynolds, W. M. (1989). *RADS manual.* Odessa, FL: Psychological Assessment Resources.

Richards, L., & Schmiege, C. (1993). Problems and strengths of single-parent families: Implications for practice and policy. *Family Relations, 42,* 277–285.

Roberts, W., Jr. (1995). Postvention and psychological autopsy in the suicide of a 14-year-old public school student. *School Counselor, 42,* 322–330.

Roth, B., & Striepling-Goldstein, S. (2003). School-based aggression replacement training. *Reclaiming Children and Youth, 12,* 138–141.

Salmon, S. (2003). Teaching empathy: The PEACE curriculum. *Reclaiming Children and Youth, 12,* 167–173.

Scheidlinger, S. (1994). A commentary on adolescent group violence. *Child Psychiatry and Human Development, 24*(1), 3–10.

Schellenbach, C. J. (1998). Child maltreatment: A critical review of research on treatment for physically abusive parents. In P. K. Trickett & C. J. Schellenbach (Eds.), *Violence against children in the family and the community* (pp. 251–268). Washington, DC: American Psychological Association.

Schmitz, C., Wagner, J., & Menke, E. (1995). Homelessness as one component of housing instability and its impact on the development of children in poverty. *Journal of Social Distress and the Homeless, 4*(6), 301–317.

Schoen, C., & Davis, K. I. (1998). *The health of adolescent boys: Commonwealth Fund survey findings.* New York: Commonwealth Fund.

Sciarra, D. T. (2004). *School counseling: Foundations and contemporary issues.* Belmont, CA: Brooks/Cole.

Seligman, M. (1998). *Learned optimism.* New York: Simon & Schuster.

Shapiro, J. P., Friedberg, R. D., & Bardenstein, K. K. (2006). *Child and adolescent therapy: Science and art.* Hoboken, NJ: John Wiley & Sons.

Sheller, B., & Watts, G. B. (1999). Helping your child cope with grief. *Faith Home for Parents.* Nashville, TN: Abingdon Press.

Shura, M. F. (1988). *The Sunday doll.* New York: Dodd Mead.

Siehl, P. (1990). Suicide postvention: A new disaster plan—What a school should do when faced with a suicide. *School Counselor, 38,* 52–57.

Soriano, M., Soriano, F., & Jimenez, E. (1994). School violence among culturally diverse populations: Sociocultural and institutional considerations. *School Psychology Review, 23*(2), 216–235.

Stefanowski-Harding, S. (1990). Suicide and the school counselor. *School Counselor, 37,* 328–336.

Stephans, R. (1994, January 15). Gangs, guns and school violence. *USA Today,* p. A7.

Strawser, S., Markos, P. A., Yamaguchi, B. J., & Higgins, K. (2000). A new challenge for school counselors: Children who are homeless. *Professional School Counseling, 3,* 162–172.

Strong, K. (1998). *Gangs and schools.* Presentation to the Governor's Conference for a Safe and Drug-Free Tomorrow, Nashville, TN.

Studer, J. (1996). Understanding and preventing aggressive responses in youth. *Elementary School Guidance and Counseling, 30,* 194–203.

Styron, T., Hanoff-Bulman, R., & Davidson, L. (2000). "Please ask me how I am": Experiences of family homelessness in the context of single mothers' lives. *Journal of Social Distress & the Homeless, 9,* 143–165.

Substance Abuse and Mental Health Services Administration. (2002). *You can help: A guide fro caring adults working with young people experiencing addiction in the family.* Retrieved January 16, 2006, from www.samhsa.gov/centers/csat/content/intermediaries

Thompson, E. A., & Eggert, L. L. (1999). Using the suicide risk screen to identify suicidal adolescents among potential high school dropouts. *Journal of the American Academy of Child and Adolescent Psychiatry, 38,* 1506–1514.

Underwood, M. (2003, December). Preventing and reducing social aggression among girls. *The Brown University Child and Adolescent Behavior Letter, 19*(12), 1–10.

U.S. Department of Health and Human Services. (2001). *Youth violence: A report of the Surgeon General.* Rockville, MD: U.S. Department of Health and Human Services, Centers for Disease Control and Prevention, National Center for Injury Prevention and Control; Substance Abuse and Mental Health Services Administration, Center for Mental Health Services; and National Institute of Mental Health, National Institutes of Health.

U.S. Department of Justice. (2005, June). *Highlights of the 2002-2003 national youth gang surveys.* Retrieved January 25, 2006, from www.ojp.usdoj.gov

U.S. Department of Justice. (2005, August). *Juvenile arrests 2003.* Retrieved January 25, 2006, from www.ojp.usdoj.gov/ojjdp

Visher, E., & Visher, J. (1995). Avoiding the mind fields of stepfamily therapy: Steps and clinical issues in remarried families. In Huntley, E. (Ed.), *Understanding stepfamilies: Implications for assessment and treatment. The Family Psychology and Counseling Series* (pp. 25–34). Alexandria, VA: American Counseling Association.

Vostanis, P., Tischler, V., Cumella, S., & Bellerby, T. (2001). Mental health problems and social supports among homeless mothers and children victims of domestic and community violence. *International Journal of Social Psychiatry, 47,* 30–41.

Wallerstein, J. (1983). Children of divorce: The psychological tasks of the child. *American Journal of Orthopsychiatry, 53,* 230–243.

Wallerstein, J. (1984). Children of divorce: Ten-year follow-up of young children. *American Journal of Orthopsychiatry, 54,* 444–458.

Wallerstein, J., & Blakeslee, S. (1989). *Second chances.* New York: Ticknor & Fields.

Wallerstein, J., & Blakeslee, S. (2003). *What about the kids?* New York: Hyperion

Wallerstein, J., & Kelly, J. (1996). *Surviving the breakup: How children and parents cope with divorce.* New York: Basic Books.

Webb, B. (1993). Counseling and therapy for the bereaved child. In B. Webb (Ed.), *Helping bereaved children* (pp. 43–58). New York: Guilford Press.

Webb, N. B., & Terr, L. (1999). *Play therapy with children in crisis.* New York: Guilford Press.

Weersing, V. R., & Brent, D. A. (2003). Cognitive-behavioral therapy for adolescent depression: Comparative efficacy, mediation, moderation, and effectiveness. In A. E. Kazdin & J. R. Weisz (Eds.), *Evidence-based psychotherapies for children and adolescents* (pp. 135–147). New York: Guilford Press.

Weisz, J. R., Southam-Gerow, M. A., Gordis, E. B., & Connor-Smith, J. (2003). Primary and secondary control enhancement training for youth depression: Applying the deployment-focused model of treatment development and testing. In A. E. Kazdin & J. R. Weisz (Eds.), *Evidence-based psychotherapies for children and adolescents* (pp. 165–186). New York: Guilford Press.

Wilson, J., & Blocher, L. (1990). The counselor's role in assisting children of alcoholics. *Elementary School Guidance and Counseling, 25,* 98–106.

Wise, A., & Spengler, P. (1997). Suicide in children younger than age fourteen: Clinical judgment and assessment issues. *Journal of Mental Health Counseling, 19*(4), 318–335.

Worden, J. (1996). *Children and grief.* New York: Guilford Press.

Yapko, M. (1993). Suggested guidelines for professional counselors. *Guidepost, 36,* 11.

Zeppa, A., & Norem, R. (1993). Stressors, manifestations of stress, and first-family/stepfamily group membership. *Journal of Divorce and Remarriage, 19,* 3–23.

19 CHAPTER | COUNSELING WITH CHILDREN WITH SPECIAL NEEDS

The miracle is not that we do this work, but that we are happy to do it.
—Mother Teresa

THE SITUATION

Children with special needs are different in some way from their peers. They deviate from what is considered to be normal or average in physical appearance, learning abilities, or behavior. They may have a mild, moderate, or severe special need, as is the spectrum of children with disabilities. Educators, parents, and other professionals emphasize meeting these children's physical, psychological, and educational needs in the least restrictive environment (outside an institution) and on providing support for the families through groups, associations, and legislation.

Being a special child presents challenges to both the parents and the child. Parents may be confused about the disability. They may have fears concerning their child's present and future life. They may experience feelings of guilt ("Did I cause this?"), self-pity ("Why did it have to happen to me?"), or even self-hate.

Hardman, et al. (1993) suggest that most parents initially react with shock, which may be accompanied by feelings of anxiety, guilt, numbness, confusion, helplessness, anger, disbelief, or denial. Realization follows and may be characterized by self-pity or self-hate and withdrawal. The parent may enter a defensive retreat stage to avoid facing reality. When parents move on to the acknowledgment stage, they are able to participate in the treatment process and may even become an advocate for the cause (Hardman et al., 1993).

HISTORY

Progress has been made toward helping children with special needs become accepted, productive members of society. The 1880s saw the first steps toward recognizing the needs of persons with disabilities with the establishment of the first schools for the deaf and the blind. In the mid-1930s, Congress passed the Crippled Children Act, authorizing financial aid to families of people with orthopedic handicaps. President Franklin D. Roosevelt, a victim of polio that caused him to be disabled, undoubtedly gave impetus to this legislation. President John F. Kennedy, who had a sister with mental retardation, urged that attention be given to children's developmental disabilities, including mental retardation and learning disabilities. In 1961, a President's Panel on Mental Retardation was established, and in 1963, a National Institute of Child Health and Human Development was founded. The child advocacy movement of the late 1960s and early 1970s resulted in the formation of the National Center for Child Advocacy. During the 1970s and 1980s, legislative appropriations and federal committees and agencies increased. In 1975, President Ford signed the Education for All Handicapped Children Act, Public Law 94–142. This law provided that all handicapped children receive free educational experiences designed to meet their particular needs. It described specific procedures for identification and placement and for designing educational programs for children with certain disabling conditions.

In 1977, the Education of the Handicapped Act was amended to define *learning disabilities,* and in 1978, the Gifted and Talented Children's Education Act provided money to states for planning, training, program development, and research. Amendments in 1983 extended the act to provide additional services to secondary school students and children from birth to 3 years old. The Education for All Handicapped Children Act was renamed Individuals with Disabilities Act (IDEA) in 1990, and two new categories of disability were added: autism and traumatic brain injury (Hardman et al., 1993). In 1990, President Bush extended the 1973 Rehabilitation Act (Section 504), which prohibited discrimination against qualified individuals in federally funded programs and protected the rights of students with disabilities to free and appropriate public education, when he signed the Americans with Disabilities Act (ADA), which prohibits discrimination against persons with disabilities in employment, transportation, public services, public accommodations, and telecommunications, regardless of federal funding (Smith & Luckasson, 1995; Hardman et al., 1993). Smith (1998) points out that Section 504 and ADA have a broader definition of disabilities than does IDEA. Section 504 and the ADA provide the "right to accommodations" to qualified persons regardless of whether they need special education. Henderson (2001) compares the purpose, eligibility requirements, educational implications, due process, placement, and evaluation procedures for the federal acts related to children with disabilities in her informative article. Currently, professionals await finalization of new regulations for providing services under the reauthorization of IDEA.

CATEGORIES OF EXCEPTIONALITY

A controversy exists over the categorizing or labeling of children. Many professionals believe that children who are so categorized may be permanently stigmatized, rejected, or prevented from developing in a healthy manner. These children, especially if they are minority children, may be assigned to inferior educational programs, institutionalized, or even sterilized because of poor diagnoses. Furthermore, classification of a child can encourage the behaviors characteristic of the label. However, classification may be necessary to obtain services for exceptional children. Children who do not neatly fit categories may have trouble obtaining diagnostic services and treatment.

Smith (1998) differentiates "classification" and "labeling," stating that classification "refers to a structured system that identifies and organizes characteristics to establish order," whereas labeling "identifies individuals or groups according to a category assigned to them" (such as a specific learning disability) (pp. 10–11). Smith admits that labeling can be stigmatizing and harmful, but also points out that it provides a common language to describe a disability. She believes that classification systems enable professionals to identify and differentiate disabilities, as well as communicate effectively about the condition; describe the disability and needs of persons with a particular condition effectively for research purposes; help citizens to form special interest groups to enhance services for persons with the disability; and facilitate planning for the treatment of a special disability.

Smith and Luckasson (1995) agree, noting that a classification system for special education "enables us to name disabilities, to differentiate one from another, and to communicate in a meaningful and efficient way about a specific disability" (pp. 9–10). In addition, a classification system is useful because it is necessary for research, for lobbying for improved services, and for relating specific treatments to specific disabilities.

The Office of Special Education Programs (OSEP) (2005) reports that in 2001, 8.9 percent of 6- to 21-year-old individuals were receiving special education services under IDEA. In IDEA, children with disabilities refers to young people who have permanent or temporary mental, physical, or emotional disabilities that interfere with their education. Thirteen categories of disabilities have been defined in IDEA under which a person 3 to 21 years old would be eligible to receive services. Although new regulations expected in the summer of 2006 may modify some of these criteria, we present a summary of the current definition of disabilities. Based on information provided by the National Information Center for Children and Youth with Disabilities (NICHCY, 2002) and a state of North Carolina manual (2000), the following section contains a list of categories and their brief descriptions:

1. *Autism:* a developmental disability that significantly affects verbal and nonverbal communication and social interaction, as well as the presence of restricted and/or repetitive behavior, interests, and activities
2. *Behaviorally-emotionally disabled:* students who have received specially designed educational support and intervention but still show patterns of

inappropriate interpersonal or intrapersonal behaviors that are long-standing and occur often; the students may not achieve adequate academic progress (not due to a learning disability); inability to maintain relationships; inappropriate or immature behavior or feeling under normal conditions; general pervasive mood of unhappiness or depression; tendency to develop physical symptoms, pains, or fears associated with problems

3. *Deaf-blindness:* the combination of hearing and visual impairments that causes severe communication and other developmental and educational problems

4. *Hearing impaired:* severe hearing loss that disables educationally and developmentally; a generic term that includes deafness and all hearing losses ranging from mild to profound

5. *Mentally disabled:* significantly subaverage general intellectual functioning and a reduced rate of learning; deficits in adaptive behavior and adverse effects on educational performance

6. *Multiple disabilities:* a pervasive primary disability that is cognitive and/or behavioral combined with one or more other disabilities; the combinations cause problems that cannot be addressed in areas that primarily focus on one area of disability, such as mental retardation-blindness

7. *Orthopedic impairment:* severe orthopedic impairment

8. *Other health impairment:* limited strength, vitality or alertness due to chronic or acute health problems; examples of such health problems are heart conditions, chronic lung disease, tuberculosis, leukemia

9. *Specific learning disability:* disorder in one or more of the processes involved in understanding or in using language that causes difficulties in listening, thinking, speaking, reading, writing, spelling, or doing mathematical calculations

10. *Speech or language impairment:* communication disorder such as stuttering, impaired articulation, or voice impairment; the disability may range in severity from mild to severe; the components of the impairment include articulation, language, voice, and fluency

11. *Traumatic brain injury:* an acquired injury to the brain caused by an external physical force that results in total or partial functional and/or psychosocial impairment

12. *Visual impairment including blindness:* impairment in vision; functionally blind children have so little vision that they use Braille for reading; partially seeing children have a loss of vision but are able to regular or large type to read (NICHCY, 2002, pp. 1–3; State of North Carolina, 2000)

Some children are not eligible for services under the criteria outlined in IDEA but may receive educational modifications under Section 504 of the Rehabilitation Act of 1973. Tarver-Behring and Spagna (2004) explain that Section 504 is a civil rights act designed to protect the rights of individuals in places that get federal funding such as schools. This act covers students whose disabilities do not affect their academic performance to the extent that they meet special education criteria, but who still need accommodations to receive an appropriate education. Under Section 504, a qualified person with disabilities has a physical or mental impairment that limits one or more major life activities (such as learning), has had the impairment for some time, and is currently exhibiting the impairment. Some eligible students include those with attention-deficit/hyperactivity disorder (ADHD), communicable diseases, behavioral disorders, physical disabilities, chronic asthma, and other impairments. The educational modifications may be reduced or modified assignments, different testing arrangements, having a teacher's aid, and many others (Tarver-Behring & Spagna, 2004).

Discussing each area of exceptionality is beyond the scope of this chapter; therefore, this chapter includes a general discussion of children who have mental retardation, learning disabilities, physical handicaps, or behavioral-emotional disorders, as well as ADHD. These conditions appear to be those counselors are most apt to encounter daily. Counselors, parents, teachers, and children may need clarification on the process that is followed to identify children who may need special education and related services. The OSEP (2002) has outlined those steps:

1. The child is referred as possibly needing services.
2. The child is evaluated in all areas related to the suspected disability.
3. A group of qualified professionals and the parents consider the results of the evaluation and determine whether the child is eligible for services.
4. If the child is found eligible, within 30 calendar days, a team meets to write an individual educational plan (IEP) for the child.
5. The IEP meeting is scheduled. Parents are invited.
6. The IEP meeting is held and the IEP is written. The plan includes accommodations, modifications, and supports to be provided to the child. Parents must consent to services and placement.
7. Services are provided. The school monitors the plan to determine whether it is being implemented as written.
8. Progress is measured and reported to the parents.
9. The IEP is reviewed at least once a year.
10. The child is re-evaluated at least every 3 years (OPEP, 2002, pp. 4–7).

We have defined *counseling* as a therapeutic relationship, a problem-solving process, a re-education, and a method for changing behavior. We have also discussed counseling as a method for helping children cope with developmental problems and as a preventive process. Children with special needs may be faced with rejection and failure. They may need an accepting relationship, someone to listen, assistance in setting present and future goals, guidance for improving interpersonal relationships, and perhaps most important, help in building a strong self-concept and confidence. Counseling with the exceptional child requires no magic formula; however, it does require counselor dedication to the philosophy that all individuals are unique and capable of growth to reach their potential.

METHODS FOR COUNSELING WITH CHILDREN WHO HAVE SPECIAL NEEDS

As is true with most counseling methods, the counseling strategies should be incorporated into a positive, accepting counseling relationship. To understand the world of the exceptional child, counselors need to have a basic knowledge of the disabling condition. What are the symptoms and general characteristics of a child with this exceptionality? What are the child's limitations? What are the child's strengths and potentials? All children have some developmental and psychological needs in common, but are there other needs specific to the exceptional condition that must be considered? The counselor does not need to become an expert in the techniques of special education, but knowledge of the needs and characteristics of these children is necessary for effective counseling.

Counselors should ask themselves if they have taken the time to get to know the child as an individual—not as a "child with a disability." The following questions are helpful:

Has my counseling assisted the child to develop good relationships with his or her classmates?

Has my counseling focused on assisting the child to solve his or her own problems?

Has my counseling helped the child to feel better about himself or herself?

Has my counseling with the parents and teachers of the child helped them to find ways of interacting that enhance the child's self-esteem and feelings of self-sufficiency?

In the professional's attempts to diagnose and find help for a child with special problems, the child as a person is sometimes forgotten in the proliferation of testing, diagnosing, and planning. These procedures that are designed to aid the child may, unfortunately, increase self-doubts and fears. Testing, diagnosing, and planning are necessary, but they cannot replace a good relationship—one in which the child feels free to express fears, anxieties, doubts, and insecurities. A person who is listened to is being respected. It may begin the process of developing or restoring a more positive self-evaluation. Building a better self-concept includes helping children see themselves as people who can and do perform and accomplish goals.

CHILDREN WITH BEHAVIORAL-EMOTIONAL DISORDERS

Behavioral-emotional disorders relate to children who have "a condition exhibiting one or more of the following characteristics over a long period of time and to a marked degree that adversely affects a child's educational performance—

A. An inability to learn that cannot be explained by other factors such as intellectual, sensory, or health problems.
B. An inability to form satisfactory interpersonal relationships with peers and teachers.

C. Inappropriate displays of feelings or behavior.
D. Pervasive unhappiness or depression.
E. A tendency to develop physical symptoms or fears associated with personal or school problems" (NICHCY, 2005)

The condition must have been present to a marked extent over a period of time and must substantially interfere with the child's educational achievement. The term includes schizophrenic children but excludes those whose problems result from social maladjustment.

In the 1999–2000 school year, 470,111 children with an emotional disturbance received services in the public schools (U.S. Department of Education, 2001). Brandenburg, Friedman, and Silver (1990) suggest that the number of children in this category receiving special education is less than one third of those who need such programs, probably because of the ambiguity of the criteria and definition.

Smith and Luckasson (1995) list the possible indicators of behavioral and emotional disorders as few or no friends, problems with family relations, problems with teacher relationships, hyperactive behavior, aggression to self or others, impulsivity, immature social skills, feelings of depression and unhappiness, withdrawal into self, anxiety or fearfulness, expression of ideas of suicide, distractibility, and inability to pay attention for an appropriate length of time. Furthermore, the authors state that the children usually have lower academic performance than expected for their age and social skills deficits, as well as the obvious behavioral problems and internal conflicts described. They recommend behavioral modification strategies, individual and family counseling, moral education, and character training. The counselor should be in contact with other professionals working with these children—teachers, medical doctors, specialists, and others—to coordinate all services for the child with behavioral-emotional disorder.

These children need love and understanding, and they need a counselor who can provide security and stability. The counselor who is effective with children who have behavioral-emotional can detect and reflect the feelings and frustrations of the children, discuss these feelings, and decide how to manage them effectively. Much of the success achieved from working with the emotionally disturbed has been due to the relationship between adult and child, as well as the technique used. These children often have experienced inconsistency in their relationships and may be suspicious of adults because of past experiences with hurtful people. The counselor needs to be strong enough to place consistent limits on the children and require them to assume responsibility for their behavior. To bring consistency and stability to the life of the child with behavioral-emotional disorders, the counselor can discuss expected and appropriate behaviors with the child. Writing out what is considered inappropriate and the consequences of this behavior is often helpful.

The counselor can define expected behaviors by such methods as contracting. The counselor, parents, teachers, and all significant people in the child's life must be willing to set limits and consistently maintain the rules. Behavior modification techniques emphasizing positive reinforcement have been effective. Relaxation exercises, talking therapy, physical activities, writing, drawing, or games may be scheduled into the child's day to provide outlets for tension and other emotions. Changes in the environment, expectations, stimulation, and conflicts should be as minimal as possible.

Some strategies help all children, and the information below could be effective with many populations. Tarver-Behring, Spagna, and Sullivan (1998) suggest that counselors help teachers with social skills strategies and classroom programs on problem solving, conflict resolutions, anger management, and making friends. Peer groups can be effective models for appropriate behavior.

The tasks of the counselor with children who have behavioral-emotional disorders can be summarized as follows:

1. Forming a counseling relationship with the child that includes well-defined responsibilities and limits
2. Working to change the child's image and expectations through counseling and consultation with family and other significant people in the child's world
3. Conducting individual and group counseling to deal with feelings and behaviors, to teach social skills, and to improve academic performance
4. Assisting parents and teachers in structuring the child's physical environment and schedule, establishing rules for behavior, and providing encouragement, reinforcement, and logical consequences for misbehavior

THE CHILD WITH A LEARNING DISABILITY

McEachern (2004) claims that almost 51 percent of children with special needs have a learning disability (LD). Learning disability is a general term for different kinds of learning problems, most often skills related to reading, writing, listening, speaking, reasoning, and doing math (NICHCY, 2002). The Learning Disabilities Association of America (2005) clarifies that types of learning disabilities are identified by the specific processing problem. The difficulties might relate "to getting information into the brain (**Input**), making sense of this information (**Organization**), storing and later retrieving this information (**Memory**), or getting this information back out (**Output**). Thus, the specific types of processing problems that result in LD might be in one or more of these four areas" (http://www.ldaamerica.us).

Boudah and Weiss (2002) state that individuals with LD usually have average or above average intelligence, yet often do not achieve on the same level as their peers. The most basic characteristic of learning disability is weaker academic achievement. The U.S. Department of Education (2001) estimates that one of every five people has a learning disability. About 3 million children with learning disabilities receive special education services in schools. The Learning Disabilities Association of America (2005) explains a learning disability as "a neurological disorder that affects one or more of the basic psychological processes involved in understanding or in using spoken or written language. The disability may manifest itself in an imperfect ability to listen, think, speak, read, write, spell or to do mathematical calculations. . ." (www.ldamerica.us). The term does not include children who have learning problems that are primarily the result of visual, hearing, or motor handicaps; of mental retardation; of emotional disturbance; or of environmental, cultural, or economic disadvantage (U.S. Office of Education, 2001). The Learning Disabilities Association of America (2005) discusses learning disabilities as an umbrella term that covers the following conditions:

- *Dyslexia:* a language and reading disability
- *Dyscalculia:* problems with arithmetic and math concepts
- *Dysgraphia:* a writing disorder resulting in illegibility
- *Dyspraxia (sensory integration disorder):* problems with motor coordination
- *Central auditory processing disorder:* difficulty processing and remembering language-related tasks
- *Nonverbal learning disorders:* trouble with nonverbal cues, for example, body language; poor coordination, clumsy
- *Visual perceptual/visual motor deficit:* reverses letters; cannot copy accurately; eyes hurt and itch; loses place; struggles with cutting
- *Language disorders (aphasia/dysphasia):* trouble understanding spoken language; poor reading comprehension

The Learning Disabilities Association of America's website (http://www.ldaamerica.us) contains information about strategies for working with children and adults with these conditions.

Children with learning disabilities usually have a measured intelligence in the normal range but are achieving academically well below an expected level. In general, the literature in this area has cited as indicators of a learning disability such characteristics as hyperactivity, distractibility, impulsiveness, motor problems, poor problem-solving skills, poor motivation, over-reliance on others for help with class assignments, poor language skills, immature social skills, and a general disorganization in learning approaches (Smith & Luckasson, 1995).

As in counseling with other children, the counselor begins by recognizing and reflecting the feelings of the young person with a learning disability. Some children with learning disabilities lack social perception and skills and perform poorly in social situations. They may lack good judgment and appear to be insensitive tattlers. They may have trouble making friends and forming good relationships in their families. Activities for building a positive body image and self-perception, sensitivity to other people, social maturity and skills, self-esteem, and emotional well-being may enhance these areas. McEachern (2004) explains their possible fear of failure and of learning reflected in their comments such as "I can't do this," "I don't know how," or "I'll never learn this."

Thompson and Littrell (1998) suggest brief solution-oriented counseling for adolescents with learning disabilities. The four-step model they use involves building rapport and then helping the student identify, describe, and define a specific problem or concern. In Step 2, the counselor and student consider what had been tried previously, what had worked, and any new possible solutions. During Step 3, the counselor helps the student decide on a specific, concrete, measurable, and attainable goal. Often, this step includes using the miracle question, "Suppose a miracle happened and the problem was solved. What would be different?" The fourth step is the generation of a specific task to help the student reach a goal. The counselors checked with the student 3 and 4 weeks later. These authors report success in 90 percent of the research participants.

Counseling goals for children with learning disabilities would include enhancing social skills, helping overcome a sense of failure, and promoting a positive attitude toward learning. McEachern (2004) recommends play techniques, art, music, and expressive writing to evoke expressions of feelings toward the disability, school, peers, and family. Cognitive-behavioral techniques to teach skills and coping strategies are suggested for older elementary and adolescent students. Brown (2005) states that music therapy that focuses on rhythm, order, and beat helps students who have cognitive disabilities. Reis and Colbert (2004) report that college students who have been identified as gifted or as learning disabled suffered negative experiences in their earlier school experiences. Reis and Colbert advocate for attention to the personal, social, and career development needs of this population. Durodoye, et al. (2004) echo that need for African American students with learning disabilities.

Boudah and Weiss (2002) have identified direct instruction of specific skills and learning strategy instruction as the best instructional practices for children with learning disabilities. The children should be taught with a step-by-step approach with appropriate modeling, practice, and feedback. Smith (1998) suggests that teachers use instructional tactics that actively involve children with learning disabilities, use advance organizers and concrete examples, demonstrate concepts as necessary, help children focus on the task at hand, teach problem-solving skills, help children understand the connection between effort and success, and teach them to predict consequences of their behavior. Because counseling is a form of teaching, these suggestions appear to be appropriate for counselors as well.

One task of a counselor working with a child with a learning disability may be to coordinate diagnostic services to pinpoint the child's specific strengths and weaknesses and plan an educational program based on these findings. A typical diagnostic evaluation includes physical, educational, and psychological assessments and perhaps the opinions of other specialists, such as speech pathologists or ophthalmologists. These data must be shared with all those working with the child to ensure a well-organized remediation plan and to avoid overlap or omission of services.

Durodoye, et al. (2004) suggest several multidisciplinary strategies for children with learning disabilities—self-motivation: self-control of academic progress; self-reinforcement of academic effort: progress and success; teaching adaptive skills; self-management for reducing problem behaviors; and teaching academic success behaviors. They stress that balancing information about children with special needs requires counseling skills that are flexible and appropriate culturally.

ATTENTION-DEFICIT/HYPERACTIVITY DISORDER AND ATTENTION DEFICIT DISORDER

The cluster of problems known as ADHD forms an extremely complex childhood problem and elicits the most frequent referrals for professional help, according to Erk (2004). The Learning Disability Association of American (2005) estimates that between 3 and 5 percent of children, or approximately 2 million children, have ADHD. The main features of this disorder are inattention, hyperactivity, and impulsivity. Children with ADHD may have trouble sitting still, controlling their behavior, and paying attention. As many as 3 to 7 of every 100 school children may have this behavioral disorder (Erk, 2004). Three types of ADHD are as follows:

- *Predominately inattentive type:* The person cannot focus or stay focused on a task or activity; the child does not pay attention to details; cannot maintain focus on play or school work; does not complete work or chores; has trouble organizing tasks and activities; gets distracted and loses things.
- *Predominately hyperactive/impulsive type:* The person is very active and often acts without thinking; the child is in constant motion, acts before thinking such as running into danger and being surprised to find themselves there; the child may fidget, squirm, run around, climb, leave seats, talk too much, have trouble playing quietly, blurt out answers, have trouble waiting for his or her turn, interrupt, and butt into games.
- *Combined type:* The person is inattentive, impulsive, and too active; these children have symptoms of both of the types described above (American Psychiatric Association [APA], 2000, p. 92).

The APA (2000) caution that for a child to be classified as hyperactive/impulsive, some symptoms must have been present before the age of 7 years, must persist for at least 6 months, must be present in multiple settings and inconsistent with the child's developmental level, and must clearly impair functioning.

Smith and Luckasson (1995) state that the condition is confusing. Not all children diagnosed as having attention deficit disorders (ADD) are in special education programs; some are diagnosed as learning disabled, and others may be classified as having behavioral disorders, emotional disturbance, or other disabilities. Erk (2004) discusses neuroanatomical abnormalities that may accompany ADHD, as well as educational and social conditions that may also be present.

A national nonprofit organization, Children with Attention Deficit Disorders, has reported that children might have ADD if they fidget, squirm, or seem restless; have trouble remaining seated, playing quietly, waiting their turn, following instructions, or sustaining attention; talk excessively; are easily distracted; blurt out answers; shift from one uncompleted task to another; interrupt others; do not seem to listen; often lose things; frequently engage in dangerous behavior; act without thinking; have low self-esteem; have frequent, unpredictable mood swings; and get angry and lose their temper easily (de la Cruz, 1994). However, many of these characteristics may be normal behaviors for a child's particular developmental level, or they could be characteristics of other problems. One must consider the intensity and duration of the symptoms, as well as how they fit into the child's overall developmental pattern.

Working with children who have ADHD requires a multidisciplinary, multitreatment model (Goldstein & Goldstein, 1990). Usually, such teams are composed of professionals such as physicians, psychologists, psychiatrists, counselors, and speech and other educational specialists. A physical examination must be a part of the diagnostic process; then professionals must supervise medications as necessary. Wicks-Nelson and Israel (2003) and the Family Doctor (2006) website state the medications of first choice for ADHD are stimulants such as methylphenidate (brand names: Concerta, Ritalin), dextroamphetamine (brand names: Dexedrine, Dextrostat), d- and l-amphetamin racemic mixture (brand name: Adderall), and pemoline (brand name: Cylert). Alternative choices include antidepressants and antihypertensives. However, these drugs have unwanted side effects for some small children, and medication as a sole treatment is not recommended by most professionals. Teachers, parents, and other adults who work with children taking medication must be aware of the treatment to provide feedback about its effects. Counselors can serve as coordinators of the many professionals working with the child during the assessment and intervention stages. In addition, they can develop referral lists that include physicians and other helping professionals familiar with ADHD, as well as local groups offering parenting classes or support groups.

According to Kottman, et al. (1995), parents of children with ADHD in their study expressed a great deal of concern about their children's self-esteem, future adjustment, and lack of social skills, and the stress of parenting these children. They called for more communication and cooperation with the school. Counselors can be the vital link between children with ADHD, their parents, and the school system. They can provide educational seminars for teachers and parents focusing on behavioral techniques to decrease impulsiveness and increase appropriate behaviors. Anastopoulos, et al. (1998) provide a comprehensive model for parent education.

Schwiebert, et al. (1995) suggest that bibliotherapy, support groups, a parent group, and family counseling may be helpful to parents, especially during the initial assessment period and while the parent is dealing with his or her feelings about the child's condition. Kottman, et al. (1995) recommend a parent training program that includes general information about ADHD, its causes, and possible treatment plans; self-esteem development suggestions; training in parent listening and encouragement skills; dealing with parent stress; suggestions for working with the child's school; and suggested means of social support for parents. Finally, Erk (1999) and Carter, et al. (2004) provide extensive, helpful suggestions for adults working with children with ADHD.

Erk (2004) reviews a collaborative multimodal study of children with ADHD (MTA Study). Children in the study were assigned to four experimental groups. The findings of that research support the integration of parent training, school intervention, child treatment, and medication management for children with ADHD. Resnick (2000) recommends a treatment menu for individual counseling with children and adolescents. The choices may include things such as understanding the diagnosis and how it can have a positive effect on a person's life, dealing with the reaction to the diagnosis, dealing with stress, dealing with lost opportunities and relationships, and coping with grief and suffering that may have been a part of their lives. Cognitive restructuring techniques may teach the child more positive ways of thinking, as well as self-monitoring of behavior. Group counseling to teach more effective social skills may be helpful at some point during treatment; however, counselors must carefully assess the child's readiness to benefit from this interaction and to function as a group member. Nigg and Rappley (2001) conclude that multimodal intervention produces the broadest benefit in ADHD. Erk (2004) recommends parent training and counseling, teacher education, individual counseling, group counseling, behavioral interventions, and self-esteem and social skills education. The services provided from different agencies and people need to be coordinated with follow-up to refresh parents on behavior management, as well as to update school plans.

THE CHILD WITH MENTAL RETARDATION

The American Association on Mental Retardation (AAMR, 2002) defines mental retardation as follows:

> Mental retardation is a disability characterized by significant limitations both in intellectual functioning and in adaptive behavior as expressed in conceptual, social, and practical adaptive skills. This disability originates before age 18.

The AAMR suggest the subgroups of mental retardation be classified according to a person's strengths and weaknesses in four areas: intellectual functioning and adaptive skills; psychological and emotional functioning; physical functioning and health; and the person's current environment and the optimal environment. The profile of the classification attends to the level of support needed by the person: intermittent or "as needed"; limited; extensive or pervasive (Wicks-Nelson & Israel, 2003). Other systems (APA, 2000) classify mental retardation by IQ scores. Those levels are mild, moderate, severe, and profound.

The limitations in skills will cause someone to learn and develop more slowly than normal (NICHCY, 2002). Newmeyer and Newmeyer (2004) list five dimensions for classification of mental retardation: intellectual abilities two standard deviations or more below the mean on standard measures of intelligence, adaptive behavior, social roles, health, and context. These should result in a profile of support needs appropriate to the person's age that are designed to enhance the well-being of the individual, as discussed previously (AAMR, 2002).

After the diagnoses, the child's functioning in four areas is studied: intellectual and adaptive skills, psychological and emotional concerns, physical functioning and health, and the current environment and the environment that would be optimal for the growth of the individual (Wicks-Nelson & Israel, 2003). Services and support are based on the level of intensity of need. Hardman et al. (1993) suggest that the child may need help with adaptive skills such as coping in school, developing interpersonal relationships, developing language skills, coping with emotional concerns, and taking care of personal needs.

The causes of mental retardation vary, and the characteristics of the children also differ. Smith and Luckasson (1995) and Smith (1998) summarize the various factors in four categories: socioeconomic and environmental factors, injury, infection and toxins, and biological causes. Poverty, with its associated factors such as pollution, poor nutrition, and inadequate health care, is the leading cause suspected in most cases with no organic basis. Head and brain injury may occur at birth or at other times (car or bicycle accidents). Mental retardation due to infection or toxin may be the result of viral infections (rubella, measles), sexually transmitted diseases (syphilis, HIV), or toxins such as alcohol, other drugs, or tobacco used by the mother during pregnancy. Down syndrome and Tay-Sachs disease are examples of mental retardation caused by biological factors. NICHCY (2002) lists the common causes as genetic conditions, problems during pregnancy, problems at birth, and health problems.

The counseling techniques in this section are geared toward those children categorized as intermittent or limited, the groups most likely to face societal problems and pressures. These children have physical and psychological needs similar to those of other children, but the added handicap of their exceptionality interferes with their adjustment. The AAMR definition suggests that children may need help in ten "adaptive skill" areas: communication (understanding and expression), self-care, home living, social interactions, understanding the community, self-direction (making choices), health and safety, obtaining functional academic skills (reading, writing, everyday mathematics), effectively using leisure time, and developing employment skills (Smith, 1998).

Counseling goals include improving social interactions, enhancing skills, developing interpersonal relationships, and promoting a positive self-image (Parette & Hourcade, 1995). Peer feedback and peer modeling can be highly effective counseling techniques. Group counseling can help the child learn and rehearse effective ways of behaving. Behavior modification techniques, such as the token system or contingency contracting, have been found to work effectively with individuals who have mental retardation. The counselor will want to be clear and concise in communications, limit the number of directions, display respect, and provide encouragement (Parette & Hourcade, 1995).

Wicks-Nelson and Israel (2003) cite behavioral techniques that help shape and strengthen adaptive skills and weaken ineffective behavior. Those authors support social skills training and functional communication training for children with mental retardation. The authors encourage counselors to be direct and set specific goals with this population. Counselors should use concrete, clear language and have short, frequent meetings with children with mental retardation.

Counselors will need to work with the parents and other significant people in the child's life to help them understand and encourage the child's abilities. Special attention should be on teaching the child independent living skills, as well as personal and social skills. The child and parents also need guidance and assistance in planning for the child's educational and vocational future.

THE CHILD WITH A PHYSICAL DISABILITY

Hardman et al. (1993) describe physical disorders as "impairments that may interfere with an individual's mobility and coordination . . . the impairments may also affect his or her capacity to communicate, learn, and adjust" (p. 340). According to NICHCY (2005), orthopedic impairment means a severe orthopedic impairment that adversely affects a child's educational performance. The term includes impairments caused by a congenital anomaly (for example, clubfoot, absence of some member, among others), impairments caused by disease (for example, poliomyelitis, bone tuberculosis, and others), and impairments from other causes (for example, cerebral palsy, amputations, and fractures or burns that cause contractures). Other Health Impairment is another IDEA category that incorporates physical disabilities. That means conditions causing limited strength, vitality, or alertness, including a heightened alertness to environmental stimuli, that results in limited alertness with respect to the educational environment, that (1) is due to chronic or acute health problems such as asthma, ADD or ADHD, diabetes, epilepsy, a heart condition, hemophilia, lead poisoning, leukemia, nephritis, rheumatic fever, and sickle cell anemia; and (2) adversely affects a child's educational performance. They may include cerebral palsy, spina bifida, spinal cord injuries, amputations, muscular dystrophy, cystic fibrosis, sickle cell anemia, adolescent pregnancy, and cocaine addiction (NICHCY, 2005).

Many children have more than one disability, and some conditions have overlapping symptoms. Knowing the characteristics, physical problems, symptoms, and prognosis of the child with a physical disability helps counselors understand the child's world. Counselors also want to know the child's strengths. Lack of knowledge and fear of the unknown can make the counselor apprehensive, which the child can sense. The children's needs vary according to the type of disability; some may need help with basic functioning and others may need help in building relationships and dealing with ridicule.

The child may have anxiety, fears, shame, or other negative feelings because of his or her disability. The children's perceptions of self and their abilities are also determined by the child's age at the time the disabling condition occurred and the severity of the condition. These reactions may reflect how the child has been treated by others, especially family. The demands for energy, time, and financial resources may add a heavy burden of stress to families. Smith (1998) points out that families of children with severe physical and health problems may experience fatigue and low vitality, a restricted social life, financial setbacks, and career interruptions, and can become preoccupied with the child's illness.

Smith and Luckasson (1995) report that the research indicates that teachers do not feel prepared to work with children with special needs in the classroom. They requested help most often with classroom management techniques. Because teachers' attitudes are critical to the success of children with disabilities, counselors should be prepared to work with them in a consultative manner to alleviate their personal concerns and anxieties about teaching children with disabilities and assist them in developing whatever skills are needed.

The counselor who works with children who have disabilities needs to be able to work with all agencies, professionals, parents, and other significant persons in the child's life. Coordinating services, rearranging physical environments, removing barriers and inconveniences, and securing special equipment and materials may be only the first step to meeting the needs of those with physical disabilities. Counselors can advocate for all services needed to help children with disabilities reach their full potential (Tarver-Behring & Spagna, 2004).

As with many other child clients, counselors would focus the goals of counseling on helping the student identify his or her strengths and encouraging the student to become a self-advocate. Counselors should focus on building feelings of self-worth and healthy attitudes. The child may need to be encouraged to express and recognize his or her feelings toward the disability, helped to learn social or personal skills, counseled in the area of independent living, and assisted in making vocational plans for the future. Adlerian counseling (see Chapter 11) may help a child recognize strengths. More important than the physical limitation is that each child is a unique individual who has capabilities and potential; the counselor's role is to facilitate growth toward reaching this potential.

GENERAL IDEAS

Simpson (1998) lauds behavior modification as one of the most effective tools in working with children with special needs. He outlines the most important features of behavior modification programs. Simpson explains the first essential task is the clear identification, definition, and measurement of an appropriate target behavior. The second step includes the identification of where, when, with whom, and under what conditions the target behavior happens. Next, the professional investigates factors that cause or maintain the target behavior. Finally, the professional uses appropriate interventions to modify the target behavior. His guidelines help counselors teach parents and teachers, as well as work with children to modify some inappropriate habits.

Deck, et al. (1999) recount some of the issues of school counselors working with students with disabilities. They discuss using small-group counseling, classroom guidance, individual counseling, after-school counseling, and collaboration with teachers and parents. Another summary of the tasks of the counselor working with any type of exceptional child might include the following:

1. Recognize that the child is a *person* first.
2. Work toward an understanding of the child's specific exceptionality and the unique social, learning, or behavioral problems that may accompany this exceptionality.
3. Counsel to enhance self-concept.
4. Facilitate adjustment to exceptionality.
5. Coordinate the services of other professionals or agencies working with the exceptional child.
6. Help the significant people in the child's life (parents and teachers especially) to understand the child's exceptionality, strengths and limitations, and special problems. Carpenter, et al. (1998) discuss teaming models for special education and the counselor's functions in those teams.
7. Assist in the development of effective, independent living skills.
8. Encourage recreational skills and hobbies.
9. Teach personal and social skills.
10. Assist in educational planning and possibly securing needed educational aids and equipment for the child.
11. Counsel with the parents.
12. Acquire a knowledge of and working relationship with professional and referral agencies.

COUNSELING WITH PARENTS OF EXCEPTIONAL CHILDREN

Interestingly, there is little research or literature for counselors who want to work with parents of exceptional children. Many parents are able to accept and adjust to their child's condition in a healthy manner; others, even though they love their child, may have trouble dealing with their feelings and the situation. Parents may experience a range of emotions: grief, shock, and disbelief; fear and anxiety about the child's future; helplessness because they cannot change the condition; and disappointment because theirs is not the perfect child they expected. They may resent the burdens the child's disability places on the family. Whatever the feelings, the counselor needs to help the parents work through them. Parents are the child's main support system, and they must be free to accept and support the child in his or her growth and development.

Counseling tasks for the counselor working with the parents of exceptional children include the following:

1. Encourage and help parents to gain knowledge about their child's exceptionality, prognosis, strengths, and limitations.

2. Assist the parents in working through feelings and attitudes that may inhibit the child's progress.
3. Advise parents concerning state, federal, or community resources available for educational, medical, emotional, or financial assistance.
4. Assist the parents in setting realistic expectations for their child.
5. Encourage the parents to view their child as a unique individual with rights and potentials and the ability to make choices about his or her own life.

Of the excellent books available to help both children and parents understand the characteristics of an exceptionality and the future of children with a particular exceptionality, those of R. A. Gardner contain a section written to parents about the disability and a section written for children to explain the disability in terms they can understand. The publications of the NICHCY have current, valuable information for parents, children, and professionals.

Parent groups are probably a good way of helping parents of exceptional youngsters. Through sharing, the parents learn that others have the feelings and problems they are experiencing. They realize they are not alone in their plight; many other parents have children who are different. Parents not only share their feelings in groups but also share methods for problem solving. Others may have lived through the particular crisis one set of parents is facing, and solutions can be discussed. Parent groups provide an atmosphere of understanding, acceptance, and support; they reassure troubled parents that they are not alone and that others care.

Counselors also may want to explore the possibilities of family therapy. Family sessions could explore feelings of anger, frustration, and shame; tendencies to scapegoat, exclude, or overprotect; communication styles or blocks; and effective and ineffective interactions and other problems of families not functioning effectively.

SUMMARY

Further research is needed on effectively counseling children with special needs. Exceptional children can learn, enjoy life, be independent and productive, and fulfill their individual potential just as surely as all other children can. They have the same rights to respect and growth as other children, and they have the same needs. Counselors who help these children celebrate their strengths and move successfully into their future roles will be richly rewarded.

Websites for Counseling with Exceptional Children

Internet addresses frequently change. To find the sites listed here, visit www.thom sonedu.com/counseling/thompson for an updated list of Internet addresses and direct links to relevant sites.

American Association for Mental Retardation (AAMR)

Children and Adults with Attention Deficit Disorders (CHADD)

National Information Center for Children and Youth with Disabilities (NICHCY)

Office of Special Education Programs (OSEP)

REFERENCES

American Association on Mental Retardation (AAMR). (2002). *Definitions*. Retrieved January 26, 2006, from http://www.aamr.org/Policies/faq_mental_retardation.shtml

American Psychiatric Association (APA). (2000). *Diagnostic and statistical manual of mental disorders* (4th ed., Rev. Ed.). Washington, DC: Author.

Anastopoulos, A. D., Smith, J. M., & Wien, E. E. (1998). Counseling and training parents. In R. A. Barley (Ed.), *Attention-deficit hyperactivity disorder*. New York: Guilford Press.

Boudah, D. J., & Weiss, M. P. (2002). Learning disabilities overview: Update 2002. *ERIC Clearinghouse on Disabilities and Gifted Education, EC Digest #E624.* Arlington, VA: ERIC.

Brandenburg, N., Friedman, R., & Silver, S. (1990). The epidemiology of childhood psychiatric disorder: Prevalence findings from recent studies. *Journal of the American Academy of Child and Adolescent Psychiatry, 29,* 76–83.

Brown, S. (2005). Art therapy urged for inclusion under IDEA: Advocates tout its effectiveness for students with disabilities. *Education Daily, 38,* 2.

Carpenter, S. L., King-Sears, M. E., & Keys, S. G. (1998). Counselors + educators + families as a transdisciplinary team = more effective inclusion for students with disabilities. *Professional School Counseling, 2,* 1–10.

Carter, D. J., Erford, B. T., & Orsi, R. (2004). Helping students with attention-deficit/hyperactivity disorder (AD/HD). In B. T. Erford (Ed.), *Professional school counseling: A handbook* (pp. 485–494). Austin, TX: ProEd.

Deck, M., Scarborough, J. L., Sferrazza, M. S., & Estill, D. M. (1999). Serving students with disabilities: Perspectives of three school counselors. *Intervention in School and Clinic, 34,* 150–156.

de la Cruz, B. (1994, May 23). Mothers go on attention deficit disorder crusade. *The Tennessean,* p. 4B.

Durodoye, B. A., Combes, B. H., & Bryant, R. M. (2004). Counselor intervention in the post-secondary planning of African American students with learning disabilities. *Professional School Counseling, 7,* 133–140.

Erk, R. R. (1999). Attention deficit hyperactivity disorder: Counselors, laws, and implications for practice. *Professional School Counseling, 2,* 318–326.

Erk, R. R. (2004). Attention-deficit/hyperactivity disorder in children and adolescents. In R. R. Erk (Ed.), *Counseling treatment for children and adolescents with DSM-IV-TR disorders* (pp. 109–154). Upper Saddle River, NJ: Merrill.

Family Doctor, Inc. (2006). Medications for ADHD. Retrieved April 6, 2006 from http://familydoctor.org/103.xml.

Goldstein, S., & Goldstein, M. (1990). *Managing attention disorders in children: A guide for practitioners*. New York: Wiley.

Hardman, M., Drew, C., Egan, M., & Wolf, B. (1993). *Human exceptionality: Society, school and family*. Boston: Allyn & Bacon.

Henderson, K. (2001). An overview of ADA, IDEA, and Section 504: Update 2001. *ERIC clearinghouse on disabilities and gifted education, ERIC EC Digest #E606.* Arlington, VA: ERIC.

Kottman, T., Robert, R., & Baker, D. (1995). Parental perspectives on attention deficit/hyperactivity disorder: How school counselors can help. *The School Counselor, 43,* 142–150.

Learning Disabilities Association of America. (2005). *Understanding learning disabilities*. Retrieved January 26, 2006, from http://www.ldaamerica.us/aboutld/teachers/understanding/ld.asp

McEachern, A. G. (2004). Students with learning disabilities: Counseling issues and strategies. In B. T. Erford (Ed.), *Professional school counseling: A handbook* (pp. 591–600). Austin, TX: ProEd.

Newmeyer, A. J., & Newmeyer, M. D. (2004). Helping students with mental retardation. In B. T. Erford (Ed.), *Professional school counseling: A handbook* (pp. 587–590). Austin, TX: ProEd.

NICHCY (National Information Center for Children and Youth with Disabilities). (2002). Factsheets. Retrieved August 8, 2002, from http://www.nichcy.org/pubs/fact-she/fs19txt.htm

NICHCY (National Information Center for Children and Youth with Disabilities). (2005). *Factsheets*. Retrieved on January 29, 2006, from www.nichcy.org/pubs/fact-she/fs5txt.htm

Nigg, J. T., & Rappley, M. D. (2001). Interventions for attention-deficit/hyperactivity disorder. In E. R. Welfel & R. E. Ingersoll (Eds.), *The mental health desk reference* (pp. 183-190). New York: John Wiley & Sons.

Office of Special Education Programs. (2002). *The basic special education process under IDEA*. Retrieved September 8, 2002, from www.ed.gov/offices/OSERS/OSEP/IEP_Guide

Office of Special Education Programs. (2005). 25th *Annual Report to Congress*. Retrieved January 29, 2006, from www.ed.gov/offices/OSERS/OSEP.

Parette, H. P., & Hourcade, J. J. (1995). Disability etiquette and school counselors: A common sense approach toward compliance with the Americans with Disabilities Act. *The School Counselor, 52,* 224–233.

Reis, S. M., & Colbert, R. (2004). Counseling needs of academically talented students with learning disabilities. *Professional School Counseling, 8,* 156–167.

Resnick, R. J. (2000). *The hidden disorder: A clinician's guide to Attention-Deficit/Hyperactivity Disorder in adults*. Washington, DC: American Psychological Association.

Schwiebert, V., Sealander, K., & Tollerud, T. (1995). Attention-deficit disorder: An overview for school counselors. *Elementary School Guidance and Counseling, 29*(4), 249–259.

Simpson, R. L. (1998). Behavior modification for children and youth with exceptionalities: Application of best practice methods. *Intervention in School & Clinic, 33,* 219–227.

Smith, D. (1998). *Introduction to special education: Teaching in an age of challenge*. Boston: Allyn & Bacon.

Smith, D., & Luckasson, R. (1995). *Introduction to special education: Teaching in an age of challenge*. Needham Heights, MA: Allyn & Bacon.

State of North Carolina. (2000). *Procedures and reference manual for exceptional children's programs*. Retrieved January 28, 2006, from http://wsfcs.k12.nc.us/academic/ecmanual/ecintro.html

Tarver-Behring, S., Spagna, M. E., & Sullivan, J. (1998). School counselors and full inclusion for children with special needs. *Professional School Counselor, 1,* 51–56.

Tarver-Behring, S., & Spagna, M. E. (2004). Counseling with exceptional children. In A. Vernon (Ed.), *Counseling children and adolescents* (pp. 189–226). Denver, CO: Love.

Thompson, R., & Littrell, J. M. (1998). Brief counseling for students with learning disabilities. *Professional School Counseling, 2,* 60–68.

U. S. Department of Education. (2001). *Twenty-third Annual Report to Congress on the Implementation of the Individual with Disabilities Education Act.* Washington, DC: U.S. Government Printing Office.

Wicks-Nelson, R., & Israel, A. C. (2003). *Behavior disorders of childhood* (5th ed.). Upper Saddle River, NJ: Prentice Hall.

CHAPTER 20

Legal and Ethical Considerations for Counselors

May you live your life as if the maxim of your actions were to become universal law.

—Immanuel Kant

Legal, ethical, moral, and professional guidelines combine in many of the issues counselors face every day. Counselors' frustration may be fueled by the lack of unequivocal answers from ethical or legal guidelines for the dilemmas created in their practice. Working with children creates particular challenges for counselors because the rights of minors may be more ambiguous than some other points of law and ethics. This chapter highlights many of the issues that often arise in counseling children and contains a survey of some of the writers in this area of counseling. Counselor education programs provide courses that incorporate a foundational understanding of legal and ethical issues, but this practice area often changes. Therefore, anyone who counsels is advised to commit to an ongoing study of legal and ethical considerations.

ETHICAL, PROFESSIONAL, AND LEGAL ISSUES

Schmidt and Meara (1984) define the differences among ethical, professional, and legal issues in counseling. Ethics is a branch of philosophy that focuses on morals and morality in their relationship to making decisions. Some authors (Fischer & Sorenson, 1996; Stone & Dahir, 2006) define ethics as the customs, mores, standards, and accepted practices of a profession. Ethical issues "arise from personal and professional standards of moral duty and obligation" (p. 56). Ethical guidelines educate professionals about principled conduct in practice, provide a means of accountability in practice, and create ways to improve the profession (Herlihy & Corey, 1996). The codes of ethics are written in broad terms and serve as starting points for making decisions (Welfel, 2006). Counselors may refer to a number of ethical codes that inform their practice. Examples include those codes of the American Counseling Association (ACA, 2005), National Board of Certified Counselors (2005), American School Counselor Association (2004), American Association for Marriage and Family Therapy (2001), American Psychological Association (2002), and National Association of Social Workers (1999). All those documents address some common issues such as competence of the practitioner, responsibilities to the person being counseled, confidentiality, cultural diversity, and potentially harmful relationships.

Professional issues are technical, procedural, or cultural standards that members of the profession are expected to accept as part of their practice. For example, Daniels (2001) provides a summary of the ways managed care affects professional issues. Finally, legal issues are related to federal, state, and municipal standards of practice as regulated by law. According to Fischer and Sorenson (1996), laws are the minimum standard that society will accept. Stone and Dahir (2006) explain that laws require that counselors act as a "reasonably competent professional would" (p. 301). That guideline refers to the "standard of care" target that may guide decisions about whether a course of action would meet that criterion (Stone & Dahir, 2006). Someone who does not follow the law faces greater punitive sanctions or penalties for not complying than for not following ethical and/or professional standards. All three sets of standards exist to guide behavior for professionals. If the standards appear contradictory in a particular situation, the counselor is left to determine the most prudent action to protect the best interest of the client. With children, those decisions become complex.

Meara, et al. (1996) have written that a code of ethics cannot contain everything one needs to know, and that codes and their interpretations change due to a changing society, technology, rules, and public policy. For these reasons, these authors argue that professionals need to be aware of principle ethics, but must also possess "virtue ethics," or character ethics. According to the authors, "proponents of virtue ethics believe that motivation, emotion, character, ideals, and moral habits situated within the tradition and practices of a culture or other group present a more complete account of moral life than actions based on prescribed rules or principles of practice . . ." (p. 24). Nystul (2003) agrees and states that virtue ethics relate to exceeding obligations and striving toward the ideals of a profession. A critical component of virtue ethics involves being sensitive to cultural issues in any decision making. The focus of principles has been on duty, laws, rules, obligations; the focus of virtue ethics, in contrast, is on the human character.

Welfel (2006) lists the following five virtues as those most commonly cited: integrity, acting consistently on personal values; prudence, acting with discernment and restraint; trustworthiness, acting and following through on commitments even in the face of difficulty; compassion, deep concern for a person's welfare; and respectfulness, avoiding action that diminishes a person's dignity or rights. Meara, et al. (1996) urge the integration of principle and virtue ethics to assist professionals in making difficult decisions and in more fully developing the ethical character of the profession.

Remley and Herlihy (2005) suggest that professional practice is built on certain basic elements that they explain as follows. One foundation is intentionality—that is, wanting to do the right thing for those being served. Another element consists of the moral principles of the helping profession. Those shared beliefs that guide our ethical reasoning include the following:

- Autonomy (respecting freedom of choice)
- Nonmaleficence (doing no harm)
- Beneficence (being helpful)
- Justice (being fair)
- Fidelity (being faithful)
- Veracity (being honest)

Other aspects Remley and Herlihy discuss include the knowledge of ethical, legal, and professional standards and the skills to apply that knowledge. These authors recommend having a decision-making model to help when encountering dilemmas. Finally, Remley and Herlihy challenge counselors to have the courage of their convictions to function in an ethical and professional manner.

DECISION-MAKING MODELS

Many scholars propose models of ethical decision making. Counselors may find useful suggestions for approaching ethical choices in the work of these authors: Cottone (2001); Forester-Miller & Davis (1995); Garcia, et al. (2003); Kitchener (1984); Meara, et al. (1996); Rave and Larsen (1995); Stadler (1986); Travydas (1987); and Van Hoose and Kottler (1985). A synthesis of these and other models that Remley and Herlihy (2005) and Welfel (2006) discuss may be helpful as counselors encounter ethical dilemmas. Those steps of decision making include the following:

1. Develop ethical sensitivity to the moral dimensions of counseling.
2. Identify and define the problem. Clarify facts, who holds a stake in the situation, and the sociocultural context of the case.
3. Think about your own emotional reactions.
4. Apply fundamental ethical principles and theories to the situation (autonomy, nonmaleficence, beneficence, justice, fidelity, veracity). Define the central issues in the dilemma and possible options.
5. Refer to professional standards, relevant laws and regulations, and current ethics literature.
6. Consult with colleagues or experts.
7. Involve the client in the decision-making process.

8. Identify desired outcomes and action to achieve those outcomes.
9. Consider different courses of action.
10. Choose and act.
11. Reflect on the actions taken (Remley & Herlihy, 2005, p. 13; Welfel, 2006, p. 22).

An example using that decision-making model can be found later in this chapter. Some tips from the Ethics Committee of the American School Counselor Association (1999–2001) may also serve as guidelines to all choices made by counselors. Following is a summary of those hints:

- Always act in the best interest of the client.
- Always act in good faith and without malice.
- Be aware of your personal values, attitudes, and beliefs.
- Refer clients to another counselor if personal characteristics interfere with your effectiveness as a helper (p. 1).

COUNSELING MINORS

Salo and Shumate (1993) write that "counseling minor clients is an ambiguous practice" (p. 1). They suggest that absolute guidelines are difficult to determine because statutes and court decisions do not always agree. In addition, conflicts arise between codes of ethics and state and federal laws. An example of the variation in state laws is the different "ages of majority," that is, the age at which a minor becomes an adult. In some states, that age is 18, in others, 19, and still others, 21 (Swenson, 1993).

Lawrence and Kurpius (2000) have traced the history of children's rights and crucial court cases that have set precedents for the interpretation of those rights. Those authors conclude that safeguarding basic rights for children involve balancing three social systems:

1. The state that must accept the imperative of maintaining the safety and rights of citizens, including children
2. The parent or family, interested in their freedom to raise their children without interference
3. The minor child "whose vested interest has been self-protection from perceived harm, preservation of privacy, and maintenance of personal dignity" (Lawrence & Kurpius, 2000, p. 132).

Lawrence and Kurpius conclude that, currently, parents and others in positions of authority over children have the balance of power. Thus, although most adults agree on the worth and dignity of children, it must be recognized that legally, minors have less rights than adults. Several sources help monitor the rights children do have in each state. Linde (2003) has identified minors' rights to ask for health care and other services. English and Kenney (2003) have generated a state-by-state description of the legal status of minors in their book *State Minor Consent Laws: A Summary.* Information in that volume outlines minors' rights to request health services. The book includes data about minors' health privacy and confidentiality statutes, disclosure to parents, and other laws that affect young people. The Guttmacher Institute (www.guttmacher.org) publishes policy briefs and summaries of laws that pertain to young people. As amended you can get to some of their reports Finally, the American Bar Association (2005) provides abbreviated information about state laws and minors on their website. Unique concerns arise when counseling children. Lawrence and Kurpius (2000) and Remley and Herlihy (2005) identify counselor competence, parental permission, confidentiality, and child-abuse reporting as ethical issues that consistently emerge when counseling children.

The ACA *Code of Ethics and Standards of Practice* (2005) outlines the responsibilities of counselors toward their clients, colleagues, workplace, and self. Most basically, the Code calls for counselors to "respect clients and their background, to recognize diversity and embrace a cross-cultural approach in support of the worth, dignity, potential, and uniqueness of people within their social and cultural contexts" (p. 1). The intent is to guide counselors through the most common problems in practice, as well as to communicate the goals of the profession. Counselors have the ethical code to guide them on ways to maintain professional behavior, to practice with the best interest of the client in mind, and to practice within the limits of their competence. The *Standards of Practice* describe the minimum behavioral expectations for carrying out the *Code of Ethics*. The following sections review the particular challenges of counseling children based on the ACA Code.

COMPETENCE

Welfel (2006) proposes a summation of competence that occurs when a person demonstrates knowledge, skill, and diligence. Knowledge includes history, theory, and research of the field and awareness of the limits of current understanding. Counselors need particular areas of skills to work with children rather than assuming they can generalize from their coursework on adults. Diligence refers to ongoing attentiveness to the needs of the client, working hard to help the person. Practitioners should participate in coursework in child counseling before working with young people. Counselors must be thoroughly familiar with child and adolescent development, developmental tasks, family dynamics, and interventions designed for a particular age and stage (Weiner & Robinson Kurpius, 1995). To be competent to counsel children, counselors must participate in specialized education, training, and supervised practice.

Detailed information can be found in the ACA *Code of Ethics,* Section C.2: Professional Competence. Generally, these guidelines refer to the following practices. To ensure professional competence, counselors should participate in continuing education not only for renewing credentials and licensure but also to stay current with best practices and updated information about client populations. Counselors should maintain accurate knowledge in their areas of expertise. Counselors accurately describe their credentials and only provide services for which they have been trained and had supervised practice.

Following those guidelines will help a counselor develop and maintain professional competence (Linde, 2003).

INFORMED CONSENT

One goal of the counseling relationship is the creation of a climate of safety and trust. Professionals assume that the protection of information obtained in that relationship increases the potential for that climate to be built. This right to privacy and confidentiality becomes complicated with minors. Informed consent presents the first complication.

The formal permission given by a client for the beginning of counseling is known as informed consent. In effect, that permission constitutes a contract that allows treatment. People who are unable to understand the contents in a consent form or who are unable to make a rational decision are also unable to give informed consent (Huey, 1996). Lawrence and Kurpius (2000) note "informed consent must be given voluntarily with sufficient knowledge of the treatment and its consequences, and the person must be competent to give it, that is, able to understand the consequences and implications of the choices being made" (p. 133). The ACA (2005) *Code of Ethics* reads as follows:

> When counseling clients who are minors or individuals who are unable to give voluntary consent, counselors seek the assent of clients to services, and include them in decision-making as appropriate. Counselors recognize the need to balance the ethical rights of clients to make choices, their capacity to give consent or assent to receive services, and parental or familial legal rights and responsibilities to protect these clients and make decisions on their behalf. (Section A.2.d)

Welfel (2006) explains that legally minors usually cannot give their informed consent for counseling services; at least one parent or guardian must provide permission instead. The impact of developmental factors relative to cognitive maturity, ethical guidelines, and legal requirements point to counselors getting the assent of minors to counseling. Welfel defines assent as involving children in decisions about their own care and in an agreement to participate in counseling. Assent is supplemental to parental consent.

Consequently, parental permission may be necessary for children to receive treatment. Remley and Herlihy (2005) explain that unless a federal or state law exists that states otherwise, school counselors do not have an obligation to attain parent's permission for counseling services. Counselors outside of school do need a parent or guardian's consent for a minor to receive counseling. Lawrence and Kurpius (2000) have discussed some situations that are exceptions to this practice. One exception is court order treatment. Another exception involves a *mature* minor, an older adolescent capable of understanding the consent. These authors note that, in some states, minors can give consent to treatment in an emergency when waiting would endanger their lives or health. A minor who is legally emancipated such as being the head of a household, being employed, being in the armed forces, or married may also be an exception (Welfel, 2006). Finally, a court order can be used to waive parental consent. The writers also caution care when working with a minor of divorced parents to obtain consent from the custodial parent. Stone and Dahir (2006) caution counselors to check the rights on the noncustodial parent who has rights as a psychological guardian even without having legal custody.

Informed consent can be made more concrete when written statements such as a disclosure letter or brochure are prepared (Muro & Kottman, 1995). At the beginning of counseling, the client should receive documents that explain confidentiality, privileged communication, and limits to either. The information should be written in simple language appropriate for the age of the child. Glosoff and Pate Jr. (2002) explain that informed consent is an ongoing, clarifying part of the counseling relationship. They recommend that counselors remind young people of the contents throughout their work. Counselors may have a simple disclosure statement for the minor client and another statement with more details for parents or guardians.

Kaplan (2001) had ideas about what to include in a disclosure statement or counseling brochure. The document should have a short description of the counselor's education, training, degrees, and work experiences. An explanation of the theory and treatment approach most often used should be included, as well as the benefits and limitations of service (Welfel, 2006). As stated earlier, a definition of confidentiality and its limits such as danger to others, reporting child abuse, maltreatment or neglect, and any agency policies that conflict with confidentiality such as filing for insurance benefits. Procedural details such as guidelines about appointments, how to contact the counselor, and approximate number of sessions can also be listed.

CONFIDENTIALITY

Stadler (1990) notes confusion concerning the terms *privacy, confidentiality,* and *privileged communication.* She states that the right to privacy ensures that people may choose what others know about them. Confidentiality refers to the professional responsibility to respect and limits access to clients' personal information. According to Stadler, issues of confidentiality are the ethical problems counselors most frequently encounter. She recommends that counselors be extremely careful to apprise their clients of their limits of confidentiality at the very beginning of counseling.

Linde (2003) provides helpful definitions about privileged communication, a legal term used to describe the privacy of the counselor–client communication. Privileged communication exists by statute and applies only to testifying in a court of law. She said, "The privilege belongs to the client, who always has the right to waive the privilege and allow the counselor to testify" (p. 52). She explains that the limits of privileged communication are determined by federal, state, and local mandates and vary in existence and parameters accordingly. Therefore, counselors must know local, state, and federal laws to understand how privileged communication applies.

One assumption on which counseling proceeds is that the promise of confidentiality helps create trust and safety both with adults and children. For example, research (Ford, et al. 1997) suggests with the promise of confidentiality adolescents are more willing to disclose personal information. Welfel (2006) has reviewed the writing of ethics scholars and concludes that "the degree to which confidentiality can be honored is directly related to the age and maturity of the minor . . . the close the young person is to the age of maturity, the greater the likelihood that he or she can be granted a fuller measure of confidentiality" (p. 90). Fundudis (2003) says four factors should be considered to determine a minor's competence:

- Chronological age, which includes developmental history and maturational progress
- Cognitive level, which includes language, memory, reasoning ability, and logic
- Emotional maturity with factors such as temperament, stability of mood, attachment, educational adjustment, and attitudinal style
- Sociocultural factors such as family values and religious beliefs

However, children may have parents or guardians who want to know the contents of counseling sessions, and those adults probably have a legal right to know (Remley & Herlihy, 2005). Stone (2004) captures the dilemma when she talked about counselors being caught between protecting the client's privacy and the parent's right to know what is happening in their child's life. Salo and Shumate (1993) contend, "When a child approaches a counselor without parental knowledge or consent, immediate tension arises between the child's right to privacy and the parent's right—on the child's behalf—to provide informed consent for the counseling" (p. 10). Obtaining parental consent is good practice for counselors unless potential danger to the minor exists. The authors point out that early communication with parents concerning the purpose of counseling can prevent later problems. The law generally supports parents who forbid counseling of their minor children unless there are extenuating circumstances. Counselors must balance offering privacy to minors with not only the rights of parents but also the therapeutic goal of engaging parents in helping children. Remley and Herlihy (2005) suggest that counselors consider these facts about children and privacy:

- Younger children have little understanding of confidentiality or a need for privacy. Huey (1996) concurs and states that young children often are much less concerned about confidentiality than is the counselor.
- Preadolescents and adolescents, in contrast, may have a heightened need for privacy due to there developmental stage.
- Some children may want their parents or guardians to know what has occurred in the counseling session(s).
- Children will sometimes disclose something to an adult hoping that the adult will intervene with other adults.
- Children's reasoning capacity may limit their ability to make decisions in their best interest.

Other authors have suggestions as well. Welfel (2006) proposes that parents will be reassured when they know that counselors will not practice outside of their competence, will make reasonable efforts to meet parents' requests, and will respect family values. She thinks that having handbooks or brochures with information about the counseling practice will help build a climate of cooperation and open communication. Huey (1996) reminds us that parents can be valuable allies in work with children. Parents are entitled to general information from the counselor about the child's progress and short updates will meet that request (Stromberg and colleagues, as cited in Corey, et al. 1998). Zingaro (1983) advises that when it is in the best interest of the child for an adult to have information, the counselor could let the adult know ways to help the minor rather than revealing specific information. Corey et al. (1998) admonish counselors to be cautious in both the kind and extent of information that is released.

To safeguard against confidentiality becoming a possible ethical or legal problem, counselors should inform the client during the first and subsequent interviews (as applicable) about confidentiality and its limits. When possible, have parents and guardians, as well as the minor, present in the first session so that all understand the parameters of therapy and limits of confidentiality. Those limits should be clearly disclosed and explained, and should include examples of legally and ethically mandated breaches of confidentiality. This disclosure should be done both verbally in language easily understood by the client and in a written professional disclosure statement (see earlier) that should be signed by the client, parents, and the counselor. All parties should keep a copy of the professional disclosure statement.

Remley and Herlihy (2005) suggest ways to cope with requests when parents want to know about counseling and the minor client has strong feelings about the disclosure not happening:

1. Discuss the request with the child and ask if the minor is willing to talk to the adult. If the child refuses, proceed with the next step.
2. Try to convince the adult that the nature of the counseling relationship and the importance of confidentiality work for the best interests of the child. Assure the adult that information concerning any danger to the child will be disclosed. If that does not convince the adult, move to the next step.
3. Hold a session with the child and the adult and act as a mediator hoping that one or the other will acquiesce. Failing that, proceed according to Step 4 or 5.
4. Inform the child beforehand, and then tell the adult the content of the counseling session to the adult who has requested the information. Or, proceed to Step 5.
5. Refuse to disclose the information after having informed your supervisor.

Mitchell, et al. (2002) add some other ideas. They encourage the counselor to use empathic skills to give the parent an opportunity to express concerns. Counselors should show respect for the parents' fears. Counselors can explain the dilemma and the role confidentiality plays in the counseling relationship. These authors recommend that children be told about the inquiry. They also encourage counselors to prepare procedures and alternatives for responses in advance of the problem situations.

As noted earlier, privileged communication is a legal concept, designed to protect the rights of the client (rather than the protection of the counselor's rights) to withhold testimony in court proceedings. Great variation exists among all fifty states, and relevant statutes must specify which professionals (for example, attorneys, clergy, psychologists, counselors) are included under the umbrella of privileged communication. Because exclusions to this privilege vary by state, it is imperative for the counselor to be thoroughly familiar with the state laws governing counseling practice. It is also the client's right to waive privileged communication that leaves the counselor with no legal grounds for withholding the requested confidential information.

However, professionals are required only to disclose the information requested to the parties specified by the client. Because the right to privileged communication is not absolute, courts may order the release of records, especially in situations in which the society's need for information overrides the client's right to privacy. In most states, the legal concept of privileged communication does not extend to groups, couples, or family counseling, nor does it cover disclosures made in the presence of third parties not specified under the umbrella of privileged communication.

Exceptions to the privileged communication right in which professionals must disclose information include the following situations:

- The professional is fulfilling a court-ordered role, such as expert witness.
- A court mandates the release of information considered to be privileged communication.
- A lawsuit against the professional is initiated by the client (for example, malpractice).
- The client uses his or her mental condition as a defense in a lawsuit.
- A professional determines the client needs hospitalization because of a mental disorder.
- A client discloses intent to commit a crime or is assessed to be dangerous to self or others.
- A client is a minor and has been or is suspected of being the victim of a crime such as child abuse (Remley & Herlihy, 2005; Welfel, 2006).

CONFIDENTIALITY OF FILES   Access to files presents another concern involving confidentiality. The federal Family Rights and Privacy Act provided parents and students of legal age the right to inspect their records and to protect unlimited access to their records (Burcky & Childers, 1976). Also known as the Buckley Amendment, the act applies to all educational records collected, maintained, or used by a school the student has attended. Personal logs, treatment records, and directory information are excluded. Personal logs are defined as records of instructional, supervisory, administrative, and associated educational personnel. The records must be in sole possession of the individual and not have been shared. Treatment records include the records of a physician, psychiatrist, psychologist, or other recognized professional acting in the professional role. The records can be used only in conjunction with the treatment of the student. Directory information includes the demographic information, grade or field of study, participation in extracurricular activities, physical descriptions, and dates of attendance (Federal Family Rights and Privacy Act, 1974; Underwood & Mead, 1995; Sealander, et al. 1999; U.S. Department of Education, 2002). The Individuals with Disabilities Education Act (IDEA) (1997) also mandates that parents have access to student files in a form they can understand.

Hughes (2001) has summarized the laws regarding the release of student information. Also, the U.S. Department of Education (2002) has clarified that schools need written permission from the parent to release information except as follows:

- To school officials with legitimate educational interests
- To a school to which a student is transferring
- Officials for auditing or evaluation purposes
- In conjunction with financial aid requests
- Organizations conducting research on behalf of the school
- Accrediting bodies
- To comply with a judicial order or subpoena
- Appropriate officials in cases of emergency
- State and local authorities in a juvenile justice system (p. 2)

Counselors need to know the types of records kept in institutional files. They may not be able to maintain confidentiality if the parents of underage children request access to such files. The counselor may maintain a personal file may be kept for confidential notes because personal files do not fall under this law. However, files that have been seen by *anyone*, except a paid secretary, or have been discussed with anyone in the process of decision making are no longer considered personal notes (Salo & Shumate, 1993).

Welfel (2006) reminds us that records of a counseling session benefit clients and professionals in providing services. She said that records help counselors be reflective and prepared. The ACA *Code of Ethics* (Section A.1.b: Records) explains maintaining, storing, and disposing of records. For the counselor's notes, Remley (1990) suggests that factual information concerning actual occurrences in the session should be kept separate from the subjective section in which the counselor records diagnoses and develops future treatment plans. Remley also recommends writing notes carefully, with the thought in mind that they could become public one day and that counselors may want to document questionable or controversial information.

Piazza and Baruth (1990) have identified six kinds of information for counseling records: identifying information; assessment data; treatment plans; case notes; termination summary; and miscellaneous information such as consent forms, correspondence, and releases. Medication information is another component of client records required by the Health Insurance Portability and Accountability Act (HIPAA) (Welfel, 2006). HIPAA protects personal health information that may be used for treatment or payment purposes and protects electronic communication systems from unauthorized access. Health care officials obtain a signature on the Notice of Privacy Practices document that signifies permission to send information to third parties for payment, to provide treatment, and to keep ordinary operation proceeding (Welfel, 2006).

BREACHING CONFIDENTIALITY   In court cases in states where the clients of counselors and psychologists (or other helpers) are not protected by a licensure law providing for privileged communication, counselors have no recourse except to reveal the information if subpoenaed. Some courts are more tolerant than others, allowing the counselor to share the privileged information with the judge in private to determine whether the information is necessary to the proceeding or whether public disclosure would be too hurtful to those involved, such as children who are a part of the case.

Examples of legally and ethically mandated breaches of confidentiality include the following situations:

- The client is younger than 18 years (or the recognized age of majority in that jurisdiction). (The parent or legal guardian then has a legal right to the child's counseling records and to be informed of the counseling content, progress, and other information.)
- The client expresses an intent to harm self, others, or property. (Court decisions such as *Tarasoff* v. *Regents of the University of California* [1974] have delineated the counselor's duty to warn and to protect others at the expense of breaking client confidentiality. Kachgian & Felthous [2004] report that in cases of clients who are dangerous, courts in many states view a breach of confidentiality as an obligation.)
- The client discloses acts (either past or present) of verbal, physical, or sexual abuse, or the counselor has reasonable suspicion that such acts occurred or are occurring.
- The counselor is court ordered to break confidentiality or to provide counseling notes or records subpoenaed or requested by the court.
- An adult client willingly provides written informed consent requesting the counselor to breach confidentiality or to release counseling records.
- The counselor is a student or is being supervised for licensure. The client's written consent to record counseling sessions must be obtained to provide the student counselor with professional supervision or consultation with treatment teams. In these cases, student counselors should disclose only as much confidential information as is required or is necessary for professional supervision or consultation.

If breaking of confidentiality is necessary, it is suggested that the counselor discuss with the client his or her intention to do so and ask the client for assistance with deciding on the best process. The counselor should explain why confidentiality must be broken, summarize what has to be done or said, and then ask the client to help resolve the dilemma. The child client might prefer to take the lead by calling parents or other authorities or by taking whatever appropriate action is necessary.

DUTY TO PROTECT   Breaching confidentiality when a counselor has a dangerous client requires extreme care. ACA *Code of Ethics,* Section B.2.a: Danger and Legal Requirements reads as follows:

> The general requirement that counselors keep information confidential does not apply when disclosure is required to protect clients or identified others from serious and foreseeable harm or when legal requirements demand that confidential information must be revealed. Counselors consult with other professionals when in doubt as to the validity of an exception.

Isaacs (1997) suggests that the *Tarasoff* case, case law in other jurisdictions, legal requirements, and ethical guidelines can confuse counselors on ways to proceed with dangerous clients. She proposes counselors develop protocols for consistency. Among other things, those protocols should include:

- Current standards of care
- List of treatment alternatives
- Full informed consent
- Consultation guidelines with parents, attorneys, school officials, and other counselors
- School and/or agency policy

Isaacs concludes that establishing protocols will prepare counselors to recognize the issues, identify their options, and have ready access to needed information. Isaacs and Stone (1999) also provide similar guidelines. Welfel (2006) explains that legal duty requires the counseling professional to take steps to protect an identifiable victim from harm such as informing the third party, notifying police, and assessing the risk for violence. That risk assessment includes client attitudes that support violence, client capacity to carry out violence, having means to complete the violent act, the intention in contrast with the idea of acting violently, responses of others to the client's plan, and the degree of client compliance with recommendations to reduce the risk. Welfel suggests consultation with other professionals when counselors are trying to determine the predictability of danger. We recommend her discussion of duty to warn and protect.

McFarland and Dupuis (2001) admonish counselors to protect gay, lesbian, bisexual, and transgendered (LGBT) students from violence by educating others, advocating for safe schools, and implementing prevention efforts. These authors cite emerging case law as mandating this protection for LGBT students.

CONFIDENTIALITY IN GROUPS   Corey (1995) was particularly concerned about confidentiality in counseling groups for minors. He urges leaders to "teach members, in terms they are capable of understanding, about the nature, purposes and limitations of confidentiality" (p. 33) and to remind members to discuss their concerns about confidentiality whenever needed. With complete information about the limits of confidentiality, members can decide how much they want to disclose. Salo and Shumate (1993) also note that "groups, by their very nature, negate the presumption of privacy" (p. 34). They advise counselors to inform all group members about the necessity for confidentiality, but also to point out that privileged communication may not apply to group discussion. Welfel (2006) states that even though group counselors cannot guarantee confidentiality, they encourage it. Having children practice keeping group communication private by role-playing situations may eliminate some complications.

CHILD ABUSE REPORTING

All states have statutes that require adults who have responsibility to care for and treat children to report suspected abuse of children (Lawrence & Kurpius, 2000). Foreman and Bernet (2000) provide clarification on state laws relative to child abuse reporting such as whether reported suspicions of abuse or incidences of abuse are mandated. Lawrence and Kurpius state that not reporting suspected abuse is one of the most common breaches of ethical standards. They hypothesize that the reporting may harm the therapeutic relationship and may destabilize the family. Rokop (2003) suggests that counselors can reduce damage to the counseling relationship by developing a strong alliance, communicating clearly about the law, expressing empathy with the client's distress, and offering support after the report is done. Lawrence and Kurpius suggest that counselors confer with professional colleagues and get legal advice before a decision is made to refrain from reporting child abuse. Welfel (2006) suggests the "well-lit room standard" in which counselors consider whether they would be proud to communicate their decision to their professional peers and expect approval of their position.

AN ETHICAL DECISION-MAKING PROCESS

Many situations have no *right* solution; the final answer depends on your counseling setting, the philosophy of your practice, the interpretation of the law by your local or state authorities, potential advantages or disadvantages of the solution, and the risks to the counselor and client. Variations in situations create nuances that impact any decision. We suggest you generate some possible ethical dilemmas and practice the process we outline in the following section. Our example from the model based on Remley and Herlihy (2005) and Welfel (2006) may be a workable way to think through ethical decision-making.

1. *Develop ethical sensitivity to the moral dimensions of counseling.* Felicity, the counselor involved, took an ethics course in her degree program and has attended several educational sessions since graduation. She also followed the advice of Welfel (2006) and has added a question about potential ethical issues to her intake form and to the outline she uses for case notes.

2. *Identify and define the problem. Clarify facts, who has a stake in the counseling outcome, and the sociocultural context of the case.* Felicity

has a 15-year-old female client, Cyndi, who has reported having an ongoing sexual relationship with an older man (Lewis), the husband of her best friend's (Janet) sister. Cyndi's parents have abandoned her and she is staying with Janet who lives with the sister and Lewis. Cyndi loves that arrangement because she has no rules to follow. She says she wants to stay with them until she can establish herself as an emancipated minor, but she also talks often about reconciliation with her parents. Cyndi's present concern is that if Janet finds out about the sexual encounters with Lewis, the girls' friendship will end.

Felicity does not know how old Lewis is, although she believes he was in high school about 4 years ago. She also is confused about what adult is currently responsible for Cyndi's well-being. Cyndi had been in foster care earlier in her life but is not in that system now. Felicity's concerns include: Is the situation one that should be reported as sexual abuse or rape or another legal duty? Depending on those answers, does the need to maintain confidentiality outweigh the potential concerns for Cyndi's safety? Felicity is uncertain whether this complex situation meets the "serious and foreseeable harm" criteria in the *Code of Ethics*.

Felicity needs information about the legal aspects and the ethical standard of what constitutes serious harm. She wants to understand more about the cultural norms of the community in which this is happening. She is familiar with other members of Cyndi and Janet's circle of friends and knows some of them are sexually active. In this situation, Felicity sees these people as stakeholders: Cyndi, Cyndi's parents, Janet, Lewis, and his wife. She recognizes that her decisions should center on Cyndi and her well-being.

3. *Think about your own emotional reactions.* Felicity recognizes that her immediate reaction is anger at all the adults involved—the parents for turning their daughter out and Lewis for exploiting Cyndi's situation.

4. *Apply fundamental ethical principles and theories to the situation (autonomy, nonmaleficence, beneficence, justice, fidelity, veracity). Define the central issues in the dilemma and possible options.* Felicity believes in this situation the moral principles of autonomy and beneficence conflict. Her understanding of autonomy would lead her to respect Cyndi's choice of living arrangements and sexual partner. However, she thinks that her understanding of the principle of beneficence would encourage intervening in this situation to protect Cyndi's health and safety.

Felicity has identified the options of calling Cyndi's parents and asking about the possibility of Cyndi moving back home, speaking with the police, or waiting to see what happens next.

5. *Refer to professional standards, relevant laws and regulations, and current ethics literature.* Felicity uncovered an informative article in *Counseling Today* titled "The End of 'Clear and Imminent Danger'" (Kaplan, 2006). She also found an article on the legal aspects of rape and sexual abuse helpful (Mitchell & Roberts, 2003). The information from

her particular state on the age of majority, emancipated minors, and minors' rights also helped clarify some of the murky guidelines.

6. *Consult with colleagues or experts.* Felicity talked about this case during her weekly supervision session. She conferred with two other people in her practice, and she asked a friend on the police force about a "hypothetical" situation that had similar characteristics. She has found the state standard requires a 6-year age difference to meet the state mandated criteria of statutory rape of a person who is 13, 14, or 15, and the ages of the people in this situation are not separated by 6 years. The legal criteria for sexual abuse has also not been met, so Felicity does not have to wrestle with whether to report to the legal system or child protective services because those guidelines have been clearly defined for her.

7. *Involve the client in the decision-making process.* The next time Felicity met with Cyndi she began, "You told me last week about you and Lewis having intercourse. You were worried about what Janet would think if she found out. Cyndi, I'm worried about you and how this affair with an older man might lead to some dangerous complications. I'd like to ask you some questions that will help me understand things better, and then together we can figure out what needs to happen to protect your health and safety."

8. *Identify desired outcomes and action to achieve those outcomes.* Felicity and Cyndi arrived at a list of desired outcomes. First, Cyndi had to have a safe place to stay. They decided to use some local resources to find Cyndi somewhere to sleep and eat until the rest of this situation could be unraveled. Cyndi agreed to contact her parents and ask them to come with her to Felicity's office to talk about the possibilities of her returning home. Cyndi did not agree to break off the affair with Lewis even though she promised she would not stay at his house again.

9. *Consider different courses of action.* Felicity sees the crux of the problem as a minor having an affair with an adult. As discussed earlier, Felicity had determined that she had no legal obligation to report this as child abuse or statutory rape. She felt she had honored the ethical principle of autonomy by helping Cyndi create a plan of action for her own well-being. Felicity decided she would see what transpired before taking any further steps.

10. *Choose and act.* Felicity has chosen to wait another week before doing anything else.

11. *Reflect on the actions taken.* As she reviews what has happened, Felicity is satisfied with the research she has done and the consultation she has sought. She has learned from the readings and the conversations. She has based her decisions on the moral principles of autonomy and beneficence as she confronted Cyndi with her concerns and helped Cyndi develop her own plan for removing herself from Lewis's environment. Felicity will continue to be directive and probing as she monitors Cyndi's living arrangements.

SUMMARY

In conclusion, Lawrence and Kurpius (2000) propose the following guidelines for counseling with minors:

1. Practice within the boundaries of your competence as defined by your education, training, and supervised practice.
2. Know state laws regarding privilege. Privileged communication does not exist unless the state has mandated it.
3. Explain your policies on confidentiality with both the child and parents at the beginning of the counseling relationship and ask them for cooperation. Provide a written informed consent that everyone signs.
4. Should you decide to work with a minor without the consent of the parent or guardian, ask the child to give informed consent in writing (Hendrix, 1991) and recognize the legal risks involved.
5. Maintain accurate and objective records.
6. Purchase adequate professional liability insurance.
7. Confer with colleagues and have access to professional legal advice when you are uncertain about how to proceed (Lawrence and Kurpius, 2000, p. 135).

WEBSITES FOR LEGAL AND ETHICAL CONSIDERATIONS FOR COUNSELORS

Internet addresses frequently change. To find the sites listed here, visit www.thomsonedu.com/counseling/thompson for an updated list of Internet addresses and direct links to relevant sites.

ACA *Code of Ethics and Standards of Practice*—Frequently Asked Questions

APA Ethical Principles of Psychologists and Code of Conduct

U.S. Department of Education

Department of Education Office for Civil Rights

National Clearinghouse on Child Abuse and Neglect Information

National Board for Certified Counselors

REFERENCES

American Association for Marriage and Family Therapy. (2001). *AAMFT code of ethics*. Retrieved January 30, 2006, from http://www.aamft.org/resources/ lrmplan/ethics/ethicscode2001.asp

American Bar Association. (2005). *Facts about children and the law*. Retrieved October 15, 2005, from http://www.abanet.org/media/factbooks/childlaw.pdf

American Counseling Association. (2005). *Code of ethics and standards of practice*. Alexandria, VA: Author.

American Psychological Association. (2002). *Ethical principles of psychologists and code of conduct*. Washington, DC: Author.

American School Counselor Association. (2004). *Ethical standards for school counselors.* Alexandria, VA: Author.

Burcky, W. D., & Childers, J. H., Jr. (1976). Buckley amendment: Focus of a professional dilemma. *School Counselor, 23,* 162–164.

Corey, G. (1995). *Theory and practice of group counseling.* Pacific Grove, CA: Brooks/Cole Publishing.

Corey, G., Corey, M. S., & Callahan, P. (1998). *Issues and ethics in the helping professions* (5th ed.). Pacific Grove, CA: Brooks/Cole.

Cottone, R. R. (2001). A social constructivism model of ethical decision making in counseling. *Journal of Counseling and Development, 79,* 39–45.

Daniels, J. A. (2001). Managed care, ethics, and counseling. *Journal of Counseling and Development, 79,* 119–122.

English, A., & Kenney, K. E. (2003). *State minor consent laws: A summary* (2nd ed.). Chapel Hill, NC: Center for Adolescent Health & the Law.

Ethics Committee of the American School Counselor Association. (1999–2001). *Ethical issues: Tips for school counselors.* Retrieved January 31, 2006, from http://www.schoolcounselor.org/content.asp?pl=325&sl=136&contentid=166

Family Educational Rights and Privacy Act, 20 U.S.C.A. §1232g (1974). [Buckley Amendment.] (1991). Implementing regulations 34 C.F.F. 99.3 Fed. Reg. 56, §117, 28012.

Fischer, L., & Sorenson, G. P. (1996). *School law for counselors, psychologists, and social workers* (3rd ed.). White Plains, NY: Longman.

Ford, C. A., Milstein, S. G., Halpern-Felscher, B. L., & Irwin, C. E., Jr. (1997). Influence of physician confidentiality assurances on adolescents' willingness to discuss information and seek future health care: A randomized controlled trial. *Journal of the American Medical Association, 278*(12), 1029–1034.

Foreman, T., & Bernet, W. (2000). A misunderstanding regarding duty to report suspected child abuse. *Child Maltreatment, 5,* 190–196.

Forester-Miller, H., & Davis T. E. (1995). *A practitioner's guide to ethical decision-making.* Alexandria, VA: American Counseling Association.

Fundudis, T. (2003). Current issues in medico-legal procedures: How competent are children to make their own decision? *Child and Adolescent Mental Health, 8,* 18–22.

Garcia, J. G., Cartwright, B., Winston, S. M., & Borzuchowska, B. (2003). A transcultural integrative model for ethical decision making in counseling. *Journal of Counseling and Development, 81,* 268–277.

Glosoff, H. L., & Pate, R. H., Jr. (2002). Privacy and confidentiality in school counseling. *Professional School Counseling, 6,* 20–27.

Hendrix, D. H. (1991). Ethics and intrafamily confidentiality in counseling with children. *Journal of Mental Health Counseling, 13,* 323–358.

Herlihy, B., & Corey, G. (1996). *ACA ethical standards casebook* (5th ed.). Alexandria, VA: American Counseling Association.

Huey, W. C. (1996). Counseling minor clients. In B. Herlihy & G. Corey, (Eds.), *ACA ethical standards casebook* (5th ed., (pp. 241–245). Alexandria, VA: American Counseling Association.

Hughes, T. (2001, Winter). Releasing student information: What's public and what's not. *School Law Bulletin, 32,* 12–29.

Individuals with Disabilities Education Act. (1997). Pub.L.No 105-17, 34 CFR 300-574.

Isaacs, M. L. (1997). The duty to warn and protect: *Tarasoff* and the elementary school counselor. *Elementary School Guidance and Counseling, 31,* 326–342.

Isaacs, M. L., & Stone, C. (1999). School counselors and confidentiality: Factors affecting professional choices. *Professional School Counseling, 2,* 258–266.

Kachgian, C., & Felthous, A. R. (2004). Court responses to *Tarasoff* statues. *Journal of the American Academy of Psychiatry and Law, 32,* 263–273.

Kaplan, D. (2006, January). The end of 'clear and imminent danger.' *Counseling Today,* 10.

Kaplan, D. M. (2001). Developing an informed consent brochure for secondary students. Retrieved October 5, 2005, from http://www.schoolcounselor.org/ethics

Kitchener, K. S. (1984). Intuition, critical evaluation, and ethical principles: The foundation for ethical decision in counseling psychology. *Counseling Psychologist, 12,* 43–55.

Lawrence, G., & Kurpius, S. E. R. (2000). Legal and ethical issues involved when counseling minors in non-school settings. *Journal of Counseling and Development, 78,* 130–136.

Linde, L. (2003). Ethical, legal, and professional issues in school counseling. In B. T. Erford (Ed.), *Transforming the school counseling profession* (pp. 39–62). Upper Saddle River, NJ: Merrill.

McFarland, W. P., & Dupuis, M. (2001). The legal duty to protect gay and lesbian students from violence in the schools. *Professional School Counseling, 4,* 171–179.

Meara, N., Schmidt, L., & Day, J. (1996) Principles and virtues: A foundation for ethical decisions, policies, and character. *Counseling Psychologist, 24*(1), 4–77.

Mitchell, C. W., Disque, J. G., & Robertson, P. (2002). When parents want to know: Responding to parental demands for confidential information. *Professional School Counseling, 6,* 156–162.

Mitchell, C. W., & Rogers, R. E. (2003). Rape, statutory rape, and child abuse: Legal distinctions and counselor duties. *Professional School Counseling, 6,* 332–338.

Muro, J. J., & Kottman, T. (1995). *Guidance and counseling in the elementary and middle schools: A practical approach.* Madison, WI: Brown & Benchmark.

National Association of Social Workers. (1999). *Code of ethics of the National Association of Social Workers.* Washington, DC: Author.

National Board of Certified Counselors. (2005). *Code of ethics.* Retrieved January 30, 2006, from http://www.nbcc.org/extras/pdfs/ethics/nbcc-codeofethics.pdf

Nystul, M. S. (2003). *Introduction to counseling: An art and science perspective* (2nd ed.). Boston: Allyn & Bacon.

Piazza, N. J., & Baruth, N. E. (1990). Client record guidelines. *Journal of Counseling and Development, 68,* 313–316.

Rave, E. J., & Larsen, C. C. (Eds.). (1995). *Ethical decision making in therapy: Feminist perspectives.* New York: Guilford Press.

Remley, T. (1990). Counseling records: Legal and ethical issues. In B. Herlihy & L. Golden (Eds.), *Ethical standards casebook* (pp. 162–169). Alexandria, VA: American Association for Counseling and Development.

Remley, T. P., & Herlihy, B. (2005). *Ethical, legal, and professional issues in counseling* (2nd ed.). Upper Saddle River, NJ: Merrill.

Rokop, J. J. (2003). The effects of CPS mandated reporting on the therapeutic relationship: The client's perspective. *Dissertations Abstracts International, 64*(5-B), 135.

Salo, M., & Shumate, S. (1993). Counseling minor clients. In T. Remley Jr. (Ed.), *The ACA Legal Series, Vol. 4.* Alexandria, VA: American Counseling Association.

Schmidt, L., & Meara, N. (1984). Ethical, professional, and legal issues in counseling psychology. In S. Brown & R. Lent (Eds.), *Handbook of counseling psychology* (pp. 56–96). New York: Wiley.

Sealander, K. A., Schwiebert, V. L., Oren, T. A., & Weekley, J. L. (1999). Confidentiality and the law. *Professional School Counseling, 3,* 122–127.

Stadler, H. A. (1986). Making hard choices: Clarifying controversial ethical issues. *Counseling and Human Development, 19,* 1–10.

Stadler, H. (1990). Confidentiality. In B. Herlihy & L. Golden (Eds.), *Ethical standards casebook* (pp. 102–110). Alexandria, VA: American Association for Counseling and Development.

Stone, C. (2004). Ethical and legal considerations for students, parents, and professional school counselors. In B. T. Erford (Ed.), *Professional school counseling: A handbook of theories, programs & practices* (pp. 57–64). Austin, TX: ProEd.

Stone, C. B., & Dahir, C. A. (2006). *The transformed school counselor.* Boston: Lahaska Press.

Stromberg, C., and his colleagues in the Law Firm of Hogan & Hartson of Washington, DC. (1993, April). Privacy, confidentiality and privilege. *The Psychologist's Legal Update.* Washington, DC: National Register of Health Service Providers in Psychology.

Swenson, L. C. (1993). *Psychology and the law for the helping professions.* Pacific Grove, CA: Brooks/Cole.

Tarasoff v. Regents of University of California. (1974). 129 Ca. 118, 13c. D177; 529 p. 2D553.

Travydas, V. M. (1987). Decision-making models in ethics: Models for increasing clarity and wisdom. *Journal of Applied Rehabilitation Counseling, 22,* 11–18.

Underwood, J. K., & Mead, J. F. (1995). *Legal aspects of special education and pupil services.* Boston: Allyn & Bacon.

U.S. Department of Education. (2002). Family educational rights and privacy act (FERPA). Retrieved March 26, 2006, from http://www.ed.gov/policy/gen/guid/fpco/ferpa/index.html

Van Hoose, W. H., & Kottler, J. A. (1985). *Ethical and legal issues in counseling and psychotherapy.* San Francisco: Jossey-Bass.

Welfel, E. R. (2006). *Ethics in counseling & psychotherapy: Standards, research, & emerging issues* (3rd ed.). Belmont, CA: Thomson.

Weiner, N., & Robinson Kurpius, S. W. (1995). *Shattered innocence: A practical guide for counseling women survivors of childhood sexual abuse.* Washington, DC: Taylor & Francis.

Zingaro, J. C. (1983). Confidentiality: To tell or not to tell. *Elementary School Guidance and Counseling, 17,* 261–267.

APPENDICES

Appendices A and B suggest techniques for intervening with specific problem behaviors, and they are included to stimulate ideas. The lists, of course, are not exhaustive, but we hope they help counselors who are attempting to develop treatment plans for children. Listed at the end of these appendices are some *Diagnostic and Statistical Manual of Mental Disorders, 4th Edition, Text Revision (DSM-IV-TR)* categories (American Psychiatric Association, 2000) that may be applicable in classifying client behaviors. Use caution in assigning classifications because the categories ordinarily describe mental disorders and are not appropriate for all problematic behaviors that are not a part of a pattern or syndrome of symptoms. The conclusion of Appendix B includes a table of psychotropic medications that may be indicated for different diagnoses. Appendix C contains computations and *T*-scores to use with goal-attainment scaling, which is explained in Chapter 2.

CHILDREN'S CONFLICTS WITH OTHERS

Alternatives For Intervention

The suggestions offered in this appendix are techniques collected from a variety of resources on counseling children with learning and social problems. Some suggestions are used directly with the child; others are consultation techniques to use with parents and teachers. In each case, the procedures must be incorporated into a therapeutic counseling or consulting atmosphere that includes caring, respect, empathic understanding, and acceptance. The techniques presented can be preventive and developmental, as well as remedial; that any given technique has one application to the exclusion of others is nearly impossible to say. In any case, the techniques should be adapted to meet the unique needs of children and their behaviors.

We thank the master's degree students in the Wake Forest University counseling program for their contributions to Appendix A. Their names appear in the section that they wrote.

CHRONIC COMPLAINING*

Emy Gamb

Chronic complaining about feeling ill gains attention or sympathy and avoids unpleasant situations. This behavior can be manifested as an exaggeration of symptoms or fantasies of diseases; for example, "I think I have cancer." Other kinds of hypochondria are consistent headaches, stomachaches, and muscle aches.

1. Recommend to the parents and child that the child be examined by a pediatrician to rule out physical illness.

---

*Reprinted with permission.

2. Try to determine the motive or goal of the chronic complainer. Are the complaints a result of feelings of inadequacy, fear of failure, a need for attention or sympathy, or an attempt to avoid an unpleasant task? Help the child find ways of meeting this need more effectively.

3. Actively listen to the child's complaints (see Chapter 6). Do not oversympathize, but tell the child you will write a note or call the parents to suggest a trip to the doctor's office to check out the complaint.

4. Encourage parents to comfort the child when they are sick but do not give the child toys or special items when they are sick. This will only reinforce for the child that being sick gets them attention (Cantor & Fallon, 1996).

5. Learn about the behavior of the child's parents. Parents are the child's number one role models. If the parent exaggerates minor illnesses, consistently misses work, or cancels social obligations, then the child may be learning it is acceptable to behave in that way (Cantor & Fallon, 1996).

6. Use of cognitive-behavioral therapy is helpful in reducing hypochondriac symptoms, attitudes, and beliefs (Barsky & Ahern, 2004).

7. Ask the children to write out their feelings or tell them to a tape recorder. A diary might help determine the circumstances under which the feelings occur (Soliday, Garofalo, & Rogers, 2004).

8. Excessive stress and tension can provoke chronic complaining. Check with parents, teachers, and other significant people in the child's life. The child may be under pressure from schoolwork, from problems within the home, or from peers. Help the other adults find ways to reduce the tension.

9. Chronic complaining may result from a lack of interest in the world around the child such as school, friends, or activities. Help these children find an interest or activity in which they can feel successful. Encourage participation in groups, children's organizations, sport teams, or neighborhood activities.

10. Enlist the aid of a buddy to encourage the complainer to become more involved in the world and to participate in friendships and activities.

11. Actively listen for clues to stresses in the child's life, and plan with the child for more constructive means of coping with the tensions (for example, relaxation techniques, physical activities, talking, writing, and play therapy).

12. Have children monitor their own behavior. Give them an index card and ask them to check it every time they become aware that they are complaining. Catching oneself in the act often increases awareness of the behavior and reduces the incidence.

13. Try to find ways for the children to assume more responsibility in their lives. Feeling competent and worthwhile reduces the need to gain attention through sickness.

REFERENCES

Barsky, A. J., & Ahern, D. K. (2004). Cognitive behavior therapy for hypochondriasis: A randomized controlled trial. *Journal of the American Medical Association, 291,* 1464–1470.

Cantor, C., & Fallon, B. A. (1996, April). Confessions of a hypochondriac. *Ladies Home Journal, 113*(4), 46.

Soliday, E., Garofalo, J. P., & Rogers, D. (2004). Expressive writing intervention for adolescents' somatic symptoms and mood. *Journal of Clinical Child & Adolescent Psychology, 33*(4), 792–802.

TATTLING*

Kate Williams

The tattler, like a gossip, is attempting to gain attention and favor, usually with an adult authority figure. Ignoring talebearers is difficult because many times they bring needed information to adults. However, the tattler is usually lonely and rejected by peers.

1. Determine the goal of tattling. Is the child attempting to gain attention, power, or revenge? Confront the child with your hypothesis; for example, "Could it be that you are telling me this to get Warren in trouble?" (See Chapter 11.)
2. Meet privately with the tattler and interpret the behavior as a cry for help to gain acceptance and recognition in the group. Discuss the reasons the child tattles and plan better ways to achieve those goals.
3. Help the child gain acceptance by capitalizing on special abilities and interests such as sports, hobbies, or special knowledge. Encourage the child to share these abilities and interests with others or to peer-teach or tutor another child.
4. The child may need help in learning social skills. Help the child find a model. Have the child list the model's admired behaviors; then rehearse and practice them.
5. Turn your attention elsewhere when the child begins a tale. Say, "Rather than discussing that now, perhaps we should . . ."
6. Use tattling as a topic for family and group discussions. Have the group consider motives for tattling and the reactions and feelings of others toward a tattler. Films, filmstrips, or stories may provide a stimulus for those discussions. List alternatives to tattling; then rehearse and practice them.
7. Use storytelling, choosing a hypothetical example similar to the child's problem, to show the consequences of tattling and the reactions of others to tattling (see Chapters 6 and 14). Ask the child questions about how the tattler must be feeling and how the child who is being tattled on must feel.
8. Instead of listening to the tattler, ask the child to write a brief note to you explaining what has happened. If multiple students are causing problems with tattling in a classroom, the teacher can begin a policy of submitting written concerns through a special mailbox that the teacher can review at his or her discretion. This way, tattling takes more effort for the student and it need not interrupt classroom instruction (Perks, 1996).
9. Ignore the tattling behavior, but praise and reinforce appropriate behaviors. Give attention to the child for the cooperation.
10. When ignoring tattling becomes impossible, draw up a contract with the child that includes rewards for not tattling.
11. Build self-esteem (see Appendix B) so that the child does not have to resort to tattling to gain attention and acceptance.
12. Pair tattlers with good role models for work and other activities. Discuss with the tattlers the behaviors they see in the role model and the positive and negative consequences of their behaviors. Encourage the child to rehearse and practice these behaviors.
13. Have children monitor their own behavior. Ask them to check an index card each time they tattle or feel the urge to tattle. Increasing awareness of the behavior may decrease the frequency.

---

*Reprinted with permission.

14. Encourage children to problem-solve. Rather than having the adult take over the situation and seek a resolution, say to the child, "I wonder what could be done to straighten this out." Assist the child in seeking alternatives.

15. Facilitate a group discussion on tattling behaviors in the child's classroom. Discuss which kind of information is appropriate to tell teachers or parents, such as reporting a matter of safety, and which information the child is mature enough to deal with by himself or herself (Kreidler, 1996).

REFERENCES

Kreidler, W. J. (1996). Caring classroom. *Instructor, 106*(3), 116–117.
Perks, C. A. (1996). Write 'em up! *Teaching PreK-8, 27*(1), 74–75.

SWEARING*

Andrea Marin

Swearing may reflect a need for attention, an effort to shock others or prove to peers that the child is "big," or it may be modeling behavior. Swearing can also be a release for pent-up aggression or tension or an expression of rebellion.

1. Determine the motive for the behavior (see Chapter 11). Is the goal a need for attention or power, an effort to cover feelings of inadequacy, or an emotional release? Does the swearing reflect a lack of social skills?

2. Confront the child, interpreting the swearing behavior as a need to shock or gain attention; for example, "Could it be that you want to shock me by using those words?" (See Chapter 11.) Work with the child to make a plan to avoid swearing in the future.

3. Offer an alternative. Instead of using a cuss word, contract with the child to use a different word in place of the swear word. If the alternative is catchy, and the child gets a positive reaction when he or she uses it, the alternative word will become reinforced over time (O'Connor, 2005; Slatalla, 2000; Vantine & Goldstein, 1998). Alternative methods of expressing emotions (physical activities, art, games, music) also can be discussed, rehearsed, and included in the contract. These ideas can be put on an index card and carried with the child for easy reference.

4. Teach children the "etiquette" of offensive language. Rather than simply saying, "No swearing!" or "Don't say that—it's a bad word!" teach children the value of being able to express themselves in acceptable ways (Vantine & Goldstein, 1998).

5. Help children learn acceptable ways to express themselves by teaching them about feeling words and reinforcing the importance of being able to share emotions using descriptive words rather than aggressive language. For instance, teach children to say, "I'm furious!" rather than allowing them to act out their frustration or anger through swear words or aggression (Vantine & Goldstein, 1998).

6. Take the fun out of swearing by making it an intellectual exercise. For instance, when a child swears, try saying, "Hmm, that's an interesting word. Where did you hear it? Do your friends use that word? Do you know what it means? How do you think people would react if you used that word?" and so on. By asking these questions, you take the emotion out of the conversation (Vantine & Goldstein, 1998).

---

*Reprinted with permission.

7. Explain that particular environments must be "swear-free zones" and elaborate on the impact of using bad words so that the reason behind having "swear-free zones" is not arbitrary (Webster, 1996). You also can remind the child that certain words are acceptable in certain places and at particular times, and some words are never appropriate.

8. Be extremely careful not to overreact to swearing. If the swearing is an attention-seeking behavior, an overreaction can actually work as reinforcement for the unwanted behavior (Webster, 1996).

9. Encourage children to be open with their emotions, particularly their frustrations, on a continual basis. If children are provided with opportunities to express themselves in healthy, acceptable manners on a regular basis, they will be less likely to allow their frustrations to build up and come out in unacceptable ways (Webster, 1996).

10. Provide as many positive role models and opportunities to engage in meaningful, "swear-free" conversation for the child as possible. Telling a child not to swear but then allowing him or her to be inundated with bad language at home or through the media, for instance, will only serve to confuse the child (O'Connor, 2005).

11. Examine the child's world. Does a certain time of day, a particular situation, or a certain event provoke the swearing? If so, attempt to reduce the frustrations by rescheduling or rearranging the environment.

12. Have the child write out some dialogue using symbols for swear words. Ask the child to substitute strong feeling words that are appropriate for the symbols.

13. Teach children stress-management techniques, such as deep breathing, to help ward off the feelings that may stimulate swearing. When a child feels an urge to swear, he or she is encouraged to breath deeply instead.

14. Use storytelling (see Chapter 14) with a hypothetical example similar to the child's problem. Ask the child to react to the story. Journaling or having the child talk into a tape recorder can also be used in conjunction with this activity or as separate methods for allowing children to vent their feelings.

15. Hold a family or group discussion focused on the motives for swearing and how others feel about the person who is swearing. Use role-playing and role rehearsal to help children see the behavior and its effects on others. Discuss and role-play alternatives to swearing. Also, as already alluded to in previous suggestions, it is important that adults also agree to eliminate swearing.

16. Small children may not be aware of the meaning of the words they use. Ask the child what they think the word means and suggest an alternative.

17. Use cognitive restructuring to help angry children who use swearing as an outlet. They may be able to reframe the situation so it does not stimulate swearing.

18. Self-monitoring may help older children become aware of their behavior. Self-reward for *not* swearing should be included in the self-management program.

19. Use confrontational techniques such as the reality questions (see Chapter 4) to encourage responsible behavior.

References

O'Connor, J. V. (2005). Kid's cussing—a step beyond sticks and stones. *Christian Science Monitor, 97,* 9.

Slatalla, M. (2000, April). My baby swears. *Time, 155,* 86.

Vantine, J., & Goldstein, L. (1998). Dealing with a dirty mouth. *Prevention, 50,* 78.
Webster, H. (1996, May). Delete those expletives. *Working Mother,* 52–56.

LYING*

Andrea Marin

As a part of their normal development, young children often lie because of their inability to distinguish fact from fantasy or because they fear disapproval and punishment. Habitual lying may be due to feelings of inadequacy, insecurity, or pressure from parents or other significant people in the child's life. It also could be a learned behavior to escape responsibility or punishment.

1. Determine what needs of the child are not being met (see Chapter 11). Is the child seeking attention or power? Is he or she attempting to evade reality or the consequences of misbehavior?
2. Arrange for successful experiences in learning and in daily interactions with peers. Feelings of success may lead to an increase in the child's self-confidence, and an increase in self-confidence may take away from the child's compulsion to lie.
3. Avoid trying to trap the child. If you have positive evidence that the child is lying, be quietly direct in your confrontation; for example, "Jeff, I know that you did not do your homework." If you do not have direct knowledge of the truth, admit to the child that you are having trouble understanding the story and ask for more details. This response lets the child know that you do not believe all that is being said and gives the child a chance to tell the truth.
4. Similarly, avoid "setups." For instance, if you catch a child hitting a classmate and you ask, "Did you just hit your friend?" the child is likely to lie and answer "no," even though he is aware that you know the truth pertaining to what happened. Instead, calmly remind the child of the rules and expectations that you have, so that he or she has an opportunity to improve and make a better choice in the future (Fredericks, 1991).
5. Children are more inclined to tell the truth when they experience or hear about the benefits of being honest than when adults provide children with negative evaluations of lying. In other words, it is more effective to emphasize the positives of telling the truth with children who are deceptive than it is to continually tell these children that it is wrong to lie (Wagland & Bussey, 2003).
6. Caregivers and parents can encourage children to take full responsibility for their errors or offenses while simultaneously encouraging them to feel proud of themselves for telling the truth (Bussey, 1992; Wagland & Bussey, 2003).
7. Adults can promote honesty and discourage lying by modeling the importance of telling the truth even at times when it is difficult to do so. Parents and caregivers must be reminded that they are important role models for their children (Fredericks, 1991).
8. The adults in the child's life should ask themselves specific questions related to the child's dishonesty. For example, if the situation is that a child continually lies about whether he did his homework, ask yourself for what reason is the child lying. For instance, is he afraid he will get in trouble if the truth is found out? Is the homework too challenging, and the child is not getting necessary assistance or tutoring? Is the homework too easy, and the child

---

*Reprinted with permission.

becomes bored and therefore does not finish assignments? In short, figure out the reason behind the lie (Kelly, 2000).

9. Narrowing down to the specific situations in which the child lies and possible reasons that he or she does so can be significant in determining how to rectify the problem. Furthermore, there may be aspects of the child's environment or circumstances that can be altered to deter him or her from lying (Kelly, 2000).

10. Children often lie to avoid punishment. Encouraging positive actions in children rather than punishing their wrongdoing may deter them from lying in the future. Also, teaching children the value in honesty can be productive and beneficial. However, punishing children for lying is not helpful and should be avoided (Kalish, 1998).

11. Separate the child from the action. If a child understands that he or she will be loved regardless of what he or she has done, the child will be more likely to tell the truth. That is, a child who feels worthwhile, loved, and successful does not have to resort to lying (see Appendix B).

12. Many contend that big lies are built on a series of little lies ("white lies"). How adults in the child's life handle small lies may play a role in whether a child moves on to tell bigger lies. This, of course, relates to that if a child sees an adult get away with telling "white lies," he or she may start to think that small lies are all right or less of an offense than big ones (Fredericks, 1991).

13. Unlike what has been said above regarding "white lies," it is all right to ignore fantasy tales that are *meaningless*. However, if you would rather not ignore the fantasy tale altogether, another possibility would be to ask the child to write the story and give it to you. Caution should be exercised not to ignore the child completely. Respond to positive behaviors.

14. Films, stories, and other materials may provide stimuli for good classroom or family discussions on lying and its consequences. Include in the discussion methods for avoiding lying and better ways of handling situations.

15. Use self-monitoring to increase awareness of the behavior. Have children keep a record of each time they told the truth when they were tempted to lie.

16. When the child continues to tell stories that are obviously fantasies, the adult may confront the child in a nonjudgmental manner, using statements such as "You know, I have never seen or heard anything like that, and I'm really having trouble imagining what you are telling me. Could we begin again?" With this technique, you do not call the child a liar, but you convey that you simply cannot accept all that is being said as the truth.

17. Note the areas in which lying appears to occur most often. Is the child lying about schoolwork, parents, money, clothes, or aggressive abilities? If the lying occurs most frequently in one area, examine the possibilities of changing the circumstances in this area to decrease the temptation or pressure to lie.

18. Talk with parents, teachers, and others close to the child. Are the expectations and pressures placed on the child too great? Do parents expect perfect behavior and the highest school marks? Are teachers demanding too much work or work that is too difficult for the child? If so, consult with these adults concerning ways of reducing pressures on the child.

19. If the problem appears to stem from excessive pressure, decrease the push toward competition with others and emphasize competition with self; for example, "You did six math problems yesterday. Let's see if you can do eight today."

20. Use the technique of storytelling (see Chapter 14). Choose a hypothetical example involving behaviors similar to those exhibited by the lying child. Ask the child to react to the story; then discuss the reactions.

21. Review the child's academic progress. Does lying compensate for a learning difficulty or cover some other real or imagined failure?

REFERENCES

Bussey, K. (1992). Lying and truthfulness: Children's definitions, standards, and evaluative reactions. *Child Development, 63,* 129–137.

Fredericks, A. D. (1991). Telling the truth. *Teaching PreK-8, 22,* 34.

Kalish, N. (1998, October). How honesty grows. *Working Mother,* 106–109.

Kelly, M. (2000, January). How can we stop our child from lying about his homework? *Family Life,* 116.

Wagland, P., & Bussey, K. (2003). Factors that facilitate and undermine truth telling about witnessed transgressive conduct. *Australian Journal of Psychology, 55,* 66.

TEASING*

Kate Williams

Teasing is attention-getting behavior with several possible motives. Children may get attention only when they misbehave, they may be showing friendship for another person, or they may have hostile motivation. Teasing is sometimes the result of a lack of knowledge about how to make friends, how to be a friend, or other social skills.

1. Determine the goal of the teasing (see Chapter 11). Is the motive attention, power, or revenge, or does the teasing come from a lack of social skills? Teasing can be a way of compensating for feelings of inadequacy or a means of covering up learning or emotional problems. Become a child watcher; listen actively to investigate all possibilities (see Chapter 6).

2. Examine the circumstances under which the child teases. What is the sequence of events? Does teasing occur most frequently in a particular time, place, or situation? If so, rearrange the environment or schedule to reduce provoking circumstances.

3. Group or family discussions may help the child see how teasing behavior affects others; these discussions also can produce suggestions and a plan for alternative ways of behaving. Peer pressure in group situations often modifies behavior of the teaser.

4. Ignore the teasing behavior as long as possible. Then use an isolation technique such as the quiet corner or the time-out room (see Chapters 9, 11, and 16). The teaser should be free to return to the group when the child has worked out a plan for behaving more acceptably.

5. Cooperatively draw up a contract to decrease teasing behaviors. Clearly define unacceptable behavior and the consequences (see Chapter 9). Rewards for appropriate behavior may also be included.

6. Help the child find other ways to get attention or acceptance. Encourage the child to pursue liked activities, interests, or hobbies and to share them with other children. Allow the child to peer-teach or tutor another child. Assign responsible tasks to the child; avoid meaningless work or drudgery jobs.

---

*Reprinted with permission.

7. Teasing is often behavior learned from a model. Check the child's environment to determine whether the teaser is modeling an admired person. Help the child find a more appropriate model, observe the model's behaviors, and rehearse new and more acceptable ways of interacting with peers.

8. Teach the child ways to interact with other children. Have him or her practice the engaging behaviors; then try those actions out and report on the reactions received.

9. Talk with the people being teased. Plan ways for these children not to reinforce the aggressor's teasing behavior. Explain to the victims of the teaser that the behavior is not as much fun if the person being teased does not respond. Explain to them that the motivation of the teaser is to get attention, even though it is negative attention. Role-play situations, teaching the victims to respond with new techniques, such as cognitive restructuring or ignoring the teasers.

10. Albert Ellis's ideas of irrational thinking may be incorporated into counseling with the person being teased. (See Chapter 8 for an explanation of cognitive restructuring.) Teach the victim to change internal thinking from "It is terrible to be teased" to "I don't like to be teased, but it is not the end of the world, and I can just ignore the teasing."

11. Children have little need to tease if they feel they are a part of their environment and successful in the world. Find ways of providing successful experiences. Capitalize on the child's interests and abilities. Encourage participation in activities at school, at home, or in the community.

12. Start a school campaign against teasing and bullying. Programs and resources are available for teachers and counselors to implement in schools (Ross, 2003).

13. Read the child an age-appropriate book that includes a character who is teased. As you read, ask questions to help the child figure out solutions for his or her situation (Freedman, 2002). Resources for children and adults can be found via the Internet at www.easingtheteasing.com/ links.html (Easing the Teasing: Strategies for Kids and Parents, 2002).

14. Teachers can make it a point to draw attention to the positive traits of the teasers and the teased in a classroom setting. This will help create a psychologically secure environment in the classroom for all students (Aho, 1998).

15. Introduce a structured learning unit to the child or affected classroom that is composed of class discussions, role plays, and writing activities intended to help children think about the boundaries between playful and hurtful behavior (Froschl, Sprung, & Mullin-Rindler, 1998; Sjostrom & Stein, 1986).

References

Aho, S. (1998). The teasers and the teased pupils at school. *Scandinavian Journal of Educational Research, 42*(3), 309–319.

Easing the Teasing: Strategies for Kids and Parents. (2002). *Erica's bibliography of fiction about bullying and teasing for children and young adults.* Retrieved December 7, 2005, from http://www.easingtheteasing.com/links.html

Freedman, J. (2002). *Easing the teasing: Helping your child cope with name-calling, ridicule, and verbal bullying.* New York: McGraw Hill.

Froschl, M., Sprung, B., & Mullin-Rindler, N. (1998). *Quit it! A teacher's guide on teasing and bullying for use with students in grades K-3.* Wellesley, MA: Wellesley Centers for Women at Wellesley College.

Ross, D. M. (2003). *Childhood bullying, teasing, and violence: What school personnel, other professionals, and parents can do* (2nd ed.). Alexandria, VA: American Counseling Association.

Sjostrom, L., & Stein, N. (1996). *A teacher's guide on teasing and bullying for use with fourth and fifth grade students.* Wellesley, MA: Wellesley Centers for Women at Wellesley College.

DISOBEDIENCE, NEGATIVISM, AND RESISTANT BEHAVIOR*

Ashley McPherson

Disobedience, negativism, and resistant behavior may be open displays of anger and antagonism toward authority figures. Children exhibiting these behaviors may be highly critical, easily irritated, and sometimes aggressive. Other times these behaviors result from the child's frustration toward an uncaring world. Finally, children may act in these uncooperative ways because they lack the skills to get along in their world and they have no one to teach them other ways of behaving.

1. Thoroughly explore the child's communication style, learning style, values, family structure, and general perception of the world to determine appropriate interventions for a disobedient and/or resistant child. Various aspects of a child's background and history may appear to be resistant behavior when this may not be the case (Scorzelli & Gold, 1999).
2. Exhibit empathy and unconditional acceptance in interaction with the child in an effort to reinforce the child's need for consistency and commitment from adult supportive figures (Harper, 1996).
3. Empower the child by allowing the individual to make choices and decisions; in this way, children will also develop an increased understanding about the responsibility associated with decision making (Harper, 1996; Landreth, 2002).
4. Determine the goals of the behavior (see Chapter 11). Actively listen to the child to learn about the child's feelings toward self, family interactions, and the school (see Chapter 6). Children tend to strike out when their needs for love and respect are not met. Recognize the child's feelings. Admit that the child has the power to disobey or resist. Avoid threatening the child. Refuse to become involved in a conflict; tell the child you will discuss the matter later.
5. Interpret the goal of the misbehavior to the child with "Could it be?" questions, but not at the time of the conflict (see Chapter 11). Later the adult might ask, "Could it be that you would like to show me that you are boss?" The question opens the door for a nonjudgmental discussion of the child's motives and for planning better ways of meeting these needs.
6. When there is no conflict, discuss with the child the consequences of the negative behavior. Plan alternative behaviors, and rehearse and practice them.
7. Avoid open confrontations of put-downs, threats, or name-calling. Try active listening to learn the reason for the negativism or disobedience (see Chapter 6).
8. Assess the environment in which the child is disobedient, negative, or resistant. Is the child receiving some reinforcement from peers or other significant persons? What circumstances provoke the behavior? Is there a time when negativism, resistance, and disobedience occur most often? Rearrangement of schedules or the environment may decrease the undesirable behavior.

*Reprinted with permission.

9. Avoid possible conflict situations by allowing the child some choices; for example, "Do you want to complete the assignment now or after lunch?" Make a list of tasks to be done, and cooperatively plan the day's schedule with the child.

10. Specify in advance the consequences for disobedience, negativism, and resistant behavior. Hold a discussion with the child in which you draw up ground rules and the consequences for breaking the rules. Rules made in cooperation with children are carried out more readily.

11. When the child misbehaves, the inappropriate behavior should be explained clearly. Children often do not understand what they have done wrong. After defining the problem, work with the child to draw up a plan or contract to change behavior (see Chapter 9). The plan may include rewards for acceptable behavior and penalties for unacceptable behavior. Rehearse and practice new behaviors to help the child meet the terms of the contract.

12. Ignore the negativism, disobedience, and resistant behavior, if possible. When ignoring the behavior becomes impossible, isolation techniques such as Seat 2, quiet corner, or time-out room may be effective in changing the behavior (see Chapter 9). Avoid physical punishment; it provides only a model of aggression for the child.

13. Disobedience, negativism, and resistant behaviors are often attempts to cover up a lack of self-confidence, lack of social skills, or inability to find success in school and other areas of life. Attempt to determine whether the unacceptable behavior is compensatory behavior for a learning problem, a lack of self-esteem, or some other problem. Look over the child's academic progress to determine whether the behavior could be related to a learning problem. Carefully watch the child's interactions with others to determine whether the problem is related to difficulties with social relationships. Listen for clues that may help you understand the child's feelings about self and others (see the discussion of active listening in Chapter 6).

14. Praise, telephone calls, or notes to the child's home about good behavior, together with other positive reinforcers, may be effective in decreasing negative behavior.

15. Discuss with the child appropriate and inappropriate behaviors. Respond to and reinforce appropriate behaviors while ignoring behavior that is unacceptable.

16. Suggest that parents or teachers leave the room for a few moments to remove themselves from the conflict. This arouses surprise and curiosity in the child about what the adult will do. The action also prevents the adult from entering into a conflict with the child (see Chapter 11).

17. Encourage the child to use constructive methods for releasing negative feelings. Suggest techniques such as talking out or writing out feelings, drawing, music, or physical exercises. Arrange for periodic emotional outlets if necessary.

18. Find the negative, resistant, or disobedient child a model or friend. Ask the child to watch the model and record admired behaviors; then rehearse and practice these behaviors with the child.

19. Encourage negative children to pursue interests, hobbies, and abilities and to become involved in activities, clubs, or other organizations in which they can feel successful. Enlist the aid of a friend or buddy to involve the child in activities.

REFERENCES

Harper, J. (1996). Interpersonal issues in counseling a resistant child: A case study. *British Journal of Guidance & Counseling, 24*(1), 129–140.

Landreth, G. L. (2002). Therapeutic limit setting in the play therapy relationship. *Professional Psychology: Research and Practice, 33*(6), 529–535.

Scorzelli, J. F., & Gold, J. (1999). The mutual storytelling writing game. *Journal of Mental Health Counseling, 21*(2), 113–124.

TANTRUMS*

Lyndsay Gross

Temper tantrums may cause parents or other adults to experience feelings of anger, frustration, and helplessness. Adults often feel they have completely lost control of the child and the situation when children throw temper tantrums. In some children, tantrums are a learned behavior for getting attention or getting their way. Other children have learned to manipulate adults by throwing tantrums. Some other children use tantrums as a way to seek revenge.

1. Determine the motive for the tantrum. Is the tantrum an effort to gain attention, to cover feelings of inadequacy, to manipulate, or to embarrass or strike out at adults? (See Chapter 11.)
2. Children throw tantrums because it is a learned behavior that works for them. They get their way or what they want. The adult can stop the behavior by not allowing it to work. Ignore the behavior whenever possible; refuse to give in. Eventually, the tantrum becomes an unrewarding behavior.
3. If ignoring the tantrum becomes impossible, quietly ask the child to leave the room and make a plan for avoiding tantrums in the future. The child should have the option of returning and behaving appropriately after a cooling-off period. Physically removing the child from the room may be necessary.
4. Provide alternative methods of venting feelings. Ask children to keep a diary of their feelings, write them out on paper, or talk to a tape recorder. Play therapy can help, and fantasy games or storytelling may provide some catharsis and insight (see Chapter 14).
5. Use active listening to understand the child's feelings and the motives behind the tantrums (see Chapter 6).
6. Investigate the possibility of the tantrums being related to a physical problem if the behavior continues over a given time period. Refer the child to a pediatrician for examination.
7. Try to determine the sequence of events before a tantrum. Investigate whether tantrums are most likely to occur at a particular time, place, or situation. Rearrange the environment or schedule to reduce the child's frustrations, if possible.
8. Avoid threats, lectures, scolding, and nagging, which can be reinforcing because they are forms of attention. Define the unacceptable behavior and the consequences for it (see Chapter 9), and consistently carry out the terms of the behavioral contract between the adult and the child.
9. Some children have temper tantrums because they feel insecure. Using techniques of isolation and other forms of strictness may tend to intensify these feelings. In such cases, some tantrum-throwing children become quiet when held affectionately and reassured.

*Reprinted with permission.

10. Peer pressure can be an effective tool for modifying children's behaviors. Group or family discussions of temper tantrums and their effects on others may help the tantrum-throwing child understand how others react to the behavior.

11. Rehearse and practice the new behaviors.

12. Help the child find a mature model. Ask the child to keep a list of the model's admired behaviors and ways in which the model handles frustrations. Rehearse and practice these ways of behaving.

13. Examine with children the self-messages that make them angry enough to throw tantrums, and try to identify more rational and helpful self-messages (see Chapter 8).

14. Teach the child to communicate his or her unhappiness through more appropriate methods such as problem-solving techniques, role modeling, or other counseling strategies.

15. To create an action plan for tantrums, consider the following questions and statements: "When do tantrums occur? Where do tantrums happen? Who is generally included? What happens before, after, and during a tantrum? Things I can do to prevent a tantrum from occurring. Ways that I can handle the tantrum when it occurs" (Oesterreich, 2003, p. 4).

REFERENCES

Oesterreich, L. (2003) Understanding children: temper tantrums. Ames, IA: Iowa State University Extension.

FIGHTING*

Jaime Ostendorf

When working with children, we often think of fighting as intense physical contact between individuals. However, there are many behaviors that fall under the umbrella of "fighting." For example, fighting can be verbal, in which yelling and screaming are involved. Parents and educators are responsible for monitoring anger and aggression. As role models, adults have the power to demonstrate appropriate ways of handling conflict. It is also important for adults to recognize the underlying causes of fighting, which could represent other difficulties within the child's life (Edwards, 1999).

1. Examine the situation that brought on the encounter. Determine the sequence of events and any particular time, place, or situation in which fights are likely to occur. Become an environmental engineer; rearrange the time schedule of the physical environment. Intervene in the sequence of events to prevent or circumvent fight-arousing conditions. This tip can be used in the home and school environments.

2. Fighting can be a compensation for feelings of inadequacy, ignorance of social skills, learned behavior from the home, or a means of covering up emotional or learning problems. Investigate these possibilities by becoming a child watcher and listening actively to the child. See Chapter 6 for more information.

3. Use group or family discussions to focus on how fighting helps or hurts the fighter, how others feel about fighting, the consequences of fighting, and ways in which the fighter could solve conflicts more effectively. Also encourage children to practice new behaviors before the group and use their feedback to

*Reprinted with permission.

improve relationships. Be certain the child has opportunities to see effective ways of resolving conflicts.

4. Determine the goal of the fighter (see Chapter 11 regarding goals of misbehavior). Is the child seeking attention, power, revenge, or free time? Is the fighting a learned behavior? Could the fighting be due to a lack of social skills? Intervene in ways that allow the child to meet these needs appropriately.

5. Students who fight typically have a great deal of anger that needs to be expressed in constructive ways. Hitting an object or person, for example, does not change the problem that is causing the anger. By finding a substitute, or something other than the thing that is desired, anger can be released in a more appropriate manner. Students can avoid fighting by finding other ways to handle their aggression. Making stress balls with balloons and rice is just one example of a creative technique (Gardner, 1990).

6. Adults need to monitor their own behavior when communicating with children. By modeling appropriate ways of expressing disappointment or anger, the adult can take advantage of this learning opportunity. Practice proper behavior such as choosing words carefully and not kicking, hitting, or even screaming. Emphasize the positive ways of solving problems and discourage violence (Edwards, 1999).

7. Parents and teachers are encouraged to discuss acceptable ways of expressing anger. Avoid telling a child what he or she can NOT do. Instead, emphasize those behaviors that are appropriate. For example, teach your students to say phrases such as "I'm so upset," rather than calling their peer a bad name. Some kids need a more action-oriented approach, which means talking with him or her will not be sufficient. Running around the block, hitting a pillow, or yelling at the wall are other ways to express anger (Edwards, 1999).

8. Children and parents or teacher may cooperatively draw up a list of ground rules concerning fighting. Each time the adult notices the child about to become involved in a fight, the adult asks, "What is the ground rule?" Have the child repeat the rule. Early and consistent intervention is necessary. A variation is to clearly define the consequences of fighting and, when fighting is about to occur, ask, "What happens when someone fights?"

9. Reinforcing the consequences of fighting will help remind the child of those behaviors that are considered appropriate. For example, a token-economy system rewards children for good behavior by giving or taking away points based on their actions. Time-outs may work for some aggressive students who are displaying poor behaviors at home and in the classroom. It is extremely important to maintain consistency to properly reinforce the negative consequences (Edwards, 1999).

10. It is not uncommon for most fighting to begin within the home environment. Students are more likely to fight with siblings than peers. Therefore, it is essential for parents to recognize and intervene during intense sibling rivalry. Have children practice sharing objects and talking calmly about their frustrations. Be consistent with the consequences of fighting (Edwards, 1999).

11. I recommend reading the book *Don't Rant and Rave on Wednesdays! The Children's Anger-Control Book* by Adolph Moser. This book includes descriptions of inappropriate behavior, as well as suggestions for alternatives. Both adults and students can benefit from this book and the effective ways to deal with anger and aggression. *Hands Are Not for Hitting* by Martine Agassi is

also a great book to use with elementary school students. This approach to fighting explores the concept of hands being used to do good things, and not when upset or frustrated (Edwards, 1999).

12. When resolving conflicts, students should remember several points: Identify the position, and state it clearly. Listen to other's points of view, and do not interrupt. Respond in positive ways. Be optimistic about the outcome. Treat others with respect and allow them the opportunity to share their point of view. Cherish the friendship, and do not give up because of a minor dispute. Be flexible in your ideas and position. Search for various alternatives to the situation. Parents and school professionals can use these tips when teaching students about conflict mediation as an alternative to fighting (Schmidt, 1997).

13. Determine the goal of the fighter. Is the child seeking attention, power, revenge, or free time? Is the fighting a learned behavior? Could the fighting be a result from the lack of social skills? Children often fight because they feel inadequate, lack social skills, learned the behavior from adult models within the home, or as a way to cover up either emotional or learning problems. Listen closely to children and watch them in the classroom for insight about their particular situation. Intervene to meet the needs of the child. What message is the child sending by engaging in these disputes?

14. Have the fighters write their sides of the story or tell it to a tape recorder. Ask the children to read their stories, or listen to the tape with them. Plan other ways to solve similar situations in the future. Let the children role-play or practice possible scenarios.

15. Peer pressure, especially in small groups, is often effective to help fighting children change their behavior. Adults should find appropriate times to encourage a group when the children are playing or working cooperatively.

16. Consider the following: Three chairs are placed in a semicircle. The adult sits between the two fighters and asks each person to describe what happened. The adult repeats what Child A says to Child B, and then Child B to Child A. This continues until the entire story has been told. Often, children will start to laugh at the situation. The adults are responsible for conveying messages, but not placing blame or making judgments about either child. Discuss how to avoid future conflicts.

17. Contract with the fighter not to fight for a short period (just a few hours or 1 day). Continue to renegotiate the contract until the behavior decreases significantly. Rewards for not fighting and consequences for fighting should be appropriate (see Chapter 9 regarding contingency contracting.)

18. Ideas for working one-on-one with a child who fights include: music therapy, relaxation techniques such as breathing, art, and play therapy with puppets.

19. Films, television programs, or stories can stimulate children to think more objectively about fighting and its consequences. Follow the film or story with a family or group discussion examining the causes and consequences of fighting and other ways the situation could have been resolved. Adults should strictly limit the amount of time children spend watching any violence on television or video games.

20. Isolation techniques such as Seat 2, the quiet corner, and time-out rooms are effective for helping children cool off. When the children feel ready to return to the family group or classroom, they may do so without lectures or blame,

provided they have a plan for staying out of fights (see Chapter 9 regarding isolation techniques).

21. The adult may quietly ask the fighters to leave the room and develop a plan for solving their conflict. The fighters would report their plan to the adult.

REFERENCES

Edwards, C. D. (1999). *How to handle a hard-to-handle kid.* Minneapolis, MN: Free Spirit Publishers.

Gardner, R. A. (1990). *The girls and boys book about good and bad behavior.* Cresskill, NJ: Creative Therapeutics.

Schmidt, J. J. (1997). *Making and keeping friends.* West Nyack, NY: Center for Applied Research in Education.

VERBAL ABUSIVENESS*

Tomica Wright

Most verbal abusiveness, such as rudeness, sarcasm, impoliteness, and name-calling, is a cover for feelings of inadequacy, a learned behavior from adults or other models, a call for attention, or a way of striking back at an unfriendly world. In this instance, the child needs interactions with adults who are calm, rational, and consistent and who behave maturely. Adults need to be on guard against allowing the child's verbal abusiveness to provoke the same behavior from them. Adults who resort to criticism, belittling, and name-calling have little chance of changing children's behaviors.

1. Determine the goal of verbal abusiveness. Could it be that the child is seeking attention, revenge, or power? (See Chapter 11.) Become a child watcher and listen attentively to determine these needs and goals. Having defined the goal, the adult can help the child find a more constructive means of meeting this need.

2. Meet privately with rude, sarcastic, impolite, or name-calling children. Interpret their behavior to them as a cry for help. Then discuss the reasons they feel it necessary to use verbal abusiveness. Help the children develop a plan for being kinder with words. Build the child's skills and vocabulary for kindness.

3. Contract with children to reduce verbal abrasiveness. Clearly define unacceptable behaviors and their consequences. The contract can also include rewards for appropriate responses (see Chapter 9).

4. Provide opportunities for success. Catch the child using nonabusive verbal behavior and comment on it; for example, "I noticed how understanding you were when Tom had his accident today. That was a nice thing to say to him."

5. Role-play or use films, filmstrips, or books to demonstrate and provide stimuli for group or family discussions. Examine what has occurred and the consequences. Discuss new and better methods of interacting. Behavior rehearsal may help children practice the new behaviors.

6. Call together the parties engaged in the verbal battle and have them write their story or tell it to a tape recorder. Read the story aloud with them or play the tape, and allow the children to discuss and evaluate what has happened. Ask them to choose three of the most hurtful statements and rewrite or eliminate those words in the story. Ask them to make a plan for avoiding future verbal battles.

---

*Reprinted with permission.

7. Encourage the teacher, parents, or other children to ignore the verbal abuser. If the behavior becomes too unacceptable to ignore, then walk away or find a quiet place. Adults may use isolation techniques such as Seat 2, quiet corner, or the time-out room (see Chapter 9).

8. Build self-esteem so the child need not resort to verbal abuse (see Poor Self-Concept section in Appendix B). Avoid criticism, name-calling, and belittling remarks. Encourage and reinforce cooperative behavior and provide opportunities for children to interact successfully.

9. Give reprimands quietly, firmly, and calmly. Do not attack the child as a person. Focus on the behavior and admit how the behavior makes you feel; for example, "I get really angry when I hear students talking like that, and I would like you to stop now."

10. Pair the child with good role models for work and other activities. Discuss with the child the behaviors the models demonstrate and the positive and negative consequences of these behaviors. Encourage the child to rehearse and practice these behaviors.

11. Teach students to use "I" messages when someone displays verbal abusiveness toward them. For example, I feel _____ when you _____ because . . .

12. Encourage the student to explore humor when faced with verbal abuse. For example: The bully says "Ugly shoes!" The student may say "Thanks! I hoped you would notice."

13. Teach peer mediation skills to empower other students to recognize verbally abusive behavior and model the behavior to help resolve conflicts.

14. Encourage students to write in a journal or complete activities to help reflect on feelings.

15. Form girl groups—"For girls only." Give girls a way to express their anger and channel it openly and positively. Invite conversations about anger and find ways to help girls build solidarity.

16. Teach children new and acceptable ways of expressing feelings and suggest other words or phrases to say in situations in which they have previously been verbally abusive.

17. Help older children develop a self-management plan. Work with them to stop the thought processes leading to irrational ideas and use the techniques of cognitive restructuring to stop the feelings that accompany verbal abusiveness. Help them develop an alternative plan for expressing their feelings.

18. For older children, try confrontational techniques such as "Could it be?" questions ("Could it be you want to hurt me by calling me names?") or Glasser's reality questions (see Chapter 4).

19. Ask the child to catch other children being courteous and report on their findings.

INFORMATION MAY ALSO BE FOUND IN THE FOLLOWING SOURCES:

Beane, A. (1999). The bully free classroom: Over 100 strategies for teachers k-8. *Free Spirit Publishing Inc., 51,* 60–62.

PBS Kids It's My Life. (n.d.) *Bullies: How to handle it.* Retrieved October 2, 2005, from http://pbskids.org/itsmylife/friends/bullies/article4.html

Vail, K. (2002). Covert aggression can be just as damaging as outright bullying and just as big a problem. *American School board Journal, 8,* 14.

PHYSICAL ABUSIVENESS*

Juleen K. Buser

The aggression and physical violence associated with bullying can stem from a host of influences that can be personal, familial, and peer related. Woods and White (2005) note that researchers have disagreed on the motivations and personalities of children who bully (p. 382). Some consider bullies to suffer from a low self-concept, depression, and unease (Marsh, Parada, Craven, & Finger, 2004), whereas others see bullies as socially adept and master manipulators who bully to gain something they desire (Pellegrini, 2004). Family factors associated with bullying behavior also covers a range of traits, including authoritarian and strict parenting; aggressive and rigid discipline; and a family climate that lacks kindness, unity, and a sense of respect among its members (Griffin & Gross, 2004; Holmes & Holmes-Lonergan, 2004). Peers also play a part in bullying, with peer response to the act of bullying serving to encourage, amplify, or even reduce the aggressive child's hostile actions (Cowie, 2004). Researchers have identified nuances in the identity of children who bully; the line between bully and victim is not always clean and absolute. Children who are called bully/victims or the provocative victims suffer the aggression of others but also instigate damaging bullying behavior with other children (Griffin & Gross, 2004). Children who fit this profile have been hypothesized to be at risk for a multitude of behavioral disorders and negative social effects and may experience more enduring harm than children who solely engage in bullying behavior or those who are only victims of bullying (Griffin & Gross, 2004; Smith, 2004). School-based interventions dominate the literature on bullying, because researchers have demonstrated that a majority of the aggressive and violent behaviors between children occur in the playground or in the classroom of the school (Fekkes, Pijpers, & Verloove-Vanhorick, 2005).

1. Implement a bullying prevention and intervention program that incorporates the whole school. Such a wide-reaching program has been documented extensively in the research as a powerful way to address bullying; consistent and ongoing antibullying efforts (Smith, 2004) that include the entire school community (Fekkes et al., 2005) have produced positive empirical results. The Olewus Bullying Prevention Programme (Olewus, 2004) includes school-, class-, and individual-level interventions. Samples (2004) has described the various levels of these interventions: at the school level, interventions include school-wide surveys that identify school needs, school rules against aggressive behavior, changes in school atmosphere, staff educational meetings, and incentives against bullying; class-level interventions include classroom rules against bullying, a curriculum that teaches anger management and conflict-resolution skills, established consequences for breaking bullying rules, and active parent involvement; and individual-level interventions include direct discussions with children who bully, communication with parents of children who bully, and role-play activities to guide responses to potentially aggressive situations (p. 206). This program cites a 52% decline in bullying conduct in a study that measured this behavior in three grades from 1999 to 2000 (Olewus, 2004, p. 25).

2. Also pay attention to school-based interventions that do not envision bullying reduction as the sole aim of the intervention. Such programs have been explored as being potentially effective and perhaps longer lasting interventions

---

*Reprinted with permission.

than methods that address bullying in a direct, insular fashion (Galloway & Roland, 2004). Studies that focus efforts on improving the school climate in general, enhancing the professional development of teachers, and influencing the behaviors of students on multiple levels has not shown as striking short-term results as certain directive whole-school interventions, but researchers have suggested that teachers may be more apt to continue to implement a wider reaching plan than one that appears to be limited specifically to addressing bullying behavior (Galloway & Roland, 2004).

3. Focus on prevention. Intervene early with children and begin addressing bullying and aggressive behavioral problems in the preschool and elementary years (Smith, 2004). Various curriculum interventions have been created for these age-groups and can be implemented in the classroom by teachers or counselors. These curriculum interventions are largely psychoeducational, because they seek to teach children to identify appropriate behavior, understand what bullying is, resolve conflicts in healthy ways, express their emotions effectively, gain compassion for victims, gain problem-solving skills, and model suitable interpersonal interactions (Samples, 2004).

4. Implement peer interventions to address bullying problems in school, because peers can learn to identify bullying behavior, successfully stop bullying behavior, and gain a support system (Cowie, 2004). Cowie provides a useful summary of various peer interventions aimed at building mutual support among children; in these groups, children feel safe to express fears, learn conflict-mediation skills, gain problem-solving abilities, and learn listening skills, and bullies and victims learn to collaborate with adults in setting up contracts and rules to avoid clashes. Fekkes at al. (2005) underscores that teaching children to speak up and react against bullying behavior, instead of remaining silent bystanders, can be an effective way to address bullying.

5. Center bullying interventions on teachers, addressing teacher knowledge, efficacy, and empathy. Research has noted the effectiveness of enhancing the knowledge of teachers regarding bullying. Newman-Carlson and Horne (2004) created Bully Busters, a curriculum to reduce bullying that focuses, in part, on instructing teachers in intervention tactics and tools to prevent and treat bullying behavior; results of their study indicate gains in knowledge and skill and a reduction in bullying (p. 266). Olewus (2004) notes that a predictor of an effective program outcome was the teacher's knowledge about bullying and potential interventions. Fekkes et al. (2005) also have documented the impact of teacher knowledge regarding bullying interventions. Augmenting the competence of teachers surrounding their perceived ability to stop bullying is another potent intervention measure, because increasing the self-efficacy of teachers in confronting bullying behavior can effectively address and reduce this behavior (Newman-Carlson & Horne, 2004; Olewus, 2004). In addition, enhancing the empathy teachers have for victims of bullying may increase their active response to bullying behavior (Olewus, 2004).

6. Explore and identify the goals of bullying behavior, because the child may be bullying for a multitude reasons; children may bully in response to a poor self-concept (Marsh et al., 2004), from a desire to gain power and status (Holmes & Holmes-Lonergan, 2004), as an aim for revenge, as a way strike out against a world perceived to be hostile or cruel, or due to learned or deficient social skills (Griffin & Gross, 2004; Holmes & Holmes-Lonergan, 2004).

7. Assist the child in learning another way to gain status, because his or her bullying behavior may be the result of a family context in which the child is consistently put down and criticized and consequently feels minimally important at home (Holmes & Holmes-Lonergan, 2004). This feeling of insignificance may be reacted against through physical aggression toward other children, as an attempt to gain a position of prominence that has eluded the bullying child at home (Holmes & Holmes-Lonergan, 2004). Explore possibilities for helping the child gain a sense of status and importance that does not involve hurting others (Holmes & Holmes-Lonergan, 2004). One way to address this status deficit may be to encourage responsibility by giving children responsible jobs at which they can feel successful—for example, delivering material or messages, watering plants, or feeding the fish. Avoid drudgery job assignments.

8. Use ideas for building a good self-concept (see Appendix B) so that the child does not resort to bullying to cover feelings of inadequacy.

9. Explore ways to teach and instill appropriate social behavior in children who bully. The method of reproof can be one method of approaching this goal. Give reprimands in a quiet, adult manner without devaluing the child as a person. Focus the reprimand on the behavior. Instead of calling the child a name, such as *bully*, admit your feelings to the child: "I get angry when I see you hit other children like that, and I would like you to stop." In addition, activities geared to elicit discussion and role-play of suitable social relationships can be effective. Sociograms are helpful in learning which children the bully likes or dislikes. Activities may be organized in which the bully is grouped with liked children and appropriate role models. Discuss with the children the behaviors they see in the models and the positive and negative consequences of these behaviors. Encourage children to rehearse and practice the appropriate behaviors.

10. Praise and reinforce friendly and cooperative behavior as another way to reinforce suitable social skills. For example, if the child helps another, verbally or physically, during play activities or during any social interaction, comment of the appropriate behavior. Catching children in good behavior is an effective intervention for many behavioral problems.

11. Include parents in the intervention, because children may report bullying behavior more frequently to parents than to teachers or other adults (Fekkes et al., 2005). Discussions with parents of children who bully or who are victims of bullying may be effective, where the counselor presents a hypothetical example similar to the bullying incident and stimulates discussion around the topic. Films, filmstrips, and stories can prompt an exploration of children's motives for bullying, the self-concepts of bullies, the peer view of bullies, and more appropriate social interactions. Role-play, rehearsal, feedback, and encouragement can then teach and reinforce new behaviors.

12. Play cooperative games with children who bully, because research has shown that cooperative games reduce aggressive behavior and increase the prosocial behavior of children, whereas overtly competitive games may have the opposite effect (Bay-Hinitz & Wilson, 2005). Another way to promote cooperative behavior is to find an interest or ability the bully has. Have the child pursue this interest or ability by helping others or sharing it with others—for instance, sharing a stamp or rock collection, building a science project.

13. Teach the child to use a method, such as stop, look, listen, and think, before taking any action.

14. Understand the role that arousal may play in the aggressive bullying behavior of children. Research has indicated that bully/victims have higher arousal levels than nonaggressive children, whereas bullies have lower than average arousal levels (Woods & White, 2005). The high arousal of bully/victims often means that these children have heightened emotions of anxiety and tension; interventions can address this high anxiety by taking children through relaxation techniques, promoting serene surroundings, teaching children coping skills, training children in self-talk, and creating a structured atmosphere where an authority such as a teacher is in control of the situation (Woods & White, 2005, p. 392). The low arousal of bullies may mean that bullies seek out commotion and aggression to increase lower than normal arousal levels; interventions to address this subdued arousal include supplying scenarios of challenge and stimulation that can provide the child with excitement and energy and replace aggressive activity (Woods & White, 2005, p. 392). Other endeavors that may energize bullying children and provide a way to gain emotional arousal appropriately include supervised activities such as running, hammering, writing out feelings, drawing pictures, playing games, or talking out feelings.

15. Observe the child's environment to determine situations that provoke bullying behavior. Try to engineer the child's activities to reduce opportunities for bullying. Rearrange time schedules or the physical environment, if possible. Intervene before the opportunity for bullying occurs.

References

Bay-Hinitz, A., & Wilson, G. (2005). A cooperative games intervention for aggressive preschool children. In L. A. Reddy, T. M. Files-Hall, & C. E. Schaefer (Eds.), *Empirically based play interventions for children* (pp. 191–211). Washington, DC: American Psychological Association.

Cowie, H. (2004). Peer influences. In C. E. Sanders & G. D. Phye (Eds.), *Bullying: Implications for the classroom* (pp. 137–157). New York: Elsevier Academic Press.

Fekkes, M., Pijpers, F., & Verloove-Vanhorick, S. (2005). Bullying: Who does what, when, and where? Involvement of children, teachers and parents in bullying behavior. *Health Education Research, 20*(1), 81–91.

Galloway, D., & Roland, E. (2004) Is the direct approach to reducing bullying always the best? In P. K. Smith, D. Pepler, & K. Rigby (Eds.), *Bullying in schools: How successful can interventions be?* (pp. 37–53). Cambridge, UK: Cambridge University Press.

Griffin, R., & Gross, A. (2004). Childhood bullying: Current empirical findings and future directions for research. *Aggression and Violent Behavior, 9*, 379–400.

Holmes, J., & Holmes-Lonergan, H. (2004). The bully in the family: Family influences on bullying. In C. E. Sanders & G. D. Phye (Eds.), *Bullying: Implications for the classroom* (pp. 111–135). New York: Elsevier Academic Press.

Marsh, H., Parada, R., Craven, R., & Finger, L. (2004). In the looking glass: A reciprocal effects model elucidating the complex nature of bullying, psychological determinants, and the central role of self-concept. In C. E. Sanders & G. D. Phye (Eds.), *Bullying: Implications for the classroom* (pp. 63–106). New York: Elsevier Academic Press.

Newman-Carlson, D., & Horne, A. (2004). Bully Busters: A psychoeducational intervention for reducing bullying behavior in middle school students. *Journal of Counseling & Development, 82*, 259–267.

Olewus, D. (2004). The Olewus Bullying Prevention Programme: Design and implementation issues and a new national initiative in Norway. In P. K. Smith, D. Pepler, & K. Rigby (Eds.), *Bullying in schools: How successful can interventions be?* (pp. 13–36). Cambridge: Cambridge University Press.

Pellegrini, A. (2004). Bullying during the middle school years. In C. E. Sanders & G. D. Phye (Eds.), *Bullying: Implications for the classroom* (pp. 203–227). New York: Elsevier Academic Press.

Samples, F. (2004). Evaluating curriculum-based intervention programs: An examination of preschool, primary, and elementary intervention programs. In C. E. Sanders & G. D. Phye (Eds.), *Bullying: Implications for the classroom* (pp. 203–227). New York: Elsevier Academic Press.

Smith, P. (2004). Bullying: Recent developments. *Child and Adolescent Mental Health, 9*(3), 98–103.

Woods, S., & White, E. (2005). The association between bullying behavior, arousal levels and behavior problems. *Journal of Adolescence, 28,* 381–395.

CRUELTY TO PEERS, ANIMALS, AND OTHERS*

Christopher Delfausse

Cruelty to people or animals is usually a sign of other problems. Children who exhibit these behaviors need immediate attention from adults to ameliorate the destructiveness. They may be desperate for someone to help them with their deep feelings of hurt. Extended counseling may be necessary to uncover the underlying reasons for the cruelty and to replace the problematic behaviors. Children who are cruel to peers or animals may be responding to punitive adults in their own lives. Severe cases may require intensive psychotherapy or even residential treatment (see also suggestions offered in Fighting and Destructiveness sections).

1. Closely supervise children in all activities.
2. Give the children releases for emotional tension—for example, varying quiet activities with physical activities frequently. Encourage constructive physical releases, such as running, playing ball, or cycling. Writing, music, art, and talking may also help. Schedule times for releases regularly throughout the day's activities.
3. Use group or family discussions that emphasize cooperation with others. Discuss the feelings and events that provoked the cruel acts, and plan ways for coping with the feelings.
4. Teach the child to train, care for, and interact in a nurturing way with animals. Being with and caring for animals will reduce any propensity children may have toward aggression and violence directed at animals. One way to do this may be to get a pet for the child and teach him or her how to raise and care for it. This idea is to increase the empathy a child has toward animals (Ascione, 2001).
5. Encourage cooperation, responsibility, and pursuit of interests by giving children responsible jobs that enable them to feel success—for example, delivering messages or filing materials. Do not place more responsibility on the child than the child can tolerate. Find areas of interest by asking the child what he or she likes to do and structure activities and jobs around them.

*Reprinted with permission.

6. Avoid physical punishment. Strong punishment produces further anger and the likelihood of aggression. It also provides a model for cruel, aggressive behavior. Limit TV viewing to nonaggressive programs. Remove as many models of aggression and cruelty as possible. Focus on the child's strengths and reinforce cooperative behaviors.

7. Diaries, play therapy, fantasy games, sentence completion, and active listening may be used as aids to understanding cruel children. Diaries and play therapy also allow children to vent their thoughts and feelings nondestructively.

8. Interpret the child's cruel behavior as a cry for help and an expression of loneliness and rejection. Ask the children to write out feelings of contempt and cruelty. Discuss the feelings and make a plan for more constructive ways of handling them. Encourage the child's appropriate behavior.

9. Ask the child to find an admired model and to keep a list of the model's behaviors for a short time. Discuss the behaviors with the child, rehearse new behaviors, and encourage the child to try out new ways of behaving.

10. With the child, draw up a behavioral contract that sets out rewards for appropriate behaviors and the consequences of cruel behavior. Clearly define acceptable and unacceptable behaviors.

11. Carefully structure the child's environment and daily activities to provide little or no opportunity for unacceptable behavior. Plan each hour's activity in cooperation with the child, if possible. A daily schedule of work, play, study time, and planned leisure time can be posted in the child's room or school desk.

12. Determine the goal of the cruel behavior. Does the child see the world as cruel? Could the child be seeking revenge or power? What needs are not being met? (See Chapter 11.)

References

Ascione, F. (September 2001). *Animal abuse and youth violence Juvenile Justice Bulletin*. (Report Number NCJ-188677). Department of Justice, Washington, DC: Office of Juvenile Justice and Delinquency Prevention.

DESTRUCTIVENESS

Destructiveness and vandalism are problems of increasing severity in our society (see also Fighting section earlier in this chapter). One of the counselor's first concerns is to find what is happening in the child's environment to cause such intense feelings and behavior. Is the child angry at someone or something (for instance, school) to the extent of having an intense need to strike out and hurt that person or place? Could the destructiveness be a result of frustration, feelings of failure, or feelings of revenge because the child feels no one cares? A second concern is gaining the child's trust to change this self-defeating behavior—a task that requires time and patience.

1. Determine the goal of the child's destructiveness. Could the motive be attention, feelings of rejection, anger, a need for power, or revenge (see Chapter 11).

2. Examine the situation that brought on the destructiveness or preceded the act. Does the destructiveness occur most often at a particular place, situation, or time? If so, become an environmental engineer, arranging the circumstances or scheduling to avoid the situations.

3. Use logical consequences (see Chapter 11) as punishment or penalty for destructive behavior. Whatever the child destroys must be paid for or the cost worked off in some manner. Refrain from harsh punishments, which may reinforce the child's idea that the world is cruel and hostile and that destructiveness is the only way of getting back at the world.

4. Have the child write a description of the destructive act; discuss and plan ways for avoiding such behavior in the future. Have the child generate multiple ways of repairing the damage caused.

5. Confront the child nonjudgmentally by interpreting the destructive behavior as a distress signal. Offer to listen and to help. Help the child make a plan to avoid destructive behaviors in the future.

6. Start a campaign of "Keep our school (home) clean!" Working together ("we" feelings) to build pride in personal areas is often helpful in preventing vandalism or destructiveness.

7. Determine the child's areas of interest and involve the destructive child in working with them—not busywork but productive tasks. Peer teaching, peer tutoring, or sharing the interest in another way may be helpful. Guiding the child in pursuing interests and special abilities may be a productive way of diverting the child's behavior toward more constructive actions and building feelings of success.

8. Encourage children to keep a diary of their feelings and thoughts or tell them to a tape recorder. Writing or talking provides a means of catharsis and gives the adult some insight into the child's world. The adult and child can then discuss these feelings and develop a plan for coping with them.

9. Play therapy with toys, Play-Doh, music, or drawing may be used in an effort to understand the feelings underlying the child's destructiveness and as a means of catharsis (see Chapter 14).

10. Hold group or family discussions focusing on the consequences of vandalism and destructiveness. Help the children look at what they are doing, the consequences, and alternative ways of behaving. Expect the child to repair damages. Use behavior rehearsal to practice new methods of handling situations.

11. Help the destructive child find a friend and model. Encouragement and peer pressure are effective in helping vandalizing children redirect their behavior into more constructive paths. Discuss the behaviors of the model and allow the children to practice and rehearse these behaviors.

12. Refrain from punishing, scolding, lecturing, moralizing, preaching, or degrading destructive children. These methods reinforce the children's thinking that the world and people are cruel and uncaring.

13. Use contracting with rewards to help the child change destructive behaviors (see Chapter 9). Be certain the child understands the rules. Define appropriate and inappropriate behaviors clearly, as well as the rewards and consequences of each. Be clear that destructiveness of any kind is unacceptable.

14. A resource person from a local law enforcement agency can discuss laws and penalties for destructiveness and vandalism with the children, but avoid scare techniques and threats.

15. Arrange the child's schedule to allow time during the day to work off energy. Vary the day's activities from quiet to physical. Encourage physical activities such as running, football or basketball, and bicycling and quiet releases such as writing, music, art, or talking.

16. Work out a plan with the child and an adult authority so that a child whose tense feelings become overwhelming can signal the adult and report to some agreed-on place to work out these feelings. For example, assisting the custodians with maintenance and cleaning might help in three ways: (1) to dissipate bad feelings, (2) to develop appreciation for the building, and (3) to create empathy for the custodian, who has to repair damage to the building.

STEALING*

Trevor J. Buser

Although many children try stealing once or twice during their developmental years, persistent, repeated acts of stealing indicate other problems and require an understanding of the motives and needs behind the behavior. Children may steal as a result of a complex web of factors, including individual, family, school, cultural, and peer-related influences (Dwivedi & Sankar, 2004). A child or adolescent, for instance, may report stealing because of the high value society places on material wealth, because of ignorance or an immature view of ownership rights, because they want to impress others, because of poor impulse control, or because they want to experience the adventure of getting away with something (Babin & Babin, 1996; Dwivedi & Sankar, 2004; Grant & Kim, 2002).

1. Maintain a balanced perspective with parents by noting that stealing is a common, albeit negative, behavior among youths (Grant & Kim, 2002; Venning, Blampied, & France, 2003). Although adults do well to address any individual act of stealing on the part of minors, it is especially important for therapists to consider the pattern of stealing behavior and developmental levels demonstrated by the client (Dwivedi & Sankar, 2004; Venning et al., 2003). If the stealing behavior of a child or adolescent is persistent, it may be one of many behaviors or symptoms indicative of more serious disorders, such as conduct disorder or kleptomania (Grant & Kim, 2002; Venning et al., 2003).
2. Counselors should address the breakdown of trust between individuals, which researchers have recognized as one of the critical difficulties put forth by stealing behavior (Pawsey, 1996). In cases involving the mere suspicion of stealing, rather than concrete evidence of its occurrence, issues of trust remain salient and treatment takes on additional complications (Tremblay & Drabman, 1997; Venning et al., 2003).
3. For cases in which detection of stealing hinges on suspicion, it is recommended that the child be required to justify the presence of the possession or money under consideration (Tremblay & Drabman, 1997). This approach, however, may cause ethical considerations, as it conflicts with the model of our judicial system, which presumes innocence until proof is offered to the contrary (Tremblay & Drabman, 1997).
4. If you have positive evidence that the child is stealing, be quietly direct in your confrontation. Ask the child for a plan to rectify the situation (see suggestion 9 later in this list) and explore ways to avoid stealing in the future.
5. Determine the motivation or goal of the behavior (see Chapter 11). Is the child seeking attention, power, or revenge? Is the behavior the result of a dare,

*Reprinted with permission.

an initiation, or peer pressure? Is the child stealing to meet basic needs for food or clothing? Actively listen to the child to try to understand the motive (Chapter 6). In cases that involve the lack of basic necessities, such as food, contact appropriate agencies to find resources for meeting those needs.

6. If peer pressure is the motivating factor for stealing, training youths in divergent thinking may lay the groundwork for the most effective refusal strategies (Wright, Nichols, Graber, Brooks-Gunn, & Botvin, 2004). Divergent thinking in social contexts has been defined as the ability to generate multiple responses to social pressure and "to adapt and modify what one says to meet the needs of the listeners" (Wright et al., 2004, p. 382). Researchers have found that adolescents who use divergent thinking in their refusal strategies demonstrate a significantly lower likelihood of engaging in stealing and other deviant behavior (Wright et al., 2004). Examples of alternative responses to peer pressure include directly saying *no,* suggesting other activities besides stealing, postponing one's answer, leaving the situation, or offering a reason for one's decision not to steal (Wright et al., 2004).

7. If stealing occurs in a group, often the children can solve the problem themselves. Present the situation to the group and ask them to draw up a plan for resolving the problem. Ask for a discussion of the plan with the entire group, avoiding accusations and blame.

8. Partner with the parents and offer parent-training programs. Behaviorally based parent-training programs have produced positive results with youths who have conduct disorders and with less serious cases involving children who steal (Dwivedi & Sankar, 2004; Venning et al., 2003). This intervention also aligns well with the research suggesting that effective parenting skills and secure attachment between parent and child serve to decrease negative behaviors in youths (Dwivedi & Sankar, 2004). Key components of applying this program with cases of stealing may include educational materials for parents on behavior modification, behavior charts for children, role plays and rehearsal of techniques to be used with children, a focus on the consequences of problem behavior, and strategy planning for anticipated setbacks (Venning et al., 2003).

9. Offer behaviorally based interventions for the child or adolescent, in addition to his or her parent(s). Tremblay and Drabman (1997) devised one such model of behavioral therapy for stealing, which incorporates steps of "confession and apology to the victim, restitution (i.e., return or replacement of the stolen object), two levels of overcorrection, and praise for alternative behavior" (p. 34). The two levels of overcorrection required the child or adolescent (1) to pay the victim a sum of money equal to the value of the stolen object, and (2) to hand over to the victim an item of equal value and use. As noted earlier, these levels of overcorrection took place in addition to the step of providing restitution (that is, returning or replacing the original item that was stolen). The second level of overcorrection, involving the forfeiture of an item of equal value, is hoped to reinforce the logical consequences of stealing, as well as ingrain within the child or adolescent a sense of empathy with the victim, who has also lost a possession of some worth. In applying this model, verbal punishments are kept to a minimum, because the steps of the model are believed to communicate the moral message regarding stealing.

10. Use preventive interventions to develop protective factors against stealing. Such interventions assist youths in the reduction of negative behaviors and may involve intensive mentoring programs, school-based peer mediation programs, and school counseling programs emphasizing social skills development, academic success, and partnerships between parents and schools (Dwivedi & Sankar, 2004). Other preventive strategies may involve helping the child or adolescent to locate and nurture an interest, hobby, or ability (for example, a stamp or rock collection, knowledge on a subject of particular interest, or sports ability). Most children who find some success in their lives and feel they belong have no need to behave inappropriately.

11. Have group or family discussions about stealing, its consequences, and the rights of ownership. Research suggests that teenagers have a relatively impoverished view of the immoral nature of stealing and tend to act more on emotion than principles (Babin & Babin, 1996). Films, music, books, and newspapers can stimulate discussion on the topic. Discuss alternatives to stealing. Plan and prepare for situations that might tempt the child to act on the impulse to steal.

12. Avoid making threats that cannot be carried out, such as "We are all going to stay here until the property is returned." Such threats inevitably end up with the adult having to withdraw the ultimatum.

13. Use storytelling (see Chapter 14), posing a hypothetical example similar to the child's problem. Ask the child for a reaction to the story. Discuss what might happen to the story's character who is involved in stealing (Dwivedi & Sankar, 2004). Such a process may be an invaluable means of assisting children in the development of empathetic behavior.

14. If stealing is a prevalent or persistent behavior, ask a local law enforcement officer to talk with the child or adolescent about the legal consequences of stealing. If the child or adolescent becomes involved in the juvenile justice system on account of stealing behavior, be attentive and sensitive to the ramifications of the child's label as a "juvenile delinquent" and monitor the impact of court appearances and associated legal activities on the family and the child or adolescent.

15. Encourage the child to focus on "reality, responsibility, right and wrong" through the techniques of reality therapy (see Chapter 4).

References

Babin, B. J., & Babin, L. A. (1996). Effects of moral cognitions and consumer emotions on shoplifting intentions. *Psychology & Marketing, 13,* 785–802.

Dwivedi, K. N., & Sankar, S. (2004). Promotion of prosocial development and prevention of conduct disorders. In P. B. Harper (Ed.), *Promoting the emotional well-being of children and adolescents and preventing their mental ill health: A handbook* (pp. 198–218), Philadelphia: Jessica Kingsley Publishers.

Grant, J. E., & Kim, S. W. (2002). Adolescent kleptomania treated with naltrexone. *European Child & Adolescent Psychiatry, 11,* 92–95.

Pawsey, R. (1996). A family behavioural treatment of persistent juvenile theft. *Australian Psychologist, 31,* 26–33.

Tremblay, G. C., & Drabman, R. S. (1997). An intervention for childhood stealing. *Child & Family Behavior Therapy, 19,* 33–40.

Venning, H. B., Blampied, N. M., & France, K. G. (2003). Effectiveness of a standard parenting-skills program in reducing stealing and lying in two boys. *Child & Family Behavior Therapy, 25,* 31–44.

Wright, A. J., Nichols, T. R., Graber, J. A., Brooks-Gunn, J., & Botvin, G. J. (2004). It's not what you say, it's how many different ways you can say it: Links between divergent peer resistance skills and delinquency a year later. *Journal of Adolescent Health, 35,* 380–391.

CHILDREN IN THE JUVENILE JUSTICE SYSTEM*

Nathaniel Ivers

The number of juveniles incarcerated in the United States has continued to increase since the late 1980s. In fact, from 1989 to 1997 the juvenile arrest rate increased 22 percent. Furthermore, many incarcerated juvenile offenders exhibit symptoms of affective disorders, behavioral and emotional problems, attention-deficit/hyperactivity disorder, as well as learning disabilities. Therefore, due to the increase in juvenile offenders in the United States and the large percentage of offenders with psychological and behavioral problems, it is requisite that counselors and other helping professionals formulate guidelines for working with children in the juvenile justice system (Granello & Hanna, 2003). A few such guidelines include:

1. Incorporate a relational group approach in treatment with female juvenile offenders. This approach helps build connections with other girls and women, while also addressing the inappropriate behaviors exhibited by the female offenders (Calhoun, Bartolomucci, & McLean, 2005).
2. Develop a peer intervention program. Peer intervention programs "facilitate group cohesiveness, interpersonal support and hope, unconditional acceptance, and the altruistic helping of others" (Brannon, Larson, & Doggett, 1991, p. 51).
3. Provide individual juvenile planning in which active and comprehensive goals and intervention strategies are planned for each youth with disabilities in the juvenile justice system (Larson & Turner, 2002).
4. Provide skill-based interventions that include group and individual counseling, social skills training, academic and vocational interventions, and life skills/multimodal approaches (Larson & Turner, 2002).
5. Offer group counseling with juvenile offenders that is problem-solution oriented and focused, as opposed to open-ended (Larson & Turner, 2002).
6. If possible, provide group counseling that is held outside of the "juvenile justice context." Research indicates that groups outside of the juvenile justice system are twice as likely to reduce recidivism in juvenile offenders (Larson & Turner, 2002, p. 7).
7. Offer individual counseling that teaches problem-solving skills and social skills as opposed to open-ended insight–based counseling approaches (Larson & Turner, 2002).
8. Use cognitive therapy with clients in which you help the juvenile offender learn to change his or her thoughts, values, attitudes, beliefs, and expectations. Social cognitive training has been found to be the single most effective treatment in reducing recidivism for juvenile offenders with learning, attention, behavioral, and emotional disabilities (Larson & Turner, 2002).

---

*Reprinted with permission.

9. Assess for social skills. This may mean assessing particular behaviors (that is, respecting authority, taking turns, or controlling one's temper) or a group of behaviors (that is, keeping friends or behaving cooperatively) (Larson & Turner, 2002).

10. Provide social skills training in which presentation of the idea (selling the skill), modeling, role-playing, corrective feedback, generalization training, coaching and reinforcement, recycle learning, and a review of progress are incorporated in the training (Larson & Turner, 2002).

11. Use advocacy skills to help juvenile offenders receive academic interventions that are tailored to the abilities of the individual. Interventions that demonstrate brevity of activities, variety, and structure have been found to be effective (Larson & Turner, 2002).

12. Advocate for vocational training (Larson & Turner, 2002).

13. Be aware of medical needs of juveniles, including substance abuse issues (Larson & Turner, 2002). "The basic components of a drug-free adolescent program include individual counseling, individual therapy, self-help groups for the patients and caretakers, substance abuse education, breathalyzer testing, family therapy and/or involvement, relapse prevention techniques, refusal techniques, educational, vocational, and social skill training, legal assistance, contingency contracting, medication, and written assignments related to the recovery process" (Larson & Turner, 2002, p. 17).

14. Implement a behavioral system that accentuates the positive in youth and helps them learn prosocial behaviors. One example is giving youth the opportunity to earn "special" incentives. For example, if the youth exhibits the desired behavior for 2 weeks, then he or she may receive radio privileges for a day, even if these privileges are not normally permitted at the security level the youth is currently on (Larson & Turner, 2002).

15. Provide family counseling that is carefully structured, that focuses on the family problems, and that teaches skills. This type of family counseling is found to be effective in reducing recidivism (Larson & Turner, 2002).

REFERENCES

Brannon, J. M., Larson, B., & Doggett, M. (1991). Peer counseling strategies: Facilitating self disclosure among sexually victimized juvenile offenders. *Journal of Addictions and Offender Counseling, 11*(2), 51–58.

Calhoun, G. B., Bartolomucci, C. L., & McLean, B. A. (2005). Building connections: Relational group work with female adolescent offenders. *Women and Therapy, 28*(2), 17–29.

Granello, P. F., & Hanna, F. J. (2003). Incarcerated and court-involved adolescents: Counseling an at-risk population. *Journal of Counseling and Development, 81*(1), 11–18.

Larson, K. A., & Turner, K. D. (2002). *Best practices for serving court involved youth with learning, attention and behavioral disabilities: Monograph series on education, disability and juvenile justice.* Washington, DC: American Institutes for Research. (ERIC Document Reproduction Service No. ED471212)

POSSIBLE *DSM-IV-TR* CODES

Conduct Disorders

Fighting, Verbal Abusiveness, Cruelty to Peers, Animals & Others, Destructiveness, Tattlers, Swearing, Lying, Disobedience, Negativism & Resistant Behavior, Stealing, Teasing, and Tantrums:

- V61.20—Parent-Relational Problem; V61.8—Sibling-Relational Problem
- V71.02—Child or Adolescent Antisocial Disorder
- 309.9.3—Adjustment Disorder with Disturbance of Conduct; 309.9—Adjustment Disorder (unspecified)
- 312.33—Kleptomania
- 312.8x—Conduct Disorder
- 312.9—Disruptive Behavior Disorder NOS
- 313.81—Oppositional Defiant Disorder

Anxiety Disorders

Chronic Complaining & Tantrums

- 300.02—Generalized Anxiety Disorder (also see other anxiety disorders such as 309.21—Separation Anxiety, 300.23—Social Phobia)
- 309.24—Adjustment Disorder with Anxiety
- 316—(Specified psychological factor) affecting . . . (indicate the general medical condition)

Reference

American Psychiatric Association. (2000). *Diagnostic and statistical manual of mental disorders* (4th ed., Rev. ed.). Washington, DC: Author.

B APPENDIX

As in Appendix A, the following techniques are derived from a variety of resources and methods for counseling with children. The procedures must be incorporated into a caring and accepting counseling or consulting atmosphere, and the techniques should be modified to meet the individual needs of children and their particular social, learning, or behavioral problems.

We appreciate the contributions of master's degree students in the counseling program at Wake Forest University. Their names appear in the section that they wrote.

SELF-HARM*

Juleen K. Buser

Referred to by alternative names including self-mutilation, self-injury, and self-abuse, the internal conflict of self-harm is broadly construed as intentional, continual, and reckless self-hurting, without an aim to commit suicide (Conterio & Lader, 1998; Zila & Kiselica, 2001). The forms of self-harm differ; children and adolescents may cut themselves, burn themselves, refuse to let wounds or scabs heal, hit themselves, carve their skin, or put objects inside their body (Conterio & Lader, 1998; Ross & Heath, 2002; Zila & Kiselica, 2001). See Chapter 18 for information on suicidal behaviors and suggestions for counseling with children exhibiting these symptoms.

Several studies, however, have documented cutting as one of the more prevalent and opportune forms of child and adolescent self-harm (Conterio & Lader, 1998; Yip, 2005; Ross & Heath, 2002). Conterio and Lader (1998) note that 1 percent of the general population falls into the category of consistent self-harmers, and that this behavior typically begins at puberty. Girls often are documented as having a higher frequency and incidence of self-harming behavior than boys (Conterio & Lader, 1998; Ross & Heath, 2002), and the literature in general shows more data and information regarding female self-harm (Zila & Kiselica, 2001). Yet, female and male reasons for self-harm have been reported to be similar (Kumar, Pepe, & Steer, 2004); consequently, many of the suggested interventions are applicable to both sexes.

---

*Reprinted with permission.

660

Understanding self-harm is a complex endeavor; the precipitating factors and reported motivations to self-harm include a host of deficits, needs, and comorbid problems. The release of tension is a common element among children's and adolescent's reasons for harming themselves; several researchers have noted an unbearable buildup of anxiety that is relieved through the act of deliberate self-harm (Crowe & Bunclark, 2000; Haines & Williams, 2003; Kumar et al., 2004). Although feelings of intense anxiety are generally agreed to be the precursor to self-harming behavior, researchers have differed on what precedes this anxiety, citing either stressful events or unexpressed feelings of hostility as triggering the intolerable anxiety (Ross & Heath, 2003). Overall, however, self-harm often serves as an affect regulator, used to bring relief when emotions become too severe and unbearable and the child or adolescent draws on self-harming activity to restore a sense of calm (Ross & Heath, 2003). One author notes the body's release of endorphins in response to physical injury, offering explanation for the sensation of relief experienced after self-harming (Galley, 2003). Other research has documented the experiences of depersonalization and disassociation that precede and persist during the self-harming behavior (Shapiro, 1987; Yip, 2005; Zila & Kiselica, 2001).

1. Determine the intention of the self-harming behavior. Adolescents will often pierce and tattoo their bodies, enduring physical pain and discomfort to gain a specific appearance and social status; these intentions are quite different from those who self-harm to regulate emotions and cope with anxiety (Froeschle & Moyer, 2004).
2. Proactively identify children and adolescents who may be self-harming, because this is often a hidden, shameful behavior and school counselors, in particular, may be the first counseling professionals to identify a self-harming child (Froeschle & Moyer, 2004). Two studies (Ross & Heath, 2002, 2003) have documented the use of a "How I Deal with Stress" questionnaire with a sample of high school adolescents. This assessment tool identifies various ways people might choose to approach stressful situations, including options ranging from deciding to shop, eat, exercise, cry, and "hurt myself on purpose" (Ross & Heath, 2003, p. 286). Adolescents are asked to rate how often they use this strategy: 0 (never), 1 (once), 2 (couple of times), or 3 (frequently) (Ross & Heath, 2003, p. 286).
3. Uncover the client's reasons for self-harming. Children and adolescents may use self-harm as a coping mechanism after troubling life events (Froeschle & Moyer, 2004; Haines & Williams, 2003; Ross & Heath, 2002) and/or as a way to feel in control of one's body (Zila & Kiselica, 2001). The Self-Injury Motivation Scale II (SIMS II) developed by Osuch has been identified by Kumar et al. (2004) as a helpful self-report measure to identify the motives for self-harming of adolescent psychiatric inpatients. In addition, Ross and Heath (2003) include a questionnaire to identify the emotions and desires of adolescents in the moments before they engaged in self-harming activity (p. 286). Recognizing the reasons for self-harming can then inform the direction of treatment.
4. Avoid blaming and labeling the self-harming adolescent (Yip, 2005; Zila & Kiselica, 2001). Common misconceptions are that all self-harming adolescents desire attention and/or want to manipulate others (Froeschle & Moyer,

2004). Although some adolescents may cut themselves in front of others for attention, many others harm themselves in secret and hope not to be discovered (Yip, 2005; Zila & Kiselica, 2001). Overall, because reasons for self-harming differ from individual to individual, inaccurate labels may enhance the stress and disturbance of adolescents and aggravate self-harming behavior (Yip, 2005).

5. To prevent blame, it is important to educate and converse with others regarding self-harming behavior. Froeschle & Moyer (2004) note the importance of informing teachers and parents about self-harm and addressing common myths surrounding the behavior so that parents can supervise behavior at home and teachers can gain empathy and insight in their interaction with these adolescents. Huband and Tantam (1999) underscore the conflict and disagreement prevalent among staff members who treat self-harming individuals in clinical settings; these authors therefore highlight the need to communicate effectively and consistently with staff in these settings.

6. Foster the support and communication of parents and peers. Unsupportive, neglectful, and/or abusive family members and the rejecting behavior of peers have been reported to increase the incidence of self-harming behavior, whereas family security and peer support may prevent and reduce self-harming behaviors (Yip, 2005).

7. Advocate for more compassionate, accepting sociocultural contexts, particularly for women. Competitive social contexts, fostering stress and pressure, may increase self-harming activity, as can social norms that objectify adolescents and hold unrealistic standards of beauty for female individuals (Yip, 2005).

8. Assess for comorbid disorders. Self-harming behavior has been linked to substance abuse, the eating disorders bulimia nervosa and anorexia nervosa, anxiety, and depression (Froeschle & Moyer, 2004; Ross & Heath, 2002; Zila & Kiselica, 2001).

9. Assess for sexual abuse and other sexual identity issues. Shapiro (1987) notes that the self-blame that victims of sexual abuse may experience is played out in acts of self-harm. Zila and Kiselica (2001) also note the connection between sexual abuse and self-harming behavior, reporting that female individuals who are abused in childhood may learn to function from a false self and deny their true self through suppressing their emotions. In addition, these authors drew attention to sexual identity confusion or ambivalence that may be also a relevant part of self-harming behavior (Zila & Kiselica, 2001).

10. Encourage the client to disclose emotions that he or she has not communicated previously; this emotional expression has been cited as a helpful technique in the clinical treatment of those who self-harm (Huband & Tantam, 1999).

11. Focus counseling interventions on enhancing the self-concept of self-harming children and adolescents. The research draws attention to the efficacy of providing opportunities for empowerment, mastery, expression, and participation to self-harming tendencies of clients, particularly female clients (Froeschle & Moyer, 2004; Sapsford, 1997; Shapiro, 1987; Yip, 2005). Yip (2005) lists interventions related to this aim, including involvement in volunteer services, creative endeavors, sport and adventure experiences, and other potentially important activities.

12. Take the developmental level of the client into account when counseling. Self-harming behavior often replaces the verbalization of emotions (Crowe & Bunclark, 2000). Therefore, because the client may consequently be operating from a preverbal level, developmentally appropriate interventions will be most helpful (Zila & Kiselica, 2001).

13. Forms of cognitive therapy have been documented as being a useful intervention with self-harming clients, because clients are assisted in identifying the thought patterns and processes that lead to their self-harming actions (Crowe & Bunclark, 2000; Zila & Kiselica, 2001).

14. Behavioral modification is another counseling technique used with this population; Zila and Kiselica (2001) refer to various behavioral interventions, including finding alternative, less physically destructive behaviors and using techniques that reinforce positive behavior and ignore self-harming behavior.

15. Various other counseling approaches have been cited as effective interventions, including methods of hypnosis therapy, assertiveness training, and modeling; both group and individual counseling can use these interventions (Froeschle & Moyer, 2004; Zila & Kiselica, 2001).

16. Some authors have documented the use of no-cutting contracts (Galley, 2003), but other researchers have argued the ineffectiveness of this technique, underscoring that intensified methods of restraint and control can be detrimental and that an effective intervention encourages the taking of personal responsibility (Crowe & Bunclark, 2000; Huband & Tantam, 1999; Zila & Kiselica, 2001).

17. Finally, be aware of the legal and ethical implications involved in treating a self-harming child or adolescent. Froeschle and Moyer (2004) note the high value self-harming clients will likely place on confidentiality and the ensuing need for counselors to carefully determine when disclosure is appropriate. If concerned that the client is at risk for serious damage, the counselor is instructed to support the client in divulging the behavior to his or her parents and, if the client refuses, to then contact the parents and other relevant people (Froeschle & Moyer, 2004).

References

Conterio, K., & Lader, W. (1998, November). *Self-Injury*. Retrieved September 19, 2005, from http://www.nmha.org/infoctr/factsheets/selfinjury.cfm

Crowe, M., & Bunclark, J. (2000). Repeated self-injury and its management. *International Review of Psychiatry, 12,* 48–53.

Froeschle, J., & Moyer, M. (2004). Just cut it out: Legal and ethical challenges in counseling students who self-mutilate. *Professional School Counseling, 7*(4), 231–235.

Galley, M. (2003). Student self-harm: Silent school crisis. *Education Week, 23*(14), 1–3.

Haines, J., & Williams, C. (2003). Coping and problem solving of self-mutilators. *Journal of Clinical Psychology, 59*(1), 1097–1106.

Huband, N., & Tantam, D. (1999). Clinical management of women who self-wound: A survey of mental health professionals' preferred strategies. *Journal of Mental Health, 8*(5), 473–487.

Kumar, G., Pepe, D., & Steer, R. (2004). Adolescent psychiatric in patients' self-reported reasons for cutting themselves. *Journal of Nervous and Mental Disease, 192*(12), 830–836.

Ross, S., & Health, N. (2002). A study of the frequency of self-mutilation in a community sample of adolescents. *Journal of Youth and Adolescence, 31*(1), 67–77.

Ross, S., & Health, N. (2003). Two models of adolescent self-mutilation. *Suicide and Life-Threatening Behaviors, 33*(3), 277–287.

Sapsford, L. (1997). Strengthening voices: A soulful approach to working with adolescent girls. *Women & Therapy, 20*(2), 75–87.

Shapiro, S. (1987). Self-mutilation and self-blame in incest victims. *American Journal of Psychotherapy, 51*(1), 46–54.

Yip, K. (2005). A multi-dimensional perspective of adolescents' self-cutting. *Child and Adolescent Mental Health, 10*(2), 80–86.

Zila, L., & Kiselica, M. (2001). Understanding and counseling self-mutilation in female adolescents and young adults. *Journal of Counseling & Development, 79*, 46–52.

CHILDHOOD OBESITY*

Lyndsay Gross

Obesity is a growing problem for children in the United States. Childhood obesity is alarming because it often results from poor eating habits and unhealthy views of food—issues that will only become more of a problem with age if not corrected in childhood.

1. Parents need to be role models for healthy eating behaviors. Parents must become aware of how food is used in the home. Children will learn the eating and exercise behaviors that are demonstrated for them; thus, parents need to be congruent with what they expect from their children (Jackson, Mannix, Faga, & McDonald, 2005).

2. Changes made to a child's eating and exercise habits need to be modifications made for the whole family (Jackson et al., 2005).

3. Parents acting hypervigilant and/or as enforcers may cause children to eat excessively when out of the parent's sight; this is linked to children being able to self-monitor food consumption (Jackson et al., 2005).

4. Parental involvement and support is key to combating obesity. Children need to know they are loved and valued. Overweight children need to be supported, to feel accepted, and to be encouraged (U.S. Department of Health and Human Services).

5. Physical activity is key. Children should get 60 minutes of moderate exercise most days of the week (Goran, Reynolds & Lindquist, 1999; U.S. Department of Health and Human Services).

6. Labeling foods "good" or "bad" is not a healthy approach to teaching about nutrition. Foods must be discussed for total diet to avoid developing unhealthy eating habits. Children need to understand how foods such as potato chips can be incorporated into a diet, which is accomplished by teaching children to look at their overall diet (Freeland-Graves & Nitzke, 2002).

7. Teach children appropriate portion sizes early on (Freeland-Graves & Nitzke, 2002).

8. Focus on the child's health and utilize their positive attributes to work toward a health goal (U.S. Department of Health and Human Services).

9. Children should not be made to feel as though their obesity makes them different. The child's obesity should not be the focus. Rather, dietary and exercise modifications need to be gradually incorporated into the family lifestyle (U.S. Department of Health and Human Services).

---

*Reprinted with permission.

10. Weight-loss diets should be lower in calories, but essential nutrients still must be present. Recommended dietary guidelines can be found via the Internet at www.health.gov/dietaryguidelines (United States Department of Health and Human Services)

11. As children grow, they often naturally lose weight as their height balances out their weight. When concerned about a child's weight, be careful investigate this possibility and consult your family physician (U.S. Department of Health and Human Services).

12. Weight loss should occur over time via diet modification and exercise. Children need to learn the healthy eating habits and exercise routines that will keep them at a normal weight and healthy for life (U.S. Department of Health and Human Services).

Works Cited

Freeland-Graves, J., & Nitzke, S. (2002). Total diet approach to communicating food and nutrition information. *American Dietetic Association Reports, 102*(1), 10–108.

Goran, M. I., Reynolds, K. D., & Lindquist, C. H. (1999). Role of physical activity in the prevention of obesity in children. *International Journal of Obesity, 23*(4), 18–33.

Jackson, D., Mannix, J., Faga, P., & McDonald, G. (2005). Overweight and obese children: Mothers' strategies. *Journal of Advanced Nursing, 52*(1), 6–13.

U.S. Department of Health and Human Services. *The Surgeon General's call to action to prevent and decrease overweight and obesity.* Retrieved October 2, 2005, from http://www.surgeongeneral.gov/topics/obesity/calltoaction/fact_adolescents.htm

POOR SELF-CONCEPT*

Jaime Ostendorf

Self-concept is the product of the beliefs and feelings people have about themselves. For many students, a poor sense of self can develop out of negative self-reflections and comments made by others in their lives. Negative feelings about themselves can affect children's motivation, work, interpersonal relationships, and future success. Unfortunately, adults reinforce these detrimental beliefs by criticizing and scolding their children. As a result, it is especially important for parents and professional educators to help students develop strong self-concepts. Following are tips for understanding those children who have negative self-concepts, as well as ways to increase positive feelings and beliefs about the self (Schmidt, 1997).

1. When correcting inappropriate behavior, adults should keep in mind this task should be done in a way so that self-concept is enhanced and not damaged. Often when a child is corrected by a parent or other adult, it is not uncommon for feelings of incompetence, shame, and even guilt to result. Remember to emphasize the child's strengths and focus less on areas of weakness during these crucial moments (See Chapter 6).

2. Students who are raised on the principles of cooperation and acceptance have a much greater chance of developing a strong self-concept. By accepting the many facets of a child's personality, the adult is reinforcing the importance of uniqueness. Working together at home or school in a way that fosters teamwork and mutual respect greatly influences the self-concept of a child (See Chapter 11).

---

*Reprinted with permission.

3. Research has shown that supportive fathers have daughters with high self-esteem and a positive sense of well-being. Not only are these girls confident in their relationships with others, but they are also better able to predict their own future happiness. A positive relationship between fathers and daughters is beneficial in many ways because it models for communication with others in the home, school, and community environments (Pipher, 1994).

4. Discuss with children what they would like to do or accomplish. Working with the children, set up realistic goals and a step-by-step program to guide them toward achieving their goals. Continue this until the children feel they can work toward their goals alone.

5. If a child believes he or she is valued by other people, then that belief becomes part of his or her self-concept. This sense of self guides the child's behavior, which is likely to be both productive and confident. A constructive pattern is likely to emerge as the individual gains from and reacts to positive value judgments from important persons in their lives (Schmidt, 1997).

6. Self-concept is greatly influenced by messages that are received by children. Send affirmative messages to students, because they are likely to create positive self-concepts as a result. In addition, showing interest in the child builds the foundation for strong self-esteem. Make the day of a child by inquiring about their likes, dislikes, and daily routines (Schmidt, 1997).

7. Self-affirmations are valuable and can benefit students; for example, "I am honest." "I am likable." "I am nice." Incorporate these statements into classroom or small group lessons. The vocalization of these self-affirmations reminds students of their positive attributes. This is similar to sending positive messages, but the power of the statement comes from within the child (Hanken & Kennedy, 1998).

8. Allow children with poor self-concepts to help someone else by arranging peer tutoring or teaching. Doing something special for someone else leads helpers to feel better about themselves.

9. Ask students to write ten positive things about themselves. Help the children find ways to use their positive attributes to increase positive feelings about themselves.

10. Children with poor self-concept may benefit from assertiveness training and involvement in group activities at home and school. Encourage participation in groups such as Boy Scouts, Girl Scouts, church groups, and community sports teams.

11. There are two kinds of fun related to self-concept. Good fun increases self-esteem and can be achieved through sports, playing games, dancing, and singing. In contrast, bad fun decreases self-esteem and should be avoided. Bad fun includes teasing, laughing, or harmful tricks. Help students identify and participate in those activities that increase self-concept (Gardner, 1990).

12. Teach the child problem-solving skills, because being able to solve one's own problems builds self-confidence.

13. Have an adult working with the child write a list of the child's strengths to help the adult form a positive conception of the child. Encourage the adult to capitalize on these strengths whenever possible to promote success in that child's life.

14. Provide opportunities for success. Encourage the child's efforts and recognize the strengths of the child at an individual level. For example, an adult can say, "You worked hard at picking up every piece of paper" (straightening the

books, throwing that ball, and so on). Keep in mind that children easily recognize artificial and forced compliments, which are ineffective.

15. Often it is helpful for adults working with these children to engage in supportive counseling as a way to understand the child. Instruction on effective parenting may also be helpful. Remind adults that inappropriate behavior often stems from a poor self-concept.
16. Use strengths exercises with children in a group situation. Give each group member a list of the names of other group members. Each child should write a positive adjective or statement beside each name. Have each child read his or her list aloud. Laminate the lists so the child can keep them for a long time.
17. Use active listening (see Chapter 6). Teach the child problem-solving skills; being able to solve one's own problems builds self-confidence.
18. Help the child change thoughts of "I can't" to "I will try." Examine the worst thing that could happen if the child attempted the task (see Chapter 8 for a discussion of cognitive restructuring). Encourage positive thinking.
19. Use diaries, drawings, incomplete sentences, fantasy games, storytelling, and play therapy as aids to understanding the child's feelings and thoughts (see Chapter 14).
20. I recommend reading books such as *Just Because I Am: A Child's Book of Affirmation* (1994) by Lauren Murphy Payne and Claudia Rohling (published by Free Spirit Publishing Inc., Minneapolis, MN) to help children ages 3 to 8 years enhance their self-concept. Many techniques for helping older children are presented by Diane Frey and Jesse Carlock in their book *Practical Techniques for Enhancing Self-Esteem* (1991; published by Accelerated Development, Inc., Publishers, Muncie, IN). Diane Frey also has a more current book, *From Human Being to Human Becoming* (1998; published by Mandela Publishers).
21. Examine the family constellation (see Chapter 11). Often children form poor self-concepts when they are compared with elder or younger siblings and feel they do not measure up. Work with families in finding ways to value each child.

References

Gardner, R. A. (1990). *The girls and boys book about good and bad behavior.* Cresskill NJ: Creative Therapeutics.

Hanken, D., & Kennedy, J. (1998). *Getting to know you.* Minneapolis, MN: Educational Media Corporation.

Pipher, M. (1994) *Reviving Ophelia: Saving the lives of adolescent girls.* New York: Ballantine Books.

Schmidt, J. (1997). *Making and keeping friends.* West Nyack, NY: Center for Applied Research in Education.

CHEATING*

Theresa Hamer

High grades and other competitive aspects of education may lead to the stress of living up to standards of excellence. Sometimes that stress may lead to cheating as a mechanism for meeting those high expectations and the pressure to achieve. School personnel and parents can place less emphasis on competition with others

---

*Reprinted with permission.

and more on cooperation with others and competition with self. School personnel and parents can also let students know that they expect honesty and demonstrate the value they place on living a life of integrity. Those preventive measures may decrease the likelihood of cheating. Some of the following suggestions may mitigate the cheating behavior that has already begun.

1. Determine the type of pressures the child may be encountering. Talk with the child and significant adults about their expectations for the child. Often parents and teachers place unrealistic pressures on children to excel in school, sports, or other areas. If this is the problem, consult with the adults and cooperatively plan ways to reduce the stress.
2. Determine the goal of the cheater (see Chapter 11). Is the child trying to impress someone, earn recognition, please parents or teachers, or cover up a learning problem?
3. Talk with cheating children concerning their study habits and preparation for work. Better study skills may increase self-confidence and reduce cheating.
4. Encourage teachers to hold class discussions with students on cheating, explore ways to reduce cheating, and draw up guidelines for consequences should the problem occur. A film, story, or hypothetical example may stimulate a rewarding discussion. Combine your discussion with a sociodrama, role-playing, or puppet play about cheating (see Chapter 14 for more information about play techniques).
5. Consult with teachers about reducing temptations to cheat by arranging classroom desks or tables to separate students.
6. Children often are asked by their friends to cheat, and many have trouble handling the situation without losing the friend. A group or family discussion focusing on the problem may help. Adults can use hypothetical questions such as "What would you do if your best friend asked you for the answer to a question during a test?" to help children find an alternative to cheating or helping their friends cheat.
7. Discuss grading procedures with teachers. What is determining the child's grade? Encourage teachers to include classroom participation, effort, and homework completion when determining a child's grade (Shore, 2003).
8. Consult with the teacher about testing procedures. Could an open book test be given? Could the teacher use alternative forms of the test? Is the teacher monitoring the test at all times?
9. If a child is caught cheating in the classroom, remove the child's paper quietly and confront the child privately. Tell the child what you saw, then discuss what consequences should be imposed. Ask that a plan be made to solve the present cheating problem and to prevent future cheating.
10. Refrain from accusing a child of cheating unless there is proof. Do not attempt to force a confession. Avoid name-calling, scolding, lecturing, moralizing, and preaching.
11. Place more emphasis on cooperative behavior and less on competition in interactions with the child. Stress competing with self rather than competing with another person.
12. Consult with teachers about handling cheating on their own. Children should not be asked to identify cheaters in their classroom. This can cause conflict between classmates (Shore, 2003).

13. Relaxation and systematic desensitization (see Chapter 9) may help a cheating child if the behavior is the result of anxiety or test phobia. Suspend competitive and punitive grading practices that create test anxiety.

14. Contract with the child to avoid cheating in the future. Clearly define cheating behavior and the consequences of the behavior.

15. Use the reality questions (see Chapter 4) to encourage responsible behavior in the cheating situation.

16. Make sure the children have an opportunity to ask questions for directions or clarification.

References

Shore, K. (2003) *Elementary teacher's discipline problem solver.* San Francisco: Jossey-Bass.

TRUANCY*

Trevor J. Buser

Truancy is defined as deliberate absence from school without valid reason or parental permission. Researchers have drawn distinctions between truancy and school refusal/phobia, where the former points to situations where the student chooses to miss school for the benefit of nonschool activities and the latter refers to situations in which students avoid school because of emotional or psychological disturbances associated with attendance, such as anxiety, fear, or rejection (Lauchlan, 2003). As Lauchlan has further explained, students who engage in truancy also tend to be involved in other negative, destructive behaviors—a tendency that comprises an additional distinguishing characteristic of truancy. It also has been noted that students may evidence signs of both truancy and school refusal, which is an important consideration for therapists to bear in mind (Kearney & Silverman, 1993; Lauchlan, 2003). This section focuses primarily on truancy, as defined earlier. School phobia is discussed later in this appendix.

1. Evaluate the frequency and pattern of truant behavior. Therapists must consider whether the presenting problem of truancy is one of several behaviors associated with more serious disorders, such as conduct disorder (Lauchlan, 2003).

2. Pinpointing the individual's reasons or motives for truancy may be difficult, but it is an essential part of the treatment process (see Chapter 11). In this vein, Kearney and Silverman (1990) stress the importance of identifying the goal or function of the student's truancy and devising strategies to address this guiding function. Research on this model of intervention, which individualizes the work of diagnosis and treatment, has demonstrated positive results in limited studies (Kearney & Silverman 1990, 1993; Lauchlan, 2003). With careful assessment, counselors are able to develop individual treatment plans and "programmes of intervention according to each pupil's needs" (Lauchlan, 2003, p. 144).

3. In forming an assessment of the individual motivations of the student, draw on the observations and intuitions of other adults in the student's life. The therapist may gain much needed insight from the parents' and teachers' experiences with the student and their sense of the student's patterns of behavior.

*Reprinted with permission.

For this reason, home visits may be a valuable tool for practitioners dealing with issues of truancy (Lauchlan, 2003).

4. Evaluate levels of anxiety in the student who is missing school. Researchers have suggested that many students miss school because of one or more forms of anxiety, including separation anxiety and situational or state-anxiety (Brandibas, Jeunier, Clanet, & Fouraste, 2004). Hence, children or adolescents may be choosing to miss school to evade situations of rejection, public humiliation, conflicts with others, or negative assessments, such as poor grades (Kearney & Silverman, 1990). If the student's anxiety levels are high, then the student may respond more positively to interventions geared for school phobia/refusal. The School Refusal Assessment Scale, devised by Kearney and Silverman (1993), may be a helpful tool in identifying the motives behind repeated absenteeism.

5. Evaluate the truant student's academic progress. Is the child experiencing learning problems, failure, or rejection? Does the child receive encouragement to attend school and find learning relevant? Does the child tend to miss a particular class period or avoid certain subject areas? Truancy often is linked with a sense of incompetence or confusion in coursework (Teasley, 2004). Children who do not achieve well or who have other learning problems are often truant because they find school unpleasant. In such cases, tutoring programs may be an important feature of the student's treatment plan. Teasley (2004), for instance, has reviewed the success of peer tutoring and mentoring programs in reducing truancy and dropout rates. Older students serving as peer counselors, tutors, or mentors help to boost academic achievement and provide additional motivation for the child to attend school.

6. Consider whether the truancy is related to family problems, responsibilities, or basic needs for money or food. Students, for example, will find it difficult to attend school if their families are requiring them to work part-time or baby-sit younger siblings. Moreover, "home dynamics such as crowded living conditions, weak parent-child relationships, and frequent relocation may negatively affect school attendance" (Teasley, 2004, p. 119).

7. Consider systemic issues particular to the school of the student. Lauchlan (2003) has reviewed a number of studies finding that certain characteristics of schools, such as authoritarian structure, large size of student body, lack of discipline and oversight of students, and antagonistic relationships between students and teachers, are associated with higher levels of truancy and absenteeism. In view of such systemic challenges, school counselors may do well to implement the Invitational Theory of Practice (Stanley, Juhnke, & Purkey, 2004), which strives to make the educational environment a safe, warm, and affirming place for children and adolescents. As Lehr, Sinclair, and Christenson (2004) argue, "caring school environments enhance opportunities for student engagement by developing supportive relationships and by increasing opportunities for success in various aspects of the school experience (e.g., academic, extracurricular, peer relations)" (p. 299).

8. Make contracts with students who are truant. These contracts emphasize the cooperative relationship between the student and adult figures in the school. Moreover, contracts serve to empower students by allowing them some degree of choice in arranging daily school activity. The implementation of contracts may be gradual in nature; for instance, the counselor may form a contract

with the student to attend school the next day. If the student fulfills this contract, then the counselor is able to renegotiate the contract, increasing days in attendance step by step. This gradual approach may be more effective than calling for 100% attendance immediately, although the counselor should bear in mind that gradual steps of implementation, as opposed to more rapid interventions, translate into additional missed class work that must be made up by the student (Lauchlan, 2003). At any rate, it is important to include a clause in the contract that implies that the child is responsible for the work that was missed. Adjustments in testing procedures or curricula, however, may be appropriate and can be included as part of the contract. Such adjustments should be made in consultation with the student's teachers. Rewards and/or penalties for attendance and nonattendance may also be worked out cooperatively with the child and described in the contract (see Chapter 9). Whenever possible and appropriate, include the student's parents and teachers in the process of contracting, so as to draw on multiple support systems in the student's life (Lauchlan, 2003).

9. Personal interest from school personnel may be an effective reinforcement strategy. Actively listen to the child for clues about what is happening in the child's life (see Chapter 6). Many students respond to special attention in the form of invitations from the teacher, other school personnel, or peers to come to the school and participate in activities. School-based group counseling opportunities and cognitive-behavioral techniques, such as social skills development, are promising ways of helping the student to build positive and strong attachments to fellow students (Lauchlan, 2003).

10. Parent-training programs may be an important way of assisting parents in establishing clear and consistent rules regarding school attendance for their children. The outcomes reported in the literature on this type of intervention, however, appear to be inconclusive; with some researchers finding favorable results and others indicating that these programs do not reduce routine absenteeism (Lauchlan, 2003).

11. Pursue community-based interventions that connect the resources of local stakeholders, such as businesses, clinics, and agencies (Cobia & Henderson, 2003; Teasley, 2004). Teasley, for instance, has drawn attention to the Office of Juvenile Justice and Delinquency Prevention (www.ojjdp.ncjrs.org) and its support of community-based programs that reduce truancy. These programs have sought to tie together the "enforcement of mandatory attendance laws, parental involvement, community involvement, meaningful sanctions for continued noncompliance, effective school-based truancy reduction programs, systematic data collection and evaluation, and community education and awareness programs" (Teasley, 2004, p. 125).

12. Implement truancy prevention programs that target elementary school–aged children who are deemed at risk for truancy in subsequent years. Longitudinal study on the Check & Connect model—a program aimed at preventing truancy and dropping out—showed reductions in student absences in subsequent years for children who were involved in the program during elementary school (Lehr et al., 2004).

13. Out-of-school suspension for truancy is seldom effective. The child who is consistently absent does not want to be in school, and suspension is no punishment. Seek ways to make school a pleasant, rewarding place. As Teasley

(2004) argues, "school-based personnel must understand that reducing truancy is a process that is better served by prosocial preventive measures than by punitive measures that do not address underlying concerns" (p. 123). It is helpful also to refrain from scolding, lecturing, and offering critical, sarcastic comments, such as "Glad to see you made it today" or "If you had been here, you would have had the assignment."

14. School counselors are advised to gather and assess school-wide data on truancy behaviors by racial/ethnic group and socioeconomic status. Such evaluations will assist in identifying and addressing cultural variables that may affect students' patterns of attendance (Cobia & Henderson, 2003).

15. Become familiar with the laws and regulations relevant to truant behavior. Teasley (2004) cautions that adults working with cases of truancy "must be familiar with the legal aspects of truancy in the states and localities where they practice, what can be done within the parameters of the law, and precedents regarding what is legally permissible" (p. 122).

References

Brandibas, G., Jeunier, B., Clanet, C., & Fouraste, R. (2004). Truancy, school refusal, and anxiety. *School Psychology International, 25,* 117–126.

Cobia, D., & Henderson, D. (2003). *Handbook of school counseling.* Upper Saddle River, NJ: Merrill Prentice Hall.

Kearney, C. A., & Silverman, W. K. (1990). A preliminary analysis of a functional model of assessment and intervention of school refusal behaviour. *Behaviour Modification, 149,* 340–366.

Kearney, C. A., & Silverman, W. K. (1993). Measuring the function of school refusal behavior: The school refusal assessment scale. *Journal of Clinical Child Psychology, 22,* 85–96.

Lauchlan, F. (2003). Responding to chronic non-attendance: A review of intervention approaches. *Educational Psychology, 19,* 133–146.

Lehr, C. A., Sinclair, M. F., & Christenson, S. L. (2004). Addressing student engagement and truancy prevention during the elementary school years: A replication study of the Check & Connect model. *Journal of Education for Students Placed at Risk, 9,* 279–301.

Stanley, P. H., Juhnke, G. A., & Purkey, W.W. (2004). Using an invitational theory of practice to create safe and successful schools. *Journal of Counseling & Development, 82,* 302–309.

Teasley, M. L. (2004). Absenteeism and truancy: Risk, protection, and best practice implications for school social workers. *Children & Schools, 26,* 117–128.

CARELESSNESS IN WORK AND WITH PROPERTY

A common complaint among teachers and parents is that children are careless with school property, books, the completion of assigned work, and personal property such as coats, sweaters, and other possessions. Lecturing, scolding, preaching, and nagging are seldom effective in changing their habits. Children need to learn responsibility for their own actions and possessions and that an adult will not always be present to assume responsibility for them.

1. Determine the reason for the carelessness. Is the behavior due to a lack of interest or motivation? Could the carelessness be an attempt to cover up learning or emotional problems or an attempt to get back at parents for some

real or imagined wrong? Actively listen to the child for clues that may indicate the motivation for carelessness (see Chapter 6).

2. The careless child can redo the work until it is correct. Children can pay for lost items or property with time or work. Parents should not hurriedly bring forgotten items such as lunches and tennis shoes. The logical consequence of carelessness, forgetting, or losing is that the child must assume responsibility—redo the work, replace the property, or do without the forgotten items (see Chapter 11).

3. Praise and reinforce responsible behavior; for example, "That paper was well written," or "You did a good job cleaning out the basement." Consistently give attention to acceptable behavior.

4. Help the careless child find a model who behaves maturely and responsibly. Pair the child with the model for activities. Ask the child to observe the model's behaviors for several days. Discuss the behaviors of the model with the careless child. Role-play and rehearse these behaviors. Make a plan for the child to try the new learning.

5. Carelessness may be due to a lack of understanding. Give clear, specific instructions to the child for proper preparation of work and other activities. Have the careless child write down the instructions to eliminate forgetting and mistakes.

6. If carelessness with homework assignments is a problem, ask the child to write down all assignments and take them home. Talk with parents to gain their cooperation in checking assigned work each night. Discontinue the procedure when the child begins to assume responsibility for homework. The parent should be available to assist the child but not do the homework for him or her.

7. If the problem appears to stem from an inability to cope with the amount of work or responsibility assigned, reduce the requirements for a time, requiring quality rather than quantity. Gradually work up to the point where the child meets the expected criteria (see Chapter 9).

8. Carelessness may reflect a difference in cultural values. The child's environment may not place a great value on achievement or the possession of property. Hold a group discussion that focuses on the value of property and of assuming responsibility for oneself. Help the children to identify acts of carelessness and their consequences, and make a plan to avoid careless acts.

9. Ask careless children to evaluate their work from your role or to assess consequences as they think you should. Discuss with them the reasons for their evaluations.

10. Encourage responsibility through the use of reality questions (see Chapter 4). Give small assignments designed for success.

UNDERACHIEVEMENT

Theresa Hamer

Underachievement usually is defined as a discrepancy between the child's ability and his or her actual achievement. It may be related to a poor self-concept, cultural deprivation, lack of family involvement and encouragement, peer pressure, learning or emotional problems, physical illness, or a lack of interest in school subjects and content.

1. Try to determine the causes contributing to underachievement. Become a child watcher and use active listening to try to understand the child (see

Chapter 6). Underachievement often is related to physical problems or other learning difficulties; therefore, a psychological evaluation and checkup with a physician may provide some insight into the problem.

2. Assess the child's academic level; then help his or her teachers build learning and class assignments from this base. Much new learning is based on old learning; the child must be able to accomplish prerequisite skills before achieving success in new ones. Once the weak link in the chain of learning is identified—for example, a past school experience, physical health, cultural background, or any other factor—counseling can begin and instructional materials can be designed to promote success.

3. Contract with the child to complete at least a small amount of work each day. Build in rewards for progress. The completion of two problems or questions is better than no progress. Renegotiate the contract periodically, increasing the amount of work expected (see Chapter 9).

4. Try peer teaching or peer tutoring. Students who are in an upper grade can tutor students in lower grades. They also can help peers who are having trouble in areas of their strengths. Both children learn and benefit from the relationship.

5. Capitalize on an area of interest or ability by relating the assignment to it. Situations in math, writing, spelling, and other subjects often can be related to the child's interests, hobbies, and skills.

6. Team teaching may be helpful. Two or more teachers are often able to generate more ideas to stimulate the child. The child may also be able to cooperate with one teacher more readily than with another.

7. Avoid lecturing, nagging, scolding, and threatening the child. Encouragement and a positive attitude produce better results. See Poor Self-Concept section earlier in this appendix for additional ideas.

8. Vary school activities from physical to quiet to prevent fatigue and boredom. Involve the child in arranging the day's work. Children who have taken part in the planning are likely to cooperate and complete the assigned tasks.

9. Underachieving children with high academic ability can benefit from an enrichment project in their area of interest. An advanced-level project that integrates a child's learning style, abilities, and a supportive student–teacher relationship can promote a student's academic growth. Self selection of a project can give a child the opportunity to demonstrate his or her hidden potential (Renzulli, Baum, Hébert, & McCluskey, 1999).

10. Teachers can consult with underachieving children for alternative ideas for completing learning objectives. Ask the child to remember a time when learning was easy, and together identify what strategies make that possible.

11. Special arrangements can be made for testing or for completing other class assignments. For example, if the child has problems in reading or writing, oral testing, tape recorders, or computers can be used.

12. Help the child find an admired friend and model. Ask the child to talk with the model about study habits and to observe the model's methods of studying. Have the child practice these procedures (see Chapter 9). Allow the two children to work and study together as much as possible.

13. Check on study skills, test-taking procedures, and place and time for studying. Help adults and the child learn ways to arrange an environment conducive to study and learning. A contract incorporating a schedule for

studying specific subjects at certain times and places will help the child plan study time more wisely and develop discipline for studying.

14. If the underachievement is related to parental pressure, counsel the parents about how to decrease the pressure yet reinforce studying. Assist parents and the child in determining an appropriate place and time to study. Make a plan to avoid or cope with things that might interfere with study times, such as small siblings, telephone calls, and peers.

15. When homework assignments are not competed at home, the logical consequence is for the child to complete the work during free time at school (see Chapter 11). Avoid nagging, scolding, or lecturing.

16. Focus on and reinforce work improvements; past faults and failures should be forgotten. Emphasize the positive; for example, "Jimmy, you did part of your homework assignment, and it was done very well. Would you be willing to work on these two additional questions?"

17. The parent–child relationship works better if parents do not teach or tutor their own children. If the child asks for help, a parent may provide assistance; however, someone outside the family is a more effective teacher or tutor.

18. For children with special learning problems, plan a consultation session with all resource persons and teachers involved. Cooperatively draw up a learning plan in which the role and the objectives of each professional are clearly defined.

19. Underachievers usually respond best to a structured environment for learning. Adults who tell children to do their best may find young people set low goals and achieve below their maximal abilities. Teachers and parents need to have high expectations but also give needed support. Give very clear directions for assignments. A check or reward system may be used for completed work. Learning contracts may be helpful to the underachiever. Some underachievers require additional time to complete all assignments; continue to encourage their completion.

20. Assist the child in setting and measuring reasonable, academic goals. Support the child and celebrate accomplished goals (Berube, 1995).

REFERENCES

Berube, B. N. (Ed.). (1995). *What educators need to know about underachievement and gifted students.* Storrs, CT: National Research Center on the Gifted and Talented.

Renzulli, J. S., Baum, S. M., Hébert, T., & McCluskey, K. W. (1999). Reversing underachievement through enrichment. *Reclaiming Children and Youth, 7,* 217–223.

DAYDREAMING

Daydreaming is not always bad; it sometimes clears confusion, solves problems, or is creative in other ways. However, excessive daydreaming or daydreaming at the wrong times—in school—can affect the child's academic progress. Adlerian theory suggests that daydreaming children are striving for superiority. These children have no faith in their abilities to achieve success in the real world; therefore, they create fantasies in which they are always great or superior.

1. Periodic eye contact between child and adult may decrease daydreaming. If one cannot make eye contact with the child, a light touch on the shoulder should bring the child back to reality.

2. Interrupt children's fantasies by calling them by name. Avoid embarrassing children by asking them to answer a question they obviously have not heard.

3. Try incomplete sentences, storytelling, diary, or play therapy to learn more about the child and the possible reason for daydreaming.

4. Channel daydreaming into constructive channels by having the child write out the daydream. The writing could be incorporated into a learning exercise. Find other opportunities to help children display their creativity.

5. Write a contract with the daydreamer for completion of assigned work (see Chapter 9). Contract for only the amount of work the child feels he or she can accomplish. Renegotiate contracts for additional work in a step-by-step plan.

6. Tape an index card to the child's desk. When the child is working on a task, place a check on the card and give verbal reinforcement for the accomplishment. A contract may be made with the child to earn rewards or privileges for a certain number of checks. Ignore the daydreaming; reward on-task behavior.

7. Plan the child's environment and schedule to vary activities from quiet to physical. Assess the day's schedule to determine whether activities are interesting, relevant, and appropriate for the child's level of maturity, interest, and ability.

8. Find the child a friend who encourages participation in groups and other activities. Encourage the teacher to include the daydreamer in group activities and projects. Counsel with the parents to plan how to reduce daydreaming at home and encourage participation in activities.

9. Often children retreat to a daydream world because the real one is too painful. Determine whether the child is having learning, social, emotional, or physical problems. A psychological evaluation and physical examination may be helpful.

10. Daydreaming may be related to a poor self-concept. See Poor Self-Concept section earlier in this appendix for additional ideas for working with these children.

SHYNESS AND WITHDRAWAL*

Christopher Delfausse

Shyness and withdrawal are attempts to avoid participation in one's surroundings. The child may fear the situation, fear failure or criticism, lack self-confidence, or fear embarrassment or humiliation. The child may also be physically ill. Unfortunately, shy and withdrawn children may be ignored because they cause less trouble than the attention-seeking child.

1. Try to determine the underlying cause for the reserved behavior. Use diaries, puppets, role-playing, incomplete sentences, drawing, storytelling, play therapy, or any similar technique to try to understand the child better. Children often express their feelings through these means when they will not verbalize them.

2. Work on developing trust and good rapport with the child. Try active listening to increase understanding of the child (see Chapter 6).

3. Tell the child about times you acted bashful. Because children look at adults as powerful figures, the children will tend to feel better about their own shy behavior (Malouff, 2002).

4. Explain to the child how they can benefit from being outgoing. Children who expect to benefit from a behavior are more likely to engage in that behavior. The most convincing way to tell children the value of being outgoing is to give

*Reprinted with permission.

personal examples. Then explain the immediate benefits of be outgoing; such as making more friends, having more fun, and enjoying school more (Malouff, 2002).

5. Involve shy or withdrawn children in small-group activities or projects with other children they like. Often a shy child is willing to talk in small groups. Encourage and reinforce these attempts to participate. Send them on errands with another child. A sociogram may determine other children who are liked.

6. Give the withdrawn child responsibilities such as carrying messages, feeding the fish, watering plants, handing out supplies, or helping the school secretary answer the phone and take messages. Avoid drudgery jobs, and do not ask the shy child to perform tasks that may be embarrassing (such as speaking in front of the class).

7. Make a list with the withdrawn child of things he or she would like to be able to do—for example, join a group of friends, speak to a particular person, or play a game. Have the child select one thing on the list and set a goal to accomplish this behavior. Use behavior rehearsal to help the child practice certain responses or behaviors. Contract with the child to try these new behaviors (see Chapter 9).

8. Avoid embarrassing shy children by teasing them about their shyness or by calling on them to perform in front of a group without first discussing and arranging the activity with them. One technique for encouraging a child to participate in class is to plan a question and answer with the child. The teacher asks the question in class and the child agrees to answer with the response. When the child feels comfortable answering rehearsed questions, the child and teacher make a contract that the teacher will call on the child only when he or she volunteers to answer. Ask the child to volunteer at least a certain number of times per week. Renegotiate periodic contracts to encourage participation in a step-by-step progression.

9. Find a model for the shy child. Ask the child to observe the model for several days and list admired behaviors. Role-play, rehearse, and contract with the child to try the new behaviors.

10. Set goals for outgoing behavior and measure behavior. The best type of goals are ones that are quantifiable; therefore, it is easier for the child to see his or her progress. It is also important to make these goals realistic.

11. Set an example of outgoing behavior, it shows the child the proper interaction between people. Children tend to learn from observing others, especially parents. Children tend to follow what parents do more than what parents say (Malouff, 2002).

12. Expose the child to unfamiliar situations. The more interaction the child gets with unfamiliar people, the sooner the shyness will go away. It is important to keep in mind that this exposure should be made gradually and at a speed at which the child is comfortable (Malouff, 2002).

13. Help the child practice interactions with others. The child may feel uncomfortable in certain situation with others, so the adult can help the child practice responses to others comments. Puppets may be used to act out interactions (Malouff, 2002).

14. Try to pair the child with another child in each new setting. With a shy child, each new person they meet in a new situation makes them more comfortable and more likely to make more friends (Malouff, 2002).

15. Read books with the child about others who have overcome shyness. Children can benefit from reading about other children who are experiencing similar problems (Malouff, 2002).
16. Teach children to identify and verbally express their emotions. Shy children can start to control their feelings of embarrassment and fear when they can start to identify and talk about their feelings (Malouff, 2002).
17. Coordinate your efforts with the other relevant adults in the child's life. Efforts to help the child will work better when all adults are on the same page (Malouff, 2002).
18. Teach extremely shy children social skills—specifically, conversational skills, asking questions, making and responding to comments, improving eye contact, and displaying warmth. Use modeling and behavior rehearsal to help the child practice new skills.
19. Use a variety of play techniques, such as hand puppets, games, art, and music, to encourage expression. Pets may be a useful adjunct to therapy.

References

Malouff, J. (2002). *Helping young children overcome shyness.* Retrieved April 12, 2006 from http://www.une.edu.au/psychology/staff/malouff/shyness.htm

EXCESSIVE TENSION AND ANXIETY*

Mary Engerer

A little tension and anxiety may motivate a child, but excessive tension and anxiety interfere with learning and performance. Excessive tension and anxiety may be situational or chronic. The symptoms include continued restlessness and movement, nail biting, tics, frequent blinking, rapid breathing, repeated throat clearing, and similar somatic complaints.

SCHOOL-RELATED TENSION AND ANXIETY

1. Tell highly anxious children that they have a right to fail. Take away the pressure to excel and to be perfect. This technique may ease the anxiety and allow further exploration of conditions causing the anxiety.
2. Highly anxious children function better with a teacher who is warm and understanding but also organized and structured. Suggest that teachers use techniques such as behavioral objectives and learning contracts so that highly anxious students know exactly what is expected of them.
3. Consult with the child's parents and teachers. Determine whether the anxiety is a result of pressures and expectations of being perfect. If so, work with the child and the adults to encourage more realistic expectations.
4. Teachers and parents may help decrease children's tension and anxiety by talking quietly to them about relaxing; for example, "Relax your neck; relax your shoulders." Deep-breathing exercises may also help the child.
5. Look over the child's schoolwork and academic progress. Anxiety often is related to learning disabilities.
6. Use cognitive-restructuring techniques to help children believe they can cope with situations. Discover the irrational, self-defeating, anxiety-provoking self-statements that the children are telling themselves, and help them formulate more positive ones.

---

*Reprinted with permission.

7. Use imagery techniques to help children visualize themselves coping with situations in a relaxed, positive manner.

8. Advise students about good test-taking procedures, such as pacing responses according to the time allotted for the test, narrowing choices by eliminating obviously wrong answers, responding first to questions to which answers are known, giving last priority to questions not known, and being aware of qualifiers such as *always* and *never.*

9. Schools can help children overcome anxiety by replacing the idea of perfection with the idea of individual excellence. Anxious children respond more favorably to the idea of "doing your best" rather than being perfect (Foxman, 2004, p. 226).

10. As the child discovers that worrying is unproductive, yet is still resistant to discontinuing this act, encourage him or her to set aside 5 to 15 minutes each day for worrying. Explain that this is the time for them to worry so the rest of the day can be used for more productive activities (Foxman, 2004, p. 227–228).

GENERAL ANXIETY

1. Some tension and anxiety may be related to fear of the unknown; for example, going to new places or being in new situations. A thorough explanation of the feared situation or a visit to a feared place with a trusted person may reduce situational anxiety.

2. Talk with anxious children and agree on methods, such as physical activities, talking, or writing, for release of these feelings. When children become highly anxious or tense, they could be allowed to signal the teacher or another adult and proceed to carry out the previously discussed plan. Counselors may suggest that anxious children come to the counseling office when they experience intense feelings.

3. Keeping a diary, writing an autobiography, drawing, playing with puppets, and other forms of play therapy may assist in determining the causes for the child's anxious feelings.

4. Children have less anxiety about situations if they feel competent. Discuss with the child the reasons for his or her anxiety and ways of handling specific situations; then rehearse the situations.

5. Relaxation methods and desensitization reduce tension and anxiety.

6. If the anxiety appears debilitating, refer the child to a medical specialist for examination.

REFERENCES

Foxman, P. (2004.) *The worried child: Recognizing anxiety in children and helping them heal.* Alameda, CA: Hunter House Publishers.

DISTRACTIBILITY/SHORT ATTENTION SPAN*

Ashley McPherson

Being able to focus one's attention on the task to be done and ignore irrelevant stimuli in the environment is necessary for learning school material and new behaviors. Although attention span and the degree of distractibility vary with the

---

*Reprinted with permission.

child and the situation, these learning problems appear to be increasing in today's classrooms. (I encourage you to refer to the Attention-Deficit/Hyperactivity Disorder section in Chapter 19 for a more detailed discussion.)

1. Determine whether the child is actually distracted easily and has a short attention span. The child's inattention may be the result of some other reason, such as the nature of the work the child is asked to do (boring or too difficult), noisy or more interesting surroundings (windows, TV, pictures, bulletin boards), or fatigue or physical illness.

2. Record the time when distractions and inattention appear to be most frequent. Rearrange the environment or schedule. Vary quiet activities with more physical ones. Limit overstimulation and distractions, including interesting bulletin boards, teachers' clothing and jewelry, mobiles, and brightly colored pictures.

3. Use seating arrangements or some method of screening the distractible child from excessive stimuli. Consider small carrels or "offices." Bookcases, movable screens, or even large moving cartons that have been painted or decorated can be used to reduce distracting stimuli.

4. Contract for the completion of short assignments. Talk with distractible children about the amount of work they believe they can accomplish—two math problems, one paragraph of English. Write a realistic contract to ensure success. Continue to renegotiate the contract, increasing the assignments as the distractibility decreases.

5. Recommend that highly distractible children be checked by a medical specialist to determine whether the behavior is a medical problem.

6. Shorten teaching time and study periods, and schedule the periods more frequently. Visual aids, games, and other teaching aids may add interest and maintain attention.

7. Use techniques such as raising or lowering your voice, placing your hand on the child's shoulder, or catching the child's eye to capture the distractible child's attention and direct it back to the task.

8. Encourage children to monitor their own behavior. Have them make a check mark on an index card when they catch themselves off-task. Next have them immediately focus on the task. Increasing awareness of the problem is often a productive technique in itself. Plan for self-reward when the child can refocus attention to the task.

9. Ensure rules and directions are as clear and brief as possible (Chesterfield County Public Schools, Department of Exceptional Education). Also, give children one directive at a time. Multiple instructions quickly become overwhelming and may be forgotten (Villegas, Hardwood, & Brozovich, 1995).

10. Prepare children for transitory periods by providing a detailed explanation of new environments and expectations (Chesterfield County Public Schools, Department of Exceptional Education).

11. Divide larger assignments and projects into smaller, more manageable sections, and encourage children to set realistic short-term goals (Chesterfield County Public Schools, Department of Exceptional Education).

12. Remain consistent in parent and educational interactions with children. This helps to establish routine behavioral expectations. Appropriate behavior and schedules will be more readily accepted and respected by children when a commitment to consistency is maintained (Villegas et al., 2005).

13. Classroom group work or group counseling with children may aid in developing social skills and positive peer interaction (Faison & Barniskis, 1993; Schwiebert & Sealander, 1995).

14. Encourage children to exercise regularly. This helps to reduce stress, because the brain releases serotonin into the body (Beal, 1998). Structured games, walking, and running are good means of exercise through a school's physical education department/curriculum. In addition, parents should encourage children to play and exercise in nonschool environments. These activities will likely involve increased social interaction with peers, another helpful intervention.

15. Help educators coordinate times when children focus most effectively: possibly early in the morning or after breakfast or lunch. More difficult tasks that require concentration and complex coursework should be scheduled to occur at this time (Beal, 1998). Children will be able to concentrate better and feel more confident in their ability to complete respective tasks.

WORKS CITED

Beal, E. (1998). *Everything you need to know about ADD/ADHD*. Retrieved October 3, 2005, from www.netlibrary.com/Reader/

Chesterfield County Public Schools, Department of Exceptional Education. (n.d.) *Elementary parent guide to attention deficit hyperactivity disorder (ADHD)*. Retrieved October 3, 2005, from http://chesterfield.k12.va.us/htm/parents_pages/ptrc/ ptrc_popups/ADHDelem.pdf

Faison, M. W., & Barniskis, E. A. (1993, March). *A systematic approach to the treatment of Attention Deficit Hyperactivity Disorder (ADHD): An intervention model*. Paper presented at the Annual Convention of the National Association of School Psychologists, Washington, DC.

Schwiebert, V. L., & Sealander, K. A. (1995). Attention-deficit hyperactivity disorder: An overview for school counselors. *Elementary School Guidance & Counseling, 29*(4), 249–261.

Villegas, O., Hardwood, T., & Brozovich, R. (1995) *Understanding attention deficit disorders*. Waterford, MI: Oakland Schools, Division of Special Education, Psychology and Learning Clinic, Instructional Services Department.

IMMATURITY AND DEPENDENT BEHAVIOR*

Nathaniel Ivers

Dependency may be the result of overprotective or critical parents who have told their children in many ways that they are incapable of functioning or thinking for themselves. Immature or dependent children usually do not achieve well in school because they are not ready to learn the subject matter presented. They may have trouble with interpersonal relationships because of their immature behavior and often become social isolates or discipline problems; alternatively, they may choose their friends from a younger group.

1. Work with the parents on strategies to help them trust the child's abilities and potentials. Suggest methods to develop independent behaviors. Books or "parent effectiveness training" (Davidson & Wood, 2004) may help parents understand their children's development and abilities.

---

*Reprinted with permission.

2. Have children identify areas in which they would like to be more independent or behaviors they would like to change. Discuss these situations and alternative ways of behaving with the child; then rehearse the situations until the child feels comfortable with new behaviors.

3. Encourage attempts to become more mature and independent. Ask the child to do jobs or assume responsibilities in the home and classroom to increase his or her confidence. Avoid assigning drudgery jobs.

4. Have the child select a model and observe the model's behavior for several days. Pair children with mature models for group activities. Ask them to keep a list of the model's behaviors they particularly like. Rehearse behaviors the children would like to acquire until they feel confident.

5. Encourage immature or dependent children to join groups such as Little League, Boy or Girl Scouts, clubs, or church groups.

6. Help children acquire the social skills necessary to have and maintain healthy friendships. Role-play different ways to begin interacting with a friend, how to cooperate in games, and how to respond to other children appropriately (Berk, 2004).

7. Advocate for the child with schools, as well as other programs in which the child may be involved (for example, Little League or Girl Scouts). For example, if the child has become involved in Boy Scouts and will be going on a week-long scout camp, after obtaining permission and a release of information, contact the scout master and inform him of ways to help reduce homesickness in the children at the scout camp. A few guidelines to give to scout masters include planning activities that help campers get to know one another, icebreakers, playing a lot of games throughout the week, informing campers of the activities for the week so that they know what to expect, establishing ground rules, keeping them busy, and so on (Smieja, 1999).

8. Give children as many choices as possible—for example, whether to complete the reading or the math assignment first, whether to wear a blue or a red shirt, and so forth.

9. Learn about the child's abilities, interests, and hobbies. Have the child peer-teach or tutor another student in one of these areas of expertise to build self-confidence. Both children will benefit from the teaching and the relationship.

10. Work with immature or dependent children to teach them problem-solving techniques. Counsel with parents and teachers to encourage these children to attempt to solve their own problems with adult guidance rather than depend on others for solutions.

11. Avoid reinforcing dependent behaviors. Encourage immature children to make decisions and accept responsibilities within their capabilities. Reinforce efforts toward more mature behavior with encouragement.

12. Use active listening to help immature and dependent children express their fears and other feelings (see Chapter 6). Help them develop realistic goals and make a systematic plan for attaining these goals.

13. Encourage parents to use active listening techniques that they may have acquired through parent effectiveness training (Davidson & Wood, 2004).

14. Because children who exhibit dependent behaviors are often victims of bullying, the school counselor should develop interventions that "change victimized children's negative opinions of themselves and that teach them to respond in non-reinforcing ways to their attackers" (Berk, 2004, p. 325).

15. If the child exhibits signs of separation anxiety with regard to attending school, a counselor may collaborate with child's parents on implementing an *in vivo* exposure technique in which the child is gradually exposed to the school environment beginning with school situations that elicit minimal anxiety in the child, and then graduating to more anxiety-provoking situations (Scott & Cully, 1995).

WORKS CITED

Berk, L. E. (2004). *Development through the lifespan* (3rd ed.). Boston: Allyn and Bacon.

Davidson, J., & Wood, C. (2004). A conflict resolution model. *Theory into Practice, 43*(1), 6–13.

Scott, J., & Cully, M. (1995). Helping the separation anxious school refuser. *Elementary School Guidance and Counseling, 29*(4), 289–297.

Smieja, C. (1999). Coping with homesickness. *Camping Magazine, 72*(3), 29–31.

PERFECTIONISTIC BEHAVIOR*

Emy Gamb

Compulsive and perfectionistic children usually perform their tasks and assignments well. They often overachieve. This behavior can inhibit everyday functioning; for example, the child takes too much time to complete assignments and feels that everything must be absolutely perfect. Perfectionistic behavior often is accompanied by symptoms of anxiety.

1. Perfectionistic children often have perfectionistic adults for models. Talk with parents and teachers to determine whether the pressures and expectations placed on the child are too great. Counsel with adults about normal growth and development and the behaviors that can be expected of the child (Basco, 1999b; A. Krain, personal communication, November 2004).
2. Determine whether the child has a stable family life. Many times perfectionistic children have stressful and hectic childhoods due to parental divorce, family financial stress, relocations, and sickness, which create an unbalanced setting. The child may try to regain control in their lives and develop perfectionistic tendencies such as keeping their bedrooms constantly clean or working incredibly hard on homework (Basco, 1999a).
3. Help the child find a balance between work and fun activities (Rosenman, 2000). Involve the children in individual and group activities that do not require perfect performance—go on family outings to the park, museums, and so on (Beam, 2001).
4. Help parents emphasize to their child that they love them unconditionally, when they succeed and when they make mistakes (Basco, 1999b; Rosenman, 2000).
5. Acknowledge the child's attempts, even if the result is not perfect (Rosenman, 2000). Be mindful when praising the child to say "Good job," not "Good boy" (Basco, 1999).
6. Encourage children to relax. Teach the child breathing exercises and other relaxation techniques (see Chapter 9).

---

*Reprinted with permission.

7. Sometimes when children struggle with perfectionism activities lose their allure. Engage the child in a conversation about the fun of learning, regardless of the result (Ehmann, 2000).

8. Encourage the child to change internal self-talk and gently challenge schemas to recognize that perfection in all areas is not essential (Basco, 1999a; A. Krain, personal communication, November 2004). "Shoulds" and "have-tos" can be changed from "I must have perfection before I can have peace of mind" to "I need to give myself credit for what I do well, even if it is not perfect" (Basco, 1999a, p. 68).

9. Encourage the child to make a list of all their accomplishments. The child may be denying themselves of acceptance (Basco, 1999a).

10. Help your child "lighten up." Allow your child to vent his or her frustrations and explain the difficulties of trying new things and making mistakes (Beam, 2001).

11. Determine whether the child's perfectionistic behavior is adaptive or maladaptive (Ashby, Kottman, & Martin, 2004).

12. Play therapy can provide a safe, nonjudging, and accepting setting to help the child challenge cognitive distortions and negative self-talk, learn new strategies to deal with anxiety, accept mistakes, and increase tolerance for risk (Ashby et al., 2004).

13. When you have to scold a child, make sure you keep the focus on the action, not the child (Basco, 1999a).

14. When it is necessary to give negative feedback, give it to the child in private and give the child an opportunity to fix the behavior. Reward improvements in their behavior (Basco, 1999a).

15. Help the child sort out those things that are important to him or her. Make two lists, one of the things they will do to the best of their ability and one of things that do not have to be perfect (Dear Highlights, 1998).

16. The overly perfectionistic child may be compensating for feelings of inadequacy. See Poor Self-Concept section earlier in this appendix for further suggestions for working with these children.

17. Perfectionistic children usually perform best in a well-structured situation where rules and expectations are clearly defined. Clearly explain all instructions and use teaching methods such as behavioral objectives and learning contracts to reduce anxiety concerning expectations.

18. Involve the children in individual and group activities that do not require perfect performance. Techniques such as creative drawing or writing de-emphasize perfection and also allow the child to express feelings.

19. Allot an amount of time for the child to finish a task. Place a timer within the child's sight. When the timer rings, review the child's progress. If the child has not made sufficient progress, contract with the child to set a new goal the next time.

20. Anxiety and tension may be related to perfectionistic behaviors. See Excessive Tension and Anxiety section earlier in this appendix for additional ideas.

WORKS CITED

Ashby, J. S., Kottman, T., & Martin, J. L. (2004). Play therapy with young perfectionists. *International Journal of Play Therapy, 13*(1), 35–55.

Basco, M. R. (1999a). *Never good enough: How to use perfectionism to your advantage without letting it ruin your life*. New York: Touchstone.

Basco, M. R. (1999b, May/June). The "perfect" trap. *Psychology Today, 32*(3), 30–36.

Beam, C. (2001, December). When your kid's a perfectionist. *Family Life*, 31.

Dear Highlights. (1998, November). *Highlights for Children, 53*(11), 42.

Ehmann, L. C. (2000, April). Why your child hobby hops. *Family Life*, 79–80.

Rosenman, E. M. (2000, September). Does your child push himself too hard? *Family Life*, 101.

SCHOOL PHOBIA*

Mary Engerer

School phobia may grow out of unpleasant or embarrassing experiences in school, failure in school, fear of separation from the security of home and parents, fear of the unknown, or other experiences that may have associated bad feelings with school.

1. Actively listen to try to understand the phobic child's underlying feelings and to establish a feeling of trust and security.
2. Explain to the child that it is perfectly natural to have fears and phobias. A child's fear needs to be validated (Heller, 1999, p. 299).
3. Explore the child's fear of school to identify the possible underlying reason the fear exists. Help the child create realistic solutions (Heller, 1999, p. 300).
4. The desensitization procedure may be used with rewards. Write a contract with the child to provide a reward for staying in school a certain amount of time (for example, 20 minutes). Renegotiate the contract for longer time periods as the child is able to stay in school an increasing length of time.
5. If one parent is reinforcing the child's anxiety about school, suggest that the other parent or another adult bring the child to school. A parent may unconsciously be encouraging school phobia by conveying anxiety to the child, verbally or nonverbally; for example, saying "Now, you call me if you get afraid while you are in school," or becoming more nervous and irritable as they approach school.
6. If the parent who experiences separation anxiety must take the child to school, he or she should be firm when leaving the child. Such parents need to practice the method of "hug and shove," meaning say good-bye to the child and then allow the child to go to school while the parent quickly leaves the area (Heller, 1999, p. 299).
7. It may be helpful for parents to tell the child where they will be during the day and to reiterate that the parents will see the child after school (Heller, 1999, p. 300).
8. Avoid placing the child in any situation that may increase fear or cause embarrassment. Clearly explain all new situations and expectations. Role-playing expected behaviors may help the child feel more confident about facing the new situation.
9. A child who fears school may find comfort in slow exposure to the school. Help the child visualize himself or herself going to school. Then have the child tour the school and meet the principal, counselor, and teachers (Heller, 1999, p. 301).
10. School phobia may be related to learning difficulties. Review the child's academic progress and provide needed help. Children who associate school with their personal failure often develop a phobia about school.

---

*Reprinted with permission.

11. Relaxation and desensitization procedures may be necessary for the extremely phobic child.

12. Often school phobia is the result of family interactions in which children become overly dependent on parents. Consultation with the family may provide some insight into the family system and suggestions for treatment.

13. Play therapy for the child with school phobia may allow the child to feel less overwhelmed and provide support while returning to school.

14. Bibliotherapy has been useful for children with school phobia. Reading about how others have overcome similar fears may help normalize the situation (Heller, 1999, p. 302).

15. Ask the teacher to involve phobic children in pleasant group projects and activities. The more pleasure the children derive from school, the more they want to attend. Successful learning, good peer relationships, pleasant teachers and other school personnel, and enjoyable activities can make school a desirable place to be, thus alleviating the child's fear.

16. Allow phobic children to phone home occasionally or at specific intervals if they feel fearful or insecure. Make arrangements with the parents so that someone is available to answer and to reassure the child.

17. Many parents include something from home in the child's lunch box or with books—for example, a picture or a favorite object.

18. See Excessive Tension and Anxiety section earlier in this chapter for more ideas for working with the phobic child.

Works Cited

Heller, S. (1999.) *The complete idiot's guide to conquering fear and anxiety.* Indianapolis, IN: Alpha.

POSSIBLE *DSM-IV-TR* CODES

Self-Destructive and Suicidal Behavior

- 296.xx—Bipolar I Disorder, Major Depressive Disorder, Bipolar II Disorder, Mood Disorder NOS
- 300.4—Dysthymic Disorder
- 309—Adjustment Disorder with Depressed Mood
- 309.81—Post-Traumatic Stress Disorder
- 311—Depressive Disorder NOS

Poor Self-Concept, Underachievement

- V61.21—Abuse of Child—Perpetrator (Physical, Sexual, Neglect)
- V62.3—Academic Problem
- V62.81—Relational Problems
- 296.20–296.36—Major Depressive Disorder
- 300.02—Generalized Anxiety
- 300.23—Social Phobia
- 300.4—Dysthymic Disorder
- 309.xx—Adjustment Disorder
- 315.3—Learning Disorder NOS
- 995.52–995.54—Abuse of Child—Victim of Abuse

Cheating, Truancy, Carelessness in Work and with Property

- V62.3—Academic Problem
- V71.02—Child or Adolescent Antisocial Behavior
- 309.3—Adjustment Disorder with Disturbance of Conduct
- 312.8x—Conduct Disorder
- 315.9—Learning Disorder NOS

Daydreaming

- V62.3—Academic Problem
- 314.xx—Attention Deficit Disorder/Hyperactivity Disorder

Shyness and Withdrawal, Excessive Tension and Anxiety, School Phobia

- V62.3—Academic Problem
- 300.00—Anxiety Disorder NOS
- 300.02—Generalized Anxiety
- 309.xx—Adjustment Disorder (309.24—Adjustment Disorder with Anxiety)
- 311—Depressive Disorder NOS

Perfectionistic Behavior

- 300.00—Anxiety Disorder NOS

Immaturity and Dependent Behavior

- V62.89—Phase of Life Problem/Borderline Intellectual Functioning

REFERENCE

American Psychiatric Association. (2000). *Diagnostic and statistical manual of mental disorders* (4th ed., Rev. ed.). Washington, DC: Author.

TABLE B-1 | MEDICATIONS THAT MAY BE INDICATED FOR CHILDHOOD DSM DIAGNOSES

Attention-Deficit/Hyperactivity Disorder (ADHD)

1. Stimulants
   - Dexedrine, Adderall (dextroamphetamine)
   - Ritalin, Metadate, Concerta, Methylin, Focalin (methylphenidate)
   - Cylert (pemoline)
2. Nonstimulants
   - Strattera (atomoxetine)
3. Antidepressants
   - Wellbutrin, Zyban (bupropion)
   - Effexor (venlafaxine)
4. Antianxiety medications
   - BuSpar (buspirone)
5. Inderal (propranolol)
6. Catapres (clonidine) (treating the severe impulsiveness of ADHD)

Major Depression

1. Serotonin reuptake inhibitors (SRIs)
   - Prozac (fluoxetine); the only selective serotonin reuptake inhibitor (SSRI) that is U.S. Food and Drug Administration (FDA)–approved for pediatric use
   - Zoloft (sertraline)
   - Paxil (paroxetine)
   - Luvox (fluvoxamine maleate, generic)
   - Effexor (venlafaxine)
   - Celexa (citalopram)
   - Lexapro (escitalopram)
2. Atypical antidepressants
   - Wellbutrin (bupropion)
   - Serzone (nefazodone)
   - Desyrel (trazodone)
   - Remeron (mirtazapine)
3. Tricyclic antidepressants (TCAs)
   - Elavil (amitriptyline)
   - Anafranil (clomipramine)
   - Tofranil (imipramine)
   - Pamelor (nortriptyline)
4. Monoamine oxidase inhibitors (MAOIs)
   - Nardil (phenelzine)
   - Parnate (tranylcypromine)

Bipolar Disorder and Mania

1. Mood stabilizers and anticonvulsants: used in treating bipolar disorder, severe mood symptoms and mood swings (manic and depressive), aggressive behavior, and impulse-control disorders
   - Lithobid, Lithostat, Eskalith (lithium carbonate)
   - Cibalith-S (lithium citrate)

- Depakote, Depakene (valproate, valproic acid) for seizures
- Tegretol (carbamazepine) for seizures
- Neurontin (gabapentin)
- Lamictal (lamotrigine)
- Topamax (topiramate)
- Trileptal (oxcarbazepine)

Mental Retardation (with severe aggression of self-injurious behavior)

1. Antipsychotic medications (see list below)
2. Inderal (propranolol)

Conduct Disorder (with aggression)

1. Inderal (propranolol)
2. Antipsychotic medications (see list below)

Schizophrenia

Antipsychotic Medications: used in the control of psychotic symptoms such as delusions and hallucinations or disorganized thinking; they also are used to treat the muscle twitches ("tics") or verbal outbursts displayed in Tourette's syndrome; in addition, they may be used in treating severe anxiety and in the reduction of extreme aggression

1. First-generation antipsychotic medications
   - Thorazine (chlorpromazine)
   - Mellaril (thioridazine)
   - Prolixin (fluphenazine)
   - Stelazine (trifluoperazine)
   - Navane (thiothixene)
   - Haldol (haloperidol)
2. Second-generation antipsychotic medications (also known as atypical or novel)
   - Clozaril (clozapine)
   - Risperdal (risperidone)
   - Seroquel (quetiapine)
   - Zyprexa (olanzapine)
   - Geodon (ziprasidone)
   - Abilify (aripiprazole)

Anxiety Disorders

Antianxiety Medications

1. Benzodiazepines
   - Xanax (alprazolam)
   - Ativan (lorazepam)
   - Valium (diazepam)
   - Klonopin (clonazepam)
2. Antihistamines
   - Benadryl (diphenhydramine)
   - Vistaril (hydroxyzine)

(Continued)

TABLE B-1 | MEDICATIONS THAT MAY BE INDICATED FOR CHILDHOOD DSM DIAGNOSES (CONCLUDED)

3. Atypical
   - BuSpar (buspirone)
   - Ambien (Zolpidem)

Obsessive-Compulsive Disorder (OCD)

1. Anafranil (clomipramine)
2. SSRIs
   - Luvox (fluvoxamine)
   - Zoloft (SSRI) sertraline

Post-traumatic Stress Disorder (PTSD)

1. Tenex (guanfacine) for "flashbacks"

Sleep Disorders

1. Antidepressants
   - Desyrel (trazodone)
2. Antihistamines
   - Benadryl (diphenhydramine)
3. Antianxiety medications
   - Ambien (zolpidem)
4. Sonata (zaleplon)

Enuresis (not due to medical disorder)

1. Tofranil (imipramine)

Tourette's Syndrome

1. Orap (pimozide)
2. Antipsychotic medications (see list above)

Eating Disorders: medications used to treat bulimia and binge-eating disorder (also used, but not as frequently, in anorexia and only after weight gain)

1. Prozac (fluoxetine)
2. Other SSRIs or serotonin noradrenaline reuptake inhibitors (SNRIs)

American Academy of Child and Adolescent Psychiatry. (2004, July).

Facts for families. *Psychiatric medications for children and adolescents part II: Types of medications*. Retrieved March 15, 2006, from http://www.aacap.org/publications/factsfam/29.htm

The Center for Health and Health Care in Schools. (2004, December). *Psychotropic drugs and children: Use, trends, and implications for schools*. Retrieved March 15, 2006, from http://www.healthinschools.org/sh/psychotropic.asp

The National Institute of Mental Health (2006, February 17). Medications. *Children's medication chart*. Retrieved March 15, 2006, from http://www.nimh.nih.gov/publicat/medicate.cfm#ptdep16

This appendix contains conversion tables for goal-attainment scales that are explained in Chapter 2.

TABLE C1 | CONVERSION TABLE FOR GOAL-ATTAINMENT SCALES WITH ONE SCORED SCALE

Sum of Scale Scores	Average Scale Score	T-score
−2	−2.00	30.00
−1	−1.00	40.00
0	0	50.00
+1	+1.00	60.00
+2	+2.00	70.00

TABLE C2 | CONVERSION TABLE FOR GOAL-ATTAINMENT SCALES WITH TWO SCORED SCALES

Sum of Scale Scores	Average Scale Score	T-score
−4	−2.00	25.19
−3	−1.50	31.39
−2	−1.00	37.59
−1	−0.50	43.79
0	0	50.00
+1	+0.50	56.21
+2	+1.00	62.41
+3	+1.50	68.61
+4	+2.00	74.81

TABLE C3 | CONVERSION TABLE FOR GOAL-ATTAINMENT
SCALES WITH THREE SCORED SCALES

Sum of Scale Scores	Average Scale Score	T-score
−6	−2.00	22.62
−5	−1.67	27.18
−4	−1.33	31.74
−3	−1.00	36.31
−2	−0.67	40.87
−1	−0.33	45.44
0	0	50.00
+1	+0.33	54.56
+2	+0.67	59.13
+3	+1.00	63.69
+4	+1.33	68.26
+5	+1.67	72.82
+6	+2.00	77.38

TABLE C4 | CONVERSION TABLE FOR GOAL-ATTAINMENT
SCALES WITH FOUR SCORED SCALES

Sum of Scale Scores	Average Scale Score	T-score
−8	−2.00	20.98
−7	−1.75	24.61
−6	−1.50	28.24
−5	−1.25	31.86
−4	−1.00	35.49
−3	−0.75	39.12
−2	−0.50	42.75
−1	−0.25	46.37
0	0	50.00
+1	+0.25	53.63
+2	+0.50	57.25
+3	+0.75	60.88
+4	+1.00	64.51
+5	+1.25	68.14
+6	+1.50	71.76
+7	+1.75	75.39
+8	+2.00	79.02

	CONVERSION TABLE FOR GOAL-ATTAINMENT
TABLE C5	SCALES WITH FIVE SCORED SCALES

Sum of Scale Scores	Average Scale Score	T-score
−10	−2.00	19.85
−9	−1.80	22.86
−8	−1.60	25.88
−7	−1.40	28.89
−6	−1.20	31.91
−5	−1.00	34.92
−4	−0.80	37.94
−3	−0.60	40.95
−2	−0.40	43.97
−1	−0.20	46.98
0	0	50.00
+1	+0.20	53.02
+2	+0.40	56.03
+3	+0.60	59.05
+4	+0.80	62.02
+5	+1.00	65.08
+6	+1.20	68.09
+7	+1.40	71.11
+8	+1.60	74.12
+9	+1.80	77.14
+10	+2.00	80.15

TABLE C6 | CONVERSION TABLE FOR GOAL-ATTAINMENT SCALES WITH SIX SCORED SCALES

Sum of Scale Scores	Average Scale Score	T-score
−12	−2.00	19.02
−11	−1.83	21.60
−10	−1.67	24.18
−9	−1.50	26.76
−8	−1.33	29.34
−7	−1.17	31.93
−6	−1.00	34.51
−5	−0.83	37.09
−4	−0.67	39.67
−3	−0.050	42.25
−2	−0.033	44.84
−1	−0.17	47.42
0	0	50.00
+1	+0.17	52.58
+2	+0.33	55.16
+3	+0.50	57.75
+4	+0.67	60.33
+5	+0.83	62.91
+6	+1.00	65.49
+7	+1.17	68.07
+8	+1.33	70.66
+9	+1.50	73.24
+10	+1.67	75.82
+11	+1.83	78.40
+12	+2.00	80.98

Name Index

Ackerman, Nathan, 347
Addison, J. D., 472
Adelman, H. S., 500
Adler, Alfred, 75, 177, 299, 300, 301, 302, 303, 304, 305, 307, 309, 310, 314, 315, 316, 322, 323, 324, 325, 327, 328, 329, 330, 331, 332, 333, 337, 341, 347, 361, 367, 395, 498, 499, 510, 513, 519
Ahn, M., 58
Aiello, B., 441
Aiken, L. R., 505
Ainsworth, M. D., 17, 21
Akos, P., 512, 525
Albon, S. L., 415, 416
Alexander, F., 105, 300
Alexander, J., 192
Alioto, J., 232
Allan, J., 442
Allen, L., 471
Allen, W., 336
Allers, C. T., 417
Al-Rashidi, B., 130
Anastopoulos, A. D., 599
Anderson, C., 202, 379
Anderson, J., 434
Ansbacher, H., 303, 314, 315
Ansbacher, R., 315
Appleton, V., 502
Ariel, S., 377, 423
Arman, J. F., 512, 551
Armistead, L., 470
Armstrong, S., 434
Arredondo, P., 459, 460, 461, 477, 478
Arthur, R., 579
Ashby, J., 436, 437
Askounis, A. C., 476
Assagioli, R., 187
Atkinson, D. R., 22, 464, 466
Axline, Virginia, 169, 175, 176, 414, 427, 440

Bachmann, G., 539
Baer-Barkley, K., 526
Bagner, D., 427
Bahl, A., 426
Bailey, D. F., 471
Baker, D., 599
Baldwin, M., 359
Balkin, R., 434
Ballou, R., 313
Bamaca, M. Y., 479
Bandura, A., 263
Banks, S., 239
Bardenstein, K. K., 458, 545, 546, 553, 555
Barker, S., 419
Barlow, D., 427
Barlow, K., 437
Barnes, M., 433, 436
Baron, A., 477
Barona, A., 466
Barrett, P., 227
Barrett-Hakanson, T., 514
Barter, J. T., 560
Bartholomew, K., 17
Bartolomeo, M., 231
Baruth, L. G., 458, 460, 461, 463, 470, 473, 478
Baruth, N. E., 619
Basham, A., 502
Bates, M., 517
Bateson, Gregory, 360
Battle, C., 176
Baumgardner, Patricia, 184
Bay-Hinitz, A., 422, 433, 575
Beamish, P. M., 557
Bean, F. D., 479
Beautrais, A. L., 558
Becicka, C., 500
Beck, A., 220, 227
Beck, A. T., 557, 560
Becvar, D., 379

Becvar, R., 379
Belgrave, F. Z., 472
Bell, C. C., 560
Bellerby, T., 573
Bemak, F., 491, 493, 500, 501, 512
Benard, B., 19, 20, 21
Bender, D., 579
Benson, P. L., 20
Berchick, R., 227
Berg, I., 135, 139, 146
Berg, I. K., 476
Bergan, J. R., 491, 493
Berger, S. N., 439
Bergin, J. J., 510, 511, 512, 517, 518, 520, 526
Berk, L. E., 17, 18, 539
Berkowitz, C., 232
Berkowitz, L., 232
Bernal, M. E., 468
Bernard, M., 220
Berne, Eric, 269, 270, 271, 275, 276, 278, 281, 282, 297, 411
Bernet, W., 622
Bernstein, Eric Lennard, 269
Berry, E. H., 19
Berry, P., 442
Berryhill-Paapke, E., 464
Beslija, A., 296
Bettelheim, Bruno, 347
Bevilacqua, L., 338
Bianchi, S., 570
Biever, J., 155
Bingham, R. P., 201
Bittner, J., 375
Black, C., 549
Blakeslee, S., 563, 564, 565, 566
Blanc, H., 426
Blewitt, P., 18
Blocher, L., 550
Blos, Peter, 75
Blount, R. L., 465

Blue, Yvonne, 239
Blum, D. J., 468
Blume, J., 552
Boggs, S., 427
Bograd, M., 355
Bolton, B., 466
Booth, P., 378, 416, 423
Bordeau, L. C., 470, 472
Borrego, J., 427
Borzuchowska, B., 611
Boster, L., 226
Boudah, D. J., 595, 597
Boutwell, D. A., 512
Bowen, Murray, 335, 337, 338, 339, 340, 341, 344, 345, 346, 360, 381
Bowlby, J., 15, 17, 21
Boyce, W., 430
Bracey, J. R., 479
Brack, C., 491
Brack, G., 328, 491
Bradley, C., 472
Bradley, L. J., 415, 435, 437, 441
Brake, K., 550
Brandenburg, N., 594
Brandt, M. A., 424
Brantley, L., 526
Brantley, P., 526
Bratton, S. C., 416, 417, 424, 425
Brazelton, T. B., 4, 6
Brechman-Toussaint, M., 227
Breen, D. T., 500
Breggin, P. R., 514
Brennan, K. A., 17
Brent, D. A., 558
Brestan, E., 426
Bretherton, I., 17
Breuer, 91
Brickell, J., 129, 130
Bridbord, K. H., 511
Briesmeister, J. M., 230, 416
Briggs, Katharine, 386, 396, 397, 402, 411, 506, 506n1
Brigman, G., 502
Broderick, P. C., 18
Brody, G., 470
Bromfield, R., 440
Bronfenbrenner, U., 10
Brown, B. M., 512
Brown, D., 458, 465, 488, 489, 490, 492, 493, 496
Brown, K., 575
Brown, L. L., 520
Brown, S., 597
Bruce, M., 135, 136, 137
Bruckner, S., 527
Bruschi, C. J., 457
Bryant, R. M., 597
Bryant, S., 500, 501
Bryne, D. F., 14
Buckley, 48
Burch, K. M., 545, 547, 548

Burcky, W. D., 618
Burley, T., 202
Burlingame, G. M., 510, 511
Burnam, M. A., 466
Burnham, S. C., 577, 579
Burton, L., 39, 98
Bush, George W., 68
Bush, M. V., 423

Cade, B., 146
Callahan, P., 617
Campbell, C. A., 196, 439
Campbell, D., 336
Campbell, J., 149, 386
Campbell, S., 35, 65, 153, 230
Canelones, P., 430
Cangelosi, D. M., 96, 414, 416, 422, 423, 438
Canino, I. A., 19
Capage, L., 426
Caplan, G., 489, 493
Caplan, R. B., 489, 493
Capuzzi, D., 45, 557, 558, 559, 560
Carao, A., 430
Cardemil, E., 176
Cardillo, J., 58
Carkhuff, R. R., 45, 54, 55, 163, 166, 168, 169
Carlson, C., 331, 332
Carlson, J., 302, 330, 499
Carlson, K., 43
Carlson, M., 330
Carmichael, K. D., 376, 423, 442
Carpenter, A., 491, 500
Carpenter, S. L., 604
Carr, A., 539, 544, 553, 554, 555
Carroll, F., 196
Carroll, M., 517
Carruthers, W., 577
Carter, D. J., 600
Carter, R. B., 440, 441
Carter, W. L., 545
Cartwright, B., 611
Casas, J. M., 459, 464
Casey, Annie E., 6
Caspar, L., 570
Casteel, Donna Maxwell, 577n1
Castes, M., 430
Cattanach, A., 434, 436
Cattani-Thompson, K., 34
Chaffin, M., 427
Chalk, R., 541
Chandler, C., 429
Chandras, K. V., 476
Chase-Vaughn, G., 472
Chasin, R., 355
Chau, I., 424
Cheatham, H. E., 461
Cherry, V. R., 472
Chesterton, G. K., 299
Childers, J. H., Jr., 618

Choate, M., 427
Choney, S. K., 464
Christopher, M., 265
Clark, A., 81
Clark, D., 227
Clark, P., 416
Clarke, C., 514
Clarke, G. N., 558
Clay, D. L., 480
Claypoole, S. D., 526
Clemente, R., 469, 470, 471, 476, 478
Clemons, D., 155
Cleveland, W. T., 500
Clinton, William J., 136
Coatsworth, D., 20
Cochran, J. L., 419
Coe, D., 431
Coffey, E. P., 64
Cohen, D., 574
Cohen, J., 231
Cohen, L., 465
Colbert, R., 597
Cole, P. M., 457
Coleman, J., 23
Coleman, M., 568, 569
Coleman, V., 419, 474
Combes, B. H., 597
Combs, A. W., 178
Connor-Smith, J., 558
Conyne, R. K., 512
Cook, J. A., 64
Cook, L., 499
Corcoran, J., 155
Corcoran, K. O., 17
Corey, G., 510, 513, 514, 515, 516, 517, 519, 522, 524, 610, 617, 621
Corey, M. S., 510, 517, 519, 524, 617
Costa, L., 555, 556
Costas, M., 416, 424
Cota, M. K., 468
Cottone, R. R., 611
Coughlin, J. W., 526
Cowen, E. L., 428, 429, 518
Cox, R., 378
Crain, W., 378
Crawford, B., 558
Crawford, T., 211
Crosbie-Burnett, M., 571
Cross, W. E., 464
Crutchfield, L. B., 525, 526
Csikszentimihalyi, M., 388
Cumella, S., 573
Cunningham, C., 435, 437
Cunningham, L., 129
Cynn, V., 477

Dacey, J., 564
Dadds, M., 227
Dagley, J. C., 517

Dahir, C. A., 609, 610, 615
Daigneault, S. D., 526
Dana, R., 466
D'Andrea, M., 265
Daniel, C., 430
Daniels, J. A., 572, 610
Danish, S. J., 177
Dansby, V. S., 512
Dattilio, F., 338
Daughhtree, C., 146, 149
Davidson, L., 571
Davis, D., 226
Davis, J., 67
Davis, K. E., 17
Davis, K. I., 544
Davis, N., 545
Davis, T. E., 611
Dawson, G., 431
Day, J., 610, 611
Deach, C., 545
DeBar, L. L., 558
Deck, M., 604
DeDomenico, G., 442
de la Cruz, B., 599
Delcampo, R., 379
DeLucia-Waack, J. L., 511, 525, 566
Demanchick, S., 427
Deming, W. Edwards, 113, 114
DeOrnellas, K., 328
DeShazer, S., 354
de Shazer, S., 134, 135, 139, 140, 150
Dettmer, P. A., 487, 501
Deutsch, Helene, 184
Diamond, G., 336
Dietrich, A., 388
Dietzel, M., 545
DiGiuseppe, R., 214, 227
DiLalla, D., 431
Diller, J., 265
Dinkmeyer, D., Jr., 315, 499
Dinkmeyer, Don, 314, 315, 329
Dishion, T. J., 465
Disque, J. G., 617
Dobson, J., 90
Dobson, K., 231
Dodge, K. A., 18
Dolliver, R., 189
Donato, T., 129
Donovan, C., 227
Dorham, C. L., 465
Dorta, D. P., 557
Dougherty, A. M., 488, 491, 492, 494, 495, 501
Douzenis, C., 526
Dowd, E., 62
Doweiko, H. E., 549
Downey, D., 570
Doyle, J., 416
Draguns, J. G., 177, 457

Dreikurs, Rudolf, 300, 311, 314, 319, 322, 331
Dreiser, Theodore, 207
Drew, C., 588, 589
Drew, N., 36
Drucker, C., 525
Drummond, P., 430
Dryden, W., 208
Duffy, A., 227
Duffy, G., 228
Duffy, J. L., 493
Dufrene, P., 474
Duncan, B., 146
Dunlap, K., 134
Dupuis, M., 621
Durodoye, B. A., 597
Dyck, N. T., 487, 501
Dye, A., 511
Dykeman, C., 502

Ecker, B., 95
Eddy, J. P., 476
Edgeworth, J., 539, 544
Edison, Thomas A., 109
Edwards, D., 328
Egan, G., 45
Egan, M., 588, 589
Eggert, L. L., 560
Einstein, Albert, 238
Eisenstadt, T., 426, 427
Eisenstein, S., 300
Elder, J., 149
Eliot, T. S., 33, 299
Elkind, D., 14
Elliot, C., 227
Elliott, S. N., 495
Ellis, Albert, 117, 189, 207, 208, 209, 210, 211, 212, 213, 214, 215, 219, 220, 223, 229, 231, 232, 233, 234, 314
Emshoff, J. G., 550
Emslie, G., 557
Engle, D., 193
English, A., 184, 612
English, H., 184
English, S., 64, 65, 66
Epp, L., 500, 501
Epstein, R., 239
Epstein, Raisa Timofeyeuna, 300
Erdman, P., 38, 39
Erford, B. T., 600
Erickson, E., 579
Erickson, Milton, 134, 351, 352, 353, 379
Erikson, E., 15, 20, 75, 84, 150, 269, 572
Erk, R. R., 598, 600
Escobar, J. I., 466
Estill, D. M., 604
Evans, K., 177, 231, 466, 467
Evans, S., 155

Eyberg, S., 426, 427
Eyseneck, Hans, 238

Faber, A., 339
Fall, M., 97, 176, 416, 435, 438
Fancher, R., 75
Farwell, G., 26
Fascoli, L., 469
Fee, V., 431
Feldman, E., 18
Felix, E., 431, 432
Felthous, A. R., 620
Ferguson, Marilyn, 183
Ferquist, R. M., 550
Ferris, J., 370
Files-Hall, T., 417, 418, 445
Fincham, F., 566
Fine, M., 568
Finn, A., 575
Fisch, R., 134
Fischer, A., 464
Fischer, J. L., 550
Fischer, L., 609, 610
Fischetti, B., 416
Fitzsimmons, M., 575
Flanagan, D., 331
Fleming, J., 146, 148, 154, 155
Follensbee, R. W., Jr., 177
Ford, C. A., 616
Ford, Gerald, 589
Forehand, R., 470
Foreman, T., 622
Forester-Miller, H., 611
Forthun, L. F., 550
Frankel, J. B., 97
Frankl, V., 134, 152, 177
Franklin, C., 155
Franklin, L. C., 423
Freed, Alvyn, 284, 287
Freed, Margaret, 284, 287
Freedman, Y., 526
Freeman, S. J., 553
Freier, M., 202
Freud, Anna, 75, 97
Freud, Sigmund, 74, 75, 76, 77, 78, 79, 80, 84, 85, 87, 90, 91, 92, 93, 94, 95, 98, 99, 105, 106, 109, 116, 130, 133, 177, 184, 208, 239, 271, 300, 301, 303, 385, 386, 387, 388, 394, 395, 396, 414
Friedberg, R. D., 230, 458, 545, 546, 553, 555
Friedman, R., 594
Friend, M., 499
Fromm, Marty, 185
Fu, V., 430
Fuertes, J., 231
Fuhriman, A. J., 510, 511
Funderbunk, B., 426, 427
Fundudis, T., 616
Fuqua, D., 488, 494, 495, 496

Furr, S. R., 512
Fusick, L., 470, 472

Gallagher, D., 149
Gallagher, N., 426, 427
Galloway, A., 212
Galpert, L., 431
Galton, Francis, 394
Ganong, L., 568, 569
Garbarino, J., 7, 51
Garcia, J. G., 611
Gardner, H., 20
Gardner, Howard, 238, 385
Gardner, R. A., 605
Gardner, Richard, 96
Garmezy, N., 20
Garner, N., 328
Garrett, M., 526
Garrett, M. T., 469, 473
Garrett, M. W., 465
Garza, C., 468
Gately, D., 567
Gazda, G. M., 517
Gerler, E., 36
Geroski, A. M., 500
Gerrity, D., 566
Getz, H., 503, 505
Ghahramanlou, M., 421
Ghandi, Mahatma, 487
Gibbons, A., 541
Gibbs, J., 479
Gibbs, J. T., 468
Gil, E., 437, 440, 441, 541
Gilbert, A., 524, 525
Gilliland, B. E., 532, 549, 551, 552, 558, 560, 562, 573, 577, 579
Gillis, A., 430
Ginott, H., 517
Ginott, H. G., 414
Ginter, E. J., 517
Giordano, M., 416
Gladding, S. T., 33, 376, 419, 423, 439, 502, 511, 513, 514, 516, 517, 522
Glaros, A., 23
Glass, G. V., 34
Glasser, William, 10, 51, 109, 110, 111, 112, 113, 114, 115, 116, 117, 118, 119, 120, 125, 126, 129, 130, 131, 133, 228, 302, 328, 345, 348, 361, 514, 530
Gloria, A. M., 477
Glosoff, H., 488
Glosoff, H. L., 615
Glover, C. J., 419
Glover, G., 425
Glover, J., 549
Goldstein, A. P., 518
Goldstein, M., 599
Goldstein, S., 599
Goleman, D., 20

Gonzalez, J., 212
Gonzalez-Mena, J., 420
Gonzo, J., 357
Gooch, Michael, 99
Goodman, Paul, 184
Goodnough, G. E., 510, 512, 526
Gordis, E. B., 558
Gordon, T., 166
Gottman, John, 357
Gould, L. J., 415, 435, 437, 441
Graf, C., 179
Graham, C., 532
Graham-Bermann, S., 572
Grant, D., 146, 149
Graves, B., 574
Grawe, K., 55
Gray, F., 472
Gray, J., 411
Green, A., 488, 544, 545
Greenberg, E., 203
Greenberg, J. M., 462
Greenberg, K. R., 516, 517, 520, 521
Greenberg, L. S., 191, 193
Greenberg, R., 433
Greenspan, S. I., 4, 6
Greig, R., 465
Grey, L., 319
Grieger, I., 463
Griffith, M., 176
Grollman, E. A., 552
Grootboom, N., 328
Gross, D. R., 45, 557, 558, 559, 560
Grotjahn, M., 300
Grünbaum, A., 105
Grych, J., 566
Guare, J., 429
Guerney, Bernard, 423
Guerney, Louise, 376, 423
Guimaraes, B., 296
Gumaer, J., 435, 436
Gunther, Bernard, 185, 359
Gutkin, T., 212
Guy, R., 284

Haffney, W., 428
Hagel, I., 430
Haley, J., 134
Haley, Jay, 348, 351, 352, 353, 354, 356, 379
Hall, C., 74, 75
Hall, G. Stanley, 75
Hall, K., 423
Halpern-Felscher, B. L., 616
Hammer, A., 397, 405
Hanes, M., 440
Hanoff-Bulman, R., 571
Happel, Clara, 184
Hardman, M., 588, 589, 601, 602
Hargaden, H., 296

Harman, L., 192
Harman, R., 202
Harper, R., 210
Harris, G., 577
Harris, Sydney J., 335
Harris, T., 282, 284
Harris, Z. L., 424, 434
Harrison, T. C., 491, 500, 501
Harter, S., 18
Hartman, J. S., 476
Harvey, Anne, 170
Harvey, S., 376, 423
Hasbrouck, J. E., 495
Haub, A. L., 519
Hauser, S. T., 20
Havey, J. M., 492
Havighurst, R., 15
Hawkins, E., 266
Hayashi, S., 177
Hayes, R. L., 501
Hays, P. A., 457
Hefferline, Ralph, 184
Heflinger, C. A., 63, 64
Heidgerken, A., 495
Heikkinen, C., 195
Helms, J. E., 458, 464, 465
Henderson, D. A., 419
Henderson, K., 589
Hendrix, D. H., 625
Henniger, M. L., 416
Henriksen, R. C., 464
Hensley, F. A., 525
Herlihy, B., 610, 611, 612, 613, 614, 616, 617, 618, 622
Hernandez, D. J., 7
Hernandez, H., 461
Herring, R. D., 441, 473, 474, 479, 562
Herschell, A., 425, 426
Hewson-Bower, B., 430
Higgins, K., 572
Hightower, A., 428
Hill, M. B., 328
Hill-Hain, A., 177
Hines, A. M., 466
Ho, M. K., 462, 464, 466, 469
Hoag, M. J., 511
Hocutt, A. M., 64
Hoffmann, T., 466
Hofstede, G., 460
Hohenshil, T. H., 503, 505
Holcomb-McCoy, C., 459, 467, 521
Holinger, P. C., 560
Holliday, D., 555, 556
Holliman, M., 193
Hollingworth, Leta, 160
Holman, M. M., 19
Holmes, J., 575
Holmes, Oliver Wendell, 74
Holmes-Lonergan, H., 575

Hood, K., 427
Horne, A. M., 517
Horney, K., 302
Horney, Karen, 184
Horowitz, L. M., 17
Hough, R. L., 466
Hourcade, J. J., 601
Houston, G., 202
Houts, R., 550
Hoven, C. W., 64
Huang, L. N., 468, 475
Hubbard, G. T., 14
Huesman, 579
Huey, W. C., 614, 616, 617
Huffstetler, B., 115
Hughes, C., 431
Hughes, D., 466
Hughes, J. N., 495
Hughes, T., 619
Hulley, L., 95
Hunt, D. E., 15
Hunt-Morse, M. C., 556
Huss, S. N., 519, 520, 521
Hutterer, R., 177
Hwang, B., 431

Ibrahim, F. A., 463
Imber-Black, E., 104
Imhof, L., 130
Ingersoll, R. E., 543
Ingraham, C. L., 493
Inhelder, B., 11, 85
Irwin, C. E., Jr., 616
Irwin, E. C., 441
Isaacs, M. L., 621
Israel, A. C., 599, 600, 601
Ivey, A., 265, 463
Ivey, M., 265

Jacknow, D., 430
Jackson, M., 473, 474
Jacob, E. J., 458
Jacobs, E., 512, 516, 522
Jacobs, J., 426
Jacobsen, E., 255
Jacobsen, H. E., 421
Jacobsen, I., 559
James, M., 283
James, R., 318, 442
James, R. K., 440, 441, 532, 549,
    551, 552, 558, 560, 562, 573,
    577, 579
James, S., 201
James, S. H., 545, 547, 548
Jang, M., 425
Jay, S., 227
Jen Der Pan, P., 379
Jenni, C., 177
Jernberg, A., 378, 416, 423
Jewel, D. L., 440
Jimenez, E., 574

Johnsen, A., 370, 378
Johnson, B., 423
Johnson, C., 474, 539
Johnson, D., 427, 428, 474, 517, 576
Johnson, D. W., 511
Johnson, F. P., 511
Johnson, J., 510, 511
Johnson, L., 176, 424
Johnson, M., 429, 430
Johnson, P., 463
Johnson, R., 576
Johnson, S., 416
Johnson, V., 327
Jome, L., 464
Jones, D., 550
Jones, D. J., 470
Jones, E., 491
Jones, E. N., 511
Jones, Ernest, 75
Jones, J. W., 550
Jones, K. D., 523
Jones, K. M., 492
Jones, L., 417, 425
Jones, S., 420, 421, 422
Jongeward, D., 283
Josephson, A., 336
Jourdan, A., 177, 180
Juhnke, G. A., 560
Jung, Carl, 75, 78, 385, 386, 387, 388,
    389, 391, 392, 393, 394, 395, 396,
    397, 401, 402, 406, 407, 408, 411

Kachgian, C., 620
Kaduson, H. G., 230, 414, 416, 422,
    423, 438
Kahn, B. B., 495
Kale, A., 424
Kalff, D. M., 441, 442
Kalodner, C. R., 526
Kant, Immanuel, 609
Kao, S., 419
Kaplan, D., 623
Kaplan, D. M., 615
Kaplan, K., 283
Karno, M., 466
Kashti, Y., 526
Kazdin, A. E., 34
Keat, D., 36
Kehoe, P., 545
Keirsey, D., 402, 403
Kelleher, K. J., 64
Kelley, B. T., 541
Kellogg, S., 193
Kelly, F., 62
Kelly, J., 563, 566
Kendall, P., 226, 227, 228
Kennedy, John F., 589
Kenney, K. E., 612
Kenny, M., 564
Kenworthy, Marian, 160
Kestenbaum, C. J., 96

Keys, S., 512
Keys, S. G., 488, 491, 493, 500, 604
Khatri, N., 231
Kim, B. S. K., 466
Kim, R., 130
Kincade, E., 177, 231, 466, 467
King, D. A., 510
King, L., 105
King, Martin Luther, Jr., 335
King-Sears, M. E., 491, 500, 604
Kingston, Maxine Hong, 183
Kirby, L., 402
Kiresuk, T., 58, 59
Kirkpatrick, L. A., 17
Kirschenbaum, H., 177, 180
Kirsner, D., 104
Kitchener, K. S., 611
Kizner, L. R., 525
Kizner, S. R., 525
Klein, Melanie, 97
Kmitta, D., 577
Knauth, D., 339
Knell, S., 416
Knell, S. M., 229, 230
Knight, G., 468
Kobak, R. R., 18
Kohlberg, L., 120
Kohn, A., 323
Koller, T. J., 378, 423
Koprowicz, C., 488
Kot, S., 429
Kottler, J. A., 611
Kottman, T., 327, 328, 415, 416,
    417, 418, 419, 433, 434, 436, 437,
    438, 469, 549, 599, 615
Kovacs, M., 557, 560
Kowalski, K., 466
Kramer, E., 439
Kratochwill, T. R., 491, 493,
    495, 512
Krautter, T., 350
Kreimer, J., 429
Krestensen, K., 375
Kris, Marianne, 75
Kroeger, O., 400
Kübler-Ross, E., 553
Kulic, K. R., 517
Kuno, T., 177
Kurpius, D., 488, 494, 495, 496
Kurpius, S. E. R., 612, 613, 614,
    622, 625
Kurtines, W., 378
Kuster, C. B., 6, 8
Kwan, K. K., 464

LaFountain, R., 328
LaFromboise, T., 473, 474
Lago, C., 176
Lambarth, C., 502
Lambert, M., 266
Lambert, M. M., 34

Lampe, R., 38, 39
Lampe, R. E., 230
Landgarten, H. B., 439
Landreth, G., 416, 419, 424, 437
Landreth, G. L., 175, 176, 414, 420, 424, 425, 433, 434, 437, 438, 442
Lane, K. S., 376, 423
Lane, P. S., 576
Lansford, Z., 406
Laor, I., 105
Larsen, C. C., 611
Lasky, G. B., 511
Lassiter, P., 328
Lau, A., 378
Lawrence, G., 612, 613, 614, 622, 625
Lawson, D., 97
Lazarus, A., 35
Lazarus, P. J., 473
Lazear, David, 504
Leben, N. Y., 439
Leblanc, M., 417
Lee, A. C., 97
Lee, C. C., 459, 460, 461, 463, 464, 466, 471, 475
Lee, J., 477, 479
Lee, M., 379
Lee, V. V., 510
Lee, W., 265
Lega, L., 231
LeGuernic, A., 276
Legum, H., 135, 140, 146
Leone, B., 579
Leong, F., 475, 477
Lepage, K. M., 493
Levenson, H., 155
LeVine, E., 11
Levinson, B., 98
Lewin, Kurt, 133
Lewinsohn, P. M., 558
Lewis, H., 431
Lewis, R. E., 20, 21
Limber, S., 575
Linarello, C., 431
Linde, L., 612, 614, 615
Lines, D., 155
Link, M., 430
Lipchik, E., 135
Lippitt, G., 494
Lippitt, R., 494
Littrell, J., 146, 155
Littrell, J. M., 525, 526, 597
Liu, W. M., 480
Lloyd, M., 378
Lobaugh, A. F., 424
Lobaugh, F. A., 424
Lochman, J., 226
Lock, J., 350
Locke, D. C., 460, 471
Lockhart, E., 488
Lockhart, E. J., 493

Loeschen, S., 368
Lojk, L., 130
Lonner, W. J., 457, 463
Lopez, R. G., 17
Lowenfeld, M., 441, 445, 446
Lowenthal, B., 20
Luckasson, R., 589, 590, 594, 596, 598, 601, 603
Luongo, P. F., 488
Lurn, W., 370
Lusky, M. B., 501
Lynch, N., 430
Lyness-Richard, D., 97, 230

MacFarland, W., 562, 564, 565, 568, 569
MacLaren, C., 208
MacLeod, I. R., 492
Madanes, Cloé, 351, 352
Majidi-Ahi, S., 471
Malcolm, W., 191, 193
Mallinckrodt, B., 17
Mander, G., 105
Maniacci, M., 322
Manikam, R., 431
Manly, L., 313
Manning, M., 478
Manning, M. L., 458, 460, 461, 463, 470, 473
Marans, S., 574
Marino, T., 64, 65, 66
Markman, H., 357
Markos, P. A., 572
Markus, H. E., 510
Marsella, A. J., 457
Martin, B., 430
Martin, J., 436
Martin, S., 62
Marvasti, J. A., 150
Maslow, A., 8, 9, 10, 20, 21, 87, 111, 161, 241, 360, 572
Mason, P. S., 440, 441
Masten, A., 19, 20, 572
Matarazzo, R., 426, 427
Matson, J., 431
Maultsby, M., 220, 221, 222, 223
Mazzetti, R., 296
McCaulley, M., 397, 405
McConnell, A. R., 566
McConville, M., 197
McDavis, R. J., 459
McDonald, L., 376, 423
McEachern, A. G., 595, 596, 597
McFadden, J., 128
McFarland, W. P., 621
McGinn, L., 221
McGinnis, E., 518
McHaney, L., 495
McKinney, J. D., 64
McLeod, E. H., 176
McNair, R., 551

McNeil, C., 425, 426, 427
McRary, A., 574
McWhirter, B. T., 559, 560, 562, 570, 571, 573, 574, 577, 578
McWhirter, E. H., 556, 559, 560, 562, 570, 571, 573, 574, 577, 578
McWhirter, J. J., 520, 559, 560, 562, 570, 571, 573, 574, 576, 577, 578
McWhirter, R. J., 559, 560, 562, 570, 571, 573, 574, 577, 578
Mead, J. F., 619
Meara, N., 81, 609, 610, 611
Mearns, D., 177
Meggert, S. S., 441, 474
Meichenbaum, D., 220
Meisgeier, C., 407, 410, 411, 506
Mellin, E. A., 557
Menke, E., 572
Mercado, M. M., 476
Michelangelo, 159
Miedema, P., 328
Mihalic, S. F., 575
Miliotis, D., 572
Miller, J. A., 466
Miller, M., 188, 189
Miller, S., 135, 476
Miller, T. I., 34
Miller-Perrin, C. L., 539, 541, 543, 544, 545
Millican, V., 328
Milliren, A., 332
Milsom, A. S., 512
Milstein, S. G., 616
Mims, S., 115
Minuchin, Salvador, 347, 348, 349, 350, 352
Mio, J. S., 461
Miranda, A., 331
Mish, F. C., 336
Mitchell, C. W., 617, 623
Moeller, J., 539
Moeller, T., 539
Moffit, K., 424
Mohr, P., 36
Molnar, A., 134, 354
Montague, M., 64
Moodley, R., 176
Moody, E. E., Jr., 526
Moore, K., 155
Moore, M., 553, 554, 555
Moreno, J. L., 360
Morgan, A., 376, 423
Morgan, D., 106
Morgan, R., 106
Morris, C., 23
Morrissey, M., 575, 576
Morten, G., 464
Mosak, Harold, 299, 301, 305, 314, 322
Mosak, M., 305, 306
Mosely-Howard, G., 331

Moustakas, C., 176, 414
Mufson, L., 557
Mulherin, M. A., 442
Mulkern, V., 64
Mullis, F., 501
Mullis, R., 502
Muro, J., 438, 549
Muro, J. J., 615
Murphy, E., 407, 411, 506
Murphy, J., 146
Murphy, K., 64
Myer, R., 318, 440, 441
Myers, Isabel, 386, 396, 397, 401, 402, 405, 406, 407, 411, 506, 506n1
Myers, K., 402
Myers, P., 402
Myers, S., 163, 179
Myrick, R., 155
Myrick, R. D., 496, 512

Nabrady, M., 296
Nader, K., 439
Nafpaktitis, M., 428
Nagata, D., 476
Nawojczyk, S., 578
Neemann, J., 572
Neil, B., 437
Nelson, J., 212
Nelson, R., 558
Neubauer, P., 97
Newcomb, K., 426
Newman, B. M., 15
Newman, P. R., 15
Newmeyer, A. J., 600
Newmeyer, M. D., 600
Newton, Isaac, 136
Nichols, C., 231
Nichols, M., 379
Niebuhr, K. E., 500
Niebuhr, R. E., 500
Nigg, J. T., 600
Nin, Anaïs, 269
Norem, R., 569
Northrup, D., 64
Notarius, C., 357
Novellino, M., 296
Nystul, M. S., 21, 23, 610

Oaklander, V., 196, 197, 438
O'Brien, M., 39, 98
O'Brien, M. U., 6, 8
Ocampo, K., 468
O'Connor, K., 421
Odum, S., 431
Offer, D., 560
Ogawa, Y., 417, 432
Ogrodniczuk, J. S., 510, 511
O'Hanlon, B., 149
O'Hanlon, W., 146
O'Hanlon, W. H., 149

O'Hara, M., 65
Ohnishi, H., 463
O'Loony, J., 499
Olson, M. E., 64
Olweus, D., 575
Omizo, M. M., 476
Omizo, S. A., 476
Oren, T. A., 619
Orlando, M., 63, 66
Orlinsky, D. E., 55
O'Rourke, K., 549, 550, 551, 552
Orsi, R., 600
Orton, G. L., 6, 414, 435, 439, 440, 513
Osawa, M., 177
Osofsky, J., 574, 576
Otwell, P. S., 501
Owens, P. C., 517
Oz, S., 125

Paisley, P. O., 14
Paivio, S., 191
Palenque, M., 430
Palm, G., 336
Palmer, David, 23
Pannu, R., 464
Papernow, P., 568, 569
Parette, H. P., 601
Parham, T., 472
Park, E., 154
Parker, L. D., 460
Parks, B. K., 55
Parks, C., 578, 579
Parmer, T., 419
Parsons, R., 575
Pate, R. H., Jr., 615
Patterson, L. E., 19, 21
Patton, M., 81
Paulson, R. I., 64
Pavlov, Ivan, 238, 254, 255
Peace, S. D., 526
Peak, T., 19
Pedersen, P., 463
Pedersen, P. B., 458, 459, 461
Pedersen, P. V., 457
Pedro-Carroll, J. L., 420, 421, 422, 427, 428, 518
Pelcovitz, D., 416
Pellar, J., 135
Perl, J., 39, 98
Perlmutter, B., 428
Perls, Fritz, 183, 184, 185, 186, 187, 188, 189, 190, 191, 195, 203, 204, 359
Perls, Laura, 185, 203, 204
Perón, Juan, 347
Persi, J., 496
Peskin, Margery, 443n1
Peters, H., 26
Petersen, G., 574, 575
Petersen, J., 112

Peterson, J. S., 525
Peterson, N., 513
Peterson, R., 422
Pew, M., 330
Pew, W., 315, 317
Pfeffer, C., 559
Phillips, L., 465
Phillips, R. D., 417
Phinney, J. S., 464, 465
Piaget, J., 11, 12, 13, 85, 119, 120, 218, 253, 319, 551
Piazza, N. J., 619
Pidcock, B., 550
Pietrzak, D., 574, 575
Pincus, D., 427
Pinderhughes, E., 231
Piper, W. E., 510, 511
Plato, 414
Plaud, J., 255
Poda, D., 284
Ponterotto, J. G., 459, 463
Pope, M., 155
Popenhagen, M., 558
Poppen, W., 47, 49, 50, 114
Popper, M., 559
Porche-Burke, L., 201
Porter, G., 500, 501
Portman, G. L., 525
Portman, T. A. A., 525
Post, P., 428
Powell, B., 66
Pressey, Sidney, 239
Price, A. W., 550
Prieto, L. R., 423
Pryzwansky, W. B., 488, 490, 492, 493, 496
Pulvino, C., 571
Purkey, William, 576
Putallaz, M., 18
Pynoos, R. S., 439
Pytluk, S. D., 464

Qian, Z., 479
Qualley, R., 558
Quenk, N., 397, 405
Quilitch, H., 422
Quinn, R., 179

Rabinowitz, I., 559
Radd, T. R., 172, 172n2, 175
Rae, W., 430
Rafferty, Y., 572
Rainey, L. M., 525
Rak, C. F., 19, 21
Ramirez, M., 572
Ramirez, M., III, 465
Ramirez, S. A., 493
Randall, R., 105
Rank, Otto, 160
Rapee, R., 227
Rappley, M. D., 600

Rasmussen, L. A., 435, 437
Rasmussen, R., 427
Rave, E. J., 611
Ray, D., 416, 417, 424, 434
Ray, K., 250
Rayfield, A., 426
Reddy, L., 417, 418, 419, 432,
    433, 445
Reeder, J., 526
Reich, Wilhelm, 184
Reis, S. M., 597
Remley, T., 611, 612, 613, 614
Remley, T. P., 616, 617, 618,
    619, 622
Resnick, R. J., 600
Reynolds, W. M., 557, 560
Rhine, T., 417, 425
Richards, L., 570
Richards, N., 434
Richardson, B., 472, 475
Richardson, T. Q., 458
Richeport-Haley, M., 379
Rickford, B., 146, 148, 154, 155
Riley, R., 380
Ringel, J. S., 63
Rio, A., 378
Ripley, V. V., 526
Ritchie, M., 417
Ritchie, M. H., 519, 520, 521
Riva, M. T., 511, 519
Robbins, R. R., 464
Robert, R., 599
Roberts, W., Jr., 561, 562
Robertson, P., 617
Robertson-Mjaanes, S., 495
Robinson, E. H., III, 523
Robinson, F. F., 511
Robinson, H., 416
Robinson, J., 296
Robinson, T., 458
Robinson Kurpius, S. W., 613
Rodgers, K. A., 500
Rodriguez, E. R., 477
Rogers, Carl, 21, 23, 45, 54, 122,
    133, 134, 159, 160, 161, 162,
    163, 164, 165, 166, 170, 175,
    177, 178, 179, 180, 189,
    213, 296
Rogers, R. E., 623
Rogers, S., 430, 431
Rokop, J. J., 622
Roll, D., 249
Romano, J., 249
Ronen, T., 228
Roosevelt, Franklin D., 589
Roth, B., 575
Roth, S., 355
Rotter, J. C., 423
Roysircar-Sodowsky, G., 463
Rozecki, T., 494, 495, 496
Rubin, J. A., 439

Russell, David L., 269
Ryan, S., 424

Sakin-Wolf, S., 330
Sallee, A., 11
Salmon, S., 575
Salo, M., 612, 616, 619, 621
Salzman, M., 473
Sanderson, W., 221
Saner, R., 201
Sanner, J., 430
Santisteban, D., 378
Satir, Virginia, 185, 357, 359, 360,
    361, 362, 363, 364, 365, 366,
    367, 368, 369, 370, 371, 372,
    375, 379, 381
Sattler, J. M., 502, 506
Saunders, A., 212
Saunders, F. W., 397
Saunders, R. C., 63
Scamardo, M., 155
Scarborough, J. L., 604
Scarupa, H. J., 541
Sceery, A., 18
Schaefer, C., 96, 414, 415, 417,
    433, 438
Schaefer, C. E., 414, 421, 422, 423
Scheidlinger, S., 578
Schein, Edward, 489, 491, 493
Schellenbach, C. J., 544
Schimmel, C., 512, 516, 522
Schmidt, L., 609, 610, 611
Schmiege, C., 570
Schmitz, C., 572
Schoen, C., 544
Schriebman, L., 431
Schuler, A., 431
Schulte, A. C., 488, 490, 492,
    493, 496
Schutz, Will, 185
Schwartz, R., 379
Schwebel, A., 567
Schwiebert, V., 599
Schwiebert, V. L., 619
Sciarra, D. T., 549, 552, 553, 557,
    558, 559, 560
Scott, Evelyn, 457
Sealander, K., 599
Sealander, K. A., 619
Selekman, M., 146, 356
Seligman, L., 33, 34
Seligman, M., 58, 557
Selman, R. L., 14
Serdahl, E., 495
Sessions, P., 64
Sexton, T. L., 34
Sferrazza, M. S., 604
Shaffer, J., 520
Shaffer, S., 462
Shahin, J., 271
Shapiro, J. P., 458, 545, 546, 553, 555

Russell, David L., 269
Shapiro, M. B., 238
Sharabani, R., 526
Shaver, P. R., 17
Shechtman, Z., 511, 517, 519, 520,
    525, 526
Shelby, J., 431, 432
Shelby, J. S., 440
Sheller, B., 552
Shen, Y.-J., 432
Shepard, M., 183
Shepard, R. E., 556
Sheridan, S. M., 493
Sherman, R., 59
Shillington, A. M., 19
Shilts, L., 139, 146
Shimizu, M., 177
Shoffner, M. F., 500
Shulman, B., 305, 306
Shumate, S., 612, 616, 619, 621
Shura, M. F., 552
Shure, M., 518
Shwery, C., 212
Siebert, A., 179, 180
Siegel, S., 227
Siehl, P., 562
Sills, C., 296
Silver, S., 594
Silverman, S., 227
Sim, A. J., 566
Simek-Morgan, L., 265
Simon, J., 149
Simon, R., 347
Simon, S., 86, 87
Simpson, R. L., 603
Simpson, Sharon, 224
Singleton, M., 155
Sink, C. A., 500
Skinner, B. F., 238, 239, 240
Skinner, C., 250
Sklare, G., 135, 139, 141,
    145, 146
Skowron, E., 339
Sladeczek, I. E., 495
Slavson, S. R., 360
Smith, A., 58
Smith, C. A., 541
Smith, D., 589, 590, 594, 596, 597,
    598, 601, 602, 603
Smith, H., 58
Smith, Helen, 574
Smith, Howard, 65
Smith, J., 370
Smith, J. M., 599
Smith, M. L., 34
Smith, R., 491
Smith, R. S., 19, 20
Smith, S., 424
Snowden, L. R., 466
Socrates, 216, 303
Sodowsky, G. R., 463, 464
Sokol, L., 227

Sokol, M., 559
Soloman, L. N., 178
Solomon, R., 559
Soltz, V., 311, 319, 322
Somers, C. L., 492
Sommers-Flanagan, J., 514
Sommers-Flanagan, R., 514
Sorenson, G. P., 609, 610
Soriano, F., 574
Soriano, M., 574
Soto-Fulp, S., 379
Southam-Gerow, M. A., 558
Spagna, M. E., 591, 592, 595, 603
Spangenberg, J., 177
Sparks, T., 545
Spaulding, D. J., 476
Speaker, K., 574, 575
Spence, S., 227, 228
Spengler, P., 559
Spurlock, J., 19
Stachowiak, J., 359
Stadler, H., 615
Stadler, H. A., 611
Stahmer, A., 431
Stanko, C. A., 525
Stanton, Elizabeth Cady, 109
Steenbarger, B., 58
Steenberger, Brett, 66
Steer, R. A., 557
Stefanowski-Harding, S., 558
Stein, B., 63, 66
Steiner, C., 282, 289, 296
Steinhardt, L., 440
Stekel, Wilhelm, 75
Stephans, R., 574
Stephenson, M., 155
Stermback, S., 442
Stiles, K., 303
Stipsits, R., 177
Stoiber, K., 512
Stoiber, K. C., 495
Stone, C., 616, 621
Stone, C. B., 609, 610, 615
Stone, I., 74, 75
Stone, Judy, 67
Stoop, D., 416
Storr, A., 387
Stott, F., 51
Strain, P., 431
Strawser, S., 572
Striepling-Goldstein, S., 575
Strong, K., 577, 578, 579
Strother, J., 437
Studer, J., 575
Sturm, R., 63
Styron, T., 571
Sue, D. W., 154, 201, 231, 378,
     459, 461, 463, 464, 470,
     471, 475
Suetake, Y., 177
Sugarman, A., 76

Sullivan, Harry Stack, 360
Sullivan, J., 430, 595
Summerton, O., 278
Sundet, R., 370, 378
Sweeney, B., 577
Sweeney, D. S., 415, 420
Swenson, L. C., 612
Szapocznik, J., 378

Talahite, A., 176
Tamang, B. L., 457
Tamura, T., 378
Tannen, D., 411
Tarasoff, 620, 621
Tares, H. L., 63
Tarver-Behring, S., 591, 592,
     595, 603
Taschman, H., 359
Taub, D. J., 525
Taylor, A., 149
Taylor, L., 500
Telles, C. A., 466
Teresa, Mother, 538, 588
Terner, J., 317
Terr, L., 541
Thebarge, R., 214
Thomas, M., 344
Thomas, Saint, 159
Thompson, C., 35, 47, 49, 50, 59, 62,
     112, 114, 115, 128, 153, 155, 230,
     239, 527
Thompson, E. A., 560
Thompson, R., 597
Thornberry, T. P., 541
Thorp, D., 431
Thuesen, J. M., 400
Thurston, L. P., 487, 501
Tischler, V., 573
Todd, T., 356
Tollerud, T., 562, 564, 565, 568,
     569, 599
Tomine, S., 475, 476
Torsteinsson, V., 370, 378
Toth, M., 276
Travydas, V. M., 611
Trevino, J., 463
Trimble, J. E., 457, 461
Trivedi, L., 39, 98
Truax, C. B., 45
Trusty, J., 458, 464, 465, 489
Tschann, J., 430
Turner, W., 336
Tyler, J. L., 439
Tyndall-Lind, A., 416, 429

Umana-Taylor, A. J., 479
Underwood, J. K., 619
Underwood, M., 575
Upchurch, J., 430
Urquiza, A., 427
Utay, J. M., 230

VanFleet, R., 230, 424
Van Hoose, W. H., 611
Van Lone, J. S., 526
Vasquez, M. J. T., 201
Vaz, K. M., 442
Veach, Laura, 63
Vinturella, L., 442
Visher, E., 569
Visher, J., 569
von Goethe, Johann Wolfgang,
     207
Vontross, C., 457, 470, 472
Vostanis, P., 573

Wachtel, E., 377
Wachtel, M., 511
Wadsworth, B., 13, 14
Wagner, J., 572
Wagner, P., 495
Wagner-Moore, L., 193
Walberg, H. J., 6, 8
Walker, R., 439
Wallerstein, J., 563, 564, 565, 566
Walter, J., 135
Wampold, B., 58
Warren, E., 434
Washington, E. D., 460, 465
Waters, V., 212, 217
Watkins, C. E., 221, 222
Watson, Goodwin, 160
Watson, J., 96
Watson, T., 250
Watts, G. B., 552
Watzlawick, P., 134
Waxer, P. H., 177
Weakland, J., 134
Webb, B., 555
Webb, L., 502
Webb, N. B., 541
Webb, W., 229
Weekley, J. L., 619
Weersing, V. R., 558
Weiling, E., 336
Weiner, N., 613
Weiner-Davis, M., 149
Weiss, M. P., 595, 597
Weissberg, R., 428, 429
Weissberg, R. P., 6, 8
Weissman, A., 560
Weisz, J. R., 558
Weitan, W., 378
Welfel, E. R., 543, 610, 611, 612,
     613, 614, 615, 616, 618, 619, 620,
     621, 622
Werner, E. E., 19, 20
West, S., 550
Westen, D., 90
Wheat, R., 443
Wheeler, G., 197
Whiston, S. C., 34
Whitaker, Robert Lee, 101

White, J., 417, 491, 502
Whitt, J., 430
Wick, D. T., 513
Wick, J. K., 513
Wicks-Nelson, R., 599, 600, 601
Wien, E. E., 599
Wilborn, B., 303
Wilde, J., 230
Williams, G., 155
Williamson, R. D., 500
Wilson, C., 526
Wilson, F. R., 517
Wilson, G., 422, 575
Wilson, J., 550
Windholtz, G., 255
Winer-Elkin, 428
Wingett, W., 332
Winnicott, D. W., 85, 89, 98, 106

Winston, S. M., 611
Wise, A., 559
Wolf, B., 588, 589
Wolfberg, P., 431
Wolpe, J., 255, 258
Wolpe, Joseph, 238
Woods, K., 278, 296
Woody, P., 227
Worchel, F., 430
Worden, J., 553
Work, W., 428
Worzbyt, J., 549, 551, 552
Wright, F., 227
Wubbolding, R., 129, 130
Wyman, P., 428

Yaccarino, M., 378
Yamada, A. M., 457

Yamaguchi, B. J., 572
Yang, P. H., 466
Yapko, M., 547
Yarbrough, J., 59, 62, 128, 155
Yasuri, M., 465
Yeh, C. J., 476
Yi, K., 104
Ying, Y., 475
Young, M., 430
Young, T. L., 63

Zaff, J. F., 465
Zebell, N., 427
Zeig, J., 353
Zeppa, A., 569
Zinck, K., 526
Zingaro, J. C., 617
Zuckerman, B., 574

TOPICAL INDEX

Abused children, 538–548
  reporting abuse, 622
Acculturation, 465–466
Achievement tests, 505
Acting out, 84
Active listening, 45–46
Adler, Alfred, 299–300. See also
  Individual psychology
Advice giving, 52–53
African-American children,
  470–472
Aggressive behavior
  cognitive-behavioral therapy, 226
  violent children. See Violent
    children
Alaskan Native children, 473–474
Alcoholics, children of, 548–551
  cognitive-behavioral therapy,
    229
American Indian children, 473–474
Anticathexis, 81
Anxiety
  cognitive-behavioral therapy, 227
  rational-emotive-behavioral
    therapy, 217, 218
Aptitude tests, 505
Archetypes, 392–394
Art therapy, 439–440
Asian-American children, 475–477
Assertiveness training, 254
Assessment tools
  achievement tests, 505
  aptitude tests, 505
  behavioral observations, 504
  case histories, 504
  intelligence tests, 504–505
  interviews. See Interviews
  projective techniques, 505
  tests, 504–506
Attention deficit disorder,
  598–600

Attention-deficit/hyperactivity
    disorder, 598–600
  cognitive-behavioral therapy, 228
Aversive conditioning, 259–260

Behavioral consultation, 491–493
Behavioral counseling. See also
    Classical conditioning
  applications of, 263–265
  assertiveness training, 254
  behavioral momentum, 249–250
  behavior analysis, 241–243
  behavior-practice groups,
    251–252
  biofeedback, 250
  case study, 260–263
  contingency contracts, 245–248
  cross-cultural applications, 265
  eating disorders, treatment of, 264
  goals, 244–245
  group counseling, 514
  homework assignments, 253–254
  human nature, 239–240
  managed health care accountability,
    266
  methods, 245–254
  modeling, 250–251
  multimodal treatment plans,
    264–265
  reinforcement schedules, 244
  response cost, 264
  role-playing, 252–253
  self-management plans, 248–249
  shaping, 249
  theory of, 240–241
  token economies, 251
Behavioral-emotional disorders,
    children with, 593–595
Behavioral momentum, 249–250
Behavioral observations, 504
Behavior-practice groups, 251–252

Bereavement, 551–556
Berne, Eric, 269–270. See also
    Transactional analysis
Bibliocounseling, 95–96
Biofeedback, 250
Bowen, Murray, 337–338. See also
    Family counseling
Brief counseling, 133–134
  cross-cultural applications, 153–154
  managed health care accountability,
    154–155
  paradoxical. See Paradoxical brief
    counseling
  solution-focused. See Solution-
    focused brief counseling

Case histories, 504
Catharsis, 91–92
Cathexis, 81
Causes of children's problems, 4–8
Changing world, 5–9
Chemically dependent families,
    children in, 548–551
Child abuse and neglect, 538–548
  reporting abuse, 622
Child development, 11
  cognitive development, 11–15
  resiliency, 19–22
  social development, 15–22
Child diversity, 468–470
  African-American children,
    470–472
  Alaskan Native children, 473–474
  American Indian children, 473–474
  Asian-American children, 475–477
  Latino children, 477–479
  multiracial children, 479–480
Children with special needs, 558
  attention deficit disorder, 598–600
  attention-deficit/hyperactivity
    disorder, 598–600

Children with special needs *(continued)*
   behavioral-emotional disorders, 593–595
   categories of, 590–592
   counseling methods, 593
   counseling techniques, 603–604
   historical backdrop, 589
   learning disabilities, 595–598
   mentally retarded children, 600–602
   parents, working with, 604–605
   physically disabled children, 602–603
Child's well-being
   barriers to, 3–4
   indicators of, 4
Child's world, 2–4
   changing world, 5–9
   personal world, 8–11
Choice theory
   counseling. See Choice theory reality therapy
   human nature, 110–115
Choice theory reality therapy, 115–116
   case study, 123–126
   counseling method, 116–120
   cross-cultural applications, 129–130
   group counseling, 513–514
   managed health care accountability, 130
   process of, 120–122
   ten-step consultation model, 126–129
Circle of irrational thinking, 209
Clarifying child's expectations, 46
Classical conditioning, 254–255
   aversive conditioning, 259–260
   counterconditioning, 259
   flooding, 258–259
   hypnosis, 259
   systematic desensitization, 255–258
Cognitive-behavioral therapy, 220–223
   aggression, treatment of, 226
   alcoholics, treatment of children of, 229
   applications of, 226–230
   attention-deficit/hyperactivity disorder, treatment of, 228
   case study, 223–226
   cross-cultural applications, 230–231
   depression, treatment of, 227–228
   managed health care accountability, 231–232
   obesity, treatment of, 228–229
   play therapy, 229–230
Cognitive development, 11–15
Collaboration, 487, 499–502
   teaming, 502
Collective unconscious, 392
Compensation, 84

Competence, 613–614
   multicultural competencies, 459
   multicultural counseling competencies. See Multicultural counseling competencies
Complementary transactions, 273
Complexes, 391
Confidentiality, 55–56, 615–618
   breaching, 620–621
   child abuse reporting, 622
   of files, 618–620
   in groups, 621–622
Conjoint family therapy, 359–360
   counseling method, 367–370
   human nature, 360–362
   key ingredients, 370
   technique, 370–373
   theory of, 362–367
Consciousness, 388
Consultation, 487, 488–489
   assessment tools. See Assessment tools
   behavioral consultation, 491–493
   consulting process, 494–496
   cross-cultural consultation, 493
   interventions, 497–499
   mental health consultation, 489, 490
   models of, 489–493, 496–497
   process consultation, 489, 491
Contingency contracts, 245–248
Counseling
   effective approaches, 33–36
   evaluation of, 58–62
   general model for, 45–48
   interviews. See Interviews
   limits, 54–55
   psychotherapy, distinguished, 23
   role of, 24–27
   seeking arrangements, 40
   termination of, 57–58
   theories, 36–39. See also specific theory
   what is, 22–24
Counseling focus scale, 26
Counseling records, 48
   confidentiality, 618–620. See also Confidentiality
Counseling theories. See also specific theory
   classification of, 36–39
Counterconditioning, 259
Covert transactions, 274
Cross-cultural applications
   behavioral counseling, 265
   brief counseling, 153–154
   choice theory reality therapy, 129–130
   cognitive-behavioral therapy, 230–231
   family counseling, 378–379
   gestalt therapy, 200–201

individual psychology, 330–332
   Jungian counseling, 411
   person-centered counseling, 176–178
   play therapy, 419–420
   psychoanalytic counseling, 104
   rational-emotive-behavioral therapy, 230–231
   transactional analysis, 295–296
Cross-cultural consultation, 493
Crossed transactions, 274
Culture. See also Child diversity; Cross-cultural applications; Multiculturalism
   acculturation, 465–466

Death and bereavement, 551–556
Defense mechanisms, 81–84
Denial, 83
Depressed children, 556–557
   cognitive-behavioral therapy, 227–228
   rational-emotive-behavioral therapy, 217
Development. See Child development
Disabilities, children with. See Children with special needs
Displacement, 82
Diversity. See Child diversity; Multiculturalism
Divorce, children of, 562–567
Dominance, 402
Dreams
   interpretation of, 92–93
   Jungian counseling, 391–392
Dreamwork, 195–196
Drug abusers, children of, 548–551
Dynamic family play therapy, 376

Early recollections, 317–318
Eating disorders
   behavioral counseling, 264
   obesity, 228–229
Ego, 79
   Jungian counseling, 388–389
Ego gatekeeper, 389–390
Ego-gram, 290
Ego states, 273
Ellis, Albert, 207–208. See also Rational-emotive-behavioral therapy
Emotional cutoff, 341
Emotionally abused children, 539
Emotionally neglected children, 539
Empty chair technique, 191–193
Ericksonian play therapy, 150
Erickson's stages, 84–86
Ethical decision-making models, 611–612
Ethical decision-making process, 622–624

Ethical issues, 609–611, 612–613
    confidentiality. See Confidentiality
Ethnic identity development, 464–465
Ethnicity. See Child diversity;
    Cross-cultural applications;
    Multiculturalism
Evaluation of counseling, 58–62
Exceptional children. See Children
    with special needs
Extinction, 241

Family counseling
    Adlerian, 328–330
    case studies, 373–375
    communications approach, 357–373
    cross-cultural applications,
        378–379
    individual counseling, distinguished,
        335–336
    managed health care accountability,
        379–380
    play therapy, 375–378
    strategic family therapy, 351–357
    structural family therapy, 346–350
    systems approach, 337–346
    what is a "family," 336–337
Family emotional systems, 345
Family projection process, 340
Fantasy, 83
Fantasy games to create awareness,
    194–195
Filial therapy, 423–425
Fixation, 83
Flooding, 258–259
Focus during counseling, 54
    group counseling, 516–519
Free association, 92
Freud, Sigmund, 74–76. See also
    Psychoanalytic theory
"Freudian" slips, 94

Game analysis, 276
Games clients play, 278–280
Gangs, 577–580
Genogram, 343
Genogram key, 342
Gestalt therapy
    case study, 197–200
    counseling method, 188–197
    cross-cultural applications,
        200–201
    group counseling, 515
    human nature, 185–187
    managed health care accountability,
        201–202
    play therapy, 196–197
    techniques, 189–196
    theory of, 187–188
Glasser, William, 109–110. See also
    Choice theory reality therapy
Goal attainment scaling, 58–62

Gottman's behavioral interview
    method, 357–359
Group counseling, 510–511
    age differences, 525–527
    case example, 528–530
    classroom meetings, 530–531
    confidentiality in groups, 621–622
    crisis intervention, 531–533
    evaluation of effectiveness, 527–528
    first session, 523–524
    group focus, 516–519
    group formation, 519–520
    group leadership skills, 515–516
    group members, 519
    group setting, 521
    group size, 521
    group stages, 521–523
    group types, 511–513
    screening interview, 520–521
    session guidelines, 523–525
    theoretically oriented, 513–515
    what is a "group," 511
Group play therapy, 420–422

Health care organizations. See
    Managed health care
    accountability
HMOs. See Managed health care
    accountability
Home environment, 6–7
Homeless children, 571–573
Human nature
    behavioral counseling, 239–240
    choice theory, 110–115
    conjoint family therapy, 360–362
    gestalt therapy, 185–187
    individual psychology, 301–309
    Jungian counseling, 386–387
    paradoxical brief counseling, 150
    person-centered counseling, 161
    psychoanalytic theory, 76–78
    rational-emotive-behavioral
        therapy, 208–210
    solution-focused brief counseling,
        134–135
    transactional analysis, 270–271
Humor, 94
Hypnosis, 259

Id, 79
Identification, 82
"I" language, 189–190
Individual psychology
    behavior, goals of, 302–303
    case studies, 324–327
    confrontation of children, 318–319
    counseling method, 314–324
    cross-cultural applications, 330–332
    early recollections, 317–318
    family atmosphere, 307–309
    family constellation, 305–307

family counseling, 328–330
    group counseling, 513
    human nature, 301–309
    lifestyle, 303
    managed health care accountability,
        332–333
    misbehavior, goals of, 311–314
    misbehavior interventions,
        319–323
    natural and logical consequences,
        323–324
    play therapy, 327–328
    social interest, 303–304
    stages of children's perspectives,
        319
    success, need for, 302
    theory of, 309–314
    "understanding" with children, 318
Individuation, 391
Information giving, 54
Informed consent, 614–615
Instinct, 81
Intellectualization, 83
Intelligence tests, 504–505
Interpretation
    of dreams, 92–93
    humor, 94
    parapraxia, 94
Interventions
    for children from chemically
        dependent families, 550–551
    consultation, 497–499
    for depression, 557–558
    for grieving children, 553, 555–556
    group crisis intervention, 531–533
    paradoxical, 351–352
    postsuicide interventions, 561–562
    for suicide, 560–561
Interviews, 502–503
    behavioral counseling, 253, 261–262
    blocked interviews, overcoming,
        56–57
    choice theory reality therapy,
        120–122, 123–125
    closing, 47–48
    cognitive-behavioral therapy,
        224–226
    family counseling, 373–375
    first interview with child, 40–45
    gestalt therapy, 197–200
    Gottman's behavioral interview
        method, 357–359
    group counseling, 520–521,
        528–530
    individual psychology approach,
        315–317, 321, 325–327
    Jungian counseling, 408–410
    person-centered counseling,
        171–172, 174–175
    play therapy, 444–445
    preparation for, 39–40

Interviews *(continued)*
    psychoanalytic counseling, 99–101
    solution-focused brief counseling,
        140, 141–142, 143–145, 147
    transactional analysis, 293–295
Isolation techniques, 498–499

Jung, Carl, 385–386. See also Jungian
        counseling
Jungian counseling
    archetypes, 392–394
    case study, 407–410
    collective unconscious, 392
    complexes, 391
    consciousness, 388
    cross-cultural applications, 411
    dominance, 402
    dreams, 391–392
    ego, 388–389
    ego gatekeeper, 389–390
    human nature, 386–387
    individuation, 391
    learning preferences, 402, 403–404
    method, 406–407
    personal unconscious, 388
    progression, 392
    psyche, 387
    psychic energy, 387–388
    psychological diversity, 404–405
    psychological types, 394–397
    regression, 392
    temperament, 402–403
    theory of, 387–396
    word association, 394

Latino children, 477–479
Learning disabilities, children with,
        595–598
    attention deficit disorder, 598–600
    attention-deficit/hyperactivity
        disorder, 598–600
Learning preferences, 402, 403–404
Legal issues, 609–611, 612–613
    confidentiality. See Confidentiality
    informed consent, 614–615
Life positions, 277–278
Life script injunctions, 275
Listening actively, 45–46

Maltreated children, 538–548
    reporting abuse, 622
Managed health care accountability,
        63–69
    behavioral counseling, 266
    brief counseling, 154–155
    cognitive-behavioral therapy,
        231–232
    family counseling, 379–380
    gestalt therapy, 201–202
    individual psychology, 332–333
    person-centered counseling, 178

play therapy, 436
psychoanalytic counseling, 105
rational-emotive-behavioral
    therapy, 231–232
reality therapy, 130
transactional analysis, 296–297
Maslow's hierarchy of needs, 9
MBHOs. See Managed health care
    accountability
Mental health consultation, 489, 490
Mental health professionals, 27–29
Mentally retarded children, 600–602
Mental Status Examination (MSE),
    503
Model for counseling, 45–48
Modeling, 250–251
Multicultural counseling competencies,
    459
    awareness, 460–461
    knowledge, 461–466
    skills, 461, 466–468
Multiculturalism, 457–459
    applications of. See Cross-cultural
        applications
    child diversity. See Child diversity
    competence, 459
    counseling competencies. See
        Multicultural counseling
        competencies
    ethnic identity development,
        464–465
Multigenerational transmission
    process, 341
Multiracial children, 479–480
Myers Briggs Type Indicator, 397–402
    theory of type development, 406
    usefulness in counseling, 405

Negative reinforcement, 241
Neglected children, 538–548
Nuclear family emotional process,
    340

Obesity, 228–229
Object relations theory, 87–90
Operant conditioning, 241. See also
    Behavioral counseling
Outcome measures, 58

Paradoxical brief counseling. See also
        Brief counseling
    case examples, 152–153
    human nature, 150
    method, 151–152
    theory of, 150–151
Paradoxical interventions, 351–352
Parapraxia, 94
Parent-child interaction therapy,
    425–427
Pavlov, Ivan, 254–255. See also
    Classical conditioning

Perls, Fritz, 183–185. See also Gestalt
        therapy
Person-centered counseling
    case study, 170–172
    cross-cultural applications, 176–178
    group counseling, 515
    human nature, 161
    managed health care accountability,
        178
    method, 164–170
    play therapy, 175–176
    self-esteem development, 172–175
    theory of, 161–164
Physically abused children, 538–548
    reporting abuse, 622
Physically disabled children, 602–603
Physically neglected children, 539,
        541, 544
Play therapy, 414
    Adlerian, 327–328
    advantages of, 415–416
    applications of, 420
    approaches to, 420–427
    art therapy, 439–440
    for autistic children, 430–431
    case study, 443–445
    for chronically ill, 429–430
    client considerations, 434–435
    cognitive-behavioral therapy,
        229–230
    cross-cultural applications,
        419–420
    for domestic violence situations,
        429
    empirical support for, 417–419
    Ericksonian, 150
    family counseling, 375–378
    filial therapy, 423–425
    gestalt therapy, 196–197
    group play therapy, 420–422
    individual psychology, 327–328
    managed health care accountability,
        436
    media and strategies, 436–443
    other interventions, in combination
        with, 432–433
    parent-child interaction therapy,
        425–427
    person-centered counseling,
        175–176
    for post-traumatic stress disorder,
        431–432
    prescriptive play therapy, 422–423
    psychoanalytic play therapy,
        97–99
    puppets, use of, 440–441
    sand, use of, 441–443
    for school adjustment difficulties,
        427–429
    skills used by therapists, 438–439
    stages of, 435–436

therapist considerations, 433–434
what is, 414–415
PMHP programs, 427–429
Positive reinforcement, 241
Prescriptive play therapy, 422–423
Process consultation, 489, 491
Professional competence, 613–614
multicultural competencies, 459
multicultural counseling
competencies. See Multicultural
counseling competencies
Professional issues, 609–611
confidentiality. See Confidentiality
Progression, 392
Projection, 82
family projection process, 340
Projective techniques, 505
Psyche, 387
Psychic energy, 387–388
Psychoanalytic counseling
case studies, 99–104
cross-cultural application, 104
managed health care accountability,
105
methods, 90–99
self-esteem development, 86–90
Psychoanalytic theory, 78–79
developmental concepts, 81–86
dynamic concepts, 81
human nature, 76–78
structural concepts, 79–81
Psychological diversity, 404–405
Psychological types, 394–397
Myers Briggs Type Indicator,
397–402, 405, 406
Psychosexual stages, 84–86
Psychotherapy, 23
Punishment, 241

Questions counselors ask, 50–52. See
also Interviews

Race. See Child diversity;
Cross-cultural applications;
Multiculturalism
Rackets, 283
Rational-emotive-behavioral
education, 219–220
Rational-emotive-behavioral therapy
counseling method, 214–220
cross-cultural applications,
230–231
group counseling, 514
human nature, 208–210
managed health care accountability,
231–232
theory of, 210–213
Rationalization, 82

Reaction formation, 82
Realty therapy. See Choice theory
reality therapy
Record keeping, 48
Regression, 83, 392
Reinforcement, 241
schedules, 244
Repression, 82
Resiliency, 19–22
Resistance analysis, 94–95
Resistance to counseling, 40–45
Response cost, 264
Rogers, Carl, 159–161. See also
Person-centered counseling
Role-playing, 252–253

Script analysis, 275–276
Self-differentiation, 339
modeling, 345–346
Self-disclosure, 48–50
Self-esteem development
person-centered counseling,
172–175
psychoanalytic counseling, 86–90
Self-management plans, 248–249
Sexually abused children, 539,
544–545
reporting abuse, 622
Shaping, 249
Sibling position, 341
Silences, 52
Single-parent homes, children in,
570–571
Skinner, B. F., 238–239. See also
Behavioral counseling
Social development, 15–22
Societal crises, 7
Societal emotional process, 341–345
Solution-focused brief counseling.
See also Brief counseling
case study, 142–146
Ericksonian play therapy, 150
goal setting, 138–142
human nature, 134–135
method, 137–138
miracle question to formulate
goals, 140–142
steps in, 146–149
theory of, 135–137
Special needs, children with. See
Children with special needs
Spousal relationships, 338–339
Stepfamilies, children in, 568–570
Storytelling, 96–97
Strategic family play therapy, 377
Strategic family therapy, 351–357
Strokes, 280–283
Structural analysis, 271–272

Structural family therapy, 346–350
Sublimation, 84
Substance abusers, children of,
548–551
Suicidal children, 558–562
Superego, 80–81
Suppression, 82
Surveys to evaluate effectiveness, 58
Systematic desensitization,
255–258
Systems approach to family therapy,
337–346

Teaming, 502
Temperament, 402–403
Termination of counseling, 57–58
Tests, 504–506
Theoretically oriented group
counseling, 513–515
Theraplay, 378
"Time-out," 498–499
Token economies, 251
Top dog/underdog, 191, 199
Transactional analysis, 273–274
case studies, 293–296
counseling method, 283–292
cross-cultural applications,
295–296
game analysis, 276
games clients play, 278–280
group counseling, 514
human nature, 270–271
life positions, 277–278
managed health care accountability,
296–297
rackets, 283
script analysis, 275–276
strokes, 280–283
structural analysis, 271–272
Transference analysis, 94
Triangulation, 340
Truth from client, 56

Unconscious
collective, 392
personal, 388
Underdog/top dog, 191, 199
Undoing, 83

Value changes, 7–8
Violent children, 573–577
gangs, 577–580

Well-being. See Child's well-being
Withdrawal, 83
Word association, 394